Managing
Human Resources

THIRD CANADIAN EDITION

Monica Belcourt
Professor
Administrative Studies
York University

George Bohlander
Professor of Management
Arizona State University

Scott Snell
Professor of Management
The Pennsylvania State University

Arthur Sherman
Professor of Psychology
California State University, Sacramento

NELSON
™
THOMSON LEARNING

Australia • Canada • Mexico • Singapore • Spain • United Kingdom • United States

NELSON

™

THOMSON LEARNING

Managing Human Resources
Third Canadian Edition

by Monica Belcourt, George Bohlander,
Scott Snell, and Arthur Sherman

Editorial Director and Publisher:
Evelyn Veitch

Acquisitions Editor:
Edward Ikeda

Marketing Manager:
Anthony Rezek

Senior Project Editor:
Karina Ten Veldhuis

Managing Production Editor:
Susan Calvert

Production Coordinator:
Hedy Sellers

Copy Editor/Proofreader:
Matthew Kudelka

Art Director:
Angela Cluer

Interior Design:
Liz Harasymczuk

Cover Design:
Linda O'Neill

Cover Image:
© Alexander Burkatowski/
CORBIS/Magma

Senior Composition Analyst:
Alicja Jamorski

Indexer:
Andrew Little

Printer:
Transcontinental Printing Inc.

**Canadian Cataloguing in
Publication Data**

Managing human resources

3rd Canadian ed.
Includes bibliographical references
and index.
ISBN 0-17-616879-6

1. Personnel management. I.
Belcourt, Monica, 1946-   .

HF5549.M3135 2001   658.3
C2001-930383-1

To Michael, Marc, and Brooker — who make family life so very interesting

To my wife, Ronnie Bohlander, and to our children, Ryan and Kathryn

To my wife, Marybeth Snell, and to our children, Sara, Jack, and Emily

To my wife, Leneve Sherman, and to our children, Judy, Beverly, and Sandy

CONTENTS IN BRIEF

PART 6: EXPANDING HORIZONS IN HUMAN RESOURCES MANAGEMENT

Chapter 17 is available on the Managing Human Resources website (**belcourt.nelson.com**).

TABLE OF CONTENTS

PART 2: MEETING HUMAN RESOURCES REQUIREMENTS

PART 3: DEVELOPING EFFECTIVENESS IN HUMAN RESOURCES

PART 4: IMPLEMENTING COMPENSATION AND SECURITY

PART 5: ENHANCING EMPLOYEE RELATIONS

PART 6: EXPANDING HORIZONS IN HUMAN RESOURCES MANAGEMENT

WWW

Chapter 17 is available on the Managing Human Resources website (belcourt.nelson.com)

PREFACE

While maintaining many of the features that have made it the leader in introductory textbooks, the new Third Canadian Edition of *Managing Human Resources* brings the changes that are occurring in management at all levels into clear focus. The role of HR managers is no longer limited to transactional services such as benefits administration and recruitment. Today, they assume an active role in the strategic planning and decision making at their organizations, with some playing key roles at the executive level. Employing human resources effectively is critical to the success of any work organization. Also, many functions that may have been done by HR specialists in the past are now done in partnership with line managers and team directors. To ensure effectiveness, HR policies and procedures must be placed into a comprehensive program that managers can use effectively in their day-to-day interactions with employees.

The Third Canadian Edition of *Managing Human Resources* will place your students at the forefront in understanding how organizations can gain sustainable competitive advantage through people. We begin with the first chapter, which explains the key challenges to HRM in developing the flexible and skilled workforce needed to compete effectively—going global, embracing new technology, managing change, developing human capital, responding to the market, and containing costs. Side by side with the competitive challenges, HRM must also address important employee concerns such as managing a diverse workforce, recognizing employee rights, and adjusting to new work attitudes. The first chapter also discusses the important partnership with line managers, and the competencies required of HR management.

The textbook continues with the introduction, explanation, and discussion of the individual practices and policies that make up HRM. We recognize the manager's changing role and emphasize current issues and real-world problems and the policies and practices HRM uses to meet them. While the focus is on the HR role of managers, we do not exclude the impact and importance of the HR department's role in developing, coordinating, and enforcing policies and procedures relating to HR functions. Whether the reader becomes a manager, an HR specialist, or is employed in other areas of the organization, *Managing Human Resources* provides a functional understanding of HR programs to enable students to see how HR affects all employees, the organization, the community, and the larger society.

Organizations in today's competitive world are discovering that it is how the individual HR topics are combined that makes all the difference. Managers typically don't focus on HR issues like staffing, training, and compensation in isolation from one another. Each of these HR practices is combined into an overall system to enhance employee involvement and productivity.

ORGANIZATION OF THE THIRD CANADIAN EDITION

This edition of *Managing Human Resources* is divided into six parts and seventeen chapters covering the following major topics:

Part 1: Human Resources Management in Perspective

The Challenge of Human Resources Management, and Equity and Diversity in Human Resources Management

Part 2: Meeting Human Requirements

Job Requirements and Employee Contributions, Human Resources Planning and Recruitment, and Selection

Part 3: Developing Effectiveness in Human Resources

Training, Career Development, and Appraising and Improving Performance

Part 4: Implementing Compensation and Security

Managing Compensation, Incentive Rewards, Employee Benefits, and Health and Safety

Part 5: Enhancing Employee Relations

Employee Rights and Discipline, The Dynamics of Labour Relations, and Collective Bargaining and Contract Administration

Part 6: Expanding Human Resources Management Horizons

International Human Resources Management

WHAT'S NEW IN THE THIRD CANADIAN EDITION

We introduce overall text improvements that more accurately reflect HR in today's business world and help students understand HR issues more effectively.

- Technology has impacted much of the way that HRM is practised. In recognition of this, there are many highlights, interviews, questions, and cases dealing with technology in areas such as e-recruiting and attracting and retaining talent in dot.com companies.

- Internet references and addresses throughout the text point students to the latest online sources for HR information and examples.

- A new section in Chapter 3 describes work-design techniques to increase employee contributions: employee empowerment and employee involvement groups. A comprehensive discussion of teams is included.

- Chapter 17, Creating High-Performance Work Systems, and the chapter feature Career Counsel appear on the Internet at the *Managing Human Resources* website (**belcourt.nelson.com**). The Career Counsel sections help students with job search strategies and value assessment and salary negotiation tactics.

- Complete update of all laws and court decisions governing HRM.

- Many new Highlights in HRM boxes present the student with up-to-date real-world examples from a variety of large and small organizations.

- Each chapter contains an interview with a Canadian functional expert. These Reality Checks not only provide a validation that the concepts presented in the chapter are applied in real organizations but also discuss the issues that practitioners are currently facing.

- Some important issues are ongoing, as the situations described in Ethics in HRM prove. Human resource management is an evolving field, and as such, some policies and practices are still being debated. Some instructors use the vignettes in Ethics in HRM to provoke discussion and debate among their students. By exposing students to ethical questions, we hope to increase their ability to think critically.

- References and examples of the policies and practices of hundreds of organizations show HRM concepts in action in the business world today.

- At the request of users and reviewers, we've increased the number of case studies to two per chapter. New comprehensive cases reinforce critical-thinking skills and problem-solving techniques. We have written six new comprehensive cases. Now the majority of the cases are about Canadian companies.

FEATURES OF THE BOOK

Designed to facilitate understanding and retention of the material presented, each chapter contains the following material:

- Learning objectives listed at the beginning of each chapter. Icons for identifying the learning objectives appear throughout the text and end-of-chapter material.

- Key terms appear in boldface and are defined in margin notes next to the text discussion. The key terms are also listed at the end of the chapter and appear in the glossary at the end of the text.

- An abundance of graphic materials, flowcharts, and summaries of research data provide a visual, dynamic presentation of concepts and HR activities. All figures are systematically referenced in the text discussion.

- Reality Check presents an interview with a Canadian expert in the field, illustrating how the material in the chapter is used in the real world.

- Ethics in HRM provokes debate and discussion among students, as they struggle with the often gray areas of Human Resources Management, such as the drug testing of employees and the electronic surveillance of the work place.

- The popular Highlights in HRM feature provides real-world examples of how organizations perform HR functions. The highlights are introduced in the text discussion and include topics such as small businesses and international issues.

- Illustrations, captioned photographs, and carefully selected cartoons reinforce points made in the text and maintain student interest.

- A chapter summary consisting of a paragraph or two for each learning objective provides a brief review of the chapter.

- Discussion questions following the chapter summary offer an opportunity to focus on each of the learning objectives in the chapter and stimulate critical thinking and discussion.

- Two case studies present current HRM issues in real-life settings that allow for student consideration and critical analysis.

- Each chapter includes references from academic and practitioner journals and books. Author notes cite some historical information as well as personal observations and experiences.

- Career Counsel on the *Managing Human Resources* Web Site (**belcourt.nelson.com**) provides a dynamic link to the Internet, enabling students to relate chapter content to job searching and career development. The Career Counsel exercises allow students to develop a career development plan.

- Website addresses are provided throughout the text for many companies and organizations.

  In addition to the features found in each of the seventeen chapters, the text provides:

- Ten comprehensive cases at the end of the main text that portray current issues and problems in HRM. Cases cover downsizing in the federal public service and its effect on recruitment, measuring human capital in the B.C. Government, the business of wellness at Canadian companies, and labour–management relations at Algoma.

- A glossary of all the key terms introduced in the text provides students with easy access to their definitions.

- Name, organization, and subject indexes and a list of websites by chapter allow the text to become a valuable reference source.

SUPPLEMENTARY MATERIALS

All printed supplementary materials were prepared by or under the direction of the text authors to guarantee full integration with the text. Multimedia and additional text supplements were prepared by experts in those fields.

For Students

- *Online Study Guide to Accompany Managing Human Resources.* In partnership with Captus Press (**www.captus.com**), Nelson Thomson Learning is pleased to offer a free on-line study guide prepared by Monica Belcourt. Complete with chapter summaries, multiple choice questions, short-answer questions, and progress checks, this supplement will enhance your learning experience.

- *Internet Course.* For students seeking extra help, a full on-line HRM course is available from Captus Press. Supplement classroom teaching by accessing the Internet server and listening to lectures given by Monica Belcourt. You can then scroll to areas of interest and access necessary information. Please contact Captus Press directly for information on the cost of these options (**www.captus.com**).

For Instructors

- *Instructor's Resource Guide.* For each chapter in the textbook, the resource guide for the Third Canadian Edition contains the following:

  — Chapter synopsis and learning objectives.

  — A detailed lecture outline, based on the textbook's chapter outline, complete with notes for incorporating the transparencies.

  — Answers to the end-of-chapter discussion questions and case studies in the textbook.

  — Solutions to the comprehensive cases in the textbook.

- *Test Bank.* The test bank includes at least 100 questions for each text chapter. Each test bank chapter includes a matrix table that classifies each question according to type and learning objective. There are true/false, multiple-choice, and essay items for each chapter, arranged by learning objective. Page references from the text are included. Each objective question is coded to indicate whether it covers knowledge of key terms, understanding of concepts and principles, or application of principles.

- *Computerized Test Bank.* The computerized testing software contains all the questions from the printed test bank, and allows the instructor to edit, add, delete, or randomly mix questions for customized tests.

- *PowerPoint Presentation Slides.* These screens will add colour and interest to your lectures.

- *Video Cassette.* Video segments from CTV news programming, featuring real companies and business situations, accompany the text chapters and were selected to help you integrate the videos with the text material. Use them to introduce a topic, cover lecture material, or stimulate discussion.

- *U.S. Transparency Acetates.* Also available with this edition is a set of transparencies. Only a few of these transparencies duplicate the figures in the textbook.

- *Applications in Human Resource Management: Cases, Exercises, and Skill Builders,* 4th Edition, by Stella M. Nkomo, Myron D. Fottler, and R. Bruce McAfee. This text supplement includes 87 new and updated cases, experiential exercises, skill builders, and term projects. These activities will supplement many of the topics covered in *Managing Human Resources,* Third Canadian Edition.

- *HRM Web Site.* A comprehensive website includes practice quizzes, chapter-specific Web links, study tips, and information on degrees and careers in human resource management. We have also included a link for instructors that contains Web-based assignments, downloadable ancillaries, updates, and teaching tips.

ACKNOWLEDGMENTS FOR THE THIRD CANADIAN EDITION

In preparing the manuscript for this edition, we have drawn not only on the current literature but also on the current practices of organizations that furnished information relating to their HR programs. We are indebted to the leaders in the field who have influenced us through their writings and personal associations. We have also been aided by our present and former students, by our colleagues at the Human Resources Professionals Association of Ontario with whom we have been associated, by HR managers, and by our academic colleagues. We want to express our gratitude to Diane White, Seneca College, for her wonderful suggestions on student exercises, several of which have been included. We would like to express our appreciation to the eight reviewers of the text:

Gordon Barnard, Durham College
Tim DeGroot, McMaster University
Robert Isaac, University of Calgary
Don MacCormac, University of PEI
Robert Oppenheimer, Concordia University
Carolin Rekar, Durham College
Sudhir Saha, Memorial University
Pat Sniderman, Ryerson Polytechnic University
Diane White, Seneca College

We appreciate the efforts of the team at Nelson Thomson Learning who helped to develop and produce this text. They include Edward Ikeda, Acquisitions Editor; Karina Ten Veldhuis, Senior Developmental Editor; and Anthony Rezek, Marketing Manager; as well as the wonderful sales representatives who have enthusiastically supported the book.

Our greatest indebtedness is to our spouses—Michael Belcourt, Ronnie Bohlander, Marybeth Snell, and Leneve Sherman—who have contributed in so many ways to this book. They are always sources of invaluable guidance and assistance. Furthermore, by their continued enthusiasm and support, they have made the process a more pleasant and rewarding experience. We are most grateful to them for their many contributions to this publication, to our lives, and to our families.

ABOUT THE AUTHORS

Monica Belcourt

Monica Belcourt is Professor, Administrative Studies, at Atkinson College, York University. She has an extensive and varied background in human resources management. After receiving a B.A. in psychology from the University of Manitoba, Winnipeg, she joined the Public Service Commission as a recruitment and selection specialist. During her tenure with the federal government, she worked in training, HRM research, job analysis, and HR planning. Dr. Belcourt obtained managerial experience as director of personnel for CP Rail, manager of Consumer Services (Quebec Region) for Consumer and Corporate Affairs, and manager of HR Development for the National Film Board.

Dr. Belcourt alternated working in HRM with graduate school, obtaining an M.A. in psychology from York University, an M.Ed. in adult education from the University of Ottawa, and a Ph.D. in management from York University. She has taught courses in management and HRM at Concordia University, McGill University, Université du Québec à Montréal, and York University. She also holds the designation of Certified Human Resource Professional (CHRP).

Dr. Belcourt's research interests include entrepreneurship and human resources. She has published over seventy articles since obtaining her Ph.D. in 1986. She is series editor for the Nelson Series in Human Resources Management, which includes the texts *Performance Management through Training and Development*, *Occupational Health and Safety*, *Human Resources Management Systems*, *Recruitment and Selection in Canada*, *Compensation in Canada*, *Strategic Human Resources Planning*, *Labour Economics*, and the forthcoming *Labour Relations*. She is the founding editor of "The Research Forum," a column in the *Human Resource Professional* and the *HRM Research Quarterly*.

Active in many professional associations and not-for-profit organizations, she is currently on the board of CIBC Insurance and the Human Resources Professionals Association of Ontario (HRPAO). She is the founding director of the Alliance for Human Resources Research, and, in this position, created distribution channels for HRM research, such as the Applied Research Stream at the HRPAO annual conference, and promoted HRM research through the establishment of awards for best theses (masters and doctoral).

George W. Bohlander

George W. Bohlander is Professor of Management at Arizona State University. He teaches undergraduate, graduate, and executive development programs in the field of human resources and labour relations. His areas of expertise include employment law, training and development, work teams, public policy, and labour relations. He is the recipient of six outstanding teaching awards at ASU and has received the Outstanding Undergraduate Teaching Excellence Award given by the College of Business at ASU. In 1996, Dr. Bohlander received the prestigious ASU Parents Association Professorship for his contributions to students and teaching.

Dr. Bolander is an active researcher and author. He has published over fifty articles and monographs covering various topics in the human resources area ranging from labour-management cooperation to team training. His articles appear in such academic and practitioner journals as *Labor Studies Journal*, *HR Magazine*,

Labor Law Journal, Journal of Collective Negotiations in the Public Sector, Public Personnel Management, National Productivity Review, Personnel, Employee Relations Law Journal, and *Journal of Individual Employment Rights.*

Before beginning his teaching career, Dr. Bohlander served as Human Resource administrator for General Telephone Company of California. His duties included recruitment and selection, training and development, equal employment opportunity, and labour relations. He was very active in resolving employee grievances and in arbitration preparation. Dr. Bohlander continues to be a consultant to both public- and private-sector organizations, and he has worked with such organizations as the U.S. Postal Service, Kaiser Cement, McDonnell Douglas, Arizona Public Service, American Productivity Center, Rural Metro Corporation, BF Goodrich, and Del Webb. Dr. Bohlander is also an active labour arbitrator. He received his Ph.D. from the University of California at Los Angeles and his MBA from the University of Southern California.

Scott A. Snell

Scott A. Snell is Professor of Management at The Pennsylvania State University. During his career, Dr. Snell has taught courses in human resources management, principles of management, and strategic management to undergraduate, graduates, and executives. In addition to his teaching duties, Dr. Snell also serves as director of research for Penn State's Institute for the Study of Organizational Effectiveness.

As an industry consultant, Professor Snell has worked with companies such as Arthur Andersen, AT&T, GE, IBM, and Shell Chemical to redesign human resource systems to cope with changes in the competitive environment. His specialization is the realignment of staffing, training, and reward systems to complement technology, quality, and other strategic initiatives. Recently, his work has centred on the development of human capital as a source of competitive advantage.

Dr. Snell's research has been published in the *Academy of Management Journal, Academy of Management Review, Human Resource Management Review, Industrial Relations, Journal of Business Research, Journal of Management, Journal of Managerial Issues, Organizational Dynamics, Organizational Studies, Personnel Administrator, Personnel Psychology, Strategic Management Journal,* and *Working Woman.* With Thomas S. Bateman, he is also co-author of *Management: Building Competitive Human Resource Management Advantage.* In addition, Dr. Snell has served on the editorial boards of *Journal of Managerial Issues, Digest of Management Research, Human Resource Management Review, Human Resource Management,* and *Academy of Management Journal.*

He holds a B.A. in psychology from Miami University (Ohio), as well as MBA and Ph.D. degrees in business administration from Michigan State University. His professional associations include the Strategic Management Society, Academy of Management, and the Society for Human Resource Management.

Arthur W. Sherman, Jr.

Arthur W. Sherman, Jr., is Professor of Psychology, California State University, Sacramento. During most of his academic career he has taught undergraduate and graduate courses in organizational psychology, personnel psychology, human resources management, psychological testing, and professional development in psychology. Dr. Sherman has served as a consultant to several organizations, including the Department of Consumer Affairs of the State of California and the Social Security Administration. He has been a participant in seminars and workshops for twelve consecutive years as a lecturer in the management development program conducted by the CSUS School of Business Administration for the federal government. For over twenty years he had a private practice as a licensed psychologist specializing in career counselling.

He has been an author of this book since its first edition as well as *Personnel Practices of American Companies in Europe*, published by the American Management Association.

As an undergraduate, Dr. Sherman attended Oberlin College and Ohio University, receiving a B.A. in psychology from The Ohio University. He received an M.A. from Indiana University and a Ph.D. in industrial and counselling psychology from Ohio State University. His professional affiliations include the American Psychological Association, the Society for Industrial and Organizational Psychology, and the Academy of Management.

After studying this chapter, you should be able to

OBJECTIVE 1
Identify how firms gain sustainable competitive advantage through people.

OBJECTIVE 2
Explain how globalization is influencing human resources management.

OBJECTIVE 3
Describe the impact of information technology on managing people.

OBJECTIVE 4
Identify the importance of change management.

OBJECTIVE 5
State HR's role in developing intellectual capital.

OBJECTIVE 6
Differentiate how TQM and re-engineering influence HR systems.

OBJECTIVE 7
Discuss the impact of cost pressures on HR policies.

OBJECTIVE 8
Discuss the primary demographic and employee concerns pertaining to HRM.

OBJECTIVE 9
Provide examples of the roles and competencies of today's HR managers.

THE CHALLENGE OF HUMAN RESOURCES MANAGEMENT

There's an old joke that goes … The organization of the future will be so technologically advanced that it will be run by just one person and a dog. The person will be there to feed the dog, and the dog will be there to make sure the person doesn't touch anything.

In the past, observers feared that machines might one day eliminate the need for people at work. In reality, just the opposite has been occurring: people are more important in today's organizations than ever before. Managers use a lot of words to describe the importance of people to their organizations. The term "human resources" implies that people have capabilities that drive organizational performance (along with other resources such as money, materials, information, and the like). Other terms such as "human capital" and "intellectual assets" all have in common the idea that people make the difference in how an organization performs. Successful organizations are especially adept at bringing together different kinds of people to achieve a common purpose. This is the essence of human resources management. **Human resources management** (HRM) is a set of interrelated functions and processes whose goal is to attract, socialize, motivate, maintain, and retain an organization's employees.

Human resources management

A set of interrelated functions and processes whose goal is to attract, socialize, motivate, maintain, and retain an organization's employees

WHY STUDY HUMAN RESOURCES MANAGEMENT (HRM)?

As you embark on this course, you may be wondering how the topic of human resources management relates to your interests and career aspirations. The answer to the question "Why study HRM?" is pretty much the same whether you plan on working in an HR department or not. Staffing the organization, designing jobs and teams, developing skilful employees, identifying approaches for improving employee performance, and rewarding employee successes—all typically labelled HRM issues—are as relevant to line managers as they are to managers in the HR department.

To work with people effectively, we have to understand human behaviour, and we have to be knowledgeable about the various systems and practices available to help us build a skilled and motivated workforce. At the same time, we have to be aware of economic, technological, social, and legal issues that either facilitate or constrain our efforts to achieve organizational goals.

Competitive Advantage through People

While people have always been central to organizations, today they have taken on an even more central role in building a firm's competitive advantage. Especially in knowledge-based industries such as software and information services, success increasingly depends on "people-embodied know-how"—on the knowledge, skills, and abilities embedded in an organization's members.[1] In fact, more and more experts are arguing that the key to a firm's success is establishing a set of **core competencies**—integrated knowledge sets within the organization that distinguish it from its competitors and deliver value to customers. McDonald's, for example, has developed core competencies in management efficiency and training. Federal Express Canada has core competencies in package routing, delivery, and employee relations. Canon Corporation has core competencies in precision mechanics, fine optics, and microelectronics.[2] Core competencies tend to be limited in number, but they provide a long-term basis for technology innovation, product development, and service delivery.

Core competencies

Integrated knowledge sets within an organization that distinguish it from its competitors and deliver value to customers

WWW

Organizations can achieve a sustained competitive advantage through people if they meet the following criteria:[3]

WWW

1. *The resources are of value.* People are a source of competitive advantage when they improve the efficiency or effectiveness of the company. Value is increased when employees find ways to decrease costs, or provide something unique to customers, or some combination of the two. Empowerment programs, total-quality initiatives, and continuous improvement efforts at companies such as Chrysler Canada and Quebec Beaucherons are intentionally designed to increase the value that employees add to the bottom line.

WWW

2. *The resources are rare.* People are a source of competitive advantage when their skills, knowledge, and abilities are not equally available to competitors. Companies such as Microsoft, Corel, and McKinsey invest a great deal to hire and train the best and the brightest employees with the goal of acquiring an advantage over their competitors.

WWW

3. *The resources are difficult to imitate.* People are a source of competitive advantage when employee capabilities and contributions cannot be copied by others. Disney and Xerox Canada are known for creating unique cultures that get the most from employees (through teamwork) and are difficult to imitate.

WWW

4. *The resources are organized.* People are a source of competitive advantage when their talents can be combined and deployed on new assignments at a moment's notice. Companies such as AT&T Canada have invested in information technology that helps them allocate and track employee assignments to temporary projects. Teamwork and cooperation are two other pervasive methods for ensuring an organized workforce.

These four criteria highlight the importance of people and show the closeness of HRM to strategic management. The number one issue keeping Canadian executives awake at night is staffing—particularly the recruitment and retention of skilled employees.[4] Because employee skills, knowledge, and abilities are among the most distinctive and renewable resources a company can draw on, the strategic management of those resources is more important than ever. Attracting and retaining skilled and motivated employees is the number one challenge facing managers today, as noted in Highlights in HRM 1. As Thomas J. Watson, founder of IBM, said: "You can get capital and erect buildings, but it takes people to build a business."[5]

WWW

HRM practices and policies must be aligned with organizational strategy. For an organization, strategy involves formulating an organization's mission, and its goals and objectives, and then developing action plans that take into consideration competitive forces and environmental influences. When banks decide to merge for competitive reasons, the impact on human resources is considerable. The acquisition of Kmart by The Bay introduced the need for HR policies and practices that would support this strategic decision. HR strategy can be viewed as a relatively passive activity when it serves merely to ensure that the right numbers of people with the right skills are in place to advance corporate objectives. Sometimes, however, HR strategy determines corporate objectives, as when a company with employees highly skilled in customer service decides to establish a new call centre division. In both cases, the organization hopes to achieve its goals by deploying its employees effectively.[6] As will be seen in Chapter 4, the role of the human resources department is critical to the achieving of organizational goals.

Highlights in HRM

1 THE WAR FOR TALENT

Employees are the number one competitive advantage. Employers are investing millions to become employers of choice and to attract skilled candidates to their doors. These recruitment strategies range from creatively designed and linked Web home pages, to the careful building up of the brand "employer of choice."

Most of us are aware that information technology employees are in high demand. What we less often realize is that labour shortages exist in most industries. For example, traditionally low-tech sectors such as construction and auto parts manufacturing are experiencing a slowdown in growth because they cannot find the 34,000 tradespeople they need. The unemployment rate is the lowest in years. Classified job ads have increased by nearly 20 percent in Alberta alone.

This battle for talent has resulted in some "unfair" fights. Companies are fighting to protect themselves from the aggressive recruiting practices of their competitors. Losing a key employee can mean losing trade secrets, knowledge, and clients. Companies such as Investors Group are suing their competitors for millions of dollars in damages, alleging that their managers and financial advisors were targeted and raided. The numbers are staggering—460 advisors left the Investors Group in 2000, and 790 quit the year before. Raiding per se is not illegal in Canada. The charges are more closely related to inducing a breach of employment contract and intent to do harm.

WWW

Source: L. Cassiani, L "Legal Action Taken in War over Talent" *Canadian HR Reporter,* October 23, 2000: 1; "Labour Shortage Stunts Manufacturing Growth," *Canadian HR Reporter,* October 23, 2000: 2.

While "competing through people" may be a theme for human resources management, the idea remains only a framework for action. On a day-to-day basis, managers focus on specific challenges and issues that pertain to human resources. Figure 1.1 provides an overall framework for human resources management. From this figure, we can see that HRM has to help blend many aspects of management; at this point we will simply classify them as either "competitive challenges" or "employee concerns." By balancing sometimes competing demands, HRM plays an important role in getting the most from employees and providing a work environment that meets their short-term and long-term needs. We will use this framework as a basis for our discussion throughout the rest of this chapter. However, remember that the purpose of all these activities and concerns is to help the organization achieve its objectives. Indeed, the framework could be expanded to include specific organizational outcomes such as profits, or efficiencies, or employee motivation or client satisfaction, depending on the specific organizational goals.

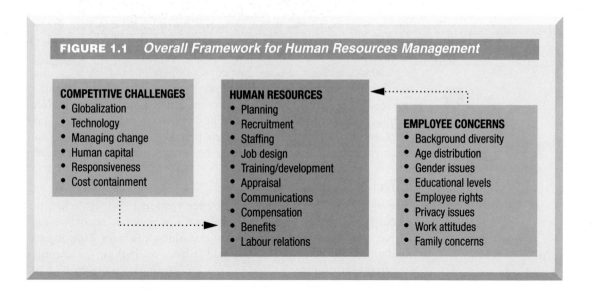

FIGURE 1.1   *Overall Framework for Human Resources Management*

COMPETITIVE CHALLENGES
- Globalization
- Technology
- Managing change
- Human capital
- Responsiveness
- Cost containment

HUMAN RESOURCES
- Planning
- Recruitment
- Staffing
- Job design
- Training/development
- Appraisal
- Communications
- Compensation
- Benefits
- Labour relations

EMPLOYEE CONCERNS
- Background diversity
- Age distribution
- Gender issues
- Educational levels
- Employee rights
- Privacy issues
- Work attitudes
- Family concerns

COMPETITIVE CHALLENGES AND HUMAN RESOURCES MANAGEMENT

WWW

For over a decade, the Society for Human Resource Management and the Commerce Clearing House have sponsored an ongoing study of the most important trends and issues facing HR. These key trends extend beyond "people issues" per se, but they all focus on the need to develop a skilled and flexible workforce in order to compete in the twenty-first century:[7]

- going global
- embracing new technology
- managing change
- developing human capital
- responding to the market
- containing costs

OBJECTIVE **2**

Challenge 1: Going Global

In order to grow and prosper, many companies are seeking business opportunities in global markets. Competition and cooperation with foreign companies have become increasingly important focal points for business since the early 1980s.

Impact of Globalization

WWW

Globalization

Trend toward opening up foreign markets to international trade and investment

By partnering with firms in other regions of the world and using information technologies to coordinate distant parts of their businesses, companies such as Motorola, General Electric, and SNC Lavalin have shown that their vision for the future is to offer customers "anything, anytime, anywhere" around the world. But **globalization** is not just something of interest to large firms. Though estimates vary widely, it is believed that 70 to 85 percent of the Canadian economy today is affected by international competition.

Efforts to lower trade barriers and to open up global markets to the free flow of goods, services, and capital among nations have created three zones of economic activity. In North America, the North American Free Trade Agreement (NAFTA) was created to facilitate commerce between Canada, Mexico, and the United States. Although some opponents of NAFTA have feared the loss of jobs to Mexico, where wages are lower, proponents of NAFTA argue that the agreement is helping remove impediments to trade and investment, and thereby creating jobs.[8] Whereas NAFTA focuses on markets in the Western Hemisphere, the European Union (EU) focuses on the integration of Europe, and the Asia Pacific Economic Cooperation (APEC) has helped establish freer trade among Pacific Rim countries. The impact of these trade agreements has been great.

WWW

Effect of Globalization on HRM

For all the opportunities afforded by international business, when managers talk about "going global," they have to balance a complicated set of issues related to different geographies, cultures, laws, and business practices. Human resource issues underlie each of these concerns and include such things as identifying capable expatriate managers who live and work overseas; designing training programs and development opportunities to enhance managers' understanding of foreign cultures and work practices; and adjusting compensation plans to ensure that pay schemes are fair and equitable across individuals in different regions with different costs of living.

So while managing across borders provides new and broader opportunities for organizations, it also represents a quantum leap in the complexity of human resources management. In fact, the international arena for HRM is so involved that we have devoted an entire chapter (Chapter 16) to discussing its competitive, cultural, and practical implications.

Challenge 2: Embracing New Technology

Advances in computer technology have enabled organizations to take advantage of the information explosion. With computer networks, unlimited amounts of data can be stored, retrieved, and used in a wide variety of ways, from simple record keeping to controlling complex equipment. In our everyday life we see bank tellers, airline reservation clerks, and supermarket cashiers using computers to perform their jobs. Nygard International, Canada's largest manufacturer of women's apparel, which produces 15 million garments annually, invested heavily in technology. This system allowed it to maintain a shipping accuracy rate of 99.9 percent (compared to 90 percent before computerization) and to reduce labour costs by 50 percent. All non-manufacturing employees spend one-third of their time on computer training.

WWW

From Touch Labour to Knowledge Workers

Knowledge workers

Workers whose responsibilities extend beyond the physical execution of work to include decision making, problem solving, and troubleshooting

Advanced technology tends to reduce the number of jobs that require little skill and to increase the number of jobs that require considerable skill. In general, this transformation is referred to as a shift from "touch labour" to "**knowledge workers**"; that is, employee responsibilities expand to include a richer array of activities such as planning, decision making, and problem solving.[9] Current employees can often be retrained to assume new roles and responsibilities. Employees who are displaced also require retraining. This is why we see pages and pages of newspaper advertisements for applicants with technical or scientific training, while large numbers of job seekers without such training register for work with employment agencies.

About 20,000 of Scotia Bank's 38,000 employees have received computer-based training, at a cost of $45 million in 1998 alone.[10]

Influence of Technology in HRM

Human resources information system (HRIS)

Computerized system that provides current and accurate data for purposes of control and decision making

Information technology has, of course, changed the face of HRM in Canada and abroad. Perhaps the central component of technology in HRM is an organization's **human resources information system** (HRIS). An HRIS provides current and accurate data for the purposes of control and decision making; in this sense it moves beyond simply storing and retrieving information to include broader applications such as producing reports, forecasting HR needs, establishing strategic plans, planning careers and promotions, and evaluating HR policies and practices (see Chapter 4). Canada Post implemented a system that allowed each of its 55,000 employees to obtain a current snapshot of pay, benefits, pension plans, and so on.[11]

One survey found that the most frequent uses of information technology include maintaining employee records, overseeing payroll operations, handling absence and vacation records, and administering recruitment and training programs.[12] BC Telecom began to use HRIS software to track employee absenteeism after discovering that as many as 700 employees out of a workforce of 17,000 were not reporting to work on any given day.[13] Federal Express recently merged its employee survey feedback process with its corporate HRIS and created an automated program that tracks 99 percent of employees throughout Canada and the United States. Alcoa's PeopleView project has integrated all human resources and payroll data worldwide into one central information system. The technology streamlines HR transactions, processes them more quickly, provides better analytical capability, and—along with other changes within HR—has saved the company more than US$40 million a year.[14]

WWW

The Internet has, of course, revolutionized our ability to access technology. A growing number of companies such as Sun Microsystems, Intel, and Hewlett-Packard (Canada) are using the Internet and company-specific "intranets," to establish home pages that allow employees and others to read current job postings and apply for positions online (see Chapter 4). Company intranets have resulted in enormous savings. Hewlett-Packard (Canada), for example, has saved $300 million over three years by distributing software through its intranet to 85,000 desktop users.[15]

WWW

Equipped with only a PC and a modem, managers can take advantage of online services designed especially for HR departments (see Highlights in HRM 2)

Each of these examples shows that technology is changing the face of HRM—altering the methods of collecting employment information, speeding up the processing of that data, and improving the process of internal and external communication.[16] In small companies in particular, managers should consider the following factors when assessing their need for an HRIS:

- initial costs and annual maintenance costs
- fit of software packages to the employee base
- ability to upgrade
- increased efficiency and time savings
- compatibility with current systems
- user-friendliness

Highlights in HRM

2   A GUIDE TO INTERNET SITES

Cyberspace offers the HR professional a large and growing set of resources for research, news, recruitment, and networking with people and organizations. Listed below are some Internet sites related to the HR field. Their addresses (URLs) are printed here for reference, but once you get started it's easier to access the rest by jumping from one of the pages that have extensive links to the Internet.

GETTING STARTED

If you're new to the Internet, the following two sites offer an introduction from an HR perspective:

WWW

- The Internet and HR: An Introduction: **www.wp.com**

This page describes the basics of getting online, including hardware requirements and Internet access providers. It provides some background on the nature of the Internet and the World Wide Web, as well as a short list of HR links.

GENERAL HR SITES

The following sites present general HR information and links to a wide range of other HR resources.

- Managing Human Resources: **belcourt.nelson.com**

This site provides up-to-date information on HR issues and links to other HR sites.

- The Human Resource Professional's Gateway to the Internet: **www.hrisolutions.com**

This site provides extensive links to HR-related WWW pages, listserv listings, and recruitment websites.

- Queen's University, Industrial Relations Centre: **www.queensu.ca**

Provides information about the centre's program and its library, and offers research links to libraries.

- Conference Board of Canada: **www.conferenceboard.c**a

Provides information about board activities and lists recent reports on economic trends.

- HR Management Resources on the Internet:
  www.nbs.ntu.ac.uk/staff/lyerj/hrm_link.htm

Developed by the Nottingham Business School, this site provides links for general HR and specific subjects, as well as links for HR publications, mailing lists, consultants, and recruitment services.

- The International Alliance for Human Resources Research: **www.yorku.ca/hrresall**

This is a global alliance of HRM experts who support research in HRM and who strive to be the catalysts for the discovery, dissemination, and application of new knowledge about HRM. Its website contains research summaries written specifically for HR practitioners.

- School of Industrial and Labor Relations: **www.ilr.cornell.edu**

Provides information about the School of Industrial and Labor Relations at Cornell University and its library, and offers information on all aspects of employer–employee relations and workplace issues. Also contains HR news and extensive research links to libraries, databases, and archives.

- Canadian Council of Human Resource Associations: **www.chrpcanada.com**

Provides information about membership, news releases, and information resources, as well as links to relevant HR sites, and has links to all the provincial human resource associations.

- Human Resources Professionals Association of Ontario: **www.hrpao.org**

Provides information about current events, conferences, and current news releases.

- The Society for Human Resource Management: **www.shrm.org**

SHRM's home page includes current events, informational resources, commercial connections, and articles from SHRM publications.

- The International Personnel Management Association–Canada: **www.ipma-canada.com**

This is a professional organization for public personnel professionals.

SPECIALIZED SITES

Here are eight sites that provide specialized HR information:

- Workplace Information Directorate: **www.hrdc-drch.gc.ca**

Provides labour statistics and information on collective bargaining, wage settlements, and emerging issues.

- Statistics Canada: **www.statcan.ca**

Provides information about hours of work, earnings, and differences by gender and province.

- Technology, HR & Communication Home Page: **www.inforamp.net/~bcroft**

This site focuses on the intersection of HR and technology. Contains pages concerning virtual reality, interactive voice response, videoconferencing, and groupware.

- Telecommuting, Teleworking, and Alternative Officing: **www.gilgordon.com**

A clearinghouse for information on telecommuting and flexible hours. Links to related sites, frequently asked questions, equipment providers, and computer linking via the Internet.

- Training & Development Homepage: **www.tcm.com/trdev**

Features a job mart, business showcase, WWW training links, frequently asked questions, and training and development listserv links.
The American Compensation Association and the Canadian Compensation Association have merged to form World at Work: **www.worldatwork.org**.

- The Workflow and Reengineering International Association: **www.waria.com**

WARIA's home page includes an article database, book and conference information, and links to related websites.

RELATED SITES
The following sites provide various types of information that can prove useful to HR:

- Canadian Human Rights Commission: **www.chrc.tcdp.gc.ca/english**

Provides information about the commission's services, and about the Employment Equity Act and the Canadian Human Rights Act.

- Human Resources Development Canada: **www.hrdc-drhc.gc.ca**

Offers information about programs and services. Contains links to related sites, including all provincial departments, and to sites that provide job search assistance, such as the Electronic Labour Exchange, the Job Bank, and Can Worknet.

- Justice Department: **Canada.justice.gc.ca**

Provides information about legal cases and settlements.

- Strategis (Industry Canada): **www.strategis.ca**

Includes industry profiles and business information.

- availability of technical support
- needs for customizing
- time required to implement
- training time required for HR and payroll

WWW

Because of these implications, HR and line managers should jointly plan for the implementation of an HRIS. Employees at Trans Alta, based in Calgary, Alberta, log into the company's Employee Self Service website to get information about their pensions.[17] Also, HR managers can provide guidance to line managers to ensure that the right technological skills are identified and sought in new employees, and to develop techno-literacy training programs. HR can also identify and evaluate the changes in organizational relationships brought about by new technology. Finally, HR should work with line managers to develop new structures that use technology to improve service, increase productivity, and reduce costs.[18]

Challenge 3: Managing Change

Technology and globalization are only two of the forces driving change in organizations and HRM. As Jack Welch, CEO of General Electric, put it: "You've got to be on the cutting edge of change. You can't simply maintain the status quo, because somebody's always coming from another country with another product, or consumer tastes change, or the cost structure does, or there's a technology breakthrough. If you're not fast and adaptable, you're vulnerable. This is true for every segment of every business in every country in the world."[19]

Types of Changes

Reactive change

Change that occurs after external forces have already affected performance

Proactive change

Change initiated to take advantage of targeted opportunities

Programs focused on total quality, continuous improvement, downsizing, re-engineering, outsourcing, and the like are all examples of organizations making changes to modify the way they operate in order to be more successful. Some of these changes are **reactive**—that is, they are made when external forces have already affected an organization's performance. Other changes are more **proactive**—that is, initiated by managers to take advantage of targeted opportunities, especially in fast-changing industries in which followers are not successful. Jack Welch, for example, recognized GE's need for change while the company was performing quite well and set in motion a series of actions to make GE a leader in all of its businesses. His goal was to bring about "boundarylessness" within the company by fostering better cooperation among parts of the business. To accomplish this goal, Welch and Steve Kerr, GE's vice president of learning, instituted a program called "Workout!" This program was designed to involve employees in instituting continuous innovation and improvement.[20] These types of change initiatives are not designed to fix problems that have arisen in the organization so much as they are designed to help renew everyone's focus on key success factors.

Managing Change through HR

In a survey, 84 percent of executives polled said they had at least one change initiative going on in their organization. Yet surprisingly, in contrast to the GE experience, only about two-thirds said that their companies had any sort of formal change-management program to support these initiatives![21] This is unfortunate since successful change rarely occurs naturally or easily. Most of the main reasons why change efforts fail come down to HR issues. Some of the top reasons are as follows:[22]

- Not establishing a sense of urgency.
- Not creating a powerful coalition to guide the effort.
- Lacking leaders who have a vision.
- Lacking leaders who communicate the vision.
- Not removing obstacles to the new vision.
- Not systematically planning for and creating short-term "wins."
- Declaring victory too soon.
- Not anchoring changes in the corporate culture.

Most employees, regardless of occupation, understand that the way things were done five or ten years ago is very different from how they are done today (or will be done five or ten years from now). Responsibilities change, job assignments change, work processes change. And this change is continuous—a part of the job—

rather than temporary. Nevertheless, people often resist change because it requires them to modify or abandon ways of working that have been successful or at least familiar to them. As Dr. Marilyn Buckner, president of National Training Systems, put it: "Nontechnical, unattended human factors are, in fact, most often the problem in failed change projects."[23] To manage change, executives and managers have to envision the future, communicate this vision to employees, set clear expectations for performance, and develop the capability to execute by reorganizing people and reallocating assets. Of course, this is easier said than done. It follows that all managers, including those in HR, have an important role in facilitating change processes, particularly in helping communicate business needs to employees and in listening to employee concerns.

Challenge 4: Developing Human Capital

The idea that organizations "compete through people" highlights the fact that success increasingly depends on an organization's ability to manage human capital. The term **human capital** describes the economic value of knowledge, skills, and capabilities. Although the value of these assets may not show up on a company's balance sheet, it nevertheless has tremendous impact on an organization's performance. According to Lewis Platt, CEO of Hewlett-Packard, "Successful companies of the 21st century will be those who do the best jobs of capturing, storing and leveraging what their employees know."[24]

Human capital

The knowledge, skills, and abilities of individuals that have economic value to an organization

Human Capital and HRM

Human capital is intangible and elusive and cannot be managed the way organizations manage jobs, products, and technologies. One of the reasons for this is that employees, not the organization, own their own human capital. If valued employees leave a company, they take their human capital with them, and any investment the company has made in training and developing those people is lost. However, the HRM systems, such as selection and training programs, that are embedded in the organization can be used to generate more human capital.[25]

To build human capital in organizations, managers must begin to develop strategies for ensuring that superior knowledge, experience, and skills are found within their workforce. Staffing programs focus on identifying, recruiting, and hiring the best and the brightest talent available. Training programs complement these staffing practices by providing skill enhancement, especially in areas that cannot be transferred to another company if an employee should leave.[26] In addition, employees need opportunities for development on the job. The most highly valued intelligence tends to be associated with competencies and capabilities that are learned from experience and are not easily taught.[27] Consequently, managers have to do a good job of providing developmental assignments to employees and making certain that job duties and requirements are flexible enough to allow for growth and learning.

Beyond the need to invest in employee development, organizations have to find ways of utilizing the knowledge that currently exists. Too often, employees have skills that go unused. According to Lief Edvinsson, director of intellectual capital for Skandia Insurance, "The value of knowledge management comes from application, not storage." At Clarica (formerly the Mutual Group) of Waterloo, Ontario, there is a pathway from the creation to the dissemination and utilization of knowledge. Bruncor (the parent company of NB Tel, New Brunswick's telecommunications company) has created the Living Lab, a think tank that pro-

WWW

duces, applies, packages and sells knowledge. Efforts to empower employees and encourage their participation and involvement more fully utilize the human capital available.[28] (Employee empowerment is discussed fully in Chapter 3.)

WWW

In companies such as Bell Canada and ORTECH Corporation, managers and employees are evaluated on their progress toward meeting developmental goals. These goals focus on skill development and on gaining new competencies and capabilities. In a growing number of instances, pay is attached to this knowledge and skill acquisition. Skill-based pay, for example, rewards employees for each new class of jobs they are capable of performing. We will discuss skill-based pay (or pay for knowledge) more in Chapter 9.

Developmental assignments, especially those involving teamwork, can also be a valuable way of facilitating knowledge exchange and mutual learning. Effective communications (whether face to face or using information technology) are instrumental in sharing knowledge and making it widely available throughout the organization. As Dave Ulrich, professor of business at the University of Michigan, noted: "Learning capability is g times g—a business's ability to generate new ideas multiplied by its adeptness at generalizing them throughout the company."[29]

WWW

HR programs and assignments are often the conduit through which knowledge is transferred among employees. Hughes Space & Communications Company, the world's largest producer of commercial communications satellites, has created a "lessons learned architecture" on the Internet where all areas of the company can store the knowledge they have learned. Through the World Wide Web, initial pieces of information and intellectual capital were posted to the company's electronic newsgroups. This information was then analyzed and consolidated by editorial teams. Employees could then access and use this new codified knowledge directly through the Internet. Executives at Hughes estimate that this form of structural capital has reduced the cost of developing a satellite by as much as US$25 million.[30]

HR managers and line managers both play an important role in creating an organization that understands the value of knowledge, documents the skills and capabilities available to the organization, and identifies ways of utilizing that knowledge to benefit the firm. We will address these issues throughout the text, but particularly in Chapters 6 and 7 on training and career development.

OBJECTIVE 6

Challenge 5: Responding to the Market

Meeting customer expectations is essential for any organization. Besides focusing on internal management issues, managers must also meet customer requirements of quality, innovation, variety, and responsiveness. These standards often separate the winners from the losers in today's competitive world. How well does a company understand its customers' needs? How fast can it develop and get a new product to market? How effectively has it responded to special concerns? "*Better, faster, cheaper ...*" These standards require organizations to constantly align their processes with customer needs. Management innovations such as total quality management (TQM) and process re-engineering are but two of the comprehensive approaches to responding to customers. Each has direct implications for HR.

Total Quality Management and HRM

Total quality management (TQM) is a set of principles and practices whose core ideas include understanding customer needs, doing things right the first time, and striving for continuous improvement. The TQM revolution took hold in the mid-

Total quality management (TQM)

A set of principles and practices whose core ideas include understanding customer needs, doing things right the first time, and striving for continuous improvement

WWW

1980s, pioneered by companies such as Motorola, Xerox, and Ford. Since that time, criteria spelled out in the Malcolm Baldrige National Quality Award have provided the impetus for both large and small companies to rethink their approach to HRM.[31]

Unfortunately, TQM programs have not been a panacea for responding to customer needs and improving productivity. Often, managers view quality as a quick fix and are disillusioned when results do not come easily.

When TQM initiatives do work, it is usually because managers have made major changes in their philosophies and HR programs. A survey of 307 executives from *Fortune* 1000 companies and 308 executives from smaller firms (twenty-plus employees) found that the most important quality-improvement techniques stressed human resources issues: employee motivation, change in corporate culture, and employee education. Organizations known for product and service quality strongly believe that employees are the key to that quality.[32]

One of the reasons HR programs are so essential to TQM is that they help balance two opposing forces. According to Laurie Broedling, senior vice president of HR and quality at McDonnell Douglas, "One set of forces (the need for order and control) pulls every business toward stagnation, while another set of forces (the need for growth and creativity) drives it toward disintegration."[33] TQM's focus on continuous improvement drives the system toward disequilibrium, while TQM's focus on customers, management systems, and the like provides the restraining forces that keep the system together. HR practices help managers balance these two forces. The 230 staff at John Deere Limited Canada won the award for quality in a large service organization for their commitment to TQM. The National Quality Institute conducted a survey among Canadian small and medium-sized enterprises and found that 33.7 percent of payroll costs were devoted to quality issues in manufacturing organizations, and 37.8 percent in service organizations.

WWW

Re-engineering and HRM

Re-engineering

Fundamental rethinking and radical redesign of business processes to achieve dramatic improvements in cost, quality, service, and speed

In recent years, organizations have gone beyond TQM programs to a more comprehensive approach to process redesign called **re-engineering**. Re-engineering has been described as "the fundamental rethinking and radical redesign of business processes to achieve dramatic improvements in cost, quality, service and speed."[34] Re-engineering often requires that managers start over from scratch in rethinking how work should be done, how technology and people should interact, and how entire organizations should be structured.[35] HR issues are central to these decisions. *First*, re-engineering requires that managers create an environment for change and, as we mentioned previously, HR issues drive change. *Second*, re-engineering efforts depend on effective leadership and communication processes, two other areas related to HRM. *Third*, re-engineering requires that administrative systems be reviewed and modified. Selection, job descriptions, training, career planning, performance appraisal, compensation, and labour relations are all candidates for change to complement and support re-engineering efforts. We will return to these issues, and discuss more directly the organizational development tools necessary for reengineering, in Chapter 7.

Challenge 6: Containing Cost

Investments in re-engineering, TQM, intellectual capital, technology, globalization, and the like are all very important for organizational competitiveness. Yet at the same time, there are increasing pressures on companies to lower costs and improve productivity to maximize efficiency. Labour costs are one of the largest expenditures of any organization, particularly in service and knowledge-intensive companies. Organizations have tried a number of approaches to lower costs, especially labour costs. These include downsizing, outsourcing and employee leasing, and productivity enhancements, each of which has a direct impact on HR policies and practices.

Downsizing

Downsizing

The planned elimination of jobs

WWW

WWW

WWW

Downsizing (or its euphemism, "rightsizing") is the planned elimination of jobs. For example, when L.L. Bean saw that sales had fallen, the company undertook a number of efforts to identify what it called "smart cost reductions." L.L. Bean's TQM activities helped the company target quality problems and saved an estimated US$30 million. But the cuts were not enough, and ultimately Leon Gorman, president of the firm, and Bob Peixotto, vice president of HR and quality, realized the company needed to eliminate some jobs. But instead of simply laying off people, L.L. Bean started early retirement and "sweetened" voluntary separation programs. In 1996, the company offered employee sabbaticals for continuing education.[36] These efforts, combined with better employee communications, helped soften the blow of layoffs at L.L. Bean.

The pain of downsizing has been widespread throughout Canada. Virtually every major corporation in the country has undergone some cycle of downsizing. A survey by Terry Wagar, an award-winning researcher at Saint Mary's University in Halifax, found that about 50 percent of employers permanently reduced their workforce over a two-year period ending in 1997, with average reduction of 12.5 percent. These results suggest that downsizing is not over.[37] The 1996 Census showed that provincial government workforces decreased by 22.5 percent (62,000 employees), and the federal public service by 14.6 percent (43,800 employees) over a ten-year period.[38]

Unfortunately, the record on downsizing's value is pretty spotty. While the stock market usually reacts positively to such announcements, only about half of the companies that have eliminated jobs have seen an increase in profits. In fact, about 20 percent of the time, profits have actually dropped after downsizing. From a human resources standpoint, these results are not especially surprising. As Dick Lidstad, vice president of HR for 3M, put it, "You don't get productivity and committed employees if at the first sign of bad times you show them they're expendable." Besides instilling poor morale among survivors, downsizing incurs additional HR costs to the company such as severance pay, accrued vacation and sick-day payouts, outplacement, pension and benefit payoffs, and administrative costs. To approach downsizing more intelligently, companies such as Chevron, Hewlett-Packard, and L.L. Bean (mentioned earlier) have made special efforts to reassign and retrain employees for new positions when their jobs are eliminated. This is consistent with the philosophy of employees as assets, as intellectual capital. According to Dick Lidstad, 3M's policy is that "HR has an obligation to help maintain the relationship between a company and its employees. Downsizing ought to be painful—you need to sweat and bleed a little before you take that last step."[39] We will return to the subject of downsizing in Chapter 4.

Outsourcing

Contracting outside the organization to have work done that formerly was done by internal employees

Outsourcing and Employee Leasing

Outsourcing simply means hiring someone outside the company to perform tasks that could be done internally. Companies often hire the services of

WWW

Employee leasing

Process of dismissing employees, who are then hired by a leasing company (which handles all HR-related activities, and contracting with that company to lease back the employees)

accounting firms, for example, to take care of financial services. Interest in outsourcing has been spurred by executives who want to focus their organization's activities on what they do best—their core competencies. Increasingly, activities such as maintenance, security, catering, and payroll are being outsourced in order to increase the organization's flexibility and to lower overhead costs. Canada Trustco, based in London, Ontario, has achieved higher service levels as a result of outsourcing its desktop support operations.[40]

There are several HR concerns with regard to outsourcing, not the least of which is that if employees are likely to lose their jobs when the work is outsourced, morale and productivity can drop rapidly. To minimize problems, line and HR managers have to work together to define and communicate transition plans, minimize the number of unknowns, and help employees identify their employment options.[41]

In some cases the outside vendors may actually hire the displaced employees. This process is known as **employee leasing** and will be discussed in more detail in Chapter 4. Nortel outsourced its payroll, employee training, and human resource information centres, along with its employee expense reimbursement scheme, to Price Waterhouse Coopers, which then hired 1,000 Nortel employees to do the work. The value of employee leasing lies in the fact that an organization can essentially maintain its working relationships but shift the administrative costs of health care, retirement, and other benefits to the vendor.[42]

Productivity Enhancements

Pure cost-cutting efforts such as downsizing, outsourcing, and leasing may prove to be disappointing interventions if managers use them as simple solutions to complex performance problems. Overemphasis on labour costs perhaps misses the broader issue of productivity enhancement.

Since productivity can be defined as the "output gained from a fixed amount of inputs," organizations can increase productivity by either reducing the inputs (the cost approach) or by increasing the amount that employees produce. It is quite possible for managers to cut costs only to find that productivity falls at even a more rapid rate. Conversely, managers may find that increasing investment in employees (raising labour costs) may lead to even greater returns in enhanced productivity. Except in extremely cash-poor organizations, managers may find that looking for additional ways to boost productivity may be the best way to increase the value of their organizations.

In absolute terms, the United States remains the world's most productive nation. The gap between the Americans and Canadians continues to grow. In 1972, Canadian factories were producing at 90 percent of the American level; in 1998, this had fallen to 72 percent. In the three-year period 1996 to 1999, output per American worker grew by 2 percent, per Canadian worker by less than 1 percent. One way to close these gaps is to invest more in technology.[43]

Employee productivity is the result of a combination of employee abilities, motivation, and work environment. When productivity falls off—or more positively, when productivity improves—the change is usually traceable to enhanced skills and motivation, or to a work environment conducive to high performance. In general, this can be summarized in the following equation:

Performance = f (ability, motivation, environment)

WWW

If any of these three dimensions is low, productivity is likely to suffer.

According to a *USA Today*/Deloitte & Touche survey, three-quarters of executives said their firms would be able to increase productivity over the next three to five years by focusing more on HR issues. Figure 1.2 shows some of the topics that we cover in this textbook relating to how managers can increase productivity in their organizations.

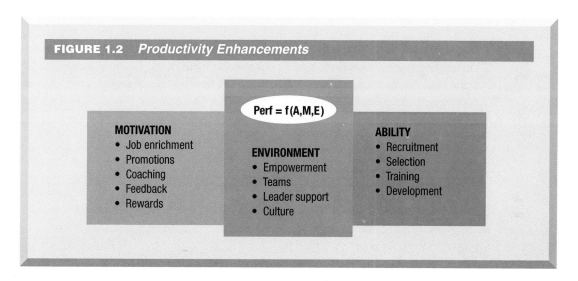

FIGURE 1.2   *Productivity Enhancements*

Perf = f(A,M,E)

MOTIVATION
- Job enrichment
- Promotions
- Coaching
- Feedback
- Rewards

ENVIRONMENT
- Empowerment
- Teams
- Leader support
- Culture

ABILITY
- Recruitment
- Selection
- Training
- Development

DEMOGRAPHIC AND EMPLOYEE CONCERNS

OBJECTIVE 8

Managers in general and HR managers in particular need to be concerned about changes in the make-up and the expectations of their employees. HRM involves being an advocate for employees, being aware of their concerns, and making sure that the exchange between the organization and its employees is mutually beneficial. Highlights in HRM 3 summarizes social concerns in HRM. We will discuss some of these issues here and address all of these issues in greater detail throughout the book.

Demographic Changes

Among the most significant challenges to managers are the demographic changes occurring in Canada. Because they affect the workforce of an employer, these changes—in employee background, age, gender, and education—are important topics for discussion.

Diversity of Backgrounds

Canadian workers will continue to be a diverse group. In the 1996 Census, more than one in ten Candians (11.2 percent) identified themselves as visible minorities.[44] The Chinese constitute the largest group (27 percent), followed by South Asians (21 percent) and blacks (18 percent).[45] Much of this growth is due to the arrival of immigrants, who often are of working age but have different educational and occupational backgrounds from those of the traditional Western European immigrant groups.

Highlights in HRM

3   SOCIAL ISSUES IN HUMAN RESOURCES MANAGEMENT

CHANGING DEMOGRAPHICS

The coming decades will bring a more diverse and more quickly aging workforce. This has major implications for all aspects of HRM as it will alter traditional experience and expectations regarding the labour pool. Among the issues in this area are

- shrinking pool of entry-level workers
- productivity
- individual differences
- retirement benefits
- skills development and flexibility in skills mix
- use of temporary employees

EMPLOYER/EMPLOYEE RIGHTS

This is clearly an important and growing area of debate and concern. To some degree, it reflects the shift in employer/employee negotiations from the bargaining table to the courtroom, as organizations and individuals attempt to define rights, obligations, and responsibilities. Among the many specific issues covered in this broad area are:

- job as an entitlement
- right to work
- concern for privacy
- AIDS
- comparable worth
- mandated benefits

ATTITUDES TOWARD WORK AND FAMILY

Because of the increase in the number of working women and in employee mobility, and a growing concern about family issues, there is increasing demand for recognition and support of family-related concerns. Among the issues in this area are:

- day care
- job sharing
- alternative work schedules
- elder care
- job rotation
- parental leave
- telecommuting
- flextime

To accommodate the shift in demographics, many organizations have increased their efforts to recruit and train a more diverse workforce. Treasury Board President Marcel Masse, in setting up a task force to determine why visible minorities are underrepresented among federal employees, made this comment: "The public service has to be more representative of the society it is working for."[46] Chapter 2 will highlight what companies are doing to manage this diversity.

Age Distribution of Employees

Past fluctuations in the birthrates of Canadians are producing abrupt changes in the makeup of the labour force. The number of older workers (age fifty-five and above) is beginning to rise as baby boomers approach retirement age. In contrast, the youth share of the labour force is projected to drop, placing a strain on those businesses looking for first-time employees entering the job market.[47]

WWW

Imbalance in the age distribution of our labour force has significant implications for employers. At Algoma Steel, for example, the average age of employees is forty-nine. It is expected that within ten years close to 50 percent of Algoma's workforce will retire.[48] On the other hand, those who constitute the population bulge are experiencing greater competition for advancement from others of approximately the same age. This situation challenges the ingenuity of managers to develop career patterns for employees to smooth out gaps in the numbers and kinds of employees.

WWW

Some employers, such as Days Inn Hotels, are making positive efforts to attract older workers, especially those who have taken early retirement. Older workers, for example, have significantly lower accident rates and absenteeism than younger workers. Furthermore, they tend to report higher job satisfaction scores. And while some motor skills and cognitive abilities may start to decline (starting around age twenty-five), most individuals find ways to compensate for this fact so that there is no discernible impact on their performance.

WWW

There is an old cliché: "You can't teach an old dog new tricks." Probably we should revise this to say, "You can't teach an old dog the same way you teach a puppy." To address the fact that seniors learn in different ways, McDonald's, a heavy recruiter of older workers, has developed its McMasters program in which newly hired seniors work alongside experienced employees so that in a matter of four weeks they are able to work on their own. The training program is designed to help seniors "unlearn" old behaviours while acquiring new skills. At Kenworth's St-Thérèse factory, a retraining program for older workers resulted in a 19 percent increase in productivity.[49] More programs like these will be talked about throughout the book.

Gender Distribution of the Workforce

WWW

According to projections by Statistics Canada, women will continue to join the Canadian labour force and are expected to account for about 48 percent of it by 2006. Employers are under constant pressure to ensure equality for women with respect to employment, advancement opportunities, and compensation. They also need to accommodate working mothers and fathers through parental leaves, part-time employment, flexible work schedules, job sharing, telecommuting, and child-care assistance. Also, because more women are working, employers are more sensitive to the growing need for policies and procedures to eliminate sexual harassment in the workplace. Some organizations have special orientation programs to acquaint all personnel with the problem and to warn potential offenders of the consequences. Many employers are demanding that managers and supervisors enforce their sexual harassment policies vigorously. The basic components of such policies will be presented in Chapter 2. Nora Spinks, an expert in work/life balance, comments on these issues in Highlights in HRM 4.

Rising Levels of Education

In recent years the educational attainment of the Canadian labour force has risen dramatically. Not coincidentally, the most secure and fastest-growing sectors of employment over the past few decades have been in those areas requiring higher levels of education. Those with more education make more money.[50] Figure 1.3 shows the average payoff in annual earnings from education. Census figures for 1996 show that 40 percent of the population had graduated from a university or other postsecondary institutions—a 29 percent increase over the 1981 figures.[51]

It is important to note that while the educational level of the workforce has continued to rise, there is a widening gap between the educated and noneducated, leading to different types of work experiences, as illustrated in Ethics in HRM. At the lower end of the educational spectrum, many employers are having to cope with individuals who are functionally illiterate—that is, unable to read, write, calculate,

Highlights in HRM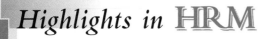

4   WORK LIFE HARMONY

www

Nora Spinks, President and CEO of Work Life Harmony, comments on the demographic issues affecting employee behaviour: "Women are in the workplace to stay; they have fewer and shorter career breaks and have more opportunities to make or influence organizational decisions. There is a high proportion of the aging 'boomer' workforce that are asking, 'What is my legacy?' They are rethinking priorities and lifestyles and reducing the number of hours they are working. At the same time, the nexus generation is entering the workforce and managerial positions with a fresh perspective and different outlook on the work experience. They see work as a means to having a life, not as life in and of itself. The boomers tend to live to work, the nexus generation work to live. Growing up, they witnessed people give up a life for the sake of a job, only to see them ultimately lose employment in periods of downsizing and restructuring. They don't want the same experience.

"A recent international study of students found that young people about to enter the workforce wanted to have a challenging career with plenty of opportunity to grow personally and professionally, *and* they wanted to be able to take advantage of those opportunities while achieving work-life balance. It is up to organizations, executives, and managers to create the kinds of environments to make that possible. It is the only way for them to meet increasing customer/client demands, meet the challenges of global competition, and reach their organizational objectives."

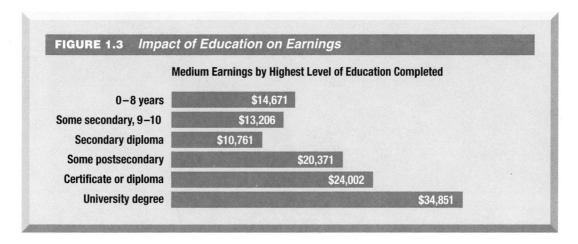

Source: Statistics Canada, Survey of Consumer Finance, 1996: 229.

or solve problems at a level that enables them to perform even the simplest technical tasks. Here are some frightening statistics: A recent study by the International Adult Literacy Survey found that one-fifth of Canadians could not understand the label on a bottle of Aspirin well enough to give the safe dosage, and only 4 out of 100 could calculate the percentage of calories in a Big Mac that came from fat.[52] A survey that tested the reading and math skills of over 5,000 employed Canadians found that as many as one in eighteen may not have the skills to do their jobs."[53]

HR managers are interested in these job trends because of their effects on all of the HRM functions. For example, given that minorities and women are increasing their share of the labour force, HR managers often analyze how each group is represented in both fast-growing and slow-growing occupations. Women, for example, are fairly well represented in fast-growing occupations such as services, but they are also represented in some slow-growth occupations such as secretarial, computer processing, and financial records processing. For some visible minorities, the data are less encouraging and have given rise to a number of efforts to encourage minority recruitment, selection, and training. (These efforts will be discussed in Chapter 2.)

But these are only the initial efforts to provide an overall environment that values and utilizes a diverse workforce. **Managing diversity** means being acutely aware of characteristics common to employees, while also managing these employees as individuals. It means not just tolerating or accommodating all sorts of differences but supporting, nurturing, and utilizing these differences to the organization's advantage. Figure 1.4 shows the results of a recent study that summarizes the major business-related reasons for managing diversity.

Managing diversity

Being aware of characteristics common to employees, while also managing employees as individuals

The Changing Nature of the Job

The era of the full-time permanent job seems to have disappeared. Nearly half of all the jobs created in the last two decades have been nonstandard—that is, part-time, temporary, or contract work. As job security erodes, so do pension plans and

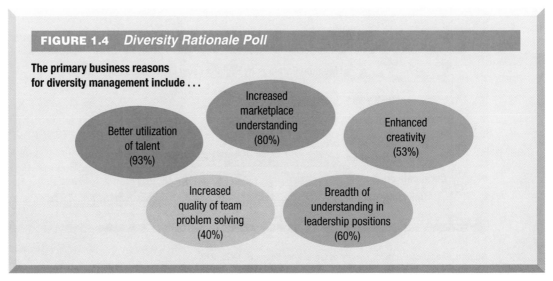

FIGURE 1.4 *Diversity Rationale Poll*

The primary business reasons for diversity management include . . .

Better utilization of talent (93%)

Increased marketplace understanding (80%)

Enhanced creativity (53%)

Increased quality of team problem solving (40%)

Breadth of understanding in leadership positions (60%)

Source: Survey data from Gail Robinson and Kathleen Dechant, "Building a Business Case for Diversity," *The Academy of Management Executive* 11, no. 3 (August 1997): 21–31. Reprinted with permission.

health care benefits, especially for part-timers. Nonstandard jobs represent about 30 percent of all employment now. The number of Canadians who are self-employed has also risen, from 10 percent in 1976 to 18 percent in 1998. As shown in Ethics in HRM, labour force participants have become increasingly polarized into haves and have-nots. We return to the subject of changing employment options in Chapter 4.

Cultural Changes

The attitudes, beliefs, values, and customs of the people in a society are an integral part of their culture. Naturally, their culture affects their behaviour on the job and the environment within the organization; these in turn influence how they react to work assignments, leadership styles, and reward systems. Like the external and internal environments of which it is a part, culture is constantly changing. HR policies and procedures therefore must be adjusted to cope with this change.

Employee Rights

Over the past few decades, federal legislation has radically changed the rules for managing employees by granting them many specific rights. For example, there are now laws granting the right to equal employment opportunity (Chapter 2), union representation if desired (Chapters 14 and 15), a safe and healthful work environment (Chapter 12), a pension plan that is fiscally sound (Chapter 11), equal pay for men and women performing essentially the same jobs (Chapter 9), and privacy in the workplace. An expanded discussion of the specific areas in which rights and responsibilities are of concern to employers and employees will be presented in Chapter 13.

Ethics in HRM

SKYWALKERS AND GROUNDWORKERS

Canadian workers can be divided into two classes: skywalkers and groundworkers. Skywalkers, those working in white-collar jobs in highrise buildings, are well educated and well trained and earn good incomes. Their jobs are secure and they receive full benefits. For these knowledge workers, the employment prospects in computer programming, financial analysis, insurance, business services, and real estate are bright. Those working in the high-rises on Bay Street, Howe Street, and rue St-Jacques earned a weekly average of $1,469 in 1996—a 62 percent increase from 1990. (The average Canadian worker earns about $604 per week.)

Below the highrise buildings toil the groundworkers. Those with little education and out-dated skills are suffering massive unemployment. Groundworkers suffer further from job insecurity and lack of benefit programs. Look for these workers in restaurants, hotels, and shops. The "McJobs" they hold in the accommodation, food, and beverage industries paid a mere $240 per week in 1996—a .005 percent increase since 1990. Those working part-time—a growing segment of the Canadian economy—fare even worse. Companies have dis-covered cost savings by replacing full-time employees with part-time workers, thereby eliminating benefits and increasing staffing flexibility. This restructuring of the job market has produced winners and losers, but many would argue that all Canadians lose when the unem-ployment rate is 9 percent and citizens feel insecure about their futures.

Source: Statistics Canada, *Statistics Canada Measures of Weekly Earnings*, Cat. No. 72-0002-XPB, 1997.

Concern for Privacy

HR managers and their staffs, as well as line managers in positions of responsibility, generally recognize the importance of discretion in handling all types of informa-tion about employees. The misuse of such information is prohibited under the Privacy Act of 1982. Privacy issues, such as electronic monitoring, drug testing, and use of employee records, have come under increasing scrutiny in recent years.[54]

WWW

Employer responses to the issue of information privacy vary widely. IBM was one of the first companies to show concern for how personal information about employees was handled. It began restricting the release of information as early as 1965 and in 1971 developed a comprehensive privacy policy. Dow Corning Corporation and Avis are two other employers that have developed privacy pro-grams.[55] We will discuss the content of such programs and present some recom-mended privacy guidelines in Chapter 13.

Changing Attitudes Toward Work

Another well-established trend is for employees to define success in terms of per-sonal self-expression and fulfilment of potential on the job. They are often less obsessed with the acquisition of wealth and now view life satisfaction as more likely to result from balancing the challenges and rewards of work with those in their personal lives. Though most people still enjoy work, and want to excel at it,

As more and more employees strive to balance the demands of their jobs with the needs of their families, employers are responding by offering greater flexibility in the workplace.

they tend to be focused on finding interesting work and may pursue multiple careers rather than being satisfied with just "having a job." People also appear to be seeking ways of living that are less complicated but more meaningful. These new lifestyles cannot help but have an impact on how employees must be motivated and managed. Consequently, HRM has become more complex than it was when employees were concerned mainly with economic survival.[56]

Balancing Work and Family

Work and the family are connected in many subtle and not so subtle social, economic, and psychological ways. Because of the new forms that the family has taken—for example, the two-income family and the single-parent family—work organizations are finding it necessary to provide employees with more family-friendly options. "Family friendly" is a broad term that may include unconventional hours, day care, part-time work, job sharing, pregnancy leave, parental leave, executive transfers, spousal involvement in career planning, assistance with family problems, and telecommuting. These kinds of programs can increase productivity by 20 percent and reduce turnover by 50 percent. Demands for work/life balance are not just coming from overstressed workers with children and aging parents. They are also driven by young workers who want a healthy balance between their personal and working lives. These issues, which have become important considerations for all managers, are discussed more fully in Chapter 11. Figure 1.5 shows some of the top concerns managers have about balancing work and home.

Some of the most progressive companies, such as Levi Strauss, PepsiCo, and the Bank of Montreal, promote flexibility throughout their organizations.[57] In general,

WWW

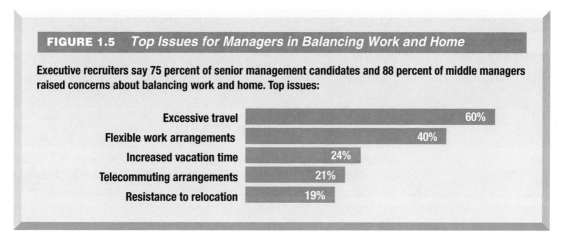

FIGURE 1.5   *Top Issues for Managers in Balancing Work and Home*

Executive recruiters say 75 percent of senior management candidates and 88 percent of middle managers raised concerns about balancing work and home. Top issues:

Excessive travel	60%
Flexible work arrangements	40%
Increased vacation time	24%
Telecommuting arrangements	21%
Resistance to relocation	19%

Source: Association of Executive Search Consultants (member survey). Used with permission of the Association of Executive Search Consultants, www.aesc.org.

WWW

these companies have calculated that accommodating individual needs and circumstances is a powerful way to attract and retain top-calibre people. Aetna Life and Casualty, for example, has cut turnover by 50 percent since it began to offer six-month parental leaves, coupled with an option for part-time work when employees return to the job. Nations Bank provides up to six weeks of paid leave for fathers. Nations Bank also encourages all of its employees to spend two hours each week visiting their children's schools or volunteering at any school—on company time. Hugh McColl, the company's chairman, sees it this way: "It may seem inconsistent that we're asking employees to work harder now, but the need to pinch pennies and reduce head count plays to the short term, while flexibility is important to our long-term health."[58]

Arthur Andersen has developed a flexible work program that allows new parents to lighten their workloads for up to three years. There are acknowledged costs, however. In professional firms, such as accounting and law, career paths and promotion sequences are programmed in a lockstep manner. Time away from work can slow down—and in some cases derail—an individual's career advancement.

THE PARTNERSHIP OF LINE MANAGERS AND HR DEPARTMENTS

OBJECTIVE
9

We have taken a good deal of time up front in this book to outline today's competitive and social challenges to reinforce the idea that managing people is not something that occurs in a back room called the HR department. Managing people is every manager's business, and successful organizations are those which combine the experience of line managers with the expertise of HR specialists to develop and utilize the talents of employees to their greatest potential. Addressing HR issues is rarely the exclusive responsibility of HR departments acting alone. Rather, HR managers work side by side with line managers to address people-related issues in the organization. And while this relationship has not always achieved its ideal, the situation is rapidly improving. HR managers are assuming a greater role in top-management planning and decision making—a trend that reflects the growing awareness among executives that HRM can make important contributions to the success of an organization. A recent issue of the *Academy of Management Journal* was devoted to research demonstrating that effective management of human resources has a clear relationship to an organization's performance.[59]

Reality Check discusses how the new HR department is structured at Air Canada.

Responsibilities of the Human Resources Manager

Although line managers and HR managers need to work together, their responsibilities are different, as are their competencies and expertise. The major activities for which an HR manager is typically responsible are as follows:

1. *Advice and counsel.* The HR manager often serves as an in-house consultant to supervisors, managers, and executives. Given their knowledge of internal employment issues (policies, labour agreements, past practices, and the needs of employees) and their awareness of external trends (economic and employment data, legal issues, and the like), HR managers can be an invaluable resource for making decisions. As in-house consultants, HR managers should concern themselves with the operating goals of the managers and supervisors. For their part, these managers must understand that the HR staff are there to help them increase their productivity rather than to raise obstacles to their goals. Thus the HR executive must be able not only to consider problems from the perspective of line managers and supervisors but also to communicate with the managers and supervisors.[60]

2. *Service.* HR managers also engage in a host of service activities such as recruiting, selecting, testing, planning and conducting training programs, managing redeployment and downsizing activities, and hearing employee concerns and complaints. Technical expertise in these areas is essential for HR managers and forms the basis of HR program design and implementation.

3. *Policy formulation and implementation.* HR managers generally propose and draft new policies or policy revisions to cover recurring problems or to prevent anticipated problems. Ordinarily, these are proposed to the senior executives of the organization, who actually issue the policies. HR managers may monitor the performance of line departments and other staff departments to ensure conformity with established HR policies, procedures, and practices. Perhaps more importantly, they are a resource to whom managers can turn for policy interpretation.

4. *Employee advocacy.* One of the enduring roles of an HR manager is to serve as an employee advocate—listening to the employees' concerns and representing their needs to managers. Effective employee relations provides a support structure when disruptive changes interfere with normal daily activities.

In the process of managing human resources, increasing attention is being given to the personal needs of the participants. Thus throughout this book we will not only emphasize the importance of the contributions that HRM makes to the organization but also give serious consideration to its effects on the individual and on society.

Reality CHECK

HR TRANSFORMATION AT AIR CANADA

WWW

As a result of the merger with Canadian Airlines International in 2000, every unit in Air Canada had to redefine itself. Air Canada was now number one in Canada—a global airline with 40 percent more activity in the world. The human resources function had to do something differently to support this.

Melissa Sonberg, formerly Director of Organizational Learning at Air Canada, was given a new job, Senior Business Unit Advisor, in the newly structured HR function. Four new groups of jobs—*Business Unit Advisors–Operations, –Corporate Strategy & Finance, –Commercial and –Customer Service*—were created to align HR interventions with strategic business objectives and organizational outcomes. The job of the business advisor was to work directly with business leaders to ensure that HR programs such as compensation and recruitment met their business needs.

The business advisors began working collaboratively with newly created functional divisions within Corporate People Services, referred to as Centres of Expertise (CoE). Their goal was to align HR with strategy, develop policies and tools to enable the realization of strategies, design measurement systems to assess the value of HR, and act as the conduit for new ideas generated by HR gurus. Sonberg states: "We need access to corporate experts and the Business Advisor role is used to jump over the evolutionary steps needed to incorporate the newest and best ideas."

Corporate People Services is building a backroom full of tools and support services, grounded in innovative ideas, to respond to business needs. All of the CoEs provide particular support and expertise. Advisors are responsible for "bundling" the right mix of expertise in support of particular business units. For example, one corporate strategy unit had the goal of identifying travel-related services to create new business.

Another unit within *Corporate People Services*, the Shared Services Centre, was created to handle all routine, repetitive transactions, and make it Web-enabled and self-service. This unit will handle routine requests, such as requests for training and for changes to personnel information. Employees will manage their own files, including their careers. Each employee will be able to track his or her own performance using a job competency profile. Included in this file will be performance appraisals identifying performance gaps, which will then be hot-linked to training opportunities.

It is interesting to note that no one has been given an HR title. Sonberg states that this was deliberate: "HR has a lot of history attached to it at Air Canada. We wanted to move away from the feeling among line managers that people issues are an HR responsibility. People issues must be incorporated in to line operations, and a business unit must be accountable for its resources. In the old model, the HR staff person would say, "Give us your needs. We'll find employees, dust them with fairy dust, and return them trained and motivated." Under the new model, business units have one-stop shopping for recruitment, selection, training, and access to decentralized resources that understand the business. We needed to move from a centralized policing department to being tightly integrated with the business."

Increasingly, employees and the public at large are demanding that employers demonstrate greater social responsibility in managing their human resources. Complaints that some jobs are devitalizing the lives and injuring the health of employees are not uncommon. Complaints of discrimination against women, visible minorities, the physically and mentally challenged, and the elderly with respect to hiring, training, advancement, and compensation are being levelled against some employers. As the workforce becomes more diverse, employees must address issues such as comparable pay for comparable work, the high cost of health benefits, day care for children of employees, and alternative work schedules.

All employers are finding that privacy and the confidentiality of employee information are serious matters and deserve the greatest protection that can be provided.

Where employees are organized into unions (see Chapters 14 and 15), employers can encounter costly collective bargaining proposals, threats of strike, and charges of unfair labour practices.

Top management generally recognizes the contributions that the HR program can make to the organization and thus expects HR managers to assume a broader role in the overall organizational strategy. HR functions must be evaluated like any others at the boardroom table. A prescription for this is outlined in Highlights in HRM 5.

Competencies of the Human Resources Manager

As top executives expect HR managers to assume a broader role in overall organizational strategy, many of these managers will need to acquire a complementary set of competencies.[61] These competencies are summarized below and shown graphically in Figure 1.6.

1. *Business mastery.* HR professionals need to know the business of their organization thoroughly. This requires an understanding of its economic and financial capabilities so that they can "join the team" of business managers. It also requires that HR professionals develop skills at external relations focused on their customers.

2. *HR mastery.* HR professionals are the organization's behavioural science experts. Prior to certification, HR professionals are required to take specified academic courses, pass competency exams, observe a code of ethics, and belong to a professional association such as the Human Resources Professionals Association of Ontario (HRPAO).

WWW

3. *Change mastery.* HR professionals have to be able to manage change processes so that HR activities are effectively merged with the business needs of the organization. This involves interpersonal and problem-solving skills, as well as innovativeness and creativity.

4. *Personal credibility.* HR professionals must establish personal credibility in the eyes of their internal and external customers. Credibility and trust are earned by developing personal relationships with customers, by demonstrating the values of the firm, by standing up for one's own beliefs, and by being fair-minded in dealing with others.

Highlights in HRM

5   THE FIVE C MODEL FOR ASSESSING HR

Executives, employees, and clients of the human resources department judge the effectiveness of this function in five ways:

1. **Compliance.** The HR department is responsible for ensuring that the organization complies with the laws that govern employee–employer relations (employment equity, health and safety, labour law, employment standards, etc). When it does this, savings are achieved in legal costs, fines, and damaging publicity.
2. **Client satisfaction.** Those external and internal clients who interact with the HR professional can be assessed on their satisfaction with services, in the same way that customers of other organizational services are measured.
3. **Culture management.** Highly effective organizations create and monitor the culture of their organizations, by surveying employee attitudes and developing programs (such as empowerment) to create the kinds of employee attitudes that result in increased motivation and productivity.
4. **Cost control.** In organizations where employees are viewed as an expense, the role of the HR department is to cut costs by reducing the labour component. Other cost control strategies include reducing turnover, absenteeism, smoking and other employee behaviours which are costly to the organization.
5. **Contribution.** Research has established that certain high-performance HR practices can have a positive effect on employee performance, by increasing knowledge, skills, and abilities, improving motivation, reducing shirking, and increasing retention of competent employees. These in turn impact organizational effectiveness.

The ability to integrate business, HR, and change competencies is essential. By helping their organizations build a sustained competitive advantage and by learning to manage many activities well, HR professionals are becoming full business partners. Forward-looking CEOs make certain that their top HR executives report directly to them and help them address key issues.

At lower levels in the organization, a rapidly growing number of companies such as Ford and Air Canada (see Reality Check) are assigning HR representatives to business teams to make certain that HR issues are addressed on the job and that HR representatives, in turn, are knowledgeable about business issues rather than simply focusing on the administrative function.

Role of the Line Manager

WWW

As much as we might say about the role of the HR department, in the final analysis managing people depends on effective supervisors and line managers. As one executive at Merck put it, "Human resources are far too important to be left to the per-

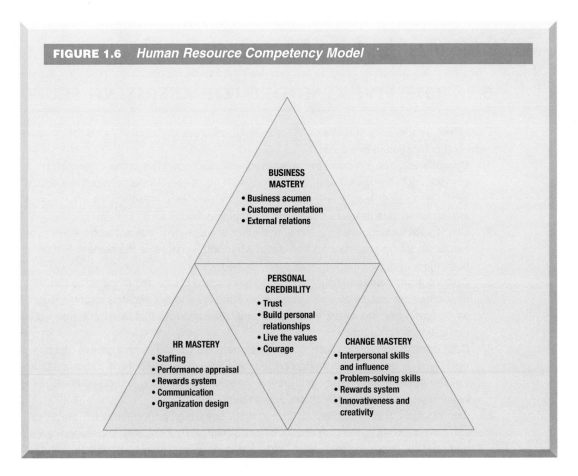

FIGURE 1.6   *Human Resource Competency Model*

BUSINESS MASTERY
- Business acumen
- Customer orientation
- External relations

PERSONAL CREDIBILITY
- Trust
- Build personal relationships
- Live the values
- Courage

HR MASTERY
- Staffing
- Performance appraisal
- Rewards system
- Communication
- Organization design

CHANGE MASTERY
- Interpersonal skills and influence
- Problem-solving skills
- Rewards system
- Innovativeness and creativity

Source: Arthur Young, Wayne Brockbank, and Dave Ulrich, "Lower Cost, Higher Value: Human Resource Function in Transformation." Reprinted with permission from *Human Resource Planning* 17, no. 3 (1994). Copyright 1994 by The Human Resource Planning Society, 317 Madison Avenue, Suite 1509, New York, NY 10017, Phone (212) 490-6337, Fax (212) 682-6851.

sonnel department." Although HR managers have the responsibility for coordinating programs and policies pertaining to people-related issues, managers and employees themselves are ultimately responsible for performing these functions.

We understand that most readers of this book will be line managers and supervisors rather than HR specialists. The text is, therefore, oriented to helping people manage people more effectively, whether they become first-line supervisors or chief executive officers. Students now preparing for careers in organizations will find that the study of HRM provides a background that will be valuable in managerial and supervisory positions. Discussions concerning the role of the HR department can to provide a better understanding of the functions performed by this department. A familiarity with the role of HR should help facilitate closer cooperation with the department's staff and utilize more fully the assistance and services available from this resource.

SUMMARY

 People have always been central to organizations, but their strategic importance is growing in today's knowledge-based industries. An organization's success increasingly depends on the knowledge, skills, and abilities of employees, particularly as they help establish a set of core competencies that distinguish an organization from its competitors. When employees' talents are valuable, rare, difficult to imitate, and organized, an organization can achieve a sustained competitive advantage through people.

 Globalization influences a significant portion of the Canadian economy and affects the free flow of trade among countries. This globalization influences the number and kinds of jobs that are available and requires that organizations balance a complicated set of issues related to managing people in different geographies, cultures, legal environments, and business conditions. HR functions such as staffing, training, compensation, and the like have to be adjusted to take into account the differences in global management.

 Advanced technology has tended to reduce the number of jobs that require little skill and to increase the number of jobs that require considerable skill—a shift we refer to as moving from touch labour to knowledge work. This displaces some employees and requires that others be retrained. In addition, information technology has influenced HRM through human resources information systems (HRIS) that streamline the processing of data and make employee information more readily available to managers.

 Both proactive and reactive change initiatives require HR managers to work with line managers and executives to create a vision for the future, establish an architecture that enables change, and communicate with employees about the processes of change.

 To "compete through people," organizations have to do a good job of managing human capital: the knowledge, skills, and capabilities that have value to organizations. Managers must develop strategies for identifying, recruiting, and hiring the best talent available; developing these employees in ways that are firm-specific; helping them to generate new ideas and generalize them through the company; encouraging information sharing; and rewarding collaboration and teamwork.

 To respond to customer needs better, faster, and more cheaply, organizations have instituted total quality management (TQM) and re-engineering programs. Each of these programs requires that HR be involved in changing work processes, training, job design, compensation, and the like. HR issues also arise when communicating with employees about the new work systems, just as with any change initiative.

 To contain costs, organizations have been downsizing, outsourcing, and leasing employees, and enhancing productivity. HR's role is to maintain the relationship between a company and its employees, while implementing the changes.

 The workforce is becoming increasingly diverse, and organizations are doing more to address employee concerns and to maximize the benefit of different kinds of employees. Demographic changes, social and cultural differences, and changing attitudes toward work can provide a rich source of variety for organizations. But to benefit from diversity, managers need to recognize the potential concerns of employees and make certain that the exchange between the organization and employees is mutually beneficial.

In working with line managers to address the organization's challenges, HR managers play a number of important roles. They are called on for advice and counsel, for various service activities, for policy formulation and implementation, and for employee advocacy. To perform these roles effectively, HR managers must contribute business competencies, state-of-the-art HR competencies, and change management competencies. Ultimately, managing people is rarely the exclusive responsibility of the HR function. Every manager's job is managing people, and successful companies are those which combine the expertise of HR specialists with the experience of line managers to develop and utilize the talents of employees to their greatest potential.

KEY TERMS

core competencies
downsizing
employee leasing
globalization
human capital
human resources information
   system (HRIS)

human resources management
   (HRM)
knowledge workers
managing diversity
outsourcing
proactive change

reactive change
re-engineering
total quality management
   (TQM)

DISCUSSION QUESTIONS

 1. Are people always an organization's most valuable asset? In teams, discuss how a company could demonstrate to you that you are its most valuable asset.

 2. Summarize the main people-related concerns you would have as you were starting a new e-commerce business.

 3. Will technology eliminate the need for human resources managers? Go to **www.ourworld.compuserve. com/ homepages/gately** and read an article titled "E HR (electronic HR)—a Walk Through a 21st Century HR Department." In its vision of the future, there are no HR managers. Is this vision realistic?

 4. What are the pros and cons of change? Does it help or hurt organizational performance? Do you like change? Explain.

 5. Can you think of a situation where, if a particular person left an organization, the organization's productivity or performance would drop rapidly?

 6. Someone once said, "TQM is like paving cowpaths." What do you suppose this means in relation to re-engineering?

 7. Do pressures on cost containment work against the effective management of people? Explain.

8. In groups, prepare to debate this issue: "Employees are an expense, and their numbers should be reduced."

9. What are the pros and cons of having a more diverse workforce? Is Canada in a better position to compete globally because of our diverse population?

10. Visit three HR departments in the same sector. Determine the roles they play (advisor, service, etc.). Is there any evidence that these HR departments are strategic partners, and are directly responsible for organizational outcomes?

CASE 1 ORGANIZATIONAL CHANGE AT HONEYWELL

WWW

Honeywell Limited is Canada's leading heating control company. It offers technology that enhances comfort, saves energy, protects the environment, and increases security and safety. Honeywell, which has operated in Canada since 1930, presently employs 2,800 people at more than fifty locations across the country. Its annual sales are $500 million.

In 1991 the main Honeywell Canada operation in Scarborough, Ontario, faced a tough challenge: it was no longer competitive, and if it did not change how it did business, every employee's job would be at risk. The traditional manufacturing operations were to be set aside, and replaced by empowered teams of skilled and motivated workers. This did not look easy at the time. The average unionized employee was forty-eight years old and had worked at his routine factory job for eighteen years. Among the plant's workers, more than fifty ethnic groups were represented.

Relations with the union were strained. However, both the Canadian Auto Workers (CAW) and management had one goal in common: to improve worker skills. This could be done by implementing work teams, which could also result in saving jobs.

Throughout the change process, the union was treated as a partner. It collaborated with management in establishing a Learning for Life program that encouraged workers to take courses in computer technology, total quality management, English as a second language, and diversity management. Today, more than 70 percent of the company's employees are taking courses. As their chairman stated: "At Honeywell, learning isn't an option; its required. Everyone is expected to complete at least forty hours of learning each year." There is a $10 milllion dollar state-of-the-art Learning Centre that each year provides an average of 31,000 student days of learning and more than 1,4000 classes.

The Honeywell plant is now organized into forty-three teams, which produce six types of heating control products. The empowered and trained workers order their own supplies, set up the machines according to established production schedules, and are responsible for quality. Employees rotate between positions and learn all aspects of production. Barriers between managers and employees have been eliminated—in other words, there are no suits, ties, or reserved parking spaces.

The results to date? Cycle times have been reduced to 1.2 hours from 80 hours; inventory has been decreased from $13.5 million to $3 million; and factory throughput per person has been increased from $85,000 to $155,000 per person. The rotating of jobs has meant a reduction in repetitive strain injuries. Because their jobs have become more technologically advanced, and require more skills, the workers are earning higher wages. The Scarborough factory now employs 400 people, and is a Honeywell Centre of Excellence for producing valves and actuators, which are exported all over the globe.

Source: Adapted from K. Dorrel, "Breaking Down the Barriers," *Plant* 56, no. 17 (November 24, 1997): 12–13. See also **www.honeywell.ca.**

Questions

1. Identify the trends affecting the management of people that Honeywell Canada faced in 1991.

2. Discuss what role the HR department played, and how it should be measured.

CASE 2

THE BUSINESS OF HR AT IBM

HR departments are typically viewed by management personnel as cost centres rather than as profit-generating centres. Until IBM underwent a major restructuring in 1992, its HR department was no exception to this. In the restructuring, IBM was divided into thirteen separate divisions, each with more autonomy than before. HR wasn't one of the thirteen new divisions; however, it was turned into a more autonomous organization through the forming of a separate company, Workforce Solutions (WFS). Hundreds of IBM HR professionals quickly joined WFS, all of them with impressive academic credentials and training, in-depth HR experience, industry association involvement, and dedication to quality and customer satisfaction.

After WFS was established, HR personnel were retained in the major divisions of IBM to provide advice and counsel and to report to line management as they always had. HR strategy, responsibility, and decision making remains in the major divisions. WFS is designed to deliver quality programs and services that support the HR strategies, plans, and functions of the major divisions. Every line still has an HR department, but now it serves only the advise and counsel function. At IBM there are roughly 700 HR employees (about 575 HR professionals and about 125 staff at WFS).

WFS is headquartered in Westchester County, New York. Operating nationwide, it provides—for a charge—the following programs and services to IBM companies:

- human resource research and consulting services
- leadership development programs
- workforce diversity programs
- equal opportunity programs and compliance monitoring
- resources planning services
- compensation and benefits programs

- recruiting and employment services
- occupational health services
- relocation programs
- international assignment services
- employee involvement and suggestion programs
- testing and assessment services

The results have been excellent: HR services delivered at a lower cost, enhancement of the commitment to HR, flexibility and responsiveness to customer needs, streamlining of HR processes, and innovative HR programs for the workplace. WFS innovations include the introduction of a world-class employee suggestion program, the design of cost-saving medical plan changes, the establishment of centralized employee benefits support using state-of-the-art technology, and increased employee involvement in the organization through incentive pay programs.

While WFS was designed mainly to provide quality, cost-effective services to the IBM community of businesses, its services are now available to outside organizations.

Source: Adapted from IBM brochure, "Workforce Solutions"; and Jennifer J. Laabs, "HR Becomes a Separate Business at IBM," *Personnel Journal* 72, no. 4 (April 1993): 25–9. **www.can.ibm.com/hr.**

Questions

1. How can the WFS concept make an HR program more cost-effective?

2. What effect is the availability of a WFS type of organization likely to have on HR personnel in their advising and counselling roles?

3. Do you foresee other companies developing similar ventures? Explain.

CAREER COUNSEL

Most students are legitimately worried about jobs and career prospects. Career Counsel is a feature at the end of each chapter designed to help students manage their working lives and to prepare for a career. The assessment exercises are designed to encourage introspection and self-discovery. We encourage you to complete these exercises on the Managing Human Resources website and compile them into a separate career planning workbook. Start by accessing **belcourt.nelson.com.**

USING THE INTERNET

WWW

HR professionals should develop core competencies that keep them abreast of changes. To stay current, visit these sites.

- The Academy of Management, HR division: **www.aom.pace.edu**
- Newsletter for the Society of Industrial Organizational Psychology: **www.siop.org**

- Human Resources Management Mega Links:
  www.hrmgt.com/hrm1.html

  For more information about how Skandia manages its human capital, check out the company's website, which has a special section on human capital: **www.skandia-afs.com**.

  Visit the following site for the most current information about TQM: **www.trainingnet.com**.

  Readers can find current information about the labour force through Statistics Canada: **www.statcan.ca/start.html**.

NOTES AND REFERENCES

1. C.K. Prahalad and G. Hamel, "The Core Competence of the Corporation," *Harvard Business Review* 68, no. 3 (1990): 79–91.

2. G. Hamel and C.K. Prahalad, *Competing for the Future* (Boston: Harvard Business School Press, 1994). See also Prahalad and Hamel, "The Core Competence of the Corporation"; J.B. Quinn, "The Intelligent Enterprise: A New Paradigm," *Academy of Management Executive* no. 4 (1992): 48–63; Corporate Leadership Council, *Vision of the Future: Role of Human Resources in the New Corporate Headquarters* (Washington, D.C.: Advisory Board Company, 1995).

3. S.A. Snell, M.A. Youndt, and P.M. Wright, "Establishing a Framework for Research in Strategic Human Resource Management: Merging Resource Theory and Organizational Learning," in G. Ferris (ed.), *Research in Personnel and Human Resource Management*, vol. 14 (Greenwich, Conn.: JAI Press, 1996): 61–90.

4. Crawley P, The Executive View, *The Globe and Mail* October 27, 1999: 1.

5. T.J. Watson, Jr., *A Business and Its Beliefs: The Ideas That Helped Build IBM* (New York: McGraw-Hill, 1963).

6. For further discussion of HRM strategy, see M. Belcourt and K. McBey, *Strategic Human Resources Planning.* (Scarborough, Ont.: ITP Nelson, in press).

7. William J. Rothwell, "Trends in HRM," Commerce Clearing House and Society for Human Resource Management.

8. "North American Free Trade Agreement," *HRMagazine*, December 1991, 85–86. See also "The Mexican Worker," *Business Week*, April 19, 1993: 84–92.

9. James W. Dean, Jr., and Scott A. Snell, "Integrated Manufacturing and Job Design: Moderating Effects of Organizational Inertia," *Academy of Management Journal* 34, no. 4 (1991): 776–804. See also Walter Kiechel III, "How We Will Work in the Year 2000," *Fortune*, May 17, 1993: 38–52.

10. J. Newman-Provost. "Learning the High Tech Way" *Canadian Banker*, 105, no. 2. March–April 1998: 34–7.

11. B. Jensen. "Canada Post Automates HR Management" *Computing Canada*, 25, no. 24, June 18, 1999: 30.

12. Colin Richards-Carpenter, "Make a Difference by Doing it Better," *People Management*, June 13, 1996: 39–40.

13. *Benefits Canada* 8, no. 8. (1994): 19.

14. Rosa V. Lindahl, "Automation Breaks the Language Barrier," *HRMagazine*, March 1996, 79–83; "Alcoa Heads toward Eliminating Administration," *Employee Benefit Plan Review*, 1996: 50.

15. T. Belford, "Hardware Solution to Soft Costs," *Financial Post* 10, no. 63 (1997): 9.

16. Colin Richards-Carpenter, "Bright Ideas from Systems Users," *Personnel Management*, February 1992: 19–20.

17. S. Felix. "Techno Benefits" *Benefits Canada*, 24, no. 1 (January 2000): 27–34.

18. Marco A. Monsalve and Arlene Triplett, "Maximizing New Technology," *HRMagazine*, March 1990: 85–7.

19. P.M. Senge, *The Fifth Discipline: The Art and Practice of the Learning Organization* (New York: Doubleday Currency, 1990); I. Nonaka, "The Knowledge Creating Company," *Harvard Business Review* 6, no. 69 (November/December 1991): 96–104; R.A. D'Aveni, *Hypercompetition: Managing the Dynamics of Strategic Maneuvering* (New York: Free Press, 1994); R. Stata, "Organizational Learning—The Key to Management Innovation," *Sloan Management Review*, 1989: 63–74.

20. Stratford Sherman, "A Master Class in Radical Change," *Fortune*, December 13, 1993: 95–6.

21. Jennifer J. Laabs, "Change," *Personnel Journal*, July 1996: 54–63.

22. John P. Kotter, "Leading Change: Why Transformation Efforts Fail," *Harvard Business Review*, March/April 1995: 59–67.

23. Lee G. Bolman and Terry E. Deal, "Four Steps to Keeping Change Efforts Heading in the Right Direction," *Journal of Quality and Participation* 22, no. 3 (May–June 1999): 6–11; Shannon Beske and Kevin Stallings, "Current Practices: Leading Strategic Change: Tools and Techniques," *Human Resource Planning* 22, no. 2 (1988):

9–10; Brenda Paik Sunoo, "Reinventing Government," *Workforce* 77, no. 2 (February 1998): 60–1; Gillian Flynn, "It Takes Values to Capitalize on Change," *Workforce* 76, no. 4 (April 1997): 27–34; Noel Tichy, "Revolutionize Your Company," *Fortune,* December 13, 1993: 115.

24. Jerry Bowles and Josh Hammond, "Competing on Knowledge," *Fortune*, September 9, 1996: S1–S18.

25. R. Amit and M. Belcourt, "Human Resources Management Processes: A Value-Creating Source of Competitive Advantage," *European Management Journal* 17, no. 2 (April 1999): 174–81.

26. Thomas A. Stewart, "Intellectual Capital," *Fortune*, October 3, 1994: 68–74.

27. Gary S. Becker, *Human Capital* (New York: Columbia University Press, 1964); S.A. Snell and J.W. Dean, Jr., "Integrated Manufacturing and Human Resource Management: A Human Capital Perspective," *Academy of Management Journal* 35, no. 3: 467–504.

28. Nick Bontis, "There's a Price on Your Head: Managing Intellectual Capital Strategically," *Business Quarterly*, Summer 1996, 41–7; Jerry Bowles and Josh Hammond, "Competing on Knowledge," *Fortune*, September 9, 1996: S1–S18.

29. Sherman, "Master Class."

30. Bowles and Hammond, "Competing on Knowledge."

31. 1998 Canada Awards for Excellence" *Canadian Business*, 71, no. 18, November 13, 1998: 33-6; Ken Scott, "Quality in Canada—We're the Best—Aren't We?" *CMA Magazine*, 72, no, 5 (June 1998): 8–10.

32. Y.K. Shetty, "The Human Side of Product Quality," *National Productivity Review* 8, no. 2 (Spring 1989), 175–82. See also Rosabeth Moss Kanter, Barry A. Stein, and Todd Jick, *The Challenge of Organizational Change—How People Experience It and Manage It* (New York: Free Press, 1991).

33. Laurie A. Broedling, "The Business of Business Is People," speech delivered to the Quality Conference, Washington Deming Study Group, George Washington University, Washington, D.C., April 8, 1996.

34. M. Hammer and J. Champy, *Reengineering the Corporation* (New York: Harper Collins, 1994).

35. David H. Freed, "The Role of the Human Resource Department in Hospital Reengineering," *Health Care Supervisor* 14, no. 3 (1996); 37–45; S. Davis and W. Davidson, *2020 Vision: Transform Your Business Today to Succeed in Tomorrow's Economy* (New York: Simon & Schuster, 1991).

36. "Up to Speed: L.L. Bean Moves Employees as Workloads Shift," *Chief Executive*, July–August 1996: 15.

37. T. Wagar, "The Death of Downsizing—Not Yet!" *Research Forum, HR Professional* 16, no. 1, (February–March 1999): 41–43,

38. J. Peters. "The Changing Face of Government" *CMA Management* 73, no. 7 (Summer 1999): 35.

39. Dawn Anfuso, "Save Jobs: Strategies to Stop the Layoffs," *Personnel Journal*, June 1996: 66–9; Jennifer J. Laabs,

"Detailing HR's Top Two Concerns in 2005," *Personnel Journal*, January 1996: 36.

40. T. Hoffman, "Landing the Best Outsourcing Deal," *Computerworld*, March 10, 1997: 65.

41. Grover N. Wray, "The Role of Human Resources in Successful Outsourcing," *Employment Relations Today*, Spring 1996: 17–23.

42. Alex Morton, "How to Cut Costs with Employee Leasing," *Folio*, 1996: 54; Sarah Bergin, "Flexible Employees: Your Most Valuable Assets," *Training and Development*, March 1996: 112–16.

43. R. Fairholm, "First, Make the Pie Bigger," *Canadian Business Economics* 8, no. 1 (Fall 2000): 3–8.

44. Canadian Human Rights Commission (**www.chrc.ca**) 2000.

45. Statistics Canada, *Employment Equity Data Program: Projections of Visible Minority Population Groups, Canada, Provinces and Regions, 1991–2016*. Cat. No. 541-XPE, Minister of Labour, January 1996.

46. D. Bueckert, "Government to Increase Visible Minority Presence in Public Service" Canadian Press newswire, April 23, 1999.

47. "Charting the Projections: 1994–2005," *Occupational Outlook Quarterly*, Fall 1995: 1–27.

48. "The Fine Print: Analysis of Algoma Steel's Latest Annual Report," *Canadian Business*, July 1996: 34–5.

49. John Southerst, "Kenworth's Grey Revolution," *Canadian Business*, September 1992: 74–9.

50. H. Drost, and R.H. Hird, *An Introduction to the Canadian Labour Market*, Toronto: Nelson Thompson Learning, 2000.

51. Statistics Canada, Labour Force Survey, 1996.

52. Statistics Canada, *Reading the Future: A Portrait of Literacy in Canada*, National Literacy Secretariat, Human Resources Development Canada, Cat. No. 889-551-XPE, September 1996, 13.

53. J. Ross, "Too Many Dumb Jobs," Canadian Press newswire, August 19, 1998.

54. Privacy Commission of Canada, "Privacy of Personal Information," Annual Report, 1988–89, Cat. No. IP30-1, 1989.

55. For practical recommendations on how to avoid lawsuits over invasion of privacy, see John Corbett O'Meara, "The Emerging Law of Employees' Right to Privacy," *Personnel Administrator* 30, no. 6 (June 1985): 159–65. See also Lee Smith, "What the Boss Knows about You," *Fortune*, August 9, 1993: 88–93; "Privacy Issues in the Workplace," *HRMagazine*, August 1992: 93–4; "Claims Gone Wrong," *HRMagazine*, January 1990: 60–2; "Debate Is Brewing over Employees' Right to Privacy," *HRFocus*, February 1993: 1–4; Michael R. Losey, "Workplace Privacy: What You Do Know May Hurt You," *Modern Office Technology*, May 1993: 56–58.

56. Brian Dumaine, "Why Do We Work?" *Fortune*, December 26, 1994: 196–204; Myron Magnet, "You Don't Have to Be a Workaholic," *Fortune*, August 9, 1993: 64.

57. Withers, P. "Central Casting" *BC Business Magazine* 28, no, 6, June 2000:18–23. Alan Deutschman, "Pioneers of the New Balance," *Fortune*, May 20, 1991: 60–8; Miller, "New Perspective."

58. Deutschman, "Pioneers"; Miller, "New Perspective."

59. For current research on the performance impact of HR, see the entire issue of *Academy of Management Journal* 39, no. 4.

60. "Building a Customer-Oriented HR Department," *HRMagazine* 36, no. 10 (October 1991): 64–6.

61. Arthur Yeung, Wayne Brockbank, and Dave Ulrich, "Lower Cost, Higher Value: Human Resource Function in Transformation," *Human Resource Planning* 17, no. 3 (1994): 1–16; David Ulrich, Wayne Brockbank, Arthur Yeung, and Dale G. Lake, "Human Resource Competencies: An Empirical Assessment," *Human Resource Management* 34, no. 4 (Winter 1995): 473–95.

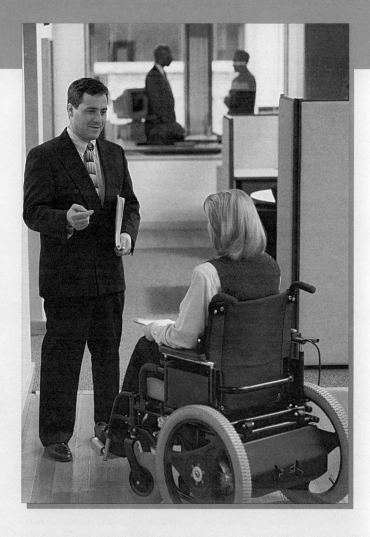

CHAPTER 2

EQUITY AND DIVERSITY IN HUMAN RESOURCES MANAGEMENT

After studying this chapter, you should be able to

OBJECTIVE 1 *Explain the reasons for employment equity legislation.*

OBJECTIVE 2 *Identify and describe the major laws affecting employment equity, and explain how they are enforced.*

OBJECTIVE 3 *Describe pay equity and strategies for implementing it.*

OBJECTIVE 4 *Discuss the Employment Equity Act in terms of its origins, its purpose, and its continued enforcement.*

OBJECTIVE 5 *Describe how employment equity is implemented in organizations.*

OBJECTIVE 6 *Discuss reverse discrimination, sexual harassment, and mandatory retirement as employment equity issues.*

OBJECTIVE 7 *Explain and give examples of diversity management.*

Employment equity

The employment of individuals in a fair and nonbiased manner

I n the field of HRM, perhaps no topic has received more attention in recent decades than employment equity. **Employment equity**, or the treatment of employed individuals in a fair and nonbiased manner, has attracted the attention of the media, the courts, practitioners, and legislators. Employment equity legislation affects all aspects of the employment relationship. When managers ignore the legal aspects of HRM, they risk incurring costly and time-consuming litigation, negative public attitudes, and damage to organization morale.

Employment equity is not only a legal topic; it is also an emotional issue. It concerns all individuals regardless of their sex, religion, age, national origin, colour, or position in an organization. Supervisors should be aware of their personal biases and how these attitudes can influence their dealings with subordinates. It should be emphasized that covert as well as blatantly intentional discrimination in employment is illegal.

In this chapter we emphasize the legislation governing employment equity, and describe the organizational response to this legislation. Today, compliance with employment equity involves managing diversity with the goal of utilizing fully the organization's human capital.

EMPLOYMENT EQUITY

Central to Canada's economic growth and prosperity in a highly competitive global marketplace will be a barrier-free environment in which all Canadians can fully explore and develop their career potential. Labour force statistics (see Chapter 1) indicated changing patterns of immigration, rising labour force participation rates for women, and an aging population with a proportionally higher incidence of disabilities. Women, visible minorities, and people with disabilities make up over 60 percent of Canada's labour force, and their numbers continue to rise. Members of designated groups entering Canada's labour pool constitute a vital resource, and their full participation in the workplace will be fundamental to an organization's ability to understand and respond to the needs of a rapidly changing marketplace. As a society, we have moved beyond principle to imperative in ensuring equal access to employment opportunities.[1]

By definition, equity means fairness and impartiality. In a legal sense, it means justice based on the concepts of ethics and fairness and a system of jurisprudence administered by courts and designed mainly to mitigate the rigours of common law. The implementation of employment equity—or "affirmative action," as it is termed in the United States—has involved establishing policies and practices designed to ensure equitable representation in the workforce and to redress past discriminations. There are four **designated groups** in Canada that have not received equitable treatment in employment.

Designated groups

Women, visible minorities, aboriginal peoples, and persons with disabilities who have been disadvantaged in employment

Status of Designated Groups

Women, aboriginal peoples, visible minorities, and people with disabilities face significant (albeit different) disadvantages in employment. Some of these include high unemployment, occupational segregation, pay inequities, and limited opportunities for career progress.

Women tend to be concentrated in occupations that are accorded lower status and pay. In 1998, women constituted 44 percent of the total workforce but were not equally represented in all occupations. For example, they held only 20 percent of upper-level management positions. Women were also underrepresented in natural science and construction, where they made up 18 percent and 3 percent of those respective workforces. Conversely, 57 percent of all service workers were women.[2]

First Nations people constitute roughly 3 percent of the population, but in western Canada they will account for a substantial portion of labour market growth. However, many Aboriginals face major barriers to employment, which are often compounded by low educational achievement and lack of job experience, as well as by language and cultural barriers. In urban centres, many Aboriginal workers are concentrated in low-paying, unstable employment. Economic self-sufficiency and participation in the economy are seen as essential to Aboriginal development. Interestingly, Native values such as cooperation and consensus decision-making have become more closely aligned with management approaches in recent years.[3]

The unemployment rate for employable people with disabilities is much higher than the national unemployment rate, which was 7.2 percent in 1999. People with disabilities face attitudinal barriers, physical demands that are unrelated to actual job requirements, and inadequate access to the technical and human support systems that would make productive employment possible. Employers seek to redress attitudinal barriers by focusing on abilities, not disabilities, as illustrated in Highlights in HRM 1.

Visible minority groups vary in their labour force profiles and in their regional distributions. Toronto has become a magnet for new immigrants, as shown in Highlights in HRM 2. Studies have shown that Latin Americans and Southeast Asians experience lower-than-average incomes, higher rates of unemployment, and reduced access to job interviews, even when they have the same qualifications as other candidates. Systemic barriers that negatively affect employment for visible minorities include culturally biased aptitude tests, lack of recognition of foreign credentials, and excessively high language requirements. Recent statistics indicate that although visible minorities—75 percent of whom are immigrants—tend to be better educated, they also have the highest unemployment rates.[4]

Between 1987 and 1995, women fared best in federally regulated organizations, as did other designated groups. Employment equity programs are responsible for this progress. Figure 2.1 shows the workforce representation of the designated groups in the Canadian labour force.[5]

Benefits of Employment Equity

Employment equity makes good business sense. It contributes to the bottom line by broadening the base of qualified individuals for employment, training, and promotions, and by helping employers avoid costly human rights complaints. Employment equity enhances an organization's ability to attract and keep the best-qualified employees, which results in greater access to a broader base of skills. It also enhances employee morale by offering special measures such as flexible work schedules and work sharing. Finally it improves the organization's image in the community.[6]

In Canada, the Charter of Rights and Freedoms, the federal Canadian Human Rights Act, and pay equity and employment equity acts are the governing pieces of legislation dealing with employment equity.

Highlights in HRM

1 FOCUS ON ABILITIES

Highlights in HRM

2 TORONTO: A REMARKABLE EXPERIMENT

"Toronto is redefining for us our image of who is a Canadian," says Myer Siemiatycki, a spokesperson for the Centre of Excellence for Research in Immigration and Settlement. Immigrants tend to cluster in large cities, and Toronto attracts by far the most immigrants in Canada. According to the 1996 census, immigrants account for 42 percent of Toronto's population, a figure that is expected to climb to 48 percent.

The cultural diversity found in Toronto is unequalled anywhere else in the world, and is perceived as a unique urban experiment. Before 1961, virtually all of Toronto's immigrant arrivals were from Europe. Now, most come from Asia, the Middle East, Central and South America, the Caribbean, and Africa. Daily life is peaceful, although the surface peace may mask intolerance. Some ethnic enclaves do exist, but conflicts are relatively rare. The kinds of ghettos found in other cities do not exist in Toronto.

The experience of one resident is typical: "I am from Guyana, and my neighbours were born in Canada, Russia, Greece, Jamaica, and India. I have always felt part of the city, never like an outsider."

Source: Alanna Mitchell, "Census Reveals Changing Face," *The Globe and Mail*, November 5, 1997: A1. Reprinted with permission from *The Globe and Mail*.

THE LEGAL FRAMEWORK

The Charter of Rights and Freedoms

The Constitution Act of 1982, which contains the Canadian Charter of Rights and Freedoms, is the cornerstone of equity legislation. The Charter guarantees some fundamental rights to every Canadian, including these:

- Fundamental freedoms (s. 2) that comprise the standard rights of freedom of speech, press, assembly, association, and religion.
- Democratic rights (ss. 3 to 5), covering franchise rights.
- Mobility rights (s. 6), concerning the right to move freely from province to province for the purposes of residence and/or employment.
- Legal rights (ss. 7 to 14), conferring standard procedural rights in criminal proceedings.
- Equality rights (s. 15), guaranteeing no discrimination by law on grounds of race, ethnic origin, colour, religion, sex, age, or mental and physical ability.
- Language rights (ss. 16 to 23).[7]

Although the Charter has offered many Canadians opportunities in terms of their own individual rights and responsibilities, it has also been a source of disap-

FIGURE 2.1 *Representation of Designated Groups in the Labour Force*

	REPRESENTATION IN THE CANADIAN POPULATION	REPRESENTATION IN THE WORKFORCE
Women	50.0%	44.57%
Aboriginals	3.0	1.29
People with disabilities	6.5	3.0
Members of visible minorities	11.0	9.68

Source: *Statistical Annual Report: Employment and Equity Act, 1997,* Canada, Human Resources Development, Labour Standards and Workplace Equity, Cat. No. LT-020-97. 1996.

pointment. The enactment of the Charter created high expectations on the part of various groups, especially unions, which believed that under Section 2 all employees would have a fundamental right to associate, to bargain collectively, and to strike. However, in 1987 the Supreme Court of Canada, in ruling on a challenge to federal public-sector laws relating to compulsory arbitration, back-to-work legislation, and wage restraint legislation, declared that Section 2 of the Charter does not include the right to bargain collectively and to strike. In the Court's view, these were not fundamental freedoms, but rather statutory rights created and regulated by legislation. As a result of this ruling, governments can weaken the collective bargaining process by limiting salary increases, legislating strikers back to work, and imposing compulsory arbitration.

Canadian Human Rights Act (CHRA)

The Canadian Human Rights Act was passed by Parliament on July 14, 1977, and became effective in March 1978. This act proclaims that

> every individual should have an equal opportunity with other individuals to make for himself or herself the life that he or she is able and wishes to have, consistent with his or her duties and obligations as a member of society, without being hindered in or prevented from doing so by discriminatory practices based on race, national or ethnic origin, colour, religion, age, sex or marital status, or convictions for an offence for which a pardon has been granted or by discriminatory employment practices based on physical handicap.[8]

The act applies to all federal government departments and agencies, to Crown corporations, and to other businesses and industries under federal jurisdiction, such as banks, airlines, railway companies, and insurance and communications companies.

For those areas not under federal jurisdiction, protection is available under provincial human rights laws. Provincial laws, although very similar to federal ones, do differ from province to province. Every province and territory has a Human Rights Act (or Code), and each has jurisdiction prohibiting discrimination in the workplace.

The prohibited grounds of discrimination in employment include race, religion, sex, age, national or ethnic origin, physical handicap, and marital status (see Figure

Bona fide occupational qualification (BFOQ)

A justifiable reason for discrimination based on business reasons of safety or effectiveness

WWW

2.2 for a complete listing). Employers are permitted to discriminate if employment preferences are based on a **bona fide occupational qualification (BFOQ)** or BFOR (bona fide occupational requirement). A BFOQ is justified if the employer can establish necessity for business operations. In other words, differential treatment is not discrimination if there is a justifiable reason. For example, adherence to the tenets of the Roman Catholic Church was deemed a BFOQ for employment as a teacher in a Roman Catholic school.[9] Business necessity also relates to the safe and efficient operation of an organization. There is an ongoing debate as to whether male guards should be allowed to work in women's prisons.

Enforcement of the Canadian Human Rights Act

The Canadian Human Rights Commission (CHRC) deals with complaints concerning discriminatory practices covered by the Canadian Human Rights Act. The CHRC may choose to act on its own if it feels that sufficient grounds exist for a finding of discrimination. It also has the power to issue guidelines interpreting the act. Highlights in HRM 3 summarizes the CHRC's enforcement procedures.

Individuals have a right to file a complaint if they feel they have been discriminated against. (The CHRC may refuse to accept a complaint if it has not been filed within a prescribed period of time, if it is deemed trivial, or if it was filed in bad faith.) The complainant must first complete a written report describing the discriminatory action. A CHRC representative reviews the facts and determines whether the claim is legitimate. Once a complaint has been accepted by the CHRC, an investigator is assigned the task of gathering more facts from both the complainant and the accused. The investigator then submits a report to the CHRC recommending a finding of either substantiation or nonsubstantiation of the allegation. If the allegation is substantiated, a settlement may be arranged in the course of the investigation. If the parties are unable to reach agreement, a human rights tribunal consisting of up to three members may be appointed to further investigate the complaint. If the tribunal finds that a discriminatory practice did take place, or that the victim's feelings or self-respect have suffered as a result of the practice, it may order the person or organization responsible to compensate the victim. Former employees of Majestic Electronics received $300,000 in compensation because they were harassed after they refused to obey the racist and sexist orders of the company president.[10]

Any person who obstructs an investigation or a tribunal, or who fails to comply with the terms of a settlement, can be found guilty of an offence, which may be punishable by a fine and/or jail sentence. If the guilty party is an employer or an employee organization, the fine can be as high as $50,000 (up to $5,000 for individuals).[11]

The Enforcement of Provincial Human Rights Laws

Provincial human rights laws are enforced in a manner very similar to that of the federal system. The major difference between the two systems is that federally regulated organizations tend to be larger and to have more sophisticated HR systems and policies as well as more experienced HR professionals. At the provincial level, the employers tend to be small and medium-sized businesses, many of which lack an HR professional who is knowledgeable about human rights legislation. Employers and employees alike may have little experience in matters of discrimination.

FIGURE 2.2 *Prohibited Grounds of Discrimination in Employment by Jurisdiction*

	Federal	British Columbia	Alberta	Saskatchewan	Manitoba	Ontario	Quebec	New Brunswick	Prince Edward Island	Nova Scotia	Newfoundland	Northwest Territories	Yukon
Race or colour	•	•	•	•	•	•	•	•	•	•	•	•	•
Religion	•	•	•	•	•	•	•	•	•	•	•	•	•
Age	•	•	•	•	•	•	•	•	•	•	•	•	•
Sex	•	•	•	•	•		•	•	•	•	•	•	•
Marital status	•	•	•	•	•	•	•	•	•	•	•	•	•
Physical/mental disability	•	•	•	•		•	•	•	•	•	•	•	•
Sexual orientation	•	•	•	•	•	•	•	•	•	•	•	•	•
National or ethnic origin*	•			•	•	•	•	•	•	•	•	•	•
Family status	•	•	•	•	•	•	•		•	•	•	•	•
Dependence on alcohol or drugs	•	•	•	•	•	•	•		•	•			
Ancestry or place of origin		•	•	•	•		•		•			•	•
Political belief		•		•			•		•	•	•		•
Based on association				•	•		•		•	•	•		•
Pardoned conviction	•	•					•						
Record of criminal conviction		•					•		•				•
Source of income				•	•	•	•		•	•			
Assignment, attachment, or seizure of pay												•	
Social condition/origin							•				•		
Language						•	•						•

*Includes linguistic background

Source: Copyright © The Canadian Human Rights Commission, "Prohibited Grounds of Employment Discrimination in Jurisdictions Across Canada," 1993. Reproduced with the permission of the Minister of Public Works and Government Services Canada, 2001.

The majority of cases are resolved at the investigation stage. If no agreement can be reached, the case is presented to the province's human rights commission. The members of the commission study the evidence and then submit a report to the minister in charge of administering human rights legislation. The minister may appoint an independent board of inquiry, which has powers similar to those of a

Highlights in HRM

3   CANADIAN HUMAN RIGHTS COMMISION ENFORCEMENT PROCEDURE

A complaint is filed by the complainant with CHRC

↓

Accused is notified of the complaint and an investigation is conducted

↓

CHRC finds reasonable cause for a finding of discrimination   ← OR →   CHRC cannot substantiate the case and case is closed

↓

CHRC attempts to get reconciliation between two parties

↓

CHRC makes a decision on the case

↓

Both parties accept CHRC's decision and the discrimination case is closed

OR

↙   ↘

If decision is appealed, appeals tribunal makes a decision

Case now goes to Supreme Court of Canada, which makes a binding decision

tribunal at the federal level. Failure to comply with the remedies prescribed by the board of inquiry may result in prosecution in provincial court. Individuals may be fined between $500 and $1,000, and organizations or groups between $1,000 and $10,000. These levies vary from province to province.

PAY EQUITY

As a result of a 1978 amendment to the Canadian Human Rights Act, pay equity became enacted as law. Pay equity law makes it illegal for employers to discriminate against individuals on the basis of job content. The goal of pay equity is to eliminate the historical wage gap between men and women and to ensure that salary ranges reflect the value of the work performed. For example, the average income of males who worked full-time in 1997 was $51,727, while women's average earnings were only $39,282, representing about 75.9 percent of what men earned.[12]

By definition, pay equity means equal pay for work of equal value. It is based on two principles. The *first* is equal pay for equal work.[13] Male and female workers must be paid the same wage rate for doing identical work. The *second* is equal pay for similar or substantially similar work (equal pay for work of comparable worth). This means that male and female workers must be paid the same wage rate for jobs of a similar nature that may have different titles (e.g., "nurse's aide" and "orderly").

Implementation of pay equity is based on comparing the work of female-dominated job classes to the value of work performed by males. Comparisons require the use of a gender-neutral, unbiased comparison system to evaluate the jobs in an establishment.[14] Comparisons must be based on the amount and type of skill, effort, and responsibility needed to perform the job and on the working conditions where it is performed. The comparison must be done in such a way that the characteristics of "male" jobs, such as heavy lifting and "dirty" working conditions, are valued fairly in comparison to the characteristics of "female" jobs, such as manual dexterity and caring for others.[15]

The federal pay equity legislation applies to that section of the workforce under its jurisdiction and covers all organizations regardless of number of employees. The federal pay equity system is complaint-based, meaning that complaints can be raised by an employee, a group of employees, or a bargaining agent.[16] A more comprehensive review of pay equity is provided in Chapter 9.

AN ACT RESPECTING EMPLOYMENT EQUITY (FEDERALLY REGULATED COMPANIES)

The Royal Commission on Equality in Employment (Abella Commission), chaired by then Ontario judge Rosalie Silberman Abella, reviewed the employment practices of federal Crown and government-owned corporations.[17] Its report, tabled in 1984, made recommendations on how four traditionally disadvantaged groups—women, Aboriginal peoples, members of visible minorities, and people with disabilities—could be brought into the mainstream of Canada's labour force. The report recommended that legislation be enacted to cover all federally regulated employers and urged provincial governments to consider developing compatible legislation. To reach employees who did not fall under federal jurisdiction, the report further recommended that a contract compliance program be included for organizations that did business with the federal government.

The Abella Commission also stressed that data collection and reporting should be an important component of compliance, since the success of an employment equity program would be measured by results. Data were to be collected on new hires, promotions, terminations, layoffs, part-time work, and other conditions of employment. Also recommended were enforceable requirements and the creation of an independent, well-resourced overseer.

In response to the findings of the Abella Commission, the federal government introduced the Employment Equity Act in 1986. It was updated in 1995.

The Employment Equity Act (1995)

Employers and Crown corporations that have 100 employees or more and that are regulated under the Canada Labour Code must implement employment equity and report on their results. Under the act, the employer is required to:

- provide its employees with a questionnaire that allows them to indicate whether they belong to one of the four designated groups;
- identify jobs in which the percentage of members of designated groups falls below their availability in the labour market;
- communicate information on employment equity to its employees, and consult and collaborate with employee representatives;
- identify possible barriers in existing employment systems that may be limiting the employment opportunities of members of designated groups;
- develop an employment equity plan aimed at promoting an equitable workplace;
- make all reasonable efforts to implement its plan;
- monitor, review, and revise its plan from time to time; *and*
- prepare an annual report on its employment equity data and activities.[18]

The concept of employment equity is rooted in the wording of federal and provincial employment standards legislation, human rights codes, and the Canadian Charter of Rights and Freedoms. Employment equity involves identifying and removing systemic barriers to employment opportunities that adversely affect women, visible minorities, Aboriginal peoples, and people with disabilities. Employment equity also involves implementing special measures and making reasonable accommodation. The purpose of the act is further defined under Section 2:

> To achieve equality in the workplace so that no person shall be denied employment opportunities or benefits for reasons unrelated to ability and in the fulfilment of that goal, to correct the conditions of disadvantage in employment experienced by women, Aboriginal peoples, persons with disabilities and visible minorities by giving effect to the principle that employment equity means more than treating persons in the same way but also requires special measures and the accommodation of differences.[19]

Under the Federal Contractors Program (FCP), contractors who bid for goods and services contracts with the federal government valued at $200,000 or more, and who employ 100 persons or more, are required to implement an employment equity program. (For a list of this program's implementation criteria, see Highlights in HRM 4.) To assist in the process, the federal government provides professional consulting services to employers throughout Canada regarding how to implement employment equity. Federally regulated employers must conduct a workforce analysis to identify underrepresentation of members of designated groups; review their employment systems, policies, and practices to identify employment barriers; and prepare a plan outlining the steps they will take to remove any identified barriers. Most provinces have similar legislation governing employment equity.

Highlights in HRM

4 IMPLEMENTATION CRITERIA FOR FEDERAL CONTRACTORS PROGRAM

1. Communication by the organization's CEO to employees, unions and/or employee associations of the commitment to achieve equality in employment through the design and implementation of an employment equity plan.
2. Assignment of senior personnel with responsibility for employment equity.
3. Collection and maintenance of information on the employment status of designated-group employees by occupation and salary levels and in terms of hiring, promotion and termination in relation to all other employees.
4. Analysis of designated-group representation within the organization in relation to their representation in the supply of qualified workers from which the contractor may reasonably be expected to recruit employees.
5. Elimination or modification of those human resource policies, practices and systems, whether formal or informal, shown to have or likely to have an unfavourable effect on the employment status of designated-group employees.
6. Establishment of goals for the hiring, training and promotion of designated-group employees. Such goals will consider projections for hiring, promotions, terminations, layoffs, recalls, retirements and, where possible, the projected availability of qualified designated-group members.
7. Establishment of a work plan for reaching each of the goals in 6 above.
8. Adoption of special measures where necessary to ensure that goals are achieved, including the provision of reasonable accommodation as required.
9. Establishment of a climate favourable to the successful integration of designated-group members within the organization.
10. Adoption of procedures to monitor the progress and results achieved in implementing employment equity.
11. Authorization to allow representatives of the CHRC access to the business premises and to the records noted in 3 above in order to conduct on-site compliance reviews for the purpose of measuring the progress achieved in implementing employment equity.

Source: Employment Equity and Immigration Canada, *Federal Contractors Program, Information for Suppliers.* Reproduced with permission from the Minister of Supply and Services, 1995.

WWW

Recent winners of merit awards for initiatives in employment equity include the Bank of Nova Scotia for increasing the number of visible minorities in its workforce to 19 percent and the Saskatchewan Wheat Pool for its partnerships with the Aboriginal community—particularly its investment in an MBA program in Aboriginal Business. In the face of threats to employment equity legislation, employers are showing willingness to keep the practice alive. As Robert Rochon, director of employment equity for National Grocer Co., puts it: "Regardless of any legislative requirement, [employment equity] is a good business decision for us. When you consider the changing face of Canada, it just makes good business sense to reflect the customers that you serve."[20]

Administration and Enforcement of the Employment Equity Act

WWW

Human Resources Development Canada is responsible for administering the Federal Contractors Program. The Canadian Human Rights Commission is mandated under the Canadian Human Rights Act[21] to prohibit discrimination in the establishments of federally regulated businesses.[22]

The CHRC is authorized to conduct on-site compliance reviews. Failure to comply may result in fines ranging from $10,000 for first offenders to $50,000 for repeat offenders.

THE IMPLEMENTATION OF EMPLOYMENT EQUITY IN ORGANIZATIONS

OBJECTIVE
5

The implementation of employment equity in an organization follows the precepts of any change management program. Thus, successful implementation must employ strategic planning, which must be incorporated into an overall business strategy. The Federal Contractors Program outlined in Highlights in HRM 4 provides a good overview of what a plan should incorporate. The process involves six main steps: senior management commitment; data collection and analysis; employment systems review; establishment of a work plan; implementation; and a follow-up process that includes evaluation, monitoring, and revision.

Step 1: Senior Management Commitment

Commitment to an employment equity plan necessitates a top-down strategy. A more supportive culture is created when the CEO or owner–operator publicly introduces written policy describing the organization's commitment to employment equity. This policy must be strategically posted throughout the organization and sent to each employee. Highlights in HRM 5 illustrates the commitment Amdahl Canada Limited has made to its employment equity effort.

WWW

An employment equity policy statement may raise many questions, so it is important to be thorough in this process in order to keep concerns to a minimum. The policy statement should be supplemented with a communiqué explaining what employment equity is, the rationale for the program, and its implications for present and future employees. Assurances must be given at this time that all information provided will be treated confidentially and will not be used to identify individuals other than for the purpose of employment equity program activities. The communiqué should also list the names of persons responsible for administering the program and outline any planned activities the employer may deem necessary to establish the program (e.g., analysis of the workforce or of policies and procedures).

Highlights in HRM

5   AMDAHL LIMITED STATEMENT OF EMPLOYMENT EQUITY

All employees of Amdahl Limited are entitled to a work environment within which individuals are treated with respect, provided with equality of opportunity based on merit and kept free of discrimination and harassment.

This commitment to employees and candidates for employment applies to all aspects of the employment relationship, including recruitment, work assignment, training opportunities, compensation, promotions, transfers and terminations.

Individuals in their employment relationship will not be unlawfully discriminated against or harassed for any reason such as their race, religion, creed, sex, marital status, age, national/ethnic origin, political belief or handicap.

Each employee is responsible for adhering to the spirit and content of this Statement. Violations of this policy constitute unacceptable behaviour and will be subject to appropriate corrective action.

Management is committed to addressing and resolving employee concerns associated with the rights described in this statement.

Source: Amdahl Limited.

Communication tools may include periodic information sessions, workplace posters, departmental or small-group meetings conducted by line management, orientation and training programs, newsletters, and vehicles such as videos, brochures, employee handbooks, and memos from the union. An innovative approach to communications was taken at the Centre de recherche industrielle du Québec (CRIQ), where employees decided to create a video to demonstrate that seemingly harmless comments and attitudes can have devastating consequences for members of designated groups. Their goal was to sensitize people without lecturing or pointing fingers. The employees acted in the video, selected its music, and directed and produced it. Its title was *Moi ... des préjugés?* (*Me ... prejudiced?*). The video depicts the experiences of a Black man, a person who is deaf, and a woman, all of whom are seeking employment with a company, and who are confronted with opinions and attitudes that have everything to do with prejudice and nothing to do with the requirements of the job.[23]

Assignment of accountable senior staff.   Senior management must place the responsibility for employment equity in the hands of a senior manager, a joint labour–management committee, and an employment equity advisory committee with mechanisms for union consultation (or, in nonunionized settings, for consultation with designated employee representatives). They must designate line management responsibility and accountability. Anyone given responsibility for employment equity must be knowledgeable about the problems and concerns of designated groups; have the status and ability needed to gain the cooperation of employees at all levels in the organization; have access to financial and human resources required to conduct planning and implementation functions; have sufficient time to devote to employment equity issues; monitor and be in a position to report to the CEO on the results of employment equity measures; and be prepared to serve as the employment equity contact person with federal and provincial government agencies.

Among the employment areas committee members may be required to review are employment practices, advertising and recruitment policies, company-sponsored training, the organization of work schedules and facilities, and systems for promotion to management positions. While committees are usually given responsibility for making recommendations and reporting on issues, ultimate authority generally rests with senior management.

Employers covered by the Employment Equity Act are legally obligated to consult with designated employee representatives or, in unionized settings, with bargaining agents. Consultation means that the employer must supply sufficient information and opportunity to employee representatives or bargaining agents to enable them to ask questions and submit advice on the implementation of employment equity.

The labour movement in Canada generally supports the concept of employment equity, so long as unions are fully informed and involved from the beginning with respect to an employer's planning process. This makes sense considering that unions are the legitimate representatives of employee interests in unionized settings. Supportive mechanisms for achieving employment equity have been reported by Human Resources Development Canada.[24] Many employers and unions have sucessfully negotiated Many employers and unions have successfully negotiated family-friendly policies such as parental leave, child care provisions, and flexible hours.

Step 2: Data Collection and Analysis

Stock data

Data showing the status of designated groups in occupational categories and compensation level

Flow data

Data that provide a profile of the employment decisions affecting designated groups

The development of an internal workforce profile is an important tool in employment equity planning. Without this information an organization would not be able to determine where it stands relative to the internal and external workforce. Profiles must be based on both stock data and flow data. **Stock data** provide a snapshot of the organization. They show where members of designated groups are employed in the organization, at what salaries and status, and in what occupations on a particular date. **Flow data** refer to the distribution of designated groups in applications, interviews, hiring decisions, training and promotion opportunities, and terminations. They provide information on the movement of employees into and through the organization. Computerized reporting systems and tracking software are available from Human Resources Development Canada to assist employers in gathering, reporting, and analyzing their internal workforce data.

Most of the information necessary for equity planning (e.g., salary, sex, access to benefits, seniority status, occupational and career history within the organization) is contained in existing personnel files. Information pertaining to the distribution of members of designated groups in the employer's organization must be accumulated by the employer through a self-identification process. Under the Employment Equity Act, employers may gather data on members of designated groups as long as employees voluntarily agree to be identified or identify themselves as members of designated groups, and as long as the data are used only for employment equity planning or reporting purposes.

Creating a climate of trust in the management of the program is a major challenge. Employers can encourage participation and confidence in the program by providing focused employment equity training to managers and by providing opportunities for managers to be recognized for their contributions to the development and administration of effective employment equity strategies. Companies such as Pratt & Whitney have introduced equity and diversity training for their supervisors.[25]

If an employer administers a self-identification questionnaire, confidentiality and a clear commitment at senior levels to the concept of employment equity should be communicated. Having employees self-identify is crucial to the success of the program, but problems may arise with self-identification. Under some provincial employment equity acts, terms such as "Aboriginal" and "racial minority" are not defined. Some employees, who have "hidden" disabilities such as epilepsy or partial deafness, may not wish to label themselves for fear of future discriminatory treatment. Some minorities, such as Aboriginals, have never disclosed their ethnic origins for similar reasons.

If too many employees with nonvisible disabilities do not identify themselves as disabled, the program could end up being designed to recruit more employees with disabilities, leaving another segment of the employee population underrepresented. Thus, because inaccurate data were accumulated on one group, the other group will not benefit from the employment equity efforts. An additional concern is that individuals with disabilities may need some form of accommodation to help them perform their jobs better. If they do not self-identify, they have denied themselves certain basic rights.

A self-identification form should contain the following:

- An explanation of the employer's employment equity policy, the purpose of the employment equity program, and the need for the information requested.
- An indication that the information supplied will be confidential and will be used only for employment equity purposes by those persons identified as responsible for the program.
- The categories for self-identification, with brief explanations and examples.
- an indication that the form has been reviewed by the relevant human rights agency.
- Space for comments and suggestions.
- The name of the contact person for information and suggestions.[26]

A self-identification form used by the City of Calgary is shown in Highlights in HRM 6.

Once the personal information forms have been completed, all occupations within the organization must be cross-referenced to the National Occupational Classification (NOC)—formerly the Standard Occupational Classification (SOC). This manual was created by Statistics Canada for use in statistical surveys and for other purposes. Personal data are organized under the four-digit NOC classifications. When building a workforce profile, employers should first refer to the four-digit unit groups and then determine which one each job belongs in. For

Highlights in HRM

6   SELF-IDENTIFICATION FORM, CITY OF CALGARY

EMPLOYMENT EQUITY IDENTIFICATION

In keeping with The City of Calgary's employment equity initiatives and outreach program, we ask that applicants provide us with the following information. Your answers are confidential, will only be used to collect data and will not affect your eligibility as an applicant as hiring decisions are based on the merit principle. Please note: the Alberta Human Rights Commission has reviewed these questions and found them acceptable.

Completion of this section is considered OPTIONAL and VOLUNTARY.

LAST NAME	GIVEN NAME	COMPETITION NUMBER

Please check the appropriate box.

Are you:

☐ Male   ☐ Female

☐ White (Caucasian)

☐ A visible minority (Black, Chinese, South Asian, etc.)

☐ Aboriginal (Canadian Indian, Métis, Inuit)

☐ Person with a disability (mobility, vision, hearing impaired, etc.)

Source: City of Calgary, Self-Identification Form, August 1995. Printed with permission.

example, secretaries and stenographers are classified in unit group 4111, which in turn can be assigned to the "clerical workers" group.

To assist employers in the storage of data and in report writing, the Employment Equity Computerized Reporting System (EECRS) has been designed.

A full workforce analysis can be generated once all the information has been loaded and the reports are complete. This utilization analysis will include a distribution of members of designated groups according to occupations and salary levels throughout the organization. Comparisons will show which designated groups exhibit **underutilization** and which groups exhibit **concentration** in specific occupations or levels, in proportion to their numbers in the labour market.[27]

Step 3: Employment Systems Review

"Employment systems" or "employment practices" are the means by which employers carry out such personnel activities as recruitment, hiring, training and development, promotion, job classification, discipline, and termination. Some of these practices are found in personnel manuals and collective agreements, while others remain more informal and based on traditional practices.

An important legal principle is that employers are accountable even when discrimination is the unintended result of employment systems that block the progress of particular groups of employees or potential employees for reasons unrelated to qualifications, merit, or business requirements. This unintentional discrimination is referred to as systemic discrimination.

Systemic barriers in employment practices.   Systemic discrimination refers to the exclusion of members of certain groups through the application of employment policies or practices based on criteria that are neither job-related nor required for the safe and efficient operation of the business. Systemic discrimination can create legal concerns for an organization. Many employment barriers are hidden, unintentionally, in the rules and the procedures and even the facilities that employers provide to manage their human resources. (See Figure 2.3 for examples of systemic barriers, along with possible solutions.) Inequity can result if these barriers encourage or discourage individuals based on their membership in certain groups rather than on their ability to do a job that the employer needs done. In one case, the Supreme Court of Canada ruled that a physical fitness test discriminated against women, and required the employer to re-instate the woman as a firefighter.[28]

Another example of systemic discrimination is when an employer's workforce represents one group in our society and the company recruits new employees by posting job vacancies within the company or by word of mouth among the employees. This recruitment strategy is likely to generate candidates similar to those in the current workforce, thereby unintentionally discriminating against other groups of workers in the labour market. A better approach might be to vary recruitment methods by contacting outside agencies and organizations. The Metropolitan Toronto Police Force has established an eight-member recruitment task force to boost its community representation, in part by educating visible minority groups about career opportunities in the force.[29]

The following employment practices and issues may need to be reviewed: job classifications and descriptions, recruitment processes, training and development, performance evaluation systems, promotions and upward mobility, levels of com-

Underutilization

Term applied to designated groups that are not utilized or represented in the employer's workforce proportional to their numbers in the labour market

Concentration

Term applied to designated groups whose numbers in a particular occupation or level are high relative to their numbers in the labour market

Systemic Discrimination

The exclusion of members of certain groups through the application of employment policies or practices based on criteria that are not job-related

FIGURE 2.3   *Employment Practices*

EXAMPLES OF SYSTEMIC BARRIERS

1. Recruitment practices that limit applications from designated groups, e.g., word of mouth, internal hiring policies.

2. Physical access that restricts those who are mobility impaired, e.g., no ramps, heavy doors, narrow passageways.

3. Job descriptions and job evaluation systems that undervalue the work of positions traditionally held by women.

4. A workplace environment that does not expressly discourage sexual or racial harassment.

EXAMPLES OF POSSIBLE SOLUTIONS

Word of mouth could be supplemented by calls to community organizations representing designated groups or to the local Canada Employment Centre.

FACILITY UPGRADING.

Rewrite job descriptions, rationalize evaluation systems, provide special training for supervisors.

Issue a company policy against these practices, with guidelines and follow-up through appraisal and discipline procedures, and develop complaint and problem-solving mechanisms for an employee to use.

Source: *Employment Equity: A Guide for Employers,* Employment and Immigration Canada, Cat. No. 143-5-91, May 1991, p. 19. Reproduced with permission from the Minister of Supply and Services, 1995.

pensation, access to benefits, termination processes, discipline procedures, facilities (i.e., building design, barrier-free access), and access to assistance.

The usual test for identifying systemic barriers involves using the following criteria to assess the policy:

- Is it job-related?
- Is it valid? (i.e., does it, or the required qualification, have a direct relationship to job performance?)
- Is it consistently applied?
- Does it have an adverse impact? (i.e., does it affect members of designated groups more than those of dominant groups?)
- Is it a business necessity?
- Does it conform to human rights and employment standards legislation?[30]

If the employee profiles indicate that certain types of people are underrepresented, then special measures may be undertaken to correct this imbalance.

Special measures and reasonable accommodation.   Special measures are initiatives designed to accelerate the entry, development, and promotion of members of designated groups from among the interested and qualified workforce. For example, some special measures may include targeted recruitment or special training initiatives aimed mainly at correcting, over a specified period of time, employment inequities stemming from past discrimination. These measures are intended to hasten the achievement of fair representation of the four designated groups in an employer's workforce.

Reasonable accommodation

Attempt by employers to adjust the working conditions or schedules of employees with disabilities or religious preferences

WWW

Reasonable accommodation involves adjusting employment policies and practices so that no individual is denied benefits, disadvantaged with respect to employment opportunities, or blocked from carrying out the essential components of a job because of race, colour, sex, or disability. Human rights tribunals across Canada have placed employers under a duty to demonstrate a degree of flexibility in meeting the reasonable needs of employees. It is no longer acceptable for employers to simply assume that all employees will "fit in" no matter what their special needs. Employers must find the means to alter systems to meet the needs of their employees as long as this does not cause "undue hardship to the employer." Reasonable accommodation may include redesigning job duties, adjusting work schedules, providing technical, financial, and human support services, and upgrading facilities. The City of Toronto developed award-winning facilities in its Barrier Free Access program, which was designed to allow people with disabilities accessible passage throughout City facilities. The Canadian military has adopted a policy that allows Native service men to wear their hair in traditional braids.

Reasonable accommodation benefits all employees. The providing of child care expenses for employees taking company-sponsored courses does more than remove a barrier to women; it also assists any employee with sole-parenting responsibilities. The flexible work schedules adopted by some companies in northern Canada benefit Aboriginal employees, who are prepared to work atypical hours in exchange for significant breaks away from the work site to take part in traditional hunting and fishing activities. Many other employees also benefit from these flexible work schedules.

FIGURE 2.4 *Suggestions for an Accessible Workplace*

- Install easy-to-reach switches.
- Provide sloping sidewalks and entrances.
- Install wheelchair ramps.
- Reposition shelves for the easy reach of materials.
- Rearrange tables, chairs, vending machines, dispensers, and other furniture and fixtures.
- Widen doors and hallways.
- Add raised markings on control buttons.
- Provide designated accessible parking spaces.
- Install hand controls or manipulation devices.
- Provide flashing alarm lights.
- Remove turnstiles and revolving doors or provide alternative accessible paths.
- Install holding bars in toilet areas.
- Redesign toilet partitions to increase access space.
- Add paper cup dispensers at water fountains.
- Replace high-pile, low-density carpeting.
- Reposition telephones, water fountains, and other needed equipment.
- Add raised toilet seats.
- Provide a full-length bathroom mirror.

Special arrangements should be made to accommodate people who are visually impaired, illiterate, or unfamiliar with the English language with tools such as Braille forms, confidential interviews, or translation. Suggestions for an accessible workplace are found in Figure 2.4.

Step 4: Establishment of a Workplan

The workforce analysis and the review of employment systems will provide the employer with a useful base from which to develop a workplan with realistic goals and timetables. A narrative statement or summary of the conclusions drawn from the examination of the workforce analysis forms part of the employment equity workplan. The summary should include any restrictions faced in hiring due to collective agreements, staff movements, or the need for specialized skills in a particular profession. The identification of restrictions helps form an overall employment equity strategy.

The plan should be considered a working tool designed to achieve results. It is a document that describes how proposed actions are to be achieved. The plan should be an integral part of the organization's overall operational plans, and must include:

- numerical goals with time frames;
- explanations about the proposed improvement in the hiring, training, and promotion of the four designated groups to increase their representation and improve their distribution throughout the organization;
- descriptions of specific activities to achieve the numerical goals; *and*
- an outline of monitoring and evaluation procedures to follow program implementation.

Numerical goals must be realistic numbers related to the workforce analysis. The goals must catalogue opportunities for hiring, training, and promotion, and must demonstrate a valid effort to correct underrepresentation or concentration of all designated groups in specific occupations or occupational categories. Nonnumerical goals include activities such as implementation of barrier-free design, targeted recruitment and advertising, modification of employment policies or practices, and provision of developmental training.

The overall goal for an organization is to achieve a representative workforce. An organization's workforce is representative when it reflects the demographic composition of the external workforce. A nonrepresentative workforce is an indicator of the need for evaluation and action to remove the barriers that block or discourage certain groups from employment and advancement. Workplan initiatives in conjunction with special measures and reasonable accommodation should contribute to the overall success of this goal.

Step 5: Implementation

The implementation of employment equity is idiosyncratic in that no two plans will be the same. Each strategy should be designed to meet the needs of the particular organization. The success of plan implementation depends on senior management's commitment to the process, how the roles and responsibilities are defined, what resources are available, the effectiveness of the communications strategy, the acceptance of plan initiatives and objectives, and the availability of training. The plan, in essence a living document, will be affected by the changes in the internal and external environment throughout the implementation period. Therefore, its strategies may be modified or eliminated when results are not achieved or if resource restraints or economic conditions necessitate a different strategy. The implementation is guided and monitored by those responsible and accountable for its outcome.

Step 6: Evaluation, Monitoring, and Revision

By monitoring progress, the employer will be able to evaluate the overall success of the equity initiatives used to achieve a representative workforce, as well as respond to organizational and environmental changes. Annual progress reports provided to all employees communicate initiatives and achievements. Interim reports on special projects heighten program visibility and acceptance; they also promote management commitment and accountability. Access the equity report at Simon Fraser University (**www.sfu.ca/employment-equity/index.html**). Research suggests that the wage gaps between white men and the designated groups are closing more rapidly in organizations with formal employment equity programs than in organizations without such programs.[31]

WWW

The monitoring activity is an essential component in the planning cycle. Only through monitoring can an employer determine whether goals are being attained and problems resolved, whether new programs are succeeding, and whether strategies have been effective. If the employer finds, upon review of the program, that there are negative results, alterations to the existing plan will have to be made with new goals. In this regard, the planning process is evolutionary, in that the achievement of employment equity involves organizational changes and builds on experience.

OTHER EMPLOYMENT EQUITY ISSUES

OBJECTIVE 6

Reverse Discrimination

In pursuing employment equity, employers may be accused of **reverse discrimination**, or giving preference to members of the designated groups to the extent that nonmembers believe they are suffering discrimination. In March 2000, an applicant for a job with the Public Service Commission was told by a receptionist that her application was not welcome because the government already had many white employees. When these charges occur, organizations are caught between attempting to correct past discriminatory practices and handling present complaints alleging that HR practices are unfair. It is exactly this Catch-22 that makes employment equity controversial. The Ontario College of Art adopted a policy of hiring only women for a ten-year period to correct a preponderance of men on its faculty.[32] Several male applicants complained that they should be interviewed and the best person be given the job. Ethics in HRM describes the concerns of white males who feel that they are victims of reverse discrimination.

Reverse discrimination

Giving preference to members of designated groups to the extent that nonmembers become the subjects of discrimination

WWW

Sexual harassment

Unwelcome advances, requests for sexual favours, and other verbal or physical conduct of a sexual nature in the working environment

Sexual Harassment

According to one study, only four of every ten Canadian women who suffer **sexual harassment** at work take any formal action, and only one out of every two women believe that a complaint would be taken seriously in their workplace.[33] This belief is reinforced by cases such as the one involving a female Sears employee who was shot to death by her manager. Fifteen months earlier, she had complained to her employer that she was being sexually harassed by her manager. The company maintained that his behaviour did not constitute sexual harassment and that he was merely a "persistent pursuer." In keeping with this position, they made no effort to stop the manager's behaviour.[34]

Many organizations are developing policies to deal with sexual harassment in the workplace. Such policies are intended as preventive measures not only against damage to reputation and employee morale, but also against the kind of litigation that Magna International faced when it was sued on the grounds that Magna employees had attempted to win contracts from purchasing officers for the Big Three automakers by wooing them with gifts and entertainment, including trips to topless bars.[35]

WWW

The sexual harrassment at policy BC Hydro focuses on avoidance and resolution rather than punishment after the fact. The Canadian Armed Forces trained 90,000 members to recognize and avoid harrassment of all kinds. Sexual situations in the work environment are not new to organizational life. Sexual feelings are a part of group dynamics, and people who work together may come to develop these kinds of feelings for one another. Unfortunately, these encounters are often unpleasant and unwelcome, as evidenced by the many reported instances of sexual harassment. Highlights in HRM 7 provides a sample of questions that can be used during a sexual harassment audit. An instrument like this one, which is essentially a test, is a valuable tool for determining what employees know and do not know about sexual harassment.

The Ontario Human Rights Code identifies three kinds of sexual harassment:

1. When someone says or does things to you of a sexual nature and you do not want or welcome it. This includes behaviour that a person should know you do not want or welcome. For example, your supervisor makes you feel

Ethics in HRM

REVERSE DISCRIMINATION

"White, Male and Worried" is the title of an article in *Business Week* that describes the unease Caucasian males feel with respect to the issue of employment equity. White males feel that they are being passed over for jobs and promotions in favour of less-qualified candidates. They complain of being blamed for everything, including all historical injustices. They are feeling threatened.

One bank manager responsible for identifying barriers to women's advancement received hate mail and was thrown out of some offices. People were saying to her: "Please stop. We have enough problems. There aren't enough jobs for the men, and you're talking about giving women more jobs and better jobs."

According to white males, members of designated groups are sometimes hired on the basis of the quota system, not the qualifications system. Merit is at the heart of the employment equity issue. Are white males the invisible victims of employment equity?

Sources: D. Flavelle, "Teaching Chiefs How to Bank on Women Workers," *Toronto Star,* May 10, 1995: E1, E3; and "White, Male and Worried," *Business Week,* January 31, 1994: 50–5.

Highlights in HRM

7   QUESTIONS ASKED IN AUDITING SEXUAL HARASSMENT

ACTIVITY.	IS THIS SEXUAL HARASSMENT?			ARE YOU AWARE OF THIS BEHAVIOUR IN THE ORGANIZATION?	
• Employees post cartoons on bulletin boards containing sexually related material.	Yes	No	Uncertain	Yes	No
• A male employee says to a female employee that she has beautiful eyes and hair.	Yes	No	Uncertain	Yes	No
• A male manager habitually calls all female employees "sweetie" or "darling."	Yes	No	Uncertain	Yes	No
• A manager fails to promote a female employee when she will not grant sexual favours.	Yes	No	Uncertain	Yes	No
• Male employees use vulgar language and tell sexual jokes that are overheard by, but not directed at, female employees.	Yes	No	Uncertain	Yes	No
• A male employee leans and peers over the back of a female employee when she wears a low-cut dress.	Yes	No	Uncertain	Yes	No
• A supervisor gives a female (male) subordinate a nice gift on her (his) birthday.	Yes	No	Uncertain	Yes	No
• Two male employees share a sexually explicit magazine while observed by a female employee.	Yes	No	Uncertain	Yes	No

uncomfortable by talking about sex all the time. The Human Rights Code says that when you show that you do not welcome or want the remarks or actions, the person must stop doing those things right away.

2. A person who has authority or power to deny you something such as a promotion or a raise makes sexual suggestions or requests that you do not want or welcome. For example, your teacher says you must have sex with him or her or you will not pass the course. Even if you do not complain about a sexual suggestion or request, it can still be sexual harassment unless it is clear that you welcome or want it.

3. A person with authority or the power to deny you something important punishes you or threatens to do something to you for refusing a sexual request. For example, your employer fires you, or threatens to fire you, because you refuse to go on a date.

WWW

York University has developed a comprehensive program to deal with sexual harassment issues. To augment its program it has published a booklet titled *Sexual Assault and Harassment on Campus*, which is intended for students and employees. This booklet provides safety tips for women and men as well as definitions of sexual harassment and other forms of harassment.[36] A pamphlet titled *Sexual Harassment and You: What Every Student Should Know* is made available to any interested person. York's policy states:

> York University strives to provide an environment wherein all students, faculty and staff are able to learn, study, teach and work, free from sexual harassment.
>
> Sexual harassment is:
>
> **1.** Unwanted sexual attention of a persistent or abusive nature, made by a person who knows or ought reasonably to know that such attention is unwanted;
>
> **2.** The making of an implied or express promise of reward for complying with a sexually oriented request;
>
> **3.** The making of an implied or express threat or reprisal, in the form of actual reprisal or in the denial of opportunity, for refusal to comply with a sexually oriented request;
>
> **4.** Sexually oriented remarks and behaviour which may reasonably be perceived to create a negative psychological and emotional environment [sometimes labelled a hostile environment] for work and study.
>
> Incidents of sexual harassment shall be investigated and dealt with by the University in accordance with guidelines and procedures put in place for that purpose from time to time.
>
> Students, faculty and staff who, it is determined, have sexually harassed another member(s) of the University community will be subject to discipline and sanctions as are appropriate in the circumstances, including but not limited to discipline and sanctions provided for in Presidential Regulations (in the case of students), and relevant collective agreements.[37]

For sexual-harassment policies to succeed, confidentiality is necessary, and so is a method for filing complaints. Without organizational commitment to zero tolerance with respect to harassment, any such policy will be meaningless. Highlights in HRM 8 presents some suggestions for an effective sexual harassment policy.[38]

Mandatory Retirement

Age is a prohibited ground of discrimination under the Human Rights Act, yet employees are forced to retire at age sixty-five. The Supreme Court recently upheld mandatory retirement, arguing that its elimination would cause monumental social upheaval.[39] However, provinces can abolish mandatory retirement within their own jurisdictions. To date, Alberta, Manitoba, and Quebec have done so.

MANAGING DIVERSITY

Managing diversity goes beyond Canadian employment equity legislation's four designated groups in addressing the need to create a fair work environment. The terms "diversity management" and "employment equity" are often used inter-

---

Highlights in HRM

8   BASIC COMPONENTS OF AN EFFECTIVE SEXUAL HARASSMENT POLICY

1. Develop a comprehensive organization-wide policy on sexual harassment, and present it to all current and new employees. Stress that sexual harassment will not be tolerated under any circumstances. Emphasis is best achieved when the policy is publicized and supported by top management.
2. Hold training sessions with supervisors to explain their role in providing an environment free of sexual harassment, and proper investigative procedures when charges occur.
3. Establish a formal complaint procedure whereby employees can discuss problems without fear of retaliation. The complaint procedure should spell out how charges will be investigated and resolved.
4. Act immediately when employees complain of sexual harassment. Communicate widely that investigations will be conducted objectively and with appreciation for the sensitivity of the issue.
5. When an investigation supports employee charges, discipline the offender at once. For extremely serious offences, discipline should include penalties up to and including discharge. Discipline should be applied consistently across similar cases and among managers and hourly employees alike.
6. Follow up on all cases to ensure a satisfactory resolution of the problem.

Diversity management

The optimization of an organization's multicultural workforce in order to reach business objectives

changeably, but there are differences. **Diversity management** is voluntary; employment equity is not. Managing diversity is a broader, more inclusive concept encompassing such factors as religion, personality, lifestyle, and education. By managing diversity, organizations hope to gain a strategic and competitive advantage by helping all employees perform to their full potential.[40]

The City of Toronto led by example when it recognized "non-Christian City of Toronto staff" by giving them two days of paid time off for religious holidays if they agreed to work Christmas Day and Good Friday (Christian holidays) at straight time.[41] Also, McDonald's Restaurants of Canada used multi-age teams and found remarkable synergy in the diversity of ages.[42]

WWW

Organizations such as CN, the Bank of Montreal, and Warner-Lambert are pioneers in the diversity movement. According to Marie Tellier, Canadian National's assistant vice-president of employment equity, the hiring and development and good management of a diverse workforce whose values and expectations are different from their managers is no longer an option—it is an economic necessity. By the year 2000, 70 to 80 percent of new arrivals on the work market will be women and nonwhites. In this context, diversity management is not only a legal obligation, but also a necessity imposed by market laws, by competition, and by the need to be the best to survive.[43]

Statistics show that the ethnocultural profile of Canada has been changing since the 1960s, and will continue to change dramatically over the next twenty years. It has been estimated that by the year 2001, visible minorities will account for 17 percent of the Canadian population.[44]

According to the 1996 Census, visible minorities represent 11.2 percent of the population. Chinese were the largest group (25 percent), followed by South Asians (21 percent) and blacks (18 percent).[45]

WWW

CEOs in Canada recognize that ethnic groups possess expertise such as language skills, knowledge of foreign cultures and business practices, and natural trade links with overseas markets that can be used to capture market share in emerging economies and new Canadian markets.[46] Ebco, a manufacturing company in

Chung Kwong Cheung, winner of a contest sponsored by the National Movement for Harmony in Canada to promote racial understanding, was able to capture the essence of the new face of Canada.[47]

Richmond, British Columbia, which has won awards for excellence in race relations, is doing business in Germany and Taiwan because it was able to tap the networks and skills of its employees, who trace their origins to forty-eight different countries. The spending power of these groups is another motivating factor. In 1991 the spending power of Canada's visible minorities was estimated to be $76 billion—a figure expected to rise to $300 billion by 2001.[48] According to Edgar Ware, ethnocultural business manager at Digital Equipment of Canada, "We have an obligation to the cultural fabric. We want to look like the people we sell to."[49] Digital's goal is to balance a diversity strategy with the organization's business plan.

WWW

Besides the moral issues surrounding diversity, there is a critical economic need for Canada to increase its share of world trade and expand its trade portfolio. In 1997, 87 percent of our export market was dominated by the United States, Japan, and the United Kingdom. If Canadian business continues to rely heavily on these markets, our export growth and standard of living may not keep pace with other international markets.[50] Third World countries in emerging markets are going to require new investments in infrastructure, public systems, and productive capital. Given the multicultural background of many of its workers, Canada is in an excellent position to provide these services.[51] Canadian companies such as Northern Telecom and SNC-Lavalin have already begun to tap the potential of these emerging markets.

WWW

Creating an Environment for Success

Transforming an organizational culture into a culture that embraces diversity can be a complex and lengthy process. Diversity initiatives should be taken slowly so that everyone can understand that this change is an evolutionary process and that expectations should be realistic. Individuals must fully understand the time, effort, commitment, and risk involved and the need for a systematic approach.[52]

Leadership is one of the most important variables in an organization's ability to successfully incorporate diversity into its business strategy. In a recent Conference Board of Canada survey, 86 percent of respondents indicated that responsibility rested with human resources.[53] The initiative should not be perceived as a human resources program or policy, but rather as a business imperative. In the words of Prem Benimadhu, vice-president of human resources research for the Conference Board, "Building a racially and culturally diverse work force has been perceived as a human resources issue. But as long as it is, it's not going to be in the mission statement of organizations."[54] Only 6 percent of firms surveyed by the Conference Board study mentioned ethnic and cultural diversity in their mission statements.

WWW

Diversity initiatives should be linked directly to the business objectives/goals of the most senior levels of management. (See Figure 2.5.) Reality Check demonstrates how the Bank of Montreal has woven its program into its organizational fabric.

Organizations seeking to incorporate the value of diversity into their corporate philosophy must make use of appropriate internally and externally focused communications. For example, the National Bank of Canada participates annually in Montreal's "La semaine des communautés culturelles," a week dedicated to the celebration of Montreal's multiculturalism. The bank believes that its visible demonstrations of commitment to ethnocultural diversity in the community it serves help raise the bank's profile.[55] Rogers Communications, a Canadian pioneer in diversity management, issued a corporate statement to communicate its commitment to diversity (see Highlights in HRM 9).

FIGURE 2.5 *Managing Diversity—A Strategic Approach*

Supportive Environment
- Strategic Plan
- Operational Plan
- Communication and Training

Measurement
- Performance Review—Employees
- Organizational Results Assessment

Highlights in HRM

9   ROGERS COMMUNICATIONS DIVERSITY MANAGEMENT PROGRAM

- Rogers employees are our single most important asset and we need to ensure that we continue to attract the highest qualified candidates to fill our current and future business needs.
- We must create an environment that celebrates the diversity of our workforce and accommodates individual needs to maximize staff morale and productivity.
- A diverse workforce will position us to take advantage and develop our business in the diverse markets and communities we serve.
- All Rogers business units need to continually seek opportunities that ensure Diversity Management plan initiatives are realistic and achievable.

Source: Courtesy of Sofia Theodorou, Director, Organizational Development, Rogers Communications Inc.

THE BANK OF MONTREAL

The Bank of Montreal, well known throughout the Canadian marketplace as an exemplary leader in diversity and equality issues, won the Catalyst Award for promoting women's careers. It was the first time a Canadian organization had won the award. (Catalyst recognizes organizations in North America for outstanding achievements in employment equity.) Johanne Totta, vice-president of workplace equality, spearheads the equity campaign from her Montreal and Toronto offices.

"One of the keys to our success is the ability to integrate our programs into the fabric of the organization. In other words, it does not become the flavour of the month. We have to really understand the issues in each of our communities across the country. We promote qualified people into senior positions, people who can make a difference and who understand their communities. In one aboriginal community, our vice president is an aboriginal with ties to his community. Working closely with the elders, he is able to find out what is going on in his business community and in that way he can better serve their needs. What might be successful in an aboriginal community might not work the same way in another community.

"To ensure that goals are met, the whole aspect of 'diversity and equality' is linked to the annual business plan. The managers are expected to understand their communities in which they provide service, so they are expected to monitor their environments and look for ways to service the communities with the appropriate staff. You can't do the right thing for the wrong reasons, so specific training is provided on how to build diversity into the business plan. As an initial step in the process, the managers must develop a plan considering the demographics and then continually build on the plan. By providing a supportive environment, managers are able to achieve the performance measurements expected. Managers must be accountable to the program through their performance appraisal.

"Communication of our program and achievements is a major component. Successes are reported through a video called 875 Live. (The term '875' is the form number for our interoffice memo.) All branches get the good news every couple of months. On a quarterly basis, the president also reports on equality initiatives. We use a National and Regional Advisory Council to learn about issues. The National Advisory Council consists of senior executives who meet to discuss the results of the business plan and ensure the plan is aggressive enough and achievable. The Regional Advisory Councils are made up of people from diversified backgrounds, including senior and junior representatives. The advisory councils are the channels whereby we find out what's really happening. We had an instance where one manager wanted everyone to go on flextime. However, the intent is not to force people to go on a program that does not meet their needs. Through the council we were able to rectify this issue.

"The ultimate goal is to meet the customer's needs. We have to understand not only their language but their culture. For example, when we set up the Asian banking strategy, we introduced a hotline number for our customers. Just before it was introduced, one of our Asian executives pointed out that we had assigned a lot of number fours. We did not realize that the number four was not acceptable to the Asian community, so we changed it immediately. To ensure our branches are more inviting to our Aboriginal communities, we use earth tones and Aboriginal artifacts.

"When our efforts toward advancement of women began in 1990, we only had 6 percent of women in executive positions; today we have 16 percent. This was achieved as a result of a Task Force on the Advancement of Women. One of the keys in any of our task forces is to repudiate myths. For example, with women, myths such as 'they have babies and quit,' 'they're too young or too old,' 'they just need more education,' and 'they don't have the right stuff' have often been used. We made efforts to show that those statements were not true. When we compared the ages of both groups, we found them to be about the same for both women and men. We also proved that although women have babies, they also had longer service records than men at the bank at every level except senior management.

"Through our strategic plan and our annual business plan, we will continue to maintain momentum, identify new issues as they arise, and survey to see if the culture is changing in any one of our business communities. It is important to remove all barriers and enhance diversity so that the program is fair to everyone. Workplace equality includes not only diversity—it also considers work and life. Providing programs that offer flexibility and opportunity to meet the needs of our employees will ultimately result in meeting the needs of our customers."

WWW

Cross-functional teams established to drive the diversity initiative are used successfully as communication vehicles by many leading edge organizations. Toronto's Sunnybrook Health Science Centre has implemented a Patient Diversity Task Force to examine and report on the barriers faced by its patients, residents, and families.[56] Other organizations seek to raise the awareness of ethnocultural diversity. Some of these initiatives are outlined in Highlights in HRM 10.

Training is essential to the success of diversity implementation. A number of companies, including Imperial Oil and Connaught Laboratories, have incorporated diversity training. Cultural etiquette is an important aspect of diversity training that aims to explain the differences, or diversity, in people.

The Department of National Defense includes diversity training in its basic officer training course.[57] A consortium of European and North American businesses is attempting to develop a global diversity standard, by which companies will be able to use software to rate the success of their diversity programs.[58]

Of even greater importance than training is the need to incorporate elements of diversity into all core training programs and to tailor those elements to meet the needs of specific business units or groups of employees.[59]

An added advantage of implementing a diversity initiative relates to its impact on employee retention. Retention of well-qualified and skilled employees is an important goal, considering the amount of resources—in both time and money—spent on recruiting and hiring new employees. Canadian organizations spend an average of 28 hours recruiting a new management or professional employee, 42 hours recruiting a new executive, and 20 hours recruiting a new technical/supervisory employee.[60] Maintaining a balanced and diversified workforce during periods of downsizing continues to be a major challenge.

Much the same as is required under employment equity, an overall review of policies and employment practices must be considered. In this regard, the use of an employee attitude survey may prove beneficial in finding areas of systemic or perceived discrimination. The evaluation criteria used most often by Canadian organizations are staff attitudes, increases in promotions for minority employees, reduction

Highlights in HRM

10   DIVERSITY AT WORK

WWW

When Apple Computer was about to market a piece of audio software called "Moof," it came close to offending 1.7 billion potential customers in the growing computer markets of India and the Middle East. Moof was a phonetic combination of "moo" and "woof." Mentioning the word "cowdog" could have proved offensive to both Hindus (to whom cows are sacred) and Muslims (to whom pigs are filthy creatures).

Quebecor Printing Inc. won a $10 million deal in the Caribbean because of one employee who was a Jamaican immigrant. Lester Garnett was able to match the region's needs with Quebecor expertise to open up a new market for the Canadian company. As a result, telephone directories for Trinidad, Bermuda, and the Bahamas are printed in Canada.

Warner-Lambert Canada had promotional materials printed in Korean and has hired an Asian representative to establish contact with current and potential accounts due to the company's high involvement with Korean small retailers in Toronto.

Caisse populaire Desjardins Cartierville has hired staff to provide service in nine languages—French, English, German, Arabic, Italian, Creole, Spanish, Portuguese, and Armenian. Select marketing and promotional materials have been translated into each of these languages. Regular information seminars are held to welcome new immigrants to the caisse system, and the caisse is an active participant in several ethnoculturally oriented organizations.

Sources: C.L. Taylor, "Dimensions of Diversity in Canadian Business: Building a Business Case for Valuing Ethnocultural Diversity," *The Conference Board of Canada, Report 143-95,* April 1995; J. Schilder, "The Rainbow Connection: Employers Who Promote Diversity May Discover a Pot of Gold," *Human Resources Professional* (April 1994): 13–15; M. Gibb-Clark, "The Payoff is Global," *The Globe and Mail,* May 16, 1995: B14.

in turnover of minority employees, reduction in number of harassment suits, recruitment statistics for minorities, and improvements in productivity.[61]

A final element in achieving success is monitoring progress and providing qualitative and quantitative evidence of change. For example, during their performance appraisals, all salaried employees at Levi Strauss & Co. (Canada) are evaluated on their ability to meet both business and aspirational goals. Aspirational goals are based on the company's core values, which include valuing diversity, following ethical management practices, and encouraging new behaviours, recognition, communications, and empowerment. These aspirations are the shared values and behaviours that will drive the company toward its mission of "sustained responsible commercial success."[62] When management measures performance as a function of diversity initiatives, values are instilled in the minds of all employees, and it is demonstrated that change and diversity are part of day-to-day business. To achieve success in diversity, it is vital to set an example and to create an atmosphere that respects and values differences. Canadian organizations have recognized the competitive advantage of embracing diversity in their business strategies. Highlights in HRM 11 describes the diversity program at Royal Bank Financial Group.

WWW

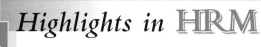

Highlights in HRM

11   LEVERAGING DIVERSITY

WWW

The Royal Bank Financial Group had already met its employment equity goals and in 1996 decided to become a leader in diversity management. It started by defining "diversity management" much more broadly than is typical for equity programs. The Royal felt that dimensions such as age, race, and gender are primarily inborn. The secondary dimensions such as education, military service, parental status, and income are acquired and can be changed or modified. They contribute to identity.

Royal wanted to harness the diversity of its 55,000 employees, and use it to gain business advantages. The diversity of its employees helps the Royal understand its customer needs. By supporting employees to fulfil their potential, the Royal fulfils its business potential.

Employee surveys revealed that the diversity effort had to have the support of managers, and that it had to be driven by business needs, and not be an HR standalone initiative. A Diversity Business Council was created and employee surveys and twenty-eight focus groups were conducted. The result was six objectives and fifteen action plans. An example of an objective was "creating a competitive advantage by making products, services, delivery channels and systems accessible to all clients and employees." Action plans included "benchmarking and sharing best practices" and "integrating diversity into business plans."

The Royal also uncovered problems. For example, one deterrent to hiring people with disabilities was that the hire could represent a significant cost to the department. The Royal established a Centralized Accommodation Budget, which managers could use to accommodate people with disabilities.

Source: L. Young, "Leveraging Diversity at the Royal Bank," *Canadian HR Reporter,* March 27, 2000: 9. N. Tombari and N. Spinks, "The Work/Family Interface at Royal Bank Financial Group: Successful Solutions—a Retrospective Look at the Lessons Learned," *Women in Management Review* 14, no. 5, 1999: 186–9.

SUMMARY

OBJECTIVE 1   Employment equity refers to the employment of individuals in a fair and nonbiased manner. Four groups in Canada—women, visible minorities, Aboriginals, and persons with disabilities—tend to be concentrated in a few occupations that are accorded lower status and pay.

OBJECTIVE 2   The Canadian Human Rights Act applies to all federally governed departments and agencies, and all organizations incorporated under federal jurisdiction. The act prohibits discrimination on the basis of grounds such as race, religion, sex, age, national or ethnic origin, physical handicap, and marital status. The Canadian Human Rights Commission enforces the act through a formal complaint procedure.

OBJECTIVE 3   Pay equity is an amendment to the Canadian Human Rights Act that makes it illegal for employers to discriminate against individuals on the basis of job content. By definition, pay equity means equal pay for work of equal value.

The Employment Equity Act requires all federally regulated employers to prepare an employment equity plan. The Canadian Human Rights Commission is mandated under the Canadian Human Rights Act to prohibit discrimination in the establishments of federally regulated businesses.

 The implementation of employment equity involves six steps: senior management support, data collection and analysis, an employment system review, establishment of a workplan, implementation, strategy, and a follow-up process that includes monitoring, reviewing, and revision.

 Reverse discrimination, sexual harassment, and mandatory retirement are among the employment equity issues undergoing continued debate.

 Managing diversity does more than incorporate employment equity. The goal of diversity management is to optimize the utilization of an organization's multicultural workforce with the goal of realizing strategic advantage.

KEY TERMS

bona fide occupational
    qualification (BGOQ)
concentration
designated groups
diversity management

employment equity
flow data
reasonable accommodation
reverse discrimination
sexual harassment

stock data
systemic discrimination
underutilization

DISCUSSION QUESTIONS

 1. Explain why employment equity is needed in organizations. What are the arguments for and against it?

 2. Identify the major federal laws that relate to employment equity, and discuss how they are enforced.

 3. Define pay equity, and discuss strategies for implementing it.

 4. Describe the purpose of the Employment Equity Act, and discuss some of its provisions.

 5. After receiving several complaints of sexual harassment, the HR department

of a city library decides to establish a sexual harassment policy. What should be included in the policy? How should it be implemented?

 6. "Discrimination against older persons does not generate the same degree of moral outrage as other forms of discrimination." Do you agree? If you find this quote offensive, read the full text of the Human Rights Commission's discussion paper on human rights for the aging (**www.ohrc.on.ca**).

 7. Describe how an organization can optimize the use of a multicultural workforce.

CASE 1

HIRING PEOPLE WITH DISABILITIES DETERMINING ATTITUDES

In Canada, 40.3 percent of people with disabilities of working age have jobs. To accommodate 75 percent of these individuals would cost organizations less than $1,000 each. A pool of talented and motivated people is available, and the accommodation costs are reasonable. Why won't more organizations hire them?

Norma Daggett, HR director for Denton Plastics, would like to introduce more diversity into the company's workforce by hiring qualified people with disabilities. Before proceeding to the hiring phase, she would like to get a sense of how the present workforce will respond to her diversity plan. To that end, she has developed the following test consisting of true/false statements that will help her determine employee attitudes toward people with disabilities.

1. Most people with disabilities do not require special work arrangements.

2. The real problem for the people with disabilities is holding a job, not getting one.

3. Employees with disabilities tend to have more accidents than other employees.

4. These employees are less likely to have a record of absenteeism.

5. People with the most severe impairments are likely to be at the top in job performance.

6. Turnover tends to be higher among employees with disabilities than among other employees.

7. Other employees tend to respond negatively when accommodations (e.g., wheelchair ramps) are made for employees with disabilities.

Questions

1. Give a true or false response to each of the above statements.

2. Refer to the correct answers (based on statistical evidence) given at the end of the chapter. For each item you answered incorrectly, ask yourself, "Where did I get that idea?" See if you can detect any personal bias toward people with disabilities.

3. Why are people with disabilities still underemployed?

CASE 2

FIGHTING FIRES

In British Columbia, the competition for firefighting jobs is fierce, with over 1,600 people applying for about sixty jobs. At one time, the provincial Ministry of Forests required all job applicants to pass this physical fitness test:

- Lift a 23 kilogram bar in an upright rowing motion 18 times.
- Carry pumps and hoses, weighting as much as 50 kilograms, over a timed distance.

● Perform a shuttle run, which involves darting back and forth at an increasingly faster pace between cones situated 20 metres apart.

WWW

The B.C. Government and Service Employees Union argued that the average man, with training, could easily pass the test, whereas the average woman, even with training, could not. Only 35 percent of women who applied for the firefighter's job passed the test; about 70 percent of the men did.

The University of Victoria scientists who designed the tests argued that most women could reach the standard, although they would have to work harder than most men to do so. Female firefighters said they had to train year round to pass the test, but they took this as a personal responsibility and as the cost of qualifying for the job. Their safety, as well as that of their colleagues and the public, depends on their strength and endurance. The B.C. Ministry of Forests spokeswoman suggested that lowering the standards would be a mistake: "Already male firefighters are asking if blazes will be designated as 'guy' fires and 'girl' fires. We want the fittest people."

Questions

1. Did the standards result in safer and more effective firefighting crews, or were they inadvertently keeping women out of a traditionally male job?

2. Was this a BFOQ? The ministry was challenged on the basis of sex discrimination. What did the Supreme Court rule, and what was their reasoning?

3. Female applicants had the chance to train and try the test at B.C. university campuses. Was this special preparation discriminatory?

4. Did the changes made fix the underlying problems? Explain.

5. What other advice would you give their managers?

CAREER COUNSEL

Find out how to handle prohibited questions during a job interview by visiting the Managing Human Resources website (**belcourt.nelson.com**).

USING THE INTERNET

WWW

The Canadian Human Rights Commission (**www.chrc–ccdp.ca**) deals with complaints concerning discriminatory practices covered by legislation.
The Neal Squire Foundation (**www.neisquire.ca**) creates opportunities for those with physical disabilities.

The Alliance for Employment Equity (www.web.net/~allforee) offers a very useful checklist on myths and facts about employment equity.

The Urban Alliance on Race Relations (**www.interlog.com/~uarr/uarr/about.html**) helps organizations develop equal access policies.

The Canadian Auto Workers (**www.caw.ca/equity.html**) provides recent statistics about designated groups.

IBM offers guidelines (**www-3.ibm.com/able/disablity.html**) about successful access to information and use of information technology by people who have disabilities.

Diversity Central (**www.diversity central.com**) is a good first stop for any information on diversity.

Another useful site is **www.diversityatwork.com**, which provides various resources, from a calendar of important cultural and religious dates and events, to a library of diversity and equity information.

CIBC's diversity policy is posted at **www.cibc.com/inside/diversitymonth.html.**

A site that provides discussion of issues on disability, as well as excellent Canadian and American links, is that of the National Institute of Disability Management and Research (**www.nidmar.ca**).

The Council of Canadians with Disabilities (**www.pcs.mbca/~ccd**) is an advocacy group.

Transition Resources and Career Services for Students with Disabilities (**tracs.csum.edu?succeedi.htm**) is an American site, but it provides a useful online publication, *Succeeding Together: People with Disabilities in the Workplace,* that outlines ways in which workplaces can accommodate those with disabilities.

NOTES AND REFERENCES

1. Human Resources Development Canada, 1998 Annual Report, Analysis of Employers' Reports, **www.hrdc-drhc.gc.ca/LEEP/Annual _Reports/98.**

2. Statistics Canada website: **www.statcan.ca/english/census 1996 table 2**

3. L. Redpath and M.O. Nielsen. "A Comparison of Native Culture, Non-Native Culture and New Management Ideology," *Canadian Journal of Administrative Studies* 14, no. 3 (1996): 327–39.

4. J. Badets and T.W.L. Chu, "Canada's Changing Immigrant Population: Focus on Canada," Statistics Canada, Ministry of Industry, Science, and Technology, Cat. No. 96-311E, 1994.

5. Annual Report, Employment Equity Act, 1996, Labour Standards and Workplace Equity, Human Resources Development Canada, Cat. No. LT-020-12-96.

6. *Employment Equity: A Guide for Employers*, Employment and Immigration Canada, Cat. No. LM-143-5-91, May 1991: 9.

7. Victor S. Mackinnon, "The Canadian Charter of Rights and Freedoms," *Public Administration: Canadian Materials* (North York: Captus Press, 1993): 179–80.

8 Canadian Human Rights Act, Canadian Human Rights Commission, 1978, Paragraph 2, Subsection (a).

9. A.P. Aggarwal, *Sex Discrimination: Employment Law and Practices*, (Toronto: Butterworths Canada, 1994).

10. "Firm Pays $300,000 in Racial Harassment Settlements," *Human Resources Management in Canada*, Report Bulletin No. 72 (Scarborough, Ont.: Prentice-Hall Canada, February 1989): 1–2.

11. Canadian Human Rights Act, Paragraph 46, Section 2(a), (b).

12. Annual Report, Employment Equity Act, 1997, Labour Standards and Workplace Equity, Human Resources Development Canada, Cat. No. LT-020-12-97.

13. Russel J.G. Juriansz, *Equal Pay Legislation and Ontario's New Pay Equity Act* (Toronto: Blake, Cassels & Graydon, 1995), 3–5.

14. Susan Riggs, "Comparing Apples and Oranges: Job Evaluations," *Worklife* 8, no. 1 (1991): 7–10.

15. "Achieving Pay Equity First Goal, But through Co-operation: Commissioner," *Pay Equity Commission Report* 1, no. 1 (March 1988): 6.

16. Morley Gunderson and Roberta Edgecombe Robb, "Equal Pay for Work of Equal Value: Canada's Experience," *Advances in Industrial and Labour Relations* 5 (1991): 151–68. See also John G. Kelly, *Pay Equity Management* (Toronto: CCH Canadian, 1988), 45–54.

17. Mme. Justice Rosalie Silberman Abella, Commissioner, *Equality in Employment: A Royal Commission Report* (Ottawa: Supply and Services Canada, 1984): 9.

18. *Introduction to Employment Equity*, Human Resources Development Canada, 1996.

19. Section 2, Employment Equity Act, 1986.

20. Kelly Toughill, "Firms Back Equity: To Some It's 'Good Business' Despite Harris's Vow to Scrap It," *Toronto Star*, June 21, 1995: A2.

21. Canadian Human Rights Act, S.C. 1976–77, c. as amended.

22. R.G.L. Fairweather, Canadian Human Rights Commission, The Standing Committee on Legal and Constitutional Affairs, May 29, 1986: 10.

23. *Towards Equity: 1993 Merit Awards*, Employment Equity Branch, Human Resources Development Canada, June 1994: 17–18.

24. *Workplace Innovations Overview—1996*, Bureau of Labour Information, Human Resources Development Canada: 1–84.

25. *Towards Equity: 1993 Merit Awards*: 11–12.

26. L. Young, "Employers Need to Scrutinize All Job Testing for Human Rights Violations, Supreme Court Rules" *Canadian HR Reporter*, October 4, 1999: 3.

27. Ibid., 18.

28. Aggarwal, *Sex Discrimination*.

29. Nicholas Keung, "Police Recruit Ethnic Officers to Boost Force," *Toronto Star*, July 25, 1997: A7.

30. *Employment Equity: A Guide for Employers*: 19.

31. Joanne Leck, Sylvie St. Onge, and Isabelle La Lancettee, "Wage Gap Changes among Organizations Subject to the Employment Equity Act," *Canadian Public Policy* 21, no. 44 (December 1995): 387–400.

32. J. Coutts, "OCA to Hire Women for Next 10 Years," *Toronto Star*, January 9, 1990: A13.

33. "Sexual Harassment," *CACSW Fact Sheet*, Canadian Advisory Council on the Status of Women, March 1993.

34. "Inquest Probes Murder-Suicide Involving Harassment Victim," *Sexual Harassment, Workplace Diversity Update* 5, no. 3 (March 1997): 4.

35. Malcolm McKillop, "A Manager's Guide to Sexual Impropriety," *The Globe and Mail*, October 7, 1997: B23.

36. Dale Hall and Siobhan McEwan, *Sexual Assault and Harassment on Campus*, York University Sexual Harassment Education and Complaint Centre, York University, 1995.

37. *Sexual Harassment and You: What Every Student Should Know*, Sexual Harassment Education and Complaint Centre, York University, 1986.

38. For a good review of sexual harassment policy, see Dana S. Connell, "Effective Sexual Harassment Policies: Unexpected Lessons from Jacksonville Shipyards," *Employee Relations Law Journal* 17, no. 2 (Autumn 1991): 191–205.

39. "Supreme Court Upholds Mandatory Retirement," *Human Resources Management in Canada*, Report Bulletin No. 95 (Scarborough, Ont.: Prentice-Hall Canada, January 1991): 1–2.

40. Christine L. Taylor, "Dimensions of Diversity in Canadian Business: Building a Business Case for Valuing Ethnocultural Diversity," *Conference Board of Canada Report 143-95*, April 1995: 1.

41. Paul Moloney, "Toronto Okays Non-Christian Holidays for Staffers," *Toronto Star*, May 17, 1995: A6.

42. Hood, S "Generational Diversity," *HR Professional*, June–July 2000: 19.

43. Jennie Constantinides, "Diversity Management: At CN, the 'Token' Will Be Broken," *Human Resources Professional* 7, no. 4 (April 1991): 29–30.

44. T.J. Samuel, *Visible Minorities in Canada* (Toronto: Canadian Advertising Foundation, 1994).

45. Anonymous, "The Diversity of Visible Minorities," *Worklife Report* 11, no. 4, 1999: 2–3.

46. Ibid.

47. Lindsay Scotton, "We Are the World: The Many Faces of Canada Come Together on Winning Images in a Contest to Depict Racial Harmony," May 19, 1995: B3. See also "Logo & Poster Design Exhibition," *Voices of Harmony* 1, no. 1 (Summer 1995): 1–7.

48. Jana Schilder, "The Rainbow Connection: Employers Who Promote Diversity May Discover a Pot of Gold," *Human Resources Professional* 11, no. 3 (April 1994): 13–15.

49. Ibid.

50. Doug Nevison, "Profiting in the Pacific Rim: Can Canada Capture Its Share?" *Conference Board of Canada Report 117-94*: 1994.

51. World Bank, 1993.

52. R. Roosevelt Thomas, Jr., "Beyond Race and Gender," *AMACOM*, 1991: 34.

53. Taylor, "Dimensions of Diversity in Canadian Business": 13.

54. John Spears, "The Many Colours of Money: Diversity Boosts Profit, Firms Told," *Toronto Star*, May 9, 1995.

55. Taylor, "Dimensions of Diversity in Canadian Business": 15.

56. *Continuing In-Patient Focused Care Excellence*, Sunnybrook Community and Public Affairs, Sunnybrook Health Science Centre, Toronto, April 1995.

57. P. Lungen, "Military Addresses Racism Issue," *Canadian Jewish News*, 30, no. 7, February 17, 2000: 6.

58. L. Young, "Global Diversity Standard in Works," *Canadian HR Reporter*, April 5, 1999: 1.

59. Claudine Kapel, "Variation Is the Theme: Organizations That Value Diversity Glimpse Profits in Improved Productivity," *Human Resources Professional* 1, no. 3 (April 1994): 9–12.

60. *Compensation Planning Outlook*, Conference Board of Canada, 1992.

61. Taylor, "Dimensions of Diversity in Canadian Business."

62. Ibid., 18.

Answers to Case Study 1

1. T	3. F	5. T	7. F
2. F	4. T	6. F	

JOB REQUIREMENTS
AND EMPLOYEE
CONTRIBUTIONS

After studying this chapter, you should be able to

Discuss the relationship between job requirements and the performance of HRM functions.

Describe the methods by which job analysis typically is completed.

Explain the various sections of job descriptions.

List the various factors that must be taken into account in designing a job.

Describe the different techniques used to maximize employee contributions.

Discuss the various job characteristics that motivate employees.

Explain the different adjustments in work schedules.

WWW

O rganizations are "re-engineering" themselves in an attempt to become more effective. Some, like Ducks Unlimited Canada and Sunnybrook Health Science Centre, are breaking into smaller units and getting flatter. There is emphasis on smaller scale, less hierarchy, fewer layers, and more decentralized work units. As organizational reshaping takes place, managers want employees to operate more independently and flexibly to meet customer demands. This requires that decisions be made by the people who are closest to the information and who are directly involved in the product or service delivered. The objective is to develop jobs and basic work units that are adaptable enough to thrive in a world of high-velocity change.

In this chapter, we discuss how jobs can be designed so as to best contribute to the objectives of the organization and at the same time satisfy the needs of the employees who are to perform them. The value of job analysis, which defines clearly and precisely the requirements of each job, will be stressed. We will emphasize that these job requirements provide the foundation for making objective and legally defensible decisions in managing human resources. The chapter concludes by reviewing several innovative job design and employee contribution techniques that increase job satisfaction while improving organizational performance. Teamwork and the characteristics of successful teams are highlighted.

RELATIONSHIP OF JOB REQUIREMENTS AND HRM FUNCTIONS

Job

A group of related activities and duties

Position

The different duties and responsibilities performed by only one employee

WWW

Job specification

Statement of the knowledge, skills, and abilities required of the person who is to perform the job

A **job** consists of a group of related activities and duties. Ideally, the duties of a job should consist of natural units of work that are similar and related. They should be clear and distinct from those of other jobs to minimize misunderstanding and conflict among employees and to enable employees to recognize what is expected of them. For some jobs, several employees may be required, each of whom will occupy a separate position. A **position** consists of the duties and responsibilities performed by only one employee. In a city library, for example, four employees (four positions) may be involved in reference work, but all of them have only one job (reference librarian).

Recruitment

Before they can find capable employees for an organization, recruiters need to know the job specifications for the positions they are to fill. A **job specification** is a statement of the knowledge, skills, and abilities required of the person performing the job. In the HR department for the City of Calgary, Alberta, the job specification for a senior personnel analyst includes the following:

1. Appropriate university degree, preferably at the master's level.

2. Four to five years of corporate management experience.

3. Working knowledge of employment equity, human rights legislation, statistical analysis, investigative procedures, and organizational development.[1]

Because job specifications establish the qualifications required of applicants for a job opening, they serve an essential role in the recruiting function. These qualifications typically are contained in the notices of job openings. Whether posted on organization bulletin boards or included in help-wanted advertisements or employment agency listings, job specifications provide a basis for attracting qualified applicants and discouraging unqualified ones.

Selection

Job description

Statement of the tasks, duties, and responsibilities of a job to be performed

In addition to job specifications, managers and supervisors will use job descriptions to select and orient employees to jobs. A **job description** is a statement of the tasks, duties, and responsibilities of a job.

In the past, job specifications used as a basis for selection sometimes bore little relation to the duties to be performed under the job description. Examples of such non–job related specifications abounded. Applicants for the job of labourer were required to have a high school diploma. Firefighters were required to be at least six feet tall. And applicants for the job of truck driver were required to be male. These kinds of job specifications discriminated against members of certain designated groups, many of whom were excluded from these jobs.

WWW

Employers must be able to show that the job specifications used in selecting employees for a particular job relate specifically to the duties of that job. In 1984, charges of discrimination were brought against the Vancouver Fire Department because it required that candidates for a firefighter's job be at least five feet nine. The Human Rights Board that heard the case could not find any correlation between the height of a firefighter and injuries or efficiencies or capacity to perform the job. The Vancouver Fire Department was found in violation of the Human Rights Act.[2] Job specifications should list the knowledge, skills, and abilities required to perform the job successfully, and should not be based on stereotypes or managerial preferences.

Training and Development

Any discrepancies between the knowledge, skills, and abilities (often referred to as KSAs) demonstrated by a job holder and the requirements contained in the description and specification for that job provide clues to training needs. Also, career development as a part of the training function is concerned with preparing employees for advancement to jobs where their capacities can be utilized to the fullest extent possible. The formal qualification requirements set forth in high-level jobs serve to indicate how much more training and development are needed for employees to advance to those jobs.

Performance Appraisal

The requirements contained in the description of a job provide the criteria for evaluating the performance of the holder of that job. The results of performance appraisal may reveal, however, that certain requirements established for a job are not completely valid. As we have already stressed, these criteria must be specific and job-related. If the criteria used to evaluate employee performance are vague and not job-related, employers may find themselves being charged with discrimination.

Compensation Management

In determining the rate to be paid for performing a job, the relative worth of the job is one of the most important factors. This worth is based on what the job demands of an employee in terms of skill, effort, and responsibility, as well as the conditions and hazards under which the work is performed. The systems of job evaluation by which this worth may be measured are discussed in Chapter 9.

JOB ANALYSIS

Job analysis

Process of obtaining information about jobs by determining what the duties, tasks, or activities associated with those jobs are

Job analysis is sometimes called the cornerstone of HRM because the information it collects serves so many HRM functions. **Job analysis** is the process of obtaining information about jobs by determining what the duties, tasks, or activities of those jobs are. The procedure involves systematically investigating jobs and then following a number of predetermined steps specified in advance of the study.[3] When completed, job analysis results in a written report summarizing the information obtained from the analysis of twenty or thirty individual job tasks or activities.[4] HR managers use these data to develop job descriptions and job specifications. These documents, in turn, are used to perform and enhance various HR functions such as developing performance appraisal criteria and designing the content of training classes.[5] The ultimate purpose of job analysis is to improve organizational performance and productivity. Figure 3.1 illustrates how job analysis is carried out, and shows the functions for which it is used.

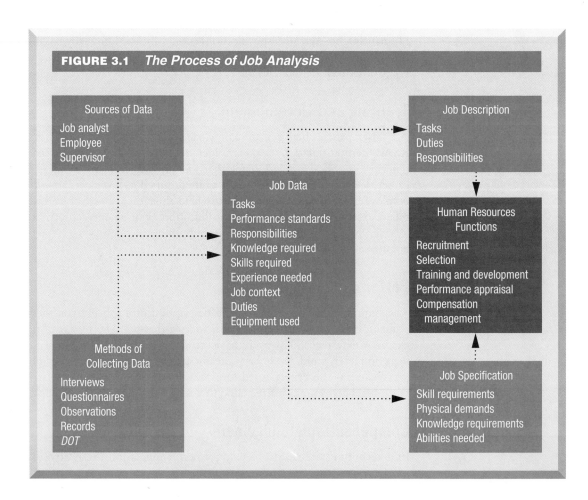

FIGURE 3.1   *The Process of Job Analysis*

Sources of Data
Job analyst
Employee
Supervisor

Job Data
Tasks
Performance standards
Responsibilities
Knowledge required
Skills required
Experience needed
Job context
Duties
Equipment used

Methods of Collecting Data
Interviews
Questionnaires
Observations
Records
DOT

Job Description
Tasks
Duties
Responsibilities

Human Resources Functions
Recruitment
Selection
Training and development
Performance appraisal
Compensation
  management

Job Specification
Skill requirements
Physical demands
Knowledge requirements
Abilities needed

In contrast with job design, which reflects subjective opinions about the ideal requirements of a job, job analysis is concerned with objective and verifiable information about the actual requirements of a job. The job descriptions and job specifications developed through job analysis should be as accurate as possible if they are to be of value to those who make HRM decisions. These decisions may involve any of the HR functions, from recruitment to termination of employees.

The Job Analyst's Responsibilities

WWW

Usually, job analysis is mainly the responsibility of the HR department. If this department is large enough to have a division for compensation management, job analysis may be performed by members of that division. For example, in the HR department at Dofasco Inc. in Hamilton, Ontario, job analysis is performed by the Compensation section.

HR staff who specialize in job analysis have the title of job analyst or personnel analyst. Since jobs with this title require a high degree of analytical ability and writing skill, they sometimes serve as entry-level jobs for college or university graduates who have chosen a career in HRM.

Although job analysts have the main responsibility for the job analysis program, they usually enlist the cooperation of the employees and managers in the departments where jobs are being analyzed. These managers and employees provide them with much of the information they need about the jobs. They may also be asked to prepare rough drafts of the job descriptions and specifications the job analysts need.

Gathering Job Information

Job data can be gathered in several ways. The common methods of analyzing jobs are interviews, questionnaires, observation, and diaries.

- *Interviews.* The job analyst questions individual employees and managers about the job under review.
- *Questionnaires.* The job analyst circulates carefully prepared questionnaires, which job holders and managers fill out individually. These forms are then used to obtain data in the following areas: job duties and tasks performed, purpose of the job, physical setting, requirements for performing the job (skill, education, experience, physical and mental demands), equipment and materials used, and special health and safety concerns.
- *Observation.* The job analyst learns about the job by observing and recording on a standardized form the activities of those who hold it. Some organizations videotape jobs for later study.
- *Diaries.* Job holders are asked to keep a diary of their work activities for an entire work cycle. Diaries are usually filled out at specific times during the work shift (e.g., every half-hour or hour) over a two- to four-week period.

Controlling the Accuracy of Job Information

If job analysis is to accomplish its intended purpose, the job data collected must be accurate. Care must be taken to ensure that all important facts are included. A job analyst should watch out for employees who tend to exaggerate the difficulty of their jobs in order to inflate their egos (and their paycheques). Ethics in HRM highlights such a case. When interviewing employees or reviewing their questionnaires, the job analyst must look for any responses that do not agree with other facts or impressions the analyst has received. Also, when job information is collected from employees, a representative group of individuals should be surveyed.

Whenever a job analyst doubts the accuracy of the information provided by employees, he or she should obtain additional information from them, from their managers, or from other individuals who are familiar with or perform the same job. It is common practice to have the descriptions for each job reviewed by the job holders and their managers. The job description summaries contained in the *National Occupational Classification* can also serve as a basis for the job analyst's review.

The *NOC* and Job Analysis

WWW

Commonly referred to as the *NOC*, the *National Occupational Classification* is compiled by the federal government. The *NOC* contains standardized and comprehensive descriptions of about 25,000 occupational titles and is now available on line (**www.worklogic.com:81/noc/NOCView.htm**). The purpose of the *NOC* is to compile, analyze, and communicate information about occupations. This information can be used for employment equity, human resource planning, and occupational supply and demand forecasts and analyses.

The *NOC* is a composite of the Canadian labour market and has helped bring about a greater degree of uniformity in the job titles and descriptions used by employers in different parts of the country. This uniformity has facilitated the movement of workers from regions that may be experiencing widespread unemployment to areas where employment opportunities are greater. Also, the *NOC* code numbers facilitate the exchange of statistical information about jobs and are useful in reporting research in the HR area, in vocational counselling, and in charting career paths through job transfers and/or advancements.[6]

Ethics in HRM

INFLATION

At some point in your working life, you will be asked to describe your job, perhaps when being interviewed by a job analyst or by answering questions on a form. Most employees have a reasonable expectation that their answers will affect their lives in significant ways. The information obtained may be used to reclassify the job to either a higher or lower pay level. Most employees believe that standards of performance may change—and the employer will expect them to work faster or to do more—although that is not the goal of job analysis.

As a result of these beliefs and expectations, employees have a vested interest in "inflating" their job descriptions, by making the job sound very important and very difficult. Thus night clerks in hotels become auditors and receptionists become administrators. Making a job sound more important than it is may reflect an employee's sincere belief in the significance of his or her contribution, or an attempt to lobby for higher pay.

WWW

Some professional associations provide a job classification system that is intended to be more current than the *NOC*. For example, the Canadian Technology Human Resources Board has established a comprehensive evaluation system that describes the major applied science and engineering technology disciplines.[7] Visit its website (**www.cthrb.ca**).

Approaches to Job Analysis

The systematic and quantitative definition of job content that job analysis provides is the foundation of many HRM practices. Specifically, job analysis serves to justify job descriptions and other HRM selection procedures. It should be emphasized that a major goal of modern job analysis is to help the organization establish the job-relatedness of its selection requirements. Several different job analysis approaches are used, each with specific advantages and disadvantages. Three of the more popular methods are functional job analysis, the position analysis questionnaire system, and the critical incident method.

Functional job analysis (FJA)

The **functional job analysis (FJA)** approach utilizes an inventory of the various types of functions or work activities that can constitute any job. FJA thus assumes that each job involves performing certain functions. Specifically, there are three broad worker functions that form the basis of this system: (1) data, (2) people, and (3) things. These three categories are subdivided to form a hierarchy of worker-function scales, as shown in Figure 3.2. The job analyst, when studying the job under review, indicates the functional level for each of the three categories (for example, "copying" under Data) and then reflects the relative involvement of the worker in the function by assigning a percentage figure to each function (e.g., 50

Functional job analysis (FJA)

Quantitative approach to job analysis that utilizes a compiled inventory of the various functions or work activities that can make up any job and that assumes that each job involves three broad worker functions: (1) data, (2) people, and (3) things

---

FIGURE 3.2 *Difficulty Levels of Worker Functions*

DATA (4TH DIGIT)	PEOPLE (5TH DIGIT)	THINGS (6TH DIGIT)
0 Synthesizing	0 Mentoring	0 Setting-up
1 Coordinating	1 Negotiating	1 Precision working
2 Analyzing	2 Instructing	2 Operating-controlling
3 Compiling	3 Supervising	3 Driving-operating
4 Computing	4 Diverting	4 Manipulating
5 Copying	5 Persuading	5 Tending
6 Comparing	6 Speaking–signalling*	6 Feeding-offbearing
	7 Serving	7 Handling
	8 Taking instructions—Helping	

* Hyphenated factors are single factors.

Source: U.S. Department of Labor, Employment and Training Administration, *Revised Handbook for Analyzing Jobs* (Washington, DC: U.S. Government Printing Office, 1991), 5.

WWW

Position analysis questionnaire (PAQ)

Quantitative approach to job analysis that utilizes a compiled inventory of the various functions or work activities that can make up any job

Critical incident method

Job analysis method by which important job tasks are identified for job success

percent to "copying"). This is done for each of the three areas, and the three functional levels must equal 100 percent. The end result is a quantitatively evaluated job. FJA can easily be used to describe the content of jobs and to assist in writing job descriptions and specifications; it is used as a basis for the *Dictionary of Occupational Titles (DOT)* code, the American equivalent of *NOC*.

The Position Analysis Questionnaire System

The **position analysis questionnaire (PAQ)** is a quantifiable data collection method covering 194 different worker-oriented tasks. Using a five-point scale, the PAQ seeks to determine the degree, if any, to which the different tasks or job elements are involved in performing a particular job.[8]

A sample page from the PAQ covering eleven elements of the Information Input Division is shown in Figure 3.3. The person conducting an analysis using this questionnaire rates each of the elements using the five-point scale shown in the upper right-hand corner of the sample page. The results obtained with the PAQ are quantitative and can be subjected to statistical analysis. The PAQ also permits dimensions of behaviour to be compared across a number of jobs and permits jobs to be grouped on the basis of common characteristics.[9]

The Critical Incident Method

The objective of the **critical incident method** is to identify critical job tasks. Critical job tasks are those important duties and job responsibilities performed by the job holder that lead to job success. Information about critical job tasks can be collected through interviews with employees or managers or through self-report statements written by employees.

Suppose, for example, that the job analyst is studying the job of reference librarian. The interviewer will ask the employee to describe the job on the basis of what is done, how the job is performed, and what tools and equipment are used. The reference librarian may describe the job as follows:

> I assist patrons by answering their questions related to finding books, periodicals, or other library materials. I also give them directions to help them find materials within the building. To perform my job I may have to look up materials myself or refer patrons to someone who can directly assist them. Some individuals may need training in how to use reference materials or special library facilities. I also give library tours to new patrons. I use computers and a variety of reference books to carry out my job.

After the job data are collected, the analyst will write separate task statements that represent important job activities. For the reference librarian, one task statement might be: "Listens to patrons and answers their questions related to locating library materials." Typically, the job analyst will write five to ten important task statements for each job under study. The final product will be written task statements that are clear, complete, and easily understood by those unfamiliar with the job. The critical incident method is an important job analysis method since it teaches the analyst to focus on employee behaviours critical to job success.

Computerized Job Analysis

Human resource information systems have greatly facilitated the job analysis process. Available today are various software programs designed specifically to ana-

FIGURE 3.3 *A Sample Page from the Position Analysis Questionnaire*

INFORMATION INPUT

	Extent of Use (U)
NA	Does not apply
1	Nominal / very infrequent
2	Occasional
3	Moderate
4	Considerable
5	Very substantial

1   INFORMATION INPUT

1.1 Sources of Job Information

Rate each of the following items in terms of the extent to which it is used by the worker as a source of information in performing his job.

1.1.1   Visual Sources of Job Information

1   U   Written materials (books, reports, office notes, articles, job instructions, signs, etc.)

2   U   Quantitative materials (materials which deal with quantities or amounts, such as graphs, accounts, specifications, tables of numbers, etc.)

3   U   Pictorial materials (pictures or picture like materials used as *sources* of information, for example, drawings, blueprints, diagrams, maps, tracings, photographic films, x-ray films, TV pictures, etc.)

4   U   Patterns/related devices (templates, stencils, patterns, etc., used as *sources* of information when *observed* during use; do *not* include here materials described in item 3 above)

5   U   Visual displays (dials, gauges, signal lights, radar scopes, speedometers, clocks, etc.)

6   U   Measuring devices (rulers, calipers, tire pressure gauges, scales, thickness gauges, pipettes, thermometers, protractors, etc., used to obtain visual information about physical measurements; do *not* include here devices described in item 5 above)

7   U   Mechanical devices (tools, equipment, machinery, and other mechanical devices which are sources of information when *observed* during use or operation)

8   U   Materials in process (parts, materials, objects, etc., which are *sources* of information when being modified, worked on, or otherwise processed, such as bread dough being mixed, workpiece being turned in a lathe, fabric being cut, shoe being resoled, etc.)

9   U   Materials not in process (parts, materials, objects, etc., not in the process of being changed or modified, which are *sources* of information when being inspected, handled, packaged, distributed, or selected, etc., such as items or materials in inventory, storage, or distribution channels, items being inspected, etc.)

10   U   Features of nature (landscapes, fields, geological samples, vegetation, cloud formations, and other features of nature which are observed or inspected to provide information)

11   U   Man-made features of environment (structures, buildings, dams, highways, bridges, docks, railroads, and other "man-made" or altered aspects of the indoor or outdoor environment which are *observed* or *inspected* to provide job information; do not consider equipment, machines, etc., that an individual uses in his work, as covered by item 7).

Source: *Position Analysis Questionnaire*, copyright 1969, 1989 by Purdue Research Foundation, West Lafayette, Indiana 47907. Reprinted with permission.

lyze jobs and to write job descriptions and job specifications based on those analyses. Typically, these programs contain generalized task statements that can apply to many different jobs. Managers and employees select those statements that best describe the job under review, indicating the importance of the task to the total job where appropriate. Advanced computer applications of job analysis combine job analysis with job evaluation (Chapter 9) and the pricing of organizational jobs. Computerized job analysis systems can be expensive to initiate, but where the organization has many jobs, the cost per job may be low.

Job Analysis in a Changing Environment

The traditional approach to job analysis assumes a static job environment in which jobs remain relatively stable apart from the incumbents who hold these jobs. Here, jobs can be meaningfully defined in terms of tasks, duties, processes, and behaviours necessary for job success. This assumption, unfortunately, discounts technological advances that are often so accelerated that jobs, as they are defined today, may be obsolete tomorrow.[10] Furthermore, downsizing, the adoption of teams, the demands of small organizations, and the need to respond to global change can alter the nature of jobs and their requirements. In a dynamic environment where job demands change rapidly, job analysis data can quickly become inaccurate, and outdated job analysis information can hinder an organization's ability to adapt to change.

For organizations that operate in a fast-moving environment, several novel approaches to job analysis may accommodate needed change. *First*, managers can adopt a future-oriented approach to job analysis. This "strategic" analysis of jobs requires that managers have a clear view of how jobs should be restructured in terms of duties and tasks in order to meet future organizational requirements.[11] *Second*, organizations can adopt a competency-based approach to job analysis in which emphasis is placed on characteristics of successful performers rather than on standard job duties and tasks.[12] These competencies would match the organization's culture and strategy and might include such things as interpersonal communication skills, decision-making ability, conflict resolution skills, adaptability, and self-motivation.[13] This technique of job analysis serves to enhance a culture of TQM and continuous improvement since organizational improvement is the stable concern. Either of these two approaches is not without its problems: managers must be able to predict future job needs accurately, job analyses must comply with employment equity legislation, and ways must be found to avoid the role ambiguity created by generically written job descriptions.

Job Descriptions

As previously noted, a job description is a written description of a job and the types of duties it includes. Since there is no standard format for job descriptions, they tend to vary in appearance and content from one organization to another. However, most job descriptions contain at least three parts: the job title, a job identification section, and a job duties section. If the job specifications are not prepared as a separate document, they are usually stated in the concluding section of the job description. Highlights in HRM 1 shows a job description for an HR employment assistant. This sample job description includes both job duties and job specifications and should satisfy most of the job information needs of managers who must recruit, interview, and orient new employees.

Job descriptions are of value to both the employees and the employer. From the employees' standpoint, job descriptions can be used to help them learn their job duties and to remind them of the results they are expected to achieve. From the employer's standpoint, written job descriptions can serve as a basis for minimizing the misunderstandings that arise between managers and their subordinates concerning job requirements. They also establish management's right to take corrective action when the duties covered by the job description are not performed as required.

Job Title

Selection of a job title is important for several reasons. *First*, the job title is of psychological importance, conferring status on the employee. For instance, "sanitation expert" is a more appealing title than "garbage collector." *Second*, if possible, the title should provide some indication of what the duties of the job entail. Titles like "meat inspector," "electronics assembler," "salesperson," and "engineer" obviously hint at the nature of the duties of these jobs. The job title also should indicate the relative level occupied by its holder in the organizational hierarchy.[14] For example, the title "junior engineer" implies that this job occupies a lower level than that of "senior engineer." Other titles that indicate the relative level in the organizational hierarchy are "welder's helper" and "laboratory assistant."

Job Identification Section

The job identification section of a job description usually follows the job title. It includes such items as the departmental location of the job, the person to whom the job holder reports, and the date on which the job description was last revised. Sometimes it also contains a payroll or code number, the number of employees performing the job, the number of employees in the department where the job is located, and the *NOC* code number. "Statement of the Job" usually appears at the bottom of this section and serves to distinguish the job from other jobs—something the job title may fail to do.

Job Duties Section

Statements covering job duties are typically arranged in order of importance. These statements should indicate the weight, or value, of each duty. Usually, but not always, the weight of a duty can be gauged by the percentage of time devoted to it. The statements should stress the responsibilities all the duties entail and the results they are to accomplish. It is also general practice to indicate the tools and equipment used by the employee in performing the job. This section is sometimes called the essential functions section.

Job Specifications Section

As stated earlier, the personal qualifications an individual must possess in order to perform the duties and responsibilities contained in a job description are compiled in the job specification. Typically the job specification covers two areas: (1) the skill required to perform the job, and (2) the physical demands the job places on the employee performing it.

Skills relevant to a job include education or experience, specialized training, personal traits or abilities, and manual dexterities. The physical demands of a job

Highlights in HRM

1   JOB DESCRIPTION FOR AN EMPLOYMENT ASSISTANT

Job Identification

JOB TITLE: Employment Assistant
Division: Western Region
Department: Human Resources Management
Job Analyst: Virginia Sasaki
Date Analyzed: 12/3/98
Wage Category: Professional
Report to: HR Manager
Job Code: 11-17
Date Verified: 12/17/98

Brief Listing of Major Job Duties

JOB STATEMENT

Performs professional human resources work in the areas of employee recruitment and selection, testing, orientation, transfers, and maintenance of employee human resources files. May handle special assignments and projects in Employment Equity, employee grievances, training, or classification and compensation. Works under general supervision. Incumbent exercises initiative and independent judgment in the performance of assigned tasks.

Essential Functions and Responsibilities

ESSENTIAL FUNCTIONS

1. Prepares recruitment literature and job advertisements for applicant placement.
2. Schedules and conducts personal interviews to determine applicant suitability for employment. Includes reviewing mailed applications and résumés for qualified personnel.
3. Supervises administration of testing program. Responsible for developing or improving testing instruments and procedures.
4. Presents orientation program to all new employees. Reviews and develops all materials and procedures for orientation program.
5. Coordinates division job posting and transfer program. Establishes job posting procedures. Responsible for reviewing transfer applications, arranging transfer interviews, and determining effective transfer dates.
6. Maintains a daily working relationship with division managers on human resource matters, including recruitment concerns, retention or release of probationary employees, and discipline or discharge of permanent employees.

7. Distributes new or revised human resources policies and procedures to all employees and managers through bulletins, meetings, memorandums, and/or personal contact.
8. Performs related duties as assigned by the human resource manager.

JOB SPECIFICATIONS

1. University degree or college diploma with major course work in human resources management, business administration, or industrial psychology; OR a combination of experience, education, and training equivalent to a degree or diploma in human resources management.
2. Considerable knowledge of principles of employee selection and assignment of personnel.
3. Ability to express ideas clearly in both written and oral communications.
4. Ability to plan and organize one's own activities independently.
5. Knowledge of human resource computer applications desirable.

refer to how much walking, standing, reaching, lifting, or talking must be done on the job. The condition of the physical work environment and the hazards employees may encounter are also among the physical demands of a job.

Problems with Job Descriptions

Managers consider job descriptions a valuable tool for carrying out HRM functions. Nevertheless, several problems are often associated with these documents, including the following:

1. If they are poorly written, using vague rather than specific terms, they provide little guidance to the job holder.

2. They are sometimes not updated as job duties or specifications change.

3. They may violate the law by containing specifications not related to job success.

4. They can limit the scope of activities of the job holder.

Some of these problems are being addressed by new approaches to job analysis (see Reality Check).

Writing Clear and Specific Job Descriptions

When writing a job description, it is essential to use statements that are terse, direct, and simply worded. Unnecessary words or phrases should be eliminated. Typically, the sentences that describe job duties begin with a present-tense verb (an action verb), with the implied subject of the sentence being the employee performing the job. The term "occasionally" is used to describe those duties that are performed once in a while. The term "may" is used in connection with those duties that are performed only by some workers on the job.

Reality CHECK

JOB ANALYSIS AT HAY McBER

The nature of job analysis is changing, as competency-based models are gaining strength in Canadian workplaces. As we focus on people, the development of job descriptions, which consider the abilities, knowledge, and skill of our "job contributors," is predominating. A job used to be a piece of paper outlining what was expected of job holders—nothing less, nothing more. Today we are seeing that piece of paper change to address the needs of a changing workforce and workplace expectations.

WWW

Dr. Charles Bethell-Fox, vice president of Hay McBer's Human Resources Planning and Development practice in New York and Toronto, works closely with organizations to help them manage change through the development of effective work processes and competencies aligned with strategic business needs.

Dr. Bethell-Fox says: "When we look at what is changing in the workplace, we see that the traditional job and the nature of work are not what they used to be. People who work for organizations increasingly find themselves performing work that may not be covered in a job description. People are working in teams, and the demands in terms of skills and knowledge change as the project changes. Functional silos are breaking down and cross-functional teams are becoming the norm. We have also seen a delayering in organizations where a part of the hierarchy—particularly middle management—is being taken away. What that means for people and jobs is that they don't fit into tidy slots within the organization.[11]

When we try to capture what people do in their jobs it is important to look at what they bring to the work situation. Knowing what they are able to do determines what they can get involved with, what strengths they bring to the team, how they can contribute. For example, look at the technical support worker who knows about a content area such as information systems. He or she is asked to work on project teams to supply a particular type of skill the team requires. Then he or she may also be asked to work on a different team with different groups of people and contribute other types of knowledge.

In addition, organizations are becoming increasingly focused on customers as a means of gaining a competitive advantage. "If you want competitive advantage, you need to leverage all internal resources to the greatest degree," states Bethell-Fox. As a job holder, if you have a particular strength you don't want to be positioned in the organization in such a way that the organization cannot gain maximum competitive advantage from your strength. The old hierarchical structures used to foster people working within functional silos, but today you want people working together. When you combine the skills of Person A with those of Person B, the two together may meet customer or market needs that could not have been achieved had you not built on the combined strengths of your people. "If people are working this way, based on what they can contribute, how can we talk about a job as if it fits into one part of the organization?" asks Bethell-Fox.

Looking at what people bring to their roles—their abilities, knowledge, and skills—is important because it helps you understand what they can contribute to the team. Bethell-Fox goes on to state, "If the measures of what an individual brings to an organization are accurate and reliable, you are in a better position to assess people and can better put them on teams where they will be able to maximize their contributions."

Clearly, job descriptions must still contain a clear description of accountabilities. But we also need to capture what competencies are expected in the job and how the person needs to do the job. For example, when we say that the individual must have five years of management experience, this tells us little about what is expected. If instead we state that the individual must be able to generate a high level of teamwork and achievement, the expectations become clearer—we can almost visualize what is expected.

Bethell-Fox further states: "If people are to maximize their contribution to the organization we need to have a clear understanding of the competencies that will deliver superior results. To deal with that we have devised are called 'Just Noticeable Difference' (JND) competency measurement scales. On these scales, different behavioural indicators of any one competency are organized into an ascending scale where behaviours known to deliver progressively higher levels of job output and performance appear at progressively higher levels on each scale."

Once the right competencies have been identified for a job or job family, the scales can be used to specify the level of behaviour required to deliver superior performance. Then current job holders and job applicants can be assessed against the scales to measure how well their demonstrated levels of competency match the requirements for superior performance. For those who do not meet the right competencies, training can be provided.

Different levels of competency lead to different job holders doing the same job in different ways and, in effect, thereby doing different jobs. For example, one job holder might be a willing participant in the team, doing his or her share of the work. Another person in the same job, however, might demonstrate more proactive team behaviours, such as actively soliciting input from other team members or taking action to calm down conflicts among other team members. Effectively, these two people are doing two different jobs because of the competencies they demonstrate. In this way, competencies define what a job means.

In closing, one of the advantages of looking at things from a competency-based point of view is that if you have a clear understanding of the competencies that drive superior performance in a role then you can integrate a whole range of human resource applications around the competency framework. In other words, selection, training and development, performance management, and even pay systems can all be built around the competency framework. This adds significant value by ensuring that you now have multiple HR programs all pointed in the same direction and closely aligned with the business strategy.

Even when set forth in writing, job descriptions and specifications can still be vague. To the consternation of many employers, today's legal environment has created what might be called an "age of specifics." Human rights legislation requires that the specific performance requirements of a job be based on valid job-related criteria. Personnel decisions that involve either job applicants or employees and are based on criteria that are vague or not job-related are increasingly being challenged successfully. Managers of small businesses, where employees may perform many different job tasks, must be especially concerned about writing specific job descriptions.

When preparing job descriptions, managers must be aware of human rights legislation. Written job descriptions must match the requirements of the job. Position descriptions may need to be altered to meet "reasonable accommodation." Reasonable accommodation is used most often in relations to religious or disability needs. The 1992 case *Renaud v. British Columbia School Board* made it clear that reasonable accommodation for religious reasons is valid.[15] Job descriptions written to match the needs for reasonable accommodation reduce the risk of discrimination. The goal is to match and accommodate human capabilities to job requirements. For example, if the job requires the job holder to read extremely fine print, to climb ladders, or to memorize stock codes, these physical and mental requirements should be stated in the job description.

Managers may find that writing job descriptions is a tedious process that distracts from other supervisory responsibilities. Fortunately, software packages are available to simplify this time-consuming yet necessary task. In one program, the user is provided an initial library of more than 2,500 prewritten job descriptions. Since the program works much like a word processor, text can be easily deleted, inserted, or modified to accommodate user demands. Various software packages can be found in HR journals such as *HRMagazine, Personnel*, and *Workforce* (formerly *Personnel Journal*), and in the HR Index published by the Human Resources Professionals Association of Ontario.

JOB DESIGN

Job design

Outgrowth of job analysis that improves jobs through technological and human considerations in order to enhance organization efficiency and employee job satisfaction

Job design is concerned with changing, modifying, and enriching jobs in order to capture the talents of employees while improving organizational performance. An outgrowth of job analysis, **job design** is concerned with structuring jobs in order to improve organization efficiency and employee job satisfaction. For example, organizations engaged in continuous improvement or process re-engineering may revamp their jobs to eliminate unnecessary job tasks or find better ways of performing work.[16] Job design should facilitate the achievement of organizational objectives and at the same time recognize the capabilities and needs of those who are to perform the job.

As Figure 3.4 illustrates, job design is a combination of four basic considerations: (1) the organizational objectives the job was created to fulfil; (2) industrial engineering considerations, including ways to make the job technologically efficient; (3) ergonomic concerns, including workers' physical and mental capabilities; and (4) employee contributions. Employee contributions are reflected in the participation of employees in making job improvements or enhancing operational decisions.

Behavioural Concerns

There are two job design methods that seek to incorporate the behavioural needs of employees as they perform their individual jobs. Both methods strive to satisfy the intrinsic needs of employees. The job enrichment model and the job characteristics model have long been popular with researchers and practitioners as ways to increase the job satisfaction of employees.

Job Enrichment

Job Enrichment

Enhancing a job by adding more meaningful tasks and duties to make the work more rewarding or satisfying.

Any effort to make work more rewarding or satisfying by adding more meaningful tasks to an employee's job is called **job enrichment**. Originally popularized by Frederick Herzberg, job enrichment is touted as a means to fulfil the motivational needs of employees, such as for self-fulfilment and self-esteem, and as leading to long-term job satisfaction and the achievement of performance goals.[17] Job enrichment, or the vertical expansion of jobs, can be accomplished by increasing the autonomy and responsibility of employees. Herzberg discusses five factors involved in enriching jobs and thereby motivating employees: achievement, recognition, growth, responsibility, and performance of the whole job versus only parts of the job. For example, managers can enrich the jobs of employees by:

- increasing the level of difficulty and responsibility of the job;
- allowing employees to retain more authority and control over work outcomes;

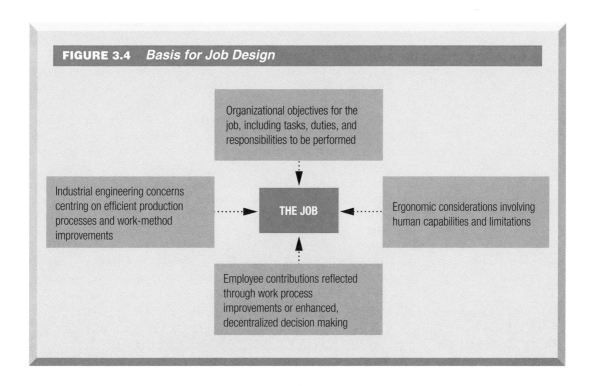

FIGURE 3.4 *Basis for Job Design*

Organizational objectives for the job, including tasks, duties, and responsibilities to be performed

Industrial engineering concerns centring on efficient production processes and work-method improvements

THE JOB

Ergonomic considerations involving human capabilities and limitations

Employee contributions reflected through work process improvements or enhanced, decentralized decision making

Some employers provide on-site day care facilities. This allows employees to maximize efficiency and provides job satisfaction.

- providing unit or individual job performance reports directly to employees;
- adding new tasks to the job that require training and growth; and
- assigning individuals specific tasks, thereby enabling them to become experts.

These factors allow employees to assume a greater role in the decision-making process and become more involved in planning, organizing, directing, and controlling their own work. Vertical job enrichment can also be accomplished by organizing workers into teams and giving these teams greater authority for self-management.

Despite the benefits to be achieved through job enrichment, it must not be considered a panacea for overcoming production problems and employee discontent. Job enrichment programs are more likely to succeed in some jobs and work situations than in others. They are not the solution to such problems as dissatisfaction with pay, with employee benefits, or with employment security. Moreover, not all employees object to the mechanical pacing of an assembly line, nor do all employees seek additional responsibility or challenge. Some prefer routine jobs because they can let their minds wander while performing their work.

Job characteristics model

Job design that purports that three factors (meaningful work, responsibility for work outcomes, and knowledge of the results of the work performed) result in improved work performance, increased internal motivation, and lower absenteeism and turnover.

Job Characteristics

Job design studies explored a new field when behavioural scientists began identifying various job dimensions that would improve simultaneously the efficiency of organizations and the job satisfaction of employees. Perhaps the theory that best exemplifies this research is the one advanced by Richard Hackman and Greg Oldham.[18] Their **job characteristics model** proposes that three psychological states of a job holder result in improved work performance, internal motivation, and lower absenteeism and turnover. The motivated, satisfied, and productive employee is one who (1) experiences meaningfulness of the work performed, (2) experiences responsibility for work outcomes, and (3) has knowledge of the results of the work performed. When these three psychological states are achieved, the employee is more strongly motivated to continue doing the job well. As Hackman and Oldham state: "The net result is a self-perpetuating cycle of positive work motivation, powered by self-generated rewards, that is predicted to continue until one or more of the three psychological states is no longer present, or until the individual no longer values the internal rewards that derive from good performance."[19]

Hackman and Oldham believe that five core job dimensions produce the three psychological states. The five job characteristics are as follows:

1. *Skill variety.* The degree to which a job entails a variety of different activities, which demand the use of a number of different skills and talents by the job holder.

2. *Task identity.* The degree to which the job requires completion of a whole and identifiable piece of work—that is, doing a job from beginning to end with a visible outcome.

3. *Task significance.* The degree to which the job has a substantial impact on the lives or work of other people, whether in the immediate organization or in the external environment.

4. *Autonomy.* The degree to which the job provides substantial freedom, independence, and discretion to the individual in scheduling the work and in determining the procedures to be used in carrying it out.

5. *Feedback.* The degree to which carrying out the work activities required by the job results in the individual being given direct and clear information about the effectiveness of his or her performance.[20]

It is important to realize that each of the five job characteristics affects employee performance differently. Employees experience the greatest motivation when all five characteristics are present, since the job characteristics combine to produce the three psychological states. Since the work of Hackman and Oldham is similar to that of Herzberg, suggestions for redesigning jobs through job enrichment also apply to the job characteristics model.

The job characteristics model seems to work best when certain conditions are met. One of these conditions is that employees must have the psychological desire for the autonomy, variety, responsibility, and challenge of enriched jobs. When this personal characteristic is absent, employees may resist the job redesign effort. Also, job redesign efforts almost always fail when employees lack the physical or mental skills, abilities, or education needed to perform the job. Forcing enriched jobs on individuals who lack these traits can result in frustrated employees.

Employee Empowerment

Employee empowerment

A technique of involving employees in their work through a process of inclusion

Job enrichment and job characteristics are specific programs that managers or supervisors can follow to formally change the jobs of employees. A less structured method is to allow employees to initiate their own job changes through the concept of empowerment. **Employee empowerment** is a technique for involving employees in their work through a process of inclusion. Empowerment encourages employees to become innovators and managers of their own work, and involves them in their jobs in ways that give them more control (see Highlights in HRM 2). Empowerment has been defined as "pushing down decision-making responsibility to those close to internal and external customers." To support high involvement, organizations must share information, knowledge, power to act, and rewards throughout the workforce.[21]

Highlights in HRM

2   EXAMPLES OF EMPLOYEE EMPOWERMENT

WWW

At Zero Knowledge Systems, a Montreal company that produces privacy software for Internet users, employees choose their own job titles. A top developer chose the title International Man of Mystery.

Canadian Marconi Company, a manufacturer of navigational systems, surveyed its employees, and as a result of their feedback designed modular benefits packages to suit employee lifestyles.

At Chrysler Corporation, a six-member design team that developed the Dodge Copperhead decided that the vehicle would have snakeskin seats and tire treads. Nobody at the top interfered.

While defining empowerment can become the first step to achieving it, in order for empowerment to grow and thrive, organizations must encourage these conditions:

- *Participation.* Employees must be encouraged to take control of their work tasks. Employees, in turn, must care about improving their work process and interpersonal work relationships.
- *Innovation.* The environment must be receptive to people with innovative ideas, and must encourage people to explore new paths and to take reasonable risks at reasonable costs. An empowered environment is created when curiosity is as highly regarded as technical expertise.
- *Access to information.* Employees must have access to a wide range of information. Involved individuals make decisions about what kind of information they need for performing their jobs.
- *Accountability.* Empowerment does not involve being able to do whatever you want. Empowered employees should be held accountable for their behaviour toward others. They must produce agreed-upon results, achieve credibility, and operate with a positive approach.[22]

Also, employee empowerment succeeds when the culture of the organization is open and receptive to change. An organization's culture is created largely through the philosophies of senior managers and their leadership traits and behaviours. In an empowered organization, effective leadership is exemplified by managers who are honest, caring, and receptive to new ideas, and who treat employees with dignity and respect and as partners in organizational success.

Industrial Engineering Considerations

Industrial engineering

A field of study concerned with analyzing work methods and establishing time standards

The study of work is an important contribution of the scientific management movement. **Industrial engineering**, which evolved with this movement, is concerned with analyzing work methods and establishing time standards. Specifically, it involves the study of work cycles to determine which, if any, elements can be modified, combined, rearranged, or eliminated to reduce the time needed to complete the cycle. Next, time standards are established by recording the time required to complete each element in the work cycle, using a stopwatch or work-sampling technique. By combining the times for each element, the total time required is determined. This time is subsequently adjusted to allow for the skill and effort demonstrated by the observed worker and for interruptions that may occur in performing the work. The adjusted time becomes the time standard for that particular work cycle. The new Autotrans automotive plant in Ingersoll, Ontario, uses a hand-controlled crane, ensuring that the operator need never bend or lift.

Industrial engineering takes a disciplined and objective approach to job design. Unfortunately, because industrial engineering focuses on improving efficiency and simplifying work methods, it may neglect the human considerations in job design. Improvements in job design and efficiency, while sound from an engineering standpoint, can sometimes be psychologically unsound. For example, the assembly line with its simplified and repetitive tasks embodies solid principles of industrial engineering, but these tasks are often not psychologically rewarding for those who must perform them. Thus, to be effective, job design must also provide for the satisfaction of human needs.

Ergonomic Considerations

Ergonomics

An interdisciplinary approach to designing equipment and systems that can be easily and efficiently used by human beings

Ergonomics attempts to accommodate the human capabilities and deficiencies of those who are to perform a job. It is concerned with adapting the entire job system—the work, the work environment, the machines, the equipment, and the processes—to match human characteristics.[23] In short, it seeks to fit the machine to the person rather than the person to the machine. Also referred to as human engineering and engineering psychology, ergonomics attempts to minimize the harmful effects of carelessness, negligence, and other human fallibilities that otherwise might cause product defects, damage to equipment, or even the injury or death of employees.

Equipment design must take into consideration the physical ability of operators to use the equipment and to react through vision, hearing, and touch to the information the equipment conveys. Designing equipment controls to be compatible with the physical characteristics and reaction capabilities of the people who must operate them, and with the environment they work in, is increasingly important. Ergonomics also considers the requirements of a diverse workforce, accommodating, for example, women who may lack the strength to operate equipment requiring intense physical force. At General Motors of Canada's newly designed transmission plant in Windsor, Ontario, mechanical assists have been installed to insulate the operators from force factors. These ergonomically designed assists use articulating arms to help operators ward off the potentially strain-causing force of the heavy parts they must lift, push, or pull.[24]

WWW

A comfortable workstation lends itself to productivity improvement and a reduction in job-related stresses and injuries.

WWW

Ergonomics contributes to productivity improvements and has been cost-effective at organizations such as Chrysler and the *Toronto Star*. The latter organization sought to minimize repetitive strain injuries (RSIs) among its employees by introducing ergonomically designed workstations and by training people in the proper use of keyboards and other office equipment.[25] Marilyn Joyce, head of Arthur D. Little's ergonomics unit, notes: "You simply have to adapt your workplace to the labour force; ignore it, and you could be sacrificing quality and productivity."[26]

The ergonomics team at Telus, Canada's second-largest telecommunications company, assessed more than 1,600 work stations to ensure that its operators worked in safe environments. Figure 3.5 provides an ergonomics checklist for computer workstations.

FIGURE 3.5 *Computer Workstation Ergonomics Checklist*

Use the following list to identify potential problem areas that should receive further investigation. Any "no" response may point to a problem.

1. Does the workstation ensure proper worker posture, such as
   - Thighs in the horizontal position?
   - Lower legs in the vertical position?
   - Feet flat on the floor or on a footrest?
   - Wrists straight and relaxed?

2. Does the chair
   - Adjust easily?
   - Have a padded seat with a rounded front?
   - Have an adjustable backrest?
   - Provide lumbar support?
   - Have casters?

3. Are the height and tilt of the work surface on which the keyboard is located adjustable?

4. Is the keyboard detachable?

5. Do keying actions require minimal force?

6. Is there an adjustable document holder?

7. Are armrests provided where needed?

8. Are glare and reflections minimized?

9. Does the monitor have brightness and contrast controls?

10. Is there sufficient space for knees and feet?

11. Can the workstation be used for either right- or left-handed activity?

Source: The National Institute for Occupational Safety and Health (NIOSH), *Elements of Ergonomics Programs: A Primer Based on Workplace Evaluations of Musculoskeletal Disorders* (Washington, D.C.: U.S. Government Printing Office, March 1997).

Designing Work for Group Contributions

Although a variety of programs have been developed to involve employees more fully in their organizations, all of these programs have two characteristics in common—they enhance collaboration, and they increase synergy. By increasing the degree of collaboration in the work environment, these techniques can improve work processes and organizational decision making. By increasing group synergy, they underline the adage that the contributions of two or more employees are greater than the sum of their individual efforts. Research has shown that working in a group setting strengthens employee commitment to an organization's goals, increases employee acceptance of decisions, and encourages a cooperative approach to workplace tasks. Two collaborative techniques are discussed here: (1) employee involvement groups, and (2) employee teams.

Employee Involvement Groups

Employee involvement groups (EIs)

Groups of employees who meet to resolve problems or offer suggestions for organizational improvement

Groups of five to ten employees doing similar or related work who meet together regularly to identify, analyze, and suggest solutions to shared problems are often referred to as **employee involvement groups (EIs)**. Also widely known as *quality circles* (QCs), EIs are used mainly to involve employees in the larger goals of the organization through their suggestions for improving product or service quality and cutting costs.[27] Generally, EIs recommend their solutions to management, which decides whether to implement them.

The employee involvement group process, illustrated in Figure 3.6, begins with EI members brainstorming job-related problems or concerns and gathering data about these issues. The process continues through the generation of solutions and recommendations, which are then communicated to management. If the solutions are implemented, results are measured and the EI and its members are usually recognized for the contributions they have made. EIs typically meet four or more hours each month. The meetings are chaired by a leader chosen from the group. The leader does not hold an authority position but instead serves as a discussion facilitator.

EIs have become an important employee contribution system, but they are not without their problems and their critics. *First*, to achieve the results desired, those participating in EIs must receive comprehensive training in problem identification and problem analysis, and in the use of various decision-making tools such as statistical analysis and cause-and-effect diagrams. Comprehensive training for EIs is often cited as the most important factor leading to their success. *Second*, managers should recognize the group when a recommendation is made, regardless of whether the recommendation is adopted. This approach encourages the group to continue coming up with ideas even when they are not all implemented by management. *Third*, some organizations have found that EIs run out of ideas, at which point management must feed them ideas to keep the process going. Other objections to EIs come from their basic design. Some critics argue that EIs do not fundamentally change the organization in which they are established. As a form of suggestion system, they may work well, but they do not alter the organization's culture. Therefore, these critics argue, the employees who participate may realize the benefits of participation, but most employees—those who are not included in EIs—will be unaffected by their efforts.

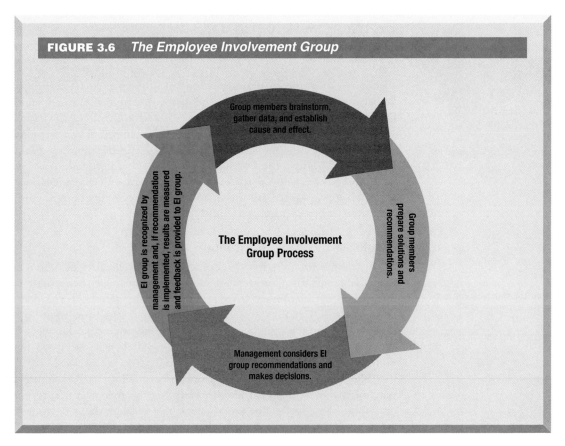

FIGURE 3.6   *The Employee Involvement Group*

Group members brainstorm, gather data, and establish cause and effect.

Group members prepare solutions and recommendations.

The Employee Involvement Group Process

Management considers EI group recommendations and makes decisions.

EI group is recognized by management and, if recommendation is implemented, results are measured and feedback is provided to EI group.

Source: The Family and Relationship Center, 7946 Ivanhoe Ave., Suite 201, La Tolla, CA, 92037.

Employee teams

An employee contributions technique whereby work functions are structured for groups rather than for individuals and team members are given discretion in matters traditionally considered management prerogatives

WWW

Employee Teams

In a survey conducted by Hewitt Associates (**www.hewitt.com**), two-thirds of 1,811 employers reported using formal teams to conduct work.[28] At Compaq Computer Corporation as many as 25 percent of the 16,000 employees are on teams that develop new products and bring them to market. At such diverse organizations as Federal Express, CIBC, Xerox Canada, Vancouver City Savings, and Abitibi-Consolidated, the benefits of employee teams have included more integration of individual skills, better performance in terms of quantity and quality, reduced turnover and absenteeism, and a sense of confidence and accomplishment among team members.[29]

Employee teams are a logical outgrowth of employee involvement and of the philosophy of empowerment. Teams are groups of employees who assume a greater role in the production or service process.[30] Teams provide a forum where employees can contribute their ideas about daily operations and identify and solve organizational problems. Employee contributions can also include joint decision making whereby employees are encouraged to share their knowledge to resolve operational concerns. Teams seek to make members of the work group share responsibility for their group's performance. Inherent in the concept of employee teams is that employees, not managers, are in the best position to contribute to workplace improvements. With work teams, managers accept the notion that the group is the logical work unit, and then apply resources to resolve organizational problems and concerns.

Teams can operate in a variety of structures, each with different strategic purposes or functional activities. Figure 3.7 describes common team forms. One form, self-directed teams, is being adopted in many organizations.[31] Self-directed teams, also called *autonomous work groups, self-managed teams,* or *high-performance teams,* are groups of employees who are accountable for a "whole" work process or segment that delivers a product or service to an internal or external customer. Team members acquire multiple skills that enable them to perform a variety of job tasks. To varying degrees, team members work together to improve their operations, handle day-to-day concerns, and plan and control their work. Highlights in HRM 3 shows the results from one study of the functions commonly performed by self-managed teams.

WWW

Self-directed teams are designed to give the team "ownership" of a product or service. In manufacturing environments, a team might be responsible for a whole product or a clearly defined segment of the production process. At Eastman Kodak Company, teams are responsible for manufacturing entire "product lines," including processing, lab work, and packaging. Similarly, in a service environment a team usually has responsibility for entire groupings of products and services, often serving clients in a designated geographic area. Providing employees with this type of ownership usually requires broader job categories and the sharing of work assignments.

FIGURE 3.7 *Forms of Employee Teams*

Cross-functional teams. A group staffed with a mix of specialists (e.g., marketing, production, engineering) and formed to accomplish a specific objective. Cross-functional teams are based on assigned rather than voluntary membership.

Project teams. A group formed specifically to design a new product or service. Members are assigned by management on the basis of their ability to contribute to success. The group usually disbands after task completion.

Self-directed teams. Groups of highly trained individuals performing a set of interdependent job tasks within a natural work unit. Team members use consensus decision making to perform work duties, solve problems, or deal with internal or external customers.

Task force teams. A task force is formed by management to immediately resolve a major problem. The group is responsible for developing a long-term plan for problem resolution that may include a charge for implementing the solution proposed.

Process-improvement teams. A group made up of experienced people from different departments or functions and charged with improving quality, decreasing waste, or enhancing productivity in processes that affect all departments or functions involved. Team members are normally appointed by management.

Virtual teams

Teams that use advanced telecommunications technology to link their members, who can be anywhere in the world

To compete in national and international markets, managers have formed **virtual teams**. Virtual teams use advanced computer and telecommunications technology to link team members who are geographically dispersed—often worldwide. Management may form a cross-functional team (see Figure 3.7) to develop a new pharmaceutical drug, and have the team operate in a virtual environment to achieve its goal. Virtual teams provide new opportunities for training, product development, and product market analysis. Importantly, virtual teams provide access to previously unavailable expertise and enhance cross-functional interactions. However, while the benefits of virtual teams are many, they are not without their problems, including language and cultural barriers and different goals and objectives across departments.

Regardless of the structure or purpose of the team, the following characteristics have been identified with successful teams:[32]

- commitment to shared goals and objectives
- consensus decision making
- open and honest communication
- shared leadership
- climate of cooperation, collaboration, trust, and support
- valuing of individuals for their diversity
- recognition of conflict and its positive resolution

Unfortunately, not all teams succeed or operate to their full potential. Therefore, in adopting the work team concept, organizations must address several issues that could present obstacles to effective team function, including overly high expectations, group compensation, training, career movement, and power. For example, new team members must be retrained to work outside their primary functional areas, and compensation systems must be constructed to reward individuals for team accomplishments. Since team membership demands more general skills, and since it moves an employee out of the historical career path, new career paths to general management must be created from the team experience. Finally, as the team members become capable of carrying out functions, such as strategic planning, that were previously restricted to higher levels of management, managers must be prepared to utilize their newfound expertise.

Another difficulty with work teams is that they alter the traditional manager–employee relationship. Managers often find it hard to adapt to the role of leader rather than supervisor and sometimes feel threatened by the growing power of the team and the reduced power of management.[33] Furthermore, some employees may have difficulty adapting to a role that includes traditional supervisory responsibilities. Another difficulty with work teams is that they must be incorporated into the organization's strategic planning process. Since work teams alter the organization structurally, they must be taken into account when organizational strategies and tactics are being established.

Finally, empirical studies of work teams suggest that teams are greater contributors to organizational performance when they operate with open and unrestricted access to information, when team membership represents diverse job functions, and when a team has a sufficient number of members to be effective.[34] Team members achieve their greatest value when participation is valued and viewed as important to success.

Highlights in HRM

3   WHAT SELF-MANAGED TEAMS MANAGE

More self-managing teams are taking on tasks that were once the purview of supervisors or managers. Among organizations with self-directed teams, the percentages indicate that teams perform these functions on their own.

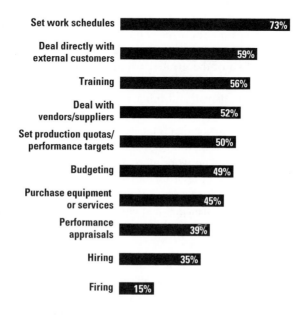

Set work schedules	73%
Deal directly with external customers	59%
Training	56%
Deal with vendors/suppliers	52%
Set production quotas/ performance targets	50%
Budgeting	49%
Purchase equipment or services	45%
Performance appraisals	39%
Hiring	35%
Firing	15%

Source: Reprinted with permission from "1995 Industry Report," *Training* 32, no. 10 (October 1995); 72. Copyright 1995. Lakewood Publicationhs, 50 S. Ninth St., Minneapolis, MN 55402.

Adjustments in Work Schedules

Adjustments in work schedules are not really a part of job design, since job tasks and responsibilities are not changed. Nevertheless, we discuss adjustments in work schedules here because they alter the normal workweek, in which all employees begin and end their workday at the same preset time (usually five 8-hour days). Employers may depart from the traditional workday or workweek in an attempt to improve organizational productivity and morale by giving employees increased control over the hours they work. The more common alternative work schedules include the compressed workweek, flextime, job sharing, and telecommuting.

The Compressed Workweek

With a compressed workweek, the number of days in the workweek is shortened by lengthening the number of hours worked per day.[35] This schedule is best illustrated by the four-day, 40-hour week, generally referred to as 4/10 or 4/40. Employees working a four-day workweek might work ten hours a day, Monday through Thursday. The 4/10 schedule is probably the best known. Other compressed arrangements include reducing weekly hours to 38 or 36 hours, or scheduling 80 hours over nine days (9/80), with one day off taken every other week.

WWW

Organizations that operate batch-processing systems (e.g., oil companies like Shell Oil) use shorter workweeks to coordinate work schedules with production schedules. Compressed workweeks can assist with scheduling arrangements by improving plant and equipment utilization. The keying of work schedules to processing time for a specific operation rather than to a standard workweek reduces startup and close-down time and often results in higher weekly output.

Two of the greatest advantages of the compressed work schedule are these: it accommodates the leisure activities of employees, and it helps employees schedule medical, dental, and other personal appointments. It also improves employee job satisfaction and morale, reduces absenteeism, and facilitates recruitment.

The major disadvantage of the compressed workweek relates to employment standards legislation governing the payment of overtime to nonsupervisory employees who work more than a specified number of hours per week. This legislation, which varies from province to province, is discussed in greater depth in Chapter 9. Another disadvantage of the compressed workweek is that it increases the amount of stress on managers and employees. Finally, long workdays can be exhausting.[36]

Flextime

Flextime

Flexible working hours that permit employees the option of choosing daily starting and quitting times, provided that they work a set number of hours per day or week

WWW

Flextime, or flexible working hours, permits employees to choose their own daily starting and quitting times, provided that they work a certain number of hours per day or week. With flextime, employees are given considerable latitude in scheduling their work. However, there is a "core period" during the morning and afternoon when all employees are required to be on the job. Flexible working hours are most common in service-type organizations—financial institutions, government agencies, and other organizations with large clerical operations. The head office of Manulife Financial has found that flextime provides many advantages for the company's employees. Royal Bank Financial Group found that about half of the nearly 4,000 users choose flexible arrangements because of family responsibilities; the rest cite other reasons such as continuing education and community involvement.

Flextime provides employees and employers with several advantages. By allowing employees greater flexibility in work scheduling, employers reduce some of the traditional causes of tardiness and absenteeism. Also, employees can adjust their work to accommodate their particular lifestyles, and in doing so gain greater job satisfaction. Employees can also schedule their working hours for the time of day when they are most productive. Variations in arrival and departure times can help reduce traffic congestion at the peak commuting hours. In some situations, employees require less time to commute, and the pressures of meeting a rigid schedule are reduced.

From the employer's standpoint, flextime can be most helpful in recruiting and retaining personnel. It has proved invaluable to organizations that wish to improve service to customers or clients by extending operating hours. Bruncor, a telecommunications company, uses flextime to keep its business offices open for customers who cannot get there during the day. Research demonstrates that flextime can have a positive impact on reliability, quality, and quantity of employee work.

There are, of course, several disadvantages to flextime. First, it is not suited to some jobs. It is not feasible, for example, where specific workstations must be staffed at all times. Second, it can create problems for managers in communicating with and instructing employees. Also, flextime schedules may also force these managers to extend their workweek if they are to exercise control over their subordinates.

Job Sharing

The arrangement whereby two part-time employees perform a job that otherwise would be held by one full-time employee is called "job sharing." Job sharers usually work three days a week, "creating an overlap day for extended face-to-face conferencing."[37] Their pay is three-fifths of a regular salary; however, job sharers usually take on additional responsibilities beyond what the original job would require. Companies that use job sharing are primarily in the legal, advertising, and financial-services businesses. Canadian banks are well known for their job-sharing programs. Employers note that without job sharing two good employees might otherwise be lost.

Job sharing is suited to the needs of families in which one or both spouses desire to work only part-time. It is also suited to the needs of older workers who want to phase into retirement by shortening their workweek. For the employer, the work of part-time employees can be scheduled to conform to peaks in the daily workload. Job sharing can also limit layoffs in hard economic times. A final benefit is that employees engaged in job sharing have time off during the week to accommodate personal needs, so they are less likely to be absent.

Job sharing does have several problems, however.[38] Employers may not want to employ two people to do the work of one, because the time required to orient and train a second employee constitutes an added burden. They may also want to avoid prorating employee benefits between two part-time employees. This problem can be addressed by permitting the employees to contribute the difference between the health insurance (or life insurance) premiums for a full-time employee and the pro rata amount the employer would otherwise contribute for a part-time employee. The key to making job sharing work is good communications between the partners, who will use a number of ways to stay in contact—phone calls, written updates, e-mail, and voice mail.

Telecommuting

Telecommuting

Use of microcomputers, networks, and other communications technology such as fax machines to do work in the home that is traditionally done in the workplace

www

One of the more recent changes, and potentially the most far-reaching, is telecommuting.[39] **Telecommuting** is the use of microcomputers, networks, and other communications technology such as fax machines to do work in the home that is traditionally done in the workplace. As technology becomes both more sophisticated and more user-friendly, employees can hook up with their offices and perform their tasks while remaining miles away.[40]

About 40 percent of employers offer work-at-home arrangements. Many organizations have developed telecommuting policies, including Bell Canada and the Bank of Montreal. The potential benefits of telecommuting are decreased production costs, increased employee satisfaction, and increased productivity. However, some managers have been reluctant to consider telecommuting because they fear they will lose control if employees are not physically present. Two provinces, British Columbia and New Brunswick, extend employer health and safety responsibility to home offices.

These flexible job arrangements have significant advantages to employers and employees, as discussed in Highlights in HRM 4.

Highlights in HRM

WWW

4   FLEX TIME AND WORK/LIFE BALANCE

Nora Spinks, president and CEO of Work-Life Harmony Enterprises, works with employers to create organizational cultures that enable employees to achieve work/life balance. The firm's goal is to develop successful work environments where individuals and organizations have the ability to reach their full potential and where employees have full and satisfying lives outside their work.

Spinks asserts that employers benefit from these family-friendly policies: "The most effective and productive employees are those who do work they enjoy, are challenged, have access to the necessary resources to meet that challenge, have control over how they work, receive recognition, rewards, and compensation based on the effort they put forth, and feel their life outside of work is respected and valued. These employees are highly resilient. In today's world of work, individual and organizational resiliency is critical for success. People in resilient, adaptable, responsive environments have the ability to change, the capacity to adapt to change, the energy to drive change and the flexibility to react positively to change, regardless of the intensity or the factors outside of their immediate control such as market forces, economic pressures and social or political circumstances."

Today's most popular employee support initiative is workplace flexibility: flextime with core hours and flexible start and end times, compressed work weeks (full workload completed in less than five days per week), and/or permanent part-time hours with equal status, pro-rated benefits, and the same development opportunities as full-time employees. Gaining in popularity are creative alternatives such as extended workweeks (full workload completed in six days) and self-funded or radical sabbaticals (setting aside a portion of pay for a period of time and taking an extended leave while collecting the banked salary (e.g., 2.5 years working at 85 percent pay and six months away from the workplace on a self-funded sabbatical).

Employees are using the time gained from workplace flexibility to fulfil family responsibilities, create a balanced lifestyle, continue their education, make a contribution to their community, or volunteer in developing countries.

Spinks argues strongly for these policies: "Establishing control over hours of work has very specific, well-documented results: reduction in illness, injury, absenteeism, presenteeism (physically present, but mentally and emotionally absent), turnover, conflict, and unhealthy lifestyles and behaviours such as smoking, drinking and drugs.

"When you work too hard or too long, you tend to rely on substances such as nicotine, caffeine, or sugar boosters to get you through the day. When you are tired all the time, your ability to solve problems and resolve conflicts is decreased significantly. When you are run down, you become uninterested and disengaged. Employees who have control over their working hours have more energy, more time, and are more engaged at home, at work, and in the community. Employers, customers, and co-workers benefit during the day, and employees, their family, friends, and community benefit at the end of the day.

"When I started in this field many years ago, employers had no understanding of the issues. I received several letters from companies saying, 'Thank you for your interest, but all our charitable dollars have been allocated for this year.' So we began to build the business case for supportive work environments. In the eighties and nineties, progressive HR departments began to implement programs and policies to address the issues. Now in 2001, employers across all sectors, from all industries, are beginning to see the strategic advantages of a family-friendly, employee supportive work environment. I now work with CEOs in boardrooms, integrating these concepts into corporate strategy.

"I think there are many reasons why employers are embracing these policies now: labour force demographics, tight labour markets, and an increasing body of evidence documenting the costs and benefits of supportive work environments and the high costs of work/life imbalance and stress in the workplace."

SUMMARY

 Job requirements reflect the different duties, tasks, and responsibilities contained in jobs. Job requirements, in turn, influence the HR function performed by managers, including recruitment, selection, training and development, performance appraisal, compensation, and various labour relations activities.

 Job analysis data can be gathered using one of several collection methods—interviews, questionnaires, observations, or diaries. Other more quantitative approaches include use of functional job analysis, the position analysis questionnaire system, and the critical incident method. It is the prevailing opinion of the courts that HRM decisions on employment, performance appraisal, and promotions must be based on specific criteria that are job-related. These criteria can be determined objectively only by analyzing the requirements of each job.

 The format of job descriptions varies widely, and often reflects the needs of the organization and the expertise of the writer. At a minimum, job descriptions

should contain a job title, a job identification section, and an essential functions section. A job specification section can also be included. Job descriptions should be written in clear and specific terms, with consideration given to their legal implications.

 Job design is a combination of four basic considerations: organizational objectives; industrial engineering concerns (i.e., analyzing work methods and establishing time standards); ergonomic considerations, which accommodate human capabilities and limitations to job task); and employee contributions.

 In the job characteristics model, five job factors contribute to increased job performance and satisfaction: skill variety, task identity, task significance, autonomy, and feedback. All factors should be built into jobs, since each factor influences different employee psychological states. When jobs are enriched through the job characteristics model, employees experience more meaningfulness in their jobs, acquire more job responsibility, and receive direct feedback from the tasks they perform.

To improve the internal processes of organizations and increase productivity, organizations are making greater efforts to involve groups of employees in work operations. Employee involvement groups are composed of employees in work units, who are charged with offering suggestions for improving product or service quality or fostering workplace effectiveness. Employee teams stress employee collaboration over individual accomplishment. Teams rely on the expertise and different abilities of their members to achieve specific objectives. Self-directed teams are characterized by their willingness to perform traditional managerial tasks.

 Changes in work schedules—which include the compressed workweek, flextime, job sharing, and telecommuting—permit employees to adjust their work periods to accommodate their particular lifestyles. Employers can select from among these HR techniques to accommodate diverse employee needs while fostering organizational effectiveness.

KEY TERMS

critical incident method
employee empowerment
employee involvement groups
   (EIs)
employee teams
ergonomics
flextime

functional job analysis (FJA)
industrial engineering
job
job analysis
job characteristics model
job description
job design

job enrichment
job specification
position
position analysis questionnaire
   (PAQ)
telecommuting
virtual teams

DISCUSSION QUESTIONS

 1. Place yourself in the position of general manager of a service department. How could formally written job requirements help you manage your work unit?

 2. Discuss the various methods for completing a job analysis. Compare and contrast these methods, noting the pros and cons of each.

 3. Working with two or three other students, collect at least five different job descriptions from organizations in your area. Compare the descriptions, highlighting similarities and differences.

 4. In small groups, write a job description for "student," with each group using a different technique. Compare and critique these job descriptions.

 5. Consider your present job or a recent job. How would you incorporate into the position the five job characteristics that motivate employees? Can all five characteristics be included?

 6. As a small business employer, explain how nontraditional work schedules might make it easier for you to recruit employees.

7. Flexible work arrangements at CIBC are labelled "Work and Lifestyle Options" and include flexible work hours, job sharing, part-time work, and telecommuting. Go to the HRDC website **(www.labour-hrdc-drhc.gc.ca/wip/ casestudies)** and search for the article "Family Friendly Policies at CIBC." Document the reasons why CIBC developed these work arrangements, and the benefits they hope to achieve. [Note that this site also contains other cases on employee empowerment and alternative work arrangements. Read about how MacMillan Bloedel used teams to acheive higher production levels and profitability, and how NB Tel redesigned work to increase organizational effectiveness.]

DUCKS UNLIMITED CANADA

Ducks Unlimited Canada, a not-for-profit environmental agency, has as its goal the protection of wetland habitat in Canada. Relying on its 100,000 members, 7,000 volunteers, and 330 employees, this charitable organization has saved over 18 million acres in Canada. Ducks Unlimited has no problem attracting biologists, scientists, and accountants, because their recruits are committed to a conservation ethic and are dedicated to protecting the environment. It has also helped recruitment that Ducks Unlimited has reorganized itself to flatten its management structure. The goal was to empower the employees and facilitate decision making. People working in the field no longer have to go up and down the power ladder to obtain approvals at every step. Field employees feel more in control of what they are doing.

The human resources administrator cites many advantages to an empowered workforce: increased retention, increased motivation, and decreased absenteeism and sick days.

Source: Adapted from Anonymous, "Taking care of the people," *Canadian Health Care Manager* 6, no. 3, April–May 1999: 5–9.

Questions

1. What arguments could be advanced both for and against the use of employee empowerment?

2. Empowerment is mainly a motivational tool, but at Ducks Unlimited the employees arrive dedicated and committed to the environmental cause. Does Ducks Unlimited need to implement empowerment?

3. How might a manager at a traditional organization react to the implementation of empowerment?

FLEXIBLE WORK ARRANGEMENTS

WWW

About 9 percent of employees across Canada work compressed work weeks. Employer benefits are reduced stress and fatigue, reduced absenteeism, a greater ability to recruit and retain valued employees, and a reduction in commuting time. A Royal Bank survey showed that 94 percent of flextime users are very satisfied,

70 percent report lower levels of stress, and 78 percent feel that their advancement opportunities are the same as or better than those of employees working the traditional work week. Also, 37 percent of managers report an increase in employee efficiency.

WWW

The City of Vancouver was the leader in flexible job arrangements. Its most popular program, the four-day compressed work week, was in place for a quarter-century. The program was started in 1976 as an experiment to reduce air pollution and traffic congestion. Employees worked the same number of hours but longer days; this provided longer service hours at City Hall. The city decided to end this service on June 1, 1999, having judged that the public would enjoy more uniform service by being able to reach the same employee any day of the week. It reasoned that most businesses work a five-day week, so the ability to provide a uniform service was important.

The union objected, citing a survey done by the city itself which claimed that 85 percent of Vancouverites and 89 percent of businesses were satisfied with the service. Over 1,000 employees will lose this flexible arrangement. A disruptive strike is being threatened.

Source: Adapted from Anonymous, "Royal Bank Survey: Flexible Work Arrangements Lessens Struggle to Juggle" *Worklife Report,* 11, no. 2, 1998: 8–9. B. Tieleman, "The Assault on the Four Day Week: Vancouver Ends Productive Scheme; Others Could Follow," *National Post,* August 17, 1999: C7.

Questions

1. What are the potential advantages and disadvantages of the compressed work week?

2. If the compressed work week was part of the job description, what legal problems might the City of Vancouver face?

3. If you were a manager, how would you explain this change to your staff?

CAREER COUNSEL

Complete the exercise on the Managing Human Resources website to find your dream job (**belcourt.nelson.com**).

USING THE INTERNET

WWW

Human Resources Development Canada (**www.worklogic.com:81/noc/home.html**) has posted a description of the *National Occupational Classification (NOC)* system, which outlines the duties, skills, interests, aptitudes, education requirements, and work settings for occupations in the Canadian labour market.

The Center for the Study of Work Teams (**www.workteams.unt.edu**) has articles on work teams that can be downloaded.

The website of the Canadian Telework Association (**www.ivc.ca**) provides a list of the benefits of teleworking and current business practices.

NOTES AND REFERENCES

1. Personal correspondence with Beth Ordoman, The City of Calgary Personnel Services Department, May 5, 1995.

2. *Canadian Human Rights Reporter/Le Babillard Canadien des Droits de la Personne*, vol. 6, 1985.

3. George T. Milkovich and Jerry M. Newman, *Compensation*, 5th rev. ed. (Homewood, Ill.: Irwin, 1996). See also Ronald A. Ash, "Job Analysis in the World of Work," in *The Job Analysis Handbook for Business, Industry, and Government*, ed. Sidney Gall (New York: Wiley, 1988): 3.

4. Richard Henderson, *Compensation Management*, 7th ed. (Englewood Cliffs, N.J.: Prentice-Hall, 1996).

5. James P. Clifford, "Job Analysis: Why Do It and How It Should Be Done," *Public Personnel Management* 23 (Summer 1994): 321–40.

6. Human Resources Development Canada, *National Occupational Classification* (Ottawa: Minister of Supply and Services, 1996).

7. Charles Brimley and Michael Brennan, "Let's Get Technical," *Canadian Business*, November 28, 1997.

8. Milkovich and Newman, *Compensation*, 68.

9. For one study on the PAQ, see James P. Clifford, "Manage Work Better to Better Manage Human Resources: A Comparative Study of Two Approaches to Job Analysis," *Public Personnel Management* 25, no. 1 (Spring 1996): 89.

10. For a thought-provoking article on the future of jobs, see William Bridges, "The End of the Job," *Fortune*, September 19, 1994: 62–74.

11. Bob Cardy and Greg Dobbins, "Job Analysis in a Dynamic Environment," *News* (Academy of Management, Human Resources Division) 16, no. 1 (Fall 1992): 4. See also Benjamin Schneider and Andrea Marcus Konz, "Strategic Job Analysis," *Human Resource Management* 28, no. 1 (Spring 1989): 51–63.

12. Steven T. Hunt, "Generic Work Behavior: An Investigation into the Dimensions of Entry-Level, Hourly Job Performance," *Personnel Psychology* 49, no. 1 (Spring 1996): 51–83.

13. Kenneth P. Carson and Greg L. Stewart, "Job Analysis and the Sociotechnical Approach to Quality: A Critical Examination," *Journal of Quality Management* 1, no. 1 (1996): 49–56.

14. Jai V. Ghorpade, *Job Analysis: A Handbook for the Human Resource Director* (Englewood Cliffs, N.J.: Prentice-Hall, 1988): 97–98.

15. Paul Wienberg, "Labour Law Overview," *Canadian Lawyer*, March 1995: 36–43.

16. For an example of process re-engineering, see Patricia A. Compton, "Process Reengineering Formula for Success for the Future," *Public Personnel Management* 25, no. 2 (Summer 1995): 257–63.

17. For Herzberg's important article on job enrichment, see Frederick Herzberg, "One More Time: How Do You Motivate Employees?" *Harvard Business Review* 46, no. 2 (January/February 1968): 53–62.

18. For the original article on the job characteristics model, see J. Richard Hackman and Greg R. Oldham, "Motivation through the Design of Work: Test of a Theory," *Organizational Behavior and Human Performance* 16, no. 2 (August 1976): 250–79.

19. Hackman and Oldham, "Motivation": 256.

20. Ibid., 257–58.

21. "Forecasting the Future of the American Workplace," *American Workplace* 1, no. 1 (September 1993): 2.

22. John H. Dobbs, "The Empowerment Environment," *Training and Development* 47, no. 2 (February 1993): 55–7.

23. Alan Fowler, "How to Conduct an Ergonomic Review," *People Management* 1, no. 8 (September 7, 1995): 45–6.

24. Personal correspondence with Dan Cerovec, Transmission Plant, GM of Canada, Windsor, Ontario, May 1995.

25. "On the Front Lines: Taming RSI," *Benefits Canada* 21, no. 3 (March 1997): 32.

26. Kenneth Labich, "Making Diversity Pay," *Fortune*, September 9, 1996: 178.

27. Robert E. Coke, Paul Bacdayan, and B. Joseph White, "Quality, Participation, and Competitiveness," *California Management Review* 35, no. 3 (Spring 1993): 68–81. See also Richard J. Magjuka, "The 10 Dimensions of Employee Involvement," *Training and Development* 47, no. 4 (April 1993): 61–7.

28. *Wall Street Journal*, December 28, 1995: A1.

29. The literature on teams is prolific. See the following: Jon R. Katzenbach and Douglas K. Smith, *The Wisdom of Teams* (Boston, Mass.: Harvard Business School Press, 1993); Donna Deeprose, *The Team Coach: Vital New Skills for Supervisors and Managers in a Team Environment* (New York: American Management Association, 1995); John H. Zenger, Ed Musselwhite, Kathleen Hurson, and Craig Perrin, *Leading Teams: Mastering the New Role* (Burr Ridge, Ill.: Irwin, 1994); and Richard S. Wellins, Dick Schaaf, and Kathy Harper Shomo, *Succeeding with Teams* (Minneapolis: Lakewood Books, 1994).

30. Paul Zuech and Nancy Finley, "Teamwork Enhances Customer Satisfaction and Manufacturing Capability at Kent-Moore," *National Productivity Review* 15, no. 2 (Spring 1996): 101–5.

31. Jack D. Orsburn, Linda Moran, Ed Musselwhite, and John H. Zenger, *Self-Directed Work Teams: The New American Challenge* (Burr Ridge, Ill.: Irwin, 1990).

32. Val Arnold, "Making Teams Work," *HRFocus* 73, no. 2 (February 1996): 12–13; Laurence Holpp and Robert Phillips, "When Is a Team Its Own Worst Enemy?" *Training* 32, no. 12 (September 1995): 71–80; and Michael A. Campion, Ellen M. Papper, and Gina J. Medsker, "Relations between Work Team Characteristics and

Effectiveness: A Replication and Extension," *Personnel Psychology* 49, no. 2 (Summer 1996): 429–52.

33. Paul W. Mulvey, John F. Veiga, and Priscilla M. Elsass, "When Teammates Raise a White Flag," *Academy of Management Executive* 10, no. 1 (February 1996): 40–9.

34. Richard J. Magjuka and Timothy T. Baldwin, "Team-Based Employee Involvement Programs: Effects of Design and Administration," *Personnel Psychology* 44, no. 4 (Winter 1991): 793–811. See also Anthony R. Montebellow and Victor R. Buzzotta, "Work Teams That Work," *Training and Development* 47, no. 3 (March 1993): 59–64; and Lewis Brown Griggs and Lemte-Louise Loow, "Breakdown or Breakthrough," *Training and Development* 49, no. 11 (October 1995): 22–9.

35. Dominic Bencivenga, "Compressed Weeks Fill an HR Niche," *HRMagazine* 40, no. 6 (June 1995): 71.

36. Gilbert Fuchberg, "Four-Day Workweek Has Become a Stretch for Some Employees," *Wall Street Journal*, August 3, 1994: A1.

37. Sue Shellenbarger, "Two People, One Job: It Really Can Work," *Wall Street Journal*, December 7, 1994: B1.

38. Elizabeth Sheley, "Job Sharing Offers Unique Challenges," *HRMagazine* 41, no. 1 (January 1996): 46–9.

39. "Telecommuting: An Idea Whose Time Has Come," *HRFocus*, November 1995: 1.

40. Julian M. Weiss, "Telecommuting Boosts Employee Output," *HRMagazine* 39, no. 2 (February 1994): 51.

After studying this chapter, you should be able to

OBJECTIVE 1

Identify the advantages of integrating human resources planning and strategic planning.

OBJECTIVE 2

Describe the basic approaches to human resources planning.

OBJECTIVE 3

Explain the advantages and disadvantages of recruiting from within the organization.

OBJECTIVE 4

Explain the advantages and disadvantages of external recruitment.

OBJECTIVE 5

Describe methods for improving the effectiveness of recruiting.

HUMAN RESOURCES PLANNING AND RECRUITMENT

I n earlier chapters we stressed that the challenges of human resources management all centre on the idea that organizations increasingly compete on the basis of the talents and capabilities of their employees. It is therefore essential that managers do a careful job of recruiting, selecting, developing, and retaining valuable employees. In this chapter we focus on how organizations can meet these needs through effective human resources planning.

Essentially, we address two closely related processes: planning and recruitment. HR planning establishes a blueprint for staffing the organization, and recruitment sets this plan in motion. Employment recruiting has acquired new importance for managers, since both manufacturing and service organizations are finding it increasingly difficult to secure qualified applicants to fill job openings. Virtually all of the available evidence suggests that employers have difficulty staffing jobs, ranging from the unskilled to the professional and highly technical; and this condition is not likely to abate in the near future.[1] No longer can managers rely solely on unsolicited applications to fill openings. Changing employment conditions mandate that managers consider a variety of recruitment alternatives to attract the right employees to the organization. The process of planning for HR needs, finding sources of applicants, and attracting applicants will be discussed in this chapter.

HUMAN RESOURCES PLANNING

Human resources planning (HRP) is the process of anticipating and making provision for the movement of people into, within, and out of an organization. Its purpose is to deploy these resources as effectively as possible, where and when they are needed, in order to accomplish the organization's goals. Other, more specific purposes of HRP include anticipating labour shortages and surpluses; providing more employment opportunities for women, minorities, and the disabled; and mapping out employee training programs. HRP provides a launching point for almost all of the activities that are subsumed under HRM.

Human resources planning (HRP)

Process of anticipating and making provision for the movement of people into, within, and out of an organization.

Importance of Human Resources Planning

Consider these facts about the Canadian labour force:

- The workforce is aging. One-third of the labour force is age 45 or older, and the group between 35 and 44 will have shrunk by more than 1 percent between 2000 and 2015. By 2030, the last of the baby boomers will be 65, and the elderly will account for one-quarter of the population.
- The fastest-growing segments of the workforce are women and Asian Canadians, the latter mainly as a result of immigration.
- Women make up 50.5 percent of the workforce (and more than 50 percent of those getting bachelor's degrees).
- Fully 18 percent of Canadians were born in another country.
- Today nearly one-third of workers are part-timers, temporary workers, or self-employed. Five percent of Canadians hold two or more jobs. The number of self-employed is around 18 percent of total employment.
- The five occupational fields expected to experience faster-than-average growth are computer services; architectural, engineering, and other scientific services; employment agencies and personnel suppliers; management

consultancy; and accounting, law, and advertising. These occupations require the highest education and skill levels.

- People between 18 and 35 represent 26 percent of the Canadian population, but hold 40 percent of the high-tech jobs.[2]

How do managers cope with all these changes? How do they make certain they have the right people at the right time doing the right things for their organizations? Dramatic shifts in the composition of the labour force require that managers become more involved in HRP, since such changes affect not only employee recruitment but also methods of employee selection, training, compensation, and motivation. Although planning has always been an essential process of management, increased emphasis on HRP becomes especially critical when organizations consider mergers, relocation of plants, downsizing, or the closing of operating facilities.

An organization can incur several intangible costs as a result of inadequate HRP—or, for that matter, no HRP. For example, inadequate HRP can lead to unfilled vacancies. The resulting loss in efficiency can be costly, especially where lead time is required to train replacements. Sometimes employees will be laid off in one department even while applicants are being hired for similar jobs in another department. The result is overhiring and the need to lay off employees who were recently hired. Finally, lack of HRP makes it difficult for employees to plan their careers or personal development. As a result, some of the more competent and ambitious ones will look for work in other organizations, where their career prospects are better.[3]

HRP and Strategic Planning

As organizations plan for their future, HR managers must concern themselves with meshing HRP and strategic planning for the organization as a whole.[4] HRP and strategic planning are linked in three main ways, discussed below.

Linking the Planning Processes

Through strategic planning, organizations set major objectives and develop comprehensive plans to achieve those objectives. Human resources planning relates to strategic planning at both the front end and the back end of this process. At the front end, human resources planning provides a set of inputs into the strategic *formulation* process in terms of what is possible—that is, whether the types and numbers of people are available to pursue a given strategy. On the back end, strategic planning and HRP are linked in terms of *implementation* concerns. Once the strategy is set, executives must make primary resource allocation decisions, including those pertaining to structure, processes, and human resources.[5]

WWW

Figure 4.1 illustrates the basic outline of how companies have begun aligning HRP and strategic planning. Companies such as British Petroleum have taken strides to combine these two aspects of management.[6] The integration of HRP and strategic planning tends to be most effective when there is a reciprocal relationship between the two processes. In this relationship, the top management team recognizes that strategic-planning decisions affect—and are affected by—HR concerns. As James Walker, noted HRP expert, has put it: "Today, virtually *all* business issues have people implications; *all* human resource issues have business implications."[7]

In the best of companies, such as Xerox, there is virtually no distinction between strategic planning and HRP; the planning cycles are the same and HR issues are seen

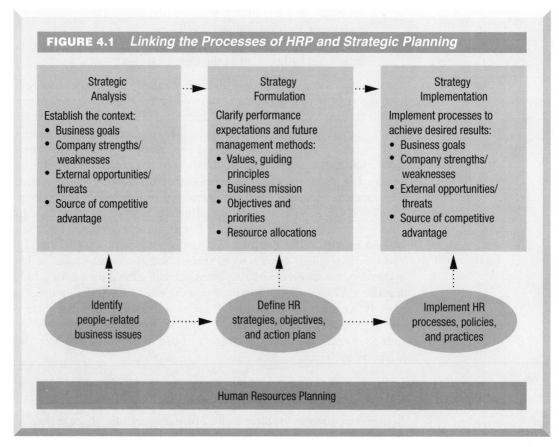

FIGURE 4.1   *Linking the Processes of HRP and Strategic Planning*

Strategic Analysis

Establish the context:
- Business goals
- Company strengths/ weaknesses
- External opportunities/ threats
- Source of competitive advantage

Strategy Formulation

Clarify performance expectations and future management methods:
- Values, guiding principles
- Business mission
- Objectives and priorities
- Resource allocations

Strategy Implementation

Implement processes to achieve desired results:
- Business goals
- Company strengths/ weaknesses
- External opportunities/ threats
- Source of competitive advantage

Identify people-related business issues

Define HR strategies, objectives, and action plans

Implement HR processes, policies, and practices

Human Resources Planning

Source: Adapted from James W. Walker, "Integrating the Human Resource Function with the Business." *Human Resource Planning* 14, no. 2 (1996). Reprinted with permission.

WWW

as inherent in the management of the business. Lucent Canada, with 800 employees, links planning and HR and uses the acronym GROWS to summarize these behaviours: G for growth, R for results, O for the obsession with customers and competitors, W for a workplace that is open, supportive, and diverse, and S for speed to market.[8] HR managers are important facilitators of the planning process and are viewed as credible and important contributors to the process of creating the organization's future. This positive linkage is made when the HR manager becomes a member of the organization's management steering committee or strategic planning group. Once this interactive and dynamic structure exists, HR managers are recognized as contributing strategic planners alongside other top managers.[9]

Mapping an Organization's Human Capital Architecture

Besides aligning the planning processes themselves, the linkage between strategy and HR today also does much to develop core competencies. Companies such as Second Cup revolutionized their industries by developing skills—core competencies—that others didn't have. These competencies helped them gain an advantage over their competitors and leverage this advantage by learning faster than others in their industries.

WWW

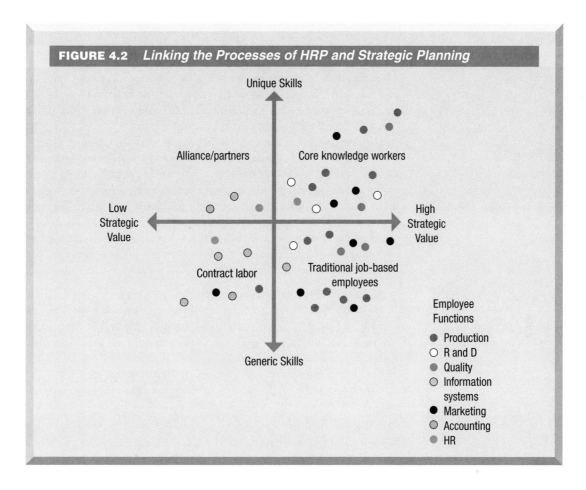

FIGURE 4.2   *Linking the Processes of HRP and Strategic Planning*

Unique Skills

Alliance/partners

Core knowledge workers

Low
Strategic
Value

High
Strategic
Value

Contract labor

Traditional job-based
employees

Generic Skills

Employee
Functions

● Production
○ R and D
● Quality
○ Information
   systems
● Marketing
○ Accounting
● HR

Underlying a firm's core competencies is a portfolio of employee skills and human capital. Figure 4.2 shows that different skill groups in any given organization can be classified according to the degree to which they create strategic value and are unique to the organization. Employment relationships and HR practices for different employees vary according to which cell they occupy in this matrix.

- *Core knowledge workers.* These employees have firm-specific skills that are directly linked to the company's strategy (e.g., R&D scientists at a pharmaceutical company, computer scientists at a software development company). These employees typically are engaged in knowledge work that involves considerable autonomy and discretion. Companies tend to make long-term commitments to these employees, investing in their continuous training and development and perhaps giving them an equity stake in the organization.

- *Traditional job-based employees.* These employees have skills that are quite valuable to a company, but not unique (e.g., salespeople in a department store, truck drivers for a courier service). These employees are employed to perform a predefined job. As it is quite possible that they could leave to go to another firm, managers often make less investment in training and development and tend to focus more on paying for short-term performance achievements.

- *Contract labour.* These employees have skills that are of less strategic value and that are generally available to all firms (e.g., clerical workers, maintenance workers, accounting and human resources staff). More and more, individuals in these jobs are being hired from outside agencies on a contract basis. The scope of their duties tends to be limited. Employment relationships tend to be transactional, and focused on rules and procedures, with very little investment in development.

- *Alliance/partners.* These people have skills that are unique but are not directly related to a company's core strategy (e.g., lawyers, consultants, and research lab scientists). Although companies perhaps cannot justify employing them in-house, given their tangential link to strategy, they have skills that are both specialized and not readily available to all firms. As a consequence, companies tend to establish longer-term alliances and partnerships with them, and to nurture an ongoing relationship focused on mutual learning. Considerable investment is made in the exchange of information and knowledge.[10]

An increasingly vital element of strategic planning for organizations that compete on competencies is determining whether people are available, internally or externally, to execute an organization's strategy. Managers have to make tough decisions about whom to employ internally, whom to contract externally, and how to manage different types of employees with different skills who contribute in different ways to the organization. HRP plays an important role in helping managers weigh the costs and benefits of using one approach to employment versus another.

Ensuring Fit and Flexibility

The third main way that HRP and strategic planning are connected is in aligning the policies, programs, and practices in HR with the requirements of an organization's strategy. In this regard, HR policies and practices need to achieve two types of fit.[11]

External fit focuses on the connection between the business objectives and the major initiatives in HR. For example, if a company's strategy focuses on achieving

A research scientist has knowledge and firm-specific skills that are directly linked to a company's strategy. Companies tend to make long-term investments in such core knwledge workers.

low cost, HR policies and practices need to reinforce this idea by reinforcing efficient and reliable behaviour. On the other hand, if the organization competes through innovation, new product development, and the like, HR policies and practices would be more aligned with the notion of creating flexibility and creativity. Highlights in HRM 1 shows the external fit between major business objectives and HR imperatives at Lucent Technologies).

This chapter deals mainly with the forecasting of supply and demand, and with managing labour surpluses and shortages. Readers interested in more strategic aspects of HR planning, such as mergers, should consult *Strategic Human Resource Planning*, by Belcourt and McBey (2000).

Internal fit means that HR practices are all aligned with one another in a mutually reinforcing configuration. For example, job design, staffing, training, performance appraisal, compensation, and the like would all focus on the same behavioural targets (such as efficiency and creativity). Unfortunately, it is all too often the case that (for example) training programs focus on teamwork and sharing, even while appraisal and compensation programs are reinforcing the ideas of individual achievement.

HRP also focuses on ensuring flexibility and agility when the environment changes. Ultimately, successful HRP helps increase **organizational capability**—the capacity of the organization to act and change in pursuit of sustainable competitive advantage.[12]

There are two main kinds of flexibility: coordination flexibility, and resource flexibility. *Coordination flexibility* is achieved through rapid reallocation of resources to new or changing needs. Through HRP, managers can anticipate upcoming events, keep abreast of changes in legal regulations, forecast economic trends, recognize competitor moves, and the like. With advanced notice, managers can move people into and out of jobs, retrain them for new skill requirements, and modify the incentives they utilize. Use of a contingency workforce composed of part-timers, temporary employees, and external partners also helps to achieve coordination flexibility.[13]

Resource flexibility, on the other hand, results from having people who can do many different things in different ways. Cross-training, job rotations, team-based work modes, and the like are all focused on establishing a flexible workforce. We will discuss each of these issues at more length throughout the text. At this point, however, we want to emphasize that the process depends on a thorough understanding of the organization's environment. And this begins with environmental scanning.

Organizational capability

The capacity to act and change in pursuit of sustainable competitive advantage

HRP and Environmental Scanning

Changes in the external environment have a direct impact on how organizations are run and people are managed. *Environmental scanning* is the systematic monitoring of the major external forces influencing the organization.[14] Managers attend to a variety of external issues; however, the following six are monitored most frequently:

1. Economic factors, including general and regional conditions.

2. Competitive trends, including new processes, services, and innovations.

3. Technological changes, including robotics and office automation.

Highlights in HRM

1 HR STRATEGY AND PLANNING MODEL FOR LUCENT TECHNOLOGIES (GLOBAL BUSINESS COMMUNICATIONS SYSTEMS)

GBCS BUSINESS PRINCIPLES	GBCS HR STRATEGIC IMPERATIVES	HUMAN RESOURCES MISSION	FOCUS AREAS	HR PLAN INITIATIVES
Make people a key priority.	I. Associates actively take ownership for the business success at all levels, individually and as teams, by improving associate value.			Learning forums, such as: • Change Management and You • GBCS Strategy Forum • PEP Workshop • Quality Curriculum
Use the Total Quality Management approach to run our business.	II. GBCS HR contributes to increased shareholder value by achieving process improvements that increase productivity and customer satisfaction.		Cultural Change	Communication Platform • Ask the President • Answer Line • All Associate Broadcasts • Bureaucracy Busters • Associate Dialogues
Rapidly and profitably globalize the business.	III. Ensuring GBCS HR readiness to expand its business initiatives into global markets, which requires a business partner that is sensitive to the unique needs of various cultures and people.	To create an environment where the achievement of business goals is realized through an acceptance of individual accountability		Diversity Platform • Pluralistic Leadership: Managing in a Global Society • Celebration of Diversity • National Diversity Council
Profitably grow by being the leader in customer-led applications of technology	IV. HR strategic plans and processes support and are integrated with GBCS's strategic and business planning processes so that the HR management system attracts, develops, rewards and retains associates who accept accountability for business success.	by each associate and by his/her commitment to performance excellence.	Rewards and Recognition	Progress Sharing Plan (PSP) Special Long-Term Plan (SLTP) Recognition Platform • Partner Platform • Trailblazers • President's Council • Achever's Club • Local Recognition Program • Touch Award

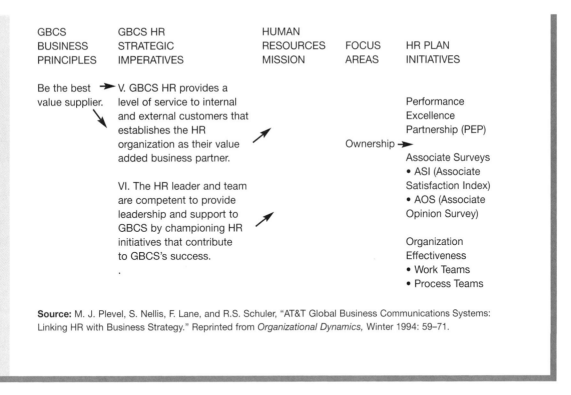

GBCS BUSINESS PRINCIPLES	GBCS HR STRATEGIC IMPERATIVES	HUMAN RESOURCES MISSION	FOCUS AREAS	HR PLAN INITIATIVES
Be the best value supplier.	V. GBCS HR provides a level of service to internal and external customers that establishes the HR organization as their value added business partner.		Ownership →	Performance Excellence Partnership (PEP)
				Associate Surveys • ASI (Associate Satisfaction Index) • AOS (Associate Opinion Survey)
	VI. The HR leader and team are competent to provide leadership and support to GBCS by championing HR initiatives that contribute to GBCS's success.			Organization Effectiveness • Work Teams • Process Teams

Source: M. J. Plevel, S. Nellis, F. Lane, and R.S. Schuler, "AT&T Global Business Communications Systems: Linking HR with Business Strategy." Reprinted from *Organizational Dynamics,* Winter 1994: 59–71.

4. Political and legislative issues, including laws and administrative rulings.

5. Social concerns, including child care and educational priorities.

6. Demographic trends, including age, composition, and literacy.

WWW

By scanning the environment for changes that will likely affect the organization, managers can anticipate their impact and make adjustments early. In a rapidly changing environment, it is extremely dangerous to be caught off guard.

In Highlights in HRM 2, David Foot, a demographer at the University of Toronto, explains why HR professionals must become more aware of the need to scan.

The labour force trends listed earlier illustrate the importance of monitoring demographic changes as a part of HRP. Such changes can affect the composition and performance of an organization's workforce. These changes are important because employment equity plans must take into account the demographic composition of the population in the area where the organization is located. Furthermore, the Canadian workforce is maturing," and HRP must consider the many implications of this demographic fact on recruitment and replacement policies. You have seen the televised ads for McDonald's and other fast food chains. Many other firms, including Tim Hortons, have made a stronger effort in recent years to hire older workers.[15] The Government of Canada, through Human Resources Development Canada, has committed $15 million to test innovative approaches to keep older workers employed.

WWW

Besides scanning the external environment, organizations such as CIBC and Nortel are careful to also scan their internal environments. Because these compa-

Highlights in HRM

2   SPOTTING TRENDS IN THE GLOBAL ECONOMY

Every human resource professional recognizes that anticipating trends is an important part of the job. Furthermore, senior HR professionals want to *influence* strategy, not just respond to strategies determined by the "real players" at the boardroom table.

David Foot of the University of Toronto, a famous Canadian economist and demographer, says that HR professionals are often ill equipped to contribute to their organization's strategy. He contends that HR people are experienced in dealing with micro issues, but often lack the big picture or macro perspective that is necessary to deal with corporate or strategic issues.

Having worked with executives and boards of directors, he is very familiar with the issues facing them and with the inability of HR managers to advance the HR view of the implications of strategic decisions. He offers this example: A company is thinking about going global—say, by expanding into Mexico. The HR person has very little knowledge about the labour market of that country (where there are many young people but relatively few seniors). Furthermore, he or she is likely to be preoccupied with important micro issues, such as how to hire employees and what the local health and safety rules are, when he ought to be considering, for example, Mexico's regional unemployment and education rates by region to determine plant location.

Other executives can think strategically when faced with changes in the environment. Foot asks: "How many HR professionals could answer the question, 'How does the exchange rate impact HR planning?' Those with a macro perspective would immediately determine: 1. How much business is internal/external? 2. Have the financial people bought insurance against exchange rate fluctuations? 3. If the Canadian dollar depreciates, and there will be more demand for our products, what are the opportunities to access labour in external markets such as Poland or Mexico? How can we recruit these people faster than other companies? This mindset is crucial to being at the board room table.

"Let me give you another example of reactionary micro thinking. Low unemployment rates traditionally result in demands from business for higher immigration levels to ease labour shortages. But this traditional HR response will become increasingly inappropriate in the new millennium because more immigrants will only compete with the children of boomers who will be entering the labour force. A proactionary macro thinking HR person will, therefore, be able to advise the CEO that this is likely to be a short-term, not a long-term labour shortage and to think internally rather than externally for new workers. This information could be crucial in influencing the company's strategic planning for the next five years."

Cultural Audits

Audits of the culture and quality of work life in an organization

nies view their employee-oriented cultures as critical to success, they conduct **cultural audits** to examine the attitudes and activities of the workforce. Sears has found that positive employee attitudes on ten essential factors—including workload and treatment by bosses—are directly linked to customer satisfaction and revenue increases.[16]

Cultural audits essentially involve discussions among top-level managers of how the organization's culture reveals itself to employees and how it can be influenced or improved. The cultural audit may include such questions as these:

- How do employees spend their time?
- How do they interact with one another?
- Are employees empowered?
- What is the predominant leadership style of managers?
- How do employees advance within the organization?

By conducting in-depth interviews and making observations over a period of time, managers are able to learn about the culture of their organization and the attitudes of its employees. With the increased diversity of the Canadian workplace, cultural audits can be used to determine whether there are different groups, or subcultures, within the organization that have distinctly different views about the nature of work, the quality of managers, and so on. Before any HR planning can take place, managers must gain a clear idea of how employees view their organization.

ELEMENTS OF EFFECTIVE HRP

Managers follow a systematic process, or model, when undertaking HRP, as shown in Figure 4.3. The three key elements of the process are forecasting the demand for labour, performing a supply analysis, and balancing supply and demand considerations. Careful attention to each factor will help top managers and supervisors meet their staffing requirements.

Forecasting Demand for Employees

A key part of HRP is forecasting the number and type of people needed to meet organizational objectives. A variety of organizational factors, including competitive strategy, technology, structure, and productivity, can influence the demand for labour. For example, as noted in Chapter 1, utilization of advanced technology is generally accompanied by less demand for low-skilled workers and more demand for knowledge workers. External factors such as business cycles—economic and seasonal trends—can also play a role. For example, Canada Post and Statistics Canada rely heavily on temporary employees at their peak periods of business.

WWW

Forecasting is often more an art than a science, in that it provides inexact approximations rather than absolute results. The ever-changing environment in which an organization operates contributes to this problem. For example, estimating changes in product or service demand is a basic forecasting concern, and so is anticipating changes in national or regional economics. A community hospital anticipating internal changes in technology, organization, or administration must consider these environmental factors in its forecasts of staffing needs. Also, the forecasted staffing needs must be in line with the organization's financial resources.

There are two approaches to HR forecasting: quantitative and qualitative. When the focus is on human resources needs, forecasting is mainly quantitative in nature and, in large organizations, is accomplished by highly trained specialists. Quantitative approaches to forecasting often employ sophisticated analytical

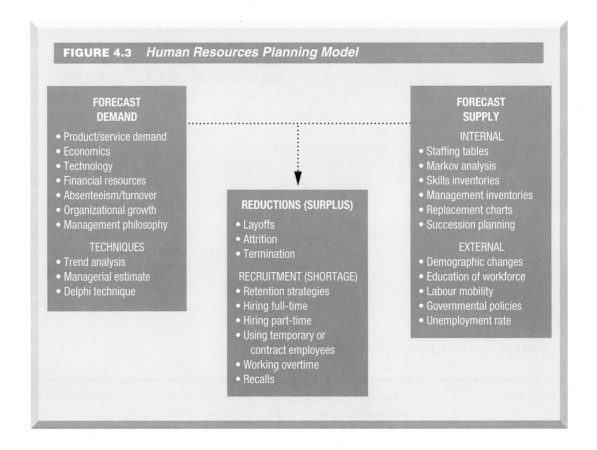

FIGURE 4.3   *Human Resources Planning Model*

FORECAST DEMAND

- Product/service demand
- Economics
- Technology
- Financial resources
- Absenteeism/turnover
- Organizational growth
- Management philosophy

TECHNIQUES
- Trend analysis
- Managerial estimate
- Delphi technique

REDUCTIONS (SURPLUS)
- Layoffs
- Attrition
- Termination

RECRUITMENT (SHORTAGE)
- Retention strategies
- Hiring full-time
- Hiring part-time
- Using temporary or contract employees
- Working overtime
- Recalls

FORECAST SUPPLY

INTERNAL
- Staffing tables
- Markov analysis
- Skills inventories
- Management inventories
- Replacement charts
- Succession planning

EXTERNAL
- Demographic changes
- Education of workforce
- Labour mobility
- Governmental policies
- Unemployment rate

models, although forecasting may be as informal as having one person who knows the organization anticipate future HR requirements. Ultimately, organizational demands will determine which technique is used. Regardless of the method, however, forecasting should not be neglected, even in relatively small organizations.

Quantitative Approaches

Quantitative approaches to forecasting involve the use of statistical or mathematical techniques; they are the approaches used by theoreticians and professional planners. One example is **trend analysis**, which forecasts employment requirements on the basis of some organizational index and is one of the most commonly used approaches for projecting HR demand.

Trend analysis usually follows several steps.

First, select an appropriate business factor. This should be the best available predictor of human resources needs. Often, sales or value added (selling price less costs of materials and supplies) is used as a predictor in trend analysis. *Second*, plot a historical trend of the business factor in relation to the number of employees. The ratio of employees to the business factor will provide a labour productivity ratio (e.g., sales per employee). *Third*, compute the productivity ratio for at least the past five years. *Fourth*, calculate human resources demand by multiplying the business factor by the productivity ratio. *Finally*, project human resources demand out to the target year. This procedure is summarized in Figure 4.4 for a building contractor.

Trend analysis

A quantitative approach to forecasting labour demand based on an organizational index such as sales

Other, more sophisticated statistical planning methods include modelling or multiple predictive techniques. Whereas trend analysis relies on a single factor (e.g., sales) to predict employment needs, the more advanced methods combine several factors, such as interest rates, gross national product, disposable income, and sales, to predict employment levels. While the costs of developing these forecasting methods used to be quite high, advances in technology and computer software have made rather sophisticated forecasting tools affordable to even small businesses.

Qualitative Approaches

In contrast to quantitative approaches, qualitative approaches to forecasting are less statistical. They attempt to reconcile the interests, abilities, and aspirations of individual employees with the current and future staffing needs of an organization. In both large and small organizations, HR planners may rely on experts who assist in preparing forecasts to anticipate staffing requirements. **Management forecasts** are the opinions (judgments) of supervisors, department managers, experts, and others who are knowledgeable about the organization's future employment needs. Various people scan conditions outside the organization for clues about what the future might hold, and then arrive at various scenarios, which the company can use in its planning. Shell Oil used management forecasts to anticipate the oil crisis in the 1970s.

Another qualitative forecasting method, the Delphi technique, attempts to decrease the subjectivity of forecasts by soliciting and summarizing the judgments of a preselected group of individuals. The final forecast thus represents a composite group judgment. The Delphi technique requires a great deal of coordination and

Management forecasts

The opinions (judgments) of supervisors, department managers, experts, and others knowledgeable about the organization's future employment needs

WWW

FIGURE 4.4 *Human Resource Competency Model*

YEAR	BUSINESS FACTOR = (SALES IN THOUSANDS)	LABOUR PRODUCTIVITY (SALES /EMPLOYEE)	Y= HUMAN RESOURCES DEMAND (NUMBER OF EMPLOYEES)
1995	$2,351	14.33	164
1996	2,613	11.12	235
1997	2,935	8.34	352
1998	3,306	10.02	330
1999	3,613	11.12	325
2000	3,748	11.12	337
2001	3,880	12.52	310
2002*	4,095	12.52	327
2003*	4,283	12.52	342
2004*	4,446	12.52	355

*Projected figures

cooperation to ensure satisfactory forecasts. This method works best in organizations where dynamic technological changes affect staffing levels.

Ideally, HRP should include the use of both quantitative and qualitative approaches. The two approaches complement each other, and when used together provide a more complete forecast by bringing together the contributions of both theoreticians and practitioners.

Forecasting Supply of Employees

Once an organization has forecast its future requirements for employees, it must determine whether it has enough employees, and the right employees, to staff anticipated openings. As with demand, this process involves both tracking current levels and making projections.

Internal Labour Supply

An internal supply analysis often begins with the preparation of staffing tables. **Staffing tables** are graphic representations of all organizational jobs, along with the numbers of employees currently occupying those jobs (and perhaps also future employment requirements derived from demand forecasts). Another technique, called **Markov analysis**, shows the percentage (and actual number) of employees who remain in each job from one year to the next, as well as the proportions of those who are promoted, demoted, or transferred, or who leave the organization. As shown in Figure 4.5, Markov analysis can be used to track the pattern of employee movements through various jobs and to develop a transition matrix for forecasting labour supply.[17]

Staffing tables

Graphic representations of all organizational jobs, along with the numbers of employees currently occupying those jobs and future (monthly or yearly) employment requirements

Markov analysis

Method for tracking the pattern of employee movements through various jobs

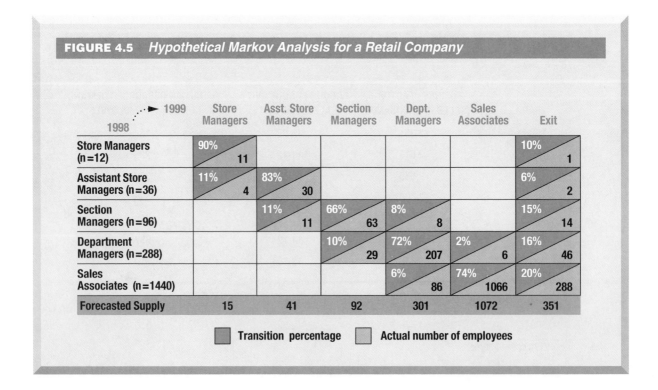

FIGURE 4.5 *Hypothetical Markov Analysis for a Retail Company*

1998 \ 1999	Store Managers	Asst. Store Managers	Section Managers	Dept. Managers	Sales Associates	Exit
Store Managers (n=12)	90% — 11					10% — 1
Assistant Store Managers (n=36)	11% — 4	83% — 30				6% — 2
Section Managers (n=96)		11% — 11	66% — 63	8% — 8		15% — 14
Department Managers (n=288)			10% — 29	72% — 207	2% — 6	16% — 46
Sales Associates (n=1440)				6% — 86	74% — 1066	20% — 288
Forecasted Supply	15	41	92	301	1072	351

■ **Transition percentage**   □ **Actual number of employees**

Forecasting the supply of human resources requires that managers have a good understanding of employee turnover and absenteeism. In an appendix to this chapter, we have included formulas for computing turnover and absenteeism rates. The calculations are easily made, and can be used by managers of both large and small organizations.

Staffing tables, Markov analysis, turnover rates, and the like tend to focus on the number of employees in particular jobs; other techniques are oriented more toward the types of employees and their skills, knowledge, and experience. **Skill inventories** can be prepared that list each employee's education, past work experience, vocational interests, specific abilities and skills, compensation history, and job tenure. Of course, confidentiality is a vital concern in setting up any such inventory. That said, well-prepared and up-to-date skill inventories allow an organization to quickly match forthcoming job openings with employee backgrounds. Organizations like Hewlett-Packard and Dupont Canada use computers and special programs to perform this task. When data are gathered on managers, these inventories are called *management inventories*.

Both skill and management inventories—broadly referred to as talent inventories—can be used to develop employee **replacement charts**, which list current job holders and identify possible replacements should openings arise. Figure 4.6 shows how an organization can develop a replacement chart for the managers in one of its divisions. This chart provides information on the current job performance and promotability of possible replacements. As such, it can be used side by side with other pieces of information for **succession planning**, which is the process of identifying, developing, and tracking key individuals so that they may eventually assume top-level positions.

In today's fast-moving environment, succession planning is often more important—and more difficult to conduct—than ever before. Canadian CEOs surveyed by William M. Mercer stated that attracting and retaining key talent was a major priority.

External Labour Supply

When an organization lacks an internal supply of employees for promotions, or when it is staffing entry-level positions, managers must consider the external supply of labour. Many factors influence labour supply, including demographic changes in the population, national and regional economics, the education level of the workforce, demand for specific employee skills, population mobility, and governmental policies. National and regional unemployment rates are often considered a general barometer of labour supply. Fortunately, labour market analysis is aided by various published documents. Unemployment rates, labour force projection rates, and population characteristics are reported by various government departments. Human Resources Development Canada (HRDC) analyzes labour markets to determine the supply and demand for labour. Also, the Canadian Occupational Forecast Program (COFOR) analyzes long-term labour market projections on a national and provincial basis. Another forecasting model, the Canadian Occupational Projection System (COPS) analyzes labour supply and demand by occupation over a ten-year period. Chambers of Commerce and various provincial development and planning agencies also may assist with labour market analysis.

Skill inventories

Files of employee education, experience, interests, skills, etc., that allow managers to quickly match job openings with employee backgrounds

WWW

Replacement charts

Listings of current job holders and persons who are potential replacements if an opening occurs

Succession planning

Process of identifying, developing, and tracking key individuals for executive positions

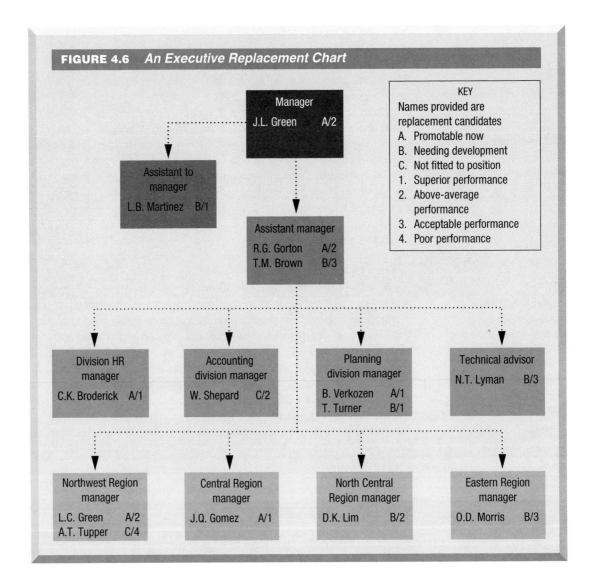

FIGURE 4.6   *An Executive Replacement Chart*

Manager
J.L. Green   A/2

Assistant to manager
L.B. Martinez   B/1

Assistant manager
R.G. Gorton   A/2
T.M. Brown   B/3

KEY
Names provided are replacement candidates
A. Promotable now
B. Needing development
C. Not fitted to position
1. Superior performance
2. Above-average performance
3. Acceptable performance
4. Poor performance

Division HR manager
C.K. Broderick   A/1

Accounting division manager
W. Shepard   C/2

Planning division manager
B. Verkozen   A/1
T. Turner   B/1

Technical advisor
N.T. Lyman   B/3

Northwest Region manager
L.C. Green   A/2
A.T. Tupper   C/4

Central Region manager
J.Q. Gomez   A/1

North Central Region manager
D.K. Lim   B/2

Eastern Region manager
O.D. Morris   B/3

Balancing Supply and Demand Considerations

Organizations strive for a proper balance between demand considerations and supply considerations. Demand considerations are based on forecasted trends in business activity. Supply considerations involve determining where and how candidates with the required qualifications are to be found to fill vacancies. Because it is so difficult to locate applicants for the increasing number of jobs that require advanced training, this aspect of planning has been receiving a great deal more attention. Greater planning effort is also needed to recruit members of designated groups for managerial jobs and technical jobs that require advanced levels of education.

To meet the demand for labour, organizations can hire full-time employees, have employees work overtime, recall laid-off workers, or use temporary employees. When HRP shows a surplus of job holders, organizations may restrict hiring, reduce work hours, institute work sharing, or consider layoffs, demotions, and/or terminations. Also, an organization may over time try to reduce its workforce by relying on attrition (a gradual reduction of employees through resignations, retirements, or deaths). Over the past decade, early retirements have become a more and more common means for organizations to reduce their excess labour supply. Organizations as diverse as health care facilities, travel companies, and colleges and universities encourage employees to accept early retirement by offering "sweetened" retirement benefits (see Chapter 11).

Organizational Downsizing

Organizational restructuring is resulting in the separation of tens of thousands of workers. In a survey of 1,140 large Canadian organizations, over half reported engaging in permanent workforce reductions in the past two years, with an average reduction of 15 percent.[18] **Restructuring** refers to any major change that occurs within an organization, and can be the result of acquisitions, retrenchments, mergers, leveraged buyouts, divestiture, plant closures or relocations, or bankruptcies. Restructuring almost always results in cutbacks, downsizing, or consolidations.

Restructuring

Any major change that occurs within an organization. It may be the result of acquisitions, retrenchments, mergers, leveraged buyouts, divestiture, plant closures or relocations, or bankruptcies

   Because of economic or competitive pressures, organizations have found themselves with too many employees or with employees who have the wrong kinds of skills. In an effort to reconcile supply and demand considerations, companies such as Safeway, the CBC, Petro-Canada, and CN Rail have eliminated literally thousands of jobs. Layoffs are not simply a result of a stagnant economy. In many cases, downsizing is part of a longer-term process of restructuring to take advantage of new technology, corporate partnerships, and cost minimization.

WWW

Making Layoff Decisions

Decisions about employee layoffs are usually based on seniority and/or performance. In some organizations, especially those with collective agreements, seniority may be the main consideration. In other organizations, such factors as ability and fitness may take precedence over seniority in determining layoffs.

   When economic conditions have brought about layoffs, employees who were let go while in good standing may be recalled to their jobs when the economic outlook brightens and job openings occur. However, these new jobs often require different sets of skills than the jobs they replace. Individuals for these jobs can be identified by searching among previous employees or among current employees who can be transferred, but often it requires searching externally in the broader labour market.[19]

   There are several options available to employers when it comes to dealing with surplus employees: layoffs, attrition, and termination.

Layoff Strategies

Employee layoff decisions are usually based on seniority and/or ability. With unionized organizations, the criteria for determining an employee's eligibility for layoff are typically set forth in the collective agreement. As a rule, job seniority receives significant weight in determining which employees are laid off first. Similar provisions in the collective agreement provide for the right of employees to be recalled for jobs they are still qualified to perform. Organizational policy as well as provisions in the collective agreement should therefore establish and define clearly the employment rights of each individual and the basis on which layoff selections will be made and re-employment effected. The rights of employees during layoffs, the conditions concerning their eligibility for recall, and their obligations in accepting recall should also be clarified. It is common for collective agreements to preserve the re-employment rights of employees laid off for periods of up to two years, provided that they do not refuse to return to work if recalled sooner.

While it has become customary for employers to recognize seniority in unionized employees, nonunion employees are not always given the same consideration. Due to the demand for a technically skilled workforce, the ability of employees to change jobs and learn new skills, as well as their performance and competencies, is given a great deal of weight in layoff decisions. The most important reason for using seniority as a basis for layoffs is the objective nature of the decision: number of years of work, not perception of ability, is the basis for the decision. The system is fair, and employees themselves can calculate their own probability of being employed.

One of the major disadvantages of overemphasizing seniority is that less competent employees receive the same rewards and security as more competent ones. The seniority system ignores talent and effort. The payroll is also higher than under other systems, because more experienced workers tend to earn more money. Also, the practice of using seniority as the basis for deciding which workers to lay off may well have a disproportionate impact on women and minority workers, who often have less seniority than other groups.

Under the umbrella of layoff strategies are several work reduction options: reduced workweek, reduced shifts, transfers to related companies, and so on. Under the reduced workweek, employees work about 20 to 30 hours per week. This option allows the organization to retain a skilled workforce, and lessens the financial and emotional impact of a full layoff, and at the same time reduces the costs of production. Some organizations have worked out arrangements so that employment insurance benefits make up most of the difference of the lost wages. However, it is sometimes difficult to predict how much work is available each week; also, overhead fixed costs such as rent and administration continue, independent of the number of hours worked.

WWW

Reduced shift work is based on a similar concept of reducing costs by reducing the number of hours worked. Some plants operate three shifts a day and may shut down the midnight to 8 a.m. shift to save money. General Motors of Canada eliminated the second shift at its assembly plant in Ste-Thérèse, Quebec, throwing 1,400 employees out of work.[20] Another approach is to reduce the number of operators per shift.

In some rare cases, organizations can transfer laid-off employees to a sister company. For example, when Dylex closed its Town and Country stores, more than 500 of its 600 laid-off Ontario employees were placed in other Dylex chain stores.[21] Shell Canada has even been known to contact other organizations that are in the hiring mode. Under this scheme, Shell employees have been re-employed within days of being laid off. Bell Canada, in the midst of laying off 5,000 employees, revamped its training courses to emphasize employability. Layoffs are the fastest way to achieve workforce reduction; attrition is the slowest.

Attrition Strategies

Some organizations have adopted a no-layoff policy. These firms view people as their most important asset, and recognize that their competencies and attitudes are valuable and cannot be easily replaced. They prefer to reduce the workforce

Attrition

A natural departure of employees from organizations through quits, retirements, and deaths

WWW

Hiring freeze

A practice whereby new workers are not hired as planned, or workers who have left the organization are not replaced

through attrition. **Attrition** refers to the "natural" departure of employees through quits, retirements, and deaths. The turnover rates of an organization vary greatly by industry and by occupation. For example, university professors rarely quit, while turnover among fast food workers can reach 300 percent a year. Most organizations can easily estimate how many people will leave the organization, and so can slowly reduce the workforce through natural means. Since 1989 Dofasco Inc. has reduced its workforce from 12,200 to 7,300 by using a number of job reduction strategies, including natural attrition, voluntary early retirement programs, and a voluntary severance program.

Attrition must be supplemented by other practices. Hiring freezes are usually implemented at the same time as the organization adopts a strategy of workforce reduction through attrition. A **hiring freeze** means that organizations will not hire new workers as planned, or will hire only in areas critical to the success of the organization. Sometimes the practice is to not replace the worker who has left or been fired.

These practices have several advantages. Organizations can control and predict compensation expenses. But the savings go beyond the salaries and benefits redeemed from departing employees. Take, for example, the costs of employing a manager earning $60,000 a year. Her benefits probably cost another $20,000. However, the costs of replacing her would include recruitment costs ($5,000), paperwork and time in hiring costs ($1,000), orientation and training expenses ($7,000), and office supplies and space ($10,000). Thus, the organization can save significantly by not replacing workers.

However, the disadvantages are significant. Present employees may be overburdened with the work of those who left; their skills may not match the skill sets of the departed workers; and, of course, no new skills or ideas are infiltrating the organization. The major disadvantage of reduction through attrition is that the organization cannot control who leaves and who stays. Valuable employees may be retiring, while less needed ones are still on the job. And the process takes a very long time compared to layoffs, which can be accomplished in days.

Some organizations attempt to accelerate attrition by offering incentives to employees to leave. These incentives include cash bonuses for people to leave during a specified time, accelerated or early retirement benefits, and free outplacement services. However, the buyout process must be carefully managed. Employees with valuable skills who can easily find another job may be the first to cash in. Key people in key positions should not be targeted for this program. Another disadvantage is that buyouts require a great deal of money up front, which may work against the goal of cost reduction. For example, Ontario Hydro paid out millions in buyouts for a few thousand employees. The buyout fiasco at Safeway Canada is described in Highlights in HRM 3. Employers must be cautious when extending offers of early retirements. An older worker was awarded $250,000 plus benefits in a wrongful dismissal suit, on the grounds that he had been forced to accept the "voluntary" early-retirement option.[22]

To sustain a no-layoffs policy, some organizations ask for volunteers to transfer into divisions where employee shortages are developing. This causes other problems. For example, highly competent employees who have years of experience, expertise, and contacts in one position may not be as productive in another division. Skill match is a recurrent problem. Mandatory transfers allow the employer to match employee skills with vacant positions more accurately. There may be associated morale problems as individuals move into jobs or divisions they do not like,

WWW

Highlights in HRM

3 BUYOUT BACKFIRES!

WWW

In Alberta, in an attempt to cut $45 million from its payroll, Safeway Canada offered a buyout package of up to $35,000 for employees who quit the company. The offer backfired when more than half the chain's workers in that province applied for the package. Safeway had estimated that up to 2,000 employees would accept the offer by the April 30 deadline. Instead, between 4,000 and 5,000 employees applied. The buyout offer had been negotiated between the company and the United Food and Commercial Workers Union. Safeway had to negotiate with the union again, to devise a way to retain some part-time workers who applied for the buyout.

Source: "News Briefs," *Human Resources Management in Canada* (Scarborough, Ont.: Prentice-Hall Canada, 1993).

WWW

or leave their team and its working style. Union contracts may forbid or inhibit these types of transfers.

Another practice, which is extremely rare in Canada but emerging in the United States, is the worker loan-out program. Recognizing that the downsizing may be temporary, or that the policy of no layoffs is sacrosanct, organizations sometimes prefer to loan employees to other (noncompeting) organizations for temporary assignments. For example, IBM pays its employees for up to two years while they work in schools or charitable institutions. These loans, while apparently expensive, actually have some economic incentives. Because organizations keep their employees, there are no costs associated with severance pay, rehiring, and training. Employees return with new skills, ideas, and contacts. The good will generated in the community and among employees may result in free press and publicity.

If the surplus of employees is deemed to be permanent, terminations may be the only option.

Termination Strategies

Termination

Practice initiated by an employer to separate an employee from the organization permanently

Termination is a practice initiated by an employer to separate an employee from the organization permanently. Termination is different from firing, in which an employee is released for such causes as poor performance, high absenteeism, or unethical behaviour. The purpose of termination is to reduce the size of the workforce, and thereby save money.

A termination strategy begins with the identification of employees who are in positions that are no longer considered useful or critical to the company's effectiveness. The managers of these employees are contacted about redeployment or termination options. Next the employee is told the news, with varying degrees of advance notice. CIBC gives three months' notice, allows the employee and the manager to prepare a redeployment plan, and allows up to six months for retraining

WWW

and repositioning.[23] At CIBC, the emphasis is on retaining competent employees whose jobs have been eliminated; the title of the program, Employment Continuity, reflects this strategy. To assist the 500 employees it laid off in 1994, Dofasco established a transition centre that provided skills development, career counselling, and tuition assistance.

Employees should be concerned about their own marketability (i.e., employability). Some suggestions for surviving rightsizing are given in Highlights in HRM 4.

Employers cannot terminate without some form of compensation to the employee. **Severance pay**, a lump-sum payment given to terminated employees, is calculated on the basis of years of service and salary. The legal minimum varies by province; for example, a clerk making $500 a week with eight years' service would receive about $4,000 in severance pay. Additional severance-pay benefits might include continued medical and dental coverage, and insurance for a specified time period. These payments, if accepted by the employee, immediately discharge the employer from further obligations. Most employers now refer to "ballpark," "reasonable range," or "reasonable offer" court decisions. The ballpark approach offers some degree of certainty to both employers and employees, and thus helps minimize costly court battles.

Severance pay

A lump-sum payment given to terminated employees

Highlights in HRM

4   SURVIVAL IN THE NEW MILLENNIUM

Professionals and managers fear the 50/50 rule: If you are over fifty years old and make more than $50,000, your job is at risk. "We don't go out to lunch, we're afraid the doors will be blocked when we get back," says one anxious manager. About one-fifth of job losses occur at the management level. Loyalty is out; it is not reciprocated by the organization. In fact, companies may not want loyal (i.e., obedient and rule-minded) employees. They may actively prefer employees who are ready to push the boundaries of the organization, instead of being dominated and intimidated by those boundaries. Loyalty is to the profession, and it means developing different attitudes toward employment. Some suggestions:

- *Develop portable skills.* Invest in training in negotiation or general management skills.
- *Build outside networks.* Be a member of a professional association. Attend conferences. Keep abreast of trends in your industry by reading all trade magazines, business sections of newspapers, and company reports. Belong to volunteer organizations and other social networks. All these strategies will serve you well should you need to search for a job.
- *Plan for transitions.* Assume that you will not be employed by one organization for a long time. Save money for these transition periods. Identify industries where your portable skills could be useful. For example, if you have always worked in marketing, consider how these skills might be useful in the not-for-profit sector of social marketing, such as adult literacy efforts.

Sources: C. Heckcher, *White Collar Blues: Management Loyalties in an Age of Corporate Restructuring* (Toronto: HarperCollins, 1995); "Monkeys in the Middle," *The Globe and Mail,* May 9, 1995: B10.

Some organizations adopt "golden parachutes," a form of severance pay, to protect their employees (especially their executives) from the downsizing effects of mergers, acquisitions, and leveraged buyouts. Golden parachutes are guarantees by the employer that detail the compensation and benefits that employees will receive in termination situations. Golden parachutes encourage managers to work actively with the company during a restructuring, and reduce the possibility of legal challenges on termination. But they are costly.

Many organizations soften the blow of termination by offering *outplacement services*. Those services, most often offered by agencies outside the corporation, ease the impact of termination by providing terminated employees with stress counselling, financial advice, career counselling, and assistance in locating another job. The job search support often includes office space, telephones and secretarial support, vocational testing, résumé writing, and feedback on interviewing skills.[24]

Some suggestions for managing the termination process are presented in Highlights in HRM 5.

Evaluating Restructuring

There are hundreds of articles dealing with downsizing. However, very few even touch on its consequences. The following section considers the consequences of downsizing on finances, organization climate, and public image.

Highlights in HRM

5   EASING TERMINATION SHOCK

Any manager who has terminated an employee will describe it as one of the worst experiences in his or her working life. Some have reported sleepless nights, stomach pains, and inability to work. There is no way to mitigate the emotional distress for the supervisor who has to terminate an employee he or she knows well. However, some experts have suggested ways to ease tensions and reduce employee retaliation:

1. Plan the termination interview early in the week, so that the employee can start an action plan with the outplacement service during the week.
2. Make sure the date does not correspond with an important date (such as a birthday) for the employee. Recently, an employee was terminated on "Take Your Daughter to Work Day." The shock and bitterness he felt at being terminated in front of his daughter—she helped him carry out his box of belongings—resulted in a lawsuit.
3. Make the interview short (less than fifteen minutes). State the reasons clearly and firmly, establishing that the decision is final, and clearly communicate all aspects of the severance package (preferably in writing).
4. Tell the employee the next steps and, if possible, give him or her the name of the outplacement counsellor.

Source: Adapted from Phyllis Macklin and Lester Minsuk, "Ways to Ease Dismissal Dread," *HRMagazine* (November 1991).

Finances

A survey of hundreds of companies that laid off workers revealed that about one-half reported improved earnings, but only one-third reported that productivity or customer service improved. Two-thirds had to hire at the same time as the layoffs because they were losing skills they needed to keep.[25]

Investors generally react negatively to an announcement of layoffs or large-scale reductions in the workforce.[26] A large-scale study of organizations in Atlantic Canada concluded that downsizing fails to meet financial goals because workforce reduction results in considerable people costs, and because the remaining personnel are less productive.[27]

Climate

Study after study shows the following effects of downsizing: surviving employees become narrow-minded, self-absorbed, and risk averse; morale sinks; productivity drops; and survivors distrust management.[28] Internally, all forms of restructuring are likely to generate fear, anxiety, and hostility. Early retirement programs and other soft attrition strategies are likely to be interpreted with less resentment than mass terminations. The organization can assume that employees anxious about the next round of terminations will suffer many stress symptoms, including reduced performance, depression, and proneness to error. The Atlantic Canada study referred to above concluded that employee commitment and morale decreased while conflict increased.

WWW

These reactions underline the growing awareness of a problem associated with restructuring: survivor sickness. Survivor sickness encompasses a range of symptoms, which may include guilt, detachment, depression, and a sense of being violated and betrayed. An expert in corporate downsizing, speaking to managers at a Conference Board of Canada meeting, used a family metaphor to describe the emotional impact of downsizing: "Imagine a family that seems to be functioning and suddenly the parents tell the four kids that they can no longer afford to support two of them. The next day at breakfast, nobody talks about the ones who have left. The father talks about how 'this will make us closer-knit, but you will have to take on your brother's chores.'"[29]

Amdahl Canada is one organization that recognizes that survivor sickness is real. In a recent downsizing, Amdahl allocated 25 percent of its strategy to the "management of mourning"—that is, mitigating the inevitable pain by communicating with honesty, directness, and respect toward fired employees.[30] The remaining 75 percent of the strategy was targeted at revitalization.

Public Image

Terminations have the most adverse impact on public perceptions. While layoffs are seen as temporary and attrition as benevolent, terminations are interpreted as cold and unfeeling, especially if the terminations affect competent employees with long tenure. One expert, speaking to the Calgary Personnel Association, said that downsizing has driven the final nail into the coffin of company loyalty.[31] Baby boomers feel a loyalty to professions, not companies, after watching their loyal parents lose the security of lifelong employment.

However, a contrarian view suggests that the era of "entitlement" is over. The attitude that regular raises, scheduled promotions, and a secure job for life were the right of every worker has been replaced by the attitude that workers must take responsibility for their own employability by continually earning their jobs and by retraining.[32]

Labour Shortages

According to demographic studies, Canada has neither the necessary population growth nor the right proportions of students entering technical and engineering schools to meet the predicted demand.[33] The result is going to be labour shortages in particular occupations, and this will affect strategic plans in certain industries. As we will discuss in Chapter 9, more and more organizations are using financial and other incentives in an effort to retain their existing staff.

Downsizing, or rightsizing, also means that alternative approaches to meeting labour needs will have to be devised. One possible strategy will be to retain a small core of permanent employees, while maintaining a fluctuating number of less permanent, quasi-employment relationships.[34] Options for obtaining labour will include leasing employees, subcontracting work, and tapping temporary help agencies, freelance professionals, part-time employees, and at-home workers. Contingent workers account for about 12 percent of all jobs in Canada—a figure that is expected to reach 25 percent by 2010.[35] Employee–employer bonds are weakening along the dimensions of physical proximity, administrative control, and duration of employment.[36] Two of the above employment options—temporary help agencies and employee leasing—are discussed later in this chapter. The ethical implications of employment contracts are addressed in Ethics in HRM.

RECRUITING WITHIN THE ORGANIZATION

Recruitment is the process of locating potential applicants and encouraging them to apply for existing or anticipated job openings. During this process, efforts are made to inform the applicants fully about the qualifications required to perform the job and the career opportunities the organization can offer its employees. Whether or not a particular job vacancy will be filled by someone from inside the organization or from outside will, of course, depend on the availability of personnel, the organization's HR policies, and the requirements of the job to be staffed.

Advantages of Recruiting from Within

Most organizations try to fill job vacancies above the entry-level position through promotions and transfers. By filling vacancies in this way, an organization capitalizes on the investment it has made in recruiting, selecting, training, and developing its current employees.

Promotion rewards employees for past performance and is intended to encourage them to continue their efforts. It also gives other employees reason to anticipate that similar efforts by them will lead to promotion; this improves morale within the organization. This is especially true for members of designated groups who have encountered difficulties in finding employment and have often faced even greater difficulty in advancing within an organization. Most organizations have integrated promotion policies as an essential part of their employment equity programs.

Ethics in HRM

THE EMPLOYMENT CONTRACT

The number of organizations substituting part-time workers for full-time employees is growing. Employees—even those with excellent track records and many years of service—are considered expendable as organizations revise their strategies to become more competitive and more profitable. When yet another reorganization occurs, management reveals the new plan with excitement. However, while management thinks it is telling employees, "We will provide you with meaningful, challenging and skill-building work that will be good for your résumé—you are responsible for your own employment," employees are hearing, "We will work you to the bone, pay you enough to prevent you from quitting, and fire you when we no longer need you. Oh, and by the way, you are our most valuable resource."

Some employment contracts are extremely one-sided, with employers determining when to hire and when to fire, without obligation or guilt. This kind of contract works when people need jobs more than organizations need employees. However, as some sectors continue to experience rapid growth, and as the labour market for certain skills becomes tighter, employees are making contractual demands that place them in the driver's seat. They are demanding signing bonuses, stock equity, retention bonuses, and sufficient notification with predetermined buyouts for termination. Furthermore, the courts are ruling that if an employee is retained for a series of uninterrupted contracts, then that contract worker is de facto an employee.

Should employees expect job security? Should employers expect employee commitment?

Source: Barbara Moses, "Loss of Loyalty Cuts Both Ways," *The Globe and Mail,* November 6, 1997: B17. Barbara Moses is author of *Career Intelligence: Mastering the New Work and Personal Realities* (Stoddart) and the *Career Planning Workbook.* Also, R.S. Echlin, "Courts Apply Smell Test in Judging Contract Workers as Long Term Employees," *The Globe and Mail,* November 22, 1999: B1.

For an organization's promotion policy to have maximum motivational value, employees must be made aware of that policy. The following is an example of a policy statement that an organization might prepare:

> "Promotion from within" is generally recognized as a foundation of good employment practice, and it is the policy of our museum to promote from within whenever possible when filling a vacancy. The job vacancy will be posted for five calendar days to give all qualified full- and part-time personnel an equal opportunity to apply.

Transfers lack the motivational value of promotions, but can sometimes protect employees from layoff, or broaden their job experiences. Furthermore, the transferred employee's familiarity with the organization and its operations can eliminate the orientation and training costs that recruitment from the outside entails. Most importantly, the transferee's performance record is likely to be a more accurate predictor of the candidate's success than the data gained about outside applicants.

Methods of Locating Qualified Job Candidates

The effective use of internal sources requires a system for locating qualified job candidates and for enabling those who consider themselves qualified to apply for openings. Qualified job candidates within the organization can be located by computerized record systems, by job posting and bidding, and by looking to those who have been laid off.

Human Resources Information Systems

WWW

Information technology has made it possible for organizations to create databases that contain the complete records and qualifications of each employee within an organization. Managers can access this information through increasingly user-friendly search engines to identify potential candidates for available jobs. Organizations such as the Royal Bank Financial Group and Manulife Financial Group have developed résumé-tracking systems that allow managers to query on-line databases of résumés. Companies such as IBM with its HR Access software (which is also used by Scotia Bank and about 450 other companies in Canada) are leaders in developing automated staffing and skills management software. These information systems, which are similar to the skills inventories mentioned earlier, allow an organization to rapidly screen its entire workforce to locate suitable candidates to fill internal openings. These data can also be used to predict the career paths of employees and to anticipate when and where promotion opportunities may arise. Since the value of the information depends on its being kept up to date, the systems typically include provisions for recording changes in employee qualifications and job placements as they occur.[37]

Job Posting and Bidding

Job posting and bidding

Posting vacancy notices and maintaining lists of employees looking for upgraded positions

WWW

Organizations often communicate information about job openings through a process referred to as **job posting and bidding**. In the past, this process consisted largely of posting vacancy notices on bulletin boards. It can also involve designated posting centres, employee publications, special handouts, direct mail, and public address messages. Increasingly, companies such as Star Data Systems are developing computerized job posting systems and maintaining voluntary lists of employees looking for upgraded positions. BMO provides a virtual place where employees can receive assistance developing their résumés. Case 3 at the end of this chapter discusses how the Calgary Stampede hires 3,000 temporary staff every year to supplement its full-time workforce of 230. When a position becomes available, the list of people seeking that position is retrieved from the computer; the records of these people are then reviewed to select the best-qualified candidate.[38]

Job posting and bidding systems can provide many benefits to an organization. However, these benefits may not be realized unless employees believe the system is being administered fairly. Furthermore, job bidding is more effective when it is part of a career development program in which employees are made aware of opportunities available to them within the organization. For example, HR departments may provide new employees with literature on job progression that describes the lines of job advancement, training requirements for each job, and the skills and abilities they will need to acquire as they move up the job progression ladder.

Limitations of Recruiting from Within

Sometimes certain jobs at the middle and upper levels that require specialized training and experience cannot be filled from within the organization and must be filled from the outside. This is especially common in small organizations. Also, for certain openings it may be necessary to hire individuals from the outside who have gained from another employer the knowledge and expertise required for these jobs.

Even when HR policy encourages job openings to be filled from within the organization, potential candidates from the outside should be considered in order to prevent the inbreeding of ideas and attitudes. Applicants hired from the outside, especially for certain technical and managerial positions, can be a source of new ideas and may bring with them the latest knowledge acquired from their previous employers. Indeed, excessive reliance on internal sources creates the risk of "employee cloning." It is not uncommon for firms in competitive fields such as high technology to try to gain secrets from competitors by hiring away their employees. In the United States, Dow recently sued GE over just such an issue.[39]

WWW

RECRUITING OUTSIDE THE ORGANIZATION

OBJECTIVE 4

Unless there is to be a reduction in the workforce, replacements must be brought in from outside to fill vacancies when job holders move to new slots in the organization. When the president or CEO of the organization retires, a chain reaction of promotions often follows. This in turn creates other managerial openings throughout the organization. The question therefore is not *whether* to bring people into the organization, but rather *at which level* they are to be brought in. Often, hiring someone from the outside is seen as essential for revitalizing an organization.[40]

The Labour Market

Labour market

Area from which applicants are to be recruited

The **labour market**, or the area from which applicants are to be recruited, will vary with the type of position to be filled and the amount of compensation to be paid. Recruitment for executives and technical personnel, who require a high degree of knowledge and skill, may be national or even international in scope. Most colleges and universities, for example, conduct national employment searches to fill top administrative positions. On the other hand, recruitment for jobs that require relatively little skill may encompass only a small geographic area. People are often reluctant to relocate; this eliminates many from employment consideration beyond the local labour market. However, by offering an attractive level of compensation and by offering to defray moving costs, employers may induce some applicants to move.[41]

Commuting times also influence the boundaries of the labour market. Insufficient public transportation or extreme traffic congestion on streets and freeways can limit the distance employees are willing to travel to work, especially to low-paying jobs. Also, population migration from the cities to the suburbs has had its effect on labour markets. Suburbanites who find suitable employment near where they live, or who can work at home, are less likely to accept or remain in jobs in the central city.

Outside Sources of Recruitment

The outside sources from which employers recruit will vary with the type of position to be filled. A computer programmer, for example, is not likely to be recruited from the same source as a machine operator. Trade schools can provide applicants for entry-level positions, though these recruitment sources are not as useful when highly skilled employees are needed.

The condition of the labour market may also determine which recruiting sources an organization will use. During periods of high unemployment, organizations may be able to maintain an adequate supply of qualified applicants from unsolicited résumés alone. A tight labour market, one with low unemployment, may force the employer to advertise heavily and/or seek assistance from local employment agencies. How successful an organization has been in developing its employment equity plan can be yet another factor determining the sources from which to recruit. Typically, an employer at any given time will find it necessary to utilize several recruitment sources. Figure 4.7 shows how 201 HR executives in one study rated the effectiveness of nine different recruiting methods.

Several studies have suggested that in both large and small organizations, an employee's recruitment source can affect his or her subsequent tenure and job performance.[42] In general, applicants who find employment through referral by a current employee tend to remain with the organization longer and give higher-quality performance than employees recruited by more formal means, such as through advertisements and employment agencies. Also, informal recruiting sources may yield higher selection rates than formal sources. Employers are cautioned, however, that relying on only one or two recruitment sources to secure job applicants could have an adverse effect on designated groups.

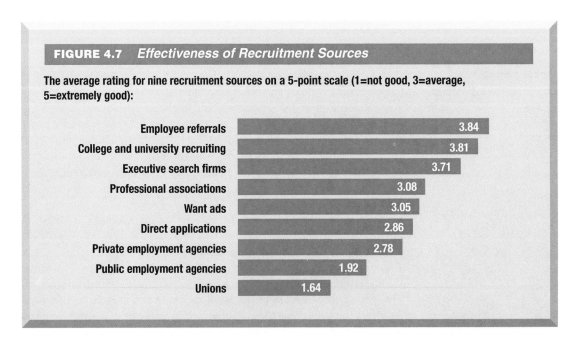

FIGURE 4.7 *Effectiveness of Recruitment Sources*

The average rating for nine recruitment sources on a 5-point scale (1=not good, 3=average, 5=extremely good):

Employee referrals	3.84
College and university recruiting	3.81
Executive search firms	3.71
Professional associations	3.08
Want ads	3.05
Direct applications	2.86
Private employment agencies	2.78
Public employment agencies	1.92
Unions	1.64

Source: "The Search for Effective Methods." Reprinted from *HRFocus,* May/1996. ©1996 American Management Association International. Reprinted by permission of American Management Association International, New York, NY. All rights reserved. http://**www.amanet.org.**

Advertisements

One of the most common methods of attracting applicants is through advertisements. Newspapers and trade journals are the media used most often; radio, television, billboards, posters, and e-mail are also utilized. Advertising has the advantage of reaching a large audience of possible applicants. Some selectivity can be achieved by using newspapers and journals directed toward particular groups of readers. Professional journals and trade journals, and publications of unions and fraternal or nonprofit organizations, fall into this category.

The preparation of recruiting advertisements is time-consuming; it also requires creativity in developing design and message content. Well-written advertisements highlight the major assets of the position while showing the responsiveness of the organization to the job and career needs of the applicants. Also, there seems to be a correlation between the accuracy and completeness of the information provided in advertisements and the recruitment success of the organization. It is typically noted in job ads that the recruiting organization is an equal opportunity employer.

Advertising can sometimes place a severe burden on an organization's employment office. Even when the specifications for the openings are described thoroughly in the ad, many applicants who know they do not meet the job requirements may still be attracted. They may apply in the hope that the employer will not be able to find applicants who do meet the specifications. Many employers choose to advertise on the Internet, through intermediaries such as Job Shark (see Highlights in HRM 6).

Unsolicited Applications and Résumés

Many employers receive unsolicited applications and résumés from individuals who may or may not be good prospects for employment (see Highlights in HRM 7, which discusses how the Toronto Blue Jays receive thousands of unsolicited résumés). Though the percentage of acceptable applicants may not be high, this source cannot be ignored. In fact, many believe that individuals who contact the employer on their own initiative are often better employees than those recruited through university or college placement services or newspaper advertisements.

Good public relations dictates that any person contacting an organization for a job be treated with courtesy and respect. If there is no possibility of employment in the organization at present or in the future, the applicant should be tactfully and frankly informed of this fact. Telling an applicant to "fill out an application, and we will keep it on file," when there is no hope for employment, is not fair to the applicant.

The Internet

According to a survey of recruiters and technology specialists from fifty-eight Canadian companies, there has been explosive growth in the use of the Internet. Over 10 million Canadians have Internet access, and by 2002, over 2.5 million résumés will be on-line. Three-quarters of university students preferred to use the Internet for their job searches. Employers claim that the Internet is faster (with some job applicants replying within thirty minutes of the posting); that it generates higher-quality candidates; and that it is cheaper (by as much as 80 percent) than advertising. Most companies use their own on-line recruiting sites. You can

Highlights in HRM

6 JOBSHARK.COM—DREAM MAKER

WWW

JobShark.com is an on-line recruitment company that helps link job seekers with jobs that match their needs and skills. According to Matt Von Teichman, co-founder and president of Job Shark, the process is fast and effective, and very, very simple for those with little time to pursue jobs.

The job seeker spends around twenty minutes completing an on-line standardized application form, giving information on skills, experience, and interests and filling out a brief personality test. Once the personality profile is entered into the system, the form is considered active. Recruiting companies post jobs, listing skills required and so on, again using a standardized format. About 1,000 new jobs are posted each month, with spring and fall being the busiest recruitment times. Jaws is the application-matching software. Within minutes of a company posting a job, notification is sent by e-mail to the job seekers whose profiles match it, giving a detailed job description, salary, and so on. The job seeker can reply by e-mail or by an internal messaging system.

In replying and indicating interest, the candidate must answer questions the company has posted—a kind of first screening interview. For example, a company might ask, "What was the last project you managed, and what software did you use?" JobShark.com has a bank of about 500 questions, including such diverse ones as, "Who is your favourite action hero and why?"

The company receives the résumés and responses (again, often within minutes), and determines whether any close matches have been made (95 percent would be considered close). The company can then communicate with the applicants by e-mail or through the internal messaging system. However, most recruiters call and arrange a face-to-face or telephone interview.

The service is free for job seekers. The companies pay a fee based on the number of jobs advertised. "In general, on-line recruitment is a great tool," says Matt Von Teichman. "It allows someone who is overloaded with work or school to be connected actively to the job market. It is a thrill to return from work and find two jobs, matched to your specifications, and you need just one click to apply. Many people have found their dream job in this way. For example, a marketing director from a packaged goods company wanted more creativity, and was looking for a culture (not money) where her contribution could be recognized and valued. She found her ideal job in a young firm that needed serious marketing. "

JobShark.com is a Canadian company, with offices throughout Canada, the United Kingdom, and South America.

visit the one for CIBC at **www.cibc.com/inside/careers/template**. A variety of websites are available where applicants can submit their résumés and potential employers can check for qualified applicants. Highlights in HRM 9 notes some of the most useful sites.

Highlights in HRM

7   BATTING A THOUSAND

WWW

The recruitment methods of major league baseball clubs are well known—that is, we all know how the position on the field are staffed. But how does a small (if very public) organization such as the Blue Jays recruit administrative staff?

The Blue Jays are a $100-million-a-year business, but employ only seventy full-time people in the office. Recruitment is very straightforward. They receive about 1,000 unsolicited résumés a year, because people are strongly attracted by the glamour of working for a baseball team. But recruitment from outside occurs very rarely—only two or three full-time staff a year. This is because the Blue Jays have an outstanding retention rate, with 40 percent of their employees having worked for them for more than fifteen years.

And they have a policy of promoting from within. Their current assistant general manager started off as a part-time ticket seller. The manager of promotions began his career in the mailroom. The Blue Jays use head-hunting firms for some executive-level positions. Baseball is a compelling sport, and this excitement helps considerably in recruiting at any level in the club.

Source: Ken Mark "Batting a Thousand," *Human Resources Professional* 11, no. 2 (March 1994): 13–15.

Highlights in HRM

8   DEVELOPING A WEBSITE THAT ATTRACTS CANDIDATES

1. Design your company website as a site visited not only by customers but also by potential employees. Work as hard building the "employer" brand as you do the product brand.
2. Market the company; don't sell the job. Talk about the vision and the opportunities.
3. Create job descriptions that talk about what the employee will be doing and the future potential. Don't simply say what the employee needs to bring to the job.
4. Link your site to other sites, anything from career sites and trade sites to game sites—anywhere your potential employee might cruise.
5. Once candidates have entered your employment site, let them join forums or connect with an employee similar to them. Give them a reason to return.

Sources: Adapted from L. Adler, "Tips for Successful Recruiting on Your Company Web Site" *Canadian HR Reporter,* April 19, 1999: 10. J. Carrol, "Hook a Job with On-Line Resume," *The Globe and Mail,* June 19, 2000: B5.

Employee Referrals

An organization's recruitment efforts can be aided by employee referrals—that is, by recommendations from current employees. Managers have found that the quality of employee-referred applicants is normally quite high, since employees are generally hesitant to recommend individuals who might not perform well. Keith Swenson, a human resources consultant with William M. Mercer, suggests several ways to increase the effectiveness of employee referral programs:

- *Up the ante.* Companies pay high commissions to employment agencies and search firms, so why not do the same thing with employees when they provide good referrals? Other recruitment incentives used by organizations include complimentary dinners, discounts on merchandise, all-expense-paid trips, and free insurance. When higher bonuses are paid for "hot" skills, employees are more likely to focus on people they know in those areas. The Playdium complexes in Burnaby. B.C., and Mississauga, Ontario, pay bounties of $200 to $1,000 to employees for hired referrals.
- *Pay for performance.* It is sometimes a good idea to save part of the referral bonus until the new hire has stayed for six months. This encourages referring employees to help the new hires succeed.
- *Tailor the program.* Companies typically need more of certain types of skills than others, but referral programs do not always reflect this. A good referral program educates employees about the kinds of people the organization wants to hire. It communicates the skills required, and also reaffirms the values and ethics sought in applicants.
- *Increase visibility.* One of the best ways to publicize a referral program is to celebrate successes. Some companies use novel approaches such as "job of the month," or "celebrity endorsements" from managers. The idea is to keep everyone thinking about bringing in good people.
- *Keep the data.* Even if a referral does not get the job, it may be a good idea to keep the résumé on file in case another vacancy arises.
- *Rethink your taboos.* Some companies are reluctant to take on certain potential hires, such as former employees, relatives, and the like. In a tight labour market, it is a good idea to broaden the search.
- *Widen the program.* Just as it may make sense to consider hiring former employees, it may make sense to ask them for referrals even if they are not candidates for the jobs themselves. Most companies have mailing lists of "corporate friends" that can be used to seek out potential candidates.
- *Measure results.* No surprise here. After the program is implemented, managers need to take a hard look at the volume of referrals, the qualifications of candidates, and the success of new hires on the job. These results are then fed back to fine-tune the program.[43]

As noted earlier, there are some negatives associated with employee referrals: inbreeding may result, and employment equity practices may be violated. Since employees and their referrals tend to have similar backgrounds, employers who rely heavily on employee referrals to fill job openings may intentionally or unintentionally screen out, and thereby discriminate against, designated groups. Furthermore, organizations may have a policy of not employing relatives of current employees. The practice of hiring relatives, referred to as **nepotism**, can invite charges of favouritism, especially in appointments to desirable positions.[44]

Nepotism

A preference for hiring relatives of current employees

Highlights in HRM

9 HOT RECRUITING SITES

- ActiJob.com
- ActiveEmploi.com
- CareerBridge.com
- CareerMosaic.com
- GlobeCareers.com

- JobShark.com
- MonsterBoard.com
- PositionWatch.com
- Workopolis.com

Executive Search Firms

WWW

Public and private employment agencies help job seekers find the right job; in contrast, executive search firms (often called "headhunters") help employers find the right person for a job. Executive search firms do not advertise in the media for job candidates, nor do they accept a fee from the individual being placed.

The fees charged by search firms range from 30 to 40 percent of the annual salary for the position to be filled. When senior executives are being recruited, this fee is paid by the client firm, whether or not the recruiting effort results in a hire. It is for this practice that search firms receive the greatest criticism.

Nevertheless, as noted earlier, it is increasingly common for CEOs to be brought in from outside the organization. Many new CEOs are being placed in their positions through the services of executive search firms. Since high-calibre executives are in short supply, a significant number of the nation's largest corporations, including Ontario Hydro and Molson Canada, are using search firms to fill their top positions. Recently, when London-based Dunlop Slazenger Corporation wanted to replace the top executives in its Maxfli business unit, it used an executive search firm to lure Bill Olsen and Edward Hughes. The tactic was designed to revitalize sales from Maxfli's position as the third-largest golf ball manufacturer.[45]

Figure 4.8 shows the results of a study by McKinsey and Company that investigated the key factors that determine the likelihood that executives will want to work for a particular company.

Educational Institutions

WWW

Educational institutions typically are a source of young applicants with formal training but relatively little full-time work experience. High schools are usually a source of employees for clerical and blue-collar jobs. Community colleges, with their various types of specialized training, can provide candidates for technical jobs. These institutions can also be a source of applicants for a variety of white-collar jobs, including those in the sales and retail fields. Some management trainee jobs are also staffed from this source. Wilfrid Laurier University holds a job fair that attracts 175 to 200 employers and 2,500 to 3,000 students, making it the largest such fair in Canada. Others schools, such as Trent University, find the Internet a

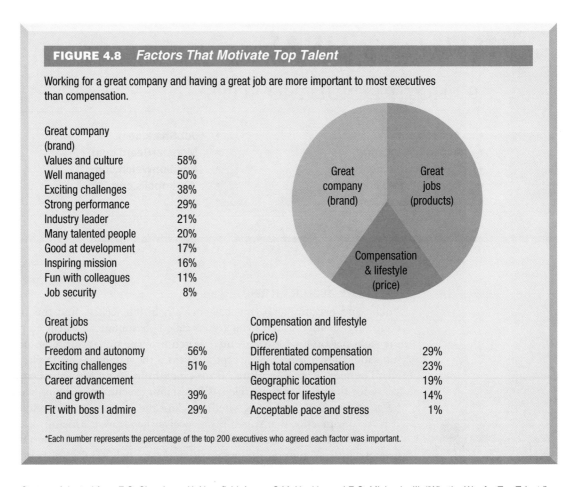

FIGURE 4.8 *Factors That Motivate Top Talent*

Working for a great company and having a great job are more important to most executives than compensation.

Great company (brand)

Values and culture	58%
Well managed	50%
Exciting challenges	38%
Strong performance	29%
Industry leader	21%
Many talented people	20%
Good at development	17%
Inspiring mission	16%
Fun with colleagues	11%
Job security	8%

Great jobs (products)

Freedom and autonomy	56%
Exciting challenges	51%
Career advancement and growth	39%
Fit with boss I admire	29%

Compensation and lifestyle (price)

Differentiated compensation	29%
High total compensation	23%
Geographic location	19%
Respect for lifestyle	14%
Acceptable pace and stress	1%

*Each number represents the percentage of the top 200 executives who agreed each factor was important.

Source: Adapted from E.G. Chambers, H. Hanafield-Jones, S.M. Hankin, and E.G. Michaels, III, "Win the War for Top Talent," *Workforce* 77, no. 12 (December 1998): 50–56. Used with permission of McKinsey & Co.

WWW

less expensive alternative, and use a system called Campus Work Link, a nonprofit Internet job posting system that is used by more than seventy colleges and universities across Canada.

For technical and managerial positions, colleges and universities are generally the primary source. However, the suitability of college and university graduates for open positions often depends on their major field of study. Humber College in Etobicoke, Ontario, offers a Human Resource Management post-diploma program. According to coordinator Pat Goodman, this twelve-course program, which includes a compulsory work placement of four weeks, has been highly effective: organizations such as Bell Mobility and Ford have employed Humber students on their work placements, and more than 90 percent of the program's participants find employment within six months after graduation.

Organizations seeking applicants in technical and professional areas are presently facing a shortage of qualified candidates. To attract graduates in areas of high demand, managers employ innovative recruitment techniques such as work/study programs, internships, low-interest loans, and scholarships.

Some employers fail to take full advantage of college and university resources.[46] Perhaps they fail to plan well, or stop following a good plan. Perhaps the recruiters they send to college and university campuses are not well trained to talk to interested candidates about career opportunities or the requirements of specific openings. Perhaps those recruiters try to visit too many campuses instead of concentrating on a carefully selected few. Perhaps they don't make thorough use of campus placement offices. Perhaps they mismanage the applicant's visits to the organization's headquarters, or fail to follow up on individual prospects or to obtain hiring commitments from higher management. All of these are common mistakes that have resulted in employers losing well-qualified prospects.

Professional Organizations

WWW

Many professional organizations and societies offer placement services to members as a benefit. Perhaps they list members seeking employment in their journals, or broadcast those lists at their national meetings. For the mutual benefit of employers and job seekers, placement centres are usually established at national meetings. For example, the Human Resources Professional Association of Ontario helps employers and prospective HR employees (who are members) come together.

Labour Unions

Labour unions can be a key source of applicants for blue-collar and some professional jobs. Some unions, such as those in the maritime, printing, and construction industries, maintain hiring halls that supply applicants, especially for short-term needs. Employers wishing to use this recruitment source should contact the local union under consideration for employer eligibility requirements and applicant availability. The Professional Institute of the Public Service (PIPS), which represents 29,000 employees ranging from computer specialists to nurses to auditors, is creating a placement agency to help its workers find jobs outside the public sector.

Five thousand applicants vie for one of 500 lucrative positions at IBM's job fair in Markham, Ontario. Four hundred prospects were identified in twenty-four hours.

Public Employment Agencies

Each province maintains an employment agency that is responsible for administering its unemployment insurance program. The agency is called the Department of Employment, or the Department of Human Resources Development, or similar, and maintains local public employment offices in most communities of any size. Individuals who become unemployed must register at one of these offices and be available for "suitable employment" before they can receive their weekly unemployment checks. This requirement means that public employment agencies are able to refer to employers with job openings those applicants with the required skills who are available for employment.

HRDC has developed a nationwide computerized job bank that lists job openings, and provincial employment offices are connected to this job bank. The computerized job bank helps facilitate the movement of job applicants to different geographic areas. Most of these offices now have a local job bank book that is published as a daily computer printout. Job openings are listed along with other pertinent information, such as number of openings, pay rates, and job specifications. The local job bank makes it possible for the agency's employment interviewers to keep a list of all the job openings in the geographic area for which the applicants assigned to them might qualify. Also, applicants looking for a specific job can review the computer printout and apply directly to the organization that has the opening. To start a job search, consult **www.worksearch.gc.ca**, which posts jobs across Canada and offers advice for finding and getting work. HRDC provides all kinds of labour market information including occupational profiles, industry profiles, and lists of potential employers.

Besides matching unemployed applicants with job openings, public employment agencies may provide employers with employment testing, job analysis, evaluation programs, and community wage surveys.

Private Employment Agencies

Charging a fee enables private employment agencies to tailor their services to the specific needs of their clients. It is not uncommon for a private employment agency to charge an employer a 25 to 30 percent fee, based on the position's annual salary, if it hires an applicant found by the agency.

Private employment agencies differ in the services they offer, their professionalism, and the calibre of their counsellors. When counsellors are paid on a commission basis, their desire to do a professional job may be offset by their desire to earn a commission. Because of this, job seekers are wise to take the time to find a recruiter who is knowledgeable, experienced, and professional. When talking with recruiters, job seekers should ask carefully about how they actually conduct their work (e.g., how they advertise, how they recruit their own staff, how they screen job seekers, and how they charge). They should try to find a recruiter who is flexible and who will consider their needs and wants.[47]

Temporary Help Agencies

The temporary services industry is one of the fastest-growing recruitment sources. The temp/contract job market is worth about $2 billion in Canada and accounts for about 10 percent of all jobs. Reflecting this, temporary services were among the strongest employers through the 1990s, and are certain to remain so in the new century.[48]

It is estimated that nine out of ten Canadian companies—both large and small—make some use of temporary employees. "Temps" are typically used for short-term assignments or to help out when managers cannot justify hiring full-time employees, such as for vacation fill-ins, for peak work periods, or to cover an employee's pregnancy leave or sick leave. More and more often, temps are being employed to fill positions once staffed by permanent employees. This practice is growing because temps can be laid off quickly, and with less cost, when work slackens. Some companies use a just-in-time staffing approach: core employees are augmented by well-trained and highly skilled supplementary workers. The use of temps has become a viable way to maintain proper staffing levels. Temps often cost less than permanent employees because they don't receive benefits and can be dismissed without the need to file Employment Insurance claims. Although used mainly in office clerical positions, they are becoming more and more common in legal work, engineering, computer programming, and other jobs that require advanced professional training.[49] Agencies often specialize in specific occupational areas or professional fields. For example, TOSI specializes in four types of jobs and labour markets (see Reality Check).

WWW

Employee Leasing

Process whereby an employer terminates a number of employees and then leases them back from another firm

Employee Leasing

Temporary help agencies supply workers only for limited periods; in contrast, employee leasing companies place their employees with subscribers on a permanent basis.

In its most common form, **employee leasing** is a process whereby an employer terminates a number of employees, who are then hired by a third party (the PEO, or professional employment organization), which then leases the employees back to the original organization. However, PEOs may also hire workers on a continual basis and lease them to requesting organizations. The leasing company performs all the HR duties of an employer—hiring, payroll, performance appraisal, benefits administration, and other day-to-day HR activities—and in return is paid a placement fee that is typically 2 to 5 percent of payroll cost plus 9 to 20 percent of gross wages to cover benefits and the PEO's profit.[50]

Improving the Effectiveness of External Recruitment

OBJECTIVE
5

With all of the uncertainties inherent in external recruiting, it is sometimes difficult to determine whether an organization's efforts to locate promising talent are effective and/or cost-efficient. However, managers can do several things to maximize the likelihood of success. These include calculating yield ratios on recruiting sources, training organizational recruiters, and conducting realistic job previews.

Yield Ratios

Yield ratio

Percentage of applicants from a recruitment source that make it to the next stage of the selection process

Yield ratios help indicate which recruitment sources are most effective at producing qualified job candidates. Quite simply, a **yield ratio** is the percentage of applicants from a particular source that make it to the next stage in the selection process. For example, if 100 résumés are obtained from an employment agency, and 17 of the applicants submitting those résumés are invited for an on-site interview, the yield ratio for that agency is 17 percent (17/100). This yield ratio can then be recalculated for each subsequent stage in the selection process (e.g., after the interview, and again after the final offer). This results in a cumulative yield ratio. By calculating and comparing yield ratios for each recruitment source, managers can figure out which sources produce qualified applicants.

Reality CHECK

TOSI PLACEMENT SERVICES

TOSI provides permanent placement services and supplies contract and temporary employees in office support, logistics, IT, and finance. Nine out of ten companies use placement agencies. Ramona Baillie, vice-president of TOSI, has worked in the placement services business for twenty-six years. "Although recruiting is a constant for both temporary and permanent staffing," she says, "we must always have a supply of skilled candidates ready to go on assignment at a moment's notice. A client may call asking for a receptionist immediately, or for desk support specialists for two months, starting Monday."

After searching their extensive database for qualified, available candidates, the placement consultants place advertisements in the newspapers, search Internet sites such as Workopolis or Monster.ca, and request referrals from other applicants. As the phone calls or résumés arrive, a first screening is done to determine whether the candidates' skills can be utilized. Then an applicant is invited to register, at which point the applicant is tested and his or her references are checked.

Ramona dispels some myths about the agency's role: "The candidate pays us no fee and makes no commitment. There is no fee taken from their hourly rates. We determine the rate of compensation, and the applicants become our employees. As employers, we pay taxes, vacation pay, statutory holidays, and workplace safety insurance, and have employment equity and training programs. We then negotiate with our clients the fee that will be charged for the services of our employees."

TOSI has many programs in place to ensure that clients are satisfied with placements. If a new employee is scheduled to arrive at the job at 9 a.m., TOSI calls at 9 a.m. to check. There is a four-hour guarantee, whereby the client assesses the performance of the temp; if not satisfied, it pays no fee for the first four hours. The first day, TOSI calls the client again to check for quality. All calls are documented, and continue on a weekly basis throughout the placement. Assignments vary by length, shift, skill, skill level, and compensation. If the client offers the temporary a permanent job, it pays TOSI a fee.

Ramona is enthusiastic about the benefits of temps for both employers and employees. Employers save money when they use temps, because they pay only for work that is performed and only hire when employees are needed. Besides handling recruitment and placement, the staffing firm provides temps with training in software upgrades. Employees benefit the most, through the training they receive and because temporary work allows them to gain new skills and experiences as they move from organization to organization. Finally, there are lifestyle benefits to being a temp: temps have freedom and flexibility in their job assignments, and this enables them to study, travel, raise their children, and so on.

Costs of Recruitment

The cost of various recruiting procedures can be computed using a fairly simple set of calculations. For example, the average source cost per hire (SC/H) can be determined by the following formula:

$$\frac{SC}{H} = \frac{AC + AF + RB + NC}{H}$$

where   AC = advertising costs, total monthly expenditure
                   (example: $28,000)
        AF = agency fees, total for the month (example: $19,000)
        RB = referral bonuses, total paid (example: $2,300)
        NC = no-cost hires, walk-ins, nonprofit agencies, etc.
                   (example: $0)
        H   = total hires (example: 119)

Substituting these numbers into the formula gives

$$\frac{SC}{H} = \frac{\$28,000 + \$19,000 + \$2,300 + \$0}{119}$$

$$= \frac{\$49,300}{119}$$

$$= \$414 \text{ (source cost of recruits per hire)}$$

Organizational Recruiters

WWW

Who performs the recruitment function depends mainly on the size of the organization. For large employers, professional HR recruiters are hired and trained to find new employees. In smaller organizations, recruitment may be done by an HR generalist; or if the organization has no HR position, recruitment may be done by managers and/or supervisors. At companies such as Steelcase Canada, members of work teams take part in the selection of new team members.

Whoever does the recruiting absolutely must have a good understanding of the knowledge, skills, abilities, experiences, and other characteristics required for the job. All too often, a new member of the HR department, or a line manager, is given a recruitment assignment, even before that person has been given interview training, or fully understands the job, or fully comprehends the values and goals of the organization.

A good recruiter has the ability to improve the applicant's perception of the job and the organization, and is often a major reason why the applicant selects a given position over other possible ones at other organizations. On this basis, we can conclude that personable, enthusiastic, and competent recruiters have an impact on the success of an organization's recruitment program.

Realistic Job Previews

Realistic job preview

Informing applicants about all aspects of the job, both desirable and undesirable

Organizations can also improve their recruitment efforts by providing job applicants with **realistic job previews (RJPs)**. An RJP informs applicants about all aspects of the job, both desirable and undesirable. In contrast, a typical job preview presents the job in only positive terms. The RJP may include a tour of the working area, as well as a discussion of health and safety considerations. Proponents of the RJP believe that applicants who are given realistic information about a position are more likely to remain on the job and be successful, because there will be fewer unpleasant surprises. Various research studies on RJP report these positive results:

- improved employee job satisfaction
- reduced voluntary turnover

- enhanced communication through honesty and openness
- realistic job expectations [51]

Like other HR practices, however, RJPs must be tailored to the needs of the organization and include a balanced presentation of positive and negative job information.

SUMMARY

 As organizations plan for their future, top management and strategic planners must recognize that strategic planning decisions affect—and are affected by—HR functions. On the one hand, HRP plays a reactive role in making certain the right numbers and types of employees are available to implement a chosen business plan. On the other hand, HRP can proactively identify and initiate programs needed for developing organizational capabilities on which future strategies can be built.

 HRP is a systematic process that involves forecasting demand for labour, performing supply analysis, and balancing supply and demand considerations. Forecasting demand involves using quantitative or qualitative methods to identify the numbers and types of people needed to meet organizational objectives. Supply analysis involves determining whether enough employees are available in the organization to meet demand, and also whether potential employees are available on the job market. Reconciling supply and demand requires a host of activities, including internal and external recruitment.

 Employers usually find it worthwhile to use internal promotions and transfers to fill as many openings as possible above the entry level. By recruiting from within,

organizations capitalize on past investments made in recruiting, selecting, training, and developing their current employees. Furthermore, internal promotions reward employees for past performance and signal to other employees that their future efforts will pay off. However, potential candidates from the outside should occasionally be considered in order to prevent the inbreeding of ideas and attitudes.

 To fill jobs above the entry level, managers must often turn to outside sources. Outside sources are a means for filling jobs with special qualifications, for avoiding excessive inbreeding, and for acquiring new ideas and technology. Which outside sources and methods are used in recruiting will depend on the recruitment goals of the organization, the conditions of the labour market, and the specifications of the jobs to be filled.

 Employers wanting to maximize the effectiveness of their recruitment programs should calculate a yield ratio, train organizational recruiters, and conduct realistic job previews.

KEY TERMS

attrition
cultural audits
employee leasing
hiring freeze
human resources planning
   (HRP)
job description
job posting and bidding

labour market
management forecasts
Markov analysis
nepotism
organizational capability
realistic job preview (RJP)
replacement charts
restructuring

severance pay
skill inventories
staffing tables
succession planning
termination
trend analysis
yield ratio

DISCUSSION QUESTIONS

1. Identify the three key elements of the human resources planning model, and discuss how they relate to each other.

2. Distinguish between the quantitative and the qualitative approaches to forecasting human resource requirements.

3. What are the advantages and disadvantages of filling openings from internal sources?

4. In what ways do executive search firms differ from the traditional employment agencies?

5. Explain how realistic job previews (RJPs) operate. Why do they seem to be an effective recruitment technique?

6. Form groups of about five people. Have each person review the websites of Internet recruitment organizations (see Highlights in HRM 9). As a group, develop a list of the features that enourage you to stay on the site, and a second list of features that encourage you to apply for a job at the company. Compare your lists to the suggestions outlined in Highlights in HRM 8 or building an effective recruitment website.

CASE 1 THE FEDERAL GOVERNMENT

In the mid-1990s the federal government undertook the largest mass layoff in Canadian history. Roughly 20,000 employees were affected. Some of the departments announcing cuts were Transport, Natural Resources, Public Works, and Human Resources.

WWW

Everyone was scrambling. Most workers did not know who would be affected. Even the president of the Public Service Alliance of Canada (PSAC) did not know which of his 165,000 were to be terminated. (The Treasury Board, which was responsible for downsizing the civil service, had refused to release names for fear of violating the Privacy Act.) The president of the PSAC complained to reporters, "We are in a hell of a position trying to find these people so we can provide them assistance or even guidance and advice. At the same time, because of that fear mentality that's out there, some of the individuals are saying,[1] If I go to the union that might hurt my chances of keeping my job.' It's absolutely ridiculous what's going on out there, and it's another reason why we need more time."

PSAC faced the difficult task of protecting its employees from the effects of a proposed bill (C-76) that would override the key job security provisions of the union's labour contracts. Under the old legislation, government employees had the right to another job in the public service if their positions were eliminated. The new legislation gives public employees whose jobs are terminated sixty days to choose between a generous buyout, a chance at another job, and early retirement.

The government expected about 15,000 workers to take the buyout and another 4,000 (over age fifty) to accept early retirement programs. The buyouts cost $1 billion. In a novel twist, PSAC wanted to open up the incentive package so that affected workers who did not want to leave the government could swap their packages with employees who wanted to leave but whose positions were not terminated. Many workers in the Ministry of Transport were transferred to the soon-to-be privatized airports and ports.

Government workers had good reason to worry. According to psychologists, people who work in huge organizations do not develop networks of external contacts that may lead to new jobs. Their skills are very narrow because of the volumes of work. For example, a clerk in the government might spend his or her entire year processing a form unique to the government. Many of these individuals have worked for only one employer and have no job search skills. Public perceptions about the easy working life of civil servants may work against their employability. And while government workers in the 1990s were waiting for the axe to fall, they were expected to continue to work.

Source: This case was developed from information in newspapers, including *The Globe and Mail*, May 2, 1995: A13, and May 26, 1995: A1.

Questions

1. What downsizing strategies did the federal government adopt? What were the limitations of these strategies?

2. What should the government have done to help laid-off workers find new jobs?

3. What should the government have done to manage survivor sickness?

4. If you were a federal employee about to be laid off, what would you do to optimize your chances of re-employment?

CASE 2

WWW

FILLING THE SHOES

Bata Ltd. is a multinational shoe company, headquartered in Canada, that has more than 55,000 employees worldwide, located in sixty-seven subsidiaries. Every single subsidiary has a succession plan in place. Each senior position has three possible successors: a person who could fill the job immediately; a second, who could be ready in two years; and a third, who could be considered in five years. There are developmental plans for each employee on the chart; these plans are contained in a master file that lists such things as the highest position the employee can be expected to attain, the training programs completed, and areas that need improvement.

The methods for developing these senior managers are varied. For example, Bata has four levels of management training: (1) for high-potential middle managers; (2) for potential company managers; (3) for executive managers who are ready to lead the company now; and (4) for existing company managers. Employees know who is on the chart.

For those not currently part of the management succession plan, there are annual opportunities to earn a place. Formal appraisal programs identify those who are doing well and make recommendations for further training. Another method for developing managers is to offer them temporary "testing" assignments. Managers can replace people on vacation for trial periods to test and upgrade their skills. A system like this one runs the risk of simply repeating the managerial styles and thinking of the previous generation. So Bata, very conscious of the need to look for new blood (i.e., new ways of thinking and acting) also identifies people who have suggested new business opportunities and who are open to divergent perspectives.

Source: Adapted from D. Brown, "You Have to Become Deputy Before You Become Sheriff," *Canadian HR Reporter,* February 14, 2000: 9.

Questions

1. Bata Ltd. has a plan for replacing senior managers. Should this plan be extended to lower levels? Would the plan be similar, or does the training of supervisors and middle managers require different selection criteria and developmental methods?

2. What are the advantages and disadvantages of making employees aware who is part of the succession chart?

CASE 3

STAMPEDE FOR TALENT

The Calgary Stampede faces unusual HR planning and recruitment challenges. The people who manage the Stampede on a full-time basis number around 230. But for the ten-day July event, an additional 3,000 employees must be hired. This small organization uses a variety of methods to attract these employees. For example, it holds a job fair that attracts thousands of job applicants. And it sends letters to about 1,800 former employees inviting them to reapply.

To track the applicants from the job fair and former employees, the Stampede has resorted to a software program called Abra HR, developed by Memotec Communications. This HRIS program enables the Stampede to track both employees and employee candidates. All the employee data are in one location, and every employee has a customized file that shows employment history, rating, and current employment status. The system enables managers to document employment history by type (e.g., full-time, part-time, year round, seasonal). Patterns in employment can be monitored to enable planners to estimate supply and demand for the next season. Managers can request reports, and employees can track their vacation pay and benefits. The benefits for this world-class rodeo include accurate and up-to-date records, a more efficient tracking system, less work duplication, and the streamlining of HR administration.

Source: Adapted from T. Berardine, "HRIS Improve Management Decision Making," *Canadian Manager* 22, no. 4 (Winter 1997): 17–18.

Questions

1. How can this system assist in HR planning?

2. Is there potential for Internet recruitment for this organization?

3. Would a system like this work for a wide range of companies of different sizes and in different industries?

CAREER COUNSEL

To learn about job search strategies, visit the Managing Human Resources website (**belcourt.nelson.com**).

USING THE INTERNET

WWW

Canada Employment Weekly (**www.mediacorp2/index**) is Canada's national career newspaper. Advertise yourself on-line, buy Canadian career books, and find interesting employment links.

Canadajobs (**www.canadajobs.com**) links you to information about jobs in Canada, including government job databases, recruiters, and companies that are hiring.

Career Edge (**www.careeredge.org**) offers links to organizations that help young people find practical work experience through paid internships.

Experience Canada (**www.experiencecanada.org**) offers young graduates the opportunity to acquire work experience in their field of study for twenty-four-week periods in a Canadian province other than their own.

NOTES AND REFERENCES

1. Adam Lawrence, "Skill Shortage and Economic Pressures Combine to Hold Back Manufacturing," *Works Management* 51, no. 3 (August 1998): 14–17; D. A. Light, "Human Resources: Recruiting Generation 2001," *Harvard Business Review* 76, no. 4 (July–August 1998): 13-16; Bill Leonard, "High Tech Boom Hits Labor Shortage Snag," *HRMagazine* 41, no. 1 (January 1996): 4; Patricia Martin, "Jobs Must Be Marketed," *Personnel Journal*, January 1996, 1–4.

2. I. Drost, *An Introduction to the Canadian Labour Market* (Toronto: ITP Nelson, 2000); M. Belcourt and K. McBey, *Strategic Human Resources Planning*, (Toronto: ITP Nelson, 2000).

3. Stephenie Overman, "Gearing Up for Tomorrow's Workforce," *HRFocus* 76, no. 2 (February 1999): 1, 15; Rick Mullin and Sylvia Pfeifer, "Hiring Becomes a Star Search," *Chemical Week* 159, no. 19 (May 14, 1997): 40–1; Douglas T. Hall, "Executive Careers and Learning: Aligning Selection, Strategy, and Development," *Human Resource Planning* 18, no. 2 (1995): 14–23.

4. Linda Gryton, "The New Rules of HR Strategy," *HRFocus* 75, no. 6 (June 1998): 13–14; Elaine McShulskis, "HR Failing to Tap the Future," *HRMagazine* 43, no. 1 (January 1998): 21; Bob Eichinger and Dave Ulrich, "Are You Future Agile?" *Human Resource Planning* 18, no. 4 (1996): 30–41.

5. Justin Hibard, "Web Service: Ready or Not," *Informationweek* 709 (November 16, 1998): 18–20; Dunstan Prial, "On-Line: Barnes & Noble Books: An IPO for Web Unit," *The Wall Street Journal*, August 21, 1998: B1; Chris Clark, "Trying to Sell Books over the Internet? Yeah, Right," *MC Technology Marketing Intelligence* 18, no. 8 (August 1998): 62.

6. Brian J. Smith, John W. Boroski, and George E. Davis, "Human Resource Planning," *Human Resource Management*, Spring–Summer 1992: 81–93. For other examples of how strategic planning and HRP are combined, see D.F. Beatty and F.M.K. Tampoe, "Human Resource Planning for ICL," *Long Range Planning* 23, no. 1 (1990): 17–28; Paul Michael Swiercz and Barbara A. Spencer, "HRM and Sustainable Competitive Advantage: Lessons from Delta Airlines," *Human Resource Planning* 15, no. 2 (1992): 35–46; Alan F. White, "Organizational Transformation at BP: An Interview with Chairman and CEO Robert Horton," *Human Resource Planning* 15, no. 1 (1992): 3–14.

7. James W. Walker, "Integrating the Human Resource Function with the Business," *Human Resource Planning* 14, no. 2 (1996): 59–77.

8. Carol Stephenson, "Corporate Values Drive Global Success at Lucent Technologies," *Canadian Speeches* 13, no. 5 (November–December 1999): 23–7.

9. Patrick Wright, Gary McMahan, Scott Snell, and Barry Gerhart, *Strategic Human Resource Management: Building Human Capital and Organizational Capability*, technical report, Cornell University, Ithaca, N.Y., 1998; Arthur Yeung and Wayne Brockbank, "Lower Cost and Higher Value: Human Resource Function in Transformation," *Human Resource Planning* 17, no. 3 (1994): 1–16.

10. D.P. Lepak and S.A. Snell, "The Human Resource Architecture: Toward a Theory of Human Capital Development and Allocation," *Academy of Management Review* 24, no. 1 (1999): 31–48.

11. P.M. Wright and S.A. Snell, "Toward a Unifying Framework for Exploring Fit and Flexibility in Strategic Human Resource Management," *Academy of Management Review* 22, no. 4 (1998): 756–72.

12. Kotaro Kuwada, "Strategic Learning: The Continuous Side of Discontinuous Strategic Change," *Organization Science* 9, no. 6 (November–December 1998): 719–36; Dave Ulrich and Robert Eichinger, "Delivering HR with an Attitude," *HRMagazine* 43, no. 7 (June 1998): 154–60; Arthur Yeung and Bob Berman, "Adding Value through Human Resources: Reorienting Human Resources Measurement to Drive Business Performance," *Human Resource Management* 36, no. 3 (Fall 1997): 321–35.

13. Terry Wagar, "Factors Affecting Permanent Workforce Reduction: Evidence from Large Canadian Organizations," *Canadian Journal of Administrative Studies* 14, no. 3 (1997): 303–14.

14. Barrie McKenna, "Axe Falls on Civil Service Jobs," *The Globe and Mail*, May 16, 1995: A1–2.

15. Jaclyn Fierman, "The Contingency Workforce," *Fortune*, January 24, 1994: 30–6; Ronald Henkoff, "Getting Beyond Downsizing," *Fortune*, January 10, 1994: 58–64; Susan Caminiti, ""What Happens to Laid-Off Managers?" *Fortune*, June 13, 1994: 68–78; Del Jones, "Kodak to Eliminate 10,000 Jobs by '96," *USA Today*, August 19, 1993: B1; Tim Jones, "Retooling Unleashes Huge Wave of Layoffs," *Chicago Tribune*, June 22, 1994.

16. Jennifer Laabs, "The HR Side of Sears' Comeback," *Workforce* 78, no. 3 (March 1999): 24–29; Odette Pollar, "A Diverse Workforce Requires Balanced Leadership," *Workforce extra* (December 1998): 4–5; Anthony Early, Jr., "A Passion for Personal Success," *Vital Speeches of the Day* 65, no. 6 (January 1, 1999): 184–87; Thomas Gilmore, Gregory Shea, and Michael Useem, "Side Effects of Corporate Cultural Transformations," *Journal of Applied Behavioral Science* 33, no. 2 (June 1997): 174–89.

17. James Ciecka, Thomas Donley, and Jerry Goldman, "A Markov Process Model of Work Life Expectancies Based on Labor Market Activity in 1994–95," *Journal of Legal Economics* 7, no. 1 (Spring 1997): 20–25; Oded Berman, Richard C. Larson and Edieal Pinker, "Scheduling Workforce and Workflow in a High Volume Factory," *Management Science* 43, no. 2 (February 1997): 158–72.

18. Terry Wagar, "Factors Influencing Permanent Workforce Reduction: Evidence from Large Canadian Companies," *Canadian Journal of Administrative Studies* 14, no. 3 (1997): 303–14.

19. "The Rebirth of IBM: Blue Is the Colour," *The Economist* 347, no. 8071 (June 6, 1998): 65–8; Ronald Henkoff, "Getting beyond Downsizing," *Fortune*, January 10, 1994: 58–64; Susan Caminiti, "What Happens to Laid-Off Managers?" *Fortune*, June 13, 1994: 68–78; Del Jones, "Kodak to Eliminate 10,000 Jobs by '96," *USA Today*, August 19, 1993: B1; Tim Jones, "Retooling Unleashes Huge Wave of Layoffs," *Chicago Tribune*, June 22, 1994: 11.

20. G. Keenan, "GM Slashing 1400 Quebec Jobs," *The Globe and Mail*, June 3, 1995: B1.

21. Linda Gutri, "Survivor Skills," *Human Resource Professional* 9, no. 3 (March 1995): 13–15.

22. Anneli Legault, "Aging Disgracefully," *Human Resources Professional* 10, no. 11 (December 1993): 10–11.

23. David McCabe, "Improvising the Future," *Human Resources Professional* 10, no. 11 (December 1993): 17–19.

24. William Soukup, Miriam Rothman, and Dennis, "Outplacement Services: A Vital Component of Personnel Policy," *SAM Advanced Management Journal*, Autumn 1987: 19–23.

25. Margot Gibb-Clark, "Survivors Also Suffer in Downsizing: Expert," *The Globe and Mail*, May 23, 1995: B5.

26. D. Worrel, W. Davidson, and V. Sharma, "Lay-off Announcements & Shareholder Wealth," *Academy of Management Journal* 34 (1991): 662–78.

27. T.H. Wagar, "Downsizing or Dumbsizing? Possible Consequences of Permanent Workforce Reduction," *Proceedings of the Administrative Sciences Association of Canada, Annual Conference* 15, no. 9, 1994.

28. W. Casco, "Downsizing? What Do We Know? What Have We Learned?" *The Executive* 7 (1993): 95–104.

29. Gibb-Clark, "Survivors Also Suffer ..."

30. Gutri, "Survivor Skills ..."

31. Bruce Tucker, "Downsizing Has Killed Loyalty," *Human Resource Management in Canada Report* 124, Scarborough: Prentice-Hall (June 1993): 17–23.

32. Chris Lee, "After the Cuts," *Training* 29, no. 7 (Jly 1992): 17–23.

33. Ibid.

34. Mary Anne L-esperance, "Strategic Staffing," *Human Resource Professional*, May 2001 (forthcoming).

35. John Kettle, "Casual Work Gets Serious," *The Globe and Mail*, November 20, 1997: B4.

36. J. Pfeiffer and J.N. Baron, "Taking the Workers Back Out: Recent Trends in the Structuring of Employment," *Research in Organizational Behavior* 10 (1988): 257–303.

37. Interested readers can check out the websites of these companies at **www.peoplesoft.com** and **www.resumix.com**. Also see Natasha Wanchek, "People Who Need PeopleSoft," *MC Technology Marketing Intelligence* 18, no. 5 (May 1998): 22–29; "Resumix Once Again Pioneers Staffing Solutions Market with Introduction of Web-Based Product," *Business Wire*, September 22, 1998; Paul Gosling, "The Computer Is Going through Your CV Now," *The Independent*, August 23, 1998: 2.

38. Gillian Flynn, "Texas Instruments Engineers a Holistic HR," *Workforce* 77, no. 2 (February 1998): 30–5; Jeannette Brown, "Amoco Taps VAR to Post Jobs Online," *Computer Reseller News* 656 (November 6, 1995): 163; Shari Caudron, "Online Job-Posting Facilitates Lateral Transfers at Household International," *Personnel Journal* 73, no. 4 (April 1994): 64J; Carol Zarrow, "People Power," *CIO* 9, no. 14 (May 1, 1996): 86.

39. Micheline Maynard and Del Jones, "Keeping Secrets: High-Tech Tools Usher in Stolen-Information Age," *USA Today*, April 10, 1997: B1, 4.

40. Rekha Balu and L. Amante, "Kellogg Co. Shakes Up Management: Financial Officer among Those Quitting," *Wall Street Journal*, March 4, 1999: B14; George Lazarus, "Pepsi Bottlers May Look Outside for New Chief," *Chicago Tribune*, February 12, 1999: 3; "Help Wanted: Creative Recruitment Tactics," *Personnel* 66, no. 10 (1989): 32–6.

41. Jennifer Laabs, "Cool Relo Benefits to Retain Top Talent," *Workforce* 78, no. 3 (March 1999): 89–94; Nancy Wong, "Do More than Make a Move," *Workforce* 78, no. 3 (March 1999): 95–7.

42. Herbert G. Heneman III and Robyn A. Berkley, "Applicant Attraction Practices and Outcomes among Small Businesses," *Journal of Small Business Management* 27, no. 1 (January 1999): 53–74; Jean Powell Kirnan, John A. Farley, and Kurt F. Geisinger, "The Relationship between Recruiting Source, Applicant Quality, and Hire Performance: An Analysis by Sex, Ethnicity, and Age," *Personnel Psychology* 42, no. 2 (Summer 1989): 293–308.

43. Keith Swenson, "Maximizing Employee Referrals," *HRFocus* 76, no. 1 (January 1999): 9–10; Thomas A. Stewart, "In Search of Elusive Tech Workers," *Fortune*, February 16, 1998: 171–2; Thomas Love, "Smart Tactics for Finding Workers," *Nation's Business*, January 1998: 20.

44. Steven Berglas, "Hiring In-laws: The Kiss of Death," *Inc.* 20, no. 16 (November 1998): 31–3; Paulette Thomas, "Workplace: An Ohio Design Shop Favors Family Ties," *Wall Street Journal*, September 8, 1998: B1; Chad Kaydo, "Does Nepotism Work?" *Sales and Marketing Management* 150, no. 7 (July 1998): 161; Brenda Paik Sunoo, "Nepotism—Problem or Solution?" *Workforce* 77, no. 6 (June 1998): 17.

45. Carrick Mollenkamp, "Dunlop Maxfli Hopes New Golf Ball Will Drive Company's Sales Higher," *Wall Street Journal*, July 15, 1998: S3. See also Thomas J. Hutton, "Increase the Odds for Successful Searches," *Personnel Journal*, November 1995, 1–5; Jacqueline M. Graves, "Bull Market for Senior Executives," *Fortune*, November 14, 1994: 14; Dave Kruger, "Executive Search Firms Riding High on Tidal Demand," *Japan Times Weekly International Edition* 36, no. 12 (March 25–31, 1996): 13.

46. "Pop Quiz: How Do You Recruit the Best College Grads?" *Personnel Journal*, August 1995: 12–18; Shannon Peters Talbott, "Boost Your Campus Image to Attract Top Grads," *Personnel Journal*, March 1996: 6–8; Holly Rawlinson, "Scholarships Recruit Future Employees Now," *Recruitment*, a supplement of *Personnel Journal*, August 1988: 14.

47. Donald A. Levenson, "Needed: Revamped Recruiting Services," *Personnel* 65, no. 7 (July 1988): 52. See also J.A. Breaugh, *Recruitment: Science and Practice* (Boston: PWS–Kent, 1992).

48. John W. Medcof and Brent Needham, "The Supra-Organizational HRM System," *Business Horizons* 41, no. 1 (January–February 1998): 43–50; Jaclyn Fierman, "The Contingency Work Force," *Fortune*, January 24, 1994: 30–6; Allison Thornson, "The Contingent Workforce," *Occupational Outlook Quarterly*, Spring 1995: 45–8; J.R. Brandstrater, "It's an Ill Wind," *Barron's*, March 25, 1996: 18–19; Michael R. Losey, "Temps: They're Not Just for Typing Anymore," *Modern Office Technology*, August 1991: 58–9. See also Louis S. Richman, "CEOs to Workers: Help Not Wanted," *Fortune*, July 12, 1993: 42–3.

49. David Lepak and Scott Snell, "The Human Resource Architecture: Toward a Theory of Human Capital Allocation and Development," *Academy of Management Review* 24, no. 1 (January 1999): 31–48; Jill E. Ellingson, Melissa I. Gruys, and Paul R. Sackett, "Factors Related to the Satisfaction and Performance of Temporary Employees," *Journal of Applied Psychology* 83, no. 6 (December 1998): 913–92; Kent Blake, "She's Just a Temporary," *HRMagazine* 43, no. 9 (August 1998): 45–52; Marianne A. Ferber and Jane Waldfogel, "The Long-Term Consequences of Nontraditional Employment," *Monthly Labor Review* 121, no. 5 (May 1998): 3–12.

50` Carolyn Hirschman, "All Aboard!" *HRMagazine* 42, no. 9 (September 1997): 80–5; "Who Is the Employer?" *HRMagazine* 42, no. 9 (September 1997): 84; Jay Finegan, "New Biz Puts 7,300 on Payroll," *Inc.* 19, no. 6 (May 1997): 17.

51. Robert D. Bretz Jr. And Timothy A. Judge, "Realistic Job Previews: A Test of the Adverse Self-Selection Hypothesis," *Journal of Applied Psychology* 83, no. 2 (April 1998): 330–7; Ben Pappas, "Accentuate the Negative," *Forbes*, December 28, 1998: 47; John P. Wanous, "Installing a Realistic Job Preview: Ten Tough Choices," *Personnel Psychology* 42, no. 1 (Spring 1989): 117–33.

CALCULATING TURNOVER AND ABSENTEEISM

Throughout this chapter we have emphasized that HRP depends on having an accurate picture of both the supply of and the demand for employees. Two factors, employee turnover and absenteeism, have a direct impact on HR planning and recruitment processes. In this appendix we discuss in depth both turnover and absenteeism, and methods for measuring them, and suggest ways to manage their impact.

EMPLOYEE TURNOVER RATES

"Employee turnover" refers simply to the movement of employees out of an organization. It is often cited as one of the reasons why Canadian productivity rates have failed to keep pace with those of foreign competitors. It is also one of the chief determinants of labour supply. Even if everything else about an organization stays the same, as employees turn over, the supply of labour goes down. This has both direct and indirect costs to the organization.

COMPUTING THE TURNOVER RATE

One formula for computing turnover rates is

$$\frac{\textbf{Number of separations during the month}}{\textbf{Total number of employees at midmonth}} \times 100$$

Thus, if there were 25 separations during a month and the total number of employees at midmonth was 500, the turnover rate would be

$$\frac{25}{500} \times 100 = 5\%$$

Turnover rates are computed on a regular basis to compare specific units (departments, divisions, work groups, etc.). Often, comparisons are made with data provided by other organizations.

Another method for computing the turnover rate reflects only the avoidable separations (S). This rate is computed by subtracting unavoidable separations (US; e.g., pregnancy, return to school, death, marriage) from all separations. The formula for this method is as follows:

$$\frac{S - US}{M} \times 100 = T \text{ (turnover rate)}$$

where M represents the total number of employees at midmonth. For example, if there were 25 separations during a month, 5 of which were US, and the total number of employees at midmonth (M) was 500, the turnover rate would be

$$\frac{25 - 5}{500} \times 100 = 4 \text{ percent}$$

In looking at the impact of turnover on HR planning and recruitment, it is vitally important to recognize that quantitative rates of turnover are not the only factor to be considered: the quality of employees who leave an organization is equally important. If poor employees leave—what experts refer to as "functional turnover"—this can benefit the organization. The costs of keeping unproductive workers may be far more than the costs of recruiting and training new, more effective performers.

DETERMINING THE COSTS OF TURNOVER

Replacing an employee is time-consuming and expensive. Costs can generally be broken down into three categories: separation costs for the departing employee, replacement costs, and training costs for the new employee. These costs are conservatively estimated at two to three times the monthly salary of the departing employee, and do not include indirect costs such as low productivity prior to quitting and lower morale and overtime for other employees because of the vacated job. Consequently, reducing turnover could result in significant savings to an organization. Highlights in HRM A1 details one organization's costs associated with the turnover of a single computer programmer. Note that the major expense is the cost involved in training a replacement.

EMPLOYEE ABSENTEEISM RATES

How often employees are absent from their work—the absenteeism rate—is also directly related to HR planning and recruitment. When employees miss work, the organization incurs direct costs of lost wages and decreased productivity. It is not uncommon for organizations to hire extra workers just to make up for the number of absences totalled across all employees. Besides these direct costs, there are indirect costs that may underlie excessive absenteeism. A certain amount of absenteeism is, of course, unavoidable. There will always be some who must be absent from work because of sickness, accidents, or serious family problems, or for other legitimate reasons. However, chronic absenteeism may signal some deeper problems in the work environment.

Highlights in HRM

A1 COSTS ASSOCIATED WITH THE TURNOVER OF ONE EMPLOYEE

Turnover costs = Separation costs + Replacement costs + Training costs

SEPARATION COSTS

1. Exit interview = Cost for salary and benefits of both interviewer and departing employee during the exit interview =
2. Administrative and record-keeping action =

     Separation costs = 1+ 2

REPLACEMENT COSTS

1. Advertising for job opening =
2. Pre-employment administrative functions and record-keeping action =
3. Selection interview =
4. Employment tests =
5. Meetings to discuss candidates (salary and benefits of managers while participating in meetings) =

     Replacement costs = 1+2+3+4+5

TRAINING COSTS

1. Booklets, manuals, and reports =
2. Education = Cost per day for new employee's salary and benefits times days for work-shops, seminars, or courses =
3. One-to-one coaching = ($/day/new employee + $/day/staff coach or job expert) $\times$ 20 days of one-to-one coaching =
4. Salary and benefits of new employee until he or she gets "up to par" = Costs per day for salary and benefits $\times$ 20 days =

     Training costs = 1+2+3+4

Total turnover costs = Separation + Replacement + Training

Source: Adapted from Michael W. Mercer, *Turning Your Human Resources Department into a Profit Center* (New York: AMACOM, 1993). Copyright 1993 Michael W. Mercer. Reproduced with permission from Michael W. Mercer, Ph.D., Industrial Psychologist, The Mercer Group, Inc., Chicago, Ill.

Computing Absenteeism Rates

Managers should determine the extent of the absenteeism problem, if any, by maintaining individual and departmental attendance records and by computing absenteeism rates. There is no universally accepted definition of "absence," nor is there a standard formula for computing absenteeism rates. However, the method most often used is

$$\frac{\text{Number of worker-days lost through job absence during period}}{\text{Average number of employees} \times \text{Number of workdays}} \times 100$$

If 300 worker-days are lost through job absence during a month having 25 scheduled working days at an organization that employs 500 workers, the absenteeism rate for that month is

$$\frac{300}{500 \times 25} \times 100 = 2.4 \text{ percent}$$

Job absence can be defined as the failure of employees to report to work when their schedules require it, whether or not such failure to report is excused. Scheduled vacations, holidays, and prearranged leaves of absence are not counted as job absence.

Comparing Absenteeism Data

The Vancouver-based Saratoga Institute regularly monitors absenteeism rates and for a fee can provide comparison rates. HR managers in a number of sectors, including health care, collect and share absenteeism rates. The Conference Board of Canada and Statistics Canada publish absenteeism data.

Costs of Absenteeism

Traditional accounting and information systems often do not generate data that reflect the costs of absenteeism. Consequently, their usefulness in HR planning is often limited. To accentuate the impact of absenteeism on organizational performance, managers should translate the data into dollar costs. A system for computing absenteeism costs for an individual organization is available. Organizations with computerized absence-reporting systems should find this additional information easy and inexpensive to generate. The cost of each person-hour lost to absenteeism is based on the hourly weighted average salary, costs of employee benefits, supervisory costs, and incidental costs.

For example, XYZ Company, with 1,200 employees, has 78,000 person-hours lost to absenteeism; the total absence cost is $560,886. When this figure is divided by 1,200 employees, the cost per employee is $467.41. (In this example, we are assuming that the absent workers are paid. If absent workers are not paid, their salary figures are omitted from the computation.) A Nova Scotia government audit of sick leave revealed that employees took an average of 10.8 sick days per year, compared to the national average of 7.3 days for public sector employees and 6.6 days for all Canadian workers. The cost of sick leave was estimated to be $25 million in one year alone. (see A. Jeffers, "Our Civil Servants Sickest in Country," Chronicle-Herald (Halifax), December 12, 1994: A1, A2; L. Kelly, "Attendance Management: An Issue of the 90's," Worklife 8, no. 5 (1992): 12–14).

ABSENTEEISM AND HR PLANNING

While an employer may find that the overall absenteeism rate and costs are within an acceptable range, it is still advisable to study the statistics to determine whether there are patterns in the data. Rarely does absenteeism spread itself evenly across an organization. It is very likely that employees in one area (or occupational group) may have nearly perfect attendance records, while others in a different area may be absent frequently. By monitoring these differential attendance records, managers can assess where problems may exist and, more importantly, begin planning ways to address underlying causes. For example, incentives could be provided for perfect attendance. Alternatively, progressive discipline procedures could be used with employees who are regularly absent.

After studying this chapter, you should be able to

Explain the objectives of the personnel selection process

Identify the various sources of information used for employee selection.

Explain the value of different types of employment tests.

Discuss the different approaches to conducting an employment interview.

Describe the various decision strategies for selection.

SELECTION

T here is perhaps no more important topic in HRM than employee selection. If it is true that organizations succeed or fail based on the talents of their employees, managers directly influence that success by the people they hire. Whether the organization is large or small, hiring the best and the brightest employees lays a strong foundation for excellence. Managers who don't recognize this point are often heard complaining about the time they spend hiring and/or fixing bad selection decisions. Also, human rights legislation and court decisions have provided an impetus for improving the selection process.

MATCHING PEOPLE AND JOBS

Selection

The process of choosing individuals who have relevant qualifications to fill existing or projected job openings

In conjunction with the recruiting process, which is designed to increase the number of applicants whose qualifications meet job requirements and the needs of the organization, **selection** is the process of choosing among those individuals who have the relevant qualifications. As Figure 5.1 shows, the overall goal of selection is to maximize hits and avoid misses. Hits are accurate predictions, and misses are inaccurate ones. The cost of one type of miss would be the direct and indirect expense of hiring an employee who turns out to be unsuccessful. The cost of the other type of miss is an opportunity cost—someone who could have been successful but didn't get a chance.

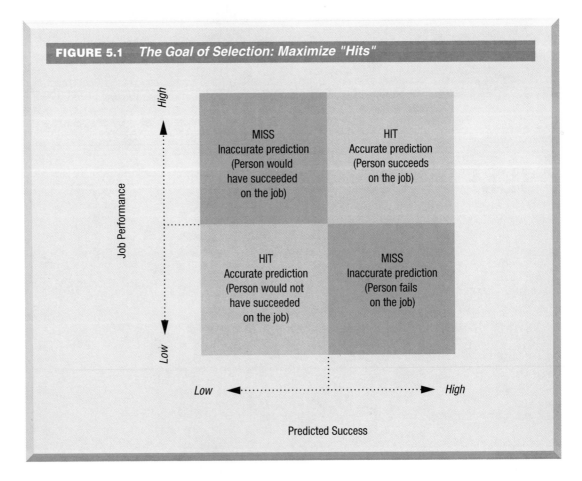

FIGURE 5.1 *The Goal of Selection: Maximize "Hits"*

Job Performance — High / Low

Predicted Success — Low / High

MISS
Inaccurate prediction
(Person would
have succeeded
on the job)

HIT
Accurate prediction
(Person succeeds
on the job)

HIT
Accurate prediction
(Person would not
have succeeded
on the job)

MISS
Inaccurate prediction
(Person fails
on the job)

While the selection program typically is the responsibility of the HR department, line managers normally make the final decision about which person to hire for their unit. It is therefore important that managers understand the objectives, policies, and practices used for selection, and that they be heavily involved from the very beginning. Those responsible for making selection decisions should have adequate information on which to base their decisions. Information about the jobs to be filled, knowledge of the ratio of job openings to the number of applicants, and as much relevant information as possible about the applicants themselves are essential for making sound decisions.

Beginning with Job Analysis

In Chapter 3 we discussed the process of analyzing jobs to develop job descriptions and specifications. Job specifications, in particular, help identify the individual competencies that employees need for success—the knowledge, skills, abilities, and other factors (KSAOs) that lead to superior performance. Having identified competencies through job analysis, managers can then use selection methods (interviews, references, psychological tests, etc.) to measure applicants' KSAOs and match these against the competencies required by both the job and the organization.[1] Research has demonstrated that complete and unambiguous specification of required competencies (via job analysis) reduces the influence of racial and gender stereotypes, and helps interviewers differentiate between qualified and unqualified applicants.[2]

Ordinarily, managers are well acquainted with all the requirements relating to jobs in their departments. Interviewers and other members of the HR department who participate in selection should work closely with the various departments in order to become thoroughly familiar with the jobs and competencies needed to perform them.

The Selection Process

In most organizations, selection is a continuous process. Turnover inevitably occurs, leaving vacancies to be filled by applicants from inside or outside the organization, or by individuals whose qualifications were assessed at an earlier time. It is common to have a waiting list of applicants who can be called as permanent or temporary positions become open.

The number of steps in the selection process and their sequence will vary, not only with the organization but also with the type and level of jobs to be filled. Each step should be evaluated in terms of its contribution. The typical steps in the selection process are shown in Figure 5.2. Not all applicants will go through all of these steps. Some may be rejected after the preliminary interview, others after taking tests, and so on.

As shown in Figure 5.2, organizations use various means to obtain information about applicants. These include application blanks, interviews, tests, and background investigations. Whichever method is used, it must conform to accepted ethical standards, including privacy and confidentiality standards, as well as to legal requirements. Above all, the information obtained must be sufficiently reliable and valid.

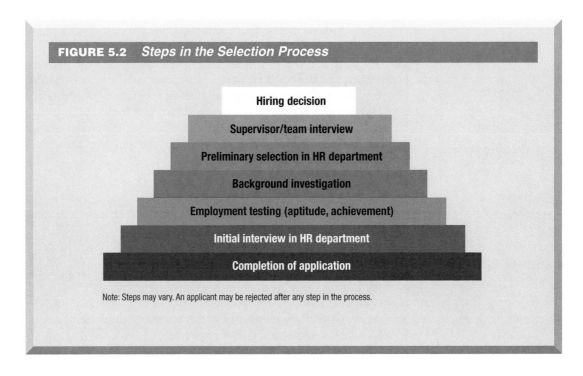

FIGURE 5.2   *Steps in the Selection Process*

Hiring decision

Supervisor/team interview

Preliminary selection in HR department

Background investigation

Employment testing (aptitude, achievement)

Initial interview in HR department

Completion of application

Note: Steps may vary. An applicant may be rejected after any step in the process.

Obtaining Reliable and Valid Information

Reliability

The degree to which interviews, tests, and other selection procedures yield comparable data over time and alternative measures

The degree to which interviews, tests, and other selection procedures yield comparable data over a period of time is known as **reliability**. For example, if interviewers judge the capabilities of a group of applicants to be different today than they were yesterday, their judgments are unreliable (i.e., unstable). Likewise, a test that gives a greatly different score when it is administered to the same individual a few days later is unreliable.

Reliability also refers to the degree to which two or more methods (e.g., interviews and tests) yield similar results or are consistent. Interrater reliability—agreement between two or more raters—is one measure of a method's consistency. The data on which selection decisions are based must be reliable, in terms of both stability and consistency, or they cannot be used as predictors.

Validity

How well a test or selection procedure measures a person's attributes

Besides pertaining to a person's suitability for a job, the information must be as valid as possible. **Validity** refers to what a test or other selection procedure measures and how well it measures it. In the context of employee selection, validity is mainly about how well the data from a procedure (e.g., an interview or test) predict job performance. Like a new medicine, a selection procedure must be validated before it is used. There are two reasons for validating a procedure. *First*, validity is directly related to increases in employee productivity, as we will demonstrate later. *Second*, employment equity regulations emphasize the importance of validity in selection procedures.[3] Although we commonly refer to "validating" a test or interview procedure, validity in the technical sense refers to the inferences made from the use of a procedure, not to the procedure itself.

Three recognized approaches to validation are criterion-related validity, content validity, and construct validity.

Criterion-Related Validity

Criterion-related validity

The extent to which a selection tool predicts, or significantly correlates with, important elements of work behaviour

The extent to which a selection tool predicts or significantly correlates with important elements of work behaviour is known as **criterion–related validity**. For example, performance on a test is compared with actual production records, supervisory ratings, training outcomes, and other measures of success that are appropriate to each type of job. In a sales job, for example, it is common to use sales figures as a basis for comparison. In production jobs, quantity and quality of output may provide the best criteria of job success.

Concurrent validity

The extent to which test scores (or other predictor information) match criterion data obtained at about the same time from current employees

There are two types of criterion-related validity: concurrent and predictive. **Concurrent validity** involves obtaining criterion data from current employees at about the same time that test scores (or other predictor data) are obtained. For example, a supervisor might be asked to rate a group of clerical employees on the quantity and quality of their performance. These employees are then given a clerical aptitude test, and the test scores are compared with the supervisory ratings to determine the relationship between them. **Predictive validity**, on the other hand, involves testing applicants and obtaining criterion data after those applicants have been hired and have been on the job for some indefinite period. For example, applicants might be given a clerical aptitude test, which is then filed away for later study. After the individuals have been on the job for several months, supervisors, who should not know the employees' test scores, are asked to rate them on the quality and quantity of their performance. Test scores are then compared with the supervisors' ratings.

Predictive validity

The extent to which applicants' test scores match criterion data obtained from those applicants/employees after they have been on the job for some indefinite period

Cross-validation

Verifying the results obtained from a validation study by administering a test or test battery to a different sample (drawn from the same population)

Regardless of the method used, cross-validation is essential. **Cross-validation** is a process in which a test or battery of tests is administered to a different sample (drawn from the same population) for the purpose of verifying the results obtained from the original validation study.

Correlational methods are generally used to determine the relationship between predictor information (such as test scores) and criterion data. The correlation scatterplots in Figure 5.3 illustrate the difference between a selection test of zero validity (A) and one of high validity (B). Each dot represents a person. Note that in scatterplot A there is no relationship between test scores and success on the job; in other words, the validity is zero. In scatterplot B, those who score low on the test tend to have low success on the job, whereas those who score high on the test tend to have high success on the job; this indicates high validity. In actual practice, we would apply a statistical formula to the data to obtain a coefficient of correlation, referred to as a *validity coefficient*. Correlation coefficients range from 0.00, denoting a complete absence of relationship, to +1.00 and to −1.00, indicating a perfect positive and perfect negative relationship, respectively.

A thorough survey of the literature shows that the averages of the maximum validity coefficients are 0.45 where tests are validated against *training* criteria and 0.35 where tests are validated against *job proficiency* criteria. These figures represent the predictive power of single tests.[4] A higher validity might be obtained by combining two or more tests or other predictors (e.g., interview or biographical data), using the appropriate statistical formulae. The higher the overall validity, the greater the chances of hiring better performers. The criterion-related method is generally preferred to other validation approaches because it is based on empirical data.

Personnel psychologists believed for several decades that validity coefficients had meaning only for the specific situation (job and organization). More recently, as a result of several research studies—many involving clerical jobs—it seems that

Validity generalization

The extent to which validity coefficients can be generalized across situations

validity coefficients can often be generalized across situations, hence the term **validity generalization**. When adequate data are available to support the existence of validity generalization, the development of selection procedures can become less costly and time-consuming. The process involves analyzing jobs and situations and, on the basis of these analyses, consulting tables of generalized validities from previous studies using various predictors in similar circumstances. It is advisable for organizations to employ the services of an industrial-organizational psychologist experienced in test validation to develop the selection procedures.

Content Validity

Content validity

The extent to which a selection instrument, such as a test, adequately samples the knowledge and skills needed to perform a particular job

When it is not feasible to use the criterion-related approach—often because samples of individuals are too small—the content method is used. **Content validity** is assumed to exist when a selection instrument, such as a test, adequately samples the knowledge and skills needed to perform a particular job.

The closer the content of the selection instrument is to actual work samples or behaviours, the greater its content validity. For example, a public service examination for accountants has high content validity when it requires candidates to solve accounting problems that are representative of those found on the job. Asking an accountant to lift a 30 kg box has content validity only if the job description states that accountants must be able to do so.

Content validity is the most direct and least complicated type of validity to assess. It is generally used to evaluate job knowledge and skill tests (see below). Unlike the criterion-related method, content validity is not expressed in correlational terms. Instead, an index that indicates the relationship between the content of the test items and performance on the job is computed from evaluations of a panel of experts.[5] While content validity does have its limitations, it has made a

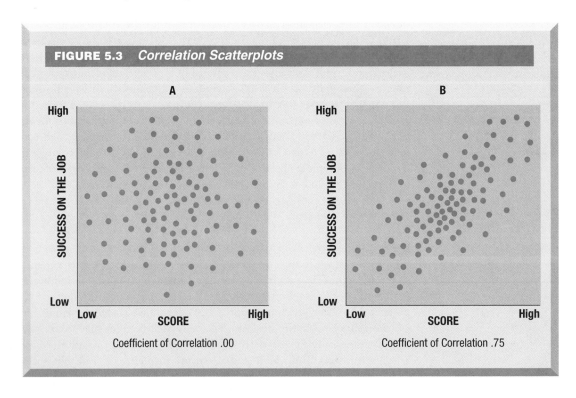

FIGURE 5.3   *Correlation Scatterplots*

A

SUCCESS ON THE JOB — High / Low
SCORE — Low / High

Coefficient of Correlation .00

B

SUCCESS ON THE JOB — High / Low
SCORE — Low / High

Coefficient of Correlation .75

positive contribution to job analysis procedures and to the role of expert judgment in sampling and scoring procedures.

Construct Validity

Construct validity

The extent to which a selection tool measures a theoretical construct or trait

The extent to which a selection tool measures a theoretical construct, or trait, is known as **construct validity**. Typical constructs are intelligence, mechanical comprehension, and anxiety. These are broad, general categories of human functions that are based on the measurement of many discrete behaviours. For example, the Bennett Mechanical Comprehension Test consists of a wide variety of tasks that measure the construct of mechanical comprehension.

Measuring construct validity requires showing that the psychological trait is related to satisfactory job performance and that the test accurately measures the psychological trait. There is a shortage of literature covering this concept as it relates to employment practices, probably because it is difficult and expensive to validate a construct and to show how it is job-related.[6]

SOURCES OF INFORMATION ABOUT JOB CANDIDATES

Many sources of information are used to provide as reliable and valid a picture as possible of an applicant's potential for success on the job. The selection process at The Bay, outlined in Reality Check, illustrates the most important sources of information. In this section we will study the potential contributions of application forms, biographical information blanks, background investigations, polygraph (or lie detector) tests, honesty and integrity tests, graphology, and medical examinations. Because interviewing plays such a major role in selection, and because testing presents unique challenges, we will discuss these sources of information in greater depth later in the chapter. Assessment centres, which are often used in managerial selection, will be discussed in Chapter 7.

Application Forms

Most organizations require application forms to be completed because they provide a fairly quick and systematic means of obtaining a variety of information about the applicant. The courts have found that many questions asked on application forms discriminate against women and minorities and often are not job-related. For example, a security firm in Ontario required applicants to fill out a form that asked for place of birth, complexion, and hair and eye colour; a board of inquiry later found that these questions discriminated against a former police officer from Guyana because of his race and place of origin.[7]

Application forms should therefore be developed with great care and revised as often as necessary.

Application forms serve several purposes. They provide information for deciding whether an applicant meets the minimum requirements for experience, education, and so on. They provide a basis for questions the interviewer will ask about the applicant's background. They also offer sources for reference checks. For certain jobs, a short application form is appropriate. The McDonald's form reproduced in Highlights in HRM 1 is quite brief but asks for information that is highly relevant to job performance. It also provides information regarding the employer's

WWW

Reality CHECK

SELECTION AT THE BAY

WWW

Canada's oldest corporation and largest department store retailer is the Hudson's Bay Company, which was established in 1670 and operates as The Bay and Zellers. Tina Peacock, human resources manager for Merchandise Services & Corporate Offices, has been with HBC for over twenty years. She helps the company achieve its goals by carefully applying selection methods to identify key potential candidates for many different positions, such as merchandise buyer, financial manager, and systems manager.

"In addition to succession planning," states Peacock, "we follow established trends, such as growth in our business units, turnover, and performance results, to identify those positions that may become vacant during the year. Through a number of training programs provided in-house, we are able to fill our positions internally. In fact, 80 percent are staffed from internal promotions. For the other 20 percent, we hire externally. As a proactive measure in anticipation of those openings, we run recruiting ads so that we always have a 'stable' of competent candidates.

"It is important that we work closely with the managers because they know what is needed to run their business. My role is to provide them with qualified candidates who possess the basic job knowledge with the right competencies to work in our fast-paced, changing environment. For instance, a number of managers are tapped into the marketplace, so they are able to get the ball rolling by identifying candidates in the industry before an ad is placed. Our role is to prescreen those candidates to ensure they have the attributes needed to successfully perform in our environment.

"We work very closely with an ad agency to assist us in preparing the ad and to provide advice on the marketing strategies of where and when to place the ad. They save you a lot of time, especially when they understand your business. Running our ads for a particular position yields us other qualified candidates for other positions we had not counted on.

"Many of our ads yield as many as 250 résumés. Based on the competencies required for a position, we prescreen the résumés. It is not uncommon for me to receive over 50 phone calls per day when an ad is running. If I can delegate some of those calls, I do; however, if they have asked me for something specific, I make an effort to call them back because they are our customers and they are important to us. Once I have determined a short list, I then conduct a pretty thorough telephone interview before bringing in any candidates. Questions regarding salary expectations, any information that may be missing on the résumé, and some very job-specific questions are reviewed. We are always looking to improve our systems. Our next ad will incorporate a Voice Response System that has been developed internally by our Information Services Department. Candidates who wish to apply to an ad will be asked to call our system and respond to some basic job-related questions. At the end of the session, the candidate will be advised whether they possess the basic requirements of the job and whether they should apply to this position.

"The questions we ask during the face-to-face interview are open-ended questions that look for behavioural attributes specific to the competencies and key job requirements. For example, we want the candidates to demonstrate how they have gone about performing their job duties in the past. For those candidates who proceed to a final interview, we ask each of them to complete a Communications Survey. Using an outside consultant, we have developed a Prediction Performance Program Profile that has identified benchmark attributes for our buyers, merchandising trainees, and store managers. The results are graphed and compared against the benchmark. This profile is not used as a basis for determining whether we should hire a candidate or not. It provides us with another opportunity to fully assess the individual's capabilities by asking more focused questions. In this way, it ensures that we have fully investigated the individual's background and credentials. We provide each of our candidates with a written assessment of the report, whether they are hired or not, and ask them to comment on the accuracy of the results. Based on these responses, the report has been assessed at an accuracy of over 90 percent."

Peacock says in closing: "Systems in the workplace will continue to change, but the bottom line is that we need the best people to technically do the job and, most importantly, they must be customer focused."

compliance with various laws and regulations. For scientific, professional, and managerial jobs, a more extended form is likely to be used.

Even when applicants come armed with elaborate résumés, it is important that they complete an application form early in the process. Individuals often exaggerate or overstate their qualifications on a résumé (see Ethics in HRM). As shown in Figure 5.4, misstatements on application forms can be pretty humorous—but they can also result in dismissal. An HR manager who misrepresented his experience in his application to Bourgault Industries, a farm equipment manufacturer in Saskatchewan, was dismissed, and the courts upheld the employer's decision. One technique for anticipating problems of misrepresentation is to ask applicants to transcribe specific résumé material onto a standardized application form. The applicant is then asked to sign a statement that the information contained on the form is true and that he or she accepts the employer's right to terminate the candidate's employment if any of the information is subsequently found to be false.[8]

WWW

Many managers don't exactly understand which questions they can ask on an application blank. Most know they should steer clear of issues such as age, race, marital status, and sexual orientation, but other issues are less clear to them. The following are some suggestions for putting together an application form:

- *Application date.* The applicant should date the application. This helps managers know when the form was completed, and gives them an idea of the time limit (e.g., one year) that the form should be on file.
- *Educational background.* The applicant should also provide grade school, high school, college, and university attendance—but not the dates attended, since that can be connected with age.
- *Experience.* Virtually any questions that focus on work experience related to the job are permissible.
- *Arrests and criminal convictions.* Questions about arrests, convictions, and criminal records are to be avoided. If bonding is a requirement, the individual can be asked if he or she is eligible.

Highlights in HRM

1   McDONALD'S RESTAURANTS EMPLOYMENT APPLICATION

McDONALD'S RESTAURANTS EMPLOYMENT APPLICATION

PERSONAL INFORMATION

Date: _____
D   M   Y

Name: _____   Phone:(_____) _____
Last   First   Middle

Present
address: _____   How long there? _____
No. & Street   City   Province   Postal Code

Position Applied for: _____   Are you presently employed? ☐ Yes ☐ No   Date of availability: _____

Have you ever worked for McDonald's before? ☐ Yes ☐ No   If so, where? _____

If you are under 16, please state your age*: _____   Referred by: _____
*Please Note: You may be required to provide proof of age prior to hire.

Have you ever been convicted of a criminal ☐ Yes ☐ No   Are you legally entitled to work in Canada? ☐ Yes ☐ No
offense for which you have not been pardoned?   (You may be required to provide proof of employment status prior to hire.)

AVAILABILITY

HOURS AVAILABLE	MONDAY	TUESDAY	WEDNESDAY	THURSDAY	FRIDAY	SATURDAY	SUNDAY
FROM							
TO							

EMPLOYMENT BACKGROUND
List your present or last position first

DATE MONTH & YEAR	COMPANY NAME & ADDRESS	TELEPHONE NUMBER INCLUDING AREA CODE	NAME AND POSITION OF SUPERVISOR	YOUR POSITION	SALARY/WAGE START I END	REASON FOR LEAVING
FROM						
TO						
FROM						
TO						
FROM						
TO						

I declare that the information contained in this application is correct to the best of my knowledge and understand that any omission or incorrect information is just cause for the rejection of my application or dismissal in accordance with the Company policy. If hired, I understand that I may be transferred to another restaurant because of promotions, training or staffing requirements. I also agree that, at all times, I will follow the rules and regulations of the Company. I authorize the Company, or its agents, to verify the information provided, and to obtain any other information relevant to this application. This information may be obtained by telephone or in writing from educational institutions, my current or former employers, financial institutions, personal information agents and my personal references. This consent is valid during the consideration of my application for employment, and if I am hired, for the duration of my employment.

SIGNATURE: _____   DATE: _____

To the applicant:
Your application will be considered active for 90 days, after which you must submit a new application. The information which you have supplied, and any other information obtained, will be used solely for the assessment of your application for employment. Your application will be kept by the Management Team and, if you are hired, it will become part of your employee file. Your file will be retained in the Manager's office, and may be accessed by Management. You may access your file by appointment with a representative of the Company. If there are mistakes in your file, you have the right to ask for them to be corrected.

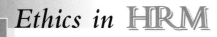

Ethics in HRM

WRITING IT WRONG

Most candidates for white-collar jobs prepare a résumé and submit it to prospective employers. They also complete the application form, answering questions required by employers for comparison purposes. Some recruitment agencies noticed during the last recession that résumé padding increased. Applicants were "stretching" the dates of their employment, misleading employers about the nature of their duties, and misrepresenting their salaries. While you are writing a résumé, adding three months to your previous employment, saying you were a night auditor instead of clerk, and adding $950 to your last salary seem like relatively harmless lies.

What are the facts? Studies of "creative" résumé writing indicate that about 30 percent of résumés report incorrect dates, 11 percent misrepresent reasons for leaving, and others exaggerate education attainments or omit criminal records. The probability is that about two-thirds of employers check references. Some former employers give only dates of employment and previous salary ranges.

Most organizations require you to sign a statement saying that the information you supply is true, and that if it is not you will be dismissed. Some cases of résumé padding have been heavily publicized. A Toronto Stock Exchange manager was dismissed for lying about having a master's degree. A member of Parliament listed an ILB on his résumé, which normally stands for International Baccalaureate of Law, but which he claimed stood for Incomplete Baccalaureate of Law. In one heart-wrenching case, a person who was ready to retire was found to have lied about his age decades earlier to get a job. On discovery, he was dismissed and lost his pension plan.

Would you pad your résumé?

Source: J. Schilder, "Trial by Hire," *Human Resource Professional 11*, no. 2 (March 1994): 21–3.

- *Country of citizenship.* Such questions are not permitted. It is allowable to ask the applicant if he or she is legally entitled to work in Canada.
- *References.* It is both permissible and advisable that the names, addresses, and phone numbers of references be provided (see below).
- *Disabilities.* Employers should avoid asking applicants if they have physical disabilities or health problems, if they have ever received psychiatric care or been hospitalized, or if they have received workers' compensation.[9]

Many of these issues will be addressed again, mainly in the section on employment interviews.

Biographical Information Blanks

One of the oldest methods for predicting job success uses biographical information about job applicants. As early as 1917, the Life Insurance Agency Management Association constructed and validated a biographical information blank (BIB) for

FIGURE 5.4 *True Lies and the Application Blank*

Some job seekers make silly mistakes or misguided attempts at humour when applying for a job. Here are some real-life examples:

In the "Intentionally/Accidentally Humorous" category:

- It's best for employers that I not work with people.
- Trustworthy references on request—if I give them a few bucks.
- Am a perfectionist and rarely if ever make mistakes.
- 1881 to 1994—Became top sales producer in office.
- You'll want me to be the Head Honcho in no time.
- Objective: Active interface with fellow Homo sapiens.
- If you hire me away from this nightmare, you'll save me thousands in therapy.

In the "Correct Spelling—Wrong Word" category:

- After receiving advice from several different angels, I decide to pursue a new line of work.
- Accounting cleric.
- As indicted, I have over five years of analyzing investments.
- I have 12 years of experience worming in the industry.
- Education: Statistics mayor.

Source: Examples are from several companies, including Robert Half International. "Beware of Resumania," *Personnel Journal,* April 1996: 28. Reprinted with permission.

life insurance salespeople. BIBs cover such issues as family life, hobbies, club memberships, sales experience, and investments. Responses to questions about these issues have been found to predict success on the job.

Like application blanks, BIBs reveal information about a person's history that may have shaped his or her behaviour. Sample questions from a BIB might include these:

- At what age did you leave home?
- How large was the town/city where you lived as a child?
- Did you ever build a model airplane that flew?
- Were sports a big part of your childhood?
- Do you play any musical instruments?

Both BIBs and application forms can be scored like tests. Because biographical questions rarely have obviously right or wrong answers, BIBs are difficult to fake. The development of a scoring system requires that the items that are valid predictors of job success be identified, and that weights be established for different responses to these items. By totalling the scores for each item, it is possible to obtain a composite score on the BIB as a whole for each applicant. Studies have shown that when BIBs and application forms are used together, and used objectively, they are one of the most accurate methods for predicting job success. This method has been useful in predicting all types of behaviour, including employee theft.[10]

Background Investigations

WWW

When the interviewer is satisfied that the applicant has possibilities, information about previous employment is investigated, as well as other information provided by the applicant. Former employers, school and college/university officials, credit bureaux, and individuals named as references may be contacted to verify pertinent information such as type of job, length of time on the job, quality of performance, highest wages, academic degrees earned, and credit rating. Most of this information is now readily available on existing computer databases.[11] Figure 5.5 shows the results of a Society for Human Resource Management (SHRM) study on how managers check applicants' backgrounds.

Checking References

Over two-thirds of Canadian employers use reference checks when hiring people for some jobs.[12] Not only are more companies checking references, but they are asking for more than the standard three references.[13] Some are asking for as many as *fifteen* from a variety of people who have interacted with the candidate: superiors, subordinates, peers, and clients. In addition, private companies that check references for a fixed fee are growing. The most common way of soliciting this information is by telephone. References are checked to confirm information provided by the applicant. For example, former employers most commonly confirm employment dates, specific job duties, previous job performance, and reason for leaving.

References are commonly used to screen and select employees, but problems can arise when they are used to predict employee performance. Written letters of reference are notorious for being inflated, and this limits their validity. Generally, telephone checks are preferable because they save time and allow for greater candour. The most reliable information usually comes from supervisors, who are best positioned to report on an applicant's work habits and performance. It is often advisable, however, to obtain written verification of information relating to job titles, duties, and pay levels from the former employer's HR office.[14]

The 1982 Canadian Charter of Rights and Freedoms gave individuals greater access to personal information about themselves. Managers are often reluctant to

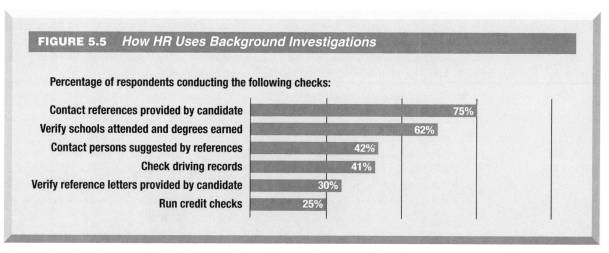

FIGURE 5.5   *How HR Uses Background Investigations*

Percentage of respondents conducting the following checks:

Contact references provided by candidate	75%
Verify schools attended and degrees earned	62%
Contact persons suggested by references	42%
Check driving records	41%
Verify reference letters provided by candidate	30%
Run credit checks	25%

Source: Reprinted with permission of the Society for Human Resource Management, Alexandria, VA.

place incriminating information in an employee's file for fear that the employee will access that information and misconstrue its intent. Since some information obtained on a reference check may not be positive, most employers prefer using the telephone to check references.

Inadequate reference checking can contribute to high turnover, employee theft, and white-collar crime. By using sources besides former employers, organizations can obtain valuable information about an applicant's character and habits. To reduce the risk of negligent hiring and to help employers screen out applicants with false résumés, several Canadian court decisions have recommended that reference checks be conducted. American courts have awarded millions of dollars in damages as a result of of slanderous statements made by former employers during reference checks; in contrast, there have been almost no cases in Canada involving defamation in employment settings. Most employers are aware that there could be a spillover of American practice into Canada, and so are cautious about how they handle reference checks. Employers who provide inaccurate and negative references may face fairly large financial penalties as a result of wrongful dismissal actions.[15] Checking is important. KPMG, in their investigations, found that in 50 percent of cases of alleged fraud, the suspect lied on the résumé.

WWW

Requiring Signed Requests for References

As a legal protection to all concerned, it is important to ask the applicant to fill out forms permitting information to be solicited from former employers and other reference sources. The Ontario Consumer Reporting Act, for example, prohibits employers from seeking references unless the candidate has provided written permission, and an employer must inform the candidate when a negative reference is provided. Understandably, many organizations are reluctant to put into writing evaluations of former employees. Firms are wary of being sued by former employees who discover that they have been given poor recommendations. As a result of such fears, some employers even hesitate to answer questions and/or verify information about former employees over the phone.

Using Credit Reports

The use of consumer credit reports by employers as a basis for establishing an applicant's eligibility for employment has become more restricted. For positions of trust, such as those involving the handling of financial instruments in banks and other financial institutions, credit reports must be used. Applicants must agree in writing to a credit report and have the right to review its contents. More important, the reason for the credit report must be job-related.

Polygraph Tests

A polygraph, or lie detector, is a device that measures the changes in respiration, blood pressure, and pulse of the person being questioned. It consists of a rubber tube around the chest, a cuff around the arm, and sensors attached to the fingers; these record the physiological changes in the examinee as the examiner asks questions that call for an answer of yes or no. Questions typically cover such items as whether a person uses drugs, has stolen from an employer, or has committed a serious undetected crime. In British Columbia, Verax Consulting uses polygraph testing for several Vancouver employers. In Ontario and New Brunswick, the use of lie detector tests for employment purposes is prohibited under the Employment

---

FIGURE 5.6 *Integrity Test Question Example*

TO TEST TENDENCY TO	DESCRIPTION
Protect	Contains items that require individuals to indicate whether they would protect friends or co-workers who had engaged in counterproductive behaviours. *Example:* I would turn in a fellow worker I saw stealing money.
Be lenient	Contains items in which test takers indicate whether they would be lenient with respect to the wrongdoings of others. *Example:* An employee should be fired if the employer finds out the employee lied on the application blank.
Admit thought	Includes items that require test takers to indicate the degree to which they would engage in counterproductive thoughts or behaviours. *Example:* I've thought about taking money from an employer without actually doing it.
Admit behaviour	Contains items in which individuals admit to directly participating in actual counterproductive behaviouurs. *Example:* Over the last three years, what's the total amount of money you've taken without permission from your employer?
Consider common	Includes items that require the individual to indicate the extent to which theft and other misbehaviours are common. *Example:* Most people I've worked with have stolen something at one time or another.
Excuse	Contains items in which individuals indicate whether there are excuses or justifications for stealing or performing other questionable behaviours. *Example:* Someone who steals because his family is in need should not be treated the same as a common thief.
Lie	Contains items that measure the extent to which the test taker is responding in a socially desirable manner.

Source: Stephen Dwight and George Alliger, "Reactions to overt integrity test items," *Educational and Psychological Measurements* 57, no. 6 (December 1997): 937–48, copyright © 1997 by Sage Publications, Inc. Reprinted with the permission of Sage Publications, Inc.

Standards Act.[16] Before considering using polygraphs, staffing officers should check provincial legislation.

Honesty and Integrity Tests

Many employers have dramatically increased their use of pencil-and-paper honesty and integrity tests. These tests are often used in settings such as retail stores, where employees have access to cash or merchandise. Common areas of inquiry include beliefs about the frequency and extent of theft in our society, the punishment for theft, and the perceived ease of theft. Payless ShoeSource has used paper-and-pencil honesty tests to reduce employee theft. When the company began its program, losses in its 4,700 stores totalled nearly US$21 million per year. Within a year of implementing its screening program, inventory shrinkage fell by 20 percent, to less than 1 percent of sales. The Nordstrom department store also uses an integrity test, called the Reid Survey, which takes about fifteen minutes to complete. Vice-president of HR Joe Demarte contends that with the Reid Survey, the company has about a 90 percent chance of screening out undesirable candidates.[17]

The Reid test is also being used in Canada, for example, by the Real Canadian Superstore in British Colombia and by Sobey's in Elmsdale, Nova Scotia. However, these tests are being challenged by both applicants and civil liberties groups. Items that might be used on an integrity test are shown in Figure 5.6. A comprehensive analysis of honesty tests reveals that they are valid for predicting job performance as well as a wide range of disruptive behaviours such as theft, absenteeism, and disciplinary problems.[18] Nevertheless, HRM specialists should use the results from these tests very cautiously and certainly in conjunction with other sources of information.

Graphology

Graphology, a term that refers to a variety of systems of handwriting analysis, is used by some employers to make employment decisions. Graphologists obtain a sample of handwriting and then examine such characteristics as the size and slant of letters, the amount of pressure applied, and the placement of the writing on the page. From their observations, graphologists draw inferences about such things as the writer's personality traits, intelligence, energy level, organizational abilities, creativity, integrity, emotional maturity, self-image, people skills, and entrepreneurial tendencies. Graphology is used extensively in France, Germany, Switzerland, Israel, and the United Kingdom in making employment decisions.[19] Companies such as Ford and General Electric have used it for selection.

Organizations that use handwriting analysis say they prefer it to typical personality tests because it only requires that job candidates take a few minutes to jot down a short essay. In contrast, a battery of personality tests and interviews with psychologists can take several hours and cost thousands of dollars. The available evidence shows that graphology is a reliable predictor of personality compared to other psychological tests. However, its predictive validity for job performance and occupational success remains questionable. In the academic community, where formal and rigorous validity studies are customary, the use of graphology for employment decisions has been viewed with considerable skepticism.[20]

EMPLOYMENT TESTS

The formal introduction of psychological selection techniques into the Canadian Army in 1941 represented both a pragmatic response to the exigencies of war and an attempt to make selection processes more democratic. Prior to 1941, entry into officer training was often based on social rank or monetary favours (as opposed to proven ability). Because of the practical need for efficiency, and to reduce selection errors, new selection procedures were adopted to optimize the use of "manpower." This in turn led to the establishment of selection and assessment centres in Canada.

Tests have played a more important part in government HR programs, in which hiring on the basis of merit is required by law. With their testing programs, government agencies have faced the same types of problems as organizations in the private sector. However, their staffs have been forced to improve their testing programs rather than abandon them. The federal government has a highly regarded testing program, which is administered by the Personnel Psychology Centre of the Public Service Commission.

Many organizations use professional test consultants to improve their testing programs and to meet human rights requirements. While it is often advisable to use consultants—especially if an organization is considering the use of personality tests—managers should have a basic understanding of the technical aspects of testing and the contributions that tests can make to the HR program.

Nature of Employment Tests

An employment test is an objective and standardized measure of a sample of behaviour that is used to gauge a person's knowledge, skills, abilities, and other characteristics (KSAOs) in relation to other individuals.[21] The proper sampling of behaviour—whether verbal, manipulative, or some other type—is the responsibility of the test author. It is also the responsibility of the test author to develop tests that meet accepted standards of reliability.[22] Data about reliability are ordinarily presented in the test manual. High reliability is essential, but offers no assurance that the test provides the basis for making valid judgments. It is the responsibility of the HR staff to conduct validation studies before adopting a test for regular use. Other considerations are cost, time, ease of administration and scoring, and the apparent relevance of the test to the individuals being tested (commonly referred to as "face validity"). Face validity is desirable but is no substitute for technical validity, described earlier in this chapter. Adopting a test just because it appears relevant is bad practice; many a "good-looking" test has poor validity.

Classification of Employment Tests

Employment tests can be classified in different ways. Generally, they are viewed as measuring either aptitude or achievement. **Aptitude tests** measure a person's capacity to learn or acquire skills. **Achievement tests** measure what a person knows or can do right now.

Aptitude tests

Measures of a person's capacity to learn or acquire skills

Achievement tests

Measures of what a person knows or can do right now

Cognitive Ability Tests

Cognitive ability tests measure mental capabilities such as general intelligence, verbal fluency, numerical ability, and reasoning ability. There are a host of paper-and-pencil tests that measure cognitive abilities, including the General Aptitude Test Battery (GATB), the Scholastic Aptitude Test (SAT), the Graduate Management Aptitude Test (GMAT), and the Bennett Mechanical Comprehension Test. Figure 5.7 shows some items that could be used to measure different cognitive abilities. The Canadian Forces use cognitive testing in selecting applicants.

Although cognitive ability tests can be developed to measure very specialized areas such as reading comprehension and spatial relations, many experts believe that the validity of cognitive ability tests simply reflects their connection to general

WWW

FIGURE 5.7   *Sample Measures of Cognitive Ability*

Verbal

1. What is the meaning of the word "surreptitious"?
   - a. covert
   - b. winding
   - c. lively
   - d. sweet

2. How is the noun clause used in the following sentence? "I hope that I can learn this game."
   - a. subject
   - b. predicate nominative
   - c. direct object
   - d. object of the preposition

Quantitative

3. Divide 50 by 0.5 and add 5. What is the result?
   - a. 25
   - b. 30
   - c. 95
   - d. 105

4. What is the value of 144^2?
   - a. 12
   - b. 72
   - c. 288
   - d. 20736

Reasoning

5. _____ is to boat as snow is to _____ .
   - a. Sail, ski
   - b. Water, winter
   - c. Water, ski
   - d. Engine, water

6. Two women played 5 games of chess. Each woman won the same number of games, yet there were no ties. How can this be?
   - a. There was a forfeit.
   - b. One player cheated.
   - c. They played different people.
   - d. One game is still in progress.

Mechanical

7. If gear A and gear C are both turning counterclockwise, what is happening to gear B?
   - a. It is turning counterclockwise.
   - b. It is turning clockwise.
   - c. It remains stationary.
   - b. The whole system will jam.

A   B   C

Answers: 1. a, 2. c, 3. d, 4. d, 5. c, 6. c, 7. b

intelligence. Measures of general intelligence (e.g., IQ tests) have been shown to be good predictors of performance across a wide variety of jobs.[23]

Personality and Interest Inventories

Cognitive ability tests measure a person's mental capacity; in contrast, personality tests measure dispositional characteristics such as extroversion, inquisitiveness, and dependability. The predictive validity of personality and interest inventories histor-

FIGURE 5.8 *Potentially Discriminatory Items on a Personality Test*

The following are items taken from an actual personality test. Used for selecting employees, the items might unintentionally discriminate against certain individuals.

1. Do you prefer to associate with people younger than yourself?

2. When you are in low spirits, do you try to find someone to cheer you up?

3. Do you ever argue a point with an older person whom you respect?

4. Do ideas run through your head so that you cannot sleep?

5. Have you ever had dizzy spells?

6. Do you tend to be radical in your political, religious, or social beliefs?

7. Do your feelings alternate between happiness and sadness without apparent reason?

8. Do you feel that marriage is essential to your present or future happiness?

9. Are you usually considered to be indifferent to the opposite sex?

10. Would you like to be a church worker?

11. Would you like to be a minister, priest, or rabbi?

12. Would you like to read the Bible as a way of having fun?

13. Would you like to have day-to-day contact with religious people?

14. Would you like to have day-to-day contact with very old people?

15. Are you concerned about philosophical problems such as religion, the meaning of life, etc.?

Source: Daniel P.O"Merara, "Personality Tests Raises Questions of Legality and Effectiveness," *HRMagazine*, January 1994, 97–100. Reprinted with permission of the Society for Human Resource Management, Alexandria, VA.

ically has been quite low.[24] And, as shown in Figure 5.8, personality tests raise problems if they inadvertently discriminate against individuals who would otherwise perform effectively. With some personality characteristics, it is not always easy to demonstrate job-relatedness and validity. The use of personality tests can also be seen as an invasion of privacy. For example, Target Stores, a retail chair, recently stopped using the Minnesota Multiphasic Personality Inventory (MMPI) and the California Psychological Inventory (CPI) as pre-employment screening devices because they asked employees questions about their political views, belief in God, homosexuality, and bodily functions.[25]

Personality and interest inventories may be most useful for helping with occupational selection and career planning. Interest tests such as the Kuder Inventory measure an applicant's preferences for certain activities over others (such as sailing versus poker).

Physical Ability Tests

Employers often need to assess a person's physical abilities. The Human Rights Code states that the test must be a bona fide occupational qualification of the job, which means that the test must duplicate the physical requirements of the job. Especially for demanding and potentially dangerous jobs like firefighter and police officer, physical abilities such as strength and endurance tend to be good predictors, not only of performance but also of accidents and injuries.[26]

WWW

Despite their potential value, physical ability tests tend to work to the disadvantage of women and people with disabilities. For example, applicants who take the RCMP's Physical Fitness Abilities Requirement Evaluation (PARE) are required to run 350 metres, complete a standing broad jump of about 2 metres, and pick up and carry a heavy bag for 15 metres. According to one RCMP officer, "If you're a bigger person, the PARE test is easier, no doubt." The fact that women fail the test in greater numbers than men has resulted in a complaint before the Canadian Human Rights Commission. The RCMP is defending the PARE test on the grounds that it simulates common police activities such as chasing a suspect on foot, carrying an injured person, and forcing open a door.[27] As with other methods for screening potential employees, the use of physical ability tests should be carefully validated on the basis of the essential functions of the job.[28]

Job Knowledge Tests

Government agencies and licensing boards usually develop job knowledge tests. These are achievement tests designed to measure a person's level of understanding about a particular job. Most public service examinations are used to determine whether the applicant possesses the information and understanding that will permit placement on the job without further training.[29] Job knowledge tests are part of the certification process for accountants and HR professionals. They should be considered as useful tools for private and public organizations.

Job Sample Tests

Job sample tests, or work sample tests, require the applicant to perform tasks that are actually a part of the work required on the job. Like job knowledge tests, job sample tests are constructed from a carefully developed outline that experts agree includes the major job functions; the tests are thus considered content-valid. They

For jobs that are physically demanding or potentially dangerous, employers need to assess the physical abilities of job candidates.

are often used to measure skills for office and clerical jobs. Job sample tests have also been devised for many diverse jobs: there are map-reading tests for traffic control officers, lathe tests for machine operators, complex coordination tests for pilots, in-basket tests for managers, group discussion tests for supervisors, judgment and decision-making tests for administrators, and spelling, punctuation, and grammar tests for copy editors. The Public Service Commission uses an in-basket test for selecting managers. This type of test is reported to be cost-effective, reliable, valid, fair, and acceptable to applicants.[30]

THE EMPLOYMENT INTERVIEW

Traditionally, the employment interview has played a very important role in the selection process—so much so that it is rare to find an employee who was hired without some sort of interview. Depending on the type of job, applicants may be interviewed by one person, by members of a work team, or by other individuals in the organization. While researchers have raised some doubts about the validity of interviews, they remain a mainstay of selection because (1) they are especially practical when there are only a small number of applicants; (2) they serve other purposes, such as public relations; and (3) interviewers maintain great faith and confidence in their judgments. The downside is that interviews can be plagued with problems of subjectivity and personal bias. In such cases, some interviewers' judgments are more valid than those of others in the evaluation of applicants.[31]

Interviewing Methods

Interview methods differ in several ways, most significantly in the amount of structure, or control, exercised by the interviewer. In highly structured interviews, the interviewer determines the course the interview will follow as each question is asked. In less structured interviews, the applicant plays a larger role in determining the course of the discussion. An examination of the different types of interviews from the least structured to the most structured will reveal the differences.

The Nondirective Interview

Nondirective interview

An interview in which the applicant is allowed the maximum amount of freedom in determining the course of the discussion, while the interviewer carefully refrains from influencing the applicant's remarks

In a **nondirective interview**, the interviewer carefully refrains from influencing the applicant's remarks. The applicant is allowed the maximum amount of freedom to determine the course of the discussion. The interviewer asks broad, open-ended questions—such as "Tell me more about your experiences on your last job"—and permits the applicant to talk freely with a minimum of interruption. Generally, the nondirective interviewer listens carefully and does not argue, interrupt, or change the subject abruptly. The interviewer uses follow-up questions to allow the applicant to elaborate, makes only brief responses, and allows pauses in the conversation. The pausing technique is the most difficult one for the beginning interviewer to master.

The greater freedom afforded to the applicant in a nondirective interview is especially valuable in bringing to the interviewer's attention any information, attitudes, or feelings that may be concealed by more structured questioning. However, because the applicant determines the course of the interview and no set procedure is followed, little information that comes from these interviews enables interviewers to cross-check agreement with other interviewers. As can be expected, the reliability and validity of the nondirective interview are minimal. This method is most often used in interviewing candidates for high-level positions and in counselling (see Chapter 13).

The Structured Interview

Structured interview

An interview in which a set of standardized questions having an established set of answers is used

More attention is being given to structured interviews as a result of employment equity requirements and a concern for maximizing the validity of selection decisions.[32] Because a **structured interview** has a set of standardized questions (based on job analysis) and an established set of answers against which applicant responses can be rated, it provides a more consistent basis for evaluating job candidates. For example, staff members of Weyerhauser Company's HR department have developed a structured interviewing process with the following characteristics:

1. The interview process is based exclusively on job duties and requirements critical to job performance.

2. It uses four types of questions: situational questions, job knowledge questions, job sample/simulation questions, and worker requirements questions.

3. There are sample answers, determined in advance, to each question, and interviewee responses are rated on a five-point scale explicitly defined in advance.

WWW

4. The process involves an interview committee so that interviewee responses are evaluated by several raters.

5. It consistently follows the same procedures in all instances to ensure that each applicant has exactly the same chance as every other applicant.

6. The interview is documented for future reference and in case of legal challenge.[33]

A structured interview is more likely to provide the type of information needed for making sound decisions. It also helps reduce the possibility of legal charges of unfair discrimination. Employers must be aware that interviews are highly vulnerable to legal attack and that more litigation in this area can be expected in the future.

Most employment interviewers tend toward either a nondirected or a structured format. However, interviewers can utilize other methods for special purposes.

The Situational Interview

Situational interview

An interview in which an applicant is given a hypothetical incident and asked how he or she would respond to it

One variation of the structured interview is the **situational interview**.[34] With this approach, an applicant is given a hypothetical incident and asked how he or she would respond to it. The applicant's response is then evaluated relative to pre-established benchmark standards. The interview can be conducted by telephone; for example, Royal Bank screens applicants by phone. Candidates replying to a newspaper ad are asked to call a telephone number; having called it, they are prompted by an electronic interactive system to answer questions about work experience, as well as situational questions such as, "Tell me about a time when you encountered a particularly difficult customer. What did you do?"

Interestingly, many organizations are using situational interviews to select new college and university graduates. Highlights in HRM 2 shows a sample question from a situational interview that is being used to select systems analysts at a chemical plant.

The Behavioural Description Interview

Behavioural description interview (BDI)

An interview in which an applicant is asked questions about what he or she actually did in a given situation

Like to a situational interview, a **behavioural description interview (BDI)** focuses on real work incidents. However, while situational interviews address hypothetical situations, the BDI format asks the job applicant what he or she actually did in a given situation. For example, to assess a potential manager's ability to handle a problem employee, an interviewer might ask, "Tell me about the last time you disciplined an employee." Such an approach to interviewing assumes that past performance is the best predictor of future performance. It may be also less susceptible to candidate faking.

The Panel Interview

Panel interview

An interview in which a board of interviewers questions and observes a single candidate

In another type of interview, a panel of interviewers question and observe a single candidate. In a typical **panel interview**, the candidate meets with three to five interviewers, who take turns asking questions. After the interview, the interviewers pool their observations to reach a consensus about the suitability of the candidate. HRM specialists using this method report that panel interviews provide several significant advantages over traditional one-to-one interviews, including higher validity because of multiple inputs, greater acceptance of the decision, and shorter decision time.[35]

Highlights in HRM

2   SAMPLE SITUATIONAL INTERVIEW QUESTION

QUESTION

It is the night before your scheduled vacation. You are all packed and ready to go. Just before you get into bed, you receive a phone call from the plant. A problem has arisen that only you can handle. You are asked to come in to take care of things. What would you do in this situation?

RECORD ANSWER

_____

_____

_____

SCORING GUIDE

Good: "I would go in to work and make certain that everything is OK. Then I would go on vacation."

Good: "There are no problems that only I can handle. I would make certain that someone qualified was there to handle things."

Fair: "I would try to find someone else to deal with the problem."

Poor: "I would go on vacation."

The Computer Interview

More and more organizations have begun using computers in the interviewing process. For example, Nike has developed expert systems to gather preliminary information and compare candidates. Typically, the system asks the candidate a series of 75 to 125 multiple-choice questions tailored to the job and then compares those responses with either an ideal profile or with the profiles developed from other candidates' responses. The computer then generates a printed report comprising the applicant's response summary, an itemized list of contradictory responses, a latency response report (time delays for each answer), a summary of potentially problematic responses, and a list of structured interview questions for the job interviewer to ask.[36]

WWW

Bell Canada used the software package E Cruiter, developed by an Ottawa-based company, Career Bridge (**www.careerbridge.com**), to organize the thousands of résumés it receives and to prescreen candidates on-line.[36]

Some research evidence suggests that applicants may be less likely to engage in "impression management" in computerized interviews than in face-to-face interviews.[37] So far, organizations have used the computer mainly as a complement to, rather than as a replacement for, conventional interviews.

Guidelines for Employment Interviewers

Employers should carefully select the people doing the interviewing. Qualities that are desirable include humility; the ability to think objectively; maturity; and poise. Given the importance of diversity in the workforce, experience in associating with people from a variety of backgrounds is also desirable.

A Review of the Best

There have been several reviews of research studies on employment interviews.[38] Each of these reviews discusses and evaluates many studies concerned with questions such as, "What traits can be assessed in the interview?" and "How do interviewers reach their decisions?" Highlights in HRM 3 presents some of the major findings of these studies. Readers who are interested in a more comprehensive survey should consult Catano et al., *Recruitment and Selection in Canada* (2000).

Figure 5.9 summarizes the variables and processes involved in the employment interview. The figure shows that the perceptions of the interviewer, and thus the hiring decision, can be influenced by a number of the applicant's characteristics. Also, many interviewer and situational factors can influence the perceptual and judgmental processes. For example, the race and sex of the applicant can shape the expectations, biases, and behaviours of an interviewer; this in turn may affect the interview's outcome. Even a limited understanding of the variables shown in Figure 5.9 can improve the effectiveness of managers and supervisors when they conduct interviews.

Interviewer Training

It has been shown that training dramatically improves the competence of interviewers. One quick source for interviewer training is Curry Business Systems' Employment Interviewer Training Course. More of a review than a training program pe se, this site (**www.curryin.com**) is divided into five modules that review

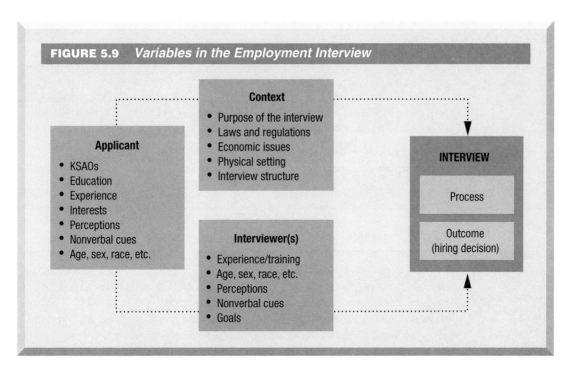

FIGURE 5.9 *Variables in the Employment Interview*

Context
- Purpose of the interview
- Laws and regulations
- Economic issues
- Physical setting
- Interview structure

Applicant
- KSAOs
- Education
- Experience
- Interests
- Perceptions
- Nonverbal cues
- Age, sex, race, etc.

Interviewer(s)
- Experience/training
- Age, sex, race, etc.
- Perceptions
- Nonverbal cues
- Goals

INTERVIEW

Process

Outcome
(hiring decision)

content, structure, planning, and legal issues. However, readers should exercise caution as it is based on American legal practices. A Canadian site that offers tips for job candidates is **www.littlegroup.com**.

Interviewer training programs should include practice interviews conducted under guidance. Practice interviews can be recorded on videotape and evaluated later in a group training session. Some variation in technique is only natural. Below are ten ground rules for employment interviews that are commonly accepted and supported by research findings. Their apparent simplicity should not lead one to underestimate their importance.

1. *Establish an interview plan.* Examine the purposes of the interview, and determine the areas and specific questions to be covered. Review job requirements, application form data, test scores, and other available information before seeing the applicant.

2. *Establish and maintain rapport.* This is accomplished by greeting the applicant pleasantly, by explaining the purpose of the interview, by displaying sincere interest in the applicant, and by listening carefully.

3. *Be an active listener.* Strive to understand, comprehend, and gain insight into what is only suggested or implied. A good listener's mind is alert, and face and posture usually reflect this fact.

4. *Pay attention to nonverbal cues.* An applicant's facial expressions, gestures, body position, and movements often provide clues to that person's attitudes and feelings. Interviewers should be aware of what they themselves are communicating nonverbally.

5. *Provide information as freely and honestly as possible.* Answer the applicant's questions fully and frankly. Present a realistic picture of the job.

Highlights in HRM

3   SOME MAJOR FINDINGS FROM RESEARCH STUDIES ON THE INTERVIEW

1. Structured interviews are more reliable than unstructured interviews.
2. Interviewers are influenced more by unfavourable than by favourable information.
3. Interrater reliability is increased when there is a greater amount of information about the job to be filled.
4. A bias is established early in the interview, and this tends to be followed by either a favourable or an unfavourable decision.
5. Intelligence is the trait most validly estimated by an interview, but the interview information adds nothing to test data.
6. Interviewers can explain why they feel that an applicant is likely to be an unsatisfactory employee, but not why the applicant may be satisfactory.
7. Factual written data seem to be more important than physical appearance in determining judgments. This increases with interviewing experience.
8. An interviewee is given a more extreme evaluation (positive/negative) when preceded by an interviewee of opposing value (positive/negative).
9. Interpersonal skills and motivation are probably best evaluated by the interview.
10. Allowing the applicant time to talk makes rapid first impressions less likely and provides a larger behaviour sample.
11. Nonverbal as well as verbal interactions influence decisions.
12. Experienced interviewers rank applicants in the same order, although they differ in the proportion that they will accept. There is a tendency for experienced interviewers to be more selective than less experienced ones.

6. *Use questions effectively.* To elicit a truthful answer, phrase questions as objectively as possible, giving no indication of what response is desired.

7. *Separate facts from inferences.* During the interview, record factual information. Later, record your inferences or interpretations of the facts. Compare your inferences with those of other interviewers.

8. *Recognize biases and stereotypes.* One typical bias is for interviewers to consider strangers who have interests, experiences, and backgrounds similar to their own to be more acceptable. Stereotyping involves forming generalized opinions of how people of a given gender, race, or ethnic background appear, think, feel, and act. The influence of sex role stereotyping is central to sex discrimination in employment. Avoid the influence of "beautyism." Discrimination against unattractive people is a persistent and pervasive form of employment discrimination. Also, avoid "halo error"—that is, judging an individual favourably or unfavourably overall on the basis of only one strong point (or weak point) on which you place high value.

9. *Control the course of the interview.* Establish an interview plan and stick to it. Provide the applicant with ample opportunity to talk, but maintain control of the situation in order to reach the interview objectives.

10. *Standardize the questions asked.* To increase reliability and avoid discrimination, ask the same questions of all applicants for a particular job. Keep careful notes; record facts, impressions, and any relevant information, including what was told to the applicant.

Types of Pre-employment Questions to Ask

The entire subject of pre-employment questioning is complex. Federal and provincial requirements sometimes vary in terms of the types of questions that may be asked during the interview. However, all jurisdictions forbid direct questions about race, sex, colour, age, religion, and national origin, and most look with disapproval on indirect questions dealing with the same topics. Some of the questions that interviewers once felt free to ask can be potentially hazardous. Human rights commissions have severely limited the areas of questioning. In general, if the question is job-related, is asked of everyone, and does not discriminate against a certain class of applicants, it is likely to be acceptable to government authorities.

Particular care has to be given to questions asked of female applicants about their family responsibilities. For example, it is inappropriate to ask, "Who will take care of your children while you are at work?" or "Do you plan to have children?" or "What is your husband's occupation?" or "Are you engaged?" In fact, it is inappropriate to ask applicants of either gender questions about matters that have no relevance to job performance.

Employers have found it advisable to provide interviewers with instructions on how to avoid potentially discriminatory questions in their interviews. The examples of appropriate and inappropriate questions shown in Highlights in HRM 4 can be used as guidelines for application forms as well as for pre-employment interviews. Complete guidelines can be developed from current information available the Canadian Human Rights Commission (**www.chrc–ccap.ca**). Once the individual is hired, the information needed but not asked for in the interview can be obtained if there is a valid need for it and if it does not lead to discrimination.

Medical Examination

A medical examination is generally given to ensure that the health and fitness of applicants is adequate to meet the job requirements. It also provides a baseline against which subsequent medical examinations can be compared and interpreted. The last objective is especially important for determining work-caused disabilities under workers' compensation law.

In the past, requirements for physical characteristics such as strength, agility, height, and weight were often determined by the employer's invalidated notions of what should be required. Many requirements that tend to discriminate against women have been questioned, and modified so as to represent typical job demands.

Medical examinations and inquiries about a candidate directed to medical professionals can be conducted only after an offer (preferably written) of employment has been made. The offer can be made conditional on the applicant's ability

Highlights in HRM

4 APPROPRIATE AND INAPPROPRIATE INTERVIEW QUESTIONS

	APPROPRIATE QUESTIONS	INAPPROPRIATE QUESTIONS
National or ethnic origin	Are you legally entitled to work in Canada?	Where were you born?
Age	Have you reached the minimum or maximum age for work, as defined by the law?	How old are you?
Sex	How would you like to be referred to during the interview?	What are your child care arrangements?
Marital status	As travel is part of the requirements of our position, would you foresee any problems meeting this obligation?	What does your spouse do for a living? Is there travel involved? Who takes care of the children when you are away?
Disabilities	Do you have any conditions that could affect your ability to do the job?	Do you use drugs or alcohol?
Height and weight	(Ask nothing)	How tall are you? How much do you weigh?
Address	What is your address?	What were your addresses outside Canada?
Religion	Would you be able to work the following schedules?	What are your religious beliefs?
Criminal record	Our job requires that our employees be bonded. Are you bondable?	Have you ever been arrested?
Affiliations	As an engineer, are you a member of the engineering society?	What religious associations do you belong to?

to perform the essential duties of the job as determined by a job-related medical examination. Any medical inquiries must be directly related to assessing the candidate's abilities to perform the essential duties of the job.[39] This allows the applicant with a disability the opportunity to be considered exclusively on merits during the selection process. Before human rights legislation was introduced, employers would screen out applicants with disabilities based on medical information requested on application forms or obtained through pre-employment medical examinations. These methods are now deemed discriminatory.

An employer may ask a candidate if she or he has any disability-related needs that would require accommodation to enable performance of the essential duties of the job. The interviewer should be cautioned about probing as to the nature of the disability. Later employment-related decisions may be perceived to be based on this information and thereby characterized as discriminatory. To ensure neutrality, and to avoid the possibility of a complaint to the Canadian Human Rights Commission, such information should remain exclusively with the examining physician, not in the personnel file.

If the employee has a disability, the employer has a duty to accommodate his or her needs. The accommodation can be accomplished either by changing some of the essential duties of the position or by providing the appropriate equipment. To determine whether an individual can do the essential duties of a particular position, the employer should conduct a physical demands analysis, checklists for which are available through most provincial ministries of labour.[40]

As mentioned earlier, requirements for physical characteristics such as height were in the past often determined by an employer's notion of what *should* be required. Under human rights legislation, employers are prohibited from imposing their own standards where it has the effect of excluding members of the designated groups, unless it can be shown that the requirements are reasonable and bona fide. Such standards are often based on the vital statistics of the average white Anglo-Saxon male. There is little evidence to demonstrate that characteristics such as height and weight constitute bona fide occupational requirements.[41]

While there is much publicity about acquired immune deficiency syndrome (AIDS), employers are prohibited from subjecting job applicants to any type of medical testing for the presence of HIV.[42] Also, employers are required to accommodate the needs of people with disabilities such as AIDS by, for example, redefining work duties and implementing temporary work reassignments. Following are three occupational situations where the employer is considered justified in treating an employee with AIDS differently from other employees:

1. The individual carries out invasive procedures, such as surgery.

2. The individual is required to travel to countries where AIDS carriers are denied entry.

3. A sudden deterioration of the brain or central nervous system would compromise public safety.

Employers are becoming sensitive to this disease. This is reflected in the employee magazine supplement about HIV and AIDS published by Procter & Gamble. The supplement, "It's Time for Education, Not Denial," outlines the corporation's policy on AIDS, provides information about the disease, and includes interviews with leading experts from Canadian hospitals.[43]

Drug Testing

WWW

The Canadian Human Rights Commission and some of its provincial counterparts have issued policies on employment-related drug testing. The complete CHRC

1999 policy on drug testing can be found at **www.chrc–ccdp.ca/
legis&poli/drgpol**. Addiction to drugs or alcohol is considered a handicap, and
the employer is to be guided by legislation and by practices such as workplace
accommodation. The medical examination cannot be conducted until a conditional offer of employment is made in writing, and the examination can determine
only the individual's ability to perform the essential duties.

WWW

If the employer has established that drug testing is job-related—typically, this
involves safety issues—the candidate must be informed that job offers are conditional on the successful passing of a drug test, and that this test will be required
during the course of employment. The employer then has the right to demand a
medical examination. If an employee refuses, he or she can be dismissed. In one situation, a Canadian Pacific conductor who had been charged by the police with
cultivating marijuana (he had received a prior conviction for possession) was asked
by his employer to submit to a drug test. He refused. He was then terminated, and
the decision was upheld by an arbitrator.[44] Toronto-Dominion Bank, Imperial Oil,
and the Federal Transport Department all use drug testing,. All three are facing
court challenges over their policies.

There is widespread opposition to drug testing in the workplace, which is why
only about 2 percent of companies in Canada do it, compared to about 80 percent
of American companies. The Canadian Civil Liberties Association takes the position that "no person should be required to share urine with a stranger" as a condition of employment.[45] Employee Assistance Programs (EAPs) play an important
role in helping employees with drug and alcohol problems. EAPs will be discussed
in Chapter 12.

Figure 5.10 shows the relative popularity of various selection methods in
Canada.

REACHING A SELECTION DECISION

OBJECTIVE
5

While all steps in the selection process are important, the most critical step is the
decision to accept or reject the applicant. Because of the cost of placing new
employees on the payroll, the short probationary period in many organizations, and
human rights considerations, the final decision must be as sound as possible. Thus
it requires systematic consideration of all the relevant information about the applicants that has been gathered. It is common to use summary forms and checklists
to ensure that all pertinent information has been included in evaluations.

Summarizing Information about Applicants

Fundamentally, an employer is interested in what an applicant *can* do and *will* do.
An evaluation of candidates on the basis of assembled information should focus on
these two factors (see Figure 5.11). The "can do" factors include knowledge and
skills, as well as the aptitude (the potential) for acquiring new knowledge and skills.
The "will do" factors include motivation, interests, and various other personality
characteristics. Both factors are essential to successful performance on the job.
Employees who have the ability (can do) but who are not motivated to use it (will
not do) are little better than employees who lack the necessary ability.

It is much easier to measure what individuals *can* do than what they *will* do.
The can-do factors are readily evident from test scores and verified information.

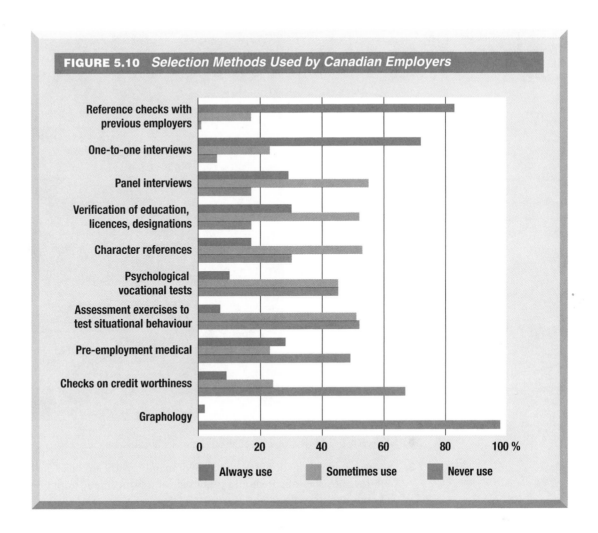

FIGURE 5.10 *Selection Methods Used by Canadian Employers*

Note: Some method percentages do not total to 100 percent because of rounding.
Source: Murray Axsmith and Associates, 1997.

What the individual will do can only be inferred. Responses to interview and application form questions can be used as a basis for making inferences about what an individual will do.

Decision Strategy

The strategy used for making personnel decisions for one category of jobs may differ from that used for other categories. For example, the strategy for selecting managerial and executive personnel will differ from the one used for selecting clerical and technical personnel. The following are only some of the questions that managers must consider:

1. Should the individuals be hired according to their highest potential or according to the needs of the organization?

Some employers use tests, such as keyboarding or Dictaphone, to help reach a selection decision.

2. At what grade or wage level should the individual be started?

3. Should initial selection be concerned mainly with an ideal match of the employee to the job, or should potential for advancement in the organization be considered?

4. To what extent should those who are not qualified but are qualifiable be considered?

5. Should overqualified individuals be considered?

6. What effect will a decision have on meeting employment equity plans and diversity considerations?

Managers must also consider which approach they will use in making hiring decisions. There are two basic approaches to selection: clinical (personal judgment) and statistical.[46]

Clinical Approach

In the clinical approach to decision making, those making the selection decision review all the data on applicants. Then, based on their understanding of the job and of the individuals who have been successful in that job, they make a decision. Different individuals often arrive at different decisions about an applicant when they use this approach, because each evaluator assigns different weights to the applicant's strengths and weaknesses. Furthermore, personal biases and stereotypes are often masked by what appear to be rational bases for acceptance or rejection.

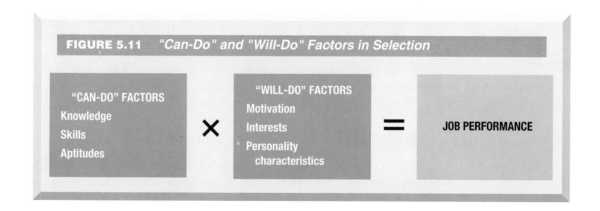

FIGURE 5.11   *"Can-Do" and "Will-Do" Factors in Selection*

| "CAN-DO" FACTORS
Knowledge
Skills
Aptitudes | × | "WILL-DO" FACTORS
Motivation
Interests
° Personality
  characteristics | = | JOB PERFORMANCE |

Statistical Approach

The statistical approach to decision making is more objective. It involves identifying the most valid predictors and weighting them through statistical methods such as multiple regression.[47] Quantified data such as scores or ratings from interviews, tests, and other procedures are then combined according to their weighted value. Candidates with the highest combined scores are then selected. A comparison of the clinical approach with the statistical approach in a wide variety of situations has shown that the statistical approach is superior. Although this superiority has been recognized for many decades, the clinical approach continues to be the one most commonly used.[48]

With a strictly statistical approach, a candidate's high score on one predictor (e.g., cognitive ability test) will make up for a low score on another predictor (e.g., the interview). For this reason, this model is called a **compensatory model**. However, it is often important that applicants achieve some minimum level of proficiency on all selection dimensions. When this is the case, a **multiple cutoff model** is used whereby only those candidates who score above the cutoff on *all* dimensions are considered. The selection decision is then made from that subset of candidates.

A variation on the multiple cutoff is the **multiple hurdle model**. This decision strategy is sequential, in that after candidates go through an initial evaluation stage, the ones who score well are provisionally accepted and are assessed further at each successive stage. This process can continue through several stages (hurdles) before a final decision is made about the candidates. This approach is especially useful when testing or training procedures are lengthy and expensive.

Each of the statistical approaches requires a decision to be made about where the cutoff lies—that point in the distribution of scores above which a person should be considered and below which the person should be rejected. The score the applicant must achieve is the cutoff score. Depending on the labour supply, it may be necessary to lower or raise the cutoff score.

While the most valid predictors should be used with any selection strategy, there is a related factor that contributes to selecting the best-qualified people. It is selectivity, or having an adequate number of applicants or candidates from which to make a selection. Selectivity is typically expressed in terms of a **selection ratio**, which is the ratio of the number of applicants to be selected to the total number of applicants. A ratio of 0.10, for example, means that 10 percent of the applicants will be selected. A ratio of 0.90 means that 90 percent will be selected. If the selection ratio is low, only the most promising applicants will normally be hired. When

Compensatory model

Selection decision model in which a high score in one area can make up for a low score in another area

Multiple cutoff model

Selection decision model that requires an applicant to achieve some minimum level of proficiency on all selection dimensions

Multiple hurdle model

A sequential strategy in which only the applicants with the highest scores at an initial test stage go on to subsequent stages

Selection ratio

The number of job applicants compared with the number of persons hired

the ratio is high, very little selectivity will be possible, since even applicants having mediocre ability will have to be hired if the vacancies are to be filled.

It should be noted that how much of a contribution any predictor will make to the improvement of a given selection process is a function not only of the validity of the predictor and the selection ratio, but also of the proportion of people who are judged successful using current selection procedures.[49]

Final Decision

After a preliminary selection has been made in the employment department, those applicants who seem to be most promising are then referred to departments that have vacancies. There they are interviewed by the managers or supervisors, who usually make the final decision and communicate it to the employment department. Because of the weight that is usually given to their choices, managers and supervisors should be trained so that their role in the selection process does not negate the more rigorous efforts of the HR department staff.

In large organizations, notifying applicants of the decision and making job offers is often the responsibility of the HR department. This department should confirm the details of the job, the working arrangements, the wages, and so on, and specify a deadline by which the applicant must reach a decision. If, at this point, findings from the medical examination are not yet available, an offer is often made contingent on the applicant's passing the examination.

In government agencies, the selection of individuals to fill vacancies is made from lists or registers of eligible candidates. Ordinarily, three or more names of individuals at the top of the register are submitted to the requisitioning official. This arrangement provides some latitude for those making a selection, and at the same time preserves the merit system.

SUMMARY

 OBJECTIVE 1 The selection process should provide as much reliable and valid information as possible about applicants so that their qualifications can be carefully matched with job specifications. The information that is obtained should be clearly job-related or predictive of success on the job and free from potential discrimination. *Reliability* refers to the consistency of test scores over time and across measures. *Validity* refers to the accuracy of measurement. Validity can be assessed in terms of whether the measurement is based on a job specification (content validity), whether test scores correlate with performance criteria (predictive validity), and whether the test accurately measures what it purports to measure (construct validity).

 OBJECTIVE 2 Interviews are customarily used in conjunction with application forms, biographical information blanks, references, background investigations, cognitive ability tests, job knowledge tests, and work sample tests.

 OBJECTIVE 3 The popularity of tests declined somewhat with the passage of human rights laws, but in recent years there has been a dramatic resurgence of testing. The value of tests should not be overlooked, since they are more objective than interviews and can provide a broader sampling of behaviour. Cognitive ability tests are especially valuable for assessing verbal, quantitative, and reasoning abilities. Personality and interest

tests are perhaps best for placement. Physical ability tests are most useful for predicting job performance, accidents, and injuries, especially for demanding work. Job knowledge and work sample tests are achievement tests and are useful for determining whether a candidate can perform the duties of the job without further training.

 Interviews are an important source of information about job applicants. They can be unstructured, with the interviewer free to pursue whatever approach and sequence of topics seems appropriate. Alternatively, they can be structured, with each applicant receiving the same set of questions, which have pre-established answers. Some interviews are situational and focus on hypothetical situations or actual behavioural descriptions of previous work experiences. Interviews can be conducted by a single individual, or by a panel, or through a computer interface. Whichever technique is chosen, those who conduct interviews should receive special training to acquaint them with interviewing techniques and human rights considerations. The training should also make them more aware of the major findings from research studies on interviews, and how they can apply those findings.

 When the hiring decision is made, all "can do" and "will do" factors should be assembled and weighted systematically so that the final decision is based on a composite of the most reliable and valid information. While the clinical approach to decision making is used more than the statistical approach, the latter is more accurate. Compensatory models allow a candidate's high score on one predictor to make up for a low score on another. Multiple cutoff and multiple hurdle approaches require a minimal competency on each of the selection criteria used. Whichever of these approaches is used, the goal is to select a greater proportion of individuals who will be successful on the job.

KEY TERMS

achievement tests
aptitude tests
behavioural description
   interview (BDI)
compensatory model
concurrent validity
construct validity
content validity

criterion-related validity
cross-validation
multiple cutoff model
multiple hurdle model
nondirective interview
panel interview
predictive validity
reliability

selection
selection ratio
situational interview
structured interview
validity
validity generalization

DISCUSSION QUESTIONS

 1. What is meant by the term "criterion" as it is used in personnel selection? Give some examples of criteria used for jobs with which you are familiar.

 2. What are some of the problems that arise in checking references furnished by job applicants? Are there any solutions to these problems?

 3. What characteristics do job knowledge and job sample tests have that often make them more acceptable to the examinees than other types of tests?

 4. Personality tests, like other tests used in employee selection, have been under attack for several decades. Why do some applicants find personality tests objectionable? On what basis could their use for selection purposes be justified? To support your arguments, check out the website **www.2h.com** for a range of tests of varying quality and legality.

5. In groups, discuss and label employment interviews that each student has experienced. How valid was each from an employer's perspective? How effective was each type in attracting you, as a candidate, to the recruiting organization?

6. In what ways does the clinical approach to selection differ from the statistical approach? How do you account for the fact that one approach is superior to the other?

SEARCHING FOR SPIES

CASE 1

The Canadian Security Intelligence Service (CSIS) is a civilian-run agency, formerly the Security Services of the RCMP. Its role is defensive—to protect Canada from terrorists and foreign spies. It does not send armed spies overseas. Selecting spies used to be a secret process. There was no public knowledge about how spies were recruited, what the job description was, and what the selection criteria and methods were.

Each year CSIS receives 3,000 unsolicited applicants for about 100 openings. However, most of these applications are from unqualified James Bond wanna-be's. CSIS wants highly qualified, well-educated, multilingual, multiskilled employees. It recruits openly, and its selection criteria and processes are public.

If you want to apply: CSIS looks for Canadian citizens who are university graduates, preferably with advanced degrees. You must have a driver's licence and be able to relocate anywhere in Canada at any time. You will have lived or studied abroad, be proficient in English and French, and have a third or fourth language. CSIS looks for generalists—people who are knowledgeable about international and political issues and who have investigative and analytical skills. As a CSIS employee, you will not be able to discuss your work with outsiders at any time.

CSIS recruits at government job fairs. As an applicant, you must go through the following selection process:

- submit a résumé
- complete a twelve-page application, which also involves writing a 500-word essay explaining why you want to become an intelligence officer
- attend a group information session, where recruiters and intelligence officers answer questions
- attend a suitability interview, where your motivation and verbal and people skills are judged
- take a battery of psychological and aptitude tests
- have your language skills tested
- attend a national assessment panel—veterans will assess your motivation, knowledge of CSIS, and general awareness of public affairs
- be submitted to security clearance procedures (including a polygraph test, fingerprints, lie detector test, credit check, criminal record check, and references back to teen years), which takes three months and costs thousands of dollars
- go to a final interview

This is a multiple hurdle model of selection. As a candidate you will have to pass each hurdle before being allowed to continue to the next. If successful, you will be on probation for five years, undergo twelve weeks of classroom training and language training, and spend two or three years at an operations desk at headquarters, before being transferred to the field under the guidance of a mentor.

Source: Adapted from J. Sallot, "The Spy Masters' Talent Hunt Goes Public," *The Globe and Mail,* June 22, 1999: A1, A10.

Questions

1. Do you think the selection system used by CSIS is valid? Using your knowledge of validity, rate each step in this process.

2. One reason CSIS went public was to increase the representation of women from 10 percent to a target of 50 percent. Are there any possible problems with discrimination in this selection system? Discuss.

CASE 2

WWW

APTITUDE TESTS AT MITSUBISHI

The Mitsubishi plant in Midland, Ontario, has begun using aptitude tests as part of its selection process. Before they will be considered for new job openings and for promotions, new candidates must pass eight different aptitude tests. One test for manual dexterity requires applicants to move small metal pegs from holes on one side of a board to holes on the other side as fast as they can. In another test, employees are shown pictures of two cows—one white and the other spotted—and asked, "Which cow would be easier to see from an airplane?"

The employees at Mitsubishi see no relationship between their jobs and the cow test; they also find it humiliating to have to move pegs on a board in order to qualify for jobs they have been doing for years. In one testing session, 80 percent of employees failed. The price of failure is exclusion from higher-paying and more desirable jobs. Even more shameful is the fact that people with less seniority and little plant experience are passing the aptitude tests.

The dispute is deeply rooted. The union feels that the tests are allowing management to replace experienced workers with new hires who work for less pay. The fact that the test results are almost always confidential has led to suspicions that the results are being manipulated in some way. After seeing their colleagues fail the tests, some workers are so discouraged that they don't even try for new jobs or promotions. Other changes that have been introduced along with the tests include twelve-hour rotating shifts, the "flexible" replacement of workers, and new computerized inspection systems.

Management defends the testing, claiming that new plants and new work methods require aptitudes such as problem solving and flexible thinking. These skills are not usually associated with the stereotype of the senior blue-collar worker. In the past, young people had no need to even graduate from high school if there was a plant in town offering big paycheques for manual labour. The tests that have been introduced discriminate against older workers with less formal education. In demand today are employees who can do many jobs, solve problems, make decisions, provide creative solutions, and function effectively as part of an empowered work team.

Source: M. Terepocki, "Testing Limits: Workplace Aptitude Tests at Mitsubishi," *Our Times* 14, no. 4 (September–October 1996): 35–7.

Questions

1. Do you see any problems with the way Mitsubishi's testing program is being managed? Discuss.

2. Suggest how the program might be modified.

3. The union is fighting to eliminate the testing. On what grounds could the union base its arguments?

4. If a Mitsubishi employee files a complaint with the Ontario Human Rights Commission on the grounds that the test discriminated against him as an older worker, what kinds of information will have to be gathered to determine the validity of his claim?

CAREER COUNSEL

The résumé preparation exercises on the Managing Human Resources website (**belcourt.nelson.com**) will help you tailor your résumé to the position.

USING THE INTERNET

WWW

You can practice reading and analyzing resumes on-line at **www.career-mosiac.com** and **www.jobcenter.com**.

Read about some of the arguments against the use of graphology at this text-heavy site: **condor.depaul.edu/ethics/hand.html**.

More information about uses for Kuder and other interest inventories can be found at **job.careernet.org/mptc/interest.htm**.

NOTES AND REFERENCES

1. "Competencies Drive HR Practices," *HRFocus*, August 1996: 15; Pat McLagan, "Great Ideas Revisited," *Training and Development*, January 1996: 60–5.

2. Bruce Meger, "A Critical Review of Competency-Based Systems," *Human Resource Professional* 9, no. 1 (January–February 1996): 22–5; Frank J. Landy and Laura J. Shankster, "Personnel Selection and Placement," *Annual Review of Psychology* 45 (Palo Alto, Calif.: Annual Reviews, 1994): 261–96. For a complete discussion of validity and reliability in selection, see V.M. Catano, S.F. Cronshaw,

W.W. Wiesner, R.D. Hackett, and L.L. Methot, *Recruitment and Selection in Canada*, 2nd edition (Toronto: Nelson Thompson Learning): 200.

3. Charlene Marmer Solomon, "Testing at Odds with Diversity Efforts?" *Personnel Journal* 75, no. 4 (April 1996): 131–40; Scott E. Maxwell and Richard D. Arvey, "The Search for Predictors with High Validity and Low Adverse Impact: Compatible or Incompatible Goals?" *Journal of Applied Psychology* 78, no. 3 (June 1993): 433–7. See also James H. Coil III and Charles M. Rice, "Managing

Work-Force Diversity in the Nineties: The Impact of the Civil Rights Act of 1991," *Employee Relations Law Journal* 18, no. 4 (Spring 1993): 547–65.

4. Frank J. Landy, "Test Validity Yearbook," *Journal of Business Psychology* 7, no. 2 (1992): 111–257. See also Edwin E. Ghiselli, "The Validity of Aptitude Tests in Personnel Selection," *Personnel Psychology* 26, no. 4 (Winter 1973): 461–77; J.E. Hunter and R.H. Hunter, "Validity and Utility of Alternative Predictors of Job Performance," *Psychological Bulletin* 96 (1984): 72–98; N. Schmitt, R.Z. Gooding, R.A. Noe, and M. Kirsch, "Meta-Analysis of Validity Studies Published between 1964 and 1982 and the Investigation of Study Characteristics," *Personnel Psychology* 37 (1984): 407–22.

5. S. Messick, "Foundations of Validity: Meaning and Consequences in Psychological Assessment," *European Journal of Psychological Assessment* 10 (1994): 1–9; Richard S. Barrett, "Content Validation Form," *Public Personnel Management* 21 (Spring 1992): 41–52.

6 Michael D. Mumford, David P. Costanza, Mary Connelly, and Julie F. Johnson, "Item Generation Procedures and Background Data Scales: Implications for Construct and Criterion-Related Validity," *Personnel Psychology* 49, no. 2 (Summer 1996): 361–98; R.D. Arvey, S.M. Nutting, and T.E. Landon, "Validation Strategies for Physical Ability Testing in Police and Fire Settings," *Public Personnel Management* 21 (1992): 301–12.

7. H.C. Jain, "Human Rights: Issues in Employment" in H.C. Jain and P.C. Wright, *Trends and Challenges in Human Resources Management* (Scarborough, Ont.: ITP Nelson, 1994), 69.

8. "Beware of Resumania," *Personnel Journal*, April 1996, 28; Marlene Brown, "Checking the Facts on a Résumé," *Personnel Journal*, January 1993, SS6–SS7. See also T. Lammers, "How to Read between the Lines: Tactics for Evaluating a Résumé," *Inc.*, March 1993, 105–7.

9. Catano et al., *Recruitment and Selection in Canada*: 48.

10. Mumford et al., "Item Generation Procedures"; Anthony F. Buono, "Biodata Handbook: Theory, Research, and Use of Biographical Information for Selection and Performance Prediction," *Personnel Psychology* 47, no. 4 (Winter 1994): 890–4; Barbara K. Brown and Michael A. Campion, "Biodata Phenomenology: Recruiters' Perceptions and Use of Biographical Information in Résumé Screening," *Journal of Applied Psychology* 79, no. 6 (December 1994): 897–908.

11. Samuel Greengard, "Are You Well Armed to Screen Applicants?" *Personnel Journal*, December 1995: 84–95; Christopher E. Stenberg, "The Role of Pre-Employment Background Investigations in Hiring," *Human Resource Professional* 9, no. 1 (January–February 1996): 19–21; L. Barani, "Background Investigations: How HR Stays on the Cutting Edge," *HRFocus* 70 (June 1993): 12.

12. S. McShane, "Most Employers Use Reference Checks But Many Fear Defamation Liability," *Canadian HR Reporter*, March 13, 1995: 4.

13. Ibid.

14. J. Schilder, "Trial by Hire," *HR Professional* 7, no. 6 (June 1991): 21–3.

15. McShane, "Most Employers Use Reference Checks."

16. "Workplace Privacy," *Ontario Commissioners Report, Worklife Report* 9, no. 3 (1994): 8–9.

17. "If the Shoe Fits," *Security Management* 40, no. 2 (February 1996): 11; Greengard, "Are You Well Armed?"; Peter Bullard, "Pre-Employment Screening to Weed Out Bad Apples," *Nursing Home* 43, no. 5 (June 1994): 29–31.

18. Malcolm C. McCulloch, "Can Integrity Testing Improve Market Conduct?" *limra's MarketFacts* 15, no. 2 (March–April 1996): 15–16. D.S. Ones, C. Viswesvaran, and F.L. Schmidt, "Comprehensive Meta-Analysis of Integrity Test Validities: Findings and Implications for Personnel Selection and Theories of Job Performance," *Journal of Applied Psychology* 78 (August 1993): 679–703.

19. Arlyn J. Imberman, "Get It in Writing," *Successful Meetings* 45, no. 5 (April 1996): 97–102.

20. Dirk D. Steiner and Stephen W. Gilliland, "Fairness Reactions to Personnel Selection Techniques in France and the United States," *Journal of Applied Psychology* 81, no. 2 (April 1996): 134–41.

21. For books with comprehensive coverage of testing, including employment testing, see Anne Anastasi and Susana Urbina, *Psychological Testing*, 7th ed. (New York: Macmillan, in press); Lee J. Cronbach, *Essentials of Psychological Testing*, 5th ed. (New York: HarperCollins, 1990).

22. Standards that testing programs should meet are described in *Standards for Educational and Psychological Tests* (Washington, D.C.: American Psychological Association, 1985). HR managers who want to examine paper-and-pencil tests should obtain specimen sets that include a test manual, a copy of the test, an answer sheet, and a scoring key. The test manual provides the essential information about the construction of the test; its recommended use; and instructions for administering, scoring, and interpreting the test. Test users should not rely entirely on the material furnished by the test author and publisher. A major source of consumer information about commercially available tests—the Mental Measurements Yearbook (MMY)—is available in most libraries. Published periodically, the MMY contains descriptive information plus critical reviews by experts in the various types of tests. The reviews are useful in evaluating a particular test for tryout in employment situations. Other sources of information about tests include *Test Critiques*, a set of volumes containing professional reviews of tests, and *Tests: A Comprehensive Reference for Assessments in Psychology, Education, and Business*. The latter describes more than 3,100 tests published in the English language. Another source, *Principles for the Validation and Use of Personnel Selection Procedures*, published by the Society for Industrial and Organizational Psychology, is a valuable guide for employers who use tests. Other publications are

available that present detailed information on how to avoid discrimination and achieve fairness in testing.

23. Patrick M. Wright, Michele K. Kacmar, Gary C. McMahan, and Kevin Deleeuw, "P 4 f(M 2 A): Cognitive Ability as a Moderator of the Relationship between Personality and Job Performance," *Journal of Management* 21, no. 6 (1995): 1129–39; Therese Hoff Macan, Marcia J. Avedon, Matthew Paese, and David E. Smith, "The Effects of Applicants' Reactions to Cognitive Ability Tests and an Assessment Center," *Personnel Psychology* 47, no. 4 (Winter 1994): 715–38; Paul R. Sackett and Daniel J. Ostgaard, "Job-Specific Applicant Pools and National Norms for Cognitive Ability Tests: Implications for Range Restriction Corrections in Validation Research," *Journal of Applied Psychology* 79, no. 5 (October 1994): 680–4; F.L. Schmidt and J.E. Hunter, "Tacit Knowledge, Practical Intelligence, General Mental Ability, and Job Knowledge," *Current Directions in Psychological Science* 2, no. 1 (1993): 3–13.

24. Seymore Adler, "Personality Tests for Salesforce Selection: Worth a Fresh Look," *Review of Business* 16, no. 1 (Summer–Fall 1994): 27–31; Schmitt, Gooding, Noe, and Kirsch, "Meta-Analysis of Validity Studies": 407–22. See also M.R. Barrick and M.K. Mount, "The Big Five Personality Dimensions and Job Performance: A Meta-Analysis," *Personnel Psychology* 44 (1991): 1–26.

25. Daniel P. O'Meara, "Personality Tests Raise Questions of Legality and Effectiveness," *HRMagazine*, January 1994, 97–100; Jeffery A. Mello, "Personality Tests and Privacy Rights," *HRFocus* 73, no. 3 (March 1996): 22–3.

26. Joyce Hogan and Ann Quigley, "Effects of Preparing for Physical Ability Tests," *Public Personnel Management* 23, no. 1 (Spring 1994): 85–104; J. Hogan, "The Structure of Physical Performance," *Journal of Applied Psychology* 76 (1991): 495–507. See also Richard D. Arvey, Timothy E. Landon, and Steven M. Nutting, "Development of Physical Ability Tests for Police Officers: A Construct Validation Approach," *Journal of Applied Psychology* 77 (December 1992): 996–1009; J. Hogan, "Physical Abilities," in M.D. Dunnette and L.M. Hough (eds.), *Handbook of Industrial and Organizational Psychology* (Palo Alto, Calif.: Consulting Psychologists Press, 1991).

27. M. Brewster, "RCMP Ease Fitness Rules for Women," *The Globe and Mail*, July 14, 1997: A4.

28. Charles Anderson, "Can Employees Physically Do the Job?" *Human Resources* 7, no. 5 (September–October 1994): 3–5; Arvey, Nutting, and Landon, "Validation Strategies," 301–12.

29. It is interesting to note that the origins of the civil service system go back to 2200 BC, when the Chinese emperor examined officials every three years to determine their fitness for continuing in office. In 1115 BC, candidates for government posts were examined for their proficiency in music, archery, horsemanship, writing, arithmetic, and the rites and ceremonies of public and private life. See Philip H. DuBois, *A History of Psychological Testing* (Boston: Allyn & Bacon, 1970), ch. 1.

30. Florence Berger and Ajay Ghei, "Employment Tests: A Facet of Hospitality Hiring," *Cornell Hotel and Restaurant Administration Quarterly* 36, no. 6 (December 1995): 28–31; Malcolm James Ree, Thomas R. Carretta, and Mark S. Teachout, "Role of Ability and Prior Job Knowledge in Complex Training Performance," *Journal of Applied Psychology* 80, no. 6 (December 1995): 721–30.

31. James M. Conway, Robert A. Jako, and Deborah F. Goodman, "A Meta-Analysis of Interrater and Internal Consistency Reliability of Selection Interviews," *Journal of Applied Psychology* 80, no. 5 (October 1995): 565–79; Malcolm Wheatley, "The Talent Spotters," *Management Today*, June 1996, 62–4; Michael McDaniel, Deborah L. Whetzel, Frank L. Schmidt, and Steven D. Maurer, "The Validity of Employment Interviews: A Comprehensive Review and Meta-Analysis," *Journal of Applied Psychology* 79, no. 4 (August 1994): 599–616.

32. Elaine D. Pulakos, Neal Schmitt, David Whitney, and Matthew Smith, "Individual Differences in Interview Ratings: The Impact of Standardization, Consensus Discussion, and Sampling Error on the Validity of a Structured Interview," *Personnel Psychology* 49, no. 1 (Spring 1996): 85–102.

33. Michael A. Campion, James E. Campion, and Peter J. Hudson, Jr., "Structured Interviewing: A Note On Incremental Validity and Alternative Question Types," *Journal of Applied Psychology* 79, no. 6 (December 1994): 998–1002.

34. Elaine D. Pulakos and Neal Schmitt, "Experience-Based and Situational Interview Questions: Studies of Validity," *Personnel Psychology* 48, no. 2 (Summer 1995): 289-308; Ivan T. Robertson, Lynda Gratton, and Usharani Rout, "The Validity of Situational Interviews for Administrative Jobs," *Journal of Organizational Behavior* 11 (January 1990): 69–76; Thung-Rung Lin, G.H. Dobbins, and Jiing-Lih Farh, "A Field Study of Race and Age Similarity Effects on Interview Ratings in Conventional and Situational Interviews," *Journal of Applied Psychology* 77 (June 1992): 363–71.

35. Amelia J. Prewett-Livingston, John G. Veres III, Hubert S. Feild, and Philip M. Lewis, "Effects of Race on Interview Ratings in a Situational Panel Interview," *Journal of Applied Psychology* 81, no. 2 (April 1996): 178–86; Philip L. Roth and James E. Campion, "An Analysis of the Predictive Power of the Panel Interview and Pre-Employment Tests," *Journal of Occupational and Organizational Psychology* 65 (March 1992): 51–60.

36. Peter C. Sawyers, "Structured Interviewing: Your Key to the Best Hires," *Personnel Journal, Special Supplement*, December 1992. See also Bob Smith, "Pinkerton Keeps Its Eye on Recruitment," *HRFocus*, September 1993, 1, 8; Elizabeth Daniele, "PC-Based Screening Passes the Test at Cigna," *Insurance & Technology* 17 (January 1992): 15, 18; Anonymous, "Bell's Getting Tuned in to On-Line Recruiting," *Computer World Canada* 14, no. 25 (December 18, 1998): 37.

37. C.L. Martin and D.H. Nagao, "Some Effects of Computerized Interviewing on Job Applicant Responses," *Journal of Applied Psychology* 74 (1989): 72–80.

38. E.C. Mayfield, "The Selection Interview—A Reevaluation of Published Research," *Personnel Psychology* 17, no. 3 (Autumn 1964): 239–60; Lynn Ulrich and Don Trumbo, "The Selection Interview since 1949," *Psychological Bulletin* 63, no. 2 (February 1965): 100–16; Orman R. Wright, Jr., "Summary of Research on the Selection Interview since 1964," *Personnel Psychology* 22, no. 4 (Winter 1969): 391–414; Neal Schmitt, "Social and Situational Determinants of Interview Decisions: Implication for the Employment Interview," *Personnel Psychology* 29, no. 1 (Spring 1976): 79–101; Richard D. Arvey and James E. Campion, "The Employment Interview: A Summary and Review of Recent Literature," *Personnel Psychology* 35, no. 2 (Summer 1982): 281–322; Michael M. Harris, "Reconsidering the Employment Interview: A Review of Recent Literature and Suggestions for Future Research," *Personnel Psychology* 42, no. 4 (Winter 1989): 691–726.

39. "Discrimination Because of Handicap," *Ontario Human Rights Commission*, Ontario Human Rights Commission, Government of Ontario, May 1991: 5.

40. See, for example, *Ontario Human Rights Commission Policy on Employment-Related Medical Information*, Ontario Human Rights Commission, Government of Ontario, March 1991: 1–2.

41. *Ontario Human Rights Commission Policy on Height and Weight Requirements*, Ontario Human Rights Commission, Government of Ontario, 1989: 1.

42. *Ontario Human Rights Commission Policy Statement on HIV/AIDS-Related Discrimination*, Ontario Human Rights Commission, Government of Ontario, April 1992: 5.

43. C. Yetman, "AIDS Awareness Promoted in P&G Employee Brochure," *Human Resources Professional* 11, no. 4 (May 1994): 7.

44. C. Hoglund, "Mandatory Drug Testing," *Human Resource Professional* 8, no. 1 (January 1992): 21–2.

45. V. Galt, "Total Ban Sought on Drug Testing by Employers," *The Globe and Mail*, February 22, 1992: A6.

46. For an in-depth discussion of these and other approaches, see Catano et al., *Recruitment and Selection in Canada*.

47. Multiple regression is a statistical method for evaluating the magnitude of effects of more than one independent variable (e.g., selection predictors) on a dependent variable (e.g., job performance) using principles of correlation and regression. See W.P. Vogt, *Dictionary of Statistics and Methodology* (Newbury Park, Calif.: Sage Publications, 1993): 146; F.N. Kerlinger, *Foundations of Behavioral Research*, 3rd ed. (Fort Worth, Tex.: Holt, Rinehart and Winston, 1986): 527.

48. P.E. Meehl, *Clinical v. Statistical Prediction* (Minneapolis: University of Minnesota Press, 1954); J. Sawyer, "Measurement and Prediction, Clinical and Statistical," *Psychological Bulletin* 66, no. 3 (September 1966): 178–200.

49. Wayne F. Cascio, *Applied Psychology in Personnel Management*, 4th ed. (Englewood Cliffs, N.J.: Prentice-Hall, 1991). Besides Cascio's book, the reader may wish to consult George F. Dreher and Daniel W. Kendall, "Organizational Staffing," in Gerald R. Ferris, Sherman D. Rosen, and Darold T. Barnum, eds., *Handbook of Human Resource Management* (Cambridge, Mass: Blackwell Publishers, 1995).

TRAINING

After studying this chapter, you should be able to

OBJECTIVE 1
List some of the characteristics of an effective orientation program.

OBJECTIVE 2
Discuss the systems approach to training and development.

OBJECTIVE 3
Describe the components of training needs assessment.

OBJECTIVE 4
Identify the principles of learning, and describe how they facilitate training.

OBJECTIVE 5
Identify the types of training methods used for managers and nonmanagers.

OBJECTIVE 6
Discuss the advantages and disadvantages of various evaluation criteria.

OBJECTIVE 7
Describe ways to optimize transfer of training.

OBJECTIVE 8
Describe the special training programs that are currently popular.

T raining has become increasingly vital to the success of modern organizations. Recall from Chapter 1 that organizations often compete on competencies—the core sets of knowledge and expertise that give them an edge over their competitors. Training plays a central role in nurturing and strengthening these competencies, and in this way has become part of the backbone of strategy implementation. Also, because technologies are changing so rapidly, employees must constantly hone their knowledge, skills, and abilities (KSAs) to cope with new processes and systems. Jobs requiring little skill are rapidly being replaced by jobs requiring technical, interpersonal, and problem-solving skills. Other trends toward empowerment, total quality management, teamwork, and international business make it necessary for both managers and employees to develop the skills that will enable them to handle new and more demanding assignments.

ORIENTATION

To get new employees off to a good start, organizations offer formal orientation programs. **Orientation** is the formal process of familiarizing a new employee with the organization, the new job, and the new work unit. It enables new employees to get "in sync" so that they start becoming productive members of the organization.

Orientation

Formal process of familiarizing a new employee with the organization, the new job, and the new work unit

Benefits of Orientation

In some organizations, formal, new-hire orientation programs are almost nonexistent or, if they do exist, are performed in a casual manner. Some readers may remember showing up the first day on a new job, being told to work, and receiving no instructions, introductions, or support. This is unfortunate, since well-run orientation programs have a number of very practical, cost-effective benefits. As reported by employers, these include the following:

- lower turnover
- higher productivity
- improved employee morale
- lower recruiting and training costs
- facilitation of learning
- reduction of the new employee's anxiety

The more time and effort an organization devotes to making new employees feel welcome, the more likely those employees are to identify with the organization and become valuable members of it. Unlike training, which emphasizes the *what* and the *how*, orientation stresses the *why*. It is designed to develop in employees a particular attitude about the work they will be doing and their role in the organization. It explains the philosophy behind the rules, and provides a framework for job-related tasks.

Cooperation between line staff and the HR department is essential to a well-integrated orientation program. Ordinarily, the HR department is responsible for coordinating orientation activities and for providing new employees with information about pay, benefits, conditions of employment, and other areas not directly under a supervisor's direction. However, the supervisor plays the most important role in the orientation program. New employees are interested mainly in what the supervisor says and does and what their new co-workers are like. Before a new employee arrives, the supervisor should inform the work group that a new worker is joining the unit. Often, supervisors or other managerial personnel recruit co-workers to serve as volunteer "sponsors" for incoming employees. Besides providing practical help to newcomers, this approach conveys an emphasis on teamwork.

Since orientation programs have an immediate and lasting impact, careful planning is essential. This planning should focus on the program goals, the topics to be covered, and the methods of organizing and presenting those topics. Organizations often provide checklists to those who conduct orientations. Highlights in HRM 1 lists items that should be included in an orientation checklist for supervisors. Orientation should focus on matters of immediate concern, such as important aspects of the job and the organization's rules for behaviour (e.g., attendance and safety).

In orientation sessions, new employees are often given a packet of materials to read at their leisure. Some of the materials these packets might include are noted in Highlights in HRM 1. It is possible that statements regarding such matters as tenure, basis for dismissal, and benefits might be viewed by employees and the courts as legally binding on the employer, so it is advisable to have the legal department review the packet and write a disclaimer to the effect that it does not constitute an employment contract.

Those who are planning an orientation program should take into account the anxiety that employees feel during their first few days on the job. It is natural to experience some anxiety, but if employees are too anxious, training costs, turnover, absenteeism, and even production costs may increase. Early in the orientation program, steps should be taken to reduce the anxiety of new employees. This can be accomplished by establishing specific times during which the supervisor will be available for questions and/or coaching. It is also worthwhile to reassure newcomers that they will attain the performance levels they are observing among their co-workers within a predetermined time frame, based on experiences with other newcomers. This reassurance is especially important for employees with limited work experience who are learning new skills.

Some employers think it does no harm to allow new employees to be oriented by their peers. But there is a danger to this practice: unsafe work practices and unacceptable behaviours that conflict with the organization's policies can be perpetuated if the supervisors themselves do not conduct the orientation. The behaviours these employees develop can undermine the organization's policies and procedures.[1]

THE SCOPE OF TRAINING

Many new employees come equipped with most of the KSAs needed to start work. Others may require extensive training before they are ready to make much of a contribution to the organization. Almost all employees need some type of training on an ongoing basis to maintain effective performance or to adjust to new ways of work.

The term "training" is often used casually to describe any effort initiated by an organization to foster learning among its members. However, many experts make a distinction between *training*, which tends to be more narrowly focused and

Highlights in HRM

1   SUPERVISORY ORIENTATION CHECKLIST

1. A formal greeting, including introduction to colleagues.
2. Explanation of job procedures, duties, and responsibilities.
3. Training to be received (when and why).
4. Supervisor and organization expectations regarding attendance and behaviour norms.
5. Job standards and production/service levels.
6. Performance appraisal criteria, including estimated time frame for achieving peak performance.
7. Conditions of employment, including hours of work, pay periods, and overtime requirements.
8. Organization and work unit rules, regulations, and policies.
9. Safety regulations.
10. Those to notify or turn to if problems or questions arise.
11. Chain of command for reporting purposes.
12. An overall explanation of the organization's operations and purpose.
13. Offers of help and encouragement, including a specific time each week (in the early stages of employment) for questions or coaching.

oriented toward short-term performance concerns, and *development*, which tends to be oriented toward broadening an individual's skills for future responsibilities. The two terms tend to be combined in a single phrase—"training and development"—in recognition that organizations use both activities to increase the skill base of their employees.

Organizations train new employees mainly in order to bring their KSAs up to the level required for satisfactory performance. As these employees continue on the job, additional training provides opportunities for them to acquire new knowledge and skills. As a result of this training, employees become even more effective on the job, and better able to perform other jobs in other areas or at higher levels.

Investments in Training

WWW

According to a Conference Board of Canada survey, Canadian businesses spend about $850 per employee each year on formal training.[2] Businesses in the financial and oil and gas sectors spend the most per employee; those in manufacturing and education spend the least. The average percentage of payroll spent on training is 1.6 percent. Consistent with the trend toward recognizing employees as the source of competitive advantage, nearly half the respondents in the Conference Board survey reported that their training budgets are increasing. Figure 6.1 outlines the types of training that organizations conduct.

FIGURE 6.1 *General Types of Trainingl*

	ORGANIZATIONS PROVIDING TRAINING (%)	NUMBER OF EMPLOYEES				
		100–489	500–999	1000–2499	2500–999	10,000 OR MORE
Computer applications	95	95	97	95	97	97
Management skills/Development	85	84	91	91	89	91
Technical skills/Knowledge	77	76	82	78	82	82
Supervisory skills	82	80	81	85	86	85
Communication skills	88	87	93	88	91	91
Customer Service	83	82	83	83	85	85
Executive development	78	77	82	84	83	89
Personal growth	67	66	72	70	71	74
Customer education	69	70	67	69	62	67
Sales	58	57	58	58	61	70

Source: "1999 Industry Report," *Training* 36, no. 10 (October 1999): 56.

Organizations also spend billions of dollars each year on informal instruction of the kind that goes on every day in every workplace. These investments are directed at a variety of programs, from basic computer skills to customer service.

A Systems Approach to Training

Since the main reason for training is to help the organization achieve its overall objectives, training programs should be developed with a focus on organizational goals and strategies. Molson Breweries has developed mandatory career development training for its employees that complements its organizational goals. Unfortunately, many organizations never make the connection between their strategic objectives and their training programs. When they don't, fads, fashions, or "whatever the competition is doing" become the main drivers of an organization's training agenda. As a result of this, the organization's investment is largely wasted—training programs are often misdirected, poorly designed, and inadequately evaluated. As a result of this, organizational performance is directly harmed.

WWW

To make certain that investments in training and development have maximum impact on individual and organizational performance, a systems approach to training should be used. The systems approach involves five phases: (1) needs assessment, (2) design, (3) implementation, (4) evaluation, and (5) transfer of training. A model that is useful to designers of training programs is presented in Figure 6.2. We will use this model as a framework for organizing the material throughout this chapter.

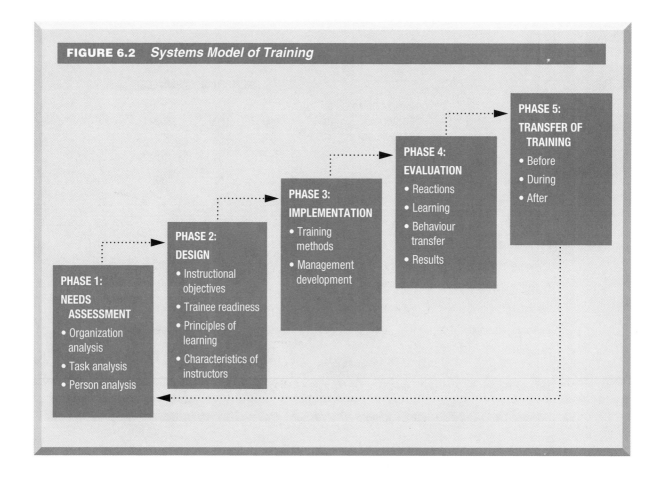

FIGURE 6.2   *Systems Model of Training*

PHASE 1:
NEEDS ASSESSMENT
- Organization analysis
- Task analysis
- Person analysis

PHASE 2:
DESIGN
- Instructional objectives
- Trainee readiness
- Principles of learning
- Characteristics of instructors

PHASE 3:
IMPLEMENTATION
- Training methods
- Management development

PHASE 4:
EVALUATION
- Reactions
- Learning
- Behaviour transfer
- Results

PHASE 5:
TRANSFER OF TRAINING
- Before
- During
- After

PHASE 1: CONDUCTING THE NEEDS ASSESSMENT

Managers and HR personnel should stay alert to the kinds of training that are needed, where they are needed, who needs them, and which methods will best deliver needed KSAs to employees. If workers consistently fail to achieve productivity objectives, this may be a signal that training is needed. Likewise, if organizations receive an excessive number of customer complaints, this may suggest inadequate training. To make certain that training is timely and is focused on priority issues, managers should approach needs assessment systematically by utilizing the three different types of analysis: organization analysis, task analysis, and person analysis (see Figure 6.3; this approach to analysis is discussed later in the chapter).

WWW

A study by the American Society for Training and Development (ASTD) made the unfortunate finding that because of the costs, expertise, and time required, organizations conduct needs assessment less than half the time before initiating a training program. Too often, managers are heard lamenting that they simply don't have time to conduct needs assessments. Ironically, as the speed of change increases, and time and resources grow more valuable, the importance of good needs assessment *increases*. The process need not be especially difficult. Highlights in HRM 2 provides some tips for doing rapid needs assessment.

Highlights in HRM

2   NOTES ON DOING NEEDS ASSESSMENT QUICK TIME

NOTE 1: Look at problem scope. Common sense suggests that small, local matters may require less information gathering than big problems with a major impact on the organization. Ask managers a series of questions about the nature of the problem and its impact on the organization, and gear your analysis accordingly.

NOTE 2: Do Organizational Scanning. To anticipate upcoming training needs, stay connected with what is going on in the organization. If a new technology is about to be launched, the need for training should take no one by surprise. In short, needs assessment isn't an event with a start-and-stop switch.

NOTE 3: Play "Give and Take." Get the information you need, but don't drag your feet with excessive analysis before reporting back to managers. Show them you are sensitive to their need for action by giving them updates on the information you have collected. If necessary, explain that better value might be gained by further analysis.

NOTE 4: Check "Lost and Found." Often, information gathered for a different purpose may bear on your training issue. Performance data (e.g., errors, customer complainants) and staffing data (e.g., proficiency tests, turnover, absenteeism) can be very helpful as starting points.

NOTE 5: Use Plain Talk. Instead of using clinical terms, such as analysis or assessment, use straight talk with managers that shows them you are (1) identifying the problem; (2) identifying alternative ways to solve the problem; (3) implementing a solution based on cost/benefit concerns; and (4) determining the effectiveness and efficiency of the solution.

NOTE 6: Use the Web. Information technology lets you communicate with others. You can use a listserv to post questions, synthesize responses, share resources, get feedback, gather information on trends, and so on.

NOTE 7: Use rapid prototyping. Often the most effective and efficient training is "just in time, just enough, and just for me." Create a rapid prototype of a program, and then evaluate and revise it as you implement it.

NOTE 8: Seek out exemplars. Find those in the organization who currently demonstrate the performance the organization wants. Bring others together with them to talk about performance issues, and let the exemplars share their experiences and insights. This avoids the risk of packaging the wrong information. The people in this process learn what they need to know from one another.

Source: Condensed from R. Zemke, "How to Do a Needs Assessment When You Don't Have Time," *Training* 35, no. 3 (March 1998): 36–44. Reprinted with permission.

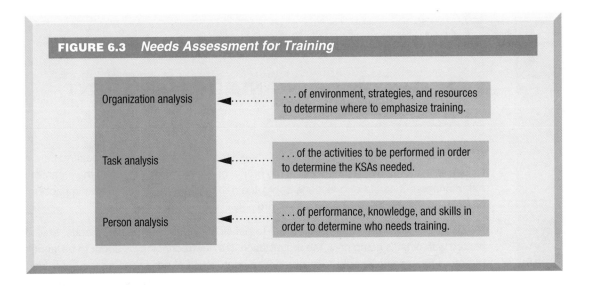

FIGURE 6.3 *Needs Assessment for Training*

Organization analysis ◄·········· ... of environment, strategies, and resources to determine where to emphasize training.

Task analysis ◄·········· ... of the activities to be performed in order to determine the KSAs needed.

Person analysis ◄·········· ... of performance, knowledge, and skills in order to determine who needs training.

Organization Analysis

Organization analysis

Examination of the environment, strategies, and resources of the organization to determine where training emphasis should be placed

The first step in needs assessment is identifying the broad forces that can influence training needs. **Organization analysis** is an examination of the environment, strategies, and resources of the organization to determine where training emphasis should be placed.

In many organizations, economic and public policy issues tend to have a widespread effect on training needs. For example, training in health and safety is often driven by laws and court decisions. Other issues tend to revolve around the strategic initiatives of an organization. For example, mergers and acquisitions often require that employees take on new roles and responsibilities and adjust to new cultures and ways of conducting business. Other issues such as technological change, globalization, re-engineering, and total quality management all influence how work is done and the types of skills needed to do it. Still other concerns may be more tactical, but no less important in their impact on training. Organizational restructuring, downsizing, empowerment, and teamwork, for example, have immediate training requirements. Finally, trends in the workforce itself affect training needs. As was mentioned in Chapter 1, employees are placing more and more value on self-development and personal growth, and this has led to an enormous desire for learning.[3]

Organization analysis involves a close examination of the resources—technological, financial, and human—that are available to meet training objectives. Typically, organizations collect data to use in the analysis—for example, information on direct and indirect labour costs, quality of goods or services, absenteeism, turnover, and number of accidents. The availability of potential replacement employees and the time required to train them are other important factors in organization analysis.

In recent years, organizations have been cutting costs, with the result that they are squeezing their training budgets—this, even while recognizing the need for more and better training. To cope with resource constraints while contributing to strategic imperatives, managers have to be more focused and efficient with their training budgets. Union Carbide has begun standardizing its safety training for all

WWW

employees (instead of customizing it for various groups), and is moving toward computer-based training and away from the more expensive classroom format.[4] To "do more with less," managers have to plan carefully where they will spend their training dollars. This means doing rigorous organization analysis.

Task Analysis

Task analysis

Process of determining what the content of a training program should be on the basis of a study of the tasks and duties involved in the job

The second step in training needs assessment is task analysis. **Task analysis** involves reviewing the job description and specification to identify the activities performed in a particular job and the KSAs needed to perform them. Often, task analysis becomes more detailed than job analysis. The overall purpose is to determine the exact content of the training program.

The *first* step in task analysis is to list all the tasks or duties included in the job. The *second* step is to list the steps performed by the employee to complete each task. Once the job is understood thoroughly, it is possible to establish the type of performance required (e.g., speech, recall, discrimination, manipulation), as well as the skills and knowledge necessary for performance. For example, in the task of taking a chest X-ray, a radiologist correctly positions the patient (manipulation), gives special instructions (speech), and checks that the X-ray tube is the proper distance from the patient (discrimination). The types of performance skills and knowledge that trainees need can be determined by observing and questioning skilled job holders and/or by reviewing job descriptions. This information helps trainers select program content and choose the most effective training method.

Competency assessment

Analysis of the sets of skills and knowledge needed for decision-oriented and knowledge-intensive jobs

Task analysis, like job analysis, seems to be emphasizing *less*, fixed sequences of tasks, and emphasizing *more*, flexible sets of competencies. As jobs change and more work is done in teams, new behaviours are required. **Competency assessment** focuses on the sets of skills and knowledge that employees need to be successful, especially for decision-oriented and knowledge-intensive jobs. Reality Check describes how Xerox Canada uses competency assessment software to identify training needs. Training programs based on work-oriented task analysis can become dated as work undergoes dynamic change. Training programs based on competency assessment are more flexible and perhaps more durable.[5] Highlights in HRM 3 provides a checklist for conducting a competency assessment.

WWW

Person Analysis

Person analysis

Determination of the specific individuals who need training

After the organization and task analyses, it is time to perform a person analysis. **Person analysis** involves determining which employees require training and (equally important) which do not. Often, performance appraisal information is used for person analysis. However, while a performance appraisal may show who is not meeting expectations, it usually doesn't show why. If performance deficiencies flow from shortfalls in ability, training may well help; if they flow from poor motivation or factors outside the employee's control, it may well not. Ultimately, managers have to sit down with employees to talk about areas for improvement and to determine with them which developmental approaches will have maximum benefit.[6]

Person analysis is important for several reasons. *First*, thorough analysis helps organizations avoid the mistake of sending all employees into training when some do not need it. *Second*, person analysis helps managers determine what prospective trainees are able to do when they enter training, so that the programs can be designed to emphasize the areas in which they are deficient.

Reality CHECK

COMPETENCY MANAGEMENT AT XEROX CANADA

Xerox Canada has evolved from a copier company into a company whose core competency is digital document management services. It has been estimated that the volume of documents flowing in and out of Canadian organizations has increased 600 percent in the past two decades. Equipping about 5,000 employees to ride the digital wave has been a challenge for Xerox's Learning and Development unit.

Director Jocelyne Traub sees her unit undertaking three roles in competency management: identifying the knowledge and skills the company needs; measuring the level of workforce preparedness necessary to achieve corporate objectives; and encouraging self-directed learning to bridge knowledge and skills gaps, thereby enabling employees to achieve their performance objectives. "When I began to explore competency management for Xerox in 1991," she recalls, "there was no blueprint. Our goal is to facilitate career resiliency and mobility of employees, in order to reach corporate objectives. Our currency is competency. The fact that you can manage a project, which is a competency that can travel from administration to marketing, is more important than the type of project managed. We talk in terms of roles, not jobs, because roles are more fluid and flexible, particularly as we work in virtual teams with transparent boundaries."

Janet Townsend, a program manager for the Learning and Development unit, is a member of the team that designed Xerox's competency management system. Included in the system is self-assessment software. Employees are presented with a profile of the competencies necessary for their job assignment, and then use the software to measure the gap between their current KSAs and the desired ones. They then develop and execute a learning plan to bridge any identified gaps. For example, for a trainer whose competencies include training delivery, the competency at level 1 might be, "Use basic training techniques (i.e., discussion and questioning) to involve learners." A level 4 competency for the same skill might be, "Coach others on alternative delivery methods and techniques." To achieve level 4, the employee would be linked to another tool that provides comprehensive learning resources, such as courses, self-study programs, and action learning plans.

The challenge for a company with expertise in technology is not to design the systems, but rather to foster a culture in which all employees are encouraged to embrace life-long learning and active utilization of available support mechanisms. Says Traub: "The idea of all employees assuming ownership for self-development and actively pursuing learning activities, in addition to formal company training, represents change for many people. The challenge is to first engage employees and then support them with tools and processes aimed at the achievement of learning goals. We all contribute to this investment in learning and we all share in the results it brings both as individuals and as an organization."

Highlights in HRM

3   TIPS FOR CONDUCTING A COMPETENCY ASSESSMENT

Learning how to perform a competency assessment can be a lengthy process. Here's a simplified approach:

- Clarify the purpose of the effort. Will you be using the competency model for training purposes only, or for other purposes as well?
- Clarify the target for the effort. Will you be constructing a competency model for the entire organization? For only part of it? For only one or several job categories, such as senior executives or middle managers?
- Network with others in your industry and in the training field. Try to find a competency model that has already been developed. (Industry associations and professional societies may have already developed models.)
- Form a panel of exemplary performers within your organization from the group targeted for assessment and from the group to which they report (such as managers and executives).
- Ask a panel of eight to twelve people in your organization to review competency studies obtained from other sources and to prioritize the competencies as they apply to success in your corporate culture.
- Verify the competency model, and secure ownership of it by encouraging input from others, such as senior executives.

Source: D.J. McNerney and A. Briggins, "Competency Assessment Gains Favor among Trainers." Reprinted from *HRFocus,* June 1995: 19. Copyright 1995 American Management Association International. Reprinted by permission of American Management Association International, New York, NY. All rights reserved. **www.amanet.org**

PHASE 2: DESIGNING THE TRAINING PROGRAM

Once the training needs have been determined, the next step is to design the learning environment. Starting a successful training programs involves more than identifying training needs. It also involves utilizing the information gained from needs analysis to design first-rate training programs. Experts suggest that training design should focus on at least these four (related) issues: (1) instructional objectives, (2) trainee readiness and motivation, (3) principles of learning, and (4) characteristics of instructors.

Instructional Objectives

As a result of conducting organization, task, and person analyses, managers will have a more complete picture of the company's training needs. On the basis of this information, they can more formally state the desired outcomes of training

Instructional objectives

Desired outcomes of a training program

through written instructional objectives. Generally, **instructional objectives** describe what the trainee will know or be able to do as a result of the training. One type of instructional objective, the performance-centred objective, is widely used because it lends itself to an unbiased evaluation of results. For example, the stated objective for one training program might be: "Employees trained in team methods will be able to perform these different jobs within six months." Performance-centred objectives typically include precise terms: "to calculate," "to repair," "to adjust," "to construct," "to assemble," and "to classify," and so on.

Robert Mager, an internationally known training expert, emphasizes the importance of instructional objectives by noting: "Before you prepare for instruction, before you select instructional procedures or subject matter or material, it is important to be able to state clearly just what you intend the results of that instruction to be. A clear statement of instructional objectives, which include 'action,' 'criteria,' and 'conditions' will provide a sound basis for choosing methods and materials and for selecting the means for assessing whether the instruction will be successful."[7]

Trainee Readiness and Motivation

Trainee readiness

The trainee's maturity and experience

Two conditions affect the success of those who are to receive training: readiness and motivation. **Trainee readiness** refers to the trainee's maturity and experience. Prospective trainees should be screened to determine that they have the background knowledge and the skills necessary to absorb what will be presented to them. Recognizing individual differences in readiness is as important in organizational training as it is in any other teaching situation. It is often desirable to group individuals according to their capacity to learn, as determined by test scores, and to provide an alternative type of instruction for those who need it.

The receptiveness and readiness of participants in training programs can be increased by having them complete questionnaires relating to why they are attending training and what they hope to accomplish. Participants can be asked to give copies of their completed questionnaires to their managers.

The other precondition for learning is trainee motivation. For optimum learning to take place, trainees must recognize their need for new knowledge or skills, and must maintain a desire to learn as training progresses. By focusing on the trainees themselves rather than on the trainer or training topic, managers can create a training environment that is conducive to learning. In this, six strategies can be essential:

1. Use positive reinforcement.

2. Eliminate threats and punishment.

3. Be flexible.

4. Have participants set personal goals.

5. Design interesting instruction.

6. Break down physical and psychological obstacles to learning.[8]

Employees are motivated by certain common needs; but they also differ from one another in the relative weight they give to those needs at a given point in time. For example, new college and university graduates are often highly ambitious, and often have established specific goals for career progression. When training objectives are clearly related to trainees' individual needs, they will be more strongly motivated to succeed in training programs.

Principles of Learning

As we move from needs assessment and instructional objectives to employee readiness and motivation, we are shifting from a focus on the organization to a focus on employees. Ultimately, training has to build a bridge between employees and the organization. One important step in this transition involves giving full consideration to the psychological principles of learning—that is, to the characteristics of training programs that help employees grasp new material, make sense of it in their own lives, and transfer it back to the job.

Because the success or failure of a training program is often related to certain principles of learning, both managers and employees should understand that different training methods and techniques vary in the extent to which they utilize these principles. All things considered, training programs are likely to be more effective if they incorporate the following principles of learning.

Goal Setting

The value of goal setting for focusing and motivating behaviour extends into training. When trainers take the time to explain the goals and objectives to trainees—or when trainees are encouraged to set goals on their own—levels of interest, understanding, and effort directed toward training are likely to increase. Often, goal setting can simply take the form of a "road map" of the course (or program), its objectives, and its learning points. A study of 150 experienced Canadian trainers by Alan M. Saks and Monica Belcourt found that few used goal setting as part of the training program.[9]

Meaningfulness of Presentation

One principle of learning is that the material to be learned should be presented in as meaningful a way as possible. In other words, trainees are better able to learn new information (from training) if they can connect it with things that are already familiar to them. Trainers often use colourful examples to which trainees can relate; these examples make the material meaningful. Also, material should be arranged so that each experience builds on the preceding ones. In this way, trainees are able to integrate experiences into a usable pattern of knowledge.[10]

Modelling

The old saying that "a picture is worth a thousand words" applies to training. Just as examples increase the meaningfulness of factual material or new knowledge in a training environment, modelling increases the salience of behavioural training. The research on social learning by Albert Bandura and others underscores the point that we learn vicariously—that is, we learn by watching. For example, if you are learning to ride a horse, it will be much easier to watch someone do it and then try it yourself, than to read a book or listen to a lecture and hope you can do it right.[11]

Modelling can take many forms. Real-life demonstrations or videotapes are often helpful; even pictures and drawings can get the visual message across. The point is that modelling demonstrates the behaviour or method to be learned. Modelling the wrong behaviour can actually be helpful sometimes, if it shows trainees what *not* to do and then clarifies the appropriate behaviour.

Individual Differences

People learn at different rates and in different ways. Some individuals can remember new information after hearing it only once (echoic memory) or seeing it only once (iconic memory). Others may have to work longer or find other techniques for retrieving the information. This may have nothing to do with their intelligence. Some students do horribly in large lecture settings but excel in small discussion classes; for other students, the reverse is true. To the extent possible, training programs should take into account these individual differences, and try to accommodate as many styles and rates of learning as possible.

Active Practice and Repetition

The things we do daily become a part of our repertoire of skills. Trainees should be given regular opportunities to practise the job tasks they are learning. A person who is being taught how to operate a machine should have an opportunity to practise on it. A manager who is being taught how to train should be given supervised practice in training.

Sometimes behaviours become second nature through practice. For example, when you first learned to drive a car, you concentrated a great deal on the mechanics: "Where are my hands, where are my feet, how fast am I going?" As you practised driving, you began to think less about the mechanics and more about the road, the weather, and the traffic. Other forms of learning are no different—by

Companies like Dale Carnegie Training offer employers training programs in valuable job skills such as teamwork.

practising, a trainee can forget about distinct behaviours and concentrate on the subtleties of how they are used.

Whole versus Part Learning

Most jobs and tasks can be broken down into parts that lend themselves to further analysis. The most effective manner for completing one part then be determined; this provides a basis for giving specific instruction. For example, keyboarding is made up of several skills that are part of the total process. The keyboarder starts by learning the proper use of each finger; eventually, with practice, the individual finger movements become integrated into a total pattern. Practice by moving individual fingers is an example of part learning. In evaluating whole-versus-part learning, you must consider the nature of the task to be learned. If it can be broken down successfully, it probably should be; otherwise, it should probably be taught as a unit.

Massed versus Distributed Learning

Another factor that determines the effectiveness of training is the amount of time devoted to one session. Should trainees be given training in five two-hour periods or in ten one-hour periods? Usually, spacing out the training results in faster learning and longer retention. This is the principle of distributed learning. Since the efficiency of the distribution will vary with the type and complexity of the task, managers should refer to the rapidly growing body of research in this area for guidance in designing a specific training situation.

Feedback and Reinforcement

Can any learning occur without feedback? Some feedback comes from self-monitoring; other feedback comes from trainers, fellow trainees, and the like. As the employee's training progresses, feedback serves two related purposes: it provides knowledge of results, and it increases motivation. Feedback helps people focus on what they are doing right and what they are doing wrong. In this way, it serves a shaping role as they approach the objectives of training. Think about when you first learned how to throw a baseball, or ride a bicycle, or swim. Someone, perhaps a parent, told you what you were doing right and what things to correct. Eventually your skills improved. Feedback also improves motivation. Progress, as determined by mistakes or successes, can be plotted on a chart, commonly referred to as a "learning curve." Figure 6.4 shows a learning curve that is commonly found when job skills are being acquired.

There are times in many learning situations when progress does not occur. These periods show up on the learning curve as plateaux. A plateau can indicate reduced motivation or ineffective methods of task performance. It is a natural phenomenon of learning, and there is usually a spontaneous recovery.

Sometimes rewards and reinforcements come in the form of approval from the manager or feelings of accomplishment; sometimes they are simply the confirmation in programmed instruction that the trainee's response is correct. (In some cases, it may be impossible to distinguish between feedback and rewards.) Generally, reinforcement is most effective when it immediately follows completion of the task.

Behaviour modification

Technique that operates on the principle that behaviour that is rewarded, or positively reinforced, will be displayed more often in the future, whereas behaviour that is penalized or unrewarded will decrease in frequency

In recent years, some work organizations have used **behaviour modification**, a technique that operates on the principle that behaviour that is rewarded—positively reinforced—will be displayed more often in the future, whereas behaviour that is penalized or unrewarded will decrease in frequency.

Characteristics of Instructors

The success of any training effort will depend greatly on the teaching skills and personal characteristics of the people conducting the training. What separates good trainers from mediocre ones? Often a good trainer is one who tries a little harder or prepares a little more carefully. However, training is also influenced by the trainer's personal manner and characteristics. Here is a short list of desirable traits:

1. *Knowledge of subject.* Employees expect trainers to know their job or subject thoroughly. They are also expected to demonstrate that knowledge. (Some experts refer to this trait as "active intelligence.")

2. *Adaptability.* Some individuals learn faster or slower than others. Instruction should be matched to the trainee's learning ability.

3. *Sincerity.* Trainees appreciate sincerity in trainers. Along with this, trainers need to be patient with trainees and demonstrate tact in addressing their concerns.

4. *Sense of humour.* Learning can be fun; very often a point can be made with a story or anecdote.

5. *Interest.* Good trainers have a keen interest in the subject they are teaching; this interest is readily conveyed to trainees.

6. *Clear instructions.* Naturally, training is accomplished more quickly and retained longer when trainers give clear instructions.

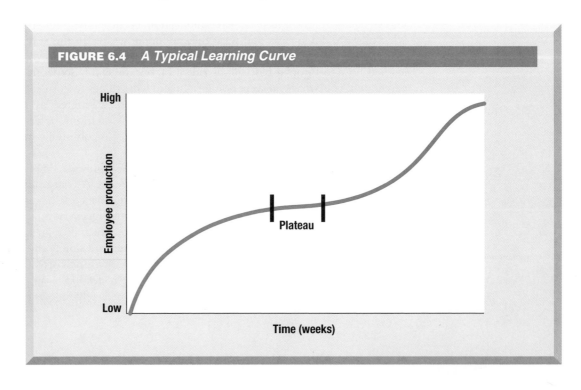

FIGURE 6.4   *A Typical Learning Curve*

7. *Individual assistance.* When training more than one employee, successful trainers always provide individual assistance.

8. *Enthusiasm.* A dynamic presentation and a vibrant personality show trainees that the trainer enjoys training. Employees tend to respond positively to enthusiastic trainers.[12]

Organizations should reward managers who are excellent trainers. Too often, managers are not recognized for their contributions to this important aspect of HRM.

PHASE 3: IMPLEMENTING THE TRAINING PROGRAM

Needs assessment, instructional objectives, principles of learning, and the like are all important to training programs. That being said, the process of choosing instructional methods is where "the rubber meets the road." In choosing among various training methods, it is of key importance to determine which ones are appropriate for the KSAs to be learned. For example, if most of the material is factual, methods such as lectures, classroom work, and programmed instruction may be fine. However, if the training has a large behavioural component, other methods such as on-the-job training, simulation, and computer-based training may work better.[13] The Belcourt–Saks study of Canadian trainers found that trainees were more likely to use their new skills in their work when a variety of methods were used, and especially when those methods closely reflected the job situation.[14]

For the following discussion, we have sorted the various training methods into two groups: those used for nonmanagerial employees, and those used for managers.

Training Methods for Nonmanagerial Employees

A wide variety of methods are available for training employees at all levels. Some of the methods have long been used. Newer methods have emerged over the years out of a greater understanding of human behaviour, particularly in the areas of learning, motivation, and interpersonal relationships. More recently, technological advances—especially in computer hardware and software—have resulted in training devices that are often more effective and economical than the traditional training methods.

On-the-Job Training

On-the-Job Training

Method by which employees are given hands-on experience with instructions from their supervisor or other trainer

The most common method for training nonmanagerial employees is **on-the-job training (OJT)**. OJT has these advantages: it offers hands-on experience under normal working conditions, and it provides opportunities for the trainer—a manager or senior employee—to build good relationships with new employees.

Although it is used by all types of organizations, OJT is often one of the most poorly implemented training methods. Three weaknesses are especially common: (1) the training environment is not well enough structured; (2) the managers lack training skills; and (3) well-defined job performance criteria are lacking. To overcome these weaknesses, training experts suggest the following:

1. Develop realistic goals and/or measures for each OJT area.

2. Plan a specific training schedule for each trainee, including set periods for evaluation and feedback.

3. Help managers establish a nonthreatening atmosphere conducive to learning.

4. Conduct periodic evaluations after training is completed, to prevent regression.[15]

Many successful trainers use a system known as *job instruction training* to acquaint managers with techniques for instructing their employees. (See Highlights in HRM 4.) Although the principles of job instruction training were developed during the Second World War, the recommended training tips are still clearly appropriate for today's organizations. Many small business managers use its basic format, or an adaptation of it, for instructing a new person on the job or a present worker on a new job.

Apprenticeship Training

Apprenticeship training

System of training in which a worker entering the skilled trades is given thorough instruction and experience, both on and off the job, in the practical and theoretical aspects of the work

An extension of OJT is **apprenticeship training**. With this method, individuals entering industry, especially in the skilled trades such as machinist, laboratory technician, or electrician, are given thorough instruction and experience, both on and off the job, in the practical and theoretical aspects of the work. Nickel producer Inco and Cambrian College recently joined forces in a maintenance training initiative.[16] Another example of an apprenticeship program is described in Highlights in HRM 5.

Apprenticeship programs originated in Europe as part of the guild system, and have since been adapted for use in Canada. Typically, these programs involve cooperation between organizations and their labour unions, or between industry and government, or between organizations and local school systems. The advantage to employees is that they are being paid to learn their trade. Magna International, the auto parts giant, pays students $8 to $15 per hour to train as millwrights and tool and die makers. Learning is offered variously in shops, laboratories, and classrooms.

WWW

Cooperative Training, Internships, and Governmental Training

Cooperative training

Training program that combines practical on-the-job experience with formal educational classes

Cooperative training programs are similar to apprenticeships, in that they combine practical on-the-job experience with formal classes. However, the term **cooperative training** is more typically used in connection with high school, college, and university programs. In recent years, educational institutions have been working harder to provide students with opportunities to combine on-the-job training with regular classroom training. For example, students at Mount Sentinel Secondary School in British Columbia participate in a Forest Workers Training Program that leads to industry-level certification.[17] Centennial College in Toronto collaborated with CIBC, AT&T Canada Enterprises, and Sun Microsystems of Canada to establish a three-semester certificate program that trains people to work in call centres.

WWW

Internship programs

Programs jointly sponsored by colleges, universities, and other organizations that offer students the opportunity to gain real-life experience while allowing them to find out how they will perform in work organizations

Internship programs are sponsored jointly by colleges, universities, and a variety of organizations, and offer students the chance to acquire real-world experience and to find out how they perform in work organizations. Organizations benefit by getting student-employees with energy, eagerness, and new ideas. Humber College in Toronto, the British Columbia Institute of Technology (BCIT) in Burnaby, and many other colleges allow students to earn college credits by performing well on placements and by fulfilling established program requirements.

Highlights in HRM

4   JOB INSTRUCTION TRAINING

Practical methods to guide you in instructing a new employee on a job—or a cureent employee on a new job or a new skill:

First, here's what you must do to get ready to teach a job:

1.   Decide what the employee must be taught in order to do the job efficiently, safely, economically, and intelligently.
2.   Have the right tools, equipment, supplies, and material ready.
3.   Have the workplace properly arranged, just as the employee will be expected to keep it.

Then you should instruct the employee according to the following four basic steps:

STEP I — PREPARATION (OF THE EMPLOYEE)

1.   Put the employee at ease.
2.   Find out what the employee already knows about the job.
3.   Get the employee interested and desirous of learning the job.

STEP II — PRESENTATION (OF THE OPERATIONS AND KNOWLEDGE)

1.   Tell, show, illustrate, and question in order to put over the new knowledge and operations.
2.   Instruct slowly, clearly, completely, and patiently, one point at a time.
3.   Check, question, and repeat.
4.   Make sure the employee really knows.

STEP III — PERFORMANCE TRYOUT

1.   Test the employee by having him or her perform the job.
2.   Ask questions beginning with *why, how, when,* or *where*.
3.   Observe performance, correct errors, and repeat instructions if necessary.
4.   Continue until you know the employee knows.

STEP IV — FOLLOW-UP

1.   Put the employee on his or her own.
2.   Check frequently to be sure the employee follows instructions.
3.   Taper off extra supervision and close follow-up until the employee is qualified to work with normal supervision.

Remember: If the employee hasn't learned, the manager hasn't taught.

Source: *The Training within Industry Report* (Washington, D.C.: Bureau of Training, Training within Industry

Highlights in HRM

5 ADVANTAGES OF COMPUTER-BASED TRAINING

1. Learning is self-paced.
2. Training comes to the employee.
3. Training is interactive.
4. New employees do not have to wait for a scheduled training session.
5. Training can focus on specific needs as revealed by built-in tests.
6. Trainees can be referred to on-line help or written material.
7. It is easier to revise a computer program than to change classroom training materials.
8. Record keeping is facilitated.
9. The computer program can be linked to video presentations.
10. CBT can be cost-effective if used for a large number of employees.

According to Pat Sniderman, professor of Organizational Behaviour and Human Resources Management, Ryerson Polytechnic University offers three innovative models for HR internships:

- HR interns shadow HR professionals, who act as mentors, for three days a week for six weeks. The interns then return to university and write a paper that integrates the research literature with their on-the-job experiences.
- Interns work full-time during the summer, and then two days a week while completing their studies.
- Interns work for an organization for a full year, typically between third and fourth year of their university degree.

To be eligible, students must have high marks, and must be interviewed by both the business school and the employer. Youth Internship Canada, a program of Human Resources Development Canada, provides funding to employers to create meaningful work experiences for unemployed youth.

The federal government and various provincial governments sponsor a multitude of training programs for new and current employees. Often these training efforts are aimed at helping people who lack marketable skills to develop those skills. Governments offer labour market adjustment programs, such as entry and re-entry training and job loss support. These support programs, which extend beyond the billions of dollars spent on unemployment insurance, lessen the impact of job loss by providing training, counselling, and information.

Of course, no single employer or government agency can solve the problems of the unemployed or soften the shattering effects of plant closures. Partnerships between governments, employers, unions, and educational institutions have been especially effective in training laid-off employees and helping them find jobs. For example, 1,300 workers at the Firestone plant in Hamilton, Ontario, benefited from an alliance between the union, the company, and the community. A highly motivated and effective adjustment committee was able to accommodate 95 percent of the laid-off workers through new jobs, retirement, and retraining.

Classroom Instruction

Most people, when they think about training, think about classrooms. There is a good reason for this. With classroom training, the minimum number of instructors can handle the maximum number of trainees. This method lends itself best to training in areas where information can be presented in lectures, demonstrations, films, and videotapes or through computer instruction. Where videotapes aren't available, audiotapes can be very valuable. For example, to instruct flight crew trainees, airlines might play a cockpit tape taken from a doomed aircraft. After listening to the tape, the trainees discuss the behaviour of the crew during the crisis. By listening to the recorded statements of others and observing their failure to operate as a team, pilot trainees develop an understanding of the need for balancing their sense of self-reliance with an ability to listen to subordinates. A special type of classroom facility is used in vestibule training. Trainees are given instruction in the operation of equipment like that found in operating departments. The emphasis is on instruction rather than production.

Programmed Instruction

One method of instruction that is especially good for allowing individuals to work at their own pace is programmed instruction. Programmed instruction—referred to more and more as self-directed learning—involves using books, manuals, or computers to break down subject matter into logical and highly organized sequences that demand continuous responses on the part of the trainee. The trainee is presented with a small segment of information and then is required to answer a question, either by writing it in a response frame or by pushing a button. If the response is correct, the trainee is told so and is presented with the next step (frame) in the material. If the response is incorrect, further explanatory information is given and the trainee is told to try again.

A big advantage of programmed instruction is that it incorporates a number of the established learning principles discussed earlier in the chapter. With programmed instruction, training is individualized, trainees are actively involved in the instructional process, and feedback and reinforcement are immediate. Programmed instruction may not increase the amount a person learns, but it usually increases the speed at which he or she learns.

Audiovisual Methods

Audiovisual equipment can be used to teach skills and procedures for many production jobs. At the simplest level, videotapes can be used to illustrate the steps in a procedure such as assembling electronic equipment or working with a problem employee. Camcorders allow trainers and trainees to view an on-the-spot recording and to get immediate feedback about progress toward learning objectives. Golf and tennis coaches often tape their students to let them see their performances.

WWW

Videodiscs take this technology further by providing trainees with immediate access to any segment of the instructional program. This is especially useful for providing employees who have different levels of knowledge and ability with individualized instruction. Videodiscs are now being used to teach doctors to diagnose illness, to help dairy farmers increase productivity, and to teach CPR trainees how to revive victims of heart attacks. More recent applications tackle the difficult managerial skills of leadership, supervision, and interpersonal relations.

Instructional programs can be transmitted to many locations at once through closed circuit television. As well, video conferencing and interactive television are bringing teletraining to life. These methods are becoming powerful tools in continuing education and in distance education. FORDSTAR, the largest satellite distance learning network in the world, shares information and provides training on multiple channels of video to 6,000 Ford and Lincoln-Mercury dealers. ReMax operates a satellite network that provides training to more than 1,000 real estate offices throughout North America.

Computer-Based Training (CBT)

With technology developing at a rapid pace and the cost of computers continuing to decline, high-tech training methods are increasedly being used in industry, academia, and the military. Computer-based training (CBT) comprises two distinct techniques: computer-assisted instruction, and computer-managed instruction. A **computer-assisted instruction (CAI)** system delivers training materials directly through a computer terminal in an interactive format. Computers offer a window for drill-and-practice, problem-solving, simulation, and gaming forms of instruction, as well as certain very sophisticated forms of individualized tutorial instruction.

Typically, a **computer-managed instruction (CMI)** system is used in conjunction with CAI. When used this way, it provides an efficient means of managing the training function. CMI uses a computer to generate and score tests and to determine trainees' proficiency levels. CMI systems can also track the performance of trainees and direct them to appropriate study materials to meet their specific needs. With CMI, the computer takes on some of the routine aspects of training; this frees the instructor to spend time on course development or individualized instruction.

When CBT is structured so as to be available to employees on the job whenever they need it, it is referred to as "just-in-time" training.[18] Most large companies, including Rogers Communications, National Grocers, and Janssen-Ortho, are engaged in computer-based training. A summary of the advantages of CBT is given in Highlights in HRM 5.

Computer-assisted instruction (CAI)

System that delivers instructional material directly through a computer terminal in an interactive format

Computer-managed instruction (CMI)

System normally employed in conjunction with CAI that uses a computer to generate and score tests and to determine the level of training proficiency

WWW

Internet Instruction

Organizations have recently begun exploring the Internet as a possible vehicle for CBT. Web pages are easy, fast, and cheap to revise. Also, using the Internet will very likely save travel and classroom costs. The downside for training may be that Internet users tend to "surf." Given the sometimes nondirect format of the Internet, it may be a challenge to focus trainee interaction. Of course, this could be an advantage as well. The Internet requires users to become adept at searching, comparing, and making sense of a large amount of information. These skills are especially important for building other skills, such as troubleshooting, problem solving, and analytical thinking. When combined with e-mail capabilities, Internet-based training can be very useful.[19]

A course in human resources management based on this text is available on the Internet. Participants can interact with one another and with the instructor via a discussion group, or they can receive private instruction via e-mail.[20]

Simulation Method

WWW

Sometimes it is either impractical or unwise to train employees on the actual equipment used on the job. An obvious example is training employees to operate aircraft, spacecraft, and other highly technical and expensive equipment. The simulation method emphasizes realism in equipment and its operation at minimum cost and maximum safety. For example, CAE Electronics worked closely with Boeing to develop flight simulators in parallel with the development of the 777 aircraft. Boeing has developed other such simulators for its aircraft and recently began using the technology to train pilots in China.[21]

The sophistication of simulations can be impressive, but as information technology becomes more powerful the distinction between simulation and the simpler CBT is beginning to blur. For example, a simulation developed by Wicat in partnership with Airbus and Singapore Airlines runs on a PC and replicates a cockpit with control displays and throttle/flap controls. Even though the PC-based simulation is relatively inexpensive, it is powerful. Pilots are taken through a self-paced program that simulates "taxi, takeoff, climb, cruise, descent, approach, landing, and go-around." These types of technologies are making it easier to offer training in new and different ways. The director of training and development for Delta Air Lines has stated that his company's goal is to deliver simulation training to employees in their homes. Using a PC and a modem, pilots will sign in and upload everything necessary for them to study the lesson. The problem at this point is delivering full-motion video. One solution might be to use remote pay-per-view training centres with video file servers fed via satellite downlinks. The possibilities seem limitless.[22]

Training Methods for Management Development

While many of the methods used to train first-level employees are also used to train managers and supervisors, there are other methods that tend to be reserved for management development. Recall that development differs somewhat from training in that its purpose is to broaden an individual's experience and provide a longer-term view of that individual's role in the organization. Over the past decade, the importance of management development has grown as organizations attempt to compete through people. About 40 percent of Canadian companies have a formal executive development policy.[23] Organizational change and strategic revitalization depend on talented leaders, managers, and supervisors. Management development is instrumental in providing managers with the skills and perspectives they need to be successful.[24]

The methods used for management development vary in terms of the principles of learning they incorporate and their appropriateness for delivering various SKAs.

On-the-Job Experiences

Some skills and knowledge can be acquired just by listening and observing or by reading. But others must be acquired through actual practice and experience. Because it presents managers with opportunities to perform under pressure and to learn from their mistakes, on-the-job development is one of the most powerful and commonly used techniques.

However, just as on-the-job training for first-level employees can lead to problems if not well planned, on-the-job management development should be well organized, supervised, and challenging to the participants.[25] Methods of providing on-the-job experiences include the following:

1. *Coaching* involves a continuing flow of instructions, comments, and suggestions from the manager to the subordinate. (Mentoring, discussed in Chapter 7, is a similar approach to personal and informal management development.)

2. *Understudy assignments* groom an individual to take over a manager's job by providing experience in handling important functions of the job.

3. *Job rotation* provides, through a variety of work experiences, the broadened knowledge and understanding required to manage more effectively.

4. *Lateral transfer* involves horizontal movement through different departments, along with upward movement in the organization.

5. *Special projects* and *junior boards* provide an opportunity for individuals to become involved in the study of current organizational problems and in planning and decision-making activities.

6. *Action learning* gives managers release time to work full-time on projects with others in the organization. Action learning is sometimes combined with classroom instruction, discussions, and conferences.

7. *Staff meetings* enable participants to become more familiar with problems and events outside their immediate area by exposing them to the ideas and thinking of other managers.

8. *Planned career progressions* (discussed in Chapter 7) utilize all these different methods to provide employees with the training and development necessary to progress through a series of jobs requiring higher and higher levels of knowledge and/or skills.

Although these methods are used most often to develop managers for higher-level positions, they also provide valuable experiences for those who are being groomed for other types of positions in the organization. And while on-the-job experiences constitute the core of management training and development, other (i.e., off-the-job) methods of development can be used to supplement these experiences.

Seminars and Conferences

Seminars and conferences, like classroom instruction, are useful for bringing groups of people together for training and development. In management development, they can be used to communicate ideas, policies, or procedures, but they are also good for raising points of debate or discussing issues (usually with the help of a qualified leader) that have no set answers or resolutions. In this regard, seminars and conferences are often used when attitude change is a goal. Other seminars, on topics ranging from communications to strategic planning, are offered by organizations such as the Human Resources Professionals of Ontario, which holds an annual conference devoted to HR topics.

Case Studies

An especially useful method for classroom learning situations is the case study. Using documented examples, perhaps developed from the actual experiences of people in their own organization, managers learn how to analyze (take apart) and synthesize (put together) facts. They also become aware of the many variables on which management decisions are based; and, in general, they improve their decision-making skills. Experienced educators and trainers generally point out that case studies are most appropriate where

1. analytic, problem-solving, and critical thinking skills are most important;

2. the KSAs are complex, and participants need time to master them;

3. active participation is desired;

4. the process of learning (questioning, interpreting, etc.) is as important as the content; *and*

5. team problem solving and interaction are possible.[26]

Useful though they may be, case studies are often mismanaged. As with any other development technique, implementation is crucial for effectiveness. Figure 6.5 provides a set of guidelines for conducting case studies. Cases are used by the the Centre for Addiction and Mental Health in Toronto as a detection and diagnostic tool.

Management Games

Training experiences have been brought to life and made more interesting through the development of management games, in which players are faced with the task of making a series of decisions affecting a hypothetical organization. The effects that decisions have on the different areas in the organization can be simulated using a computer programmed for the game. A big advantage of this technique is that it requires a high degree of participation.

Games are now in wide use as a training method. Many of them have been designed for general use. Recently, more industry-specific games have been developed, so simulations are now available for a wide variety of industries.[27] More and more organizations are using simulations of organization dynamics as tools for change. For example, General Electric uses a three-day simulation to wrap up its management development program. This is a customized computerized simulation that teaches managers to balance such variables as profit, cost, turnover, product schedules, and personnel changes.[28] Practitioners in the management training have come to realize that extensive preparation, planning, and debriefing are needed to realize the potential benefits of this method.

The game method does not always require a computer. TD Bank uses a simulation called Desert Kings to encourage more open communication, increase levels of team performance, and increase commitment to both internal and

FIGURE 6.5 *Guidelines for Using Case Studies*

1. Be clear about learning objectives, and list possible ways to achieve the objectives.
2. Decide which objectives would be best served by the case method.
3. Identify available cases that might work, or consider writing your own.
4. Set up the activity, including the case materials, the room, and the schedule.
5. Follow the principles of effective group dynamics.
6. Provide a chance for all learners to take part, and try to keep the groups small.
7. Stop for process checks, and be ready to intervene if group dynamics get out of hand.
8. Allow for different learning styles.
9. Clarify the trainer's role.
10. Bridge the gap between theory and practice.

Source: Adapted from Albert A. Einsiedel, Jr., "Case Studies: Indispensable Tools for Trainers," *Training and Development,* August 1995: 50–53.

external customer service. Extensive preparation, planning, and debriefing are needed to realize the potential benefits of management games.

Role Playing

In role playing, the participants assume the attitudes and behaviours of other people—in other words, they *play* other people. Often these other people are a supervisor and a subordinate who are having a particular problem with each other. By acting out other people's positions, participants can increase their empathy for others, and learn to see situations from a different perspective. Often, role playing also helps them learn how to counsel others. Role playing is used widely in training health care professionals to be sensitive to the concerns of patients. It is also used widely in training managers to handle employee issues relating to absenteeism, performance appraisal, and conflict situations.

Participants are sometimes hesitant to try role playing. Successful role play takes planning. Instructors should do the following:

1. Ensure that members of the group are comfortable with one another.

2. Select and prepare the role players by introducing a specific situation.

3. To help participants prepare, ask them to describe potential characters.

4. Realize that volunteers make better role players.

5. Prepare the observers by giving them specific tasks (e.g., evaluation, feedback).

6. Guide the role-play enactment through its bumps (since it is not scripted).

7. Keep it short.

8. Discuss the enactment and prepare bulleted points of what was learned.[29]

Role play is applicable to a variety of training experiences. Planned and implemented correctly, role play can bring realism and insight into dilemmas and experiences that otherwise might not be shared.

Behaviour Modelling

One technique that combines several different training methods, and therefore multiple principles of learning, is **behaviour modelling**, which has four basic components:

Behaviour modelling

Approach that demonstrates desired behaviour and gives trainees the chance to practise and role-play those behaviours and receive feedback

1. *Learning points.* At the beginning of instruction, the essential goals and objectives of the program are laid out. Sometimes the learning points are a sequence of behaviours to be taught. For example, the learning points might describe the recommended steps for giving employees feedback.

2. *Model.* Participants view films or videotapes in which a model manager is portrayed dealing with an employee in an effort to improve his or her performance. The model shows specifically how to deal with the situation and demonstrates the learning points.

3. *Practice and role play.* Trainees extensively rehearse the behaviours demonstrated by the models. Most of the training time is spent in these skill practice sessions.

4. *Feedback and reinforcement.* As the trainee's behaviour increasingly resembles that of the model, the trainer and other trainees provide social reinforcers such as praise, approval, encouragement, and attention. Videotaping behaviour rehearsals provides feedback and reinforcement. Throughout the training period the emphasis is on transferring the training to the job.

Does behaviour modelling work? Several controlled studies have shown it to be successful in helping managers interact with employees, handle discipline, introduce change, and increase productivity.[30]

Many of the methods used for management development focus on changing attitudes as well as skills. Culture management programs such as empowerment are designed to increase employee commitment to organizational goals. However, some individuals object to giving their "souls" as well as their bodies to the corporate world, and especially resent any program content that is not consistent with their personal morality or religious beliefs. Ethics in HRM illustrates the need to investigate the underlying philosophies of training programs.

PHASE 4: EVALUATING THE TRAINING PROGRAM

OBJECTIVE
6

Training, like any other HRM function, should be evaluated to determine its effectiveness. A variety of methods are available to assess whether training programs have stimulated learning, affected behaviour on the job, and improved the bottom-line performance of the organization. Unfortunately, few organizations adequately evaluate their training programs. In many ways this goes beyond poor management: it is poor business practice. Given the considerable financial stake that organizations have in training, managers should want to maximize the return on that investment.

There are four basic criteria for evaluating training: (1) reactions, (2) learning, (3) behaviour, and (4) results. Some of these criteria are easier to measure than others, but each is important in that it provides different information about the worth of a given training program. When these criteria are combined, managers have a total picture of the program, and can start making decisions about whether the program is viable, and if it is, how to improve it.[31]

Ethics in HRM

MIND MANIPULATION

WWW

Half of the twenty-four employees of SaskTel who participated in a training program on process re-engineering required in its aftermath psychological counselling, or stress leave, or both. Trainees said they were subjected to a greenhouse environment: windows were papered over, employees were not allowed to communicate with one another, and all were subjected to verbal abuse from the training consultants. As the president of the Ontario Society for Training and Development commented: "That's not training, that's assault."

Seagulls Pewter and Silversmiths of Pugwash, Nova Scotia, sent its employees to seminars based on the controversial Est therapy. Employees complained to their union that the seminars, in which participants were encouraged to delve into painful emotions, often drove participants to breakdowns.

A large insurance company hired a consultant to conduct management training for hundreds of supervisors and managers. The company did not realize that the consultant was a member of L. Ron Hubbard's Church of Scientology and was teaching management principles developed by scientologists. Critics contend that scientology is a cult, not a religion. Employees resented being subjected to psychological concepts based on "tones" that catalogue emotions; to the ruthless devotion to ferreting out and firing problem employees; and to "religious scriptures."

The employees in these organizations were required to participate in programs that caused them undue stress and sometimes violated their moral or religious beliefs. Those who organized the programs believed that employees with the "right" attitudes would be more effective. Do organizations have a right to influence the motivations, attitudes, and beliefs of employees?

Sources: Edward Kay, "Trauma in Real Life," *The Globe and Mail Report on Business Magazine,* November 1996: 82–92; J. Saunders, "How Scientology's Message Came to Allstate," *The Globe and Mail,* April 24, 1995: B1; R. Sharpe, "Agents of Intimidation," *The Globe and Mail,* March 28, 1995: B8.

Criterion 1: Reactions

One of the simplest and most common approaches to training evaluation involves assessing participants' reactions. Happy trainees are more likely to want to utilize what they learned during the program. However, participants can do more than just tell you whether they liked the program or not. They can suggest which content and techniques they found most useful. They can critique the instructors, and make suggestions about participant interactions, feedback, and the like.

While evaluation methods based on reactions are beginning to improve, too many conclusions about training effectiveness are still based on broad satisfaction measures that lack specificity. It should also be noted that positive reactions are no guarantee that the training was successful. It is easy to collect glowing comments from trainees; but gratifying as this information may be to management, the training has served no purpose unless it leads to improved behaviour and job performance. Better than five out of six organizations in Canada measure trainee reaction.[32] Yet the Belcourt–Saks study of Canadian trainers mentioned earlier in this chapter found no link between participants' reactions and the later utilization of learned skills and knowledge on the job.[33] In the final analysis, reaction measures should not stop with assessing the training's entertainment value.

Criterion 2: Learning

Beyond what participants thought about the training, it might be a good idea to see whether they actually learned anything. Some organizations have figured this out; 42 percent of Canadian companies measure learning.[34] Some of them test trainees' knowledge and skills before the training program starts, to establish a baseline. Trainees are then measured again after the training program to determine whether their skills and/or knowledge improved as a result of it. Another approach is to test individuals in a control group and compare their results with those in the group being trained. This helps the organization learn whether improvements were a result of training, as opposed to some other factor (such as change in jobs, or compensation, or something else). The control group should comprise employees who have not received the training but who match the trainees in such areas as experience, past training, and job level.[35]

Criterion 3: Behaviour

Transfer of training

Effective application of principles learned to what is required on the job

You might be surprised to learn that much of what employees learn in a training program never gets used back on the job. It's not that the training was necessarily ineffective. In fact, on measures of employee reactions and learning, the program might score quite high. But for various reasons, trainees may not demonstrate behaviour change back on the job. **Transfer of training** refers to the effective application of principles learned to what is required on the job. Only 23 percent of Canadian organizations assess whether behaviour on the job changes as a result of training, and only 16 percent of all Canadian organizations link this finding to organizational results.[36] Transfer of training is discussed in more depth in a later section.

Criterion 4: Results

WWW

In an American Society of Training and Development (ASTD) study, roughly two-thirds of training managers reported that they were being pressured more and more to show that their programs were producing "bottom-line" results.[37] Some of the results-based criteria used in evaluating training include increased productivity, fewer employee complaints, decreased costs and waste, and profitability. Dofasco sent employees to three different companies in France and England to learn how to fortify the ladles they use to carry molten lead. Each trip cost about $20,000, but a million dollars will be saved for every ladle that does not break because of what was learned on these study trips.

Utility and Return on Investment

Many organizations are beginning to think of training programs in terms of utility. *Utility* refers to the benefits derived from training relative to the costs incurred. If the cost of training is high and the benefits are low, or if employees leave their jobs for other ones, the utility of training may be low.[38] Those training managers who do measure results have found the transfer of KSAs to the job to be both more extensive and more enduring.[39]

Increasingly, organizations with sophisticated training systems are looking to training to support long-term strategy and change; for these firms, short-term financial returns are not the point of training. Instead of looking for a "payback," organizations such as Motorola and Arthur Andersen view training in terms of its "pay-forward"—that is, the extent to which the training provides knowledge and skills that create a competitive advantage and a culture that is ready for continuous change.[40]

Benchmarking

Benchmarking

Process of measuring one's own services and practices against the recognized leaders in order to identify areas for improvement

Training and development are increasingly being viewed from a strategic standpoint. Parallel with this is a growing interest in **benchmarking** developmental services and practices against those of recognized leaders in industry. While no single model for exact benchmarking exists, the simplest models are based on the late W. Edwards Deming's classic four-step process. The four-step process advocates that managers do the following:

1. *Plan*. Conduct a self-audit to define internal processes and measurements; decide on areas to be benchmarked, and choose the comparison organization.

2. *Do*. Collect data through surveys, interviews, site visits, and/or historical records.

3. *Check*. Analyze data to discover performance gaps, and communicate findings and suggested improvements to management.

4. *Act*. Establish goals, implement specific changes, monitor progress, and redefine benchmarks as a continuous improvement process.

To use benchmarking successfully, managers must define clearly the measures of competency and performance and then objectively assess the current situation and identify areas for improvement. To this end, experts in this area are attempting to work out ways of measuring what training departments do. Three broad areas that most HR training and developmental practitioners consider essential to measure are:

1. *Training activity*. How much training is occurring?

2. *Training results*. Do training and development achieve their goals?

3. *Training efficiency*. Are resources utilized in the pursuit of this mission?

The American Society for Training and Development and its Institute for Workplace Learning, along with the Saratoga Institute in Canada, have established a project that allows organizations to measure and benchmark training and development activities against one another. This benchmarking forum compares data on training costs, staffing, administration, design, development, and delivery of training programs. Initiatives such as these help organizations evaluate their training programs; in addition, the process serves as a feedback loop for reinitiating needs assessment and design of future training.[41]

PHASE 5: OPTIMIZING TRANSFER OF TRAINING

Transfer of training, or the implementation (and maintenance) in the work environment of the skills acquired during the training program, has been a long-standing subject of concern to organizations that are looking for a better return on their training dollars.[42]

The Belcourt–Saks survey of Canadian trainers found that in the immediate aftermath of a training program, two-thirds of employees were effective in implementing the skills they had acquired; however, this figure had dropped to about one-third by a year later.[43] Prescriptions for achieving optimum transfer before, during, and after a training program are discussed below.

Before Training

Training effectiveness is influenced by organizational activities years before an actual program begins. Effective transfer begins with the creation of an organizational learning culture in which knowledge and skills acquisition are highly valued and are considered to be the responsibility of every employee; in which job assignments are challenging; in which there are formal mechanisms for rewarding the acquisition of new skills; and in which informal networks support learning and its application. Simply put, a learning culture values learning and its application.

In the period before training begins, trainers and supervisors should identify trainee needs and solicit trainee input about the program content. Pretraining reading, activities, and course assignments have been found to increase the probability of effective transfer. When supervisors set goals with the trainees in advance of the training program, they are sending a powerful signal that training is important.[44]

During Training

As we have seen, trainers have a wide variety of methods from which to choose. The choice of training method is based on factors such as cost, time, implementation difficulty, and learning objectives. The best methods for optimizing transfer are those in which the trainee is highly involved. Also, the more the training situation resembles the job, the more likely transfer will occur. Training methods that provide job approximation and encourage trainee involvement include on-the-job training, one-on-one training, and simulations; somewhat less effective in this are role playing, behaviour modelling, self-study, case studies, and multimedia. A combination of methods generally works best. When the training method cannot be matched exactly to the work environment, trainers often stress the learning principles behind the training instead of focusing on rote behaviour.

After Training

One way to ensure that trainees do not abandon the KSAs learned in the training program is to have them apply self-management techniques. On returning to work, trainees will face obstacles that may frustrate successful transfer. Relapse-prevention training can provide them with strategies for coping with any post-training hurdles they encounter.[45] Trainees can be trained to manage post-course relapses by setting their own goals (written behavioural contracts).

Booster sessions, in which trainees discuss their training experiences and support one another, have also had a positive effect on transfer; so has the submission of post-training progress reports by trainees. Supervisors can reinforce transfer by providing trainees with opportunities to practise their recently acquired KSAs, and by offering positive feedback when they do. The organization can use promotions or bonuses to reward and motivate trainees who successfully implement the KSAs.[46] For discussions on excellence in training, consult **www.extrain.com**.

SPECIAL TOPICS IN TRAINING AND DEVELOPMENT

While we have focused almost exclusively on the processes underlying a systems model of training—needs assessment, principles of learning, implementation methods, evaluation—it may be useful to discuss some of the more popular topics that are covered in these training programs. As we noted in Figure 6.1, there are a wide variety of training programs. A lot of training addresses the KSAs that reflect the demands of a particular job; besides this kind, many employers develop training programs to meet the needs of a broader base of employees. In this final section, we summarize some of these programs, including basic skills training, team training, and diversity training. Global training will be covered in Chapter 16.

Basic Skills Training

Surveys have shown that between 30 and 40 percent of Canadian workers cannot read simple directions or do the basic mathematics required to total a restaurant bill or complete a mail order invoice.[47] These findings have important implications for society at large and for organizations that must work around employees' skill deficiencies. Advances in technology make weaknesses in basic skills that much more noticeable. Basic skills have become essential occupational qualifications; they have profound implications for product quality, customer service, internal efficiency, and workplace and environmental safety.

WWW

While there are different possible approaches to the problem, in-house basic skills programs have come increasingly into favour.[48] Here are just a few examples: Ford offers reading courses at twenty-five of its plants; Domino's Pizza uses a videodisc program to teach reading and math (and making pizza dough); Polaroid United Technologies and AT&T have developed remedial training programs in math, English, and spelling. In Canada, companies like Abitibi-Consolidated have discovered the benefits of investing in literacy projects.[49] Figure 6.6 lists ten basic skills for the workplace.

Grown-ups don't learn the way kids do, so many of the traditional basic skills training techniques are not successful with adults. To implement a successful program in basic and remedial skills, managers should

- explain to employees why and how the training will help them in their jobs;
- relate the training to the employees' goals;
- respect and consider participant experiences, and use these as a resource;
- use a task-centred or problem-centred approach so that participants "learn by doing"; *and*

FIGURE 6.6 *Human Resource Competency Model*

TEN BASIC SKILLS FOR THE WORKPLACE

1. Reading
2. Writing
3. Computing
4. Speaking
5. Listening

6. Solving problems
7. Managing oneself
8. Knowing how to learn
9. Working as part of a team
10. Leading others

- give feedback on progress toward meeting learning objectives.

The key to developing a successful basic skills program is *flexibility*. The principle of individual differences should be reinforced; the realities of work and family constraints should be acknowledged.[50]

Team Training

As we discussed in Chapter 3, organizations rely on teams to achieve strategic and operational goals. Whether it be an air crew, a research team, or a manufacturing or service unit, how much the team contributes is a function not only of the KSAs of the individuals in it, but also of how well those individuals interact. The teamwork behaviours of effective teams are shown in Figure 6.7. The skills required involve both process dynamics and behavioural dynamics. These behaviours are observable and measurable, which provides a basis for training team members to function more effectively in the pursuit of their goals.[51] Over a three-year period, 6,700 employees at Dofasco participated in four-day workshops on interpersonal and group skills.[52]

WWW

Coca-Cola's Fountain Manufacturing Operation (the 104-person plant that makes syrup for Coke and Diet Coke) recently worked with consultants from Moving On! to develop team training for its manufacturing employees. This program focuses on three skill categories: (1) technical, (2) interpersonal, and (3) team action. The *technical* component is called Four-Deep Training, which implies that each individual should learn four different jobs to allow for team flexibility. The *interpersonal skills* component is called Adventures in Attitudes, and focuses on listening, conflict resolution, influence, and negotiation. *Team action* training focuses on team leadership, management of meetings, team roles, group dynamics, and problem solving—all skills needed to function effectively as a team. The training has increased quality and customer satisfaction, and has also helped reduce costs. Furthermore, it has been used to set up a model for preparing employees for the future.[53]

In the past few years, other organizations have developed exercises to generate enthusiasm and enhance team participation. Managers who want to design team training for their organization should remember the following:

1. Team building is a difficult and comprehensive process. Since many new teams are under pressure to produce, there is little time for training. You cannot cover everything in a twenty-four-hour blitz. Team training works best when it is provided over time and parallels team development.

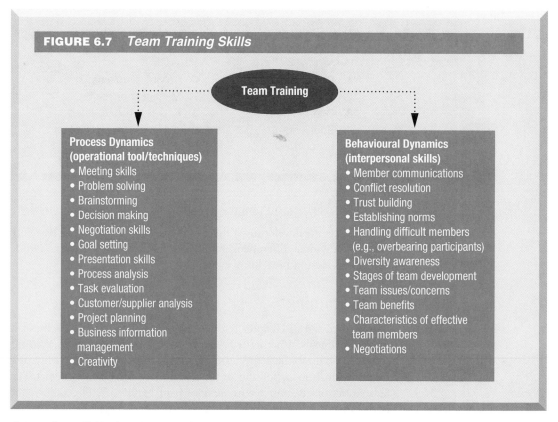

FIGURE 6.7 *Team Training Skills*

Team Training

Process Dynamics (operational tool/techniques)
- Meeting skills
- Problem solving
- Brainstorming
- Decision making
- Negotiation skills
- Goal setting
- Presentation skills
- Process analysis
- Task evaluation
- Customer/supplier analysis
- Project planning
- Business information management
- Creativity

Behavioural Dynamics (interpersonal skills)
- Member communications
- Conflict resolution
- Trust building
- Establishing norms
- Handling difficult members (e.g., overbearing participants)
- Diversity awareness
- Stages of team development
- Team issues/concerns
- Team benefits
- Characteristics of effective team members
- Negotiations

Source: George Bohlander and Kathy McCarthy, "How to Get the Most from Team Training," *National Productivity Review,* Autumn 1996: 25–35.

2. Team development is not always a linear sequence of "forming, storming, norming, and performing." Training initiatives can help a team work through each of these stages, but managers must be aware that lapses can occur.

3. Additional training is required to assimilate new members. Large changes in membership may result in teams reverting to a previous developmental stage.

4. Behavioural and process skills need to be acquired through participative exercises. Team members cannot internalize subjects such as conflict resolution through passive listening. Hands-on experiences are much better.[54]

A website devoted to team training is **www.mrg.ab.ca/tbindex.htm**.

Diversity Training

Many large organizations sponsor some sort of diversity training. This emphasis is sparked by an awareness of the varied demographics of the workforce, the challenges of employment equity, the dynamics of stereotyping, the changing values of the workforce, and the potential competitive payoffs from bringing different people together for a common purpose. There are basically two types of diversity training: (1) awareness building, which helps employees appreciate the benefits of diversity, and (2) skill building, which provides the KSAs necessary for working with people who are different. For example, a skill-building diversity program might teach managers how to conduct performance appraisals with people from different cultures, or teach male supervisors how to coach female employees toward better career opportunities. All of the diverse dimensions—race, gender, age, disabilities, lifestyles, culture, education, ideas, and backgrounds—should be considered in the design of a diversity training program.[55]

WWW

Connaught Laboratories has won a host of awards for its diversity training program. About 800 employees participated in a three-hour program that covered topics such as government policies, trends in demographics, terminology, designated groups, and the benefits of a new work environment. Managers attended a one-day workshop on learning to manage diversity.

Not all diversity training is independently designed. Increasingly, diversity training is being combined with other training programs. Some believe this represents the "mainstreaming" of diversity with other strategic issues facing organizations. For example, Honeywell subsumes diversity training within a week-long advanced management program and as part of its sales training programs. General Electric trains mentors and protégés in a program that isn't explicitly a diversity initiative but nevertheless clearly helps women and ethnic minorities.[56]

Organizations that have been successful with diversity training realize that such training is a long-term process that requires the highest level of skill. Ineffective training in this area can cause more problems than it solves. Unfortunately, many consulting firms have added diversity training to their list of programs without adequate personnel to handle the assignment. To avoid the pitfalls of substandard diversity training, managers will want to do the following:

1. *Forge a strategic link.* Begin by establishing the reasons for diversity training. Clarify the links between diversity and business goals in order to provide a context for training. Employment equity and valuing diversity are not the same thing. Ultimately, diversity enhances differences and unites those differences toward a common goal.

2. *Check out consultants' qualifications.* Recognize that there are no certification criteria for consultants, so make certain they are qualified. Background and experience checks are essential.

3. *Don't settle for "off the shelf " programs.* Each company has somewhat different goals, and the training should reflect this.

4. *Choose training methods carefully.* Most diversity training is really education (awareness building). Managers may hope they are developing skills, but this requires more in-depth training. Employees often benefit from both awareness building and skill building, but these are not the same thing.

5. *Document individual and organizational benefits.* Diversity training, when done well, enhances communications, improves responsiveness to social issues, reduces lawsuits, creates a climate of fairness, improves productivity on complex tasks, and increases revenues and profits.

Good diversity training programs extend beyond employment equity goals and support the competitive capability of the organization.[57]

SUMMARY

 Today we find that organizational operations cover a broad range of subjects and involve personnel at all levels, from orientation through to management development. Besides providing the training needed for effective job performance, employers offer training in such areas as personal growth and wellness.

 Training begins with orientation and continues throughout an employee's service with an organization. By participating in a formal orientation program, employees acquire the knowledge, skills, and attitudes that increase the probabilitiy that they will succeed with the organization. For an orientation to be effective there should be close cooperation between the HR department and other departments in all phases of the program, from initial planning through to follow-up and evaluation.

For effective training programs, the systems approach is recommended. This approach consists of five phases: (1) needs assessment, (2) program design, (3) implementation, (4) evaluation, and (5) optimization of transfer of training.

 Needs assessment begins with organization analysis. Managers must establish a context for training by deciding where training is needed, how it connects with strategic goals, and how organizational resources can best be used. Task analysis is used to identify the knowledge, skills, and abilities that are needed. Person analysis is used to identify which people need training.

 In designing a training program, managers must consider the two fundamental preconditions for learning: readiness and motivation. In addition, principles of learning should be considered in order to create an environment that is conducive to learning. These principles include goal setting, meaningfulness, modelling, individual differences, active practice, whole-versus–part learning, distributed learning, feedback, and rewards and reinforcement.

 For training nonmanagerial personnel, a wide variety of methods are available. On-the-job training is one of the most commonly used methods because it provides the advantage of hands-on experience and an opportunity to build a relationship between supervisor and employee. Apprenticeship training and internships are especially effective because they provide both on- and off-the-job experiences. Other off-the-job methods include the conference or discussion method, classroom training, programmed instruction, computer-based training, simulation, closed-circuit TV, teletraining, and interactive videodisc. All of these methods can make a contribution to the training effort at relatively little cost vis-à-vis the number of trainees that can be accommodated.

A wide variety of training methods are also used for developing managers. On-the-job experiences include coaching, understudy assignment, job rotation, lateral transfer, project and committee assignments, and staff meetings. Off-the-job experiences include analysis of case studies, management games, role playing, and behaviour modelling.

 Evaluations of training programs should focus on several criteria: participant reactions, learning, behaviour change on the job, and bottom-line results.

 Transfer of training is measured by examining the degree to which trained skills are demonstrated back on the job. Benchmarking and utility analysis help evaluate the impact of training and provide the information for further needs assessment. Organizations can optimize transfer of training by adopting particular strategies before, during, and after the training program.

 Special issues in training involve those programs that are important to a broad range of employees. Basic skills training, team training, and diversity training are critically important in today's organizations.

KEY TERMS

apprenticeship training
behaviour modelling
behaviour modification
benchmarking
competency assessment
computer-assisted instruction
  (CAI)

computer-managed instruction
  (CMI)
cooperative training
internship programs
on-the-job training (OJT)
organization analysis

orientation
person analysis
task analysis
trainee readiness
transfer of training

DISCUSSION QUESTIONS

 1. Why is employee orientation an important process? What are some benefits of a properly conducted orientation program?

 2. A new employee is likely to be anxious the first few days on the job.
  a. What are some possible causes of this anxiety?
  b. How can the anxiety be reduced?

 3. Providing training to employees is a significant retention tool in a tight labour market. In groups, discuss the benefits of training for individuals and organizations. Debate this resolution: "Employees should be required to repay education program benefits if they leave the organization before a specific amount of time (one year)."

 4. What analyses should be made to determine the training needs of an organization? After the needs are determined, what is the next step?

 5. Which principles of learning do you see demonstrated in your own class? In what ways might you bring other principles into the class?

 6. Indicate which training methods you would use for each of the following jobs. Give reasons for your choices.
  a. File clerk
  b. Computer operator
  c. Automobile service station attendant
  d. Pizza maker
  e. Nurse's aide

 7. Compare computer-assisted instruction with the lecture method in regard to the way the two methods involve the different psychological principles of learning.

 8. You are the manager of an accounts receivable unit in a large company. You are switching to a new system of billing and record keeping and need to train your three supervisors and twenty-eight employees in the new procedures. What training method(s) would you use? Why?

 9. Participants in a training course are often asked to evaluate the course by means of a questionnaire. What are the pros and cons of this approach? Are there better ways of evaluating a course?

10. You have been asked to design a training program to teach supervisors methods of performance feedback. What techniques would you include to ensure that the training material is applied on the job?

11. Make a list of those behaviours that would improve performance as a team member. For each behaviour, suggest one or two training methods that would be appropriate for the learning of that skill.

JUST-IN-TIME ORIENTATION

The normal practice for most organizations is to hold orientation programs once a month, or when sufficient numbers of new employees have been hired to warrant a session. What is needed is just-in-time (or as-needed) orientation. Ontario's Ministry of Education and Training (MET) developed an on-line orientation program to solve this problem, and also to save money. Other benefits of this on-line orientation program include these: material can be kept current; the message delivered is consistent; access is simple, regardless of time or employee location; the employee can choose which sections to review intensively, depending on interests; and fewer staff are required to conduct orientations. This orientation program consists of the following:

WWW

- a welcome letter from the CEO
- the ministry vision, purpose, and values
- the organization chart
- the role of the ministry
- links to other sites containing information about benefits, the union, the government, etc.

WWW

The MET Orientation Experience uses graphics and themes from the Orient Express. You can see a sample of this program at **www.worksearch.gc.ca/hrof-fice/stat/orientation_e.html**. There is an interactive test that quizzes employees about their knowledge of the ministry. The site even offers a chance to enter a draw, the prize being a trip on the Orient Express.

Ernst & Young, a professional consulting firm, operates differently. Months before candidates arrive for work, the firm sends them letters and newsletters and invites them to drop by for informal chats. Also, at the orientation, E&Y provides an overview of the firm; an administrative checklist of tasks to be conducted before the employee starts; a binder documenting the firm's vision, values, strategies, and structures; computer and voice mail training; and a form for employee feedback. As well, managers are provided with an orientation map to guide them through the first six months of hiring.

Source: C. Gibson, "On-line Orientation: Extending a Welcoming Hand to New Employees" *Canadian HR Reporter,* November 30, 1998: 22–3; A. McCauly, "The Long and Winding Road," *Canadian HR Reporter,* November 16, 1998: 10–11.

Questions

1. Compare the MET orientation program and the E&Y orientation program to the suggested checklist found in this chapter.

2. Many advantages of on-line orientation are listed. What are the limitations of such a program?

3. As a new employee, which of these two sessions would you prefer, and why? Compare your response to others in your group or class.

CASE 2

CHATEAU WHISTLER

WWW

The Chateau Whistler in Whistler, British Columbia, is one of the world's leading hotels, and has been named the number one ski resort in North America for the past eight years. The 557-room hotel opened in 1989, and currently has 650 full-time employees.

The orientation program for new employees at the Chateau Whistler reflects the same standards that guests enjoy at the hotel. New recruits have raw talents such as energy and enthusiasm, but have to be trained quickly in the art of service excellence.

On Day One of the orientation program an "Orientation Game" is played; then the employees are introduced to the hotel (the types of rooms, the amenities, etc.). Then the following are discussed:

- salary and benefits, including health care, pension plan, discounted ski passes, staff meals, food discounts, discounted rates at other properties, and health club access
- employment standards, human rights, and labour relations (although the hotel is not unionized)
- health and safety, including WHMIS (Workplace Hazardous Material Information System) and MSDS (Material Safety Data Sheets) and the environmental program
- harassment policy
- the wellness program
- the incentive program

New employees also receive a tour of the town of Whistler, so that they can talk to guests about the key attractions and establish a network of friends.

Day Two is devoted to the Service Plus Program. The Service Plus Code is:

S	support
E	empathy
R	responsiveness
V	valuing differences
I	interdependence
C	caring
E	expectations

The Day Two program focuses on the guest–employee interaction, and strives to teach employees how to provide excellent service, deal empathetically and effectively with problems reported by guests, and solve problems creatively. Training consists of role plays such as "handling the difficult guest." Specifically, the new recruits gain an understanding of the CP Hotel's mission statement and commitment to service, the changing service culture, and the high service expectations of the guests.

The third component of the orientation program is "Guest for a Night," during which employees who have been working at the hotel for three months eat at the restaurants, enjoy the facilities, and spend one night in the hotel as a guest. According to David Roberts, the hotel's general manager, the goal of the Guest for a Night program is to ensure that employees can talk knowledgeably about guest rooms, restaurants, and other facilities, and understand the level of quality that the hotel provides.

As part of this program, employees are asked to fill out a feedback survey, just like a guest. Also at this time, employees are invited to be part of a focus group to express concerns and provide feedback about their work experiences.

Through these orientation and training programs, employees develop knowledge and skills in service excellence. More importantly, they develop a commitment to the company. At a ten-year reunion party given for 600 people, 599 said it was the best working experience of their lives.

Questions

1. Compare the Chateau Whistler's orientation program to the list of activities presented in Highlights in HRM 1. Would you add anything?

2. The hospitality sector has high turnover rates among employees. Why does the Chateau Whistler invest so much time, money, and energy into its orientation program?

3. Describe the activities in the orientation and training programs that would ensure a high degree of transfer of training to the job.

4. How would you measure the success of this program? What results criteria would you try to measure?

CAREER COUNSEL

Complete the training list on the Managing Human Resources website (**belcourt.nelson.com**).

USING THE INTERNET

The following sites have information about training:

- WebCT (**www.webct.com/webct/–**). This was developed by Murray Goldberg at the University of British Columbia. This site provides an integrated and versatile training environment, and has attracted some 2 million university and college users.
- Lotus Learning Space (**www.lotus.com/learningspace**)
- Blackboard CourseInfo (**www.blackboard.com**)
- Top Class (**www.wbtsytstems.com**)

The Office of Learning Technologies is part of Human Resources Development Canada. It acts as a catalyst for innovation in technology-enabled learning and skills development (**www.hrdc.drhc.gc.ca**).

The Facilitator's Tool Box (**www.oac.uoguelph.ca/~pi/pdrc/facbox**) offers ideas for trainers, including descriptions of games, tips on classroom techniques, and exercises in creativity.

Motorola is a high-tech firm, and much of its training uses multimedia technology. To read how Motorola University has extended training worldwide through the Internet and CD-ROM technologies; visit **www.mot.com**.

Siemens now has apprenticeship programs at several American locations, and several more are planned. Some of the programs include college coursework. You can learn the latest details at **www.sea.siemens.com/training/apprenticeship.html**.

The focus of GE's committment to leadership development is GE Crotonville, the world's first major corporate business school. Information about the development programs offered at Crotonville can be found at **www.ge.com/ibcroa18.htm**

NOTES AND REFERENCES

1. For an interesting discussion of the importance of orientation of younger employees, see James W. Sheehy, "New Work Ethic Is Frightening," *Personnel Journal* 69, no. 6 (June 1990): 51–5.

2. Jean-Pascale Saigue, "Focus on Competencies: Training and Development Practices, Expenditures, and Trends," *Conference Board of Canada Report 177–96*, December 1996.

3. Sam McClelland, "Gaining Competitive Advantage through Strategic Management Development," *Journal of Management Development* 13, no. 5 (1994): 4–13.

4. Marc Hequet, "Doing More with Less—1995 Industry Report," *Training* 32, no. 10 (October 1995): 77–82; B. Filipczak, "Training Cheap," *Training* 33, no. 5 (May 1996): 28–34.

5. Donald J. McNerney and Angela Briggins, "Competency Assessment Gains Favor among Trainers," *HRFocus*, June 1995: 19. See also William J. Rothwell, *Effective Succession Planning: Ensuring Leadership Continuity and Building Talent from Within* (New York: amacom, 1994); Edward E. Lawler III, "From Job-Based to Competency-Based Organizations," *Human Resource Management* 15, no. 1 (1994): 3–15; Juan I. Sanchez, "From Documentation to Innovation: Reshaping Job Analysis to Meet Emerging Business Needs," *Human Resource Management Review* 4, no. 1 (1994): 51–74.

6. Geary Rummler, "In Search of the Holy Performance Grail," *Training and Development* 50, no. 4 (April 1996): 26–32.

7. Robert F. Mager, *Making Instruction Work, or, Skillbloomers* (London: Kogan Page, 1990). See also Robert F. Mager,

What Every Manager Should Know about Training (Belmont, Calif.: Lake Publishing, 1992); Elwood F. Holton III and Curt Bailey, "Top-to-Bottom Curriculum Redesign," *Training and Development* 49, no. 3 (March 1995): 40–4.

8. Jeffrey D. Facteau, Gregory H. Dobbins, and Joyce E. Russell, "The Influence of General Perceptions of the Training Environment on Pretraining Motivation and Perceived Training Transfer," *Journal of Management* 12, no. 1 (Spring 1995): 1–25. See also Kimberly A. Smith-Jentsch, Florian G. Jentsch, Stephanie C. Payne, and Eduardo Salas, "Can Pretraining Experiences Explain Individual Differences in Learning?" *Journal of Applied Psychology* 81, no. 1 (February 1996): 110–16; "Learn to Transform Your Business," *Journal of Management Development* 14, no. 9 (1995): 14–16.

9. Alan M. Saks and Monica Belcourt, "Post-Training Activities and the Transfer of Training," *Canadian Learning Journal*, April 1998.

10. Monica Belcourt and Alan M. Saks, "Training Methods and the Transfer of Training," *Canadian Learning Journal*, February 1998.

11. The classics by Albert Bandura here include *Social Foundations of Thought and Action: A Social Cognitive Theory* (Englewood Cliffs, N.J.: Prentice-Hall, 1986) and *A Social Learning Theory* (Englewood Cliffs, N.J.: Prentice-Hall, 1977).

12. For recent discussions on the desired characteristics of trainers as well as their effects on training, see Kathryn Tyler, "Simon Says, 'Make Learning Fun,'" *HRMagazine* 41, no. 6 (June 1996): 162–8; Dale Ballou and Michael

Podgursky, "Education Policy and Teacher Effort," *Industrial Relations* 34, no. 1 (January 1995): 21–39; Andy Hubbard, "People and Money," *Mortgage Banking* 55, no. 4 (January 1995): 91–2.

13. Alan Fowler, "How to Decide on Training Methods," *People Management* 1, no. 25 (December 21, 1995): 36–7.

14. Belcourt and Saks, "Training Methods and Transfer of Training."

15. Polly A. Phipps, "On-the-Job Training and Employee Productivity," *Monthly Labor Review*, March 1996: 33; Reed Neil Olsen and Edwin A. Sexton, "Gender Differences in the Returns to and the Acquisition of On-the-Job Training," *Industrial Relations* 35, no. 1 (January 1996): 59–77; W.H. Weiss, "Techniques for Training and Instructing Manufacturing Plant Employees," *Supervision* 55, no. 10 (October 1994): 18–20.

16 "Plant Partnering for the Future: An Industrial Giant and an Educational Institution Team Up for a Maintenance Training Initiative," *Plant* 56, no. 7 (May 1997): 20.

17. Conference Board of Canada News Release, May 4, 1997.

18. Suzanne Kapner, "Virtual Training Takes Food Service into the Future," *Nation's Restaurant News* 30, no. 15 (April 15, 1996): 7; Carolyn Spitz, "Multimedia Training at Hewlett-Packard," *Training and Development* 46, no. 6 (June 1992): 39–41; Joanne Irish, "Anatomy of a Multimedia Project," *Training* 32, no. 7 (July 1995): 44–9; Leslie Goff, "Just-In-Time Training: More Timely Than Ever," *Computerworld* 29, no. 37 (September 11, 1995): 96.

19. "Web-Based Training in the Future?" *Computerworld*, December 18, 1995: 81; Donald Forlenza, "Computer-Based Training," *Professional Safety* 40, no. 5 (May 1995): 28–9.

20. For information about the course, see the preface of this text or visit www.captus.org.

21. Bruce D. Nordwall, "CAE about to Ship First 777 Full Flight Simulator," *Aviation Week and Space Technology* 140, no. 25 (June 20, 1994): 22; Michael Mecham, "Boeing Extends Training Help to China's Airlines," *Aviation Week and Space Technology* 143, no. 1 (July 3, 1995): 51.

22. Danna K. Henderson, "Virtual Work," *Air Transport World* 33, no. 4 (April 1996): 69–71; "Where Will You Be in 10 Years?" *Training and Development* 50, no. 4 (April 1996): 14.

23 "Executives Untrained," *The Globe and Mail*, September 15, 1997: B15.

24. Robert M. Fulmer and Albert Vicere, *Executive Education and Leadership Development: The State of the Practice* (State College, Pa.: Penn State Institute for the Study of Organizational Effectiveness, 1995). See also Albert Vicere, Maria Taylor, and Virginia Freeman, "Executive Development in Major Corporations: A Ten-Year Study," *Journal of Management Development* 13, no. 1 (1994): 4–22.

25. Darcy Hitchcock, "Learning from Chaos," *Journal for Quality and Participation* 19, no. 1 (January/February 1996): 42–5.

26. Albert A. Einsiedel, Jr., "Case Studies: Indispensable Tools for Trainers," *Training and Development*, August 1995, 50–3. See also Alan Fowler, "How to Decide on Training Methods," *People Management* 1, no. 25 (December 21, 1995): 36–7.

27. David C. Lane, "On a Resurgence of Management Simulations and Games," *Journal of the Operational Research Society* 46, no. 5 (May 1995): 604–25. For more information on a variety of commercially available management games, see "Handbook of Management Games," *HRFocus* 71, no. 5 (May 1994): 20.

28. Kim Slack, "Training for the Real Thing," *Training and Development* 47, no. 5 (May 1993): 79–89.

29. Sandra J. Balli, "Oh No ... Not Role Play Again," *Training and Development*, February 1995: 14–15.

30. Jon M. Werner, Anne O'Leary-Kelly, Timothy T. Baldwin, and Kenneth N. Wexley, "Augmenting Behavior-Modeling Training: Testing the Effects of Pre- and Post-Training Interventions," *Human Resource Development Quarterly* 5, no. 2 (Summer 1994): 169–83.

31. Donald Kirkpatrick, "Great Ideas Revisited: Revisiting Kirkpatrick's Four-Level Model," *Training and Development* 50, no. 1 (January 1996): 54–7. For an opposing view on this model, see Elwood F. Holton III, "The Flawed Four-Level Evaluation Model," *Human Resource Development Quarterly* 7, no. 1 (Spring 1996): 5–21.

32. Saigue, "Focus on Competencies."

33. Saks and Belcourt, "Post-Training Activities and Transfer of Training."

34. Saigue, "Focus on Competencies."

35. Robert R. Haccoun and Thierry Hamtiaux, "Optimizing Knowledge Tests for Inferring Learning Acquisition Levels in Single Group Training Evaluation Designs: The Internal Referencing Strategy," *Personnel Psychology* 47, no. 3 (Autumn 1994): 593–604.

36. Saigue, "Focus on Competencies."

37. A.P. Carnevale and E.R. Schulz, "Evaluation Practices," *Training and Development* 44 (1990): S23–S29. See also Anthony R. Montebello and Maureen Haga, "To Justify Training, Test, Test Again," *Personnel Journal* 73, no. 1 (January 1994): 83–7.

38. Jeff Moad, "Calculating the Real Benefit of Training," *Datamation* 41, no. 7 (April 15, 1995): 45–7; Jac Fitz-enz, "Yes ... You Can Weigh Training's Value," *Training* 31, no. 7 (July 1994): 54–8.

39. Saks and Belcourt, "Post-Training Activities and Transfer of Training."

40. Richard Lee, "The 'Pay-Forward' View of Training," *People Management* 2, no. 3 (February 8, 1996): 30–2; Nancy Dixon, "New Routes to Evaluation," *Training and Development* 50, no. 5 (May 1996): 82–5.

41. Leslie F. Overmyer Day, "Benchmarking Training," *Training and Development*, November 1995, 26–30; Donald J. Ford and Catherine Fisk, "Benchmarking HRD," *Training and Development* 47, no. 6 (June 1993): 37–41; Samuel Greengard, "Discover Best Practices through

Benchmarking," *Personnel Journal*, November 1995: 62–73.

42. T.T. Baldwin and R.J. Magjuka, "Organizational Training and Signals of Importance: Linking Pretraining Perceptions to Intentions to Transfer," *Human Resource Development Quarterly*, Spring 1991: 25–36.

43. Alan M. Saks and Monica Belcourt, "Transfer of Training in Canadian Organizations," *Update*, September 1997, 9–10.

44. Monica Belcourt and Alan Saks, "Effects of Pre-Training Activities and a Learning Culture on the Transfer of Training," *Update*, December 1997: 2.

45. Monica Belcourt and Alan M. Saks, "Training Methods and Transfer of Training," *Canadian Learning Journal*, February 1998: 3.

46. Saks and Belcourt, "Post-Training Activities and Transfer of Training."

47. G. Geis, *As Training Moves toward the Next Decade*, (Toronto: Ontario Training Corporation, 1991).

48. Erica Gordon Sorohan, "Basic Skills Training on the Rise," *Training and Development* 49, no. 5 (May 1995): 12–13. See also David Stamps, "Solutions 101," *Training* 32, no. 12 (December 1995): 38; Patrick J. O'Connor, "Getting Down to Basics," *Training and Development* 47, no. 7 (July 1993): 62–4; Edward E. Gordon, Judith A. Ponticell, and Ronald R. Morgan, *Closing the Literacy Gap in American Business: A Guide for Trainers and Human Resource Specialists* (New York: Quorum Books, 1991).

49. "Case Studies in Literacy," *Canadian Business Review* 18, no. 1 (Spring 1991).

50. Teresa L. Smith, "The Basics of Basic-Skills Training," *Training and Development* 49, no. 4 (April 1995): 44–6; Teresa L. Smith, "Job Related Materials Reinforce Basic Skills," *HRMagazine*, July 1995: 84–90.

51. "How to Get the Most from Team Training," *HRFocus* 72, no. 3 (March 1995): 20; Steven Crom and Herbert France, "Teamwork Brings Breakthrough Improvements in Quality and Climate," *Quality Progress* 29, no. 3 (March 1996): 39–42.

52. J. Mayberry, "Big Steel Responds," *The Globe and Mail Report on Business Magazine*, October 1997: 10.

53. Sandra N. Phillips, "Team Training Puts Fizz in Coke Plant's Future," *Personnel Journal* 75, no. 1 (January 1996): 87–92.

54. George W. Bohlander and Kathy McCarthy, "How to Get the Most from Team Training," *National Productivity Review*, Autumn 1996: 25–35.

55. Patricia L. Nemetz and Sandra L. Christensen, "The Challenge of Cultural Diversity: Harnessing a Diversity of Views to Understand Multiculturalism," *Academy of Management Review* 21, no. 2 (April 1996): 434–62; William Beaver, "Let's Stop Diversity Training and Start Managing for Diversity," *Industrial Management* 37, no. 4 (July–August 1995): 7–9; Mikel Hogan Garcia, "An Anthropological Approach to Multicultural Diversity Training," *Journal of Applied Behavioral Science* 31, no. 4 (December 1995): 490–504.

56. Jack Gordon et al., "Is Diversity Training Heading South?" *Training* 33, no. 2 (February 1996): 12–14.

57. Leslie E. Overmyer Day, "The Pitfalls of Diversity Training," *Training and Development* 49, no. 12 (December 1995): 24–9; Sara Rynes and Benson Rosen, "A Field Survey of Factors Affecting the Adoption and Perceived Success of Diversity Training," *Personnel Psychology* 48, no. 2 (Summer 1995): 247–70; "Quick-Fix Diversity Efforts Are Doomed," *Training*, January 1995, 18–19; Dawn Anfuso, "All Colgate Asks for Is a Little Respect," *Personnel Journal* 74, no. 10 (October 1995): 49.

CHAPTER 7

CAREER DEVELOPMENT

After studying this chapter, you should be able to

OBJECTIVE 1

Explain how a career development program integrates individual and organizational needs.

OBJECTIVE 2

Describe the conditions that help make a career development program successful.

OBJECTIVE 3

Discuss how job opportunities can be inventoried and employee potential assessed.

OBJECTIVE 4

Describe the methods used for identifying and developing managerial talent.

OBJECTIVE 5

Cite the ways that employers can facilitate the career development of women.

OBJECTIVE 6

Cite the ways that employers can facilitate the career development of members of minority groups and of dual-career couples.

OBJECTIVE 7

Describe the various aspects of personal career development that should be considered.

W e have noted at several points in this text—and in several ways—that the ground rules for managing people are changing dramatically in today's working world. To be competitive over the long run, organizations have to be adaptive. Jobs are becoming more flexible to cope with change, and organizations are embracing alternative ways of designing work that take into account the diverse interests and backgrounds of potential employees. The need for innovation and technological change means that skills that are valuable today may be obsolete tomorrow. Flatter organization structures mean that there are fewer positions for promotion, so individuals must look for advancement opportunities outside the firm. At the same time, increased competition for talent means that some individuals will be lured away to work for other firms. The booming economy of the past decade, coupled with extremely low unemployment rates, means that individuals have more employment opportunities from which to choose. The upshot of this is that individuals are less likely to work in the same job for extended periods and that most, in fact, are unlikely to spend their entire careers with only one firm.[1]

All of these changes are going on at once, so it's small wonder that career management is one of the most important topics for new employees, old employees, and those of you who are just starting to think about entering the workforce. The desire to make the most of one's knowledge and skills is something that individuals and organizations have in common. On the one hand, the task has perhaps never been more challenging. On the other hand, organizations and employees are more focused on it than ever before. In this chapter we cover career development as an HRM function, and provide some suggestions for you to consider in your own career development.

ELEMENTS OF CAREER DEVELOPMENT PROGRAMS

Organizations have long engaged in human resources planning and development. As we noted in Chapter 4, this activity involves charting the moves of large numbers of employees through various positions in an organization and identifying future staffing and development needs. Career development programs, with their greater emphasis on the individual, introduce a personalized aspect to the process.

A common approach to establishing a career development program is to integrate it with the existing HR functions and structures in the organization. Integrating career development with other HR programs creates synergies in which all aspects of HR reinforce one another. Figure 7.1 illustrates how HR structures relate to some of the essential aspects of the career management process. For example, in planning careers, employees need organizational information— information that strategic planning, forecasting, succession planning, and skills inventories can provide. Similarly, as they obtain information about themselves and use it in career planning, employees need to know the career paths within the organization and how management views their performance.[2]

The Goal: Matching Individual and Organizational Needs

In the final analysis, career development should be viewed as a dynamic process that matches the needs of the organization with the needs of employees.

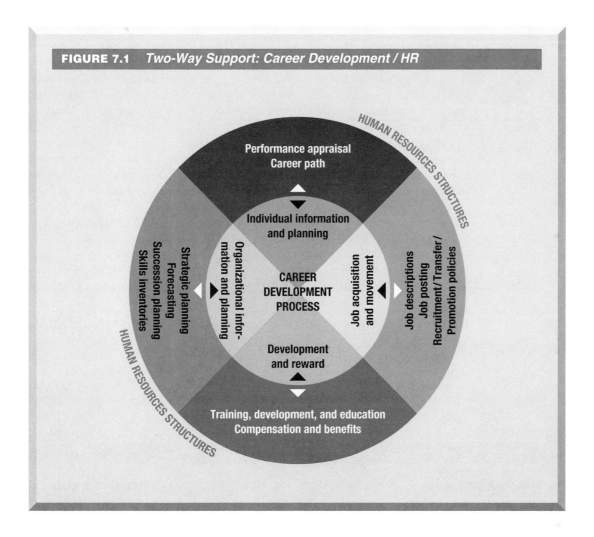

FIGURE 7.1 Two-Way Support: Career Development / HR

Source: Zandy B. Leibowitz, Caela Farren, and Beverly L. Kaye, *Designing Career Development Systems* (San Francisco: Jossey-Bass, 1986), 41. Reproduced with permission of Jossey-Bass, Inc., a subsidiary of John Wiley & Sons.

The Employee's Role

In today's organizations, individuals are responsible for initiating and managing their own career planning. It is up to each individual to identify his or her own knowledge, skills, abilities, interests, and values and seek out information about career options in order to set goals and develop career plans. Managers should encourage employees to take responsibility for their own careers, offering continuing assistance in the form of feedback on individual performance and making available information about the organization, about the job, and about career opportunities that might be of interest.

The organization is responsible for supplying information about its mission, policies, and plans and for providing support for employee self-assessment, training, and development. Significant career growth can occur when individual initiative combines with organizational opportunity. Career development programs benefit managers by giving them increased skill in managing their own careers, by helping them retain valued employees, by increasing their understanding of the organization, and by enhancing their reputations as people developers. As with other HR programs, the inauguration of a career development program should be based on the organization's needs as well.

Needs assessment should take a variety of approaches (surveys, informal group discussions, interviews, etc.), and should involve personnel from different groups, such as new employees, managers, plateaued employees, minority employees, and technical and professional employees. Identifying the needs and problems of these groups provides the starting point for the organization's career development efforts. As shown in Figure 7.2, organizational needs should be linked with individual career needs in a way that joins personal effectiveness and satisfaction of employees with the achievement of the organization's strategic objectives.

The Organization's Role: Establishing a Favourable Context

If career development is to succeed, it must receive the complete support of top management. Ideally, senior line managers and HR department managers should work together to design and implement a career development system. The system should reflect the goals and culture of the organization, and the HR philosophy should be woven throughout. An HR philosophy can provide employees with a clear set of expectations and directions for their own career development. For a program

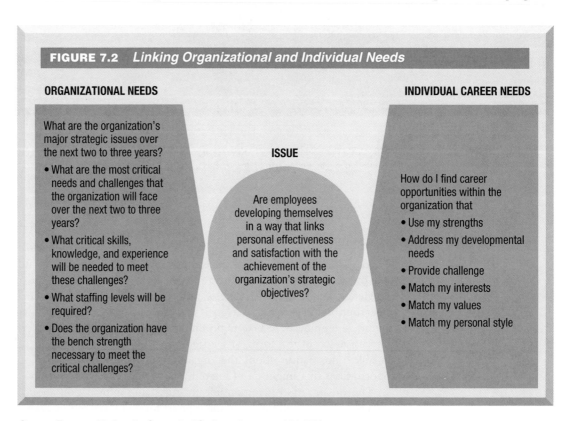

FIGURE 7.2 *Linking Organizational and Individual Needs*

ORGANIZATIONAL NEEDS

What are the organization's major strategic issues over the next two to three years?

• What are the most critical needs and challenges that the organization will face over the next two to three years?

• What critical skills, knowledge, and experience will be needed to meet these challenges?

• What staffing levels will be required?

• Does the organization have the bench strength necessary to meet the critical challenges?

ISSUE

Are employees developing themselves in a way that links personal effectiveness and satisfaction with the achievement of the organization's strategic objectives?

INDIVIDUAL CAREER NEEDS

How do I find career opportunities within the organization that

• Use my strengths

• Address my developmental needs

• Provide challenge

• Match my interests

• Match my values

• Match my personal style

Source: Forrer and Leibowitz, Conceptual Systems, Inc., copyright 1992.

to be effective, managerial personnel at all levels must be trained in the fundamentals of job design, performance appraisal, career planning, and counselling.

One of the most important indicators of management support comes in the form of mentoring. This is true whether it is done formally as part of an ongoing program, or informally as merely a kind gesture to a less experienced employee. Dealing with uncertainty is one of the biggest challenges any individual faces in his or her career. Receiving advice and council from someone who has gone through similar experiences can be invaluable to employees. We discussed mentoring briefly in Chapter 6 (Training and Development), and devote an entire section to the topic later in this chapter.

Blending Individual and Organizational Goals

Before individuals can engage in meaningful career planning, they must be aware of the organization's philosophy, and must also have a good understanding of the organization's more immediate goals. Otherwise, they may plan for personal change and growth without knowing whether or how their own goals match those of the organization. For example, if the technology of a business is changing and new skills are needed, will the organization retrain to meet this need, or will it hire new talent? Is there going to be growth, stability, or decline in the number of employees needed? How will turnover affect this need? Clearly, an organizational plan that answers these kinds of questions is essential to support individual career planning.

At the same time, individuals can't be expected to establish their career goals with *perfect* understanding of where they are going or—for that matter—where the organization is going. People change over time, and because they do, so do their needs and interests. Similarly, organizations change direction and adjust their strategies to cope with that change. So while goal setting is critical, building in some flexibility is probably a good idea.

Identifying Career Opportunities and Requirements

While career development integrates a number of related HR activities, the process has to keep a steady watch on the needs and requirements of the organization. This involves analyzing the competencies required for jobs, the progression among related jobs, and the supply of ready (and potential) talent available to fill those jobs.

Competency Analysis

It is important for an organization to study its jobs carefully in order to identify and assign weights to the knowledge and skills that each one requires. This can be achieved through job analysis and evaluation systems, such as those used in compensation programs. The system used at Sears measures three basic competencies for each job: know-how, problem solving, and accountability. Know-how is broken down into three types of job knowledge: technical, managerial, and human relations. Problem solving and accountability also have several dimensions. Scores for each of these three major competencies are assigned to each job; a total value is then computed for each job. For any planned job transfer, the amount of increase (or decrease) the next job represents in each of the skill areas, as well as in the total point values, can be computed. This information is then used to make certain that a transfer to a different job is a move that requires growth on the part of the employee.

Sears designs career development paths to provide the following experiences: (1) an increase in at least one skill area on each new assignment, (2) an increase of at least 10 percent in total points on each new assignment, and (3) assignments in several different functional areas.[3]

Job Progressions

Job progressions

Hierarchy of jobs a new employee might experience, ranging from a starting job to jobs that successively require more knowledge and/or skill

Once the skill demands of jobs are identified and weighted according to their importance, it is then possible to plan **job progressions**. A new employee with no experience is typically assigned to a "starting job." After a period of time in that job, the employee can be promoted to one that requires more knowledge and/or skill. While most organizations concentrate on developing job progressions for managerial, professional, and technical jobs, progressions can be developed for all categories of jobs. These job progressions then can serve as a basis for developing **career paths**—the lines of advancement within an organization—for individuals.

Career paths

Lines of advancement in an occupational field within an organization

Figure 7.3 illustrates a typical line of advancement in the human resources area of a large multinational corporation. It is apparent that to advance very far in HRM with this firm, one must be prepared to move geographically. This is also true of other career fields in the organization.

Many organizations prepare interesting and attractive brochures to describe the career paths that are available to employees. General Motors has prepared a career development guide that groups jobs by fields of work such as engineering, manufacturing, communications, data processing, financial, HR, and scientific. These categories give employees an understanding of the career possibilities in the various fields.

Although these analyses can be quite helpful to employees—and are perhaps essential for organizations—a word of caution is appropriate here. Many successful careers are not this methodical, nor do they proceed in a lockstep manner. In today's working world, careers often progress less through rational planning than through creating and capitalizing on arising opportunities. So while it is a good idea for organizations to map out career paths, and while individuals would do well to establish a strategy for advancement, many successful individuals readily admit that their career paths were very much a function of circumstance. These people often note that they were lucky to be "in the right place at the right time." Of course, others describe these people as being extremely career savvy.

Lots of Possibilities

It used to be that career development and planning systems focused mainly on promotions and hierarchical advancement. In today's flatter organizations and more dynamic work environment, an individual's career advancement can occur along several different paths: transfers, demotions—even exits—as well as promotions. HR policies have to be flexible enough to adapt as well as helpful enough to support the career change.

Promotion

Change of assignment to a job at a higher level in the organization

As illustrated in Figure 7.3, a **promotion** is a change of assignment to a job at a higher level in the organization. The new job normally provides an increase in pay and status and demands more skill or carries more responsibility. Promotions enable an organization to utilize the skills and abilities of its personnel more effectively. And of course the chance of promotion serves as an incentive for good per-

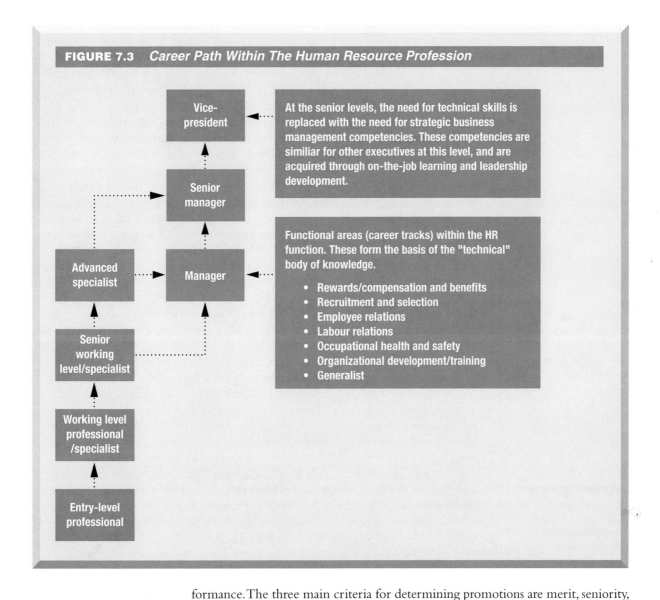

FIGURE 7.3 *Career Path Within The Human Resource Profession*

Vice-president

At the senior levels, the need for technical skills is replaced with the need for strategic business management competencies. These competencies are similiar for other executives at this level, and are acquired through on-the-job learning and leadership development.

Senior manager

Manager

Functional areas (career tracks) within the HR function. These form the basis of the "technical" body of knowledge.

- Rewards/compensation and benefits
- Recruitment and selection
- Employee relations
- Labour relations
- Occupational health and safety
- Organizational development/training
- Generalist

Advanced specialist

Senior working level/specialist

Working level professional /specialist

Entry-level professional

formance. The three main criteria for determining promotions are merit, seniority, and potential. Often the problem involves determining how much consideration to give to each factor. A common problem in organizations that promote mainly on past performance and seniority is the Peter Principle. This refers to situations where individuals are promoted as long as they have done a well in their previous job. The trouble is, this continues until someone does poorly in his or her new job. Beyond that point they are no longer promoted. In effect, people are promoted to their level of incompetence.[4]

In flatter organizations, there are fewer promotional opportunities and many individuals have found career advancement through lateral moves. A **transfer** is the placement of an employee in another job for which the duties, responsibilities, status, and remuneration are approximately equal to those of the previous job (although as an incentive, organizations may offer a salary adjustment). Individuals who look forward to change or who want a chance to learn more may seek out

Transfer

Placement of an individual in another job for which the duties, responsibilities, status, and remuneration are approximately equal to those of the previous job transfers. Also, transfers often provide a broader foundation for individuals to prepare them for an eventual promotion. Sometimes a transfer requires the employee to change his or her work group, workplace, work shift, or organizational unit; it may even require moving to another geographic area. Through transfers, an organization can place its employees in jobs where their services are needed more, and where they can acquire new knowledge and skills.

A downward transfer, or *demotion*, moves an individual into a lower-level job that can provide developmental opportunities. Although such a move is ordinarily considered unfavourable, some individuals actually may request it in order to return to their "technical roots." For example, it is not uncommon for an organization to appoint a temporary team leader, with the proviso that that individual will be able to step down from this position to reassume a former position.

Transfers, promotions, and demotions require individuals to adjust to new job demands and usually to a different work environment. A transfer that involves moving to a new location in Canada or abroad places greater demands on an employee, because it requires that employee to adapt not only to a new work environment but also to new living conditions. An employee who has a family has the added responsibility of helping its members adjust to the new living arrangements. Some employers provide all types of **relocation services**—for example, they cover moving expenses, help the employee sell a home, and provide cultural orientation and language training—but there is always some loss of productive time. It has been suggested that pretransfer training, whether it be related to job skills or lifestyle, is one of the most effective ways to reduce lost productivity.

When one considers the numerous changes that can accompany a career move in an organization, it should come as no surprise that many people are opting to accept career changes that involve exiting the organization. Given the limited career opportunities in firms, and the need for talent in other companies, many individuals are discovering that their best career move may be to switch companies.

Some employees leave voluntarily; some are forced out. Many organizations now provide **outplacement services** to help terminated employees find work elsewhere. These services can be used to enhance a productive employee's career, or to terminate an unproductive employee. If an organization cannot meet its career development responsibilities to its productive workers, HR policy should be to provide them with help in finding more suitable career opportunities elsewhere. Jack Welch, CEO of General Electric, was one of the first executives to make a commitment to employees that while the company could no longer guarantee lifetime employment, it would try to ensure employability. That is, GE has committed itself to providing employees with the skills and support they would need to find jobs in other organizations.[5]

Relocation services

Services provided to an employee who is transferred to a new location

Outplacement services

Services provided by organizations to help terminated employees find a new job

WWW

Dual Career Paths

One of the most obvious places where career paths have been changing is in the technical and professional areas. One of the ironies of organizations has been that the most successful engineers, scientists, and professionals are often promoted right out of their area of specialization into management. Instead of doing what they are good at, they are promoted into a job they often don't understand or enjoy. It has become apparent that there must be another way to compensate these people without elevating them into management. The solution has been to develop dual career paths, or tracks, that provide for progression in special areas such as finance, marketing, and engineering, with compensation that is comparable to that received by managers at different levels.[6]

WWW

Many organizations have found that this is the solution to keeping employees with valuable knowledge and skills performing tasks that are as important to the organization as those performed by managers. Highlights in HRM 1 shows the dual career path devised by Xenova Corporation, a biopharmaceutical company, to recognize both the scientific and the managerial paths of employees.

OBJECTIVE 4

Gauging Employee Potential

Besides mapping career opportunities and requirements within their organizations, managers must establish a clear understanding of the talent base they have at their disposal. This typically begins—though it does not end—with the use of performance appraisals.

Using Performance Appraisals

Performance appraisals are discussed in more depth in Chapter 8. For our purposes here, we note that managers measure and evaluate employee performance for several reasons, of which none is more important than making developmental and career decisions. Successful performers are often good candidates for a promotion. In contrast, poorly performing employees may need—and benefit from—a transfer to another area or even a demotion.

Identifying and developing talent in individuals is a task that all managers should take seriously. As they conduct formal appraisals, they should watch for any potential their employees may have to succeed in managerial or advanced technical jobs, and encourage their growth in that direction. The immediate manager should not be the only person doing this; there should be others in the organization who have the power to evaluate, nominate, and sponsor employees with promise.

Inventorying Management Talent

As we discussed in Chapter 4, talent inventories are an important tool in succession planning. These inventories indicate the skills employees have as well as their interests and experiences. They help managers pay better attention to the developmental needs of employees, regarding both their present jobs and the managerial jobs to which they may be promoted. An equally important part of this process is identifying high-potential employees who may be groomed as replacements for managers who leave for whatever reason.

WWW

Unfortunately, many companies do a poor job of managing their talent. In a study conducted by McKinsey and Company, three-quarters of corporate officers said their companies were chronically short of talent. At the same time, half of the respondents to a similar survey acknowledged that they were not doing effective succession planning and were unprepared to replace key executives.[7]

WWW

Organizations that make a deliberate point of developing human assets as well as turning a profit typically have the talent they need and some to spare. Some companies—Xerox, Intel, and Proctor and Gamble, to name three—have become "academy" companies that unintentionally provide a source of talented managers to organizations that lack good management career development programs of their own.

Highlights in HRM

1 ROLES WITHIN THE XENOVA SYSTEM

SCIENTIST (RS 1/2)

Plans and undertakes laboratory work to achieve agreed project goals, using inputs from colleagues, the external scientific community, literature, and suppliers.

SENIOR SCIENTIST (RS 3/4)

Plans and undertakes experimental programs and laboratory work to achieve agreed project or scientific goals, using inputs from and providing outputs to colleagues, community, and suppliers.

RESEARCH ASSOCIATE (RS 5/6)

Provides expertise and direction to programs and projects through in-depth understanding of a scientific specialism; leads or forms part of a scientific team with the main purpose of providing a specialist's expertise in a scientific discipline.

PRINCIPAL SCIENTIST (RS 7/8)

Provides scientific expertise and understanding of the highest level to ensure scientific leadership and direction; maintains a personal standing as a world-recognized and highly respected scientist and uses this to further the aims of the company through science.

SECTION LEADER (SM 4/5)

Leads and manages a team of scientists from both a science and an operational management standpoint; makes a significant contribution to the management of groups of scientists and the general management of the department.

DEPARTMENT HEAD (SM 3)

Leads and manages a department of scientists to provide Xenova with a well-managed and motivated scientific resource; makes a significant contribution to the general management of the company or division of the company.

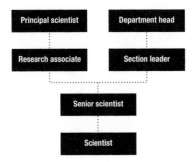

Source: Adapted from Alan Garmonsway and Michael Wellin, "Creating the Right Natural Chemistry," *People Management* 1, no. 19 (September 21, 1995): 36–9.

WWW

Assessment centre

Process by which individuals are evaluated as they participate in a series of situations that resemble what they might be called on to handle on the job

In-basket training

Assessment centre process for evaluating trainees by simulating a real-life work situation

Leaderless group discussion

Assessment centre process that places trainees in a conference setting to discuss an assigned topic, either with or without designated group roles

Using Assessment Centres

There are other very effective ways to assess a person's career potential. Assessment centres were pioneered in the mid-1950s by Douglas Bray and his colleagues at AT&T, and are considered one of the most valuable methods for evaluating personnel. An **assessment centre** is a process (not a place) by which individuals are evaluated as they participate in a series of situations that resemble what they might be called on to handle on the job. The popularity of assessment centres can be attributed to two things: (a) they improve an organization's ability to select employees who will perform successfully in management positions; and (b) they help employees develop the skills they use in their present positions. These centres use in-basket exercises, leaderless group discussions, and the various approaches discussed in the previous chapter.

In-basket training   In this method, a problem situation is simulated. The participants are given several documents, each describing some problem or situation requiring an immediate response. They are thus forced to make decisions under the pressure of time and also to determine what priority to give each problem.

Leaderless group discussions   Trainees are gathered in a conference setting to discuss an assigned topic, with or without designated group roles. The participants are given little or no instruction in how to approach the topic, nor are they told what decision to reach. Leaderless group trainees are evaluated on their initiative, leadership skills, and ability to work effectively in a group setting.

The various activities of the Public Service Commission assessment centre are discussed in Highlights in HRM 2. Participation in these activities provides samples of behaviour that are representative of what is required for advancement. At the end of the assessment centre period, the assessors' observations are combined and integrated to develop an overall picture of the strengths and needs of the participants. Usually, a report is then submitted to senior management, and feedback is given to the participants.

More and more attention is being paid to the validity of assessment centre procedures. As with employment tests, the assessments provided must be valid. Before the assessment centre is run, the characteristics or dimensions to be studied should be determined through job analyses. The exercises used in the centre should reflect the job for which the person is being evaluated—that is, the exercises should have content validity. While the assessment centre method lends itself readily to content validation, predictive validity has also been observed often. A strong positive relationship is found between assessments and future performance on the job.[8]

While assessment centres have proved quite valuable in identifying managerial talent and in helping individuals in their development, it should also be noted that the method tends to favour those who have strong interpersonal skills and the ability to influence others. Some people find it difficult to perform at their best in a situation that for them is as threatening as taking a test. How assessment centre personnel conduct the exercises and provide feedback to the participants does much to determine how individuals react to the experience.

Career Development Initiatives

Although career management involves a great deal of analysis and planning, the bottom line is that it has to provide tools that will help employees gauge their

Highlights in HRM

2 THE ASSESSMENT CENTRE PROGRAM OF THE PUBLIC SERVICE COMMISSION

WWW

The first step in the use of an assessment centre is to work with managers, who are asked by psychologists to keep a diary of their daily activities and problems. They are then questioned about their work in order to identify the major problems that a manager might face. The focus is on identifying the abilities needed to resolve these problems. This information is used to develop the simulation exercises.

Candidates for managerial positions, playing the role of a manager, are asked to respond to a series of letters, memos, and variance reports. They then present, in oral and written forms, the approach they would use to resolve the problem. These approaches include the establishment of priorities, plans, solutions, and decisions.

The selection board, composed of the hiring manager, at least one outside manager, and a staffing officer, is trained to understand the simulation and the various effective approaches. The candidates are evaluated on how well they got their ideas across and on how well they plan, monitor, and control programs.

Everyone involved strongly identifies with the realistic nature of the simulation. Candidates get so involved in the simulation that they forget it is a test, and managers feel they can actually visualize these people at work. Even unsuccessful candidates claim they learn about themselves in the process.

Source: The Personal Psychology Centre, Public Service Commission, Government of Canada, Ottawa.

potential for success in the organization. To this end, supervisors and HR staff often resort to informal counselling. Also, many organizations give their employees information on educational assistance, employment equity programs and policies, salary administration, and job requirements. Career planning workbooks and workshops are also popular means of helping employees identify their potential and the strength of their interests.[9]

Career Planning Workbooks

WWW

Some organizations prepare workbooks to help their employees systematically assess their own values, interests, abilities, goals, and personal development plans. Ontario Hydro uses assessment tools such as the Barbara Moses Career Planning Workbook and the Strong Campbell Interest Inventory. A computer-based program called Discovery contains a self-assessment component that provides information on occupations, skill requirements, and educational institutions. Employees can also make use of a reference library that contains books on careers and job search strategies.

Some organizations prefer to use workbooks that were written for the general public. A popular one is Richard N. Bolles, *What Color Is Your Parachute?* Andrew

H. Souerwine's *Career Strategies: Planning for Personal Growth,* John Holland's *Self-Directed Search,* and John W. Slocum and G. Scott King's *How to Pack Your Career Parachute* are used often as well.[10] These same books are recommended to students as aids to career planning. Many electronic career-planning products, such as Career Cruising and Career Explorer, are also available.

Career Planning Workshops

Workshops offer experiences similar to those provided by workbooks. However, they have the advantage of providing a chance to compare and discuss attitudes, concerns, and plans with others in similar situations. Some workshops focus on current job performance and development plans. Others deal with broader life and career plans and values.

As mentioned earlier, employees should be encouraged to assume responsibility for their own careers. A career workshop can help them do that. It can also help them learn how to make career decisions, set career goals, create career options, and seek career planning information; at the same time, it can help them build confidence and self-esteem.[11] Highlights in HRM 3 describes a workshop used by Marriott Corporation.

Career Counselling

Career counselling

Process of discussing with employees their current job activities and performance, their personal job and career goals, their personal skills, and suitable career development objectives

Career counselling involves talking with employees about their current job activities and performance, their personal and career interests and goals, their personal skills, and suitable career development objectives. While some organizations make counselling a part of the annual performance appraisal, career counselling is usually voluntary. Career counselling may be provided by HR staff, managers and supervisors, specialized staff counsellors, or outside consultants. The federal government, through the Human Resources Development Department, offers many job search and career counselling services. Access the HRDC website at **www.hrdc–drhc.gc.ca** and look for programs such as the University of Waterloo Career Manual.

Most provincial governments offer career planning help. For example, New Brunswick Human Resources Development has opened a centre in Miramichi, New Brunswick, that provides bilingual assistance for career planning to people who are physically and/or intellectually challenged. Several techniques for career counselling are outlined at the end of this chapter. You can create your own career plan by completing the Career Counsel excercises, found at the end of each chapter on the Nelson website.

As employees approach retirement, they may be encouraged to participate in preretirement programs, which often include counselling along with other helping activities. Preretirement programs will be discussed in Chapter 11.

The obligations of employees to return the corporate investment in their development are discussed in Ethics in HRM.

Determining Individual Development Needs

Because the requirements of each position and the qualifications of each person are different, no two individuals will have identical developmental needs. For one individual, self-development may consist of developing the ability to write reports, give talks, and lead conferences. For another, it may require developing interpersonal skills in order to communicate and relate more effectively with a diverse

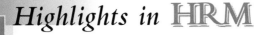

Highlights in HRM

WWW

3   CAREER DEVELOPMENT WORKSHOPS AT THE MARRIOTT

Given the business realities of a highly competitive hotel industry, Marriott Corporation executives know that they can no longer take a paternalistic approach to career management. To provide managers and supervisors with assistance in managing their own careers—and the careers of their employees—Marriott has developed a workshop called "Partners in Career Management." The workshop is based on a four-step model that helps managers focus on the following questions:

- Who am I? The program helps employees identify their skills, values, and interests.
- How am I seen? The program offers ongoing feedback to help employees understand how others view their contribution.
- What are my career objectives? The workshop helps employees create a set of realistic career goals.
- How can I achieve my goals? The workshop helps individuals develop action plans that focus on leveraging their abilities and experiences to achieve their goals.

By training its managers to help company employees learn about career opportunities and resources, Marriott is moving toward shifting responsibility for career management away from the company and to the employee. At Marriott, employees are responsible for

- Assessing their own skills, values, interests, and developmental needs
- Determining long- and short-term career goals
- Creating with their managers career development plans to reach their goals
- Following through with their plans
- Learning about career management resources such as the online job posting system
- Meeting with their managers on a regular basis for career development discussions
- Recognizing that career discussions imply no promises or guarantees
- Recognizing that their development will depend directly on Marriott's organizational needs and opportunities as well as their own performance

Source: Shari Caudron, "Marriott Trains Managers to Become Partners in Career Management," *Personnel Journal,* April 1996: 28. Reprinted with permission.

workforce. Periodic performance appraisals can provide a basis for determining each manager's progress. Conferences in which these appraisals are discussed are an essential part of self-improvement efforts.

In helping individuals plan their careers, it is important for organizations to recognize that younger employees today seek meaningful training assignments that are interesting and involve challenge, responsibility, and a sense of empowerment. They also have a greater concern for the contribution that their work in the

Ethics in HRM

WHOSE CAREER IS IT?

WWW

Organizations like Procter & Gamble and IBM invest a great deal of time and money in developing their professional sales staff and management personnel. Similarly, the federal government offers new university recruits up to six months of language training and tuition-paid university courses, as well as several weeks of skills training, within the first two years on the job.

Other organizations refuse to invest in the long-term development of their employees. They cite statistics suggesting that over one-third of university recruits will quit within the first year. In addition, they argue that other corporations will raid these highly trained personnel.

Do employees who have received the benefit of extensive development programs at the employer's expense have an obligation to remain with the organization so that it can realize a return on its investment? Revenue Canada thinks that the employee benefits from these courses and is taxing the individual, a decision under appeal.

organization will make to society. Unfortunately, they are often given responsibilities they view as rudimentary, boring, and composed of too many "make work" activities. Some organizations are attempting to retain young managers with high potential by offering a **fast track program** that lets them advance more rapidly than those with less potential. A fast-track program may provide for a relatively rapid progression—lateral transfers or promotions—through a number of managerial positions requiring exposure to different organizational functions; it may also provide opportunities to make meaningful decisions.

Fast track program

Program that encourages young managers with high potential to remain with an organization by letting them advance more rapidly than those with less potential

WWW

Career Self-Management Training

In response to the growing view that employees should assume greater responsibility for their own career management, many organizations such as Montreal-based DMR Consulting are establishing training programs for employees on how they can engage in *career self-management.* This training focuses on two main objectives: (1) helping employees learn to continuously gather feedback and information about their careers, and (2) encouraging them to prepare for mobility.

The training is not geared toward skills and behaviours associated with a specific job, but rather toward individuals' long-term personal effectiveness. Employees typically undergo self-assessments to increase awareness of their own career attitudes and values. Also, they are encouraged to widen their point of view beyond the next company promotion to broader opportunities in the marketplace. Many have not seen these external opportunities as viable options, much less something the company would acknowledge. Participants might be encouraged to engage in career networking, or to identify other means to prepare for job mobility, such as hearing reports from employees who made transitions to new job opportunities both within and outside the organization.[12]

Mentors

Executives who coach, advise, and encourage individuals of lesser rank

Mentoring

When people talk about their employment experiences, they often mention individuals at work who influenced them. Often, these are immediate managers who were especially helpful as career developers. But they also mention others higher in the organization who guided and supported them in their career development. Executives and managers who coach, advise, and encourage employees of lesser rank are called **mentors**. A survey of Canadian executives found that 95 percent of them feel that mentors are critical for those beginning their careers.[13]

People often define "mentor" too narrowly. The top ten myths about mentors are listed in Figure 7.4. Actually, informal mentoring goes on every day in every

---

FIGURE 7.4 *Top Ten Mentor Myths about Mentors*

Myth 1: *Mentors exist only for career development.* Sometimes the mentor focuses on formal career development. Sometimes the mentor is teacher, counsellor, or friend. Some mentors assume all these roles. This enhances both personal and professional development.

Myth 2: *You only need one mentor.* You can have multiple mentors in your life. Different mentors provide different things and tap different facets of our lives.

Myth 3: *Mentoring is a one-way process.* Learning flows both ways. The mentor often learns from the protégé, so that growth is reciprocal.

Myth 4: *A mentor has to be older than the protégé.* Age does not matter: experience and wisdom do matter. Don't deprive yourself of the chance to learn from others who have rich experiences.

Myth 5: *A mentor has to be the same gender and race as the protégé.* The purpose of mentoring is to learn. Don't deprive yourself. Seek mentors who are different from you.

Myth 6: *Mentor relationships just happen.* Being in the right place at the right time can help, but the key to selecting a good mentor is what (not who) you need. Don't be afraid to actively seek a mentor.

Myth 7: *High-profile people make the best mentors.* Prestige and success can be good, but communication skills, leadership styles, work ethics, and the like vary among individuals. A good mentor will challenge you according to your needs, readiness, and aspirations.

Myth 8: *Once a mentor, always a mentor.* Over time, the mentor should pull back and let the protégé go his or her own way. Although the two may maintain contact, the relationship changes over time.

Myth 9: *Mentoring is a complicated process.* The most complicated part is getting out of a bad mentor relationship. If the relationship is not productive, find a tactful way to disengage.

Myth 10: *Mentor-protégé expectations are the same for everyone.* People seek mentors for the same reasons: resources, visibility, enhanced skills, and counsel. But each individual brings different expectations. The key is understanding where the protégé is now, not where he or she should be.

type of organization. Generally, the mentor initiates the relationship, but sometimes an employee will approach a potential mentor for advice. Most mentoring relationships develop over time on an informal basis. However, in proactive organizations there is an emphasis on formal mentoring plans, in which mentors are assigned to employees who are being considered for promotion. Under a good mentor, learning focuses on goals, opportunities, expectations, standards, and fulfilling one's potential.[14]

Figure 7.5 lists the most effective features of mentors as well as those being mentored. In general, mentoring functions can be divided into two broad categories: career functions, and psychosocial functions. *Career functions* are those aspects of the relationship that enhance career advancement. *Psychosocial functions* are those aspects that enhance the protégé's sense of competence, identity, and effectiveness. Both functions are viewed as critical to management development.[15]

Imperial Oil, the Ontario Public Service Commission, and the Bank of Montreal all have formal mentoring programs. IBM Canada formally mentored 600 people in 2000, under five different mentoring programs: skills mentoring, career mentoring, diversity mentoring, new hire mentoring, and certification mentoring (this last one to help employees qualify for industry certifications).

WWW

Given the importance of mentoring, a number of organizations devoted to it have been springing up. When done well, mentoring helps both the pupil and the mentor. Not surprisingly, mentoring is also being done over the Internet. This process, known as e-mentoring, is mediated through websites that bring experienced business professionals together with individuals seeking counselling. Following are a few examples:

- *TheMentors* is the mentoring subsidiary of SIBCAN, an organization of Canadian oil industry specialists.
- *Communitech* is a technology association covering the Kitchener, Waterloo, Cambridge, and Guelph area. It encourages mentoring by forming peer-to-peer groups.
- *Wired Woman Society and the Women in Trades and Technology National Network* is based in Vancouver. It has an online career resource centre that provides mentoring as one of its services.
- *Webgrrls* is primarily a mentoring organization.

Even though participants in e-mentoring typically never meet in person, many form long-lasting e-mail connections that come to be very beneficial. Still, most par-

---

FIGURE 7.5 *Mentoring Functions*

CAREER FUNCTIONS	PSYCHOSOCIAL FUNCTIONS
Sponsorship	Role modelling
Exposure and visibility	Acceptance and confirmation
Coaching	Counselling
Protection	Friendship
Challenging assignments	

Source: Kathy E. Kram, *Mentoring at Work,* University Press of America, Lanham, Md., 1988. Reprinted with permission.

Webgrrls.com provides a forum for women in or interested in new media and technology to mentor and teach each other.

ticipants see these connections as supplements to—rather than substitutes for—in-company mentors. Highlights in HRM 4 describes one mentoring relationship that went online.

Another new form of mentoring is Take Our Kids to Work Day. This is a business/government venture in which about 400,000 grade nine students join a parent or sponsor on the job. At Scotia Bank, they inspect the bank vault and trading floor; at DeHavilland, they observe an airplane being built.[16]

CAREER DEVELOPMENT FOR A DIVERSE WORKFORCE

Today some organizations offer extensive career development programs. These often include programs geared to specific groups such as women, minorities, and dual-career couples. Let's examine some of these special programs more closely.

Career Development for Women

In Chapter 4 we discussed the current trend toward employing women in fields that were once considered men's domains. At one time, management was one of those domains. Nowadays, as a result of employment equity and the need for strong

Highlights in HRM

4   E-MAIL MENTORING

Virtual mentoring is often an excellent way for busy mentors (and equally busy protégés) to deal with time constraints. Those who are comfortable with e-mail and the Internet say that both have many advantages over real-time meetings. Because there are no geographic boundaries to e-mentoring (i.e., no need for the mentor and the protégé to be in the same city), a wider range of possible mentors is accessible. Scheduling is easier, since either party can log on at any time to ask questions or offer counsel. Because the mentor can take time to consider the answers to questions, the individual being mentored gets more reasoned responses. People seeking advice often maintain a log of their questions and the answers to them; these can be shared later with others in similar situations. Because e-mentoring is more efficient in many ways, mentors can advise more people. The technology can even help match mentors and protégés.

IBM Canada is running a pilot e-mentoring program in which forty girls from grades seven and eight have been matched with computer programmers, sales personnel, and administrators, the goal being to stimulate their interest in technology careers.

The downside is that e-mentoring uses 'flat' technology and so cannot convey emotions or facial expressions that in a face-to-face interaction often alert the mentor to underlying problems. That being said, the advantages of e-mentoring—quick feedback, well-considered responses, and more informal communication—make it one of the more popular ways for employees to build organizational know-how.

leadership, organizations are making pointed efforts to increase the proportion of women they employ as managers.

Eliminating Barriers to Advancement

Women have been at a disadvantage in management because they have not been part of the "old boys' network"—that is, the informal network that traditionally enabled senior (male) members of organizations to pass along news of advancement opportunities and other career tips to junior (male) members. Women have typically been outside that network, and have lacked role models to serve as mentors. Recognizing the importance of networking, women in organizations are creating their own networks. At the Bank of Montreal, there is now a women's network that any female employee can join; it serves as a system for encouraging and fostering women's career development. Figure 7.6 lists some of the do's and don'ts of networking.

WWW

General Motors of Canada has established a woman's advisory council to integrate and promote women. The number of women in senior management levels at GM from 9 to 30 percent during the three-year tenure of Maureen Kempston Darkes as president of GM Canada.

FIGURE 7.6 *Rules of Networking*

Barbara Moses, president of BBM Human Resource Consultants and the author of *Career Intelligence: Mastering the New Work and Personal Realities*, states that networking is an increasingly important career skill. Networking is not about using someone to get ahead; rather, it is about expanding relationships and developing mutually supportive ones. Here are some do's and don'ts of networking:

- Don't call once a year, feigning friendship and concern, when it is obvious that the rest of the year you don't care if this person exists.
- Do keep in touch throughout the year, giving information about mergers or moves, or anything that might benefit the other person.
- Don't approach everyone you meet as a potential business lead. People you meet at parties or on planes should be appreciated for their characteristics, not for what they can do for you. Make new friends, not new contacts. Too often, people hang out in herds, actors with actors; bankers with bankers. Parties and planes offer the opportunity to add breadth to your world.
- Don't use information interviewing. Some guru suggested that calling someone and saying "I am currently exploring careers. Can I meet with you to discuss your business?" is now seen as the transparent and tired job-search technique that it is. Volunteer work and internships will impress an employer more.

Source: Adapted from Barbara Moses, "The Right and Wrong Ways to Network," *The Globe and Mail,* September 4, 1997, B10.

Women's advancement in management has been hindered by various stereotypes. Some of the more corrosive myths about working women were discussed in Chapter 4. Fortunately, there is substantial evidence that stereotyped attitudes toward women are changing. As women pursue career goals assertively and attitudes continue to change, the climate for women in management will grow even more favourable. Research has shown that newer male managers tend to be more receptive to the idea of promoting of women managers.

The good news for women is that in the past decade they have made substantial progress in securing mid- and lower-level management positions. Figure 7.7 shows how women are presently represented in the labour force, including management positions.

WWW

Even so, there is much left to do to break the glass ceiling—that invisible web of attitudes, prejudices, and old-boy networks that prevents women from advancing to important positions. Some organizations, such as BC Tel, are trying to increase the number of women by ensuring that every senior executive has a career development strategy in place for women, and by linking their variable compensation to the success of this plan.

Glass Ceiling Audits

The glass ceiling can be described as "those artificial barriers based on attitudinal or organizational bias that prevent qualified individuals from advancing upward in

> **FIGURE 7.7** *Women at Work*
>
> 51 percent of the Canadian population
> 57 percent of graduate degree holders
> 45 percent of the labour force
> 32 percent of managers
> 6 percent of corporate directors

Source: R. McIroy, "The Glass Ceiling,"" *HR Professional,* 17, no. 4 (August 2000): 31–35.

their organizations into management level positions."[17] Glass ceiling reviews, a form of corporate review, can be conducted to identify practices that seem to be hindering the upward mobility of qualified women (and minorities) and to be limiting their access to:

- upper-level management and executive training
- rotational assignments
- international assignments
- opportunities for promotion
- opportunities for executive development programs at universities
- desirable compensation packages
- opportunities to participate on high-profile project teams
- upper-level special assignments

These audits can document any ceilings, and the reasons they exist. Self-audits are one step toward tapping the potential of a diversified workforce.

Preparing Women for Management

As noted earlier, opportunities for women to move into management positions are definitely improving. But developing women as managers involves more than breaking down the barriers to advancement—it also includes achieving a better understanding of women's needs and of the requirements of the management world.

Companies committed to equal opportunities for women and men will undoubtedly keep the best talent available. A list of actions organizations can take to maximize the human resource represented by women is presented in Highlights in HRM 5.[18]

Many employers now offer special training to women who are on a management career path. They may use their own staff or outside firms to conduct this training. Opportunities are also available for women to participate in seminars and workshops that provide instruction in, and experiences with, a wide variety of management topics.

In the past few years, considerably more women have enrolled in college and university degree programs in management. At the same time, more women trained in management have joined management department faculties at business schools. All of this has created an environment that fosters the mentoring and development of women as professionals capable of assuming higher-level positions in work organizations.

Highlights in HRM

5 MAXIMIZING THE HUMAN RESOURCES OF FEMALE MANAGERS

1. Ensure that women receive frequent and specific feedback on their job performance. Women need and want candid reviews of their work. Clearly articulated suggestions for improvement, standards for work performance, and plans for career advancement make women feel more involved in their jobs and make them better employees.

2. Accept women as valued members of the management team. Include them in every kind of communication. Listen to their needs and concerns, and encourage their contributions.

3. Give talented women the same opportunities as talented men to grow, develop, and contribute to company profitability. Give them responsibility for directing major projects and for planning and implementing systems and programs. Expect them to travel and relocate and to make the same commitment to the company as their ambitious male counterparts.

4. Regarding career advancement opportunities, give women the same level of counselling as men.

5. Identify women as potential managers early in their careers, and help them advance through training and other developmental activities.

6. Help women strengthen their assertion skills. Reinforce strategic career planning to encourage their long-term commitment to their careers.

7. Either formally or informally, accelerate the development of qualified women through fast-track programs. This will provide them with the exposure, knowledge, and positioning for career advancement.

8. Provide opportunities for women to develop mentoring or sponsoring relationships with employees. Too often, women do not have equal or easy access to senior employees. The overall goal should be for knowledgeable, senior-level men and women to provide advice, counsel, and support to promising female employees.

9. Encourage company co-ed management support systems and networks. Sharing experiences and information with other men and women who are managers provides invaluable support to peers. These activities enable women to meet and learn from men and women in more advanced stages of their careers—a helpful way of identifying potential mentors or role models.

10. Consider whether it would be feasible to increase women's participation in company-sponsored planning retreats. Also, encourage them to use company facilities, attend company social functions, and so on. With some notable exceptions, men are still generally more comfortable with other men; as a result, women miss many of the career and business opportunities that arise during social functions. Also, women may not have access to the company's informal political and social systems. Encourage male managers to include women when socializing with other business associates.

Source: Adapted from R.M. Wentling, "Women in Middle Management: Their Career Development and Aspirations." Reprinted from *Business Horizons,* January/February 1992, copyright 1992 by the Foundation for the School of Business at Indiana University. Used with permission.

Besides all this, books and magazines are providing today's women with a wealth of information and guidance. The business sections of bookstores are heavily stocked with books written especially for women who want a better idea of the career opportunities available to them. Many books are devoted to the pursuit of careers in specific fields.[19]

Accommodating Families

A big problem women managers are facing today is how to balance their career with their family. Women managers with young children often experience conflict between their responsibility to the children and their duty to the employer. For some, the conflict becomes too painful, and they abandon their careers, at least temporarily.

WWW

In recent years many employers, including Alco Railings (Langley), Handprint Research (Toronto), and Merak Projects (Calgary), have launched programs that are mutually advantageous to the career-oriented woman and the employer. These programs, which include alternative career paths, extended leave, flextime, job sharing, and telecommuting, offer new ways to balance career and family. For example, 30 percent of the Royal Bank's 40,000 employees are on some sort of flexible work schedule.

Yet there is still a fairly sharp debate about the "mommy track"—that separate track designed to help women be productive but not necessarily upwardly mobile.[20] Many women as well as men criticize the use of this separate track as perpetuating a double-standard and as pitting women against women—those with children against those without. On the other hand, there are those who believe that this approach at least gives women choices.

Career Development for Minorities

OBJECTIVE 6

Many organizations have specific career planning programs for minority employees. These programs are intended to equip employees with career planning skills and development opportunities that will help them compete effectively for advancement.

We observed in Chapter 4 that many employers make a special effort to recruit minorities. Once individuals from minority groups are on the job, it is important for employers to provide opportunities for them to move ahead in the organization as they improve their job skills and abilities.

Advancement of Minorities to Management

The area of employment that has been the slowest to respond to employment equity programs is the advancement of minorities to middle and top management positions. For example, while visible minorities constitute approximately 11 percent of the Canadian labour force (Statistics Canada, 2000), they are not equivalently represented in the managerial and executive ranks.

Visible minorities who aspire to senior management commonly find that their careers rise like rockets till they reach the middle ranks, at which point they confront a barrier that makes it very difficult to move higher. Given the shortage of talent in most industries, few organizations can afford to neglect the development of potential managers.

Minority managers do play a part in creating a better climate for groups that are discriminated against in advancement opportunities. Even so, top management and the HR department still have the main responsibility for creating conditions that are favourable for recognizing and rewarding performance on the basis of objective, nondiscriminatory criteria.

Dual-Career Couples

Dual-career partnerships

Couples in which both member follw their own careers and actively support each other's career development

Two-career families have become a way of life in North America. Economic necessity and social forces have encouraged this, to the point that over 80 percent of all marriages are now **dual-career partnerships**, in which both members follow their own careers and actively support each other's career development.

The dual-career arrangement has both positives and negatives. Many organizations are aware of the problems facing dual-career couples and have programs to assist them. Flexible working schedules are the most common organizational accommodation to these couples. Other arrangements include leave policies where either parent can stay home with a newborn, policies that allow work to be done at home, day care on the organization's premises, and job sharing.

The difficulties that dual-career couples face include time demands, emotional stress, and the need for quality child care. However, the main problem these couples face is the threat of relocation. Many large organizations now offer some kind of job-finding assistance for spouses of employees who are relocated; often, for example, they pay the fees charged by employment agencies, job counselling firms, and executive search firms. Organizations are also developing networking relationships with other employers to find jobs for the spouses of their relocating employees. These networks are a means to "share the wealth and talent" in a community while simultaneously assisting in the recruitment efforts of the participating organizations.[21]

Employers often must relocate dual-career couples to foreign facilities. This is a major issue. Fewer employees are willing to relocate unless the organization is willing to provide assistance to their spouses. Many employers have developed ways to integrate the various allowances typically paid for overseas assignments when husband and wife work for the same employer. Far more complex are the problems that arise when couples work for two different employers. The problems associated with overseas assignments of dual-career couples will be examined in greater detail in Chapter 16.

PERSONAL CAREER DEVELOPMENT

There are many ways that an employer can contribute to an employee's career development and at the same time meet its own HR needs. Though the organization can be a positive force in the development process, the primary responsibility for personal career growth still rests with the individual. One's career often begins before a period of employment with an organization, and often continues after it. To help employees achieve their career objectives, managers and HRM professionals should have an understanding of the stages involved in developing a career and the actions people should take to be successful.

Stages of Career Development

People's knowledge, skills, abilities, attitudes, and career aspirations change as they mature. The work individuals do in different occupations varies considerably, but the challenges and frustrations they face in the different stages of their careers are remarkably similar. A model of career stages is shown in Figure 7.8. The stages are (1) preparation for work, (2) organizational entry, (3) early career, (4) midcareer, and (5) late career. The typical age range and the major tasks at each stage are also presented in this figure.

FIGURE 7.8 *Stages of Career Development*

STAGE 1: PREPARATION FOR WORK

Typical age range: 0–25

Major tasks:	Develop occupational self-image, assess alternative occupations, develop initial occupational choice, pursue necessary education.

STAGE 2: ORGANIZATIONAL ENTRY

Typical age range: 18–25

Major tasks:	Obtain job offer(s) from desired organization(s), select appropriate job based on accurate information.

STAGE 3: EARLY CAREER

Typical age range: 25–40

Major tasks:	Learn job, learn organizational rules and norms, fit into chosen occupation and organization, increase competence, pursue goals.

STAGE 4: MID-CAREER

Typical age range: 40–55

Major tasks:	Reappraise early career and early adulthood, reaffirm or modify goals, make choices appropriate to middle adult years, remain productive in work.

STAGE 5: LATE CAREER

Typical age range: 55–retirement

Major tasks:	Remain productive in work, maintain self-esteem, prepare for effective retirement.

Source: Adapted from *Career Management* by Jefferey H. Greenhouse and Gerard Callanan, copyright © 1993 by Harcourt, Inc. Reproduced by permission of the publisher.

Stage 1—preparation for work—encompasses the period prior to entering an organization, which often extends to age twenty-five. During this period, individuals must acquire the knowledge, abilities, and skills they will need to compete in the marketplace. This is also the time when careful planning, based on sound information, should be the focus. Reality Check describes a service that helps new entrants obtain their first job experiences. Stage 2—typically from eighteen to twenty-five—is devoted to soliciting job offers and selecting an appropriate job. During this period people may also be involved in preparing for work. Stages 3, 4, and 5 entail fitting into a chosen occupation and organization, modifying goals, making choices, remaining productive, and, finally, preparing for retirement. For the rest of this chapter we examine some Stage 1 activities, since these are the ones that students are most concerned about. Retirement planning will be discussed in Chapter 11.

Developing Personal Skills and Competencies

In planning a career, one must do more than simply acquire specific job knowledge and skills. While job know-how is clearly essential, there are other skills that one must develop to be successful as an employee. To succeed as a manager, one must achieve a still higher level of proficiency in various important areas: communication, time management, self-motivation, interpersonal relations, and—in its broadest sense—leadership.

Hundreds of self-help books have been written on these topics, and myriad opportunities to participate in workshops are available, often under the employer's sponsorship.[22] One should not overlook sources of valuable information such as articles in general interest magazines and professional journals.

Choosing a Career

Many years ago, when Peter Drucker was asked about career choice, he said: "The probability that the first job choice you make is the right one for you is roughly one in a million. If you decide your first choice is the right one, chances are that you are just plain lazy."[23] The implications of this statement are just as true today. One must often do a lot of searching and changing to find a career path that is psychologically and financially satisfying.

Use of Available Resources

A variety of resources are available to help individuals choose a satisfying career. Counsellors at colleges and universities, as well as those in private practice, are equipped to help individuals evaluate their aptitudes, abilities, interests, and values as they relate to career selection. Many business schools have shown an interest in career planning and development. Finally, many colleges and universities run placement offices and continuing education centres that offer career planning assistance.

Accuracy of Self-Evaluation

Successful career development depends partly on the individual's ability to conduct an accurate self-evaluation. In making a self-evaluation, one needs to consider those factors which are personally significant. The most important *internal* factors are one's academic aptitude and achievement, occupational aptitudes and skills, social skills, communication skills, leadership abilities, and interests and values. Salary level, status, and opportunities for advancement and for growth on the job should all be considered. *External* factors to be assessed include family values and expectations, economic conditions, employment trends, job market information, and the perceived effect of physical or psychological disabilities on success.[24]

Significance of Interest Inventories

Psychologists who specialize in career counselling typically administer a battery of tests (see Chapter 5 for a discussion of these). The Strong Vocational Interest Blank (SVIB), developed by E.K. Strong Jr, was one of the first interest tests to be developed.[25] Somewhat later, G. Frederic Kuder developed inventories to measure the subject's degree of interest in various activities: mechanical, clerical, scientific, persuasive, and so on. Strong's and Kuder's inventories have both been used widely in vocational counselling.

Reality CHECK

WWW

CAREER EDGE MAKING A DIFFERENCE

Career Edge is an innovative internship program for university and college graduates. For recent graduates with no work experience, obtaining that first job can be difficult. They are caught in the cycle of "no experience, no job; no job, no experience." Career Edge helps graduates obtain that first job, which then leads, in the most cases, to a permanent job. Career Edge contacts host organizations, who agree to provide an internship combining four elements: employment experience, learning, coaching, and networking. Because the interns are employed by Career Edge, employers do not have to fight for additional positions (a very difficult task in any organization), but can employ the interns from contract budgets. The interns are paid a stipend of $16,200 per annum.

All job posting is done electronically. Employers post internships on the Career Edge website (**www.careeredge.org**). Underemployed or unemployed graduates can sign on and search for internships by sector, company, educational discipline, recency, city, length of internship desired, and so on. When a fit is found, the full job description is made available. The site also offers information on job search skills such as résumé and interview preparation.

Frances Randle, the president and CEO of Career Edge, says: "The contact is made directly between the candidate and the host organization, because these students have to learn how to market themselves, and companies have to commit to the intern directly. Interns are looking for practical experience, increased confidence in their abilities, learning about their fields, getting experience in that field, having challenging work, developing a network, and getting feedback on performance, in that order. Companies want recent university graduates who are enthusiastic, flexible, interested in learning, yet with some technical skills and the ability to communicate."

Since opening for business in October 1996, when the youth unemployment rate was nearly 18 percent, Career Edge has placed 4,500 interns at 425 companies. About 85 percent of the interns find full-time work in their chosen field.

Strong found that people's interests vary substantially between occupations, and that a person's interest pattern tends to remain quite stable, especially after age twenty-one. By taking his test, now known as the Strong Interest Inventory, one can learn how closely one's interests correspond with those of successful people in a wide range of occupations. Personality type can also be obtained by applying a special scoring key on the Strong Interest Inventory answer sheet. This key, developed by John Holland, provides scores on six personality types: (1) realistic, (2) investigative, (3) artistic, (4) social, (5) enterprising, and (6) conventional. These categories characterize not only a type of personality, but also the type of working environment a person would find the most satisfying. When Holland's theory is actually applied, combinations of the six types are examined. For example, a person might be classified as realistic-investigative-enterprising (RIE). Jobs in the RIE category include mechanical engineer, lineperson, and air traffic controller. To facilitate the search for occupations that match one's category, such as RIE, Holland has devised a series of tables that correlate the Holland categories with jobs in the *Dictionary of Occupational Titles (DOT)*.[26]

Another inventory that measures both interests and skills is the Campbell Interest and Skill Survey (CISS).[27] The CISS can be used to help employees explore career paths and options, and also to help organizations develop their employees or reassign them in the wake of major organizational changes. When completing the inventory, individuals report their levels of interest and skill by applying a six-point response scale to 200 interest items and 120 skill items. The responses are translated into seven orientations: influencing, organizing, helping, creating, analyzing, producing, and adventuring. They are then further categorized into twenty-nine basic scales, such as leadership and supervision. Finally, occupations are identified that reflect today's workplace.

Highlights in HRM 6 shows a sample profile for one individual. Note that at the top of the profile the range of scores is from 30 to 70, with 50 in the midrange. Corresponding verbal descriptions of scores range from very low to very high. Also note that on the profile, two types of scores are profiled: interest (a solid diamond) and skill (an open diamond). The interest score shows how much the individual likes the specified activities; the skill score shows how confident the individual feels about performing these activities.

In HRM 6 there are four combinations of interest and skill worth noting: pursue, develop, explore, and avoid. For the individual whose scores are profiled in HRM 6, one would interpret the scores on the seven orientation scales (as shown in the right-hand column of the profile) as follows:

Influencing	Pursue
Organizing	Indeterminate
Helping	Pursue
Creating	Avoid
Analyzing	Avoid
Producing	Indeterminate
Adventuring	Develop

On the basis of such profiles, individuals can see how their interests and skills compare with those of a sample of people happily employed in a wide range of occupations. Completed answer sheets can be mailed to a scoring centre, or software is available for in-house scoring.

Highlights in HRM

6 CAMPBELL INTEREST AND SKILL SURVEY: INDIVIDUAL PROFILE

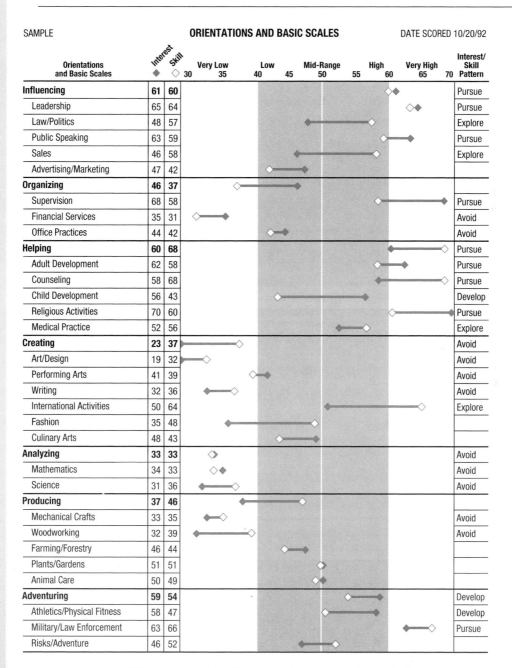

SAMPLE   **ORIENTATIONS AND BASIC SCALES**   DATE SCORED 10/20/92

Orientations and Basic Scales	Interest	Skill		Interest/Skill Pattern
Influencing	61	60		Pursue
Leadership	65	64		Pursue
Law/Politics	48	57		Explore
Public Speaking	63	59		Pursue
Sales	46	58		Explore
Advertising/Marketing	47	42		
Organizing	46	37		
Supervision	68	58		Pursue
Financial Services	35	31		Avoid
Office Practices	44	42		Avoid
Helping	60	68		Pursue
Adult Development	62	58		Pursue
Counseling	58	68		Pursue
Child Development	56	43		Develop
Religious Activities	70	60		Pursue
Medical Practice	52	56		Explore
Creating	23	37		Avoid
Art/Design	19	32		Avoid
Performing Arts	41	39		Avoid
Writing	32	36		Avoid
International Activities	50	64		Explore
Fashion	35	48		
Culinary Arts	48	43		
Analyzing	33	33		Avoid
Mathematics	34	33		Avoid
Science	31	36		Avoid
Producing	37	46		
Mechanical Crafts	33	35		Avoid
Woodworking	32	39		Avoid
Farming/Forestry	46	44		
Plants/Gardens	51	51		
Animal Care	50	49		
Adventuring	59	54		Develop
Athletics/Physical Fitness	58	47		Develop
Military/Law Enforcement	63	66		Pursue
Risks/Adventure	46	52		

Scale ranges: Very Low 30, 35 | Low 40, 45 | Mid-Range 50, 55 | High 60 | Very High 65, 70

Evaluation of Long-Term Employment Opportunities

In making a career choice, try to determine the long-term opportunities in the fields you are considering. While even the experts can err in their predictions, pay at least some attention to the opinions that are available. One source of information with a good track record is *Job Futures*, a Human Resources Development Canada (HRDC) publication that provides Canadians with information about the current world of work, as well as projections for the future (**www.hrdc-drhc.gc.ca/JobFutures**). Occupational Outlooks provides information on 211 occupational groups, representing all jobs in Canada. Also, many libraries have publications that provide details about jobs and career fields. In recent years, a considerable amount of computer software has been developed to help people access information about career fields and match their abilities, aptitudes, interests, and experiences with the requirements of various occupational areas.

WWW

Choosing an Employer

Once you have made a career choice, even if only tentatively, the next big step is deciding where to work. The choice of employer may be based mainly on location, or on whether a position is immediately available, or on starting salary, or on other basic considerations. However, a college or university graduate who has prepared for a professional or managerial career is likely to have more sophisticated concerns. Douglas Hall suggests that people often choose an organization on the basis of its climate and how it appears to fit their needs. According to Hall, people with a high need for achievement often choose aggressive, achievement-oriented organizations. In contrast, power-oriented people often pick influential, prestigious, power-oriented organizations, while affiliative people tend to pick warm, friendly, supportive organizations. We know that people whose needs fit with the organization's climate are rewarded more and are more satisfied than those who fit in less well, so it is natural to reason that fit should also be a factor in your choice of organization. In the changing world of employment, it is becoming more and more unlikely that individuals will remain with one organization for their entire career. The old model of "the organization man," who starts and stays with the same company, is giving way to a more flexible career model that Hall refers to as "protean" (after the Greek god Proteus, who could change shape at will).[28]

The Plateauing Trap

Career plateau

Situation in which for either organizational or personal reasons the probability of moving up the career ladder is low

Judith Bardwick was the first to label the plateauing phenomenon.[29] A **career plateau** is a situation in which for either organizational or personal reasons the probability of moving up the career ladder is low. According to Bardwick, only 1 percent of the labour force will not plateau at some point in their working lives. There are three types of plateaux: structural, content, and life. A *structural plateau* marks the end of promotions, so that one has to leave the organization to find new opportunities and challenges. A *content plateau* occurs when a person has learned a job too well and is bored with day-to-day activities. According to Susan Brooks, a *life plateau* is more profound, and may feel like a midlife crisis.[30] People who experience life plateaux often have allowed work or some other major factor to become the most significant aspect of their lives, and experience a loss of identity and self-esteem when they stop achieving success in that area. Organizations can help indi-

Becoming an entrepreneur can lead to great personal satisfaction as the business grows and prospers.

viduals cope with plateaux by providing opportunities for lateral growth where opportunities for advancement do not exist.

Becoming an Entrepreneur

Entrepreneur

One who starts, organizes, manages, and assumes responsibility for a business or other enterprise

No discussion of careers is complete without a discussion of entrepreneurship. To be an **entrepreneur**—one who starts, organizes, manages, and assumes responsibility for a business or other enterprise—is to embrace a personal challenge, and many individuals find accepting that challenge preferable to being an employee. Most small businesses are run by entrepreneurs, who accept the personal financial risks that go with owning a business but who also benefit directly when the business succeeds.[31]

Small businesses are a big employer. In fact, the majority of Canadian workers are employed by companies with fewer than twenty people on the payroll. Put another way, small businesses pay over half of the wages and salaries in this country. Two decades ago, 13 percent of Canadians were self-employed; today the figure is 20 percent (Statistics Canada, 2000).[32]

If you are considering starting a small business, you can get help from various federal and provincial sources. For example, the Canada-Ontario Business Service Centre (COBSC) provides a single point of access to information about all aspects of starting a business (**www.sbsc.org**). Before starting, you should consider it essential to obtain as much information as possible from the SBA, from libraries, and from organizations and individuals who are knowledgeable about the type of business you are considering.

For an overview of HR issues in small business, there are many how-to books you can consult.[33]

Keeping a Career in Perspective

Work is central the quality of most people's lives. It provides a setting for satisfying almost the entire range of human needs, and in that sense is of considerable value to individuals. That being said, people should learn to keep their careers in perspective so that they don't neglect other areas of life.

Off-the-Job Interests

Life satisfaction is the product of many forces. Some of the more important ingredients of a well-rounded life are physical health, emotional well-being, financial security, harmonious interpersonal relationships, freedom from too much stress, and the achievement of personal goals. While a career can provide some of the satisfaction that one needs, most people find it necessary to have interests and activities outside their career. Off-the-job activities provide a respite from daily work responsibilities; they also offer satisfaction in areas unrelated to work.

Marital and/or Family Life

For both individuals and organizations, career development plans must take into account the needs of spouses and children. As we mentioned earlier, relocation often poses a strong threat to family needs. When there is a conflict between the desire to advance in one's career and the desire to stay in one place, disaster can result. Many employers now provide assistance in this area, including relocation counselling, in an effort to reduce the pain that can accompany relocations.

Besides the need to relocate, there are other potential sources of conflict between career and family—for example, a heavy work load, compulsory overtime, and the demands of shift work. Poor leadership on the job, the disappointment of not meeting one's own expectations, and general dissatisfaction with the job itself can affect an individual's life away from work. Then there are various family-related sources of conflict, which include the spouse's employment patterns, dissonance between the partners' career orientations, and the need to spend an unusually large amount of time dealing with family concerns.[34]

Planning for Retirement

If you are just starting your career, retirement must seem a long way off. Even so, it is never too early to start planning for it. If you want to enjoy your retirement, you should start paying careful attention now to your health, your finances, your family, and your interpersonal relationships, and continue to do so throughout your adult life. It is your own individual responsibility to set the stage for a healthy and satisfying retirement as free as possible from worries—especially the ones that could have been avoided or minimized by acting earlier. Most larger organizations have preretirement programs; unfortunately, many of the participants, while they find these programs helpful, are too close to retirement to gain much from them. As we will see in Chapter 11, such programs are no substitute for personal initiative in this area.

Maintaining a Balance

Some people are "married" to their work to such an extent that they fail to provide the attention and caring essential to marriage and family relationships. These people lack an appreciation for the balance that a satisfying life requires. Always remember that "to be a success in the business world takes hard work, long hours, persistent effort, and constant attention. To be a success in marriage takes hard work, long hours, persistent effort, and constant attention. The problem is giving each its due and not shortchanging the other."[35]

Figure 7.9 lists some of the work–family balancing strategies that have been adopted by women managers.

FIGURE 7.9 *Work-Family Balancing Strategies Adopted by Women Managers*

Employed outside services for domestic help	84%
Curtailed personal interests	71
Relied on supportive spouse or partner	65
Used in-home child care services	47
Developed strong interpersonal networks outside of work	28
Used external child care services	26
Postponed having children	26
Pursued personal interests	21
Took leave of absence for personal reasons	16
Decided not to have children	15
Worked at home	13
Delayed marriage	10
Worked part-time or flexible hours	10

Source: "Closing the Gap," *Conference Board of Canada Report*, December 1997. The Conference Board of Canada is a membership-based, not-for-profit, independent applied research organization.

SUMMARY

OBJECTIVE 1 A career development program is a dynamic process that should integrate the individual's employee needs with those of the organization. It is the responsibility of the employee to identify his or her own KSAs as well as interests and values, and to seek out information about career options. The organization should provide information about its mission, policies, and plans, and about what it will provide in the way of training and development for the employee.

OBJECTIVE 2 To succeed, a career development program must have the support of top management. The program should reflect the goals and the culture of the organization, and managerial personnel at all levels must be trained in the fundamentals of job design, performance appraisal, career planning, and counselling. Employees should be aware of the organization's philosophy and goals; when they aren't, they have no way of knowing whether their own goals match

those of the organization. HRM policies, especially those relating to rotation, transfers, and promotions, should be consistent with the organization's goals. The objectives and opportunities of the career development program should be broadcast widely throughout the organization.

 Job opportunities can be identified by studying various jobs and determining the knowledge and skills each one requires. It is then possible to plan job progressions. These progressions can serve as a basis for developing career paths. Once career paths have been developed and employees have been identified on the career ladders, the jobs can be inventoried to determine where individuals with the required skills and knowledge are needed or will be needed.

 All managers are responsible for identifying and developing managerial talent. Besides immediate superiors, there should be others in the organization who can nominate and sponsor employees with promise. Many organizations use assessment centres to identify managerial talent and recommend developmental experiences that will enable individuals to reach their full potential. Mentoring is invaluable for providing guidance and support to potential managers.

 The first step in facilitating the career development of women is to eliminate barriers to advancement. By encouraging the formation of women's networks, providing special training for women,

accepting women as valued members of the organization, providing mentors for women, and accommodating families, organizations can do much to foster women's career development.

 Minority groups are an important part of any diversified workforce. Many organizations, besides creating conditions that recognize and reward performance, have established special programs (such as internships) that provide hands-on experience and special training for minority workers. Another group that management must pay attention to is dual-career couples, who often require flexible working schedules.

 In choosing a career, you should use all available resources. You should consider internal factors such as your academic aptitude and achievement, occupational aptitudes and skills, communication skills, leadership abilities, and interests and values. You must also consider external factors such as economic conditions, employment trends, and job market information. In choosing a career, you should make use of interest and skill inventories. You should assess the long-term employment opportunities in various occupational fields by reading various publications, including those offered by the government. It is also important to keep your career in perspective, to ensure a balanced life. Work has a big impact—often the biggest—on overall quality of life; even so, you should pay proper attention to your physical health and your family and interpersonal relationships, and to interests and activities outside your career.

KEY TERMS

assessment centre	entrepreneur	mentors
career counselling	fast track program	outplacement services
career paths	in-basket training	promotion
career plateau	job progressions	relocation services
dual-career partnerships	leaderless group discussions	transfer

DISCUSSION QUESTIONS

1. Give some reasons for the trend toward increased emphasis on career development programs.

2. The TD Bank maintains a special suite of offices at its world headquarters in Toronto for its retired executives. Several of the bank's former chief executives use their offices regularly.
   a. Of what value is this arrangement to the corporation? To the individuals?
   b. How might retired executives in any organization assist in the career development of current employees?

3. What contributions can a career development program make to an organization that is forced to downsize its operations?

4. Over 50 percent of all MBAs leave their first employer within five years. While this may mean career growth for individuals, it represents a loss to employers. What are some likely reasons why an MBA would leave his or her first employer?

5. List some of the barriers to advancement that women often face in organizations.

6. How are the career challenges of minorities both similar to and different from those of women?

7. CIBC has instituted a number of practices to make its workplaces more family-friendly. Go to **labour.hrdc-drhc.gc.ca/wip**, which brings you to the Workplace Innovations web page; then click on Publications and scroll down to Innovative Work Place Practices: Case Studies; then click on Family Friendly Policies at CIBC. In groups, discuss why the CIBC is implementing these programs, and the problems involved in gaining commitment to family-friendly workplaces.

8. What personal characteristics do employers look for when they consider individuals for long-term employment and probable advancement? To what extent can these characteristics be developed?

9. One recruiter has said, "Next to talent, the second most important factor in career success is taking the time and effort to develop visibility." How can visibility be developed?

CASE 1

MANAGING THE ORGANIZATION CAREER PIPELINE

WWW

Organizations have several good reasons to concern themselves with their employees' career development: they want highly motivated and capable employees, and they want a deep pool of talent on which to draw. The University of Toronto's MBA graduates for 2000 are willing to work brutal hours in return for top dollars, but only for a while. These graduates see themselves as free agents running their own micro-businesses. They do not plan to work for any organization for twenty years. They are looking for organizations that offer flexibility in working arrangements—for example, that will allow them to work from home, or to work in other divisions to learn new skills, or to work internationally.

In various ways, the following employers are accommodating the career development needs of this generation:

WWW

- Oasis, an IT company that develops e-payment systems, supports its employees through an employee knowledge advancement system (EKAP), which provides a forum where generalists and specialists can share knowledge and training on-site on a daily basis. This encourages mobility and growth within the corporate structure.
- Statistics Canada is one of six recipients (and the only one from Canada) of the Work in America Institute's Award for Excellence. It earned this award for its work/life program, a career development program it developed that includes training, long-term career development, and positive a work environment (including a no-layoff policy and the opportunity to take sabbaticals).
- Through a campaign called Xerox Total Value, Xerox Canada lets its employees know that it values them. Each employee receives a customized package that includes information on salaries, bonuses, and career development. The company spends thousands of dollars on training for each employee. It sees career development as a retention tool.
- KPMG offers a unique service to its clients: a confidential career development and coaching service, which offers career counselling to the employees of other organizations who are considering leaving their present job. Sometimes a focused career plan, articulated to the employer, is enough to keep an employee. Although the names of the employees are not given to their employers, the employers are charged $2,500 for each employee who receives counselling about the right career path. If even one out of ten counselled employees decides to stay with the employer, then the cost is worth it.

Sources: Adapted from Anonymous, "Award for Stats Canada," *Work Life Report* 11, no. 4 (1999): 16. G. Crone, "The Corporate War for Talent," *Financial Post* 1, no. 76 (January 25, 1999): C9. V. Galt, "Great Expectations of Today's MBAs," *The Globe and Mail* (November 16, 2000); P. Khanna, "If Workers Quit, Let Them Go," *Computer World Canada* 15, no. 16 (August 13, 1999): 22, 23.

Questions

1. Employees rarely leave just for money. Companies such as those listed in this case are using career development as a retention strategy. Comment on its possible effect on employees. Would a career plan keep you at an organization?

2. List all the practices organizations can use to help employees manage their careers. How can organizations tell if their career management systems are working?

3. Should career development be outsourced to providers such as KPMG?

4. Some organizations develop their employees to be marketable, as they cannot guarantee job security. Comment on this strategy.

CASE 2

CAREERS—DEAD OR ALIVE

The management of a career can be a full-time job in itself. Here is some advice on how to manage a career:

- *Competence counts.* It's not who you know but what you know. Until you can prove your ability to do the work, and are seen as adding value, there is no point in discussing transfers or promotions.
- *Establish a network.* It's not only what you know, after all, but who you know.
- *Do what you love.* Work is focusing more and more on issues broader than money. Once you have determined what motivates you, your career will evolve. A career does not simply mean getting ahead, or moving vertically up a career ladder.
- *Volunteer in not-for-profit organizations.* This will help you kick-start your career and establish a network. The number of volunteers from the 15 to 24 age group increased from 18 percent in 1987 to 33 percent in 1997. These people say they learned job skills and gained experience by working as volunteers.

Questions

1. Mergers, downsizings, and bankruptcies demonstrate dramatically that jobs are not forever. Is career management a dead concept?

2. The advice given by career experts and managers is often contradictory: "It's who you know" versus "It's what you know"; "Become a generalist" versus "Stay a specialist"; "Work hard and focus on your own job" versus "Act strategically with your eye on the next job." Why does advice vary so much? List some factors (demographic, labour market, sector, etc.) that influence the advice given to those seeking to develop a career plan.

CAREER COUNSEL

Visit the Managing Human Resources website (**belcourt.nelson.com**).

USING THE INTERNET

WWW

Ford Motor Company provides an excellent illustration of the dual-career path. See the description of the Ford Technical Specialist Program at **www.ford.com/default.asp**.

Many organizations today realize the importance of families to both men and women managers. To see how quality-of-life and family resource programs are included in career planning at DuPont, visit **www.dupont.com/careers/you/work/html#family**.

NOTES AND REFERENCES

1. Valentin Fernandez, "Career Strategies for the 21st Century," *Executive Speeches* 13, no. 6 (Jun–July 1999): 20-3; Brent B. Allred, Charles C. Snow, and Raymond E. Miles, "Characteristics of Managerial Careers in the 21st Century," *Academy of Management Executive* 10, no. 4 (1996): 17–27; Stephen A. Laser, "Employees, Careers, and Job Creation: Developing Growth-Oriented Human Resource Strategies and Programs," *Personnel Psychology* 49, no. 2 (Summer 1996): 504–8.

2. Ellen Ernst Kossek, Karen Roberts, Sandra Fisher, and Beverly Demarr, "Career Self-Management: A Quasi-experimental Assessment of the Effects of a Training Intervention," *Personnel Psychology*, 51, no. 4 (Winter 1998): 935–62; Ann G. Colby, "Making the New Career Development Model Work," *HRMagazine* 40, no. 6 (June 1995): 150–2; Shari Caudron, "HR Revamps Career Itineraries," *Business Credit* 97, no. 9 (September 1995): 20–7.

3. Peg O'Herron and Peggy Simonsen, "Career Development Gets a Charge at Sears Credit," *Personnel Journal* 74, no. 5 (May 1995): 103–6. See also Jules Abend, "Behind the Scenes at: Sears," *Bobbin* 39, no. 11 (June 1998): 22–6; Shari Caudron, "The De-Jobbing of America," *Industry Week* 243, no. 16 (September 5, 1994): 30–6; Edward E. Lawler III, "From Job-Based to Competency-Based Organizations," *Journal of Organizational Behavior* 15, no. 1 (January 1994): 3–15.

4. Laurence J. Peter and Raymond Hull, *The Peter Principle* (Cutchogue, NY: Buccaneer Books, 1996).

5. Sumantra Ghoshal, Christopher A. Bartlett, and Peter Moran, "A New Manifesto for Management," *Sloan Management Review* 40, no. 3 (Spring 1999): 9–20.

6. Ann M. Thayer, "Dual Career Ladders," *Chemical & Engineering News* 76, no. 44 (November 2, 1998): 51–5; Alan Garmonsway and Michael Wellin, "Creating the Right Natural Chemistry," *People Management* 1, no. 19 (September 21, 1995): 36–9; Shari Caudron, "Downshift Yourself," *Industry Week* 245, no. 10 (May 20, 1996): 126–30; Jerome A. Katz, "Which Track Are You On?" *Inc.* 17, no. 14 (October 1995): 27–8.

7. Robert J Grossman, "Heirs Unapparent," *HRMagazine* 44, no. 2 (February 1999): 36–44; Amy Barrett, "How to Keep Rising Stars from Straying," *Business Week*, (June 7, 1999): 80.

8. Peter Carrick and Richard Williams, "Development Centres—a Review of Assumptions," *Human Resource Management Journal* 9, no. 2 (1999): 77–92; Maria M Chapham, "A Comparison of Assessor and Self Dimension Ratings in an Advanced Management Assessment Centre," *Journal of Occupational and Organizational Psychology* 71, no. 3 (September 1998): 193–203; Harold W. Goldstein, Kenneth P. Yusko, Eric P. Braverman, D. Brent Smith, and Beth Chung, "The Role of Cognitive Ability in the Subgroup Differences and Incremental Validity of Sssessment Centre Exercises," *Personnel Psychology* 51, no. 2 (Summer 1998): 357–74; Amos S. Engelbrecht and Hermann Fischer, "The Managerial Performance Implications of a Developmental Assessment Center," *Human Relations* 48, no. 4 (April 1995): 387–404; Robert G. Jones and Mark D. Whitmore, "Evaluating Developmental Assessment Centers as Interventions," *Personnel Psychology* 48, no. 2 (Summer 1995): 377–88.

9. Lisa A. Burke, "Developing High-Potential Employees in the New Business Reality," *Business Horizons* 40, no. 2 (March–April 1997): 18–24.

10. For up-to-date career information and guidance as well as an opportunity for self-analysis, see Richard Boles, *What Color is Your Parachute 1999: A Practical Manual for Job-Hunters & Career-Changers*; James D. Porterfield, *Business Career Planning Guide* (Cincinnati, Oh.: South-Western Publishing, 1993); and Julie Griffin Levitt, *Your Career—How to Make It Happen*, 3d ed. (Cincinnati, Oh.: South-Western Publishing, 1995). Those who are interested might also wish to obtain a copy of the video *Planning Your Career*, TMW/Media Group (September 2, 1998) (run time: 22 minutes).

11. Shari Caudron, "Marriott Trains Managers to Become Partners in Career Development," *Personnel Journal* 73, no. 4 (April 1994): 641 [also published as "Marriott Trains Managers to Become Partners in Career Development," *Business Credit* 97, no. 9 (September 1995): 22]. See also Shari Caudron, "HR Revamps Career Itineraries," *Business Credit* 83, no. 4 (April 1994): 35; Jean R. Haskell, "Getting Employees to Take Charge of Their Careers," *Training and Development* 47, no. 2 (February 1993): 51–4.

12. Ellen Ernst Kossek et al., "Career self-management," *Personnel Psychology* 51, no. 4 (Winter 1998): 935–62.

13. Grace Casselman, "Someone to Watch Over Me," *Computer World Canada* 15, no. 2 (January 29, 1999): 14–16.

14. Matt Starcevich and Fred Friend, "Effective Mentoring Relationships from the Mentee's Perspective," *Workforce*, supplement (July 1999): 2–3; Samuel Aryee, Thomas Wyatt, and Raymond Stone, "Early Career Outcomes of Graduate Employees: The Effect of Mentoring and Integration," *Journal of Management* 33, no. 1 (January 1996): 95–118.

15. Kathryn H. Dansky, "The Effects of Group Mentoring on Career Outcomes," *Group and Organization Management* 21, no. 1 (March 1996): 5–21; Stephen G. Green and Talya N. Bauer, "Supervisory Mentoring by Advisors: Relationships with Doctoral Student Potential, Productivity and Commitment," *Personnel Psychology* 48, no. 3 (Autumn 1995): 537–61. Kathy Kram, *Mentoring at Work*, University Press of America, Lanham, MD, 1988.

16. John McKay, "Across Canada, It's Kids Day at Work," Canadian Press newswire, November 2, 1999.

17. A host of reports on glass ceiling issues can be found on the U.S. Department of Labor's website: **www.dol.gov**.

18. Rose Mary Wentling, "Women in Middle Management: Their Career Development and Aspirations," *Business Horizons* 35, no. 1 (January–February 1992): 47–54. See also Harris Collingwood, "Women as Managers: Not Just Different—Better," *Working Woman* 20, no. 11 (November 1995): 14; Elyse Mall, "Why Getting Ahead Is (Still) Tougher for Women," *Working Woman* 19, no. 7 (July 1994): 11.

19. The interested reader should find the following books very informative: Johanna Hunsaker and Phillip Hunsaker, *Strategies and Skills for Managerial Women* (Cincinnati, Oh.: South-Western Publishing, 1991); and Helen Gurley Brown, *Having It All* (New York: Simon and Schuster, 1982).

20. Theodore Gideonse, "Mommy Track at the Times," *Newsweek* 131, no. 22 (June 1, 1998): 61; Yvonne Benschop and Hans Doorewaard, "Covered by Equality: The Gender Subtext of Organizations," *Organization Studies* 19, no. 5 (1998): 787–805; "Why Law Firms Cannot Afford to Maintain the Mommy Track," *Harvard Law Review* 109, no. 6 (April 1996): 1375–92.

21. Valerie Frazee, "Expert Help for Dual-Career Spouses," *Workforce* 4, no. 2 (March 1999): 18–20; Charlene Marmer Solomon, "One Assignment, Two Lives," *Personnel Journal* 75, no. 5 (May 1996): 36–74; Gillian Flynn, "Heck No— We Won't Go!" *Personnel Journal* 75, no. 3 (March 1996): 37–43.

22. A selection of self-help publications on a variety of topics can be found in any bookstore. College and university bookstores typically have a wide selection in their trade or general books department. Two recent popular books by Stephen R. Covey that present a principle-centred approach to time management are *First Things First Everyday* (New York: Fireside, 1997) and *The 7 Habits of Highly Effective People: Powerful Lessons in Personal Change* (New York: Fireside, 1990).

23. Mary Harrington Hall, "A Conversation With Peter Drucker," *Psychology Today* 1, no. 10 (March 1968): 22.

24. Candace Jones and Robert J. DeFillippi, "Back to the Future in Film: Combining Industry and Self-Knowledge to Meet the Career Challenges of the 21st Century," *Academy of Management Executive* 10, no. 4 (November 1996): 89–104; Walter Kiechel III, "A Manager's Career in the New Economy," *Fortune*, April 4, 1994: 68–72.

25. E.K. Strong Jr of Stanford University was active in the measurement of interests from the early 1920s to the time of his death in 1963. Since then his work has been carried on by the staff of the Measurement Research Center, University of Minnesota. The Strong Interest Inventory is distributed by Consulting Psychologists Press, Inc., P.O. Box 60070, Palo Alto, Calif. 94306, to qualified persons under an exclusive licence from the publisher, Stanford University Press.

26. Gary D. Gottfredson and John L. Holland, *Dictionary of Holland Occupational Codes*, Psychological Assessment Resources, December 1996.

27. The *Campbell Interest and Skill Survey* (copyright 1992) is published and distributed by NCS Assessments, P.O. Box 1416, Minneapolis, Minn. 55440. For recent research in this area, see David Lubinski, Camilla P. Benbow, and Jennifer Ryan, "Stability of Vocational Interests among the Intellectually Gifted from Adolescence to Adulthood: A 15-Year Longitudinal Study," *Journal of Applied Psychology* 80, no. 1 (February 1995): 196–200.

28. Douglas T. Hall and Jonathan E. Moss, "The New Protean Career Contract: Helping Organizations and Employees Adapt," *Organizational Dynamics* 26, no. 3 (Winter 1998): 22–37. Also see Douglas T. Hall, *The Career Is Dead, Long Live the Career: A Relational Approach to Careers* (San Francisco: Jossey-Bass, 1996); Douglas T. Hall, "Protean Careers of the 21st Century," *Academy of Management Executive* 10, no. 4 (1996): 8–16; Douglas T. Hall and Associates, *Career Development in Organizations* (San Francisco: Jossey-Bass, 1986).

29. Judith Bardwick, *The Plateauing Trap* (New York: AMACOM, 1986). See also Judith Bardwick, *Danger in the Comfort Zone: From Boardroom to Mailroom—How To Break the Entitlement Habit That's Killing American Business* (New York: AMACOM Book Division, 1995).

30. Susan Sonnesyn Brooks, "Moving Up Is Not the Only Option," *HRMagazine* 39, no. 3 (March 1994): 79–82. See also Michel Tremblay, Alain Roger, and Jean-Marie Toulouse, "Career Plateau and Work Attitudes: An Empirical Study of Managers," *Human Relations* 48, no. 3 (March 1995): 221–37.

31. Abraham Sagie and Dov Abraham, "Achievement Motive and Entrepreneurial Orientation: A Structural Analysis," *Journal of Organizational Behavior* 20, no. 3 (May 1999): 375–87; Eleni T. Stavrou, "Succession in Family Businesses: Exploring the Effects of Demographic Factors on Offspring Intentions to Join and Take Over the Business," *Journal of Small Business Management* 37, no. 3 (July 1999): 43–61. To read about the HR issues facing small business owners, see M. Butteris, *Help Wanted: The Complete Guide to Human Resources for Canadian Entrepreneurs*, John Wiley & Sons, Toronto, 1999

32. Statistics Canada 2000, "Labour, Employment and Unemployment": **www.statcan.ca/english/pgdb/people/labour.htm**.

33. To read about the HR issues facing small business owners, see M. Butteris, *Help Wanted: The Complete Guide to Human Resources for Canadian Entrepreneurs*, John Wiley & Sons, Toronto, 1999.

34. Charlene Marmer Solomon, "Workers Want a Life! Do Managers Care?" *Workforce* 78, no. 8 (August 1999): 54–8; Katherine J. Sweetman, "Family and Careers," *Harvard Business Review* 73, no. 4 (July–August 1995): 14–15.

35. Christopher Caggiano, "Married ... with Companies," *Inc.* 17, no. 6 (May 1995): 68–76; Andrew E. Scharlach and Janice K. Stanger, "Mandated Family and Medical Leave:

Boon or Bane?" *Compensation and Benefits Management* 11, no. 3 (Summer 1995): 1–9; Timothy A. Judge, John W. Boudreau, and Robert D. Bretz Jr, "Job and Life Attitudes of Male Executives," *Journal of Applied Psychology* 79, no. 5 (October 1994): 767–82; Samuel Aryee and Vivienne Luk, "Balancing Two Major Parts of Adult Life Experience: Work and Family Identity among Dual-Earner Couples," *Human Relations* 49, no. 4 (April 1996): 465–87; Stewart L. Stokes Jr., "A Line in the Sand: Maintaining Work–Life Balance," *Information Systems Management* 13, no. 2 (Spring 1996): 83–85; Gillian Flynn, "Hallmark Cares," *Personnel Journal* 75, no. 3 (March 1996): 50–3.

After studying this chapter, you should be able to

Explain the purposes of performance appraisals and the reasons they fail.

Identify the characteristics of an effective appraisal program.

Describe the different sources of appraisal information.

Explain the various methods used for performance evaluation.

Outline the characteristics of an effective performance appraisal interview.

APPRAISING AND IMPROVING PERFORMANCE

I n the preceding chapters we have discussed some of the most effective methods available to managers for acquiring and developing top-notch employees. But talented employees are not enough—a successful organization is especially adept at engaging its workforce to achieve goals that benefit both it and its employees. In this chapter we turn to performance appraisal programs. These are some of the most helpful tools an organization has to maintain and enhance productivity and make progress toward strategic goals. While we will focus mainly on formal procedures, they can be informal as well. All managers monitor how employees work and assess their performance against organizational needs. They form impressions about the relative value of employees to the organization, and seek to maximize every individual's contribution. Yet while these ongoing informal processes are vitally important, most organizations also have a formal performance appraisal once or twice a year.

The success or failure of a performance appraisal program depends on the philosophy underlying it, its connection with business goals, and the attitudes and skills of those responsible for its administration. Many different methods can be used to gather information about employee performance. However, gathering information is only one step in the appraisal process. The information must be evaluated in the context of organizational needs, and then communicated to employees so that it will result in high levels of performance.[1]

PERFORMANCE APPRAISAL PROGRAMS

Performance appraisal programs have spread to large and small organizations in the public and private sectors. Advocates see these HR programs as excellent ways to appraise, develop, and use the knowledge and abilities of employees. However, more and more observers are pointing out that performance appraisals often fall short of their potential.[2]

For example, interest in total quality management (TQM) has led many organizations to rethink how they approach performance appraisal. While most managers still recognize the benefits of performance appraisals, TQM challenges some long-standing assumptions about how they should be conducted.[3] Motorola, Merrill Lynch, and Procter & Gamble have modified their appraisal systems to place more emphasis on quality of performance (in addition to quantity), teamwork (in addition to individual accomplishments), and process improvements (in addition to performance outcomes).[4] Each of these issues is discussed at greater length in the chapter.

WWW

Purposes of Performance Appraisal

It might seem at first glance that performance appraisals have a rather narrow purpose—to evaluate who is doing a good job (or not). But in reality, performance appraisals are among the most versatile tools available to managers, and can serve many purposes that benefit both the organization and the employee whose performance is being appraised. The following are just a sample of these:

1. They give employees the opportunity to discuss performance and performance standards regularly with their supervisor.

2. They provide the supervisor with a means of identifying the strengths and weaknesses of an employee's performance.

3. They provide a format that enables the supervisor to recommend a specific program designed to help the employee improve performance.

4. They provide a basis for salary recommendations.

Figure 8.1 shows the most common uses of performance appraisals, according to a survey of 202 Canadian HR managers. In general, these can be classified as either administrative or developmental.

Administrative Purposes

From the standpoint of administration, appraisal programs provide input that can be used for the entire range of HRM activities. Performance appraisals are used most often as a basis for compensation decisions.[5] The practice of "pay for performance" is found in all types of organizations. Performance appraisal is also directly related to a number of other important HR functions, such as promotion, transfer, and layoff decisions. Performance appraisal data can also be used in HR planning, to determine the relative worth of jobs under a job evaluation program and as criteria for validating selection tests. Performance appraisals also provide a "paper trail" for documenting HRM actions that may result in legal action. Because of employment equity programs, employers should maintain accurate and objective records of employee performance; that way, they will be able to defend themselves against possible charges of discrimination in connection with HRM actions such as promotion, salary determination, and termination. Finally, it is important to recognize that the success of the entire HR program depends on knowing how the performance of employees compares with the goals established for them. This knowledge is best derived from a carefully planned and administered HR appraisal program. Appraisal systems are capable of influencing employee behaviour and can lead directly to an improvement in organizational performance.

Developmental Purposes

From the standpoint of individual development, appraisal provides the feedback that is essential when discussing an employee's strengths and weaknesses with the goal of improving performance. Whatever the employee's level of performance, the appraisal process provides an opportunity to identify issues for discussion, to eliminate any potential problems, and to set new goals for achieving high performance.

FIGURE 8.1 *Reasons for Performance Appraisal*

LEVEL OF EMPLOYEE	ADMINISTRATIVE		DEVELOPMENTAL
	Pay increase	Promotion	Professional Development
Blue collar	9.7%	26.5%	51.2%
Lower management	68.7	62.7	88.0
Upper management	60.8	47.6	74.3

Source: S. Way and J.W. Thacker, "Trends in Canadian Human Resource Practices," *HR Professional* 17, no. 4 (August 2000): 41–3,

Newer approaches to performance appraisal emphasize training, development, and growth plans for employees. A developmental approach to appraisal recognizes that the purpose of a manager is to improve job behaviour, not simply to evaluate past performance. One of the major benefits of an appraisal program is that it provides a sound basis for improving performance.

WWW

For example, Monsanto has recently changed its performance appraisal system (referred to as the Performance Enhancement Process) to manage the context in which performance occurs, rather than simply "calling the fouls." By focusing on employee development, Monsanto hopes to change the manager's role in performance appraisal from that of judge to one of a coach.[6]

Why Appraisal Programs Sometimes Fail

In actual practice, and for a number of reasons, formal performance appraisal programs sometimes yield disappointing results. Figure 8.2 indicates the main reasons why. For example, if an appraisal program is used to provide a written appraisal for salary action and at the same time to motivate employees to improve their work, the administrative and developmental purposes may be in conflict. In situations like this, the appraisal interview easily becomes a discussion about salary during which the manager seeks to justify the action taken. As an end result, the discussion may have little influence on the employee's future job performance.

FIGURE 8.2 *Top Ten Reasons Performance Appraisals Can Fail*

1. Manager lacks information concerning an employee's actual performance.

2. Standards by which to evaluate an employee's performance are unclear.

3. Manager does not take the appraisal seriously.

4. Manager is not prepared for the appraisal review with the employee.

5. Manager is not honest/sincere during the evaluation.

6. Manager lacks appraisal skills.

7. Employee does not receive ongoing performance feedback.

8. Insufficient resources are provided to reward performance.

9. There is ineffective discussion of employee development.

10. Manager uses unclear/ambiguous language in the evaluation process.

Source: Adapted with permission from Clinton O. Longnecker and Denise R. McGinnis, "Appraising Technical People: Pitfalls and Solutions," *Journal of Systems Management,* December 1992, 12–16; and Clinton O. Longnecker and Stephen J. Goff, "Why Performance Appraisals Still Fail," *Journal of Compensation and Benefits* 6, no. 3 (November/December 1990): 36–41. Copyright 1992 and 1990 by Warren, Gorham & Lamont, Park Square Building, 31 St. James Avenue, Boston, MA 02116-4112. 1-800-950-1216. All rights reserved. See also Clinton O. Longnecker and Dennis A. Gioia, "The Politics of Executive Appraisals," *Journal of Compensation and Benefits* 10, no. 2 (September/October 1994): 5–11; Ken Blanchard, "Performance Appraisals," *Executive Excellence* 11, no. 10 (October 1994): 15–16; Allan J. Weber, "Making Performance Appraisals Consistent with a Quality Environment," *Quality Progress* 28, no. 6 (June 1995): 65–69; Paul Falcone, "The Integrated Performance Appraisal," *Management Review* 84, no. 12 (December 1995): 46; "Seven Deadly Sins of Performance Appraisals," *Supervisory Management* 39, no. 1 (January 1994): 7–8.

As with all HR functions, if the support of top management is lacking the appraisal program will not succeed. Even the best-conceived program will not work in an environment where appraisers are not encouraged by their superiors to take the program seriously. To underscore the importance of this responsibility, top management should announce that effectiveness in appraising subordinates is a standard by which the appraisers themselves will be evaluated.

Other reasons why performance appraisal programs sometimes fail to yield the desired results include the following:

1. Managers feel that little or no benefit will be derived from the time and energy spent in the process.

2. Managers dislike the face-to-face confrontation of appraisal interviews.

3. Managers are not sufficiently adept in providing appraisal feedback.

4. The judgmental role of appraisal conflicts with the helping role of developing employees.

In many organizations, performance appraisal is a once-a-year activity in which the appraisal interview becomes a source of friction for both managers and employees. An important principle of performance appraisal is that continual feedback and employee coaching must be a positive daily activity. The annual or semi-annual performance review should be a logical extension of the day-to-day supervision process.

For employees who are being appraised, one of the main concerns is that the system be fair, since it is central to so many HRM decisions. Employees who believe it isn't may consider appraisal interviews a waste of time and leave those interviews feeling anxious or frustrated. Also, they may pay only perfunctory attention to the system and play only a passive role during interviews. When the issue of fairness is carefully addressed during the planning stages of appraisal, the program will help the organization reach its goals.[7]

Finally, organizational politics can introduce a bias even in fairly administered employee appraisals.[8] For example, managers may inflate evaluations because they desire higher salaries for their employees or because higher subordinate ratings make them look good as managers. Alternatively, managers may want to get rid of troublesome employees, passing them off to another department by inflating their ratings. A survey of over 2,000 Canadian workers indicated that only 60 percent understood the measures being used to evaluate their performance, 57 percent thought their performance had been evaluated fairly, and even fewer (39 percent) found that the performance review was helpful. The next section describes how performance appraisal processes can be improved.[9]

DEVELOPING AN EFFECTIVE APPRAISAL PROGRAM

The HR department ordinarily has the main responsibility for overseeing and coordinating appraisal programs. Managers from the operating departments must also be actively involved, especially in helping establish the program's objectives. Furthermore, employees are more likely to accept and be satisfied with the performance appraisal program when they have the chance to participate in its development. Their concerns about fairness and accuracy in determining raises, promotions, and the like tend to be alleviated somewhat when they have been involved at the planning stages and have helped develop the performance standards themselves.

What Are the Performance Standards?

Before appraisals are conducted, the standards by which performances are to be evaluated must be clearly defined and communicated to the employees. These standards should be based on job-related requirements derived from job analysis and reflected in the job descriptions and job specifications (see Chapter 3). When performance standards are properly established, they help translate organizational goals and objectives into job requirements that convey acceptable and unacceptable levels of performance to employees.[10]

As shown in Figure 8.3, there are four basic considerations in establishing performance standards: strategic relevance, criterion deficiency, criterion contamination, and reliability.

Strategic Relevance

Strategic relevance refers to the extent to which standards relate to the strategic objectives of the organization. For example, if a TQM program has established a

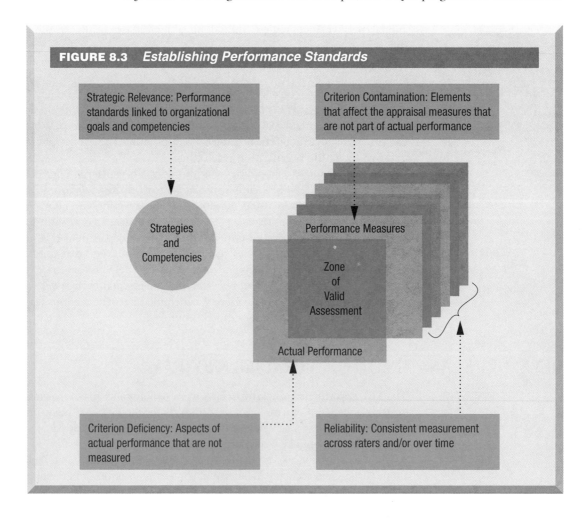

FIGURE 8.3   Establishing Performance Standards

Strategic Relevance: Performance standards linked to organizational goals and competencies

Criterion Contamination: Elements that affect the appraisal measures that are not part of actual performance

Strategies and Competencies

Performance Measures

Zone of Valid Assessment

Actual Performance

Criterion Deficiency: Aspects of actual performance that are not measured

Reliability: Consistent measurement across raters and/or over time standard that "95 percent of all customer complaints are to be resolved in one day," then it is relevant for the customer service representatives to use such a standard for their evaluations. Companies such as 3M and Rubbermaid have strategic objectives that 25 to 30 percent of their sales are to be generated from products developed in the past five years. These objectives are translated into performance standards for their employees.[11]

Criterion Deficiency

A second consideration in establishing performance standards is the extent to which those standards capture the entire range of an employee's responsibilities. When performance standards focus on a single criterion (e.g., sales revenues) to the exclusion of other important but less quantifiable performance dimensions (e.g., customer service), the appraisal system is said to suffer from criterion deficiency.[12]

Criterion Contamination

Performance criteria can be "contaminated." In other words, there are factors outside an employee's control that can influence his or her performance. Thus, the performance appraisals of production workers should not be contaminated by the fact that some use newer machines than others. In the same vein, the performance appraisals of travelling salespeople should not be contaminated by the fact that territories vary in sales potential.

Reliability

Reliability refers to the stability or consistency of a standard, or the extent to which individuals tend to maintain a certain level of performance over time (see Chapter 5). Reliability can be measured by correlating two sets of ratings made by a single rater or by two different raters. For example, two managers can rate the same individual and estimate his or her suitability for a promotion. Their ratings can then be compared to determine interrater reliability.

Performance standards permit managers to specify and communicate precise information to employees about the quality and quantity of their output. When performance standards are written, they should be defined in quantifiable and measurable terms. For example, "ability and willingness to handle customer orders" is not as good a performance standard as "all customer orders will be filled in four hours with a 98 percent accuracy rate." When standards are expressed in specific terms, and the employee's performance is measured against a clear standard, a more justifiable appraisal results.

Legal Issues

Since performance appraisals are used as one basis for HRM actions, they must meet certain legal requirements. HR professionals and their lawyers often face the situation where a manager has fired an employee for poor performance, but has also left a paper trail of glowing performance reviews over the years. In circumstances like this it is difficult for the employer to argue that the employee was dismissed for cause. As a common result, the employer much assume legal liability for wrongful dismissal.

An employer can also face a legal challenge to its appraisal system when an appraisal indicates acceptable or above-average performance but the employee is later passed over for promotion, or disciplined for poor performance, or discharged, or laid off. In these situations a performance appraisal can undermine the legitimacy of the later personnel decision. Intel was recently taken to court by a group of former employees on the grounds that the performance appraisal system (used for layoff decisions) was unreliable and invalid. In light of court cases like this one, performance appraisals should meet the following guidelines:

- Performance ratings must be job-related, with performance standards developed through job analysis.
- Employees must be given a written copy of their job standards in advance of appraisals.
- Managers who conduct the appraisal must be able to observe the behaviour they are rating. This involves having a measurable standard against which to compare employee behaviour.
- Supervisors should be trained to use the appraisal form correctly. They should be instructed in how to apply appraisal standards when making judgments.

Appraisals should be discussed openly with employees. Counselling or corrective guidance should be offered to help poor performers improve their performance.

There should be an appeals procedure to enable employees to express disagreement with the appraisal.[13]

Employers must make sure that managers and supervisors document appraisals and reasons for subsequent HRM actions (see Chapter 12 on documentation). This information may prove decisive should an employee take legal action. An employer's credibility is strengthened when it can support performance appraisal ratings by documenting instances of poor performance.

Who Should Appraise Performance?

WWW

Just as there are multiple standards for evaluating performance, so are there multiple candidates for appraising performance. Given the complexity of today's jobs, it is often unrealistic to expect one person to fully observe and evaluate a given employee's performance. As shown in Figure 8.4, raters can include supervisors, peers, team members, subordinates, customers, and the employee (i.e., self-evaluation). Each of these alternatives has at least some relevance to the administrative and developmental purposes we discussed earlier. Canadian Tire, the Canadian Institute of Chartered Accountants, and the Ontario Ministry of Northern Development and Mines have begun using multiple-rater approaches (i.e., 360 degree appraisal) to evaluate employee performance.[14] We will talk more about 360 degree appraisal at the end of this section.

Manager/Supervisor Appraisal

Manager and/or supervisor appraisal

Performance appraisal done by an employee's manager and often reviewed by a manager one level higher

Manager and/or supervisor appraisal has been the traditional approach to evaluating an employee's performance. Typically, supervisors are in the best position to perform this function, although it may not always be possible for them to do so. Managers often complain that they do not have the time to fully observe the performance of their employees. These managers must then rely on performance records to evaluate an employee's performance. When reliable and valid measures are not available, the appraisal may well be less than accurate. (Recall our earlier discussion of criterion deficiency and contamination.)

When a supervisor appraises employees independently, those appraisals are often reviewed by the supervisor's superior. This reduces the likelihood of superficial or biased evaluations. Generally, reviews by superiors are more objective than appraisals by immediate supervisors, and provide a broader perspective of employee performance. For the managerial perspective on performance appraisals, see Reality Check.

Self-Appraisal

Self-Appraisal

Performance appraisal done by the employee being evaluated, generally on an appraisal form completed by the employee to the performance review

Sometimes employees are asked to evaluate themselves on a self-appraisal form. **Self-appraisal** can be useful when managers are trying to increase the employee's involvement in the review process. A self-appraisal system requires the employee to complete the appraisal form before the performance interview. At a minimum, this gets the employee thinking about his or her strengths and weaknesses; this in turn can lead to discussions about barriers to effective performance. During the performance interview, the manager and the employee discuss job performance and agree on a final appraisal.

This approach can work well when the manager and the employee jointly establish future performance goals or employee development plans. Critics of self-appraisal argue that self-raters are more lenient than managers in their assessments and tend to present themselves in a highly favourable light. For this reason, self-appraisals may be best for developmental purposes rather than for administrative decisions. When used in conjunction with other methods, self-appraisals can be a valuable source of appraisal information.[15]

Electronic Performance Monitoring

The most controversial practice in performance appraisal is electronic performance monitoring. Nowadays it is easy to track workers by audiotaping their conversations, videotaping their activities, counting their computer keystrokes electronically, and so on. Employee performance can be measured objectively by these means. However, employees must be told they are being monitored, and all dimensions of job performance should be included in the performance appraisal.

FIGURE 8.4 *Alternative Sources of Appraisal*

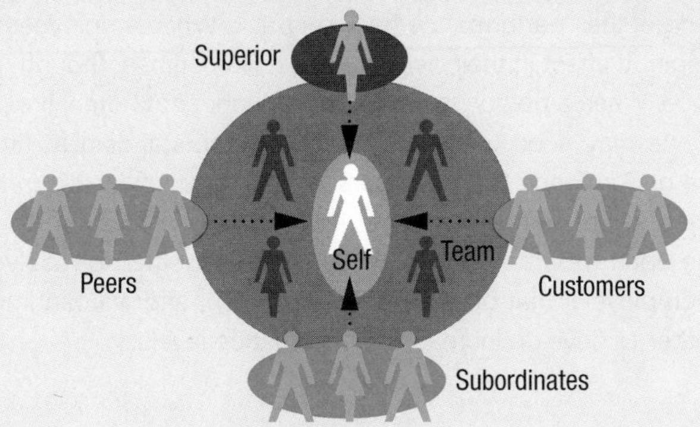

Reality CHECK

PERFORMANCE APPRAISAL AT TRANSLOGIC

TransLogic Limited, based in Mississauga, Ontario, is a leading supplier of computerized material transport systems in Canada, with installations worldwide. Paul Collings is the president, with additional responsibility for international business development. His goal is to motivate his staff to perform their functions professionally and successfully.

"In my opinion the technical aspects of a performance appraisal system should be tailored to suit each particular circumstance," states Collings. "The system has to be dynamic so that it meets the needs of our changing and diverse operations. There must be some structure in place such as filling out the appropriate paperwork, timing, follow-up, and so forth, but it must also be flexible enough to deal with the different groups of employees that work within our organization, and deal with 'people as people.'

"For instance, in order to tie the results of our sales staff to the overall business plan, we knew we had to deviate from our standard performance appraisal system and adopt a unique program geared to measure the direct results of our sales staff. Using the standard format that we had used for so many years had not addressed the particular competencies that mattered most to value-added selling, such as sourcing new clients, selecting the right client to match the profile of our organization, or the ability to read situations that would help to close sales. The system we have devised is geared to measure the direct, day-to-day results that we expect of our sales staff. In fact, the paperwork that we have to complete is a summary of little talks we have had along the way. The real issue surrounding performance is how we deal with it on a daily basis. When employees achieve a milestone, we let them know how proud we are, just the same as letting them know when an area requires improvement. We work together with employees to ensure that they have full support as a means of achieving results. It doesn't do an employee any good to let things slide—you need to deal with issues as they occur.

"Because we deal with performance on a daily basis, it cuts down on the annual anxieties sometimes felt, because there are no surprises. All issues, positive or otherwise, are dealt with as they occur."

Collings approaches employee issues in a positive fashion. "I believe the basic premise is that employees want to do a good job, accomplish goals, be as successful as they can, and be acknowledged for their results. They also want to know when improvement is needed so they can get their performance back on track. When employees are successful on the job, there is a spinoff effect in their personal lives. Sometimes, though, personal issues can affect performance. When a person is not happy at work or at home, it can become a vicious circle. Therefore, we may need to be a little more understanding at times and accept less than acceptable performance to help a person work through issues in the short term. In the long term, the job still needs to get done. If employees are having personal problems, I expect them to be open with me so that we can work together to resolve these situations. I try to show our employees that objectives are common, and we can improve outcomes when we work together to develop increased performance levels."

Subordinate Appraisal

Subordinate appraisal

Performance appraisal of a superior by an employee, which is more approriate for developmental than for administrative purposes

Some organizations use **subordinate appraisal** to give managers feedback on how their subordinates view them.[16] Subordinates are in a good position to evaluate their managers, since they are in frequent contact with them and occupy a unique position from which to observe many performance-related behaviours. The performance dimensions judged most appropriate for subordinate appraisals include leadership, oral communication, delegation of authority, coordination of team effort, and interest in subordinates. The manager at the Langley Memorial Hospital in Langley, B.C., arranged such a "reverse appraisal" and learned how to communicate more effectively with her team.[17] However, dimensions related to managers' specific job tasks, such as planning and organizing, budgeting, creativity, and analytical ability, are not usually appropriate for subordinate appraisal.

Since subordinate appraisals give employees power over their bosses, managers may be hesitant to endorse such a system, especially when it might be used as a basis for compensation decisions. However, when the information is used for developmental purposes, managers tend to be more open to the idea. Available evidence suggests that when managers heed the advice of their subordinates, their own performance can improve substantially. Nevertheless, to avoid potential problems, subordinate appraisals should be submitted anonymously and combined across several individual raters.[18]

WWW

Peer Appraisal

Peer appraisal

Performance appraisal done by one's fellow employees, generally on forms that are compiled into a single profile for use in the performance interview conducted by the employee's manager

Individuals of equal rank who work together are being asked more and more often to evaluate one another. A **peer appraisal** often differs to some degree from a supervisor's appraisal, since peers see different dimensions of performance. Peers can readily identify a co-worker's leadership and interpersonal skills, along with various other strengths and weaknesses. A desk sergeant asked to rate a foot patrol officer on a dimension such as "dealing with the public" may not have had much opportunity to observe it. Fellow officers will have had the opportunity to observe this behaviour regularly.

One advantage to peer appraisals is that they often furnish more accurate and valid information than appraisals by superiors. The supervisor often sees employees putting their best foot forward; those who work with their fellow employees on a regular basis will have gained a more realistic picture. With peer appraisals, co-workers complete an evaluation on the employee. The forms are then usually compiled into a single profile, which is given to the supervisor for use in the final appraisal.[19]

Despite evidence that peer appraisals are possibly the most accurate method of judging employee behaviour, there are reasons why they are not used more often.[20] These reasons are commonly cited:

1. Peer ratings are simply a popularity contest.

2. Managers are reluctant to give up control over the appraisal process.

3. Those receiving low ratings might retaliate against their peers.

4. Peers rely on stereotypes in ratings.

When peers are in competition with one another (e.g., sales associates), peer appraisals may not be advisable for administrative decisions such as those relating to salary or bonuses. Also, employers who use peer appraisals must make sure to safeguard confidentiality in handling the review forms. A breach of confidentiality can create interpersonal rivalries or hurt feelings and foster hostility among fellow employees.

Team Appraisal

Team appraisal

Performance appraisal, based on TQM concepts, that recognizes team accomplishment rather than individual performance

An extension of the peer appraisal is the **team appraisal**. Peers of equal standing often do not work closely together. In a team setting it may be nearly impossible to separate out an individual's contribution. Advocates of team appraisal argue that individual appraisal can be dysfunctional in a team environment, since it detracts from the critical issues of the team.

A company's interest in team appraisals is often driven by its commitment to TQM principles and practices. At its root, TQM is a control system that involves setting standards (based on customer requirements), measuring performance against those standards, and identifying opportunities for continuous improvement. In this regard TQM and performance appraisal are perfectly complementary. However, a basic tenet of TQM is that performance is best understood at the level of the system as a whole, whereas performance appraisal traditionally has focused on individual performance. Team appraisals represent one way to break down barriers between individuals and to encourage their collective effort.[21] Often, the system is complemented by team incentives or group variable pay (see Chapters 10 and 17).

Customer Appraisal

Customer appraisal

Performance appraisal, which, like team appraisal, is based on TQM concepts and seeks evaluation from both internal and external customers

More and more organizations are using internal and external **customer appraisal** as a source of performance appraisal information. This form of appraisal is also driven by TQM concerns. External customers' evaluations have long been used to appraise restaurant personnel. However, companies such as Sears have begun utilizing external customers as well. Sears customers receive a coupon asking them to call a 1-800 number within a week of making a purchase. In exchange for

Team appraisals are one way a company can practise TQM, break down barriers between individuals, and encourage collective effort.

answering prerecorded questions on a touchtone phone, the customers receive $5 off their next purchase. Each call can be linked to a particular transaction (and sales associate) based on the receipt number. With 468 million transactions a year, enough survey data are generated for each sales associate to provide meaningful feedback on performance measures such as service and product knowledge.

Managers establish customer service measures (CSMs) and set goals for employees that are linked to company goals. Often the CSM goals are linked to employee pay through incentive programs. Customer survey data are then incorporated into the performance evaluation. By including CSMs in their performance reviews, companies hope to produce more objective evaluations, more effective employees, more satisfied customers, and better business performance.[22]

There are also *internal* customers. These include anyone inside the organization who depends on an employee's work output. For example, managers who rely on the HR department for selection and training services are candidates for conducting internal customer evaluations of that department. For both developmental and administrative purposes, internal customers can provide extremely useful feedback about the value being added by an employee or team of employees.[23]

Putting It All Together: 360 Degree Appraisal

As mentioned earlier, many companies are combining various sources of performance appraisal information to create multirater—or 360-degree—appraisal and feedback systems. Jobs are multifaceted, and different people see different things. As the name implies, 360 degree feedback is intended to provide employees with as accurate a view of their performance as possible by getting input from all angles: supervisors, peers, subordinates, customers, and the like. Although in the beginning, 360 degree systems were purely developmental, and were restricted mainly to management and career development, they have migrated to performance appraisal and other administrative applications. Because the system combines more information than a typical performance appraisal, it can become administratively complex. For that reason, organizations have recently begun using Web technology (the Internet, intranets) to compile and aggregate the information.[24]

Figure 8.5 lists some pros and cons of 360 degree appraisal. Although 360 degree feedback can be useful for both developmental and administrative purposes, most companies start with an exclusive focus on development. Often, employees are understandably nervous about people ganging up on them in their evaluations. When an organization starts with only developmental feedback (i.e., feedback that isn't tied to compensation, promotions, and the like), its employees become accustomed to the process and learn to value the input they get from various parties.

When Intel established a 360 degree system, it followed these safeguards to ensure maximum quality and acceptance:

WWW

- *It ensured anonymity.* It made certain that no employee ever knew how any evaluation-team member responded. (The supervisor's rating was an exception to this rule.)
- *It made respondents accountable.* Supervisors were instructed discuss each evaluation team member's input, letting each member know whether she or he used the rating scales appropriately, whether their responses were reliable, and how other participants rated the employee.

FIGURE 8.5 *Pros and Cons of 360 Degree Appraisal*

PROS

- The system is more comprehensive in that responses are gathered from multiple perspectives.

- Quality of information is better. (Quality of respondents is more important than quantity.)

- It complements TOM initiatives by emphasizing internal/external customers and teams.

- It may lessen bias/prejudice since feedback comes from more people, not one individual.

- Feedback from peers and others may increase employee self-development.

CONS

- The system is complex in combining all the responses.

- Feedback can be intimidating and cause resentment if employee feels the respondents have "ganged up."

- There may be conflicting opinions, though they may all be accurate from the respective standpoints.

- The system requires training to work effectively.

- Employees may collude or "game" the system by giving invalid evaluations to one another.

- Appraisers may not be accountable if their evaluations are anonymous.

Sources: Compiled from David A. Waldman, Leanne E. Atwater, and David Antonioni, "Has 360 Feedback Gone Amok?" *Academy of Management Executive* 12, no. 2 (May 1998): 86–94; David Antonioni, "Designing an Effective 360-Degree Appraisal Feedback process," *Organizational Dynamics* 25, no. 2 (Autumn 1996): 24–38; Mark Edwards and Ann J. Ewen, "How to Manage Performance and Pay with 360 Degree Feedback," *Compensation and Benefits Review* 28, no. 3 (May/June 1996): 41–46; Mary N. Vinson, "The Pros and Cons of 360 Degree Feedback: Making It Work," *Training and Development* 50, no. 4 (April 1996): 11–12.

- *Steps were taken to prevent "gaming" the system.* Some individuals will try to help or hurt an employee by giving either too high or too low an evaluation. Or team members will attempt to collude with one another by agreeing to give each other uniformly high ratings. Supervisors were instructed to check for obviously invalid responses.

- *It used statistical procedures.* Weighted averages or other quantitative approaches were applied to combine evaluations. Supervisors were careful about using subjective combinations of data that might undermine the system.

- *It identified and quantified biases.* Prejudices or preferences related to age, gender, ethnicity, or other group factors were checked for.[25]

WWW

Based on the experiences of companies like Dominion Directory in Burnaby, B.C, 360 degree feedback can be a valuable approach to performance appraisal. Its success, as with any appraisal technique, depends on how managers use the information and how fairly employees are treated.

Training Appraisers

A weakness of many performance appraisal programs is that managers and supervisors are not adequately trained for the appraisal task and provide little meaningful feedback to subordinates. Because they lack precise standards for appraising subordinates' performance and have not developed the necessary observational and feedback skills, their appraisals become nondirective and meaningless. It follows that the performance appraisal task can be vastly improved by training appraisers.

Establishing an Appraisal Plan

Training programs are most effective when they follow a systematic process that begins with explaining the objectives of the performance appraisal system.[26] It is important for the rater to know what the appraisal is to be used for. For example, using the appraisal for compensation decisions rather than development purposes may affect how the rater evaluates the employee, and may change the rater's opinion of how the appraisal form should be completed. The mechanics of the rating system—how often the appraisals are to be conducted, who will conduct them, what the standards of performance are, and so on—should also be explained. In addition, appraisal training should alert raters to the weaknesses and problems of appraisal systems so they can be avoided.

Eliminating Rater Error

Appraisal training should focus on eliminating subjective errors in the rating process. Gary Latham and Kenneth Wexley stress the importance of performance appraisal training by noting:

> Regardless of whether evaluations are obtained from multiple appraisers or from only the employee's immediate superior, all appraisers should be trained to reduce errors of judgment that occur when one person evaluates another. This training is necessary because to the degree to which a performance appraisal is biased, distorted, or inaccurate, the probability of increasing the productivity of the employee is greatly decreased. Moreover, wrong decisions could be made regarding whom to promote, retain, or replace, which in turn will penalize the organization's bottom line. In addition, when a performance appraisal is affected by rating errors, the employee may be justified in filing a discrimination charge.[27]

With any rating method, certain types of errors can arise that should be considered. The "halo error" (see Chapter 5) is common with respect to rating scales, especially those which do not include carefully developed descriptions of the employee behaviours that are being rated.[28] Provision for comments on the rating form tends to reduce halo error.

Some types of rating errors are *distributional errors*, in that they involve a group of ratings given to a number of employees. For example, raters who are reluctant to assign either extremely high or extremely low ratings commit the **error of central tendency**. As a result, they rate all employees about average. It is a good idea to explain to these raters that among large numbers of employees, one should expect to find significant differences in behaviour, productivity, and other characteristics.

It is also common for some raters to give unusually high or low ratings. For example, a manager may erroneously assert, "All my employees are excellent," or

Error of central tendency

Performance rating error in which all employees are rated about average

Leniency or strictness error

Performance rating error in which the appraiser tends to give employees either unusually high or ununually low ratings

Recency error

Performance rating error in which the appraisal is based largely on the employee's most recent behaviour rather than on the behaviour throughout the appraisal period

Contrast error

Performance rating error in which an employee's evaluation is biased either upward or downward because of comparison with another employer just recently evaluated

Similar-to-me error

Performance rating error in which an appaiser inflates the evaluation of an employee because of a mutal personal connection

"None of my people are good enough." These beliefs give rise to what is called **leniency or strictness error**.[29] One way to reduce this error is to clearly define the characteristics or dimensions of performance and to provide meaningful descriptions of behaviour, known as "anchors," on the scale. Another approach is to require ratings to conform to a *forced distribution*. Managers appraising employees under a forced distribution system are required to place a certain percentage of employees into various performance categories. For example, it may be required that 10 percent of ratings be poor (or excellent). This is similar to the requirement in some schools that instructors grade on a curve. However, while a forced distribution may solve leniency and strictness error, it may also create other errors in the accuracy of ratings—especially if most employees are performing above standard.

Some rating errors are *temporal* in that the performance review is biased either favourably or unfavourably, depending how performance information is selected, evaluated, and organized by the rater over time. For example, when the appraisal is based largely on the employee's recent behaviour, good or bad, the rater has committed the **recency error**. Managers who give higher ratings because they believe an employee is "showing improvement" may unwittingly be committing recency error. Without work record documentation for the entire appraisal period, the rater is forced to recall recent employee behaviour to establish the rating. Having the rater routinely document employee accomplishments and failures throughout the whole appraisal period can minimize the recency error. Rater training also helps reduce this error.

Contrast error occurs when an employee's evaluation is biased either upward or downward because of another employee's performance that was evaluated just previously. For example, an average employee can appear especially productive when compared with a poor performer; yet that same employee can appear unproductive when compared with a star performer. Contrast errors are most likely to occur when raters are required to rank employees from best to poorest. Employees are evaluated against one another, usually on the basis of some organizational standard or guideline. For example, they may be compared on the basis of their ability to meet production standards or on their "overall" ability to perform their job. As with other types of rating error, contrast error can be reduced through training that focuses on using objective standards and behavioural anchors to appraise performance.

Similar-to-me error occurs when appraisers inflate the evaluations of people with whom they have something in common. For example, if both the manager and the employee are from small towns, the manager may unwittingly have a more favourable impression of the employee. The effects of a similar-to-me error can be powerful, and when the similarity is based on race, religion, gender, or some other protected category, it may result in discrimination.

Furthermore, raters should be aware of any stereotypes they may hold toward particular groups (e.g., male/female, white/black), because the observation and interpretation of performance can be clouded by these stereotypes. Results from a study examining how stereotypes of women affect performance ratings suggested that women evaluated by raters who hold traditional stereotypes of women are at a disadvantage when it comes to obtaining merit pay increases and promotions.[30] This problem is aggravated when employees are appraised on the basis of poorly defined performance standards and subjective performance traits.

Avenor, a Montreal-based pulp and paper company, developed formal training programs to reduce the subjective errors commonly made during the rating process. This training can pay off, especially when participants have the opportu-

WWW

nity to (1) observe other managers making errors, (2) actively participate in discovering their own errors, and (3) practice job-related tasks to reduce the errors they tend to make.[31]

Feedback Training

Finally, a training program for raters should provide some general points to consider for planning and conducting the feedback interview. The interview not only provides employees with knowledge of the results of their evaluation, but also allows the manager and employee to discuss current problems and set future goals.

Training in specific skills should cover at least three basic areas: communicating effectively, diagnosing the root causes of performance problems, and setting goals and objectives.[32] Supervisors can use a checklist to help them prepare for the appraisal interview. A checklist suggested by AT&T is provided in Highlights in HRM 1. The AT&T checklist reflects the growing tendency of organizations to have employees assess their own performance prior to the appraisal interview. Performance appraisal interviews will be discussed in more depth later in the chapter.

WWW

PERFORMANCE APPRAISAL METHODS

OBJECTIVE 4

In the discussion that follows, we examine in some detail some methods that have found widespread use, and we briefly touch on other methods that are used less often. Broadly speaking, performance appraisal methods measure traits, or behaviours, or results. *Trait* approaches are still the most popular despite their inherent subjectivity. *Behavioural* approaches provide more action-oriented information to employees and for that reason may be best for development. *Results-oriented* approaches are gaining popularity because they focus on the measurable contributions that employees make to the organization.

Trait Methods

Trait approaches to performance appraisal are designed to measure the extent to which an employee possesses certain characteristics—dependability, creativity, initiative, leadership, and so on—that are viewed as important for the job and for the organization in general. Trait methods are the most popular mainly because they are so easy to develop. However, if they are not designed carefully on the basis of job analysis, they can be severely biased and subjective.

Graphic Rating Scales

Graphic rating scale method

A trait approach to performance appraisal whereby each employee is rated according to a scale of characteristics

In the **graphic rating scale method**, each trait or characteristic to be rated is represented by a scale on which a rater indicates the degree to which the employee possesses that trait or characteristic. An example of this type of scale is shown in Highlights in HRM 2. There are many variations of the graphic rating scale. The differences lie mainly in (1) the characteristics or dimensions on which individuals are rated, (2) the degree to which the performance dimensions are defined for the rater, and (3) how clearly the points on the scale are defined. In Highlights in HRM 2 the dimensions are defined briefly, and some attempt is made to define the points on the scale. Subjectivity bias is reduced somewhat when the dimensions

Highlights in HRM

1 SUPERVISOR'S CHECKLIST FOR THE PERFORMANCE APPRAISAL

SCHEDULING

1. Schedule the review and notify the employee ten days or two weeks in advance.
2. Ask the employee to prepare for the session by reviewing his or her performance, job objectives, and development goals.
3. Clearly state that this will be the formal annual performance appraisal.

PREPARING FOR THE REVIEW

1. Review the performance documentation collected throughout the year. Concentrate on work patterns that have developed.
2. Be prepared to give specific examples of above- or below-average performance.
3. When performance falls short of expectations, determine what changes need to be made. If performance meets or exceeds expectations, discuss this and plan how to reinforce it.
4. After the appraisal is written, set it aside for a few days and then review it again.
5. Follow whatever steps are required by your organization's performance appraisal system.

CONDUCTING THE REVIEW

1. Select a location that is comfortable and free of distractions. The location should encourage a frank and candid conversation.
2. Discuss each item in the appraisal one at a time, considering both strengths and shortcomings.
3. Be specific and descriptive, not general or judgmental. Report occurrences rather than evaluating them.
4. Discuss your differences and resolve them. Solicit agreement with the evaluation.
5. Jointly discuss and design plans for taking corrective action for growth and development.
6. Maintain a professional and supportive approach to the appraisal discussion.

Source: Adapted from "The Performance-Management Process, Part 1 and 2," *Straight Talk* (AT&T) 1, nos. 8 and 9 (December 1987).

on the scale and the scale points are defined as precisely as possible. This can be achieved by training raters and by including descriptive appraisal guidelines in a performance appraisal reference packet.[33]

Also, the rating form should provide sufficient space for comments on the behaviour associated with each scale. These comments improve the accuracy of the appraisal because they require the rater to think in terms of observable employee

Highlights in HRM

2   GRAPHIC RATING SCALE WITH PROVISION FOR COMMENTS

Appraise employee's performance in PRESENT ASSIGNMENT. Check (✔) most appropriate square. Appraisers are urged to freely use the "Remarks" sections for significant comments descriptive of the individual.

1. KNOWLEDGE OF WORK: Understanding of all phases of his/her work and related matters	Needs instruction or guidance		Has required knowledge of own and related work		Has exceptional knowledge of own and related work
	☐	☐	☐	☑	☐
	Remarks: *Is particularly good on gas engines.*				

2. INITIATIVE: Ability to originate or develop ideas and to get things started	Lacks imagination		Meets necessary requirements		Unusually resourceful
	☐	☑	☐	☐	☐
	Remarks: *Has good ideas when asked for an opinion, but otherwise will not offer them. Somewhat lacking in self-confidence.*				

3. APPLICATION: Attention and application to his/her work	Wastes time Needs close supervision		Steady and willing worker		Exceptionally industrious
	☐	☐	☑	☐	☐
	Remarks: *Accepts new jobs when assigned.*				

4. QUALITY OF WORK: Thoroughness, neatness, and accuracy of work	Needs improvement		Regularly meets recognized standards		Consistently maintains highest quality
	☐	☐	☐	☐	☑
	Remarks: *The work he turns out is always of the highest possible quality.*				

5. VOLUME OF WORK: Quantity of acceptable work	Should be increased		Regularly meets recognized standards		Unusually high output
	☐	☐	☑	☐	☐
	Remarks: *Would be higher if he did not spend so much time checking and rechecking his work.*				

behaviours and also provide specific examples to discuss with the employee during the appraisal interview.

Mixed-Standard Scales

Mixed-standard scale method

A trait approach to performance appraisal similar to other scale mehtods but based on comparison with (better than, equal to, or worse than) a standard

The **mixed standard scale method** is a modification of the basic rating scale method. Instead of evaluating traits according to a single scale, the rater is given three specific descriptions of each trait. These descriptions reflect three levels of performance: superior, average, and inferior. After the three descriptions for each trait are written, they are randomly sequenced to form the mixed standard scale. As shown in Highlights in HRM 3, supervisors evaluate employees by indicating whether their performance is better than, equal to, or worse than the standard for each behaviour.

Highlights in HRM

3   EXAMPLE OF MIXED STANDARD SCALE

DIRECTIONS: Please indicate whether the individual's performance is above (+), equal to (0), or lower (–) than each of the following standards.

1. _____   Employee uses good judgment when addressing problems and provides workable alternatives; however, at times does not take actions to prevent problems. (*medium PROBLEM SOLVING*)

2. _____   Employee lacks supervisory skills; frequently handles employees poorly and is at times argumentative. (*low LEADERSHIP*)

3. _____   Employee is extremely cooperative; can be expected to take the lead in developing cooperation among employees; completes job tasks with a positive attitude. (*high COOPERATION*)

4. _____   Employee has effective supervision skills; encourages productivity, quality, and employee development. (*medium LEADERSHIP*)

5. _____   Employee normally displays an argumentative or defensive attitude toward fellow employees and job assignments. (*low COOPERATION*)

6. _____   Employee is generally agreeable but becomes argumentative at times when given job assignments; cooperates with other employees as expected. (*medium COOPERATION*)

7. _____   Employee is not good at solving problems; uses poor judgment and does not anticipate potential difficulties. (*low PROBLEM SOLVING*)

8. _____   Employee anticipates potential problems and provides creative, proactive alternative solutions; has good attention to follow-up. (*high PROBLEM SOLVING*)

9. _____   Employee displays skilled direction; effectively coordinates unit activities; is generally a dynamic leader and motivates employees to high performance. (*high LEADERSHIP*)

Forced Choice Method

The **forced choice method** requires the rater to choose from statements, often in pairs, that appear equally favourable or equally unfavourable. The statements, however, are designed to distinguish between successful and unsuccessful performance. The rater selects one statement from the pair without knowing which statement correctly describes successful job behaviour. For example, forced choice pairs might include the following:

1. _____ a) Works hard.   _____ b) Works quickly.
2. _____ a) Shows initiative   _____ b) Is responsive to customers.
3. _____ a) Produces poor quality. _____ b) Lacks good work habits.

The forced choice method is not without limitations, the main one being that it is expensive to establish and to maintain its validity. Because it has been a source of frustration to many raters, it has sometimes been eliminated from appraisal programs. Also, it is not as good as some other methods at helping employees develop their skills and strengths.

Essay Method

Rating scale methods provide a structured form of appraisal; in contrast, the **essay method** requires the appraiser to compose a statement that best describes the employee being appraised. The appraiser is usually instructed to describe the employee's strengths and weaknesses and to make recommendations for his or her development. Often the essay method is combined with other rating methods. Essays can provide additional descriptive information on performance that is not obtained with a structured rating scale, for example.

The essay method provides an excellent opportunity to point out the unique characteristics of the employee being appraised. This aspect of the method is heightened when the supervisor is instructed to describe specific points about the employee's promotability, special talents, skills, strengths, and weaknesses. A major limitation of the essay method is that composing an essay that covers all of an employee's essential characteristics is a very time-consuming task (though when combined with other methods, this method does not require a lengthy statement). Another disadvantage of the essay method is that the quality of the performance appraisal may be influenced by the supervisor's writing skills and composition style. Good writers often produce more favourable appraisals. A final drawback of this appraisal method is that it tends to be subjective and may not focus on relevant aspects of job performance.

Behavioural Methods

As mentioned earlier, one of the potential drawbacks of trait-oriented performance appraisals is that traits tend to be vague and subjective. We discussed earlier that one way to improve a rating scale is to have descriptions of behaviour along a scale, or continuum. These descriptions permit the rater to readily identify the point where a particular employee falls on the scale. Behavioural methods have been developed to state specifically which actions should (or should not) be exhibited on the job. These methods are often more useful for providing employees with developmental feedback.

Forced-choice method

A trait approach to performance appraisal that requires the rater to choose from statements designed to distinguish between successful and unsuccessful performance

Essay method

A trait approach to performance appraisal that requires the rater to compose a statement describing employee behaviour

Critical Incident Method

Critical incident method

Job analysis method by which important job tasks are identified for job success

The **critical incident method**, described in Chapter 3 in connection with job analysis, is also used as a method of appraisal. Recall that a critical incident occurs when employee behaviour results in unusual success or unusual failure in some part of the job. Example of a *favourable* critical incident: A janitor observed that a file cabinet containing classified documents had been left unlocked at the close of business. The janitor called the security officer, who took the necessary action to correct the problem. Example of an *unfavourable* critical incident: A mail clerk failed to deliver an Express Mail package immediately, instead putting it in with regular mail to be routed two hours later.

One advantage of the critical incident method is that it covers the entire appraisal period (and therefore may guard against recency error). And because the behavioural incidents are specific, they can facilitate employee feedback and development. However, unless both favourable and unfavourable incidents are discussed, employees who are appraised may have negative feelings about this method. Some employees have been known to refer to it as the "little black book" approach. Perhaps its greatest contribution is in developing job specifications and in constructing other types of appraisal procedures (see below).

Behavioural Checklist Method

One of the oldest appraisal techniques is the behavioural checklist method, which consists of the rater checking those statements on a list that he or she believes are characteristic of the employee's performance or behaviour. A checklist developed for computer salespeople might include a number of statements such as the following:

_____ Is able to explain equipment clearly.
_____ Keeps abreast of new developments in technology.
_____ Tends to be a steady worker.
_____ Reacts quickly to customer needs.
_____ Processes orders correctly.

Behaviourally Anchored Rating Scale (BARS)

Behaviourally anchored rating scale (BARS)

A behavioural approach to performance appraisal that consists of a series of vertical scales, one for each important dimension of job performance

A **behaviourally anchored rating scale (BARS)** consists of a series of five to ten vertical scales, one for each important dimension of performance identified through job analysis. These dimensions are anchored by behaviours identified through a critical incidents job analysis. The critical incidents are placed along the scale and are assigned point values according to the opinions of experts. A BARS for the job of firefighter is shown in Highlights in HRM 4. Note that this particular scale is for the dimension described as "Firefighting Strategy: Knowledge of Fire Characteristics."

Typically, a BARS is developed by a committee that includes both subordinates and managers.[34] The committee's task is to identify all the relevant characteristics or dimensions of the job. Behavioural anchors in the form of statements are then established for each of the job dimensions. Several participants are asked to review the anchor statements and indicate which job dimension each anchor illustrates. The only anchors retained are those which at least 70 percent of the group agree belong with a particular dimension. Finally, anchors are attached to their job dimensions and placed on the appropriate scales according to values that the group assigns to them.

Highlights in HRM

4   EXAMPLE OF BARS FOR MUNICIPAL FIRE COMPANIES

FIREFIGHTING STRATEGY: Knowledge of Fire Characteristics. This area of performance concerns the ability of a firefighter to use his or her knowledge of fire characteristics to develop the best strategy for fighting a fire. It involves the following activities: Observe fire and smoke conditions and locate source of fire. Size up fire and identify appropriate extinguishing techniques and ventilation procedures. Consult preplan reports. Apply knowledge of heat and fluid mechanics to anticipate fire behaviour. Identify and screen or saturate potential exposures using direct or fog streams or water curtains. Identify and remove or protect flammable or hazardous materials.

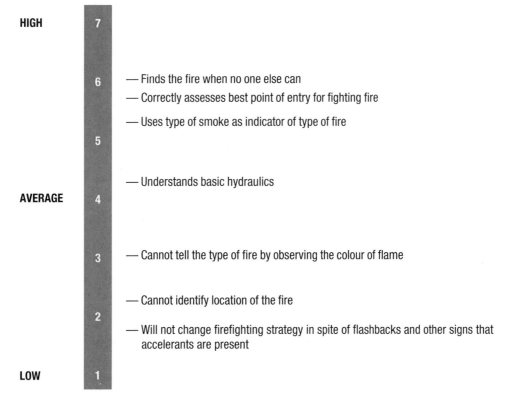

HIGH   7

6   — Finds the fire when no one else can
— Correctly assesses best point of entry for fighting fire

— Uses type of smoke as indicator of type of fire

5

— Understands basic hydraulics

AVERAGE   4

3   — Cannot tell the type of fire by observing the colour of flame

— Cannot identify location of the fire

2
— Will not change firefighting strategy in spite of flashbacks and other signs that accelerants are present

LOW   1

Source: Adapted from Landy, Jacobs, and Associates.

At present there is no strong evidence that a BARS reduces all of the rating errors mentioned earler. However, some studies have shown that scales of this type can yield more accurate ratings.[35] One major advantage of a BARS is that personnel outside of the HR department participate with HR staff in its development. Employee participation can lead to greater acceptance of the performance appraisal process and of the performance measures it uses.

WWW

Also, the procedures followed in developing a BARS result in scales with a high degree of content validity. Canadian Pacific Hotels launched a performance management system called REACH, in which each job skill was described at each of three levels: developing, succeeding, and mastering. An employee at the developing level of customer service might miss opportunities to improve service, while one at the mastering level might anticipate future guests' needs.[36] The main disadvantage of a BARS is that it requires considerable time and effort to develop. Also, because the scales are specific to particular jobs, a scale designed for one job may not apply to another.

Behaviour Observation Scales (BOS)

Behaviour observation scale (BOS)

A behavioural approach to performance appraisal that measures the frequency of observed behaviour

A **behaviour observation scale (BOS)** is similar to a BARS in that both are based on critical incidents. However, as Highlights in HRM 5 shows, rather than asking the evaluator to choose the most representative behavioural anchor, BOS is designed to measure how often each of the behaviours has been observed.

The value of BOS is that it enables the appraiser to play the role of observer rather than judge. In this way, he or she can more easily provide constructive feedback to the employee. Users of the system often prefer it over BARS or trait scales for (1) maintaining objectivity, (2) distinguishing good from poor performers, (3) providing feedback, and (4) identifying training needs.[37]

Results Methods

Rather than looking at the traits of employees or the behaviours they exhibit on the job, many organizations evaluate employee accomplishments—the results they achieve through their work. Advocates of results appraisals contend that they are more objective and empowering for employees. Looking at results such as sales figures, production output, and the like is less subjective and so may be less open to bias. Furthermore, results appraisals often give employees responsibility for their outcomes, while giving them discretion over the methods they use to accomplish them (within limits). This is empowerment in action.

Productivity Measures

A number of results measures are available to evaluate performance. Salespeople are evaluated on the basis of their sales volume (both the number of units sold and the dollar amount in revenues). Production workers are evaluated on the basis of the number of units they produce and perhaps on the scrap rate or number of defects that are detected. Purchasing agents at Gaines Pet Foods in Cobourg, Ontario, use performance measurements such as managing the purchasing cycle time. Executives are often evaluated on the basis of company profits or growth rate. Each of these measures directly links what employees accomplish to results that benefit the organization. In this way, results appraisals can directly align employee and organizational goals.

Highlights in HRM

5 SAMPLE ITEMS FROM BEHAVIOUR OBSERVATON SCALE

Instructions: Please consider the sales representative's behaviour on the job in the past rating period. Read each statement carefully, then circle the number that indicates the extent to which the employee has demonstrated this effective or ineffective behaviour.

For each behaviour observed, use the following scale:

5 represents *almost always*	95–100% of the time	
4 represents *frequently*	85–94% of the time	
3 represents *sometimes*	75–84% of the time	
2 represents *seldom*	65–74% of the time	
1 represents *almost never*	0–64% of the time	

SALES PRODUCTIVITY	ALMOST NEVER				ALMOST ALWAYS
1. Reviews individual productivity results with manager	1	2	3	4	5
2. Suggests to peers ways of building sales	1	2	3	4	5
3. Formulates specific objectives for each contact	1	2	3	4	5
4. Focuses on product rather than customer problem	1	2	3	4	5
5. Keep account plans updated	1	2	3	4	5
6. Keeps customer waiting for service	1	2	3	4	5
7. Anticipates and prepares for customer concerns	1	2	3	4	5
8. Follows up on customer leads	1	2	3	4	5

But there are some problems with results appraisals. First of all, recall our earlier discussion of criteria contamination. Results appraisals are easily contaminated by external factors that employees cannot influence. Sales representatives who have extremely bad markets and production employees who can't get the materials will not be able to perform up to their abilities. It may be unfair to hold these employees accountable for results that are contaminated by circumstances beyond their control.

Furthermore, results appraisals may inadvertently encourage employees to "look good" on a short-term basis, while ignoring the long-term ramifications. For example, line supervisors may let their equipment suffer to reduce maintenance costs. If the appraisal focuses on a narrow set of results criteria to the exclusion of other important process issues, the system may suffer from criterion deficiency and may unintentionally foster the attitude that "what gets measured gets done." In fact, in any job involving interaction with others, it is not enough to simply look at production or sales figures. Factors such as cooperation, adaptability, initiative, and concern for human relations may be important to job success. If these factors are important job standards, they should be added to the appraisal review. In sum, to be realistic, both the results and the methods or processes used to achieve them should be considered.

Management by Objectives

Management by objectives (MBO)

Philosophy of management that rates performance on the basis of employee achievement of goals set by mutual agreement of employee and manager

One method that attempts to overcome some of the limitations of results appraisals is **management by objectives (MBO)**. MBO is a philosophy of management first proposed by Peter Drucker in 1954 that has employees establish objectives (e.g., production costs, sales per product, quality standards, profits) through consultation with their superiors and then uses these objectives as a basis for evaluation.[38] MBO is a system involving a cycle (Figure 8.6) that begins with setting the organization's common goals and objectives and ultimately returns to that step. The system acts as a goal-setting process whereby objectives are established for the organization (step 1), departments (step 2), and individual managers and employees (step 3).

As Figure 8.6 illustrates, a significant feature of the cycle is that specific goals are established by the employee, but those goals are based on a broad statement of employee responsibilities prepared by the supervisor. Employee-established goals are discussed with the supervisor and jointly reviewed and modified until both parties are satisfied with them (step 4). The goal statements are accompanied by a detailed account of the actions the employee proposes to take in order to reach the goals. During periodic reviews, as objective data are made available, the progress the employee is making toward the goals is assessed (step 5). Goals can be changed at this time as new or additional data are received. After a period of time (usually six months or one year), the employee makes a self-appraisal of what she or he has accomplished, substantiating the self-appraisal with factual data wherever possible. The "interview" is an examination of the employee's self-appraisal by the supervisor and the employee together (step 6). The final step (step 7) is reviewing the connection between individual and organizational performance.

MBO programs should be viewed as part of a total system for managing, not as merely an addition to the manager's job. Managers must be willing to empower employees to accomplish their objectives on their own, giving them discretion over the methods they use but also holding them accountable for outcomes. The following guidelines can be especially helpful:

1. Managers and employees must be willing to establish goals and objectives together. Goal setting has been shown to improve employee performance, typically by 10 to 25 percent. Goal setting works because it helps employees focus on important tasks and makes them accountable for completing these tasks. It also establishes an automatic feedback system that aids learning, since employees can regularly evaluate their performance against their goals.[39]

2. Objectives should be quantifiable and measurable for the long and short term. However, goal statements should be accompanied by a description of how that goal will be accomplished.

3. Expected results must be under the employee's control. Recall our early discussion of criterion contamination.

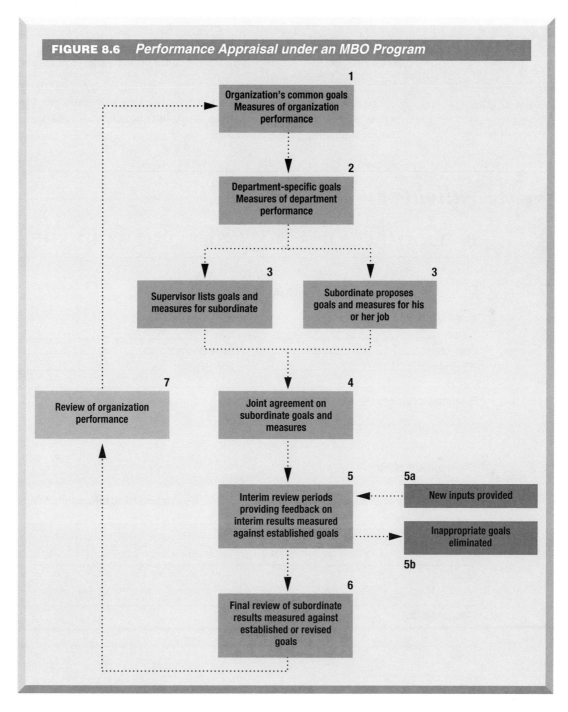

FIGURE 8.6   *Performance Appraisal under an MBO Program*

Source: Adapted from George S. Odiorne, *Management by Objectives* 11 (Belmount, CA: David S. Lake Publishers, 1979).

4. Goals and objectives must be consistent for each level (top executive, manager, and employee).

5. Managers and employees must establish specific times when goals are to be reviewed and evaluated.

Highlights in HRM 6 presents the goal-setting worksheet used by Universal Service Corporation. Note that this worksheet contains sections for setting goals and for evaluating goal achievement.

Highlights in HRM

6 EXAMPLE OF A GOAL-SETTING WORKSHEET

UNIVERSAL SERVICE CORPORATION

Employee's Rating Record

Name _____   Date _____

Job Title _____   Department _____

Appraised by _____   Date Started _____

Summary of Appraisal

Development Needs

Major Responsibilities and Period Goals	**Evaluation of Attainment of Goals**
Responsibility	
Goal	
Responsibility	
Goal	
Responsibility	
Goal	

WWW

MBO is used extensively in the "Big Six" public accounting firms (Arthur Andersen, Ernst & Young, Coopers & Lybrand, Deloitte & Touche, KPMG, Peat Marwick, and Price Waterhouse). Usually, the systems are designed to help situate partners' actions in the larger context of the organization as a whole. When firm, office, and individual goals are arranged in a hierarchical structure, each partner's objectives can be nested in the firm's overall plans. Consistent with the prescriptions of MBO advocates, periodic counselling sessions are held between supervisors and subordinates to discuss areas for performance improvement. MBO programs are usually integrated with mentoring systems. In addition, companies have integrated their MBO systems with measures of customer satisfaction; this provides yet another means for merging TQM initiatives with MBO.[40]

Which Performance Appraisal Method to Use?

The choice of method should be based largely on the purpose of the appraisal. Figure 8.7 lists some of the strengths and weaknesses of trait, behaviour, and results approaches to appraisal. Note that the simplest and least expensive techniques often yield the least accurate information. However, research has not always supported a clear choice among appraisal methods.[41] While researchers and HR managers generally believe that the more sophisticated and more time-consuming methods offer more useful information, this may not always be the case. Managers must make cost-benefit decisions about which methods to use.

The bigger picture here focuses on how the performance appraisal systems are used. Having a first-rate method does no good if the manager simply "shoves it in a drawer." Alternatively, even a rudimentary system, when used properly, can initiate a discussion between managers and employees that genuinely drives superior performance. These issues are discussed below under the topic of performance appraisal interviews.

APPRAISAL INTERVIEWS

OBJECTIVE
5

The appraisal interview is perhaps the most important part of the entire performance appraisal process. The appraisal interview gives a manager the opportunity to discuss a subordinate's performance record and to explore areas of possible improvement and growth. It also provides an opportunity to identify the subordinate's attitudes and feelings more thoroughly and thus to improve communication.

The interviewer can become overburdened by attempting to discuss too much, such as the employee's past performance and future development goals. Dividing the appraisal interview into two sessions, one for the performance review and the other for the employee's growth plans, can alleviate time pressures. Moreover, by separating the interview into two sessions, the interviewer can give each session the proper attention it deserves. It can be difficult for a supervisor to perform the role of both evaluator and counsellor in the same review period. Dividing the sessions can also improve communication between the parties, thereby reducing stress and defensiveness.

The format for the appraisal interview is determined in large part by the purpose of the interview, the type of appraisal system used, and the organization of the interview form. Most appraisal interviews attempt to give feedback to employees on how well they are performing their jobs and on planning for their future devel-

FIGURE 8.7 *Summary of Various Appraisal Methods*

	ADVANTAGES	DISADVANTAGES
Trait methods	1. Are inexpensive to develop 2. Use meaningful dimensions 3. Are easy to use	1. Have high potential for rating errors 2. Are not useful for employee counselling 3. Are not useful for allocating rewards 4. Are not useful for promotion decisions
Behavioural methods	1. Use specific performance dimensions 2. Are acceptable to employees and superiors 3. Are useful for providing feedback 4. Are fair for reward and promotion decisions	1. Can be time-consuming to develop/use 2. Can be costly to develop 3. Have some potential for rating error
Results method	1. Has less subjectivity bias 2. Is acceptable to employees and superiors 3. Links individual performance to organizational performance 4. Encourages mutual goal setting 5. Is good for reward and promotion decisions	1. Is time-consuming to develop/use 2. May encourage short-term perspective 3. May use contaminated criteria 4. May use deficient criteria

opment. Interviews should be scheduled far enough in advance to allow the interviewee, as well as the interviewer, to prepare for the discussion. Ten days to two weeks is usually enough lead time.

Three Types of Appraisal Interviews

The individual who has studied different approaches to performance appraisal interviews most thoroughly is probably Norman R.F. Maier. In his classic book *The Appraisal Interview*, he analyzes the cause-and-effect relationships in three types of appraisal interviews: tell-and-sell, tell-and-listen, and problem solving.[42]

Tell-and-Sell Interview

The skills required in the tell-and-sell interview include the ability to persuade an employee to change in a prescribed manner. This may require the development of new behaviours on the part of the employee and skilful use of motivational incentives on the part of the appraiser/supervisor.

Tell-and-Listen Interview

In the tell-and-listen interview the skills required include the ability to communicate the strong and weak points of an employee's job performance during the first part of the interview. During the second part of the interview, the employee's feelings about the appraisal are thoroughly explored. The supervisor is still in the role of appraiser, but the method requires listening to disagreement and coping with defensive behaviour without attempting to refute any statements. The tell-and-listen method assumes that the opportunity to release frustrated feelings will help to reduce or remove those feelings.

Problem-Solving Interview

The skills associated with the problem-solving interview are consistent with the nondirective procedures of the tell-and-listen method. Listening, accepting, and responding to feelings are essential elements of the problem-solving interview. However, this method goes beyond an interest in the employee's feelings. It seeks to stimulate growth and development in the employee by discussing the problems, needs, innovations, satisfactions, and dissatisfactions the employee has encountered on the job since the last appraisal interview. Maier recommends this method, since the objective of appraisal is normally to stimulate growth and development in the employee.

Managers should not assume that only one type of appraisal interview is appropriate for every review session. Rather, they should be able to use one or more of the interview types, depending on the topic being discussed or on the behaviour of the employee being appraised. The interview should be seen as requiring a flexible approach.[43]

Conducting the Appraisal Interview

While there are probably no hard-and-fast rules for how to conduct an appraisal interview, there are some guidelines for increasing the employee's acceptance of the feedback, satisfaction with the interview, and intention to improve in the future. Many of the principles of effective interviewing discussed in Chapter 5 apply to performance appraisal interviews as well. Here are some other guidelines that should also be considered.

Ask for a Self-Assessment

As noted earlier in the chapter, it is useful to have employees evaluate their own performance prior to the appraisal interview. Even if this information is not used formally, the self-appraisal starts the employee thinking about his or her accomplishments. Self-appraisal also ensures that the employee knows which criteria he or she is being evaluated against; this eliminates any potential surprises.

Recent research evidence suggests that employees are more satisfied and view the appraisal system as providing more *procedural justice* when they have input into the process. When the employee has evaluated his or her own performance, the interview can be used to discuss those areas where the manager and the employee have reached different conclusions—not so much to resolve the "truth," but to work toward a resolution of problems.[44]

Invite Participation

The core purpose of a performance appraisal interview is to initiate a dialogue that will help the employee improve her or his performance. The more the employee is an active participant in that discussion, the more likely it is that the root causes and obstacles to performance will be uncovered, and the more likely it is that constructive ideas for improvement will be raised. Research suggests that participation is strongly related to the employee's satisfaction with the appraisal feedback, to the extent to which that feedback is perceived as fair and useful, and to the strength of the employee's intention to improve performance.[45] As a rule of thumb, supervisors should spend only about 30 to 35 percent of their time talking during the interview. The rest of the time they should be listening to employees respond to questions.

Express Appreciation

Praise is a powerful motivator, and especially in an appraisal interview, employees are seeking positive feedback. It is often beneficial to start the appraisal interview by expressing appreciation for what the employee has done well. In this way, he or she may be less defensive and more likely to talk about aspects of the job that are not going so well. However, try to avoid obvious use of the "sandwich technique," in which positive statements are followed by negative ones, which are then followed by positive ones. This approach may not work for several reasons. Praise often alerts the employee that criticism will be coming. Positive comments following the criticism then suggest to the employee that no more negative comments will be coming for a while. If managers follow an appraisal form, the problem of the sandwich technique can often be avoided. Furthermore, if employees are kept informed of their behaviour on a regular basis, there will be no need for this appraisal technique to be used.

Specific, measurable job standards help remove vagueness and subjectivity from performance appraisals.

Minimize Criticism

Employees who have a good relationship with their managers may be able to handle criticism better than those who do not. However, even the most stoic employees can absorb only so much criticism before they start to get defensive. If an employee has many areas in need of improvement, managers should focus on those few objective issues that are most problematic or most important to the job. Some tips for using criticism constructively include the following:

- *Consider whether it is really necessary.* Frustration with performance problems sometimes leads to criticism that is little more than a manager "letting off steam." Make certain that the criticism focuses on a recurrent problem or a consistent pattern of behaviour.
- *Don't exaggerate.* Even managers who dislike criticizing may find that once they get started, they tend to overdo it. Sometimes we overstate problems in order to be convincing or to demonstrate our concern. Try to keep criticism simple, factual, and to the point. Avoid using terms like "always, completely, or never."
- *Make improvement your goal.* "Laying it on the line" is not likely to be useful unless it clarifies a path to improved performance. Criticism needs to be complemented with managerial support. This point is elaborated on below.[46]

Change the Behaviour, not the Person

Managers often try to play psychologist, to "figure out" why an employee has acted a certain way. When dealing with a problem area in particular, remember that it is not the person who is bad, but the actions exhibited on the job. Avoid suggestions about personal traits to change; instead suggest more acceptable ways of performing. For example, instead of focusing on the employee's "unreliability," the manager might focus on the fact that the employee "has been late to work seven times this month." It is difficult for employees to change who they are; it is usually much easier for them to change how they act.

Focus on Solving Problems

In addressing performance issues, it is often tempting to get into the "blame game," in which both manager and employee enter into a potentially endless discussion of why a situation has arisen. Solving problems often requires an analysis of the causes; but ultimately the appraisal interview should be directed at devising a solution to the problem.

Be Supportive

One of the better techniques for engaging an employee in the problem-solving process is for the manager to ask, "What can I do to help?" Employees often attribute performance problems to either real or perceived obstacles (such as bureaucratic procedures or inadequate resources). By being open and supportive, the manager conveys to the employee that he or she will try to eliminate external roadblocks and work with the employee to achieve higher standards.

Establish Goals

Since a major purpose of the appraisal interview is to make plans for improvement, it is important to focus the interviewee's attention on the future rather than the past. In setting goals with an employee, the manager should observe the following points:

- Emphasize strengths that the employee can build on rather than weaknesses to overcome.
- Concentrate on opportunities for growth that exist within the framework of the employee's present position.
- Limit plans for growth to a few important items that can be accomplished within a reasonable period of time.
- Establish specific action plans that spell out how each goal will be achieved. These action plans can include lists of contacts and resources as well as timetables for follow-up.
- Some supervisors may be tempted to establish difficult goals with their subordinates. The ethical issues surrounding unreasonable goals are discussed in Ethics in HRM.

Follow Up Day to Day

WWW

Ideally, performance feedback should be an ongoing part of a manager's job. Feedback is most useful when it is immediate and specific to a particular situation. Unfortunately, both managers and employees are often happy to finish the interview and file away the appraisal form. A better approach is to have informal talks periodically to follow up on the issues raised in the appraisal interview. Levi Strauss recently redesigned its performance appraisal system to explicitly include informal feedback and coaching sessions on an ongoing basis. The changes, referred to as the Partners in Performance Program, help Levi Strauss managers adopt more of a coaching role (as opposed to that of a judge) and are designed to enhance continuous improvement and business objectives.[47]

Improving Performance

The appraisal interview often provides the basis for noting deficiencies in employee performance and for making plans for improvement. Unless these deficiencies are brought to the employee's attention, they are likely to continue until they become quite serious. Sometimes underperformers may not understand exactly what is expected of them. However, once their responsibilities are clarified, they are in a position to take the corrective action needed to improve their performance.

Identifying Sources of Ineffective Performance

Performance is a function of several factors, which perhaps can be boiled down to three primary ones: ability, motivation, and environment. Every individual has a unique pattern of strengths and weaknesses that play a part. But talented employees with low motivation are not likely to succeed. Also, other factors in the work environment—or even in the external environment, which includes personal, family, and community concerns—can impact performance positively or negatively. Figure 8.8 suggests how these three factors (ability, motivation, and environment) can influence performance.

It is recommended that a diagnosis of poor employee performance focus on these three interactive elements. For example, if an employee's performance is not up to standards, the cause could be a skill problem (knowledge, abilities, technical competencies), an effort problem (motivation to get the job done), and/or some

Ethics in HRM

STRETCH GOALS

WWW

Employees are being asked to set performance goals, labelled "stretch goals," that ask them to double sales or increase response time to customers threefold. Research has shown that the establishment of goals results in higher productivity. So if goals are good, are super goals better?

"Not necessarily," says Steve Kerr, General Electric's chief learning officer. In his opinion, most managers don't know how to manage stretch targets. Companies set ambitious goals for their employees but fail to provide them with the resources they need to achieve them. They are saying, in effect, "We aren't going to give you any more people or money, so your solution is to work smarter and be creative." The only resource left to employees is their personal time, and so North Americans are working harder than employees in any other developed country. They are working evenings and weekends, with fewer vacations. "That's immoral," says Kerr. "Companies have a moral obligation to provide the tools to meet tough goals."

How should stretch goals be managed? The goal must be seen as achievable, and not provoke a reaction of "you've got to be kidding." People must also realize that creative energy can be increased. For example, in one innovation training program, teams are given an orange and told that each person must handle the orange, but that the orange must end up in the hands of the person who started with it. All teams start by throwing the orange to team members; this takes nine seconds. They try to reduce the time to seven seconds by throwing faster or in tighter circles. When told that it is possible to do this task in one second, they get creative: they stack their hands and the first person drops the orange through the stacked but open hands and catches it at the bottom.

If the stretch goals aren't achieved, then punishment should not be used. Be careful with high achievers who are already stretching, or these winners will feel like losers if they can't meet impossible goals. Provide the tools; asking people to double their quota without ensuring backup is demoralizing. Finally, share the wealth. If the achievement results in additional funds flowing to the organization, split the incremental savings or gains.

Some employees, masters at the politics of organizations, play games with stretch goals. They negotiate hard for modest, achievable goals, while arguing that these are stretch targets. Others, with high needs for achievement, accept the stretch targets. At bonus time, the modest goal setters have met or surpassed their goals, and receive merit increases. Having failed to achieve impossible targets, the less Machiavellian employees receive nothing.

In your job, would you accept a stretch goal? Would you negotiate hard to make it sound impossible, but be achievable?

Source: Adapted from S. Sherman, "Stretch Goals: The Dark Side of Asking for Miracles," *Fortune,* November 13, 1995, 231.

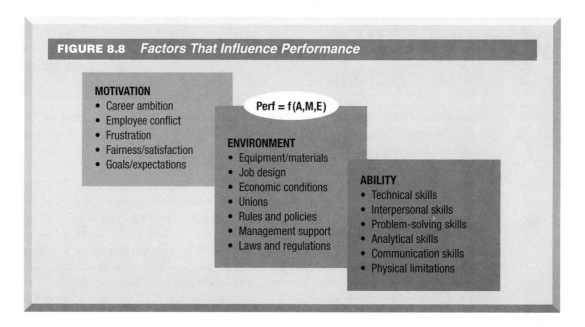

FIGURE 8.8 *Factors That Influence Performance*

MOTIVATION
- Career ambition
- Employee conflict
- Frustration
- Fairness/satisfaction
- Goals/expectations

Perf = f(A,M,E)

ENVIRONMENT
- Equipment/materials
- Job design
- Economic conditions
- Unions
- Rules and policies
- Management support
- Laws and regulations

ABILITY
- Technical skills
- Interpersonal skills
- Problem-solving skills
- Analytical skills
- Communication skills
- Physical limitations

problem in the external conditions of work (poor economic conditions, supply shortages, difficult sales territories).[48] Any one of these problem areas could cause performance to suffer.

Managing Ineffective Performance

Once the sources of performance problems are known, a course of action can be planned. This action may lie in providing training in areas that would increase the knowledge and/or skills needed for effective performance. A transfer to another job or department might give an employee a chance to become a more effective member of the organization. In other situations, greater attention may have to be focused on ways to motivate the individual.[49]

If ineffective performance persists, it may be necessary to transfer the employee, take disciplinary action, or discharge the person from the organization. Whatever action is taken to cope with ineffective performance, it should be done with objectivity, fairness, and a recognition of the feelings of the individual involved.

A final word of caution when it comes to managing performance problems: Research consistently shows that managers often attribute poor performance to characteristics of the individuals (ability or motivation), while employees themselves typically make external attributions for their miscues. This can establish a negative cycle if not handled properly. Managers who assume that employees are not motivated or not capable may begin to treat them differently (perhaps supervising them too closely or watching for their next mistake). This can actually reduce an employee's motivation and cause him or her to withdraw. This in turn may confirm the manager's initial belief that the employee does not "measure up." As you can see, this "set up to fail" syndrome can be self-fulfilling and self-reinforcing. We hope that the ideas and suggestions we have given in this chapter will help managers accurately identify who is performing well (and why), and give them some focus for improving employee productivity.[50]

SUMMARY

 Performance appraisal programs serve many purposes, which in general terms fall into two categories: administrative and developmental. *Administrative purposes* relate to who will be promoted, transferred, or laid off, and compensation decisions. *Developmental purposes* relate to improving and enhancing an individual's capabilities (e.g., identifying a person's strengths and weaknesses, eliminating external performance obstacles, and establishing training needs). These two purposes of performance appraisal reflect HRM's larger role, which is to integrate the individual with the organization.

 In many organizations, performance appraisals are seen as a necessary evil. Many managers avoid conducting appraisals because they dislike playing the role of judge. As a consequence, they conduct appraisals reluctantly once a year and then forget about them. As a result, they do not develop good feedback skills. Furthermore, when managers are not adequately trained, subjectivity and organizational politics can distort the reviews.

The success of an organization depends heavily on how well its people perform. If the contributions of each individual are to be determined accurately, a formal appraisal program with clearly stated objectives must be established. Carefully defined performance standards that are reliable, strategically relevant, and free from both criterion deficiency and contamination are essential foundations for evaluation. Appraisal systems must also comply with the law. Appraisals should be treated with the same concerns for validity as selection tests are. For example, ratings must be job-related, employees must understand their performance standards in advance, appraisers must be able to observe job performance, appraisers must be trained, feedback must be given, and an appeals procedure must be established.

 It is often a good idea to use multiple raters, because different individuals see different facets of an employee's performance. For example, supervisors have legitimate authority over their employees and are well positioned to tell whether they are contributing to the goals of the organization. Peers and team members, on the other hand, often have an unfiltered view of an employee's work activity, especially as it relates to issues such as cooperation and dependability. Subordinates often provide good information about whether an employee is facilitating their work, and customers (both internal and external) can suggest how well an employee is adding value and meeting their requirements. Self-appraisal is useful if for no other reason than it encourages employees to think about their strengths, weaknesses, and future goals. More and more organizations are using multiple raters—or 360 degree appraisal—to get a more comprehensive picture of employee performance. Whatever the source of the appraisal information, appraisers should be thoroughly trained in the particular methods they use in evaluating their subordinates. Participation in developing rating scales, such as a bars, automatically provides such training.

 Several methods can be used for performance appraisal. These include trait approaches (graphic rating scales, mixed standard scales, forced choice forms, and essays), behavioural methods (critical incident ratings, checklists, BARS, and BOS), and results methods (MBO). Which method is chosen depends on the purpose of the appraisal. Trait appraisals are simple to develop and complete, but have problems of subjectivity and are not useful for feedback. Behavioural methods provide more specific information for feedback but can be time-consuming and costly to develop. Results appraisals are more objective and can link individual performance to the organization as a whole, but they may encourage a short-term perspective (e.g., annual goals) and may not include subtle yet important aspects of performance.

 The degree to which the performance appraisal program benefits the organization and its members is directly related to the quality of the appraisal interviews. Interviewing skills are best developed through instruction and supervised practice. Research suggests that while there are various approaches to interviews, employee participation and goal setting exercises lead to higher satisfaction and improved performance. It is also helpful to discuss problems, show support, minimize criticism, and reward effective performance. In the interview, deficiencies in employee performance can be discussed and plans for improvement can be made.

KEY TERMS

behaviourally anchored rating scale (BARS)

behaviour observation scale (BOS)

contrast error

critical incident method

customer appraisal

error of central tendency

essay method

forced choice method

graphic rating scale method

leniency or strictness error

management by objectives (MBO)

manager and/or supervisor appraisal

mixed standard scale method

peer appraisal

recency error

self-appraisal

similar-to-me error

subordinate appraisal

team appraisal

DISCUSSION QUESTIONS

 1. What are the major purposes of performance appraisal? In what ways might these purposes be contradictory?

 2. Describe how performance appraisal and selection, training, and development relate to one another.

 3. How can performance appraisals be adjusted to include the principles underlying total quality management?

 4. Describe the characteristics of the ideal appraisal system.

 5. What guidelines must performance appraisals follow if they are to be legally defensible?

 6. What sources could evaluate the performance of people working in the following jobs?

   a. sales representative
   b. TV repairer
   c. director of nursing in a hospital
   d. HR manager
   e. air traffic controller

 7. In many organizations, evaluators submit ratings to their immediate superiors for review before discussing them with the individual employees they have rated. What advantages are there to this procedure?

 8. What are the pros and cons of trait, behaviour, and results appraisals?

 9. Three types of appraisal interviews are described in this chapter.
   a. What different skills are required for each type of appraisal interview? What reactions can one expect to the use of these different skills?

b. How can one develop the skills needed for the problem-solving type of interview?

c. Which method do you feel is the least desirable? Explain.

10. A hotel's receiving department is responsible for checking deliveries of food and beverages, checking what has been received against what has been ordered, and verifying the quality of the merchandise received. In May 2000 an employee of the Westin Ottawa failed to check a case of vegetables, which had started to rot. The receiver, who had been with the hotel for seventeen years, admitted that he had not checked the vegetables. As a result, his supervisor gave him a written warning. The employee grieved, stating that he was too busy because the work load was excessive.

There was an investigation, which indicated that the grievor had not worked any overtime, nor had he requested permission to work any overtime. It was also noted that during the receiver's vacation period, the replacement worker had been able to perform the job without any difficulty. There was also evidence that the receiver was taking excessive breaks.

As a result of this investigation, the grievance was denied. In addition, the employee was sent a letter reminding him of his job responsibilities and of the need to restrict himself to the scheduled breaks. As a last step he was given a procedure to follow if he believed that the work was becoming excessive.

Discuss how a performance appraisal system might have prevented this grievance. Which performance appraisal method would you recommend for this type of job?

CASE 1

360 DEGREE APPRAISAL AT JOHNSON & JOHNSON

WWW

To provide a broader perspective for performance appraisal and to encourage employee development, Johnson & Johnson Advanced Behavioral Technology (JJABT), based in Denver, Colorado, has instituted a 360 degree feedback system. This new system allows employees to compare their own perceptions with those of superiors, peers, subordinates, and external customers.

According to company executives, the most important consideration in the system is choosing the correct individuals to be raters. To assemble the rating group, JJABT employees develop a list of key internal and external customers with whom they interact and then recommend five to ten individuals to serve as raters. Each employee's supervisor is still ultimately responsible for the appraisal and ensures that the appropriate raters are selected. This helps prevent ratees from stacking the deck with supportive customers or colleagues who will give high ratings.

After managers have decided who will do the rating, the criteria by which the ratee will be evaluated are made clear. Since the supervisor is most aware of the work tasks and goals of the individual being rated, the various raters ideally evaluate the ratee only on the behaviours or work incidents that they have directly observed. The JJABT 360 degree appraisal form includes items such as these: Does the employee

- Follow up on problems, decisions, and requests in a timely fashion?
- Clearly communicate his or her needs and expectations?
- Share information or help others?

- Listen to others?
- Establish plans to meet future needs?
- Adhere to schedules?

Raters score these items on a scale ranging from 1 (needs improvement) to 5 (outstanding). Space is also provided for the raters to make written comments.

The employee's supervisor is responsible for summarizing the data and determining the final performance rating. This represents a combination of the comments and ratings from the various raters and the supervisor's own feedback on the ratee's performance. Typically, managers include a mean score and distribution range for each item.

On the basis of the company's experience so far, it seems clear that feedback can't always be taken at face value. For instance, care must be exercised when one rater has given highly negative or positive feedback. JJABT managers stress that the key is to look for trends or patterns in the data. If there are questions or ambiguities in the raters' feedback, supervisors will often solicit additional feedback from the same or new raters. After summarizing the data, the supervisor conducts the formal appraisal interview with the ratee.

To ensure fairness, raters are provided the option of being anonymous or open in their feedback. If the rater requests anonymity, the supervisor must not reveal his or her identity to the ratee when discussing the performance review. However, if the rater is willing to be open, the supervisor may refer the ratee with questions about his or her feedback to the rater. In this way, it is hoped that the 360 degree appraisal can become less an evaluative tool and more a comprehensive system for enhancing communication, facilitating self-development, and improving performance.

Source: John F. Milliman, Robert A. Zawacki, Carol Norman, Lynda Powell, and Jay Kirksey, "Companies Evaluate Employees from All Perspectives," *Personnel Journal* (November 1994): 99–103.

Questions

1. What are the advantages and disadvantages of Johnson & Johnson's 360 degree appraisal?

2. Do you think the rating system is useful? How might you suggest improving it?

3. What are your views on the anonymity issue? Should raters be encouraged to be open? Explain.

CASE 2

HOW DOES THE BANK OF MONTREAL KEEP SCORE ON SUCCESS?

WWW

In 1990, when Matthew W. Barrett became the Bank of Montreal's chairman and Tony Comper became its president, they had one main goal: to focus the entire workforce on success. It's a simple idea, but not so easy to execute. How would they get entry-level tellers to think of their work not just as a means to a paycheque, but as a direct contribution to BMO shareholders? How would they remind corporate executives that their jobs were not just to boost the bottom line, but to charm entire communities?

The answer was what BMO executives call a balanced scorecard approach. To be competitive, executives decided, the bank had to meet the needs of four stakeholders: BMO shareholders, customers, employees and communities.

Executives translated that idea into four goals: shareholders needed a return on equity, customers needed good service, employees needed to feel loyal and satisfied, and communities needed to feel that the bank made a difference in their neighbourhoods. Return on Investment would determine satisfaction for shareholders; surveys and feedback would determine satisfaction for customers, employees, and communities.

So far, so good. But every single department and every employee in every department had to understand how their work contributed to achieving those four goals. So each employee's and department's performance ratings now are dependent on their contribution toward each goal. Employees in the customer service department, for instance, are rated by their return on equity (judged by their cost-effectiveness), their customer satisfaction (judged by customer feedback), and their community involvement (judged by any outreach programs or increase in customers).

Departments may be assigned a specific stakeholder. HR is charged with the employee piece—that is, with providing competent, committed workers in a cost-effective way. Harriet Stairs, senior vice-president of HR, uses training and education to ensure competency, and work/life and career development programs to boost commitment. Knowing that she's rated on the cost-effectiveness of all this, she also keeps her eye on the price tag: "It encourages everyone to do his or her job with the exact same issues in mind," she says.

At the end of the year, the scores from everyone's performance ratings are translated into indexes, with ratings from 1 to 10. The index for the employee stakeholder piece is determined by ratings for competency, commitment, and cost-effectiveness. The four indexes—for BMO shareholders, customers, employees, and communities—are then rolled up into one figure of merit. At the end of each year, these results are presented to the board of directors, who use them to determine bonuses.

Source: "How the Bank of Montreal Keeps Score on Success" by Gillion Flynn, copyright December 1997. Used with permission of ACC Communications/Workforce, Costa Hesa, CA. Website at **http://www.workforce.com.** All rights reserved.

Questions

1. What are the strengths and weaknesses of a balanced scorecard approach to performance appraisal?

2. Do you think such an approach would integrate well with an MBO system? Explain.

3. Do you believe that a balanced scorecard approach would be more effective for the administrative or developmental purposes of appraisal?

CAREER COUNSEL

Obtain a rating of your performance by consulting **belcourt.nelson.com.**

USING THE INTERNET

WWW

You can experience a 360 degree feedback system by accessing **www.panoram-icfeedback.com**, the website of Panoramic Feedback.

Visit **www.sales.org** for a list of skills and capabilities that can be used to measure a sales force.

At **www.workteams.unt.edu80/proceed/jwax.htm** you will find a detailed description of how one manufacturing facility implemented a peer appraisal system in conjunction with self-directed work teams.

Visit **www.performdb.com** for a demonstration of the forced choice method.

Software used in preparing 360 degree appraisal systems is available from a number of companies. The website of Organizational Universe Systems (**www.ours.use.net/msasbro.htm**) not only sells that company's software but also provides an interesting discussion of 360 degree feedback.

Historical background on the development of BARS can be found at **www.wissago.uwex.edu/test/joe/1897winter/a5.html**.

NOTES AND REFERENCES

1. Brian D. Cawley, Lisa M. Keeping, and Paul E. Levy, "Participation in the Performance Appraisal Process and Employee Reactions: A Meta-analytic Review of Field Investigations," *Journal of Applied Psychology* 83, no. 4 (August 1998): 615–33; Mike Deblieux, "Encouraging Great Performance," *HRFocus* 75, no. 1 (January 1998): 13; Birgit Benkhoff, "Ignoring Commitment Is Costly: New Approaches Establish the Missing Link Between Commitment and Performance," *Human Relations* 50, no. 6 (June 1997): 701–26.

2. Schofield, Philip, "Do Appraisals Need Review?" *Works Management* 52, no. 2 (February 1999): 24–6; Marilyn Moats Kennedy, "The Case Against Performance Appraisals," *Across the Board* 36, no. 1 (January 1999): 51–2; Gillian Flynn, "Employee Evaluations Get So-So Grades," *Personnel Journal* 74, no. 6 (June 1995): 21–3.

3 For recent work on performance appraisal and TQM, see Simon S.K. Lam and John Schaubroeck, "Total Quality Management and Performance Appraisal: An Experimental Study of Process versus Results and Group versus Individual Approaches," *Journal of Organizational Behavior* 20, no. 4 (July 1999): 445–57; Allan J. Weber,

"Making Performance Appraisals Consistent with a Quality Environment," *Quality Progress* 28, no. 6 (June 1995): 65–9; Jai Ghorpade, Milton M. Chen, and Joseph Caggiano, "Creating Quality-Driven Performance Appraisal Systems: Executive Commentary," *Academy of Management Executive* 9, no. 1 (February 1995): 32–41.

4. Ann Monroe, "Compensation: How Merrill Rewards Its Team Players," *Investment Dealers Digest* 62, no. 22 (May 27, 1996): 15; Nancy K. Austin, "It's Time for Your Review," *Incentive* 168, no. 3 (March 1994): 19.

5. Matt Bloom, "The Performance Effects of Pay Dispersion on Individuals and Organizations," *Academy of Management Journal* 42, no. 1 (February 1999): 25–40; Donald J. Campbell, Kathleen M. Campbell, and Ho-Beng Chia, "Merit Pay, Performance Appraisal, and Individual Motivation: An Analysis and Alternative," *Human Resource Management* 37, no. 2 (Summer 1998): 131–46; Robert H Woods, Michael Sciarini, and Deborah Breiter, "Performance Appraisals in Hotels," *Cornell Hotel and Restaurant Administration Quarterly* 39, no. 2 (April 1998): 25–9.

6. Jon Younger and Kurt Sandholtz, "Helping R&D Professionals Build Successful Careers," *Research Technology Management* 40, no. 6 (November–December 1997): 23–8; Thomas W. Jones, "Performance Management in a Changing Context: Monsanto Pioneers a Competency-Based Developmental Approach," *Human Resource Management* 34, no. 3 (Fall 1995): 425–42; "Performance Management: What's Hot—What's Not," *Compensation and Benefits Review* 26, no. 3 (May–June 1994): 71–5.

7. Ronald J Deluga, "The Quest for Justice on the Job: Essays and Experiments," *Journal of Occupational and Organizational Psychology* 72, no. 1 (March 1999): 122–4; Brian D. Cawley, Lisa M Keeping, and Paul E Levy, "Participation in the Performance Appraisal Process," *Journal of Applied Psychology* 83, no. 4 (August 1998): 615–33.

8. Robert Bookman, "Tools for Cultivating Constructive Feedback," *Association Management* 51, no. 2 (February 1999): 73–9; Clinton O. Longnecker and Dennis A. Gioia, "The Politics of Executive Appraisals," *Journal of Compensation and Benefits* 10, no. 2 (September–October 1994): 5–11; Aharon Tziner, Gary P. Latham, Bruce S. Price, and Robert Haccoun, "Development and Validation of a Questionnaire for Measuring Perceived Political Considerations in Performance Appraisal," *Journal of Organizational Behavior* 17, no. 2 (March 1996): 179–90.

9. T. Davis and M.J. Landa, "A Contrary Look at Performance Appraisal," *Canadian Manager* 24, no. 3 (Fall 1999): 18, 19.

10. David C. Martin and Kathryn M. Bartol, "Performance Appraisal: Maintaining System Effectiveness," *Public Personnel Management* 27, no. 2 (Summer 1998): 223–30; William H. Bommer, Jonathan L. Johnson, Gregory A. Rich, Philip M. Podsakoff, and Scott B. Mackenzie, "On the Interchangeability of Objective and Subjective Measures of Employee Performance: A Meta-Analysis," *Personnel Psychology* 48, no. 3 (Autumn 1995): 587–605.

11. "Strategic Planning Viewed from the Bottom Up," *The Futurist* 32, no. 4 (May 1998): 46; Anthony Johnson, "Performance Monitoring and Policy-Making: Making Effective Use of Evaluation Strategies," *Total Quality Management* 9, nos. 2/3 (May 1998): 259–67; Tracy B. Weiss and Franklin Hartle, *Reengineering Performance Management: Breakthroughs in Achieving Strategy Through People* (1997): St. Lucie Press; Milan Moravec, Ron Juliff, and Kathleen Hesler, "Partnerships Help a Company Manage Performance," *Personnel Journal* (January 1995): 104–8.

12. Gregory D. Streib and Theodore H. Poister, "Assessing the Validity, Legitimacy, and Functionality of Performance Measurement Systems in Municipal Governments," *American Review of Public Administration* 29, no. 2 (June 1999): 107–23; Margaret A. McManus and Steven H. Brown, "Adjusting Sales Results Measures for Use as Criteria," *Personnel Psychology* 48, no. 2 (Summer 1995): 391–400.

13. Werner and Bolino, "Explaining U.S. Courts of Appeals Decisions," *Personnel Psychology* 50, no. 1 (Spring 1997): 1–24; "Legalities of Documenting Performance," *Credit Union Executive* 35, no. 6 (November–December 1995): 11–12; John Edward Davidson, "The Temptation of Performance Appraisal Abuse in Employment Litigation," *Virginia Law Review* 81, no. 6 (September 1995): 1605–29. For an informative video on performance appraisal issues in the courtroom, see *The Legal Side of Performance Appraisal: You Be the Judge*, produced by the Bureau of Business Practice (24 Hope Road, Waterford, Conn., 06386).

14. Clive Fletcher, "The Implication of Research on Gender Differences in Self-Assessment and 360 Degree Appraisal," *Human Resource Management Journal* 9, no. 1 (1999): 39–46; David A. Waldman and David E. Bowen, "The Acceptability of 360 Degree Appraisals: A Customer-Supplier Relationship Perspective," *Human Resource Management* 37, no. 2 (Summer 1998): 117-29; James M. Conway, "Analysis and Design of Multitrait-Multirater Performance Appraisal Studies," *Journal of Management* 22, no. 1 (1996): 139–62.

15. Adrian Furnham and Paul Stringfield, "Congruence in Job-Performance Ratings: A Study of 360 Degree Feedback Examining Self, Manager, Peers, and Consultant Ratings," *Human Relations* 51, no. 4 (April 1998): 517–30; Shaul Fox, Tamir Caspy, and Avner Reisler, "Variables Affecting Leniency, Halo, and Validity of Self Appraisal," *Journal of Occupational and Organizational Psychology* 67, no. 1 (March 1994): 45–56; Paul E. Levy, "Self-Appraisal and Attributions: A Test of a Model," *Journal of Management* 19 (Spring 1993): 51–62.

16. Jerrell D. Coggburn, "Subordinate Appraisals of Managers: Lessons from a State Agency," *Review of Public Personnel Administration* 18, no. 1 (Winter 1998): 68-79; Stephanie Gruner, "Turning the Tables," *Inc.* 18, no. 6 (May 1996): 87–9; David Littlefield, "Halifax Employees to Assess Management," *People Management* 2, no. 3 (February 8, 1996): 5.

17. L. Berglund, "So, You Think You're a Good Manager ... Find Out for Sure with a Reverse Appraisal of Your Staff," *Modern Purchasing* 40, no. 5 (May 1998): 32.

18. Alan G. Walker and James W. Smither, "A Five-Year Study of Upward Feedback: What Managers Do with Their Results Matters," *Personnel Psychology* 52, no. 2 (Summer 1999): 393–423; Michael K. Mount; Timothy A. Judge, Steven E. Scullen, Marcia R. Sytsma, and Sarah A. Hezlett, "Trait, Rater and Level Effects in 360-Degree Performance Ratings," *Personnel Psychology* 51, no. 3 (Autumn 1998): 557–76.

19. Donald B. Fedor, Kenneth L. Bettenhausen, and Walter Davis, "Peer Reviews: Employees' Dual Roles as Raters and Recipients," *Group & Organization Management* 24, no. 1 (March 1999): 92–120.

20. Vanessa Urch Druskat and Steven B. Wolff, "Effects and Timing of Developmental Peer Appraisals in Self-

Managing Work Groups," *Journal of Applied Psychology* 84, no. 1 (February 1999): 58–74; Kenneth L. Bettenhausen and Donald B. Fedor, "Peer and Upward Appraisals: A Comparison of Their Benefits and Problems," *Group & Organization Management* 22, no. 2 (June 1997): 236–63.

21. Leslie B Hammer and Karen M Barbera, "Toward an Integration of Alternative Work," *Human Resource Planning* 20, no. 2 (1997): 28–36; Patricia K. Zingheim and Jay R. Schuster, "Supporting Teams with Multi-Rater Performance Reviews," *Compensation and Benefits Management* 11, no. 3 (Summer 1995): 41–5.

22. Michelle A. Yakovac, "Paying for Satisfaction," *HRFocus* 73, no. 6 (June 1996): 10–11; John Milliman, Robert A. Zawacki, and Brian Schultz, "Customer Service Drives 360-Degree Goal Setting," *Personnel Journal* 74, no. 6 (June 1995): 136–42; Margaret Kaeter, "Driving toward Sales and Satisfaction," *Training* (August 1990): 19–22.

23. George Eckes, "Practical Alternatives to Performance Appraisals," *Quality Progress* 27, no. 11 (November 1994): 57–60; James P. Muuss, "Security and the Surrogate Shopper," *Security Management* 39, no. 12 (December 1995): 55–7. Benjamin Schneider, Paul J. Hanges, and Harold W. Goldstein, "Do Customer Service Perceptions Generalize? The Case of Student and Chair Ratings of Faculty Effectiveness," *Journal of Applied Psychology* 27, no. 4 (April 1994): 65–9.

24. David W Bracken, Lynn Summers, and John Fleenor, "High-tech 360," *Training & Development* 52, no. 8 (August 1998): 42–5.

25. David A. Waldman, Leanne E. Atwater, and David Antonioni, "Has 360 Feedback Gone Amok?" *The Academy of Management Executive* 12, no. 2 (May 1998): 86–94; David Antonioni, "Designing an Effective 360-Degree Appraisal Feedback Process," *Organizational Dynamics* 25, no. 2 (Autumn 1996): 24–38.

26. Gary E. Roberts, "Perspectives on Enduring and Emerging Issues in Performance Appraisal," *Public Personnel Management* 27, no. 3 (Fall 1998): 301–20; William Hubbartt, "Bring Performance Appraisal Training to Life," *HRMagazine* 40, no. 5 (May 1995): 166, 168.

27. Gary P. Latham and Kenneth N. Wexley, *Increasing Productivity through Performance Appraisal*, 2nd ed. (Reading, Mass.: Addison-Wesley, 1994): 137.

28. Andrew L Solomonson and Charles E Lance, "Examination of the Relationship between True Halo and Halo Error in Performance Ratings," *Journal of Applied Psychology* 82, no. 5 (October 1997): 665–74; Charles E. Lance, Julie A. LaPointe, and Amy M. Stewart, "A Test of the Context Dependency of Three Causal Models of Halo Rater Error," *Journal of Applied Psychology* 79, no. 3 (June 1994): 332–40; Keven Murphy, Robert A. Jako, and Rebecca L. Anhalt, "Nature and Consequences of Halo Error: A Critical Analysis," *Journal of Applied Psychology* 78, no. 2 (April 1993): 218–25.

29. Deidra J. Schleicher and David V. Day, "A Cognitive Evaluation of Frame-of-Reference Rater Training: Content and Process Issues," *Organizational Behavior and Human Decision Processes* 73, no. 1 (January 1998): 76–101; Jeffrey S. Kane, John H. Bernardin, Peter Villanova, and Joseph Peyrefitte, "Stability of Rater Leniency: Three Studies," *Academy of Management Journal* 38, no. 4 (August 1995): 1036–51.

30. Sandy Wayne and Robert Liden, "Effects of Impression Management on Performance Ratings: A Longitudinal Study," *Academy of Management Journal* 38, no. 1 (February 1995): 232–60.

31. Gary E. Roberts, "Perspectives on Enduring and Emerging Issues in Performance Appraisal," *Public Personnel Management* 27, no. 3 (Fall 1998): 301–20; David J. Woehr, "Understanding Frame-of-Reference Training: The Impact of Training on the Recall of Performance Information," *Journal of Applied Psychology* 79, no. 4 (August 1994): 525–34.

32. Terry Gillen, "Why Appraisal Should Climb the Skills Agenda," *People Management* 2, no. 9 (May 2, 1996): 43.

33. Stephen C. Behrenbrinker, "Conducting Productive Performance Evaluations in the Assessor's Office," *Assessment Journal* 2, no. 5 (September–October 1995): 48–54.

34. Joseph Maiorca, "How to Construct Behaviorally Anchored Rating Scales (BARS) for Employee Evaluations," *Supervision* 58, no. 8 (August 1997): 15–18; Jeffrey M. Conte, Frank J. Landy, and John E. Mathieu, "Time Urgency: Conceptual and Construct Development," *Journal of Applied Psychology* 80, no. 1 (February 1995): 178–85.

35. For a comprehensive review of the research on BARS, see Chapter 6 in H. John Bernardin and Richard W. Beatty, *Performance Appraisal: Assessing Human Behavior at Work* (Boston: Kent, 1984). Also see Gary Latham and Kenneth N. Wexley, *Increasing Productivity through Performance Appraisal* (Reading, Mass.: Addison-Wesley, 1994); Kevin R. Murphy and Jeanette N. Cleveland, *Understanding Performance Appraisal*, Thousand Oaks, Calif.: Sage, 1995).

36. S. Nador, "A Properly Crafted Performance Management Program Aids Professional Development," *Canadian HR Reporter* (May 17, 1999): 10.

37. Latham and Wexley, *Increasing Productivity through Performance Appraisal* (Reading, Mass.: Addison-Wesley, 1994); Aharon Tziner, Richard Kopelman, and Christine Joanis, "Investigation of Raters' and Ratees' Reactions to Three Methods of Performance Appraisal: BOS, BARS, and GRS," *Revue Canadienne des Sciences de l'Administration* 14, no. 4 (December 1997): 396–404.

38. Peter F. Drucker, *The Practice of Management* (New York: Harper & Brothers, 1954). Reissued by HarperCollins in 1993.

39. E. Locke and G. Latham, *A Theory of Goal Setting and Task Performance* (Englewood Cliffs, N.J.: Prentice-Hall, 1990). See also John J Donovan and David J Radosevich, "The Moderating Role of Goal Commitment on the Goal Difficulty-Performance Relationship: A Meta-analytic Review and Critical Reanalysis," *Journal of Applied Psychology* 83, no. 2 (April 1998): 308–15; Don

VandeWalle, Steven P Brown, William L Cron, and John W Slocum Jr, "The Influence of Goal Orientation and Self-Regulation Tactics on Sales Performance: A Longitudinal Field Test ," *Journal of Applied Psychology* 84, no. 2 (April 1999): 249–59.

40. Mark A. Covaleski, Mark W. Dirsmith, James B. Heian, and Sajay Samuel, "The Calculated and the Avowed: Techniques of Discipline and Struggles over Identity in Big Six Public Accounting Firms," *Administrative Science Quarterly* 43, no. 2 (June 1998): 293–327. For an example of how Roberts Express has integrated its MBO system with TQM and customer requirements, see Jack Pickard, "Motivate Employees to Delight Customers," *Transportation and Distribution* 34, no. 7 (July 1993): 48. See also Jim M. Graber, Roger E. Breisch, and Walter E. Breisch, "Performance Appraisal and Deming: A Misunderstanding?" *Quality Progress* 25, no. 6 (June 1992): 59–62; Dennis M. Daley, "Pay for Performance, Performance Appraisal, and Total Quality," *Public Productivity and Management Review* 16, no. 1 (Fall 1992): 39–51.

41. Deloris McGee Wanguri, "A Review, An Integration, and a Critique of Cross-Disciplinary Research on Performance Appraisals, Evaluations, and Feedback," *Journal of Business Communications* 32, no. 3 (July 1995): 267–93; Peter Allan, "Designing and Implementing an Effective Performance Appraisal System," *Review of Business* 16, no. 2 (Winter 1994): 3–8; Wiersma, Vane Den Berg, and Latham, "Dutch Reactions."

42. Norman R.F. Maier, *The Appraisal Interview* (New York: John Wiley, 1958); Maier, *The Appraisal Interview—Three Basic Approaches* (San Diego: University Associates, 1976).

43. John F. Kikoski, "Effective Communication in the Performance Appraisal Interview: Face-to-Face Communication for Public Managers in the Culturally Diverse Workplace," *Public Personnel Management* 28, no. 2 (Summer 1999): 301–22; Howard J. Klein and Scott A. Snell, "The Impact of Interview Process and Context on Performance Appraisal Interview Effectiveness," *Journal of Managerial Issues* 6, no. 2 (Summer 1994): 160–75.

44. David E. Bowen, Stephen W. Gilliland, and Robert Folger; "HRM and Service Fairness: How Being Fair with Employees Spills over to Customers," *Organizational Dynamics* 27, no. 3 (Winter 1999): 7–23; Audrey M. Korsgaard and Loriann Roberson, "Procedural Justice in Performance Evaluation: The Role of Instrumental and Non-Instrumental Voice in Performance Appraisal Discussions," *Journal of Management* 21, no. 4 (1995): 657–69; Susan M. Taylor, Kay B. Tracy, Monika K. Renard, J. Kline Harrison, and Stephen J. Carroll, "Due Process in Performance Appraisal: A Quasi-Experiment in Procedural Justice," *Administrative Science Quarterly* 40, no. 3 (September 1995): 495–523.

45. Martin Geller, "Participation in the Performance Appraisal Review: Inflexible Manager Behavior and Variable Worker Needs," *Human Relations* 51, no. 8 (August 1998): 1061–83; Brian D. Cawley, Lisa M. Keeping, and Paul E. Levy, "Participation in the Performance Appraisal Process and Employee Reactions: A Meta-analytic Review of Field Investigations," *Journal of Applied Psychology* 83, no. 4 (August 1998): 615–33.

46. Ted Pollock, "Make your Criticism Pay Off," *Automotive Manufacturing & Production* 110, no. 6 (June 1998): 10; Helaine Olen, "The Pitfalls of Perfectionism," *Working Woman* 21, no. 3 (March 1996): 55–7; Ted Pollock, "The Positive Power of Criticism," *Automotive Production* 108, no. 5 (May 1996): 13.

47. "Levi Strauss and Company Implements New Pay and Performance System," *Employee Benefit Plan Review* 48, no. 7 (January 1994): 46–8.

48. Scott A. Snell and Kenneth N. Wexley, "Performance Diagnosis: Identifying the Causes of Poor Performance," *Personnel Administrator* 30, no. 4 (April 1985): 117–27.

49. Robert Crow, "You Cannot Improve My Performance by Measuring It!" *Journal of Quality and Participation* 19, no. 1 (January–February 1996): 62–4; Allan M. Mohrman and Susan Labers Mohrman, "Performance Management Is 'Running the Business,'" *Compensation and Benefits Review* 27, no. 4 (July–August 1995): 69–75.

50. Jean François Manzoni and Jean-Louis Barsoux, "The Set-Up-to-Fail Syndrome," *Harvard Business Review* 76 no2 (March–April 1998): 101–13.

MANAGING

COMPENSATION

After studying this chapter, you should be able to

OBJECTIVE 1
Explain employer concerns in developing a strategic compensation program.

OBJECTIVE 2
Identify the various factors that influence the setting of wages.

OBJECTIVE 3
Discuss the mechanics of each of the major job evaluation systems.

OBJECTIVE 4
Explain the purpose of a wage survey.

OBJECTIVE 5
Define the wage curve, pay grades, and rate ranges as parts of the compensation structure.

OBJECTIVE 6
Identify the major provisions of the federal and provincial laws affecting compensation.

OBJECTIVE 7
Discuss the current issues of equal pay for comparable value, pay compression, and low-wage budgets.

A n extensive review of the literature indicates that important work-related variables leading to job satisfaction include challenging work, interesting job assignments, equitable rewards, competent supervision, and rewarding careers.[1] It is doubtful, however, whether many employees would continue working if it were not for the money they earn. Employees want compensation systems that are fair and that reflect their skills and expectations. Pay is a major consideration in HRM because it provides employees with a tangible reward for their services, and with recognition as well. Employee compensation includes all forms of pay and rewards that employees receive for performing their jobs. Direct compensation includes employee wages and salaries, incentives, bonuses, and commissions. Indirect compensation includes the many benefits supplied by employers. Nonfinancial compensation includes employee recognition programs, rewarding jobs, and flexible work hours to accommodate personal needs.

Both managers and scholars agree that compensation decisions send a message about what management considers to be important. Furthermore, payroll constitutes a sizable operating cost to employers. In manufacturing firms, compensation is seldom as low as 20 percent of total expenditures; in service enterprises, it often exceeds 80 percent. It follows that a strategic compensation program is essential if pay is to motivate employee production sufficiently to keep labour costs at acceptable levels. This chapter is about compensation programs and job evaluation systems, and about how to establish structures for determining compensation. Also included is a discussion of the legislation that affects wage and salary rates. Chapter 10 will review financial incentive plans for employees. Employee benefits that are part of the total compensation package are discussed in Chapter 11.

STRATEGIC COMPENSATION PLANNING

What is strategic compensation planning? Simply stated, it is the compensation of employees in ways that enhance motivation and growth while, at the same time, aligning their efforts with the objectives, philosophies, and culture of the organization. Strategic compensation planning goes beyond determining what market rates to pay employees—although market rates are one element of compensation planning—to purposefully link compensation to the organization's mission and general business objectives.[2]

Strategic compensation planning also serves to mesh the monetary payments made to employees with specific functions of the HR program. For example, when new employees are being recruited, the rate of pay for jobs can increase or limit the supply of applicants. Employers have adopted special pay strategies to attract job applicants with highly marketable skills, such as welders (in Alberta's oil and gas boom), high-tech workers, and engineers and scientists with financial knowledge. Howard W. Risher, a compensation specialist, notes: "The linkage of pay levels to labour markets is a strategic policy issue because it affects the caliber of the workforce and the organization's relative payroll costs."[3] Organizations also use compensation to retain scarce skills. According to a Conference Board of Canada study of 365 Canadian companies, the following retention strategies are often used: rewards (55 percent), variable compensation (9 percent), and special incentives (31 percent).[4] Many fast food restaurants—traditionally low-wage employers—have had to raise their starting wages to attract enough applicants to meet their staffing requirements. When rates of pay are high, a large pool of applicants is created, and

WWW

organizations can raise their selection standards and hire better-qualified employees. This in turn can reduce employer training costs. When employees perform at exceptional levels, their performance appraisals may justify an increase in pay. For these reasons and others, an organization should develop a formal HR program to manage employee compensation.

In this chapter we will discuss two important aspects of strategic compensation planning: linking compensation to organizational objectives and the motivating value of compensation.

Linking Compensation to Organizational Objectives

When organizations undertake to downsize, restructure, outsource, or re-engineer, their intention is to become leaner and flatter; the point of this is to gain flexibility and respond more quickly to ever-changing customer demands. Organizations with fewer employees must manage their compensation programs in such a way that those who remain are motivated to make value-added contributions while assuming ownership of their jobs.[5] An outcome of today's dynamic business environment is that managers have needed to change their pay philosophies so that they no longer pay for a specific position or job title and instead reward employees on the basis of their individual contributions to the organization's success.[6] In sum, a compensation program must be tailored to the needs of the organization and its employees.

Compensation specialists are speaking more and more often about value-added compensation. A *value-added compensation* program—also called *value chain compensation*—is one in which the components of the compensation package (benefits, base pay, incentives, etc.) both separately and in combination create value for the organization and its employees. In taking a value-added perspective, managers ask questions such as, "How does this compensation package benefit the organization?" Payments that fail to advance either the employee or the organization are removed from the compensation program.[7]

It is not uncommon for an organization to establish very specific goals when joining its organizational objectives to its compensation program.[8] Formalized compensation goals serve as guidelines for managers to ensure that wage and benefit policies achieve their intended purpose.[9] The more common goals of a strategic compensation policy include the following:

1. To reward employees' past performance.

2. To remain competitive in the labour market.

3. To maintain salary equity among employees.

4. To mesh employees' future performance with organizational goals.

5. To control the compensation budget.

6. To attract new employees.

7. To reduce unnecessary turnover.

If an organization is to achieve these goals, it must establish policies that will guide its managers in the decisions they make. Formal statements of compensation policy typically include the following:

1. The rate of pay within the organization, and whether it is to be above, below, or at the prevailing community rate.

2. The ability of the pay program to gain employee acceptance while motivating employees to perform to the best of their abilities.

3. The pay levels at which employees will be recruited, and the pay differentials between new and more senior employees.

4. The intervals at which pay raises are to be granted, and the extent to which merit and/or seniority will influence the raises.

5. The pay levels needed to facilitate the achievement of a sound financial position in relation to the products or services offered.

The Motivating Value of Compensation

Pay constitutes a quantitative measure of an employee's relative worth. For most employees, pay has a direct bearing not only on their standard of living, but also on the status and recognition they enjoy both on and off the job. Since pay is a reward the employee receives in exchange for his or her contributions, it is essential, according to the equity theory, that the pay be equitable in terms of those contributions. It is essential as well that the employee's pay be equitable in terms of what other employees are receiving for their contributions.

Pay Equity

Equity can be defined as anything of value earned through the investment of something of value. Equity theory—from which pay equity is derived—is a motivation theory that explains how employees respond to situations in which they feel they have received less (or more) than they deserve.[10] Central to the theory is the role of perception in motivation and the fact that individuals make comparisons. The theory states that in a given situation, individuals form a ratio of their inputs (abilities, skills, experiences) to their outcomes (salary, benefits). They then compare the value of that ratio with the value of the input/output ratios for other individuals in a similar class of jobs either inside or outside the organization. If the value of their ratio equals the value of another's, they perceive the situation as equitable, and no tension exists. However, if they perceive their input/output ratio as inequitable relative to others', tension is created and they are motivated to eliminate or reduce the inequity. The strength of their motivation is proportional to the magnitude of the perceived inequity. Figure 9.1 illustrates pay equity and feelings of being fairly paid.

Pay equity

An employee's perception that compensation received is equal to the value of the work performed

Employees achieve **pay equity** when the compensation received is equal to the value of the work performed. Research clearly demonstrates that employees' perceptions of pay equity, or inequity, can dramatically affect their motivation as it relates to both work behaviour and productivity. Managers must therefore develop strategic pay practices that are both internally and externally equitable. Compensation policies are internally equitable when employees believe that the wage rates for their jobs approximate the job's worth to the organization.

Perceptions of external pay equity exist when the organization is paying wages that are relatively equal to what other employers are paying for similar types of work.

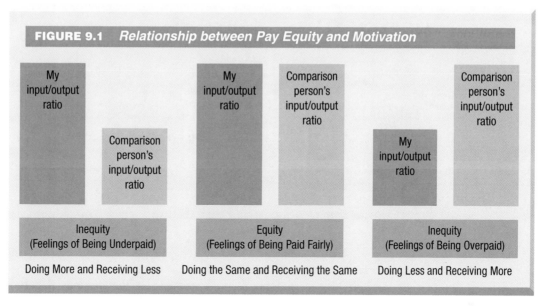

The greater the perceived disparity between my input/output ratio and the comparison person's input/output ratio, the greater the motivation to reduce the inequity.

Expectancy Theory and Pay

The expectancy theory of motivation predicts that one's level of motivation depends on the attractiveness of the rewards sought and the probability of obtaining those rewards.[11] The theory has developed from the work of psychologists who consider humans as thinking, reasoning beings who have beliefs and anticipations concerning future life events. Expectancy theory thus holds that employees will work harder if they have reason to expect that doing so will result in a reward that is valued.[12] To inspire this effort, the value of any monetary reward should be attractive. Employees also must believe that good performance is valued by their employer and will result in their receiving the expected reward.

Figure 9.2 illustrates the relationship between compensation and the expectancy theory of motivation. The model predicts that high effort will lead to high performance (expectancy), and high performance in turn will lead to monetary rewards that are appreciated (valued).

Clearly, how employees view compensation can be an important factor in determining the motivational value of compensation. Furthermore, when employers communicate pay information effectively, and when the organization's environment elicits the trust of employees in management, employees will have more accurate perceptions of their pay. The perceptions that employees develop concerning their pay are influenced by the accuracy of their knowledge and by their understanding of the compensation program's strategic objectives.

Pay Secrecy

Misperceptions by employees concerning the equity of their pay and its relationship to performance can be created by secrecy about the pay that others receive. There is reason to believe that secrecy can generate distrust in the compensation system, reduce employee motivation, and inhibit organizational effectiveness. Yet

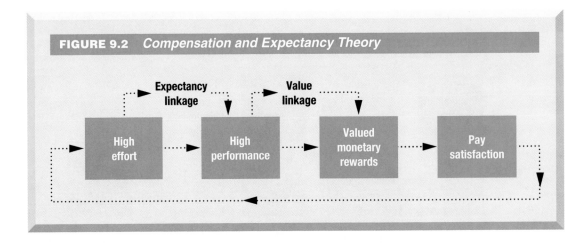

FIGURE 9.2   *Compensation and Expectancy Theory*

pay secrecy seems to be an accepted practice in many organizations in both the private and the public sector.

Managers sometimes justify secrecy on the grounds that most employees prefer to have their own pay kept secret. Another big reason for pay secrecy—one that managers may be unwilling to admit—is that it gives organizations greater freedom in compensation policy. After all, when pay decisions are not disclosed, there is no need to justify or defend them. Employees who are not supposed to know what others are being paid have no objective basis for pursuing complaints about their own pay. Secrecy also helps hide inequities in the internal pay structure. Furthermore, it can lead employees to believe that there is no direct relationship between pay and performance.

The Bases for Compensation

Hourly work

Work paid on an hourly basis

Piecework

Work paid according to the number of units produced

In most private, public, and not-for-profit organizations, work has traditionally been compensated on an hourly basis. It is referred to as **hourly work**, in contrast to **piecework**, in which employees are paid according to the number of units they produce. Hourly work is far more prevalent than piecework as a basis for compensating employees.

Employees compensated on an hourly basis are classified as *hourly employees*, or wage earners. Those whose compensation is computed on the basis of weekly, biweekly, or monthly pay periods are classified as *salaried employees*. Usually, hourly employees are paid only for the time they work. Salaried employees, in contrast, are generally paid the same for each pay period, even though they occasionally may work more hours or fewer than the regular number of hours in a period. They also usually receive certain benefits not provided to hourly employees.

Employment practices are a provincial jurisdiction, and each province has its own employment standards act. Each of these acts contains a provision that requires the employer to reimburse the employee at a specified rate after he or she has worked the minimum required hours. This rate is usually 1.5 times the employee's base hourly rate of pay. A number of employers offer overtime pay that is more generous than what the act specifies. Some acts provide for time in lieu of overtime; thus, four hours of overtime paid at 1.5 would be the equivalent of six hours in either pay or time off in lieu of payment. Supervisory and management personnel are not usually paid overtime; still other personnel work overtime for free (see Ethics in HRM). Each of the employment standards acts includes a list of people who are exempt from the overtime provision.

Because so many American companies are operating in Canada, the terms *exempt* and *nonexempt* are often heard, although neither has any relevance in Canadian legislation. These terms are used specifically to denote *supervisory* and *nonsupervisory*. U.S. legislation stipulates that only nonexempt (i.e., nonsupervisory) workers are entitled to overtime pay.

COMPONENTS OF THE WAGE MIX

A number of *internal* and *external* factors influence directly or indirectly, and typically in combination, the rates at which employees are paid. These factors constitute the wage mix (see Figure 9.3). For example, the area wage rate for administrative assistants (AAs) might be $10.50 per hour. However, one employer may elect to pay its AAs $12.25 per hour because of their excellent performance. The impact of government legislation on the wage mix will be discussed later in the chapter.

Internal Factors

Internal factors that influence wage rates include the employer's compensation policy, the worth of the job, the employee's relative worth in meeting job requirements, and the employer's ability to pay.

Employer's Compensation Policy

WWW

Highlights in HRM 1 illustrates the compensation objectives of two organizations, CIBC and Hewlett-Packard. The pay objective of Hewlett-Packard is to be an industry pay leader; CIBC seeks to be wage-competitive. Both employers strive to promote a compensation policy that is fair and competitive.

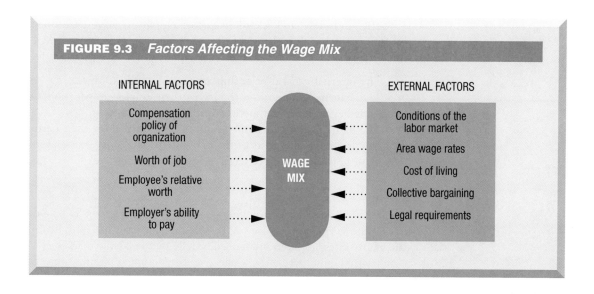

FIGURE 9.3   *Factors Affecting the Wage Mix*

INTERNAL FACTORS

- Compensation policy of organization
- Worth of job
- Employee's relative worth
- Employer's ability to pay

WAGE MIX

EXTERNAL FACTORS

- Conditions of the labor market
- Area wage rates
- Cost of living
- Collective bargaining
- Legal requirements

Ethics in HRM

WORKING FOR FREE

Two restaurants in Ontario, one in Port Hope and the other in Belleville, were benefiting from the services of more than twenty people (called volunteers or agents) who were not being paid wages. The province's Employment Standards Act stipulated that waiters must be paid $5.95 an hour (less than the minimum wage, due to tips), and that every employer must pay a minimum wage. The restaurants argued that they provided a location where workers could act as service agents and do their business. Were the waiters working for free?

Elaine Chu worked at a local fast food restaurant to earn enough money to support herself while she attended university part-time. Her job title was night manager, and she worked the 4 p.m. to 11 p.m. shift. During this shift she was the only employee on duty, and she did much of the food preparation, serving, and cleanup. Most nights, customers arrived after the movies (around 11 p.m.), and Chu was expected to work into the next shift until the crowd dispersed. She received no overtime pay for these extra hours because employers were not required to pay overtime for managers. Did Chu's employer misuse the title "manager" in order to circumvent its obligations with respect to overtime pay? To be deemed a true manager, an individual should have staff reporting to him or her, should have responsibility for a major aspect of the business, and should provide counselling to more junior staff through performance appraisal. Was Chu working for free?

According to a Statistics Canada survey, one-fifth of all employees put in extra hours at work, and 60 percent of these are unpaid, with workers averaging nine unpaid hours per week. White-collar employees are working for free, and they know why: they are afraid of losing their jobs.

Sources: Bruce Little, "Canadians Work Overtime for Free," *The Globe and Mail*, July 14, 1997: B6; Susan Bourette, "Volunteer Waiters Work Only for Tips," *The Globe and Mail*, July 27, 1997: A7.

CIBC and Hewlett-Packard, like other employers, have established numerous compensation objectives that affect the pay their employees receive. At a minimum, employers of whatever size should set pay policies that consider the following:

- The internal wage relationship among jobs and skill levels.
- The external competition (i.e., what their employees get should reflect to some degree what competitors' employees are getting).
- The basic notion that employees will be rewarded for their performance.
- Administrative elements of the pay system such as overtime premiums, payment periods, and short-term or long-term incentives.[13]

Worth of a Job

Organizations without formal compensation programs generally base the worth of jobs on the subjective opinions of people familiar with the jobs. In these circumstances, pay rates are often influenced heavily by the labour market or—in the case of unionized employees—by collective bargaining. Organizations with formal

Highlights in HRM

1   COMPENSATION OBJECTIVES AT CIBC AND HEWLETT-PACKARD

CIBC

- Align with objectives and key performance measures
- Encourage teamwork and positive relations
- Provide rewards for excellent performance
- Ensure strong link between pay and performance
- Be market-competitive
- Attract, retain, and motivate high-caliber employees
- Ensure fair treatment

HEWLETT-PACKARD

- Help H-P continue to attract creative and enthusiastic people who contribute to its success
- Pay employees at top end of pay scale
- Reflect sustained contribution of unit, division, and H-P
- Be open and understandable
- Ensure fair treatment
- Be innovative, competitive, and equitable

Sources: Personal correspondence with Gail Cohen, CIBC Insurance, 1995; George T. Milkovich and Jerry M. Newman, *Compensation*, 5th ed. (Chicago: Irwin, 1996). Used with permission.

compensation programs are more likely to rely on job evaluation systems to determine pay rates. Even when rates are subject to collective bargaining, job evaluation can help an organization maintain some control over its wage structure.

WWW

Job evaluations are widely used in all sectors, both public and private. The City of Mississauga and Star Data Systems use job evaluations to establish wage structures. Job evaluation is used most often in the clerical, technical, and various blue-collar sectors; it is least often found in managerial and top executive sectors.

Employee's Relative Worth

In both hourly and salaried jobs, employee performance can be recognized and rewarded through promotion and by means of various incentive systems. (The most common incentive systems are discussed in the next chapter.) Employers can also reward superior performance by granting merit raises on the basis of steps within a rate range established for a job class. However, for merit raises to work as intended, they must be determined by an effective performance appraisal system

How would you rate the worth of a rescue worker's job?

that differentiates between employees who deserve the raises and those who do not. Moreover, this system must provide a visible and credible relationship between performance and any raises received.[14] Unfortunately, too many so-called merit systems provide for raises to be granted automatically. As a result, employees tend to be rewarded more for merely being present than for being productive.

Employer's Ability to Pay

In the public sector, the amount of pay and benefits employees can receive is limited by the funds budgeted for this purpose and by the willingness of taxpayers to provide those funds through taxes. In the private sector, on the other hand, pay levels are limited to the financial resources available to employers—which of course includes profits. Thus, an organization's ability to pay is determined in part by the productivity of its employees. This productivity is a result not only of their performance, but also of the amount of capital the organization has invested in labour-saving equipment. Generally, increases in capital investment reduce the number of employees required to perform the work and increase an employer's ability to provide higher pay for its employees.

Economic conditions and competition can also significantly affect the rates that employers are able to pay. Competition and recessions can force prices down, thereby reducing the income from which compensation payments are drawn. In these situations, employers have little choice but to reduce wages and/or lay off employees—or, even worse, go out of business.

External Factors

External factors that influence wage rates include labour market conditions, area wage rates, cost of living, collective bargaining (if the employer is unionized), and legal requirements.

Labour Market Conditions

The labour market reflects the forces of supply and demand for qualified labour in a given area. These forces influence the wage rates required to recruit and retain competent employees. Remember, however, that various counterforces can reduce the full impact of supply and demand on the labour market. For example, the economic power of unions may prevent employers from lowering wage rates even when unemployment is high among union members. As well, government regulations may prevent an employer from paying at a market rate less than an established minimum. In regions where unemployment is high, workers may be willing to accept lower wages in exchange for the assurance of stable employment. For example, letter carriers in Saint John, New Brunswick, accepted a contract with a modest 1 percent pay increase because it included a no-layoff clause and a guarantee that employees would not be relocated outside a 40 km radius.

Area Wage Rates

WWW

A formal wage structure should provide rates that are in line with those being paid by other employers for comparable jobs in the area. Data pertaining to area wage rates can be obtained at minimal cost from local area wage surveys. Wage survey data can also be obtained from compensation consulting firms such as Mercer Management Consulting and Robert Half Canada. Smaller employers use government or local board of trade surveys to establish rates of pay for new and senior employees. Many organizations conduct their own surveys. Others engage in a cooperative exchange of wage information, or rely for these data on various professional associations such as the Human Resources Professionals Association of Ontario. Most wage information is inexpensive—under $100—and so is available to all employers, regardless of size. The Conference Board of Canada conducts an annual compensation survey. In 1999, workers in the high-demand sector of computer software received the highest increases (over 6 percent), while Canadian employees in general received an average increase of about 3 percent.[15]

Data from area wage surveys can be used to prevent the rates for certain jobs from drifting too far above or below those of other employers in the region. When rates rise above existing area levels, an employer's labour costs can become excessive. Conversely, when they drop too far below area levels, it can be difficult to recruit and retain competent personnel. Wage survey data must also take into account indirect wages paid in the form of benefits.

Cost of Living

Escalator clauses

Clauses in collective agreements that provide for quarterly cost-of-living adjustments in wages, basing the adjustments on changes in the consumer price index

Consumer price index (CPI)

Measure of the average change in prices over time in a fixed "market basket" of goods and services

Because of inflation, compensation rates must sometimes be adjusted upward to help employees maintain their purchasing power. This can be achieved through **escalator clauses**, which are found in a number of collective agreements. These clauses provide for quarterly cost-of-living adjustments (COLAs) in wages based on changes in the **consumer price index (CPI)**. The CPI is a measure of the average change in prices over time in a fixed "market basket" of goods and services.[16] The most common adjustments are 1 cent per hour for each 0.3 or 0.4 point change in the CPI.

WWW

The CPI is largely used to set wages. It is based on a bundle of prices: food, clothing, shelter, and fuels; transportation fares; charges for medical services; and prices of other goods and services that people buy for day-to-day living. Statistics Canada collects price information on a monthly basis and calculates the CPI for Canada as a whole and for various Canadian cities. Separate indexes are published by size of city and by region of the country. Employers in a number of communities monitor changes in the CPI as a basis for compensation decisions.

Changes in the CPI can have a major impact on pay rates. When wage increases are granted solely on the basis of the CPI, pay rates are compressed within the pay structure; this creates inequities among those receiving the wage increase. Inequities also result from the fact that adjustments are made on a cent-per-hour rather than a percentage basis. For example, a cost-of-living adjustment of 50 cents represents a 10 percent increase for an employee earning $5 per hour, but only a 5 percent increase for one earning $10 per hour. Unless adjustments are made periodically in employee base rates, the desired differential between higher- and lower-paying jobs will gradually be reduced. The incentive to accept more demanding jobs will also be reduced.

Collective Bargaining

Real wages

Wage increases larger than rises in the consumer price index

One of the main functions of a labour union is to bargain collectively over conditions of employment, the most important of which is compensation (see Chapter 14). In each negotiation the union's goal is to achieve increases in **real wages**—that is, wage increases larger than the increase in the CPI—and thereby increase the purchasing power and standard of living of its members. This goal includes gaining wage settlements that equal if not exceed the pattern established by other unions in the area.

Agreements negotiated by unions tend to establish rate patterns in the labour market. As a result, wages are generally higher in areas where organized labour is strong. To recruit and retain competent personnel and avoid unionization, nonunion employers must either meet or exceed these rates. The "union scale" also becomes the prevailing rate that all employers must pay for work performed under government contract. The impact of collective bargaining thus extends beyond the segment of the labour force that is unionized.

JOB EVALUATION SYSTEMS

OBJECTIVE
3

Job evaluation

Systematic process of determining the relative worth of jobs in order to establish which jobs should be paid more than others within an organization

As we noted earlier, one important component of the wage mix is the worth of the job. Organizations formally determine the value of jobs through a process of job evaluation. **Job evaluation** is the systematic process of determining the relative worth of jobs; the goal is to establish which jobs should be paid more than others within the organization. Job evaluation helps establish internal equity between various jobs. The relative worth of a job can be determined by comparing it with others inside the organization or by comparing it with a scale that has been constructed for this purpose. Whichever method is used, the comparison can be made on the basis of the jobs as a whole or on the basis of the parts that constitute the jobs.

FIGURE 9.4   *Different Job Evaluation Systems*

BASIS FOR COMPARISON	SCOPE OF COMPARISON	
	JOB AS WHOLE (NONQUANTITATIVE)	JOB PARTS OR FACTORS (QUANTITATIVE)
Job vs. job	Job ranking system	Factor comparison system
Job vs. scale	Job classification system	Point system

Four methods of comparison are shown in Figure 9.4. They provide the basis for the main systems of job evaluation. We will begin by discussing the simpler, nonquantitative approaches, and conclude by reviewing the more popular, quantitative systems. Whichever method is used, it is important to remember that all job evaluation methods require varying degrees of judgment on the part of managers.

Job Ranking System

Job ranking system

Simplest and oldest system of job evaluation by which jobs are arrayed on the basis of their relative worth

The simplest and oldest system of job evaluation is the **job ranking system**, which arrays jobs on the basis of their relative worth. One technique used to rank jobs consists of having the raters arrange cards listing the duties and responsibilities of each job in order of the importance of the jobs. Job ranking can be done by a single individual knowledgeable about all jobs or by a committee composed of management and employee representatives.

Another common approach to job ranking is the paired comparison method. Raters compare each job with all other jobs by means of a paired comparison ranking table that lists the jobs in both rows and columns, as shown in Figure 9.5. To use the table, raters compare a job from a row with the jobs from each of the columns. If the row job is ranked higher than a column job, an X is placed in the appropriate cell. After all the jobs have been compared, raters total the Xs for row jobs. The total number of Xs for a row job will establish its worth relative to other jobs. Differences in rankings should then be reconciled into a single rating for all jobs. After jobs are evaluated, wage rates can be assigned to them through use of a salary survey, discussed later in the chapter.

The basic weakness of the job ranking system is that it does not provide a very refined measure of each job's worth. Since the comparisons are usually made on the basis of the job as a whole, it is quite easy for one or more factors in a given job to bias the ranking given to it, especially if the job is complex. This weakness can be partially eliminated by having the raters agree before the evaluation process on one or two important factors with which to evaluate jobs and the weights to be assigned these factors. Another disadvantage of the job ranking system is that the final ranking of jobs merely indicates the relative importance of the jobs, not the differences in the degree of importance that may exist between jobs. A final limitation of the job ranking method is that it can be used only with a small number of jobs, probably no more than fifteen. Its simplicity, however, makes it ideal for smaller employers.

FIGURE 9.5 *Paired-Comparison Job Ranking Table*

Row Jobs \ Column Jobs	Senior administrative secretary	Data entry operator	Data processing director	File clerk	Systems analyst	Programmer	Total
Senior administrative secretary	—	X		X		X	3
Data entry operator		—		X			1
Data processing director	X	X	—	X	X	X	5
File clerk				—			0
Systems analyst	X	X		X	—	X	4
Programmer		X		X		—	2

Directions: Place an X in cell where the value of a row job is higher than that of a column job.

Job Classification System

In a **job classification system**, jobs are classified and grouped according to a series of predetermined grades. Successive grades reflect increasing amounts of job responsibility, skill, knowledge, ability, or other factors. For example, Grade GS-1 from the U.S. federal government grade descriptions reads as follows:

> GS-1 includes those classes of positions the duties of which are to perform, under immediate supervision, with little or no latitude for the exercise of independent judgment (A) the simplest routine work in office, business, or fiscal operations; or (B) elementary work of a subordinate technical character in a professional, scientific, or technical field.

The descriptions of each of the job classes constitute the scale against which the specifications for the various jobs are compared. Managers then evaluate a given job by comparing its description with those of different wage grades; the goal of this exercise is to "slot" the job into the appropriate grade. This system has the advantage of simplicity, but is less precise than the point and factor comparison systems (discussed in the next sections), because the job is evaluated as a whole.

Point System

Point system

Quantitative job evaluation procedure that determines the relative value of a job by the total points assigned to it

WWW

The **point system** is a quantitative job evaluation procedure that determines a job's relative value by totalling the points assigned to it. It has been used successfully by high-visibility organizations such as Boeing and Honeywell, and by many other public and private organizations of all sizes. Although point systems are rather complicated to establish, once in place they are relatively simple to understand and use. The principal advantage of point systems is that they provide a more refined basis for making judgments than ranking or classification systems, and so produce results that are more valid and less easy to manipulate.

With a point system, jobs are evaluated quantitatively on the basis of factors or elements—commonly called compensable factors—that constitute the job. The skills, responsibilities, and working conditions that a job usually entails are the more common major compensable factors; these serve to rank various jobs as more or less important than others. How many compensable factors an organization uses depends on the nature of the organization and of the jobs to be evaluated. Once selected, compensable factors are assigned weights according to their relative importance to the organization. For example, if responsibility is considered extremely important to the organization, it might be assigned a weight of 40 percent. After this is done, each factor is divided into a number of degrees. Degrees represent the different levels of difficulty associated with each factor.

A point system requires the use of a point manual. This is a type of handbook that contains descriptions of compensable factors and the degrees to which these factors may exist in the jobs. The manual will also indicate—usually by means of a table (see Highlights in HRM 2)—the number of points allocated to each factor and to each of the degrees into which these factors are divided. The point value assigned to a job represents the sum of the numerical degree values of each compensable factor that the job possesses.

Developing a Point Manual

A variety of point manuals have been developed by organizations, trade associations, and management consultants. An organization that seeks to use one of these existing manuals should make certain that the manual is suited to its particular jobs and operating conditions. If necessary, the organization should modify the manual or develop its own to suit its needs.

WWW

The job factors listed in Highlights in HRM 2 represent the ones covered by the American Association of Industrial Management point manual. Each of the factors listed in this manual has been divided into five degrees. However, the number of degrees into which the factors in a manual are to be divided can be more or less than this number, depending on the relative weight assigned to each factor and the ease with which the individual degrees can be defined or distinguished.

After the job factors in the point manual have been divided into degrees, a statement must be prepared defining each of these degrees, as well as each factor as a whole. The definitions should be concise, yet should also distinguish the factors and each of their degrees. Highlights in HRM 3 represents another portion of the point manual used by the American Association of Industrial Management; this one describes each of the degrees for the job knowledge factor. These descriptions enable those conducting a job evaluation to determine the extent to which the factors exist in each job being evaluated.

Highlights in HRM

2 POINT VALUES FOR JOB FACTORS OF THE AMERICAN ASSOCIATION OF INDUSTRIAL MANAGEMENT

FACTORS	1ST DEGREE	2ND DEGREE	3RD DEGREE	4TH DEGREE	5TH DEGREE
SKILL					
1. Job knowledge	14	28	42	56	70
2. Experience	22	44	66	88	110
3. Initiative and ingenuity	14	28	42	56	70
EFFORT					
4. Physical demand	10	20	30	40	50
5. Mental or visual demand	5	10	5	20	25
RESPONSIBILITY					
6. Equipment or process	5	10	15	20	25
7. Material or product	5	10	15	20	25
8. Safety of others	5	10	15	20	25
9. Work of others	5	10	15	20	25
JOB CONDITIONS					
10. Working conditions	10	20	30	40	50
11. Hazards	5	10	15	20	25

Source: Developed by the National Metal Trades Association. Reproduced with permission of the American Association of Industrial Management, Springfield, Mass.

The final step in developing a point manual is to determine the number of points to be assigned to each factor and to each degree within these factors. Although the total number of points is arbitrary, 500 points is often the maximum.

Highlights in HRM

3 DESCRIPTION OF JOB KNOWLEDGE FACTORS AND DEGREES OF THE AMERICAN ASSOCIATION OF INDUSTRIAL MANAGEMENT

1. JOB KNOWLEDGE

This factor measures the knowledge or equivalent training required to perform the position duties.

1st Degree Use of reading and writing, adding and subtracting of whole numbers; following of instructions; use of fixed gauges, direct reading instruments, and similar devices where interpretation is not required.

2nd Degree Use of addition, subtraction, multiplication, and division of numbers including decimals and fractions; simple use of formulas, charts, tables, drawings, specifications, schedules, wiring diagrams; use of adjustable measuring instruments; checking of reports, forms, records, and comparable data where interpretation is required.

3rd Degree Use of mathematics together with the use of complicated drawings, specifications, charts, tables; various types of precision measuring instruments. Equivalent to one to three years applied trades training in a particular or specialized occupation.

4th Degree Use of advanced trades mathematics, together with the use of complicated drawings, specifications, charts, tables, handbook formulas; all varieties of precision measuring instruments. Equivalent to complete accredited apprenticeship in a recognized trade, craft, or occupation; or equivalent to a two-year technical college education.

5th Degree Use of higher mathematics involved in the application of engineering principles and their performance of related practical operations, together with a comprehensive knowledge of the theories and practices of mechanical, electrical, chemical, civil, or like engineering field. Equivalent to complete four years of technical college or university education.

Source: Developed by the National Metal Trades Association. Reproduced with permission of the American Association of Industrial Management, Springfield, Mass.

Using the Point Manual

Job evaluation under the point system is accomplished by comparing the job descriptions and job specifications, factor by factor, against the various factor-degree descriptions contained in the manual. Each factor in the job being evaluated is then assigned the number of points specified in the manual. Once the points for each factor have been determined from the manual, the total point value for the job as a whole can be calculated. The relative worth of the job is then determined from the total points that have been assigned to that job.

Factor Comparison System

Factor comparison system

Job evaluation system that permits the evaluation process to be accomplished on a factor-by-factor basis by developing a factor comparison scale

A **factor comparison system**, like a point system, permits the job evaluation process to be accomplished on a factor-by-factor basis. It differs from a point system in that the compensable factors of the jobs to be evaluated are compared against the compensable factors of key jobs in the organization, which serve as the job evaluation scale. Key jobs can be defined as those which are important for wage-setting purposes and are widely known in the labour market. Key jobs have the following characteristics:

1. They are important to employees and the organization.

2. They vary in terms of job requirements.

3. They have relatively stable job content.

4. They are used in salary surveys for wage determination.

Key jobs are evaluated against five compensable factors: skill, mental effort, physical effort, responsibility, and working conditions. The result is a ranking of the different factors for each key job. Usually a committee is selected to rank the criteria across key jobs. Committee members must also assign monetary rates of pay to each compensable factor for each key job. Once this task is completed, a factor comparison scale is developed to be used for evaluating all other jobs. The appendix at the end of this chapter shows the calculations of the factor comparison system in greater detail. Highlights in HRM 4 describes how one company used this system to achieve its compensation objectives.

Job Evaluation for Management Positions

WWW

Hay profile method

Job evaluation technique using three factors—knowledge, mental activity, and accountability—to evaluate executive and managerial positions

Because management positions are more difficult to evaluate and involve certain demands not found in jobs at the lower levels, some organizations do not attempt to include them in their job evaluation programs. Those employers that do evaluate these positions can extend their regular evaluation systems to include such positions, or they can develop a separate evaluation system for management positions.

Several systems have been developed especially for evaluating executives, managers, and professionals. One of the better known is the **Hay profile method**, developed by Edward N. Hay. The three broad factors that constitute the evaluation in the "profile" include knowledge (or know-how), mental activity (or problem solving), and accountability.[17] The Hay method uses only three factors because it is assumed that these factors represent the most important aspects of all executive and managerial positions. The profile for each position is developed by determining the percentage value to be assigned to each of the three factors. Jobs are then ranked on the basis of each factor, and point values that make up the profile are assigned to each job on the basis of the percentage-value level at which the job is ranked.

THE COMPENSATION STRUCTURE

Job evaluation systems provide for internal equity and serve as the basis for wage rate determination. They do not in themselves determine the wage rate. The evaluated worth of each job in terms of its rank, class, points, or monetary worth must

Highlights in HRM

4   PROVEN METHODS IN JOB EVALUATION

Star Data Systems of Markham, Ontario, currently employs around 500 people. The company is a growing presence in its market. To facilitate Star Data's growth, the director of human resources implemented a job evaluation program as a means of "paying people fairly and equitably, complying with pay equity legislation, and being able to attract high-caliber candidates."

Following proven models, all employees were required to complete job questionnaires. The process involved having the employees answer questions that related to the compensable factors chosen for the job evaluation process. Of the 92 descriptions prepared, 47 were deemed benchmark positions and 45 were deemed nonbenchmark positions. Examples of benchmark positions at Star Data included marketing coordinator, network support technicians, assistant controller, and shipper/receiver. Among the nonbenchmark positions were exchange reporter, product specialist, and technical sales analyst.

To ensure fairness and equity in the evaluation process, Star Data formed a job evaluation committee comprising employees from various levels in the organization. An outside consultant was hired to train committee members to evaluate positions in an unbiased manner. Job evaluation was used to determine the relative value placed on all positions in the organization. A point-factor method was applied. The focus of the evaluations was the requirements of the job. Each job was measured against four compensable factors: skill, which included the subfactors of knowledge and experience; working conditions, which involved consideration of work environment factors; responsibility, which focused on interpersonal skills/contact/communications, complexity/judgment/problem solving, scope of responsibility, and impact of results; and effort. All of these compensable factors, along with their subfactors, were tailor-made to fit Star Data's business needs.

Weightings were determined for each of the compensable factors in the evaluation process based on the value of the particular factor to the organization, the value placed on the factors by other companies in the industry, the requirements of pay equity legislation, and input from the consulting group. Since working conditions/effort were not deemed to be a deterrent for completing the work, only a 5 percent weight was assigned to that factor; in contrast, skill received a 40 percent weighting.

Having completed their evaluation of the positions, the committee assigned a point total to each position, which allowed a hierarchy to be developed. Based on the point totals, the positions were divided into groups to form twelve salary grades. Using the benchmark positions found in each salary grade, salary and pay information was collected from competitors and other organizations to arrive, via salary surveys, at an average market salary as the midpoint. This methodology ensured that the plan was competitive with the external marketplace.

Star Data, with a new salary grade format, was in a position to analyze internal salaries against the new ranges and to review any pay equity issues. All employees in the organization knew their own salary ranges, their position within the range, and whether salary adjustments would be necessary.

In the future, Star Data will ensure that the system is maintained in a bias-free manner, that the salary administration program remains competitive with the external marketplace, and that salaries are administered fairly and consistently. The company plans to remain competitive by participating in annual surveys and by making necessary salary and range adjustments as conditions warrant. The ultimate responsibility rests with the managers to provide constructive and timely performance reviews and salary increases that are tied directly to performance.

be converted into an hourly, daily, weekly, or monthly wage rate. The compensation tool used to help set wages is the wage and salary survey.

Wage and Salary Surveys

Wage and salary survey

Survey of the wages paid to employees of other employers in the surveying organization's relevant labour market

A **wage and salary survey** is a survey of the wages paid by employers in an organization's relevant labour market—local, regional, or national, depending on the job. The labour market is often defined as the area from which employers obtain certain types of workers. The labour market for office personnel would be local, whereas the labour market for engineers would be national. A wage and salary survey permits an organization to maintain external equity—that is, to pay its employees wages equivalent to the wages similar employees earn in other establishments.

When job evaluation and wage survey data are used jointly, they serve to link the likelihood of both internal and external equity. Although surveys are conducted mainly to gather competitive wage data, they can also collect information on employee benefits or organizational pay practices (e.g., overtime rates or shift differentials).

Collecting Survey Data

While many organizations conduct their own wage and salary surveys, a variety of "preconducted" pay surveys are available to satisfy the requirements of most public and not-for-profit or private organizations.

WWW

Many provinces and cities conduct surveys and make them available to employers. Besides these government surveys, boards of trade and professional associations conduct special surveys tailored to their members' needs. Employers with global operations can purchase international surveys through large consulting firms. The overseas compensation survey offered by TPF&C reports on the payment practices in twenty countries. While all of these third-party surveys provide certain benefits to their users, they also have various limitations. There are two problems with all published surveys: they are not always compatible with the user's jobs; and the user cannot specify which data to collect. To overcome these problems, organizations may collect their own compensation data.

Employer-Initiated Surveys

Employers wishing to conduct their own wage and salary survey must first select the jobs to be used in the survey and identify the organizations with which they actually compete for employees. Since it is not feasible to survey all the jobs in an organization, usually only key jobs—also called benchmark jobs—are used. The survey of key jobs is usually sent to ten or fifteen organizations that represent a valid sample of other employers likely to compete for the employees of the surveying organization. A diversity of organizations should be selected—large and small, public and private, new and established, union and nonunion—since each classification of employer is likely to pay different wage rates for surveyed jobs.[18]

After it has identified the key jobs and the employers to be surveyed, the surveying organization must decide what information to gather on wages, benefit types, and pay policies. For example, when requesting pay data, it is important to specify whether hourly, daily, or weekly pay figures are needed. In addition, those conducting surveys must state whether the wage data are needed for new hires or for senior employees. Precisely defining the compensation data needed will greatly increase the accuracy of the information received and the number of purposes for which it can be used. Once the survey data are tabulated, the compensation structure can be completed.

Wage Surveys and Virtual Jobs

Jobs are constantly changing to match the dynamic needs of the organization and its customers. As a result, compensation specialists are asking questions like these: "How do you conduct salary surveys when there are no stable jobs?" "How do you match jobs when there are no jobs to match?" "How should internal and external pay equity be addressed?" These questions can be answered by developing creative pay surveys to match the organization's compensation strategy. For example, when organizations pay on the basis of employee competencies and skills, pay surveys will need to address the compensation of core competencies that span all work and jobs. Maturity curves can also be used to compensate for ever-changing job content. These have traditionally been used to compensate scientific and technical personnel, but they can also be used to compensate employees on the basis of a relationship between market value and experience (see Chapter 10).

The Wage Curve

OBJECTIVE 5

Wage curve

Curve in a scattergram representing the relationship between relative worth of jobs and wage rates

The relationship between the relative worth of jobs and their wage rates can be represented by means of a **wage curve**. This curve can indicate the rates currently being paid for jobs in an organization, or the new rates resulting from job evaluation, or the rates for similar jobs currently being paid by other organizations in the labour market. A curve can be constructed graphically by preparing a scattergram consisting of a series of dots that represent the current wage rates. As shown in Figure 9.6, a freehand curve is then drawn through the cluster of dots in such a way as to leave a roughly equal number of dots above and below the curve. The wage curve can be relatively straight, or it can be curved. This curve can be used to determine the relationship between the value of a job and its wage rate at any given point on the line.

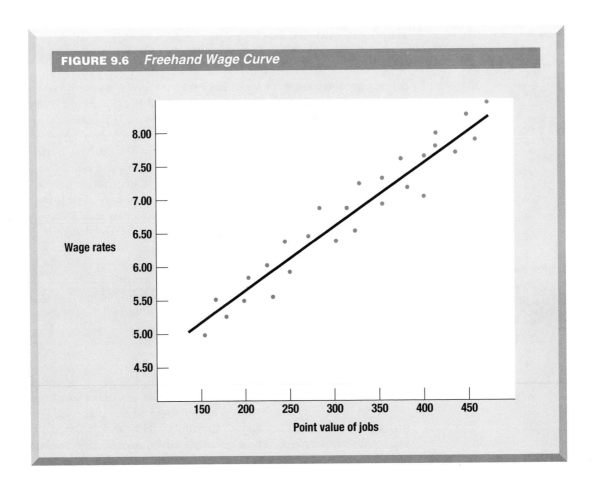

FIGURE 9.6   *Freehand Wage Curve*

Pay Grades

Pay grades

Groups of jobs within a particular class that are paid the same rate for rate range

From an administrative standpoint, it is generally preferable to group jobs into **pay grades** and to pay all jobs within a particular grade the same rate or rate range. When the classification system of job evaluation is used, jobs are grouped into grades as part of the evaluation process. When the point and factor comparison systems are used, however, pay grades must be established at selected intervals that represent either the point or the evaluated monetary value of these jobs. Figure 9.7 illustrates a series of pay grades designated along the horizontal axis at 50 point intervals.

The grades within a wage structure may vary in number. The number is determined by such factors as the slope of the wage curve, the number and distribution of the jobs within the structure, and the organization's wage administration and promotion policies. The number utilized should be sufficient to permit difficulty levels to be distinguished, but not so great as to make the distinction between two adjoining grades insignificant.

Rate Ranges

A single rate can be created for each pay grade (see Figure 9.7), but it is more common to provide a range of rates for each pay grade. The rate ranges can be the

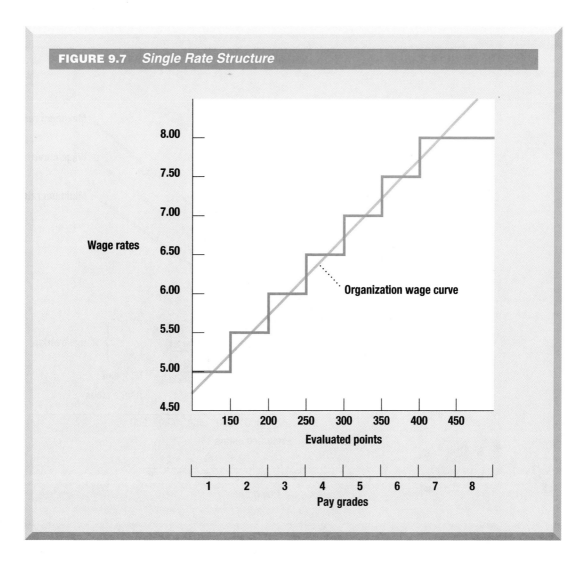

FIGURE 9.7   *Single Rate Structure*

same for each grade, or they can be proportionately greater for each successive grade (see Figure 9.8). Rate ranges constructed on the latter basis provide a greater incentive for employees to accept a promotion to a job in a higher grade.

Rate ranges generally are divided into a series of steps that permit employees to receive increases up to the maximum rate for the range on the basis of merit or seniority or a combination of the two. Most salary structures provide for the ranges of adjoining pay grades to overlap. The purpose of the overlap is to permit an employee with experience to earn as much as or more than a person with less experience in the next-higher job classification.

The final step in setting up a wage structure is to determine the appropriate pay grade into which each job should be placed on the basis of its evaluated worth. Traditionally, this worth has been determined on the basis of job requirements, without regard to the performance of the person in that job. Under this system, the performance of those who exceed the requirements of a job can be acknowledged by merit increases within the grade range or by promotion to a job in the next-higher pay grade.

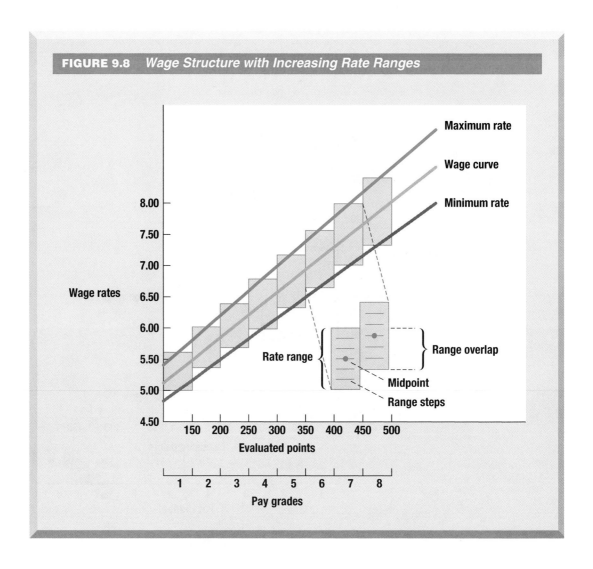

FIGURE 9.8 *Wage Structure with Increasing Rate Ranges*

Organizations may pay individuals above the maximum of the pay range when employees have high seniority or when promotional opportunities are scarce. Wages paid above the range maximum are called *red circle rates*. Because these rates are exceptions to the pay structure, employers often "freeze" these rates until all ranges are shifted upward through market wage adjustments.

Alternatives to Traditional Job-Based Pay

Job-based systems still predominate in employee compensation. Unfortunately, these systems often fail to reward employees for their skills or for the knowledge they possess; nor do they always encourage them to learn new job-related skills. Also, job-based pay systems may not reinforce an organizational culture that stresses employee involvement, or provide increased employee flexibility to meet overall production or service requirements. For these reasons, organizations such as Frito-Lay, Northern Telecom, Sherwin-Williams, and Honeywell have introduced skill-based pay plans.

WWW

Skill-based pay

Pay based on how many skills employees have or how many jobs they can perform

Skill-based pay, also referred to as knowledge-based pay, pay for knowledge, competency-based pay, or multiskill-based pay, compensates employees according to the different skills or increased knowledge they possess rather than the specific job categories they belong to. Whatever they are called, these pay plans encourage employees to earn higher base wages by learning and performing a wider variety of skills (or jobs) or by displaying an array of competencies that can be applied to a variety of the organization's requirements. Organizations grant an increase in pay after each skill has been mastered and can be demonstrated according to a predetermined standard. Skill-based pay is often used where employees are part of autonomous work groups or employee teams. Skill-based pay systems represent a fundamental change in management attitudes regarding how work should be organized and how employees should be paid for their efforts.[19] The most frequently cited benefits of skill-based pay include these: greater productivity, increased employee learning and commitment to work, improved staffing flexibility to meet production or service demands, and reduced effects of absenteeism and turnover (since managers can assign employees where and when needed).[20] Skill-based pay also encourages employees to acquire training when the organization needs new or updated skills.

Unfortunately, skill-based pay plans have some long-term drawbacks. Some plans limit the amount of compensation employees can earn, regardless of the new skills or competencies they acquire. Thus, after achieving the top wage, employees may be reluctant to continue their educational training. Furthermore, employees

Continuous training and upgrading of skills has become a necessity in today's labour market.

can become discouraged when they acquire new abilities but find there are no higher-rated jobs to which they can transfer. Unless all employees have the opportunity to increase their pay by attaining new skills, employees who are not given this opportunity may feel disgruntled.

Broadbanding

Organizations that adopt skill-based pay systems often use broadbanding to structure their compensation payments to employees. Broadbanding simply collapses many traditional salary grades into a few wide salary bands.[21] Banding encourages lateral skill-building; it also addresses the need to pay employees performing multiple jobs with different skill-level requirements. According to one authority, "Broadbands help eliminate the obsession with grades and, instead, encourage employees to move to jobs where they can develop in their careers and add value to the organization."[22] When organizations pay employees through broadbands, they consider job responsibilities, individual skills and competencies, and career mobility patterns when assigning employees to those bands. About 20 percent of Canadian organizations use broadbanding, and another 32 percent are considering it.[23] Current trends in compensation are discussed in Reality Check.

GOVERNMENTAL REGULATION OF COMPENSATION

Compensation management, like the other areas of HRM, is subject to provincial and federal regulations. In each province there is an employment standards act that establishes minimum requirements with respect to wages, hours of work, and overtime. Provincial as well as federal minimum requirements can be obtained by contacting the appropriate federal or provincial office.

The Canada Labour Code

Part III of the Canada Labour Code and the Canada Labour Standards Regulations set minimum labour standards for all employees and employers in works or undertakings that fall within federal jurisdiction, including interprovincial highway and rail transportation, pipelines, telecommunications, air transport, fishing, and banking. Federal Crown corporations are covered by the Canada Labour Code, but federal public service employees are not. Employees working under these classifications are subject to a forty-hour workweek. Managerial and professional employees are not covered by the hours-of-work provisions and may be required to exceed those hours. Revisions are constantly being made to these standards; HR managers must keep abreast of these changes to ensure compliance in the workplace.

Employment Standards Acts

The Employment Standards Acts of each province and territory establish minimum standards with a view to protecting both employees and employers in certain employment situations. Collective agreements are permitted to override the provisions of these acts as long as employees are not being provided with less than what the acts have stipulated, and as long as these overrides benefit the employee.

Reality CHECK

TRENDS IN COMPENSATION

WWW

According to Suzanne Payette, Director of Workplace Information, Human Resources Development Canada, the most dramatic recent change in compensation has been the move away from the label of compensation management to talking about a total rewards approach. The American Compensation Association, a well-known organization with a strong brand, just renamed itself World at Work. The total rewards perspective recognizes that the organization context, the work content, and opportunities for personal development are part of rewards. People look for challenge, not only money. Organizations must provide work environments that attract, motivate, and retain, because money alone does not do this, and money can be matched. Money is important, but it is not the sole element of the total rewards package.

The use of variable compensation is on the rise. More and more organizations are offering it, and it is forming part of compensation for more and more employees. About 80 percent of all Canadian organizations (about 95 percent in the private sector) have some kind of variable compensation plan. The most prevalent of such plans is the bonus (individual, team, or organization). As Suzanne states: "The complexities and variations in the plans make them unique or specific to each organization. Another trend is to rewarding teams, not just individuals, and the performance target to be achieved reflects this. For example, the goal might be that 90 percent of customers report a satisfaction level of 90 percent, regardless of who is servicing them." A close second, and increasing rapidly, is the various kinds of stock ownership plans. Stock ownership and stock options make employees more productive and help companies retain workers with critical skills.

The increasing use of measurement is another trend: "A lot of lip service was paid to measurement in the past, but now the amount of information available is greater, and the ability to crunch numbers faster is enhanced. We have the tools to measure, so we are measuring more. The increased use of benchmarking is another trend, and this results in the cross-fertilization of general organizational practices."

The detailed measurement of employee performance is not controversial, provided that employees perceive that the program is fair. The key to a fair system lies in determining how each unit in the organization contributes to the organization's overall targets. Obviously, this easier in some situations than in others. The key is to involve employees in identifying relevant measures, determining methods of assessment, and implementing the system. Employees need to believe that the system is designed and being implemented fairly. Their trust in it is best secured through an open book approach and through employee participation.

Employers who operate in more than one province must become fully informed of the different requirements that exist in each province. This information is generally available on the Internet.

Each province's act contains a provision that stipulates that an overtime rate of 1.5 times the base rate must be paid for all hours worked in excess of the set minimum prescribed in the province. For example, if an employee works 45 hours in a province that legislates the minimum workweek as 40 hours, he or she is entitled to overtime for the extra five hours at 1.5 times his or her base rate. Particular groups, including lawyers, doctors, engineers, and managers, are exempt from overtime requirements.

Child Labour Provisions

In all provinces, legislation has been passed to prevent the abuse of children in work situations. For instance, in Ontario, where some of the strictest laws exist, persons under sixteen cannot work during school hours unless they have completed secondary schooling or its equivalent. The province has also legislated the following age restrictions:

MINIMUM AGE	OPERATION
16	Logging operation or mining
15	Factory or construction work
14	Any industry
18	Underground or surface mines

People under sixteen cannot be employed in workplaces to which the public has access from 9 p.m. to 6 a.m.

Other Legislation

Employment equity is under federal jurisdiction for all federally regulated companies, as well as for companies not covered under the Canada Labour Code that have dealings with federally legislated companies. Pay equity is covered provincially where applicable. As we discussed in Chapter 2, legislation relating to employment equity and pay equity is designed to ensure that fair employment practices are applied to all members of designated groups.

SIGNIFICANT COMPENSATION RULES

As with other HR activities, compensation management operates in a dynamic environment. For example, as managers strive to reward employees in a fair manner, they must consider controls over labour costs, legal issues regarding wages paid to male and female employees, and internal pay equity concerns. Each of these concerns is highlighted in four important compensation issues: equal pay for comparable value, wage rate compression, low-salary budgets, and two-tier wage systems. Only three are discussed: equal pay for comparable value; measuring comparability, and wage rate compression...

Equal Pay for Comparable Value

One of the most important gender issues in compensation is equal pay for equal value. The issue stems from the fact that jobs performed predominantly by women are paid less than those performed by men. This practice results in what critics term institutionalized sex discrimination, in the sense that women are receiving less pay for jobs that are different from but comparable in worth to those performed by men. The issue of **comparable value** goes beyond whether women and men should be paid the same for doing the same work—that is, whether a female nurse should be paid the same as a male nurse. Of course she should. Rather, the argument for comparable value is that jobs held by women are not compensated the same as those held by men, even though both job types may contribute equally to the organization's success.

Comparable value

The concept that male and female jobs that are dissimilar, but equal in terms of value or worth to the employer, should be paid the same

Measuring Comparability

Advocates of comparable value argue that men's and women's wage rates are so different because occupations traditionally held by women have traditionally been undervalued. To remedy this situation, they propose that wages be made equal for jobs that are "somehow" of equal value to the organization. Unfortunately, there is no consensus on a comparable value standard by which to evaluate jobs, nor is there agreement on whether present job evaluation techniques can remedy the problem.[24] Indeed, organizations may dodge the comparable value issue by using one job evaluation system for clerical and secretarial jobs and another system for other jobs. The advocates of comparable value also contend that current job evaluation techniques simply continue the differences in pay between the sexes. However, others believe that job evaluation systems can be designed to measure different types of jobs, in the same way that apples and oranges can be compared (see Figure 9.9).

The argument over comparable value is likely to remain a HR issue for many years to come. Unanswered questions such as the following will keep the issue alive:

1. If comparable value is adopted, who will determine the value of jobs, and by what means?

2. How much would comparable value cost employers?

3. Would comparable value reduce the wage gap between men and women caused by labour market supply-and-demand forces?

4. Would comparable value reduce the number of employment opportunities for women?

Organizations that have implemented comparable value policies have raised women's wages. In one public sector study of the impact of comparable value on men's and women's earnings, the researcher concluded that when comparable value is implemented through special wage increases, public sector wages move ahead of local prevailing wages and male/female wage differentials are greatly reduced.[25]

Wage Rate Compression

Wage rate compression

Compression of differentials between job classes, particularly the differential between hourly workers and their managers

Earlier, when we discussed the compensation structure, it was noted that the main purpose of pay differentials between the wage classes is to provide an incentive for employees to prepare for and accept more demanding jobs. Unfortunately, this incentive is being significantly reduced by **wage rate compression**—the reduc-

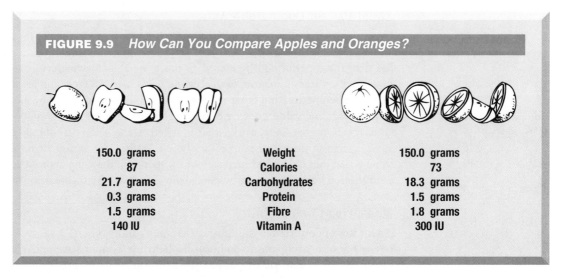

FIGURE 9.9   *How Can You Compare Apples and Oranges?*

150.0 grams	Weight	150.0 grams
87	Calories	73
21.7 grams	Carbohydrates	18.3 grams
0.3 grams	Protein	1.5 grams
1.5 grams	Fibre	1.8 grams
140 IU	Vitamin A	300 IU

Sources: M. Belcourt, "Human Resource Management" in *Introduction to Canadian Business*, edited by J. Plinuissen (Toronto: McGraw-Hill Ryerson and Captus Press, 1994), 410.

tion of differences between job classes. Wage rate compression is largely an internal pay equity concern. The problem arises when employees perceive that there is too narrow a difference between their compensation and that of colleagues in lower-rated jobs.

HR professionals acknowledge that wage rate compression is a widespread organizational problem that affects diverse occupational groups: white-collar and blue-collar workers, technical and professional employees, and managerial personnel. It can cause low employee morale, which in turn can lead to reduced employee performance, higher absenteeism and turnover, and even delinquent behaviour such as employee theft.

There is no single cause of wage rate compression. It can occur when unions negotiate across-the-board increases for hourly employees but managerial personnel are not granted corresponding wage differentials. These increases often result in part from the COLAs provided for in collective agreements. Other inequities have resulted from the scarcity of applicants in computer, engineering, and other professional and technical fields. Job applicants in these fields are often offered starting salaries not far below those paid to employees with considerable experience and seniority. Wage rate compression often results when organizations grant pay adjustments for lower-rated jobs without providing commensurate adjustments for occupations at the top of the job hierarchy.

Identifying wage rate compression and its causes is far easier than implementing organizational policies to alleviate its effects. Organizations that want to minimize the problem can incorporate the following ideas into their pay policies:

1. Give larger compensation increases to more senior employees.

2. Emphasize pay for performance, and reward employees for merit.

3. Limit the hiring of new applicants seeking exorbitant salaries.

4. Design the pay structure to allow a wide spread between hourly and supervisory jobs, or between new hires and senior employees.

5. Provide equity adjustments for selected employees hardest hit by pay compression.

Other options include permitting more flexibility in employees' work schedules, including four-day work weeks and work at home.

SUMMARY

 When establishing compensation programs, organizations of any size must consider specific goals—for instance, employee retention, compensation distribution, and adherence to a budget. Compensation must both reward employees for past efforts (pay for performance) and motivate their future efforts. Employees' attitudes toward a pay program are affected by their perceptions of its fairness, both within the organization and relative to other organizations. Organizations must heed their employees' concerns about fairness while remaining competitive. When an organization can attract qualified employees and at the same time control labour costs, it is more likely to remain viable in the domestic and international markets.

 How compensation payments are determined and administered can significantly affect employee productivity and the achievement of organizational goals. *Internal* influences on wage rates include the employer's compensation policy, the worth of the job, the performance of the employee, and the employer's ability to pay. *External* factors include labour market conditions, area wage rates, the cost of living, the outcomes of collective bargaining, and legal requirements.

 Organizations use one of four basic job evaluation techniques to determine the relative worth of jobs. A *job ranking system* arranges jobs in numerical order according to the importance of the employee's duties and responsibilities. A *job classification system* slots jobs into pre-established grades. Higher-grade jobs involve heavier responsibilities, more difficult working conditions, and more extensive duties. A *point system* of job evaluation uses a point scheme based on these compensable job factors: skill, effort, responsibility,

and working conditions. The more compensable factors a job possesses, the more points are assigned to it. Jobs with higher accumulated points are considered more valuable to the organization. A *factor comparison system* evaluates jobs on a factor-by-factor basis against key jobs in the organization.

 Wage surveys determine the external equity of jobs. Data obtained from surveys help an organization establish its wage policy while ensuring that it does not pay more, or less, than needed for jobs in the relevant labour market.

 The wage structure is composed of a wage curve, pay grades, and rate ranges. It depicts graphically the pay rates assigned to jobs within each pay grade. Pay grades represent the grouping of similar jobs on the basis of their relative worth. Each pay grade includes a rate range. Rate ranges have a midpoint and minimum and maximum pay rates for all jobs in the pay grade.

 Compensation is regulated by the federal and provincial governments through the Canada Labour Code, employment standards acts, child labour provisions, and employment equity/pay equity legislation.

 Comparable value policies seek to overcome the fact that jobs held by women are compensated at a lower rate than those performed by men. This happens even though the respective jobs of men and women may contribute equally to organizational productivity. *Wage rate compression* largely affects managerial and senior employees. It typically arises when the pay given to new employees or the wage increases gained through collective agreements close the pay gap betwen higher and lower ranks in an organization.

KEY TERMS

comparable value
consumer price index (CPI)
escalator clauses
factor comparison system
Hay profile method
hourly work

job classification system
job evaluation
job ranking system
pay equity
pay grades
piecework

point system
real wages
skill-based pay
wage and salary survey
wage curve
wage rate compression

DISCUSSION QUESTIONS

1. Tomax Corporation has 400 employees and wants to develop a compensation policy that corresponds to its dynamic business strategy. The company wishes to employ a high-quality workforce that is capable of responding to a competitive business environment. Suggest different compensation objectives to match Tomax's business goals.

2. Since employees vary in terms of their job performance, would it not be more feasible to determine the wage rate for each employee on the basis of each employee's relative worth to the organization?

3. What is job evaluation? Describe the two nonquantitative and two quantitative approaches to job evaluation.

4. Describe the basic steps in conducting a wage and salary survey. What are some factors to consider?

5. One of the problems with granting wage increases on a percentage basis is that the lowest-paid employees, who are having the most trouble making ends meet, get the smallest increases, while the highest-paid employees get the largest increases. Is this objection valid?

6. Federal laws governing compensation raise important issues for both employers and employees. Discuss the following:
   a. The effects of mandatory overtime
   b. The effects of raising the minimum wage

7. What are some of the problems with developing a pay system based on equal pay for comparable value?

WWW

CANADA POST

Canada Post Corporation has 67,000 workers, which makes it one of Canada's largest employers. In 1997 it revised its job evaluation system for postmasters and assistants. The old system, which had been in place since 1976, did not take into account changes that had arisen since 1981, when Canada Post became a Crown corporation.

A human resources consulting firm, Watson Wyatt Worldwide, was hired to assist with the entire process. According to Linda Tremblay of Organization Planning and Development, Canada Post, the job evaluation system was revised to incorporate employee input, to be responsive to federal pay equity legislation, and—most importantly—to reflect corporate culture and values.

The new job evaluation system measured the content and relative value of jobs. The system evaluated jobs according to their "typical" or "normal" components—that is, tasks that were done on a regular basis. These compensable factors were a function of the job itself, not of the performance of the person doing the job.

The four factors considered and their relative weights were as follows:

A   Responsibilities—What type of responsibilities does the job entail?   60%
B.   Skills—What particular skills are needed to accomplish the job?   25
C   Working Conditions—What working conditions apply to the job?   11
D.   Effort—What amount of effort does the job require?   <u>4</u>
     Total   100%

An example of an item under C: Working Conditions:

This factor measures the surroundings or physical conditions under which your work must be done and the extent to which they make your job disagreeable. Consider whether elements such as those listed are present, and the relative amount and continuity of exposure:
Place a checkmark besides all those that apply:

- adverse weather conditions
- confined work space
- dirt/dust
- fumes
- inadequate lighting
- lack of privacy
- noisy conditions
- temperature extremes
- verbal abuse/public harassment
- other

Job evaluation criteria, such as in the above example, were used in each of the four areas, and summarized as below:

JOB EVALUATION CRITERIA

Compensable factors	Components
Responsibilities	Internal and External contacts
	Decision making
	Supervision of employees
	Responsibility for Property Maintenance
	Responsibility for Rural Routes, Suburban Services and/or Stage Services
	Points of Call
	Responsibility for Contractor Invoices
	Responsibility for a Till and/or Authorized Allowance
Skills	Knowledge areas (such as budget process, collective agreement, contacted services in mail operations or property management, financial practices, procedures knowledge, product knowledge, primary sortation, final sortation, sales and customer service techniques, personnel management techniques)
	Job Related experience
Working conditions	Physical Work Environment
	Travel
Effort	Physical Effort
	Multiple Demands

Employees completed the Job Evaluation Questionnaire for their own jobs. The completed questionnaires were then reviewed by supervisors, managers, and human resources staff.

Total points were then allocated to each job, which corresponded to one of six job bands. Collective agreement negotiations then were used to set the rates of pay for each of the six job bands.

Source: Interview and correspondence with Linda Tremblay, Canada Post Corporation.

Questions

1. What type of job evaluation system did Canada Post use?

2. What are the advantages and limitations of this system?

3. If you were asked to review both the questionnaire and the process used to obtain the job information, what recommendations would you make?

CASE 2

WWW

PAY DECISIONS AT PERFORMANCE SPORTS

Katie Perkins's career objective while attending Durham College was to earn a degree in small business management and then start her own business. Her ultimate desire was to combine her love of sports with her strong interest in marketing and start a mail-order golf equipment business aimed specifically at beginning golfers.

WWW

In February 1998, after extensive development of a strategic business plan and a loan of $75,000 from the Federal Business Development Bank, she established Performance Sports. Based on a marketing plan that stressed fast delivery, error-free customer service, and deep discount pricing, the company grew rapidly. At present, Performance Sports employs sixteen people: eight customer service reps earning between $9.75 and $11.25 per hour; four shipping and receiving associates earning between $8.50 and $9.50 per hour; two clerical staff, each earning $8.75 per hour; an assistant manager earning $13.10 per hour, and a general manager with a wage of $15.00 per hour. Both the manager and the assistant manager are former customer service representatives.

Perkins intends to create a new managerial position, purchasing agent, to handle the complex duties of purchasing golf equipment from the company's many suppliers. Also, the mail order catalogue from Performance Sports will soon be expanded to handle a complete line of tennis equipment. Since the position of purchasing agent is new, Perkins isn't sure how much to pay this person. She wants to employ someone with between five and eight years' experience in sports equipment purchasing.

While attending an equipment manufacturers' convention in Vancouver, Perkins learns that a competitor, East Valley Sports, pays its customer service reps on a pay-for-knowledge basis. Intrigued by this approach, Perkins asks her assistant manager, George Balkin, to research the pros and cons of this payment strategy. This request has become a priority, since only last week two customer service representatives expressed dissatisfaction with their hourly wage. Both complained that they felt underpaid relative to the large amount of skills and knowledge needed to provide excellent customer service.

Questions

1. What factors should Perkins consider when setting the wage for the purchasing agent position? What resources are available for her to consult when establishing this wage?

2. Suggest some advantages and disadvantages of a pay-for-knowledge policy for Performance Sports.

3. Suggest a new payment plan for the customer service representatives.

CAREER COUNSEL

To find out what compensation you can expect to receive in your career, visit the Managing Human Resources website (**belcourt.nelson.com**).

USING THE INTERNET

WWW

Summaries of compensation reports can be found at **www.conferenceboard.ca**, the website of the Conference Board of Canada.

Human Resources Development Canada publishes summaries of wage settlements. You can find the wage rates of specific jobs in your region at **www.hrdc-drhc.gc.ca**.

The University of British Columbia has posted its job evaluation system at **www.hr.ubc.ca**.

Every province has posted its Employment Standards Act on the Web, often under the Department of Labour, or "Labour Laws," or "Employment Standards." For Ontario, go to this address: **www.gov.on.ca/LAB/es/ese.htm**.

Management consulting firms often provide summary compensation data. Check these sites: **www.kpmg.com**, **www.watsonwyatt.com**, **www.hjewittassoc.com**, **www.wmmercer.com**, and **www.haygroup.com**.

NOTES AND REFERENCES

1. Robert Kreitner and Angelo Kinicki, *Organizational Behavior*, 3rd ed. (Burr Ridge, Ill: Irwin, 1995), Chapter 6.
2. Peter V. LeBlanc and Paul W. Hurley, "How American Workers See the Rewards of Work," *Compensation and Benefits Review* 30, no. 1 (January–February 1998): 24–8.
3. Kathryn Tyler, "Compensation Strategies Can Foster Lateral Moves," *HRMagazine* 43, no. 5 (April 1998): 64–71.
4. N.B. Carlyle and S. Payette, *Compensation Planning Outlook 1998*, Conference Board of Canada, October 1997.
5. Edward G. Vogeley and Louise J. Schaeffer, "Link Employee Pay to Competencies and Objectives," *HRMagazine* 40, no. 10 (October 1995): 75–81.
6. Vogeley and Schaeffer, "Link Employee Pay": 75.
7. Terry M. Newman and Frank Krzystofiak, "Value-Chain Compensation," *Compensation and Benefits Review* 30, no. 3 (May–June 1998): 60–6.
8. For frequently referenced books on strategic compensation planning, see Richard J. Long, *Compensation in Canada* (Scarborough, Ont.: ITP Nelson, 1998) and Edward E. Lawler III, *Strategic Pay: Aligning Organizational Strategies and Pay Systems* (San Francisco: Jossey-Bass, 1990); Bill Leonard, "New Ways to Pay Employees," *HRMagazine* 39, no. 2 (February 1994): 61.
9. "Stay for Pay: A Retention Solution," *HRFocus* 75, no. 9 (September 1998): 57.
10. For one of the classic articles on equity theory, see J. Stacey Adams, "Integrity in Social Exchange," in L. Berkowitz, ed., *Advances in Experimental Social Psychology*.
11. Victor H. Vroom, *Work and Motivation* (San Francisco: Jossey-Bass, 1994). This landmark book, originally published in 1964, integrates the work of hundreds of researchers seeking to explain choice of work, job satisfaction, and job performance.
12. Andrew DuBrin, *Fundamentals of Organizational Behavior: An Applied Approach* (Cincinnati, Ohio: South-Western Publishing, 1997).
13. George T. Milkovich and Jerry M. Newman, *Compensation*, 5th ed. (Chicago: Irwin, 1996): 11–14.
14. Glenn Bassett, "Merit Pay Increases Are a Mistake," *Compensation and Benefits Review* 26, no. 2 (March–April 1994): 20–2.
15. A. Davies, "Who Wants to Be a Millionaire?" *Benefits Canada* 24, no. 1 (January 2000): 7.
16. *CPI Detailed Report*, May 1996 (Washington, D.C.: U.S. Department of Labor, Bureau of Labor Statistics, May 1996): 94.
17. Richard I. Henderson, *Compensation Management*, 7th ed. (Reston, Va.: Reston Publishing, 1996).
18. Robert L. Heneman, "Finding the Right Salary Survey," *HRFocus* 75, no. 7 (July 1998): 10.
19. Darrell J. Cira and Ellen R. Benjamin, "Competency-Based Pay: A Concept in Evolution," *Compensation and*

Benefits Review, September–October 1998: 21–8; see also Gail Grib and Susan O'Donnell, "Pay Plans That Reward Employee Achievement," *HRMagazine* 40, no. 7 (July 1995): 49–50; Vogeley and Schaeffer, "Link Employee Pay."

20. Edward E. Lawler III, Gerald E. Ledford, Jr., and Lei Chang, "Who Uses Skill-Based Pay and Why?" *Compensation and Benefits Review* 25, no. 2 (March–April 1993): 22–6.

21. Susan Haslett, "Broadbanding: A Strategic Tool for Organizational Change," *Compensation and Benefits Review* 27, no. 6 (May 1995): 40–6; Gary I. Bergel, "Choosing the Right Pay Delivery System to Fit Banding," *Compensation and Benefits Review* 25, no. 4 (July–August 1994): 34–8;

"Despite Success, Companies Are Skeptical about Broadbanding," *HRFocus* 72, no. 5 (May 1995): 14.

22. Larry Reissman, "Nine Common Myths about Broadbands," *HRMagazine* 40, no. 8 (August 1995): 79–86.

23. Carlyle and Payette, *Compensation Planning Outlook*, 3.

24. Susan Gardiner, "Implementing Comparable Worth/Pat Equity: Experience of Cutting Edge States," *Public Personnel Management* 27, no. 4 (Winter 1998): 475–89.

25. G. Hundley, "The Effects of Comparable Worth in the Public Sector on Public/Private Occupational Relative Wages," *Journal of Human Resources* 28, no. 2 (Spring 1993): 310–40. See also Elaine Sorensen, "Effect of Comparable Worth Policies on Earnings," *Industrial Relations* 26, no. 3 (Fall 1987): 227–39.

JOB EVALUATION: THE FACTOR COMPARISON SYSTEM

The factor comparison system is a quantitative technique for evaluating jobs. The process is geared toward developing a factor comparison scale to evaluate, and pay, all jobs in the organization. Developing the system is a complex task, but once that has been done it is relatively easy to use. There are four basic steps in developing and using a factor comparison scale: (1) select and rank key jobs, (2) allocate wage rates for key jobs across compensable factors, (3) set up a factor comparison scale, and (4) evaluate all other jobs.

Step 1: *Select and rank key jobs on the basis of compensable factors.* Key jobs are normally ranked against five factors: skill, mental effort, physical effort, responsibility, and working conditions. It is normal for the ranking of each key job to be different because of the different requirements of jobs. The ranking of three key jobs is shown in Figure A.1. Usually, a factor comparison scale comprises fifteen to twenty key jobs.

Step 2: *Allocate wage rates for key jobs.* Then determine the proportion of the current wage being paid on a key job to each of the factors of which the job is composed. Thus, the proportion of a key job's wage rate allocated to the skill factor will depend on the importance of skill in comparison with mental effort, physical effort, responsibility, and working conditions. It is important that the factor rankings in step 1 be consistent with the wage apportionment rankings in step 2. Figure A.2 illustrates how the rate for three key jobs has been allocated according to the relative importance of the basic factors that make up these jobs.

Step 3: *Set up the factor comparison scale.* After the wages for each key job have been apportioned across the factors, the data are displayed on a factor comparison scale (see Figure A.3). The location of the key jobs on the scale, and the compensable factors for these jobs, provide the benchmarks against which other jobs are evaluated.

Step 4: *Evaluate all other jobs.* We are now ready to compare other jobs against the key jobs in the columns of Figure A.3. As an example of how the scale is used, let's assume that the job of screw machine operator is to be evaluated by means of the factor comparison scale. Having compared the skill factor for screw machine operator with the skill factors of the key jobs on the table, we decide that the skill demand of the job places it about halfway between those of storekeeper and punch press operator. The job is therefore placed at the $5.55 point on the scale. The same procedure is used to place the job at the appropriate point on the scale for the remaining factors.

FIGURE A.1 *Ranking Key Jobs by Compensable Factors*

JOB	SKILL	MENTAL EFFORT	PHYSICAL EFFORT	RESPONSIBILITY	WORKING CONDITIONS
Machinist planner	1	1	3	1	3
Punch press operator	2	2	1	3	2
Storekeeper	3	3	2	2	1

FIGURE A.2 *Wage Apportionment for Each Factor*

JOB	TOTAL	SKILL	MENTAL EFFORT	PHYSICAL EFFORT	RESPONSIBILITY	WORKING CONDITIONS
Machinist planner	$13.00	$6.50 (1)	$3.50 (1)	$0.50 (3)	$1.60 (1)	$0.90 (3)
Punch press operator	11.30	6.20 (2)	1.60 (2)	1.00 (1)	0.80 (3)	1.70 (2)
Storekeeper	9.85	4.90 (3)	1.30 (3)	0.70 (2)	1.20 (2)	1.75 (1)

Using the Factor Comparison Scale

The evaluated worth of the jobs added to the scale is computed by adding up the money values for each factor as determined by where the job has been placed on the scale for each factor. Thus the evaluated worth of the screw machine operator would be determined by totalling the monetary value for each factor as follows:

Skill	$5.55
Mental effort	1.35
Physical effort	0.82
Responsibility	0.60
Working conditions	<u>1.40</u>
	<u>$9.72</u>

FIGURE A.3 *Human Resource Competency Model*

HOURLY RATE	SKILL	MENTAL EFFORT	PHYSICAL EFFORT	RESPONSIBILITY	WORKING CONDITIONS
6.50	• Machinist planner				
6.25	• Punch press operator				
6.00					
5.75					
5.50	• *Screw mach. operator*				
5.25					
5.00	• Storekeeper				
4.75					
4.50					
4.25					
4.00					
3.75					
3.50		• Machinist planner			
3.25					
3.00					
2.75					
2.50					
2.25					
2.00					• Storekeeper
1.75		• Punch press operator		• Machinist planner	• Punch press operator
1.50		• *Screw mach. operator*		• Storekeeper	• *Screw mach. operator*
1.25		• Storekeeper		• Punch press operator	• Machinist planner
1.00			• Punch press operator	• *Screw mach. operator*	
0.75			• *Screw mach. operator*		
0.50			• Storekeeper • Machinist planner		

Note: If this scale contained the fifteen to twenty key jobs that typically constitute a factor comparison scale, the gaps between jobs on the scale would be reduced substantially.

INCENTIVE

REWARDS

After studying this chapter, you should be able to

OBJECTIVE 1
Discuss the basic requirements for the successful implementation of incentive programs.

OBJECTIVE 2
List the types of incentive plans for nonmanagement employees, and the reasons for implementing them.

OBJECTIVE 3
Explain why merit raises may fail to motivate employees adequately, and discuss ways to increase their motivational value.

OBJECTIVE 4
State and identify the advantage of each of the principal methods used to compensate salespeople.

OBJECTIVE 5
Differentiate how gains may be shared with employees under the Scanlon, Rucker, Improshare, and earnings-at-risk gainsharing systems.

OBJECTIVE 6
Explain what profit-sharing plans are and the advantages and disadvantages of these programs.

OBJECTIVE 7
Describe the main types of ESOP plans, and discuss the advantages of ESOPs to employers and employees.

I n the previous chapter we emphasized that the worth of a job is a significant factor in determining the pay rate for that job. However, pay based solely on this measure may fail to motivate employees to perform to their full capacity. Unmotivated employees are likely to meet only minimum performance standards. Recognizing this fact, organizations such as CIBC, Delta Inns, and BFGoodrich offer some form of incentive to workers.[1] These organizations are attempting to get more motivational mileage out of employee compensation by tying it more clearly to organizational objectives and employee performance.

WWW

Managers at Magma Copper Company have noted that incentive linked with output "causes workers to more fully apply their skills and knowledge to their jobs while encouraging them to work together as a team." Marshall Campbell, vice-president of human resources at Magma, remarks, "If we increase production of ore extraction, and tie output to employee compensation, we operate with lower costs and that makes us more competitive in the national and international marketplace."[2] In their attempts to raise productivity, managers are focusing on the many variables that help determine the effectiveness of pay as a motivator.

THE PAY-FOR-PERFORMANCE STANDARD

Pay-for-performance standard

Standard by which managers tie compensation to employee effort and performance

WWW

To raise productivity and reduce labour costs in today's competitive economic environment, organizations are increasingly setting compensation objectives based on a **pay-for-performance standard**. It is agreed that managers must tie at least some reward to employee effort and performance. Without this standard, motivation to perform with greater effort will be low, resulting in higher wage costs to the organization.

The term "pay for performance" refers to a wide range of compensation options, including merit-based pay, bonuses, salary commissions, job and pay banding, team or group incentives, and various gainsharing programs.[3] Each of these compensation systems seeks to differentiate between the pay of average performers and that of outstanding performers. When Star Data Systems of Markham, Ontario, implemented its compensation program, its objectives were "to fairly and equitably manage salaries, to establish compensation practices that are fairly and consistently applied internally and to ensure compliance with legislative requirements."[4] Productivity studies show that employees increase their output by 15 to 35 percent when an organization installs a pay-for-performance program.

Unfortunately, designing a sound pay-for-performance system is not easy. Consideration must be given to the following: how employee performance will be measured, what monies will be allocated for compensation increases, which employees will be covered, the payout method, and when (i.e., how often) payments will be made. A critical issue is the size of the monetary increase and its perceived value to employees. While opinion varies as to how large a wage or salary increase must be before employees perceive it as meaningful, a pay-for-performance program will not achieve its full potential if pay increases only approximate rises in the cost of living.

In this chapter, we discuss incentive plans in terms of the objectives they hope to achieve and the various factors that affect their success. We also attempt to identify which plans are most effective in motivating different categories of employees to achieve these objectives. For discussion purposes, we have grouped the incen-

FIGURE 10.1 *Types of Incentive Plans*

INDIVIDUAL	GROUP	ENTERPRISE
Piecework	Team compensation	Profit sharing
Standard hour plan	Scanlon Plan	Stock options
Bonuses	Rucker Plan	Employee stock ownership plans
Merit pay	Improshare	
Lump-sum merit pay	Earnings at risk plans	
Sales incentives		
Maturity curves		
Executive compensation		

tive plans into two broad categories: individual incentive plans, and group incentive plans (see Figure 10.1).

REASONS AND REQUIREMENTS FOR INCENTIVE PLANS

WWW

A clear trend in strategic compensation management is the growth of incentive plans—also called variable pay programs—for employees throughout the organization. According to a survey conducted by KPMG, variable pay programs are being used more and more; roughly two-thirds of nonmanagerial employees now benefit from them.[5] According to a Conference Board of Canada study of compensation practices in 365 organizations, 70 percent of organizations have established variable pay plans.[6]

Incentive plans operate outside the merit (base pay) increase system, and extend their reach into nontraditional groups.[7] They create an operating environment that champions a philosophy of shared commitment as well as the belief that every individual contributes to organizational performance and success.

Incentive Plans as Links to Organizational Objectives

Over the years, organizations have implemented incentive plans for a variety of reasons: high labour costs, competitive product markets, slow technological advances, and high potential for production bottlenecks. While these reasons are still cited, contemporary arguments for incentive plans focus on pay-for-performance and link compensation rewards to organizational goals. Managers believe that by meshing compensation and organizational objectives, employees will assume "ownership" of their jobs, and thereby increase their effort and improve their overall performance. Incentives are designed to encourage employees to put out more effort to complete their job tasks—effort they might not be motivated to expend under hourly and/or seniority-based compensation systems. Financial incentives are intended to improve or maintain high levels of productivity and quality; when they work well, the global market improves for Canadian goods and

---

FIGURE 10.2 *Advantages of Incentive Pay Programs*

- Incentives focus employee efforts on specific performance targets. They provide real motivation that leads to important employee and organizational gains.
- Incentive payouts are variable costs linked to the achievement of results. Base salaries are fixed costs largely unrelated to output.
- Incentive compensation is directly related to operating performance. If performance objectives (quantity and/or quality) are met, incentives are paid. If objectives are not achieved, incentives are withheld.
- Incentives foster teamwork and unit cohesiveness when payments to individuals are based on team results.
- Incentives are a way to distribute success among those responsible for producing that success.

---

services. Figure 10.2 summarizes the major advantages of incentive pay programs as noted by researchers and HR professionals.

Do incentive plans work? Various studies have demonstrated a measurable relationship between incentive plans and improved organizational performance. The typical incentive program yields organizational productivity increases between 5 and 50 percent.[8] In the area of manufacturing, productivity often improves by as much as 20 percent after an incentive plan is adopted. Improvements, however, are not limited to goods-producing industries. Service organizations and not-for-profit and government agencies also show productivity gains when incentives are linked to organizational goals. After beginning an incentive pay program, Sun Life of Canada reduced its unit costs of business service (i.e., its per unit costs of processing claims) and improved customer service. Taco Bell Corporation reduced food costs and improved customer service after it began an employee bonus program.[9]

WWW

However, incentive plans have not always led to organizational improvement, for several reasons. *First*, incentive plans sometimes fail to satisfy employee needs. *Second*, management may have been less than successful in designing and implementing the plan.[10] *Third*, the success of an incentive plan depends on the organization's internal environment. A plan is more likely to work when morale is high, employees believe they are being treated fairly, and there is harmony between employees and management.

Requirements for a Successful Incentive Plan

For an incentive plan to succeed, employees must want it. Whether they do will depend on how successful management is in introducing the plan and convincing employees of its benefits. When employees are encouraged to participate in developing and administering the plan, they will be more willing to accept it.[11]

Employees must be able to make a clear connection between the incentive payments they receive and their job performance.[12] This connection is more visible when they can judge their performance by objective quality or quantity standards. For the plan to succeed, the employees must be committed to meeting these standards. This requires mutual trust and understanding between employees and their supervisors, which can only be achieved through open, two-way channels of communication. Management should never allow incentive payments to be seen as entitlements. Instead, employees should perceive these payments as a reward that must be earned through effort. This perception can be strengthened if the incentive money is distributed to employees by separate cheques. Compensation specialists note that successful plans also have these characteristics:

- Financial incentives are linked to valued behaviour.
- The incentive program seems fair to the employees.
- Productivity and quality standards are challenging but achievable.
- Payout formulas are simple and understandable.

SETTING PERFORMANCE MEASURES

Measurement is key to the success of incentive plans because it communicates the importance of the organization's established goals. What gets measured and rewarded gets attention. For example, if the organization desires to be a leader in quality, performance indexes might focus on customer satisfaction, timeliness, or being error-free. If being a low-priced producer is the goal, then the emphasis will probably be on cost reductions, or on increased productivity with lower acceptable levels of quality. A variety of performance options are available; however, most of them focus on quality, cost control, or productivity. Highlights in HRM 1 describes how customer satisfaction measures (CSMs), which are a new kind of performance measure, can be linked with customer service goals.

One authority on incentive plans has noted that when a plan fails, that failure can usually be traced to the choice of performance measures.[13] The best measures are simple and quantitative and are structured to show a clear relationship to improved performance. Measures that are too complex or too quantitative are to be avoided. Also, when selecting a performance measure, one must ask how much the employees can actually influence the measurement. Finally, employers must guard against "ratcheting up" performance goals (i.e., constantly trying to exceed earlier results). This eventually leads to employee frustration and to the perception that the standards are unattainable. The result will be a loss of trust in management and a backlash against the entire incentive program.

ADMINISTERING INCENTIVE PLANS

While incentive plans based on productivity can reduce direct labour costs, for an organization to achieve their full benefit they must be carefully designed, implemented, and maintained. A cardinal rule is that thorough planning must be combined with a "proceed with caution" approach. Compensation managers repeatedly stress a number of points related to the effective administration of incentive plans. Three of the more important points, by consensus, are these:

1. Incentive systems are effective only when managers are willing to grant incentives based on differences in individual, team, or organizational performance. When incentive payments become automatic, the purpose of the plan is defeated. Incentive plans are not supposed to pay off in almost all circum-

Highlights in HRM

1 SETTING PERFORMANCE GOALS THROUGH CUSTOMER SATISFACTION MEASURES (CSMS)

WWW

Organizations are relying more and more on customer opinion to gauge their success. Parallel with this has been a growing interest in using customer satisfaction measures (CSMs) as the basis for performance reviews and compensation rewards. According to a study by Walker Information, at least six winners of the Malcolm Baldrige National Quality Award—Federal Express, Xerox, AT&T Network Systems, Granite Rock, IBM Rochester, and AT&T Universal Card—used CSMs as a basis for employee compensation. The following three reasons were cited: they demonstrate a commitment to the customer; they hold employees accountable; and they foster change. Perhaps the most compelling reason for establishing CSMs is that they focus employees on the all-important goal of giving careful attention to each and every customer interaction. Organizations can tie CSMs to reward systems in a variety of ways, but the process generally follows the following format:

- The organization collects survey data that identify the key factors related to the customer's purchase satisfaction. It then conducts a survey across customers to quantify the organization's current performance levels in those areas.
- The organization sets CSM goals. These goals identify the areas for improvement, the levels of improvement expected, and the time frame to achieve those improvements. The targets may be fixed (e.g., "Improve customers' rating of product quality by two percentage points in 2002"), or they may call for continuous improvements for each quarter or year.
- CSM goals are linked to incentive pay; anywhere from 10 to 100 percent of the employee's total potential bonus can be based on whether the CSM goals are achieved.
- The organization communicates the goals to its employees and develops supporting action plans. These plans determine how the participants will go about achieving the objectives.
- At the end of the period, the organization surveys its customers again and remeasures its performance in the targeted areas. It then incorporates the results into performance reviews, which give the employees an objective look at how their work affects customers. One benefit of a CSM program is that it replaces the traditionally "soft" process used to measure customer satisfaction with quantified results. The cycle continues with the setting of new CSM goals.

stances; the point of them is to motivate performance. In sum, if the plan is to succeed, poor performance must go unrewarded.

2. Annual salary budgets must be large enough to reward and reinforce exceptional performance. When compensation budgets are set to ensure that pay increases do not exceed certain limits (often established as a percentage of payroll or sales), these constraints may work against rewarding outstanding individual or group performance.

3. The overhead costs associated with implementing and administering the plan must be determined. These may include the cost of establishing performance standards and the cost of additional record keeping. The time consumed in communicating the plan to employees, answering questions, and resolving any complaints about it must also be included in these costs.[14]

INDIVIDUAL INCENTIVE PLANS

In today's competitive world, when organizations are designing incentive plans for their nonmanagement employees, flexibility is everything. Technology, job tasks and duties, and/or the organization's goals (e.g., being a low-cost producer) all affect the organization's choice of incentive pay programs. Also, when employees work in teams, a team incentive plan may be preferred, since the team's total effort may not be easy to break down into individual efforts. Managers often note that when individual employees are rewarded for the entire group's effort, rivalries are reduced, cooperation is strengthened, and concern increases for the unit's overall performance. In addition, in highly competitive industries such as foods and retailing, low profit margins tend to place a cap on the amount of money available for incentive payouts. All these considerations suggest that tradition and philosophy, as well as economics and technology, govern the design of nonmanagement incentive systems. The various gainsharing plans discussed later in this chapter are typically offered to both nonmanagement and management employees.

Straight piecework

Incentive plan under which employees receive a certain rate for each unit produced

WWW

Differential piece rate

Compensation rate under which employees whose production exceeds the output receive a higher rate for all of their work than the rate paid to those who do not exceed the standard amount

Piecework

One of the oldest incentive plans is based on piecework. Under **straight piecework**, employees receive a certain rate for each unit produced. Their compensation is determined by the number of units they produce during a pay period. At Steelcase, a maker of office furniture, employees can earn more than their base pay—often as much as 35 percent more—through piecework for each slab of metal they cut or chair they upholster. Under a **differential piece rate**, employees whose production exceeds the standard output receive a higher rate for all of their work than the rate paid to those who do not exceed the standard.

Employers who include piecework in their compensation strategy, do so for several reasons. The wage payment for each employee is simple to compute, and the plan permits the organization to predict its labour costs with considerable accuracy, since these costs are the same for each unit of output. The piecework system is more likely to succeed when units of output can be measured easily, when the quality of the product is less critical, when the job is fairly standardized, and when a constant flow of work can be maintained.

Computing the Piece Rate. Time standards establish the time required to perform a given amount of work, but do not by themselves determine what the incentive rate should be. An incentive rate must be based on the hourly wage rate that would otherwise be paid for the type of work being performed. As an example, let us say that the standard time for producing one unit of work in a job paying $7.50 per hour is set at twelve minutes. The piece rate will be $1.50 per unit, computed as follows:

$$\frac{60 \text{ (minutes per hour)}}{12 \text{ (standard time per unit)}} = 5 \text{ units per hour}$$

$$\frac{\$7.50 \text{ (hourly rate)}}{5 \text{ (units per hour)}} = \$1.50 \text{ per unit}$$

Piecework: The Drawbacks

Piecework systems have some obvious advantages, a big one being that they are linked directly to a pay-for-performance philosophy. But they also have a number of disadvantages. For many types of jobs, the production standards on which piecework must be based can be difficult to develop. Jobs in which individual contributions are difficult to distinguish or measure, or in which the work is mechanized to the point that employees exercise very little control over output, are often unsuited to piecework. Importantly, piecework incentive systems can work against an organization's attempts to promote cooperation, creativity, and problem solving, since each of these can infringe on an employees' time and productivity and, it follows, their total pay.

One of the biggest weaknesses of piecework (and of other incentive plans based on individual effort) is that it may not always be an effective motivator. Employees who believe that their fellow workers would disapprove of them increasing their output may avoid exerting maximum effort because their desire for peer approval outweighs their desire for more money (here, the co-workers are engaging in "rate busting").[15] Also, the standards on which piece rates are based tend to loosen over time, either because of peer pressure to relax the standards or because employees discover ways to do the work in less than standard time. In either situation, the employees are not required to exert as much effort to receive the same amount of incentive pay; as a result, the incentive value is reduced.[16]

Some union leaders fear that management will use piecework or similar systems to speed up production, getting more work from employees for the same amount of money. Piecework may also be inappropriate where

- quality is more important than quantity;
- technology changes frequently; *and*
- cross-training is desired to promote scheduling flexibility.

Standard Hour Plan

Standard hour plan

Incentive plan that sets rates based on the completion of a job in a predetermined standard time

Another common incentive technique is the **standard hour plan**, which sets incentive rates on the basis of a predetermined "standard time" for completing a job. If employees finish the work in less than the expected time, their pay is still based on the standard time for the job multiplied by their hourly rate. For example, if the standard time to install an engine in a half-ton truck is five hours and the

Piecework incentive programs have been used for many years in the garment industry.

mechanic completes the job in four-and-a-half hours, the payment will still be the mechanic's hourly rate times five hours. Standard hour plans are well suited to long-cycle operations, and to jobs or tasks that are nonrepetitive and require a variety of skills.[17]

WWW

The Wood Products Southern Division of Potlatch Corporation has successfully used a standard hour plan to produce various wood products. The incentive payment is based on the standard hours for producing and packaging 1,000 feet of wood panelling. Employees who produce the panelling in less time than the standard are paid an incentive that is based on the percentage improvement. For example, if the standard is 1,000 hours and the wood panelling is completed in 900 hours, a 10 percent incentive will be paid. Each employee's base hourly wage will be increased by 10 percent and then multiplied by the hours worked.

Standard hour plans can motivate employees to produce more; however, employers must ensure that equipment maintenance and product quality do not suffer as employees strive to do their work faster to earn more income.

Bonuses

Bonus

Incentive payment that is supplemental to the base wage

WWW

A **bonus** is an incentive payment that is supplemental to the basic wage. It is often given at the end of a year and does not become part of base pay. Bonuses provide employees with more pay for exerting greater effort; at the same time, the employees still have the security of their basic wage. Bonus payments are already common among managers and executives, and are becoming more common for employees throughout organizations. For example, IBM Canada's 17,000 employees receive bonuses averaging about 10 percent of their pay. Depending on who is to receive the bonus, the incentive payment can be determined on the basis of cost reduction, quality improvement, or performance criteria established by the organization. At the executive level, performance criteria might include earnings growth or enterprise-specific objectives. At the Royal Bank of Canada, bonuses are given for meeting financial performance goals.

For hourly employees, the bonus payment can be based on the number of units an individual produces, as in the case of piecework. For example, at the basic wage rate of $7 an hour plus a bonus of 15 cents per unit, an employee who produces 100 units during an eight-hour period is paid $71, computed as follows:

(Hours × wage rate) + (number of units × unit rate)   = Wages

   8   × $7)   +   (100 × 15¢)   = $71

At Inco, hourly bonuses are given based on operating profits.

When some special employee contribution is to be rewarded, a **spot bonus** is used. A spot bonus, as the name implies, is given "on the spot," typically for some employee effort not directly tied to an established performance standard. For example, a customer service representative might receive a spot bonus for working long hours to fill a new customer's large order.

Spot bonus

Unplanned bonus given for employee effort unrelated to an established performance measure

Merit Pay

A merit pay program (merit raises) links an increase in base pay to the employee's success at his or her job. The increase is usually given on the basis of some objective performance standard—although the superior's subjective evaluation of the subordinate's performance may play a large part in the determination. Merit raises can be useful if employees see them as related to performance. At present, as many as 90 percent of large public and private sector organizations have merit pay programs for one or more of their employee groups.[18]

Behavioural science research and various motivation theories provide the rationale for merit pay plans and for other pay-for-performance programs. But if employees are to see the link between pay and performance, their performance must be evaluated in light of objective criteria. If their superiors add subjective judgment to the mix, employees must have confidence in the validity of this judgment. Most important, any increases granted on the basis of merit should be distinguishable from employees' regular pay and from any cost-of-living or other general increases. Where merit increases are based on pay for performance, merit pay should be withheld when performance declines.[19]

Problems with Merit Raises

Merit raises do not always achieve their intended purpose. Unlike bonuses, merit raises may be perpetuated year after year even after performance starts to decline. In these situations, employees come to expect the increases and to see them as unrelated to performance. Also, employees in some organizations are opposed to merit raises because (among other reasons) they do not really trust management. Merit raises too easily evolve into increases based on seniority or favouritism, or raises to accommodate increases in cost of living or in area wage rates.[20]

Two compensation specialists have noted: "Some subordinates have better political connections within the company than others. Subordinates who are politically, socially, and familially connected inside and outside the organization, who carry clout, and who can hurt the supervisor in some way are likely to receive a larger share of the merit pie than their performance might warrant."[21] Even when merit raises are determined by performance, the employee's gains may be offset by inflation and higher income taxes. Compensation specialists also recognize the following problems with merit pay plans:

1. Money available for merit increases may be inadequate to satisfactorily raise employees' base pay.

2. Managers may have no guidance in how to define and measure performance; there may be vagueness regarding merit award criteria.

3. Employees may not believe that their compensation is tied to effort and performance; they may be unable to differentiate between merit pay and other types of pay increases.

4. Employees may believe that organizational politics plays a significant part in merit pay decisions, despite the presence of a formal merit pay system.

5. There may be a lack of honesty and cooperation between management and employees.

6. "Overall" merit pay plans sometimes do not result in higher levels of employee performance.[22]

A major weakness of merit raises relates to the performance appraisal system on which the increases are based. Performance can be difficult to measure even when the system is effective. When it isn't effective, the entire merit pay plan can be compromised. Moreover, the performance appraisal objectives of employees are often at odds with those of their employers. Most employees want to maximize their pay increases; most superiors merely want to reward employees in an equitable manner on the basis of their performance. Employees who are too combative can do their careers more harm than good, if their performance appraisals haven't been written yet.

While there are no easy solutions to these problems, organizations with true merit-pay plans often base the raises they award on **merit guidelines**, which are tied to performance appraisals. Highlights in HRM 2 shows a guideline chart for awarding merit raises. The percentages may change from year to year, depending on various internal or external factors such as profit levels and economic indicators (such as the CPI). Under the illustrated merit plan, to prevent all employees from being rated outstanding or above average, managers may be required to distribute performance ratings according to some pre-established formula (e.g., only 10 percent can be rated outstanding). Also, when setting merit percentage guidelines, organizations should consider individual performance along with such factors as training, experience, and current earnings.

Lump-Sum Merit Pay

To make merit increases more flexible and visible, almost half of Canadian organizations have implemented a **lump-sum merit program**.[23] Under this type of plan, each employee receives a single lump-sum increase at the time of performance review—an increase that is not added to base salary. Barring promotions, the employees' base salaries are essentially frozen.[24]

Lump-sum merit programs offer several advantages. For one, they enable employers to keep a lid on annual salary expenses. Put another way, merit increases granted on a lump-sum basis do not drive up base salary levels. Also, lump-sum programs help employers contain employee benefit costs, since the levels of benefits are usually calculated from current salary levels. There are also advantages for employees. A lump-sum merit payment provides a clear link between pay and per-

Merit guidelines

Guidelines for awarding merit raises that are tied to performance objectives

Lump-sum merit guidelines

Plan under which each employee receives a single lump-sum increase at the time of performance review

Highlights in HRM

2   MERIT PAY GUIDELINES CHART

A merit pay guidelines chart is a "look up" table for awarding merit increases on the basis of (1) employee performance, (2) position in the pay range, and, in a few cases, (3) time since the last pay increase. Most merit pay guidelines charts are designed to move new job holders relatively quickly up to the midpoint of their pay range (see Chapter 9) once they can competently perform the work. The purpose of getting employees' pay to the midpoint is to ensure that they are competitively compensated and are not tempted to move to other employers that pay higher wages or salaries. Another feature of the chart is that it slows the employees' progress in the pay range above the midpoint to ensure that only top performers move toward the upper limit of the range. If too many employees are paid above the midpoint, the organization is paying a premium for labour, and top performers who are at the top of the pay range cannot receive pay increases unless the pay range is adjusted.

The merit pay guidelines chart below shows the pay range for each pay grade as divided into five levels (quintiles), with 1 at the bottom of the pay range and 5 at the top. On the left, employee performance (as determined by the annual appraisal) is arranged in five levels from high (outstanding) to low (unsatisfactory). An employee's position in his or her salary range and performance level indicates the percentage pay increase to be awarded. For example, a person at the top of the pay range (5) who gets a performance rating of "outstanding" will be awarded a 6 percent pay increase. However, an outstanding performer at the bottom of the pay range (1) will receive a 9 percent increase.

Because the purpose of the guidelines chart is to balance conflicting pay goals, it compromises, by design, the relationship between merit increases and performance appraisal ratings. The highest-rated performers will not always be the employees with the highest percentage increase. Notice that a superior performer in quintiles 1, 2, and 3 can receive a percentage increase as much as or more than that of an outstanding performer in quintile 5. As a result, employees are likely to learn that pay increases are not determined just by performance. However, as we learned in Chapter 9, if money is to serve as a motivator, expectancy theory specifies that employees must believe there is a link between performance and pay increases if performance is to remain at a high level.

MERIT PAY GUIDE CHART

QUINTILE (POSITION IN RANGE), %

Performance Level	1	2	3	4	5
Outstanding (5)	9	9	8	7	6
Superior (4)	7	7	6	5	4
Competent (3)	5	5	4	3	3
Needs improvement (2)	0	0	0	0	0
Unsatisfactory (1)	0	0	0	0	0

Source: Adapted from K. Dow Scott, Steven E. Markham, and Michael J. West, "The Influence of a Merit Pay Guide Chart on Employee Attitudes toward Pay at a Transit Authority," *Public Personnel Management* 25, no. 1 (Spring 1996): 103–15. Reprinted with permission.

formance. For example, a 6 percent merit increase granted to an industrial engineer earning $42,000 a year translates into a weekly increase of $48.46—a figure that looks small compared with a lump-sum payment of $2,520.

Organizations with lump-sum merit programs will want to adjust base salaries upwards from time to time. They can do this yearly or after several years. These adjustments should keep pace with the rising cost of living and with increases in the general market wage.

Sales Incentives

Sales work almost always demands high enthusiasm and drive. Add to this that the work is highly competitive, and you will understand why financial incentives are so common to the field. Whatever incentive plan salespeople are offered, it must motivate them and elicit their cooperation and trust. Motivation is especially important for salespeople away from the office, who cannot be supervised closely and who, as a result, must exercise a high degree of self-discipline.

Unique Needs of Sales Incentive Plans

WWW

Incentive systems for salespeople are complicated by the fact that there are so many different types of sales jobs.[25] Department store clerks who ring up customer purchases are salespeople, but so are the industrial salespeople from McGraw-Edison who provide consulting and various high-tech services to their clients. The performance of salespeople can be measured by the dollar volume of their sales, or by the number of new accounts they land, or by their ability to promote new products or services, or by the various forms of customer service they offer (even when these do not immediately produce sales revenues).

But performance standards for sales employees are difficult to develop because their sucess or failure can be deeply affected by external factors they don't control.[26] Economic and seasonal fluctuations, sales competition, changes in demand, and the nature of the assigned sales territory can all affect an individual's sales. In other words, sales volume alone may not provide an accurate picture of the effort they have expended.

In developing incentive plans for salespeople, managers must consider how to reward extra sales effort and at the same time compensate sales employees for activities that do not contribute directly or immediately to sales. A final point: sales employees must be able to enjoy some degree of income stability.

Types of Sales Incentive Plans

Straight salary plan

Compensation plan that permits salespeople to be paid for performing various duties that are not reflected immediately in their sales volume

Straight commission plan

Compensation plan based on a percentage of sales

A compensation plan for sales employees can be a straight salary plan, or a straight commission plan, or a combination salary and commission plan.[27] With a **straight salary plan**, salespeople are paid for performing various duties that don't have an immediate impact on their sales volume. A plan like this lets them devote more time to providing services and building up customer goodwill without jeopardizing their income. The main limitation of the straight salary plan is that it may not motivate salespeople to maximize their sales volume.

A **straight commission plan** is based on a percentage of sales. It provides maximum incentive and is easy to compute and understand. Organizations that pay a straight commission based on total volume might use one of the following simple formulas:

$$\text{Total cash compensation} = 2\% \times \text{total volume}$$

or

$$\text{Total cash compensation} = 2\% \times \text{total volume up to quota}$$
$$+ 4\% \times \text{volume over quota}$$

Straight commission plans have the following disadvantages:

1. They emphasize sales volume rather than profits.

2. Customer service after the sale is likely to be neglected.

3. Earnings tend to fluctuate widely between good and poor periods of business, and turnover of trained sales employees tends to increase in poor periods.

4. Salespeople are tempted to grant price concessions.

Combined salary and commission plan

Compensation plan that includes a straight salary and a commission

When a **combined salary and commission plan** is used, the percentage of cash compensation paid out in commissions (i.e., incentives) is called "leverage." Leverage is usually expressed as a ratio of base salary to commission. For example, a salesperson working under a 70/30 combination plan receives total cash compensation paid out as 70 percent base salary and 30 percent commission. The amount of leverage is determined after considering the constraining factors affecting performance discussed earlier and the sales objectives of the organization. The combination salary and commission plan is widely used for the following reasons:[28]

1. The right kind of incentive compensation, if linked to salary in the right proportion, has most of the advantages of both the straight salary and the straight commission forms of compensation.

2. A salary-plus-incentive compensation plan offers greater design flexibility and can therefore be more readily set up to maximize company profits.

3. The most favourable ratio of selling expense to sales can be developed.

4. The field sales force can be motivated to achieve specific company marketing objectives in addition to sales volume.

Maturity Curves

Like other salaried workers, professional employees—engineers, scientists, and lawyers, for example—can be motivated through bonuses and merit increases. In some organizations, unfortunately, professional employees cannot advance beyond a certain point in the salary structure unless they are willing to take on administrative work. After they are promoted, their professional talents are no longer utilized fully. Too often, the organization loses a good professional employee and gains a poor administrator. To prevent this from happening, some organizations have extended the salary range for professional positions so that it equals or nearly equals the one for administrative positions. When a "double track" wage system is offered, professionals who do not aspire to become administrators can still earn comparable salaries. Such a system was illustrated in Chapter 7.

Career curves (maturity curves)

Experience or performance bases for providing salary increases for professional employees

Organizations also use **career curves** or **maturity curves** as a basis for providing salary increases to professional employees. These curves, such as the ones shown in Figure 10.3, provide for the annual salary rate to be based on experience and per-

Commission is one tool employers use to motivate salespeople

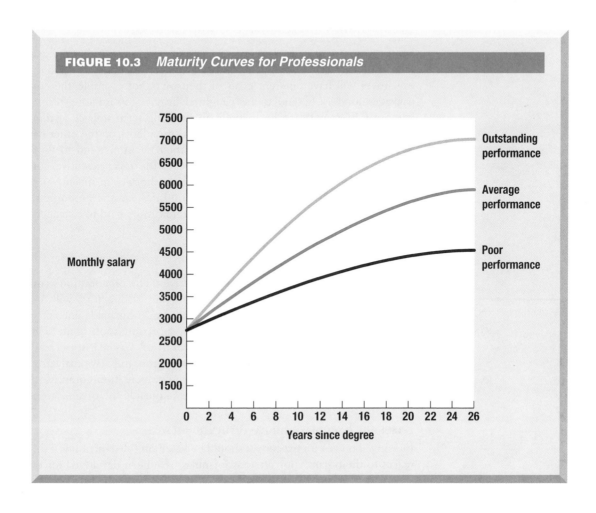

FIGURE 10.3   *Maturity Curves for Professionals*

Monthly salary

Outstanding performance

Average performance

Poor performance

Years since degree

formance. Separate curves are established to reflect different levels of performance and to provide for annual increases. The curves representing upper levels of performance tend to rise higher and faster than the curves representing lower performance levels.

Professional employees can receive compensation beyond base pay. For example, scientists and engineers employed by high-tech firms can be included in performance-based incentive programs such as profit sharing and stock ownership. These plans encourage greater levels of individual performance. Cash bonuses can be awarded to those who complete projects on or before deadline dates. Also, payments can be given to individuals who have been elected to professional societies, or who have been granted patents, or who have met professional licensing standards.[29]

EXECUTIVE COMPENSATION

A major function of incentive plans for executives is to motivate them to develop and use their abilities and contribute their energies to the fullest possible extent. Incentive plans should also make it easier to recruit and retain competent executive employees. This can be accomplished with plans that enable executives to accumulate a financial estate and to shelter a portion of their compensation from current income taxes.

Components of Executive Compensation

Most organizations have more than one compensation strategy for executives. This reflects the fact that most organizations have more than one goal, and that different executives will have different goals of their own. For example, the compensation packages for CEOs tend to be weighted heavily toward long-term incentives, because CEOs ought to be focused on the long-term impact of their decisions rather than the short-term ones. Group vice-presidents, on the other hand, may be offered more short-term incentives, since their decisions tend to focus more on six- to twelve-month turn-arounds. Whatever the mix, executive compensation plans have four basic components: base salary; short-term incentives or bonuses; long-term incentives or stock plans; and perquisites. Another important element in compensation strategy is the compensation mix to be paid to managers and executives accepting overseas assignments.

Bases for Executive Salaries

WWW

Executive base salaries tend to be market-driven. The organization's compensation committee (usually a subcommittee of the board of directors) will order a salary survey to find out what executives are earning in comparable enterprises. In 1999 Peter Munk, chairman of Barrick Gold Corporation, took home \$38.9 million, which made him Canada's highest-paid executive.[30] Comparisons can be based on organization size, sales volume, or industry grouping. By analyzing published studies and self-generated salary surveys, the compensation committee can determine the equity of the compensation package outside the organization.[31]

Bases for Executive Short-Term Incentives

Incentive bonuses for executives should be based on the contribution the individual makes to the organization. Various formulas have been developed for this purpose.

Incentive bonuses can be based on a percentage of the company's total profit or on a percentage of its profits in excess of a specific return on the shareholders' investment. Or the bonus can be tied to an annual profit plan, with the amount to be determined by the extent to which an agreed-on profit level is exceeded. Payments can also be based on performance ratings or on the achievement of specific objectives established by agreement between the executive and the board of directors.

WWW

In a continuing effort to monitor the pulse of the marketplace, more organizations are tying operational yardsticks to the traditional financial gauges when computing executive pay. Called *balanced scorecards*, these yardsticks often measure things like customer satisfaction, the ability to innovate, or product or service leadership. Notes David Cates, a compensation principal with Towers Perrin, a balanced scorecard "allows companies to focus on building future economic value, rather than be driven solely by short-term financial results."[32]

A bonus payment can also take the form of cash or stock. Furthermore, the timing of the bonus payment can vary. It can be immediate (it often is), or it can be deferred for a short time, or it can be deferred until retirement.

Most organizations pay their short-term incentive bonuses in cash (in the form of a supplemental cheque), in keeping with their pay-for-performance strategy. By providing the reward soon after the performance, they link it to the effort it is based on. When given this way, cash bonuses can be a significant motivator.

A deferred bonus can be used to provide the sole source of retirement benefits or to supplement a regular pension plan.[33] An executive who is in a lower tax bracket when the deferred benefits are ultimately received—which is not always the case—can realize income tax savings. Also, interest will be accumulating on the deferred amount, which won't be taxed until received. By the same token, deferred income funds do become a part of the company's indebtedness, and may be lost in part or in total should the company become insolvent. Also, if these funds do not grow faster than the inflation rate, the participant may effectively suffer a loss.

Bases for Executive Long-Term Incentives

WWW

Short-term incentive bonuses are criticized for encouraging top executives to focus on quarterly profit goals at the expense of long-term survival and growth objectives. This is why corporations such as Sears and Starbucks have adopted compensation strategies that tie executive pay to long-term performance measures. Each of these organizations recognizes that while incentive payments for executives may be based on the achievement of specific goals relating to their positions, the plans must also take into account the performance of the organization as a whole. Important to shareholders are performance results such as growth in earnings per share, return on shareholders' equity, and, ultimately, stock price appreciation. For this reason, a variety of incentive plans have been developed to tie rewards to these performance results, especially over the long term.

Stock options are the main long-term incentive offered to executives; 85 percent of Canadian CEOs have a stock option plan. The basic principle behind stock options is that executives should have a stake in the business so that they have the same perspective as the owners (i.e., the shareholders).[34] The major long-term incentives fall into three broad categories:

- stock price appreciation grants
- restricted stock and restricted cash grants
- performance-based grants

Each of these broad categories includes various stock grants or cash incentives linked to executive performance. See Figure 10.4 for definitions of the various grant types. Stock options are heavy contributors to executives' million-dollar compensation packages.

Executive Perquisites

Perquisites

Special benefits given to executives; often referred to as "perks"

Besides incentive programs, executive employees are often given special benefits and perquisites. **Perquisites**, or "perks," are a means of demonstrating the executives' importance to the organization while giving them an incentive to improve their performance. Perks also serve as status symbols both inside and outside the organization. Perquisites can also provide a tax saving to executives, since some are not taxed as income. Some of the more common perks offered to executives are company cars, country club memberships, mobile phones, and company-paid parking. Highlights in HRM 3 lists the more common perks offered to executives. Most companies use a variety of incentive plans and perks, as described in Reality Check.

Executive Compensation: The Issue of Amount

Consider the size of the following financial payments, drawn in 1998:

Peter Munk, Chairman, CEO, Barrick corp	$38.9 million
Richard Currie, President, Loblaws Cos and Westons Ltd	34.1 million
Frank Stronach, chairman, Magna	26.1 million
Frank Hasenfratz, Chairman, CEO, Linamar	21.4 million
Galen Weston, Chairman, Weston Ltd. and Loblaw Cos	15.2 million

While the majority of total executive compensation is received in bonuses and long-term incentives, many people ask this question: "Are top executives worth the salaries and bonuses they receive?" The answer depends on whom you ask.[35] Corporate compensation committees justify big bonuses in the following ways:

1. Large financial incentives are a way to reward superior performance.

2. Business competition is pressure-filled and demanding.

3. Good executive talent is in great demand.

4. Effective executives create shareholder value.

Others justify high compensation as a fact of business life, reflecting market compensation trends.[36] Some of these issues are raised in Ethics in HRM.

Nevertheless, in an era of massive downsizing, stagnant wage increases, and heavier workloads for layoff survivors, corporations are being heavily criticized for paying their senior executives too much.[37] Cries for openness and for performance accountability are beginning to abound.[38] Compensation professionals fully expect that in the coming years, the following issues will come to a head:

1. Performance measurement techniques will have to be refined to reflect individual contributions. The measurement and rewarding of executive performance will require creative compensation approaches.

FIGURE 10.4 *Types of Long-Term Incentive Plans*

STOCK PRICE APPRECIATION PLANS

Stock options	Rights granted to executives to purchase shares of their organization's stock at an established price for a fixed period of time. Stock price is usually set at market value at the time the option is granted.
Stock appreciation rights (SARs)	Cash or stock award determined by increase in stock price during any time chosen by the executive in the option period; does not require executive financing.
Stock purchase	Opportunities for executives to purchase shares of their organization's stock valued at full market or a discount price, often with the organization providing financial assistance.
Phantom stock	Grant of units equal in value to the fair market value or book value of a share of stock; on a specified date the executive will be paid the appreciation in the value of the units up to that time.

RESTRICTED STOCK/CASH PLANS

Restricted stock	Grant of stock or stock units at a reduced price with the condition that the stock not be transferred or sold (by risk of forfeiture) before a specified employment date.
Restricted cash	Grant of fixed-dollar amounts subject to transfer or forfeiture restrictions before a specified employment date.

PERFORMANCE-BASED PLANS

Performance units	Grants analogous to annual bonuses except that the measurement period exceeds one year. The value of the grant can be expressed as a flat dollar amount or converted to a number of "units" of equivalent aggregate value.
Performance shares	Grants of actual stock or phantom units. Value is contingent both on predetermined performance objectives over a specified period of time and the stock market.
Formula-value grants	Rights to receive units or the gain in value of units determined by a formula (such as book value or an earnings multiplier) rather than changes in market price.
Dividend units	Rights to receive an amount equal to the dividends paid on a specified number of shares; typically granted in conjunction with other grant types, such as performance shares.

2. Organizations will face heavier government regulation of executive compensation. In the United States, salaries are monitored by the Securities and Exchange Commission (SEC); in Canada, regulations governing the disclosure of executive compensation vary between provinces. For example, the Ontario Securities Commission requires the disclosure of executive compensation, including base pay, bonuses, and long-term incentives; it also permits shareholders to propose and vote to limit executive compensation.

WWW

Highlights in HRM

3   THE SWEETNESS OF EXECUTIVE PERKS

PREVALENT PERKS

- Company car
- Company plane
- Financial consulting
- Company-paid parking
- Estate planning
- First-class air travel

- Physical exams
- Mobile phones
- Large insurance policies
- Income tax preparation
- Country club membership
- Luncheon club membership

LESS PREVALENT

- Chauffer service
- Children's education
- Spouse travel

- Personal home repairs
- Legal counselling
- Vacation cabins

3. Executive compensation practices will need to support global value-creating strategies with well-considered incentive pay programs. Hard questions to be answered will include these: "What exactly are the implications of global competitiveness and of the corresponding strategies required to improve Canadian corporations' effectiveness?" "How do these new strategies affect organizations and their compensation systems?"

GROUP INCENTIVE PLANS

With the increasing emphasis on cost reduction and total quality management, many organizations are implementing group incentive plans. These plans let employees share the benefits of improved efficiency; they also encourage a cooperative (as opposed to individualistic) spirit among employees and reward them for their total contribution to the organization. Group incentive plans are especially desirable when the type of work being done makes individual performance difficult or impossible to measure.

Team or group incentive plan

Compensation plan where all team members receive an incentive bonus payment when production or service standards are met or exceeded

Team Compensation

Production has become more automated; teamwork and coordination have become more important; and the contributions of those engaged only indirectly in production or service tasks have increased. For all these reasons, **team incentive**

Reality CHECK

INCENTIVES IN THE DOT.COM WORLD

WWW

Large corporations have been restructuring and downsizing hundreds of employees; yet at the same time, many small dot.com companies have been ramping up, hiring hundreds of employees in a very short time. Derivion, an e-billing application service provider (ASP) that leverages the power of the Internet to automate bill delivery and payment systems for companies, will be tripling its staff in the next year. Jon Hamovitch, Derivion's VP of human resources, says it's important to practise disciplined human resources management in an environment where process is often seen as a dirty word. He works with line managers to show them the difference between process and bureaucracy, and that following the right process will ensure that the right employees will be selected, and motivated once hired.

How does Derivion attract and retain employees and distinguish itself from its competitors? According to Hamovitch, Derivion tries for the right mixture of base salary and incentives. It has its own system for calculating base salaries: "We are engaged in timely, live salary surveys. We go directly to job sites, such as Monster.com, and look at competitors' jobs and what they are paying. We also scan résumés to determine the salary expectations of the kinds of employees we want to hire. These are good ways of staying current. We also subscribe to an on-line salary survey, which is updated daily."

All dot.com companies use stock options to attract and retain employees, but Derivion's option plan is unique. Hamovitch continues: "At Derivion our stock options are available to all employees, not just designers or executives, and are aligned directly with the impact employees have on company performance. In dot.com companies, employees are really the only ones who can impact share value in direct ways, such by as delivering a product on time, and selling it. Bonuses are based on performance: 50 percent based on individual performance, 50 percent on company performance."

Incentives at dot.com companies are very important, and include soft factors like culture: "We promote a great culture—it is casual and informal. Employees wear jeans, play fooz ball. We value innovation and creativity and don't punish mistakes, not the first time. There are negatives, like long and irregular hours. But these occur in peaks and valleys, so when in a valley, we tell employees to take time off, and give them extra tickets to events."

Derivion, like other high-tech companies, works in a tight labour market, but finds that creating the right compensation system attracts, motivates, and retains the kinds of employees that enable timely product development and delivery.

plans have become more popular. These plans reward team members with an incentive bonus when they exceed agreed-on performance standards.

The catch, since all teams are not alike (see Chapter 3), is that managers cannot adopt a uniform measurement standard or payout formula for team pay. According to Steven Gross, Hay manager, "Each type of team requires a specific pay structure to function at its peak."[39] Unfortunately, teams may fail because their pay structures do not support their goals.

Ethics in HRM

THE ETHICS OF EXECUTIVE COMPENSATION

WWW

The average annual compensation for Canadian CEOs is $1 million. That is more than 150 times what the average worker makes. In the United States, the ratio is 200 to 1. The CEO of BCE, Jean Monty, was booed by striking employees at the company's annual general meeting when union members contrasted his $17 million pay package with the company's offer of $19 per hour to telephone operators. Is any effort—especially when it cannot be attributed to one individual—worth the $38 million that Peter Munk gets? What makes this issue especially sensitive is the widening gap between executive salaries and workers' wages. Bank managers are receiving millions of dollars in compensation, while bank tellers are making slightly more than the minimum wage. Executives and head hunters defend these rates on the basis of what executives contribute to their organizations.

A study of compensation practices by KPMG reveals that 35 to 40 percent of the companies listed on the Toronto Stock Exchange tie executive compensation to corporate performance. However, corporate fortunes are often beyond the control of any one individual, and are more likely to be determined by external factors, including global economic conditions, new players, and changing technologies.

The bottom line on executive compensation is competition. Organizations pay market rates to hire the kind of executive talent they need.

This caveat aside, organizations typically use a three-step approach to establishing team incentive payments.[40]

- *First*, they set performance measures on which the incentive payments will be based. Improvements in efficiency or product quality, or reductions in material or labour costs, are common benchmark criteria. For example, if labour costs for a team represent 30 percent of the organization's sales dollars, and the organization pays a bonus for labour cost savings, then whenever team labour costs are less than 30 percent of sales dollars, those savings will be paid as an incentive bonus to the team members. Information on the size of the incentive bonus is reported to employees on a weekly or monthly basis, along with the reasons why incentive pay was or was not earned.
- *Second*, the size of the incentive bonus is determined. At one insurance company, health insurance underwriters can receive team incentive bonuses of up to 10 percent of base salary; however, the exact level of incentive pay depends on overall team performance and on the company's performance over one year. Team incentives are paid annually.[41]
- *Third*, a payout formula is established and fully explained to employees. Team bonuses can be distributed to employees equally, or in proportion to their base pay, or on the basis of their relative contributions to the team. Using discretionary formulas, managers or in some cases the team members themselves agree on the payouts to individual team members. Figure 10.5 presents the commonly stated advantages and disadvantages of team incentive pay.[42]

Gainsharing Incentive Plans

Gainsharing plans

Programs under which both employees and the organization share the financial gains according to a predetermined formula that reflects improved productivity and profitability

Gainsharing plans are designed to increase productivity or decrease labour costs, and then share the monetary gains with employees. They allow employees to share in the benefits of improved efficiency realized by the organization or by major units within it. Many of these plans cover managers and executives as well as hourly workers. The plans encourage teamwork among all employees and reward them for their total contribution to the organization. These plans are especially desirable when working conditions make individual performance difficult or impossible to measure.

Gainsharing involves establishing effective structures and processes of employee involvement as well as fair means of rewarding overall improvement in performance. The employees involved improve productivity by using labour, capital, and raw materials more effectively and then share the financial gains according to a formula which reflects that improved productivity (and profitability).

Although gainsharing is now a widely accepted reward system, it doesn't always work. Highlights in HRM 4 discusses how to establish an effective gainsharing program.[43]

OBJECTIVE 5

Four Unique Bonus Plans

In this section, four bonus plans are highlighted: the Scanlon, the Rucker, the Improshare, and the earnings-at-risk. They share the same intent, which is to provide employees with bonuses for maximum effort and cooperation. None of them,

---

FIGURE 10.5   *The Pros and Cons Team or Group Incentive Plans*

PROS

- Team incentives support group planning and problem solving, thereby building a team culture.
- The contributions of individual employees depend on group cooperation.
- Unlike incentive plans based solely on output, team incentives can broaden the scope of the contribution that employees are motivated to make.
- Team bonuses tend to reduce employee jealousies and complaints over "tight" or "loose" individual standards.
- Team incentives encourage cross-training and the acquisition of new interpersonal competencies.

CONS

- Individual team members may perceive that "their" efforts contribute little to team success or to the attainment of the incentive bonus.
- Conflicts may arise within the group. For example, some members may be pressured to limit their performance (if the other team members are afraid these stalwarts could make them look bad). There is also the "free-ride" effect (when one individual puts in less effort than the others but shares equally in team rewards).
- Complex payout formulas can be difficult for team members to understand.

Highlights in HRM

4 LESSONS LEARNED: DESIGNING EFFECTIVE GAINSHARING PROGRAMS

Will your gainsharing program be successful? While there are no precise keys to success, proponents of gainsharing cite the following as important components of a meaningful gainsharing plan:

- Enlist total managerial support for the gainsharing effort. While the support of top management is critical, without the encouragement of middle- and lower-level managers (i.e., those directly involved in implementing the program), gainsharing will invariably fail.
- When developing new programs, include representatives from all the groups affected by the gainsharing effort—labour, management, and employees. Inclusion builds trust as well as understanding of the program's intent and operation.
- Keep gamesmanship out of the program. Some involved parties may be more interested in preserving their self-interest than in supporting the group effort. When corporate politics are allowed to enter—as when the bonus calculation is manipulated to keep payouts down—the gainsharing program will almost certainly fail.
- Bonus payouts must be seen as fair, must be easy for employees to calculate, must be frequent, and must be large enough to encourage future employee effort. The goal is to create a pay-for-performance environment.
- Establish effective, fair, and precise measurement standards. Standards must encourage increased effort without being unreasonable.
- Be certain that employees are predisposed to a gainsharing reward system. Is there a "cultural readiness" for gainsharing? If changes are indicated, what needs to be done? Will employees need additional skills training or training in other competencies in order to make anticipated organizational improvements?
- Launch the plan during a favourable business period. Business downturns jeopardize payments. A plan is likely to fail if it does not pay out under normal conditions in its first two or three years of operation.

however, is tied to profit fluctuations. The Scanlon and Rucker plans are named after the people who developed them (Joe Scanlon and Alan W. Rucker). They share the same basic philosophy: participative management is a good thing, and costs should be reduced by sharing the resulting savings with employees. However, the formulas on which the resulting bonuses are based are somewhat different. The third plan, Improshare, is a gainsharing program based on the number of finished goods that employee work teams complete in an established period. The fourth plan, earnings-at-risk, encourages employees to achieve higher output and quality standards by placing a portion of their base salary at risk of loss.

The Scanlon Plan

Scanlon plan

Bonus incentive plan using employee and management committees to gain cost-reduction improvements

The philosophy behind the **Scanlon plan** is that employees should offer ideas and suggestions to improve productivity and should then be rewarded for their constructive efforts. The plan requires good management, leadership, and trust, as well as respect between employees and managers and a workforce dedicated to responsible decision making. When correctly implemented, the Scanlon plan can result in improved efficiency and profitability for the organization, and in steady employment and high compensation for employees.

According to its proponents, effective employee participation—which includes the use of committees on which employees are represented—is the most significant feature of the Scanlon Plan.[44] This plan provides employees with the opportunity to communicate their ideas and opinions and to exercise some degree of influence over decisions affecting their work and their welfare in the organization. Employees become managers of their own time and energy, of the equipment they use, of the quality and quantity of their production, and of other factors related to their work. When this plan is followed, workers accept changes in production methods more readily and volunteer new ideas. The Scanlon plan encourages greater teamwork and sharing of knowledge at the lower levels. It demands more efficient management and better planning as workers try to reduce overtime and to work smarter rather than harder or faster.

The main mechanisms for employee participation in the Scanlon plan are shop committees, which are established in each department. (See Figure 10.6 for an illustration of the Scanlon plan suggestion process.) These committees consider production problems and make suggestions for improvement within their respective departments to an organizationwide screening committee. The screening committee oversees the operation of the plan, acts on suggestions received from the shop committees, and reviews the data on which monthly bonuses are to be based. This committee is also responsible for consulting with and advising top management, which retains decision-making authority. Both the shop committees and the screening committee are composed of equal numbers of employees and managers.

Usually, financial incentives under the Scanlon plan are offered to all employees on the basis of an established formula. This is a significant feature of the plan. The formula is based on increases in employee productivity as determined by a norm that has been established for labour costs. The norm, which is subject to review, reflects the relationship between labour costs and the sales value of production (SVOP). The SVOP includes sales revenue and the value of goods in inventory. Figure 10.7 illustrates how the two figures are used to determine the Scanlon plan incentive bonus.

The plan also provides for the establishment of a reserve fund, into which 25 percent of every earned bonus is paid to cover deficits during the months when labour costs exceed the norm. After the reserve portion has been deducted, the rest of the bonus is distributed, with 25 percent going to the organization and 75 percent to the employees. At the end of the year, any surplus that has been accumulated in the reserve fund is distributed to employees according to the same formula.

The Scanlon plan (and variations of it) has become a fundamental way of managing, if not a way of life. The Xaloy Corporation, a major manufacturer of bimetallic cylinders, uses a modified Scanlon program based on the following four principles:

WWW

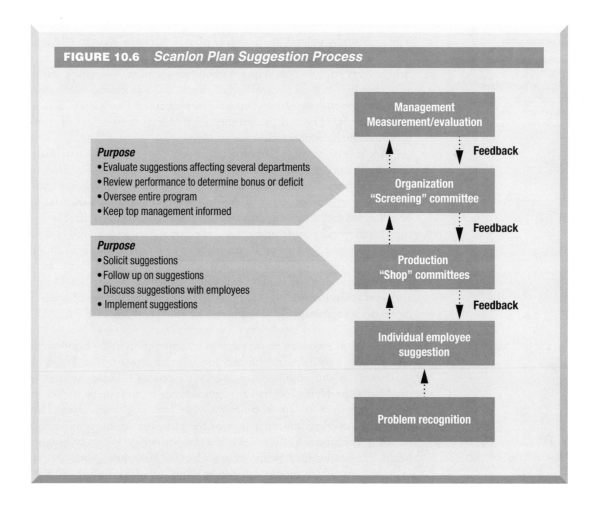

FIGURE 10.6 *Scanlon Plan Suggestion Process*

1. *Identity.* Employee involvement is linked to the company's mission and purpose statement.

2. *Competence.* A high level of competence is expected from employees.

3. *Participation.* A suggestion process taps into employee ideas.

4. *Equity.* Success is based on a partnership forged among employees, customers, and investors.

Rucker Plan

Bonus incentive plan based on the historical relationship between the total earnings of hourly employees and the production value created by the employees

The Rucker Plan

The share-of-production plan (SOP), or Rucker plan, usually covers just production workers, but it can be expanded to cover all employees. As with the Scanlon plan, committees are formed to elicit and evaluate employee suggestions. The Rucker plan, however, uses a far less elaborate participatory structure. As one authority noted: "It commonly represents a type of program that is used as an alternative to the Scanlon plan in firms attempting to move from a traditional style of management toward a higher level of employee involvement."[45]

FIGURE 10.7 *Determining the Monthly Scanlon Plan Incentive Bonus*

1.	Sales revenue		= $100,000
2.	Plus value of goods in iventory		10,000
3.	Sales value of production (SVOP)		$110,000
4.	Target payroll cost (40% of no. 3)	$44,000	
5.	Minus actual labour costs	35,000	
6.	Available incentive bonus		$9,000
7.	Deficit reserve	2,250	
8.	Company share	2,250	
9.	Employee share	4,500	

Employee bonus (percent of actual payroll) = 12.8% ($4,500/$35,000)

The financial incentive of the Rucker plan is based on the historical relationship between the total earnings of hourly employees and the production value that employees create. The bonus is based on any improvement in this relationship that employees are able to realize. Thus, for every 1 percent increase in production value that is achieved, workers receive a bonus of 1 percent of their total payroll costs.[46]

Lessons from the Scanlon and Rucker Plans

Perhaps the most important lesson to be learned from the Scanlon and Rucker plans is that if management wants to gain the cooperation of its employees in improving efficiency, it must find ways to get them involved psychologically as well as financially in the organization. They must identify with the organization. This cannot come out of the traditional manager–subordinate relationship. Employee cooperation is essential to the successful administration of the Scanlon and Rucker plans; at the same time, the plans themselves do not necessarily stimulate this cooperation. The attitude of management is of paramount importance to the success of either plan. For example, where managers show little confidence and trust in their employees, the plans tend to fail.

Improshare

Gainsharing program under which bonuses are based on the overall productivity of the work team

Improshare

Improshare—improved productivity through sharing—is a gainsharing program developed by Mitchell Fain, an industrial engineer with experience in traditional individual incentive systems. Whereas individual production bonuses are typically based on how much an employee produces above some standard amount, Improshare bonuses are based on the overall productivity of the work team. Improshare output is measured by the number of finished products a work team produces in a given period. Both production (direct) employees and nonproduction (indirect) employees are included in the determination of the bonus.[47] Since a cooperative environment benefits all, Improshare promotes increased interaction and support between employees and management.

The bonus is based not on dollar savings, as in the Scanlon and Rucker plans, but on the productivity gains that result from reducing the time it takes to produce a finished product. Bonuses are determined monthly by calculating the difference between standard hours (Improshare hours) and actual hours, and dividing the result by actual hours. The employees and the company each receive payment for 50 percent of the improvement. Companies such as Hinderliter Energy Equipment Corporation pay the bonus as a separate cheque to emphasize that it is extra income.

Earnings-at-Risk Plans

Earnings-at-risk plans

Incentive pay plans placing a portion of the employee's base pay at risk, but giving the opportunity to earn income above base pay when goals are met or exceeded

WWW

As the name implies, **earnings-at-risk plans** place a portion of the employee's base pay at risk. The philosophy behind these programs is that employees should not expect substantial rewards without assuming some risk for their performance. These plans allow employees to recapture lower wages and to reap additional income above full base pay when quality, service, or productivity goals are met or exceeded. An employee's base pay might be set at 90 percent (i.e., 10 percent below market value—the risk part), the loss to be regained through performance. For example, at Saturn Corporation, employee total compensation is made up of base pay, risk pay, and reward pay. Team members earn their risk pay back and receive reward pay as standards are exceeded. Interestingly, at Saturn, employees' base salaries are tied directly to organizational goals.[48]

ENTERPRISE INCENTIVE PLANS

Enterprise incentive plans differ from individual and group incentive plans in that all of the organization's members participate in the plan's compensation payout. Enterprise incentive plans reward employees on the basis of the success of the organization over an extended time—usually one year, but sometimes longer. Enterprise incentive plans seek to create a "culture of ownership" by fostering a culture of cooperation and teamwork among all the organization's members. Common enterprise incentive plans include profit sharing, stock options and employee stock ownership plans (ESOPs).

OBJECTIVE 6

Profit-Sharing Plans

Profit sharing

Any procedure by which an employer pays, or makes available to all regular employees, in addition to base pay, special current or deferred sums based on the profits of the enterprise

WWW

Probably no incentive plan has been the subject of more widespread interest, attention, and misunderstanding than profit sharing. **Profit sharing** is any procedure by which an employer pays, or makes available to all regular employees, special current or deferred sums based on the organization's profits. As defined here, profit sharing represents cash payments made to eligible employees at specified time periods; it is thus distinct from profit sharing in the form of contributions to employee pension funds.

The intention of profit-sharing plans is to give employees the opportunity to increase their earnings by contributing to the growth of their organization's profits. In 2000, Dofasco, a steel maker in Hamilton, Ontario, distributed $53.3 million to 7,000 employees in a profit-sharing plan. These contributions can be directed toward improving product quality, reducing operating costs, improving work methods, and building good will rather than just increasing rates of production. Profit sharing can stimulate employees to think and feel more like partners in the enterprise, and to concern themselves with the welfare of the organization as a whole. Its purpose is to motivate a total commitment from employees rather than simply to have them contribute in specific areas.

WWW

A popular example of a highly successful profit-sharing plan is the one in use at Lincoln Electric Company, a manufacturer of arc-welding equipment and supplies.[49] This plan was started in 1934 by J.F. Lincoln, president of the company. Each year the company distributes a large percentage of its profits to employees in accordance with their salary levels and merit ratings. In recent years the annual bonus has ranged from a low of 55 percent to a high of 115 percent of annual wages. In addition, Lincoln's program includes a piecework plan with a guarantee, cash awards for employee suggestions, a guarantee of employment for 30 hours of the 40-hour work week, and an employee stock purchase plan.

The success of Lincoln Electric's incentive system depends on a high level of contribution by each employee. The performance evaluations that employees receive twice a year are based on four factors—dependability, quality, output, and ideas and cooperation. There is a high degree of respect among employees and management for Lincoln's organizational goals and for the profit-sharing program.

Variations in Profit-Sharing Plans

The variations in profit-sharing plans relate mainly to the proportion of profits shared with employees and to how those profits are distributed. The amount shared with employees can range from 5 to 50 percent of net profit. In most plans, however, about 20 to 25 percent of the net profit is shared. Profits can be distributed to all employees on an equal basis, or can be based on regular salaries or on some formula that takes into account seniority and/or merit. The payments can be disbursed in cash, or deferred, or combine cash and deferred.

Weaknesses of Profit-Sharing Plans

Profit-sharing plans have certain weaknesses. The profits shared with employees may be the result of inventory speculation, luck with weather, economic conditions, national emergencies, or other factors over which employees have no control. Conversely, losses may occur during years when employee contributions have been at a maximum. When profit-sharing payments are made only once a year or are deferred until retirement, their motivational value is less. If a plan fails to pay off for several years in a row, both productivity and employee morale can suffer.

Stock Options

Stock ownership plans for employees have existed in some organizations for many years. These programs are sometimes implemented as part of an employee benefit plan or as part of a corporate culture that links employee effort to stock performance. Organizations that offer stock ownership programs to employees do so in the belief that these programs have some incentive value. The theory is that when employees are allowed to buy the company's stock, they feel like partners in the organization, so their productivity increases, so the stock price rises.

WWW

Under many plans, employees are entitled to purchase stock on an instalment basis through payroll deductions (i.e., without having to pay brokerage fees). Stock ownership plans serve as productivity incentives for booksellers at Borders, baggage handlers at Delta Airlines, and baristas at Starbucks[50] (a barista at Starbucks who was earning $20,000 in 1991 would have been able to cash in his or her options in 1996 for $50,000). Stock ownership programs have become a popular way to boost the morale of disenfranchised employees caught in mergers, acquisitions, and downsizing.

Employee Stock Ownership Plans (ESOPs)

Employee stock ownership plans (ESOPs) have grown significantly in the past ten years. Canadian Tire and Sears Canada have established ESOPs. Companies such as Canadian Pacific Express and Transport have been rescued by ESOP-financed employee buyouts, and Polaroid and Chevron have used ESOPs to fight hostile takeover bids.[51] ESOPs can be used to generate funds to purchase an organization's stock otherwise available to outside raiders. By providing employees with the opportunity to share ownership, ESOPs can serve as a motivating force. According to a Toronto Stock Exchange study, ESOP companies enjoy higher growth and profits, and higher employee productivity.

ESOPs take two basic forms: a stock bonus plan, and a leveraged plan. With a *stock bonus plan*, each year the organization gives stock to the ESOP or gives cash to the ESOP to buy outstanding stock. The ESOP holds the stock for the employees, who are routinely informed of the value of their accounts. Stock allocations can be based on employee wages or seniority. When employees leave the organization or retire, they can sell their stock back to the organization, or they can sell it on the open market if it is traded publicly. *Leveraged* ESOPs are similar to stock bonus plans, the difference being that the ESOP borrows money from a bank or other financial institution to purchase stock. The organization then makes annual tax-deductible payments to the ESOP, which in turn repays the lending institution. An organizations can also place its stock in an ESOP trust and use it as collateral for a bank loan. As the loan is repaid, the stock used as collateral is allocated to employee accounts. Payments of both the principal and interest can be deducted from the organization's income tax liability.

Federal support for ESOPs is available through labour-sponsored venture capital funds. Employees who invest in labour funds are eligible for a 30 percent federal tax credit on their investment (the maximum yearly investment is $3,500). There is no federal legislation in Canada that deals exclusively with employee share ownership; the legislation that governs deferred profit sharing plans (DPSPs) and employee stock options is used as a guide.

Advantages of ESOPs

Encouraged by favourable federal income tax provisions, employers utilize ESOPs as means of providing retirement benefits for their employees. Tax incentives permit a portion of earnings to be excluded from taxation if that portion is assigned to employees in the form of shares of stock. Employers can thus provide retirement benefits for their employees at relatively low cost: in effect, their stock contributions are being subsidized by the federal government. As noted, ESOPs can also increase employees' pride of ownership in the organization, and act as an incentive for them to increase productivity and help the organization prosper and grow. Some promoters of ESOPs even claim that these plans are making Canadian organizations more competitive in world markets. The plans, they maintain, are increasing productivity, improving employee–management relations, and promoting economic justice.[52] About one-third of Canadian companies have established ESOPs.[53]

OBJECTIVE

7

Employee stock ownership plans (ESOPs)

Stock plans in which an organization contributes shares of its stock to an established trust for the purpose of stock purchases by its employees

WWW

Problems with ESOPs

Generally speaking, ESOPs are more likely to serve their intended purposes in publicly held companies than in privately held ones. A major problem with private-company ESOPs is that the company may not be able to purchase back the stock of its employees when they retire. These employees do not have the option to dispose of their stock on the open market. Even large organizations have suffered financial difficulties that have lowered the value of the their stock and, it follows, the value of their employees' retirement plans. This problem is eliminated when the organization establishes a sinking fund to be used exclusively for repurchasing stock.

Other problems with ESOPs include the following:

- The more an employee's pension is based on an ESOP, the more the eventual payout is going to depend the price of the company's stock. Future retirees are vulnerable to stock market fluctuations as well as to management mistakes.
- Traditional pension plans are guaranteed by legislation. ESOP contributions are not. So employee pensions could vanish if the company does, or even if it simply suffers setbacks.
- When all pension funds are allocated to the company's stock, employees can no longer diversify their retirement options—a basic principle of investing. The risk for employees is that the ESOP will be worthless if the employer fails.[54]
- Finally, though studies show that productivity improves when ESOPs are implemented, these gains are not guaranteed. ESOPs help little unless managers are willing to involve employees in organizational decision making. Unfortunately, ESOPs are sometimes set up in ways that restrict employees' access to decision making, and that expose the ESOP to risk.

SUMMARY

The success of an incentive pay plan depends on the organizational climate in which it must operate, employee confidence in it, and its suitability to employee and organizational needs. Importantly, employees must view their incentive pay as being equitable and related to their performance. Performance measures should be quantifiable and easily understood and should bear a demonstrated relationship to organizational performance.

Piecework plans pay employees a given rate for each unit satisfactorily completed. Employers implement these plans when output is easily measured and when the production process is fairly standardized.

Bonuses are incentive payments above base wages paid on either an individual or team basis. A bonus is offered to encourage employees to exert greater effort. Standard hour plans establish a standard time for job completion. An incentive is paid for finishing the job in less than the pre-established time. These plans are popular for jobs with a fixed time for completion.

Merit raises will not motivate employees when they are seen as entitlements, which happens when these raises are given yearly without regard to changes in employee performance. Merit raises are not motivational when they are given because of seniority or favouritism or when merit budgets are inadequate to sufficiently reward employee performance. To be motivational, merit raises must be such that employees see a clear relationship between pay and performance, and the salary increase must be large enough to exceed inflation and higher income taxes.

 Salespeople may be compensated by a straight salary, by a combination of salary and commission, or by a commission only. Paying employees a straight salary allows them to focus on tasks other than sales, such as service and customer good will. A straight commission plan causes employees to emphasize sales goals. A combination of salary and commission provides the advantages of both the straight salary and the straight commission form of payments.

 The Scanlon, Rucker, Improshare, and earnings-at-risk gainshare plans pay bonuses to employees unrelated to profit levels. Each of these plans encourages employees to maximize their performance and cooperation through suggesteions offered to improve organizational performance. The Scanlon Plan pays an employee a bonus based on saved labour cost measured against the organization's sales value of production. The bonus under the Rucker Plan is based on any improvement in the relationship between the total earnings of hourly employees and the value of production that employees create. The Improshare bonus is paid when employees increase production output above a given target level. With earnings-at risk programs, employees earn bonuses when production quotas are met or exeeded, as well as wages that had been put at risk.

 Profit-sharing plans pay to employees sums of money based on the organization's profits. Cash payments are made to eligible employees at specified times, typically yearly. The main purpose of profit sharing is to provide employees with additional income through their participation in organizational achievement. Employee commitment to improved productivity, quality, and customer service will contribute to organizational success and, in turn, to their compensation. Profit-sharing plans may not achieve their stated gains when employee performance is unrelated to organizational success or failure. This may happen because of economic conditions, other competition, or environmental conditions. Profit-sharing plans can have a negative effect on employee morale when plans fail to consistently reward employees.

 With a stock bonus ESOP, each year the organization contributes stock or cash to buy stock, which is then placed in an ESOP trust. With a leveraged ESOP, the organization borrows money from a lending institution to purchase stock for the trust. Under either plan, the ESOP holds the stock for the employees until they either retire or leave the company, at which time the stock is sold back to the company or through a brokerage firm. Employers receive tax benefits for qualified ESOPs; they also hope to receive their employees' commitment to organizational improvement. Employees, however, may lose their retirement income should the company fail or stock prices fall. Another drawback to ESOPs is that they are not guaranteed by any legislation.

KEY TERMS

bonus
career curves (maturity curves)
combined salary and
   commission plan
differential piece rate
earnings-at-risk incentive plans
employee stock ownership plans
   (ESOPs)

gainsharing plans
Improshare
lump-sum merit program
merit guidelines
pay-for-performance standard
perquisites
profit sharing
Rucker Plan

Scanlon Plan
spot bonus
standard hour plan
straight commission plan
straight piecework
straight salary plan
team or group incentive plan

DISCUSSION QUESTIONS

1. Working individually or in groups, identify the factors necessary for a successful incentive plan.

2. Contrast the differences between straight piecework, differential piece rate, and standard hour plans. Explain where each plan might best be used.

3. A common complaint about merit raises is that they do little to increase employee effort. What are the causes of this belief? Suggest ways to increase the motivating value of merit raises.

4. What are the reasons underlying the different payment methods for sales employees?

5. Because of competitive forces in your industry, you have decided to implement a profit-sharing plan for your employees.

Discuss the advantages of profit sharing, and identify specific characteristics that will ensure success for your plan.

6. What are the reasons for the success of the Scanlon and Rucker plans?

7. What are some of the reasons for the rapid growth of ESOPs? Cite some of the potential problems concerning their use.

8. Go to the Career Counsel website for this chapter and complete the excercise. Then form groups in your class, along different characteristics such as age, gender, family status, and career stage, and see if the incentives that appeal to you differ by any demographic factors. Discuss in groups why you chose what you did.

CASE 1

INCENTIVES IN A TIGHT LABOUR MARKET

High-tech knowledge workers are in huge demand, and companies are inventing all kinds of incentives to retain them. As one IT manager put it: "Our inventory has legs, and we are competing with everyone, and we want employees to stay." These people are not motivated by the prestige symbols (big offices, luxury cars) of the previous generation; they want to be free to be themselves, express their style. Employers have to make the workplace intoxicating.

"My company is the coolest" was the reaction of the employees of Zero Knowledge, based in Montreal, when the company reserved a cinema for an opening day screening of *Star Wars: Episode I, The Phantom Menace*, and invited employees to invite up to ten friends. Dress code at this company? No pyjamas. Zero Knowledge offers a gym and a relaxation room, and allows employees to choose their own job titles.

MacDonald Dettwiler & Associates (an aerospace firm) offers scholarships that enable employees to pursue graduate degrees, and professional development dollars printed in vouchers that can be exchanged for books, or to purchase a day off work to attend an outside course.

Price Waterhouse Coopers has a concierge program, whereby employees can call someone to pick up their laundry or service their car. There is also a bonus for employees who agree to accept travel assignments of longer than three months. This firm also allows employees to work a five-day assignment in four days, thus only be away three nights if travelling.

Source: Adapted from H. Davidson, "Hip CEOs Are Pulling Out All the Stops to Reshape Their Workplaces and Keep Employees for Life," *Profit* 18, no. 7 (November 1999): 46–52; R. Maxwell, "Companies Use Innovation to Combat Shortage," *Computer World Canada* 15, no. 3 (February 12, 1999): 45.

Questions

1. Do these perks retain employees? In groups, discuss the kinds of perks that would ensure you would stay with an employer.

2. Perks can be useful for retention, but are they effective at motivation? Explain. What are the best ways to motivate an employee to work harder or smarter?

CASE 2

TO MERIT OR NOT TO MERIT

In January 1993, Centennial Hospital implemented a formal performance appraisal program for its 127 staff nurses. The program originally met with some resistance from a few nurses and supervisors, but generally the system was welcomed as an objective way to appraise nursing performance. Complaints centred around the increase in time it took to complete the appraisal review process and the fact that supervisors disliked having to confront nurses who disagreed with their performance review. Nursing supervisors are required to appraise employee performance annually and to forward to the HR department a copy of each appraisal form.

In July 1995, Thomas Tittle, HR manager for the hospital, reviewed all nurses' appraisals on file since the beginning of the program. From this study, he concluded that the great majority (82 percent) of nurses were evaluated as performing at an "average" level, as indicated by a global rating at the bottom of the form. Roughly 10 percent were rated "above average" or "superior," and the remainder received "below standard" performance reviews. As a response to these findings, Tittle decided to base the annual raises for all nurses on the consumer price index for the hospital's metropolitan area. This, he concluded, would allow the nurses to maintain their standard of living while guaranteeing all nurses a yearly raise. For the past three years, nurses have received their annual wage increase according to this policy.

As part of the hospital's employee involvement program, Tittle holds quarterly meetings with groups of employees to solicit their feelings about hospital policy and their jobs. Both positive and negative opinions are expressed at these gatherings. These opinions are used to modify hospital policy. At meetings in the past year, a number of nurses, both junior and senior, have expressed dissatisfaction with the across-the-board pay policy for annual raises. The biggest complaint centres on the lack of motivation to increase output, since all nurses are paid the same regardless of individual performance. These comments have been numerous enough that Tittle has considered changing the nurses' compensation policy. In the past seven months, nine of the better nurses have quit to take jobs with area hospitals that award annual increases on a merit or pay-for-performance basis.

Questions

1. What are the advantages of adopting a merit pay plan for hospital nurses? Are there any disadvantages to starting a merit pay program?

2. What problems might arise with a supervisor's appraisals of nurses?

3. Develop a merit pay guideline chart based on the following levels of performance evaluation: superior, above average, average, below average, and poor. Use current cost-of-living figures for your area, or salary survey data available to you, to guide your merit percentage increases.

4. It is not uncommon for hospital nurses to work in teams. Explain how a team-based incentive program for nurses might be developed. What criteria might be used to evaluate team performance?

CAREER COUNSEL

Take the Incentive Survey on the Managing Human Resources website (**belcourt.nelson.com**) to discover what motivates you in your career.

USING THE INTERNET

WWW

Check the World at Work website (**www.worldatwork.com**) for trends in compensation.

Access the Society for Human Resources Management (**www.shrm.org/hrlinks**), and explore the Compensation and Benefits icon.

Quality Digest Magazine provides extensive coverage of quality and productivity issues. For information on the Scanlon, Rucker, and Improshare plans, visit **www.qualitydigest.com/jul/gainshre.html**.

NOTES AND REFERENCES

1. Gillian Flynn, "Why Rhino Won't Wait 'til Tomorrow," *Personnel Journal* 75, no. 7 (July 1996): 36–43. See also Garry M. Ritzky, "Incentive Pay Programs That Help the Bottom Line," *HRMagazine* 40, no. 4 (April 1995): 68–74; and John L. Morris, "Bonus Dollars for Team Players," *HRMagazine* 40, no. 2 (February 1995): 76–83.

2. Ongoing productivity and compensation research conducted by one of the authors with Magma Copper Company, Tucson, Arizona.

3. Craig T. Cantoni, "Learn to Manage Pay and Performance Like an Entrepreneur," *Compensation and Benefits Review* 29, no. 1 (January–February 1997): 52–8.

4. Kathleen A. Guinn and Robert J. Corona, "Putting a Price on Performance," *Personnel Journal* 10, no. 5 (May 1991): 72.

5. "Hope for Higher Pay: The Squeeze on Incomes is Gradually Easing Up," *Maclean's*, November 25, 1996: 100–1.

6. "Incentive Pay Rising," *The Human Resources Advisor Newsletter*, September–October 1999: 3; N.B. Carlyle, *Compensation Planning Outlook 1999*, Conference Board of Canada, October 1998.

7. David Beck, "Implementing a Gainsharing Plan: What Companies Need to Know," *Compensation and Benefits Review* 24, no. 1 (January–February 1992): 23.

8. Nina Gupta and Jason D. Shaw, "Financial Incentives Are Effective," *Compensation and Benefits Review* 30, no. 2 (March–April 1998): 26–32.

9. Bill Leonard, "Creating Opportunities to Excel," *HRMagazine* 40, no. 2 (February 1995): 47–51; Shari Caudron, "Variable-Pay Program Increases Taco Bell's Profits," *Personnel Journal* 72, no. 6 (June 1993): 64.

10. "Perception versus Reality with Variable Pay Success," *HRFocus* 75, no. 6 (June 1998): 7.

11. Robert H. Heeneman, Julie A. Fox, and Don E. Eskew, "Using Employee Attitude Surveys to Evaluate a New Incentive Pay Program," *Compensation and Benefits Review* 30, no. 1 (January–February 1998): 40 ff.

12. John G. Belcher, Jr, *How to Design and Implement a Results-Oriented Variable Pay System* (New York: American Management Association, 1996).

13. Beck, "Implementing a Gainsharing Plan": 23.

14. Don Barksdale, "Leading Companies through the Variable Pay Jungle," *HRMagazine* 43, no. 8 (July 1998). See also Kenan S. Abosch, "Variable Pay: Do We Have the Basics in Place?" *Compensation and Benefits Review* 30, no. 4 (July–August 1998): 12–22.

15. George T. Milkovich and Jerry M. Newman, *Compensation*, 5th ed. (Chicago, Ill.: Irwin, 1996): 328.

16. Thomas B. Wilson, "Is It Time to Eliminate the Piece Rate Incentive System?" *Compensation and Benefits Review* 24, no. 2 (March–April 1992): 43–49.

17. Milkovich and Newman, *Compensation*: 328.

18. Carlyle, "Compensation Planning Outlook 1998."

19. Barry L. Wisdom, "Before Implementing a Merit System … Know the Environment and Situations That Demand Caution," *Personnel Administrator* 34, no. 10 (October 1989): 46–9.

20. Glenn Bassett, "Merit Pay Increases Are a Mistake," *Compensation and Benefits Review* 26, no. 2 (March–April 1994): 20–5. See also Lena B. Prewitt, J. Donald Phillips, and Khalad Yasin, "Merit Pay in Academia: Perceptions from the School of Business," *Public Personnel Management* 20, no. 4 (Winter 1991): 409–16.

21. Nina Gupta and G. Douglas Jenkins, Jr., "The Politics of Pay," *Compensation and Benefits Review* 28, no. 2 (March–April 1996): 23–30.

22. J. Edward Kellough and Haoran Lu, "The Paradox of Merit Pay in the Public Sector: Persistence of a Problematic Procedure," *Public Personnel Administration* 13, no. 2 (Spring 1993): 45–61. See also Herbert G. Heneman and I. Phillip Young, "Assessment of a Merit Pay Program for School District Administrators," *Public Personnel Management* 20, no. 1 (Spring 1991): 35–46.

23. Carlyle, "Compensation Planning Outlook 1998."

24. R. Bradley Hill, "A Two-Component Approach to Compensation," *Personnel Journal* 72, no. 5 (May 1993): 154–61.

25. Bill O'Connell, "Dead Solid Perfect: Achieving Sales Compensation Alignment," *Compensation and Benefits Review* 28, no. 2 (March–April 1996): 41.

26. John K. Moynahan, *The Sales Compensation Handbook* (New York: Amacom, 1991).

27. To promote higher sales efforts, organizations can also offer special cash incentives and noncash incentives such as merchandise, travel awards, and status and recognition awards. One study showed that the majority of responding organizations use noncash incentives in addition to their standard compensation plan. See Alfred J. Candrilli, "Success through a Quality-Based Sales Incentive Program," *Compensation and Benefits Review* 22, no. 5 (September–October 1990): 54–59; Jerry McAdams, "Rewarding Sales and Marketing Performance," *Personnel* 64, no. 10 (October 1987): 8–16.

28. John Tallitsch and John Moynahan, "Fine-Tuning Sales Compensation Programs," *Compensation and Benefits Review* 26, no. 7 (March–April 1994): 34–7.

29. J. Goodings, "Rising Pay Heightens Employee Expectations," *Canadian HR Reporter*, May 17, 1999: 1.

30. Mark MacKinnon, "Barrick's Munk Leads Parade 38.9 Million," Canadian Press newswire, April 26, 1999.

31. William L. White, "Managing the Board Review of Executive Pay," *Compensation and Benefits Review* 24, no. 6 (November–December 1992): 35.

32. "Balancing the 'Score' in Executive Pay," *HRFocus* 73, no. 3 (June 1996): 17.

33. Kenneth L. Powell and Mark G. Bosswick, "Deferred-Compensation Plans Make a Comeback," *The National Law Journal*, November 13, 1995: C-6.

34. Frederick W. Cook, "How Much Stock Should Management Own?" *Compensation and Benefits Review* 22, no. 5 (September–October 1990): 20–8. See also John D. England, "Don't Be Afraid of Phantom Stock," *Compensation and Benefits Review* 24, no. 5 (September–October 1992): 39–46.

35. Charles F. Schultz and N. Elizabeth Fried, "Fending Off Unreasonable Compensation Attacks," *HRMagazine* 37, no. 6 (June 1992): 49–54.

36. Nandini Rajagopalah and John E. Prescott, "Determinants of Top Management Compensation: Explaining the Impact of Economic, Behavioral, and Strategic Constructs and the Moderating Effects of Industry," *Journal of Management* 16, no. 3 (1990): 515–38.

37. Byrne, "How High Can CEO Pay Go?": 100. See also John A. Byrne, "Gross Compensation?" *Business Week*, March 18, 1996, 32–3; and "What Keeps CEO Pay Down?" *Business Week* (February 3, 1997): 30.

38. John F. Boschen, "You Can Pay Me Now and You Can Pay Me Later," *Journal of Business* 68, no. 4 (October 1995): 577–608.

39. Steven E. Gross, "When Jobs Become Team Roles, What Do You Pay For?" *Compensation and Benefits Review* 29, no. 1 (January–February 1997): 48–51.

40. Steven E. Gross, *Compensation for Teams*, New York: American Management Association, 1996.

41. Donald J. McNerney, "Rewarding Team Performance and Individual Skill Building," *HRFocus* 72, no. 1 (January 1995): 3–5.

42. Information on team incentive plans is readily available. For example, see Steven E. Gross and Jeffrey Blair, "Reinforcing Team Effectiveness through Pay," *Compensation and Benefits Review* 27, no. 5 (September 1995): 34–38; Robert L. Heneman and Courtney Von Hippel, "Balancing Group and Individual Rewards: Rewarding Individual Contributions to the Team," *Compensation and Benefits Review* 27, no. 4 (July 1995): 63–8; John L. Morris, "Bonus Dollars for Team Players," *HRMagazine* 40, no. 2 (February 1995): 76–83; and Anne M. Saunier and Elizabeth J. Hawk, "Realizing the Potential of Teams through Team-Based Rewards," *Compensation and Benefits Review* 26, no. 4 (July–August 1994): 24–33.

43. Robert Masternak, "How to Make Gainsharing Successful: The Collective Experience of 17 Facilities," *Compensation and Benefits Review* 29, no. 5 (September–October 1997): 43–52.

44. Steven E. Markham, K. Dow Scott, and Walter G. Cox, Jr., "The Evolutionary Development of a Scanlon Plan," *Compensation and Benefits Review* 24, no. 2 (March–April 1992): 50–6.

45. Edward Ost, "Gain Sharing's Potential," *Personnel Administrator* 34, no. 7 (July 1989): 94.

46. The Rucker Plan uses a somewhat more complex formula for determining employee bonuses. For a detailed example of the Rucker bonus, see Milkovich and Newman, *Compensation*, 338.

47. The standard of Improshare's measurement system is the base productivity factor (BPF), which is the ratio of standard direct labour hours produced to total actual hours worked in a base period. The productivity of subsequent periods is then measured by enlarging standard direct labour hours earned by the BPF ratio to establish Improshare hours (IH). The IH is then compared with actual hours worked in the same period. If earned hours exceed actual hours, 50 percent of the gain is divided by actual hours worked in order to establish a bonus percentage for all employees in the plan.

48. Stephenie Overman, "Saturn Teams Working and Profiting," *HRMagazine* 40, no. 3 (March 1995): 72–4.

49. Kenneth W. Chilton, "Lincoln Electric's Incentive System: A Reservoir of Trust," *Compensation and Benefits Review* 25, no. 6 (November 1994): 29–34.

50. Kerry Capell, "Options for Everyone," Business Weekk July 22, 1996: 80–8.

51. S. Lebrun, "ESOP Saves the Day," *Canadian HR Reporter*, November 17, 1997: 1.

52. William Smith, Harold Lazarus, and Harold Murray Kalkstein, "Employee Stock Ownership Plans: Motivation and Morale Issues," *Compensation and Benefits Review* 22, no. 5 (September–October 1990): 37–47.

53. "Reality Cheques: Here's How BC Companies are Starting to Change the Way They Pay," *BC Business* 22, (February 1994): 28–38.

54. Ronald M. Mano and E. DeVon Deppe, "The ESOP Fable: Employees Beware!" *Compensation and Benefits Review* 26, no. 6 (November–December 1994): 44–8.

EMPLOYEE BENEFITS

After studying this chapter, you should be able to

OBJECTIVE 1

Describe the characteristics of a sound benefits program.

OBJECTIVE 2

Recognize management concerns about the costs of employee benefits, and discuss ways to control those costs.

OBJECTIVE 3

Explain the employee benefits required by law.

OBJECTIVE 4

Discuss ways to control the costs of health care programs.

OBJECTIVE 5

Describe those benefits which involve payment for time not worked.

OBJECTIVE 6

Discuss recent trends in retirement policies and programs.

OBJECTIVE 7

Describe the major factors involved in managing pension plans.

OBJECTIVE 8

List the types of service benefits employers can provide.

C ompensation surveys indicate that most employees are unable to name accurately the benefits they receive, and that between 40 and 60 percent of employees underestimate the value of their benefits.[1] Though benefits are largely undervalued and misidentified, they are still an important issue for both employers and employees. Benefits are not a "fringe"; they are in fact an integral part of compensation packages. Almost 80 percent of benefits are provided voluntarily by employers. Benefits represent both a significant cost and an employment advantage for employers. At the same time, they provide important psychological and physical assistance to employees. The importance of benefits to both sides cannot be overstated.

Virtually all employers provide a variety of benefits to supplement the wages or salaries they pay their workers. These benefits, some of which are required by law, must be considered a part of total compensation. In this chapter we look at the characteristics of employee benefits programs. We examine the types of benefits required by law; we also discuss the major discretionary benefits that employers offer, the employee services they provide, and the retirement programs in common use. We conclude the chapter with a discussion of popular work/life benefit programs.

EMPLOYEE BENEFITS PROGRAMS

Employee benefits are an indirect form of compensation; they are meant to improve employees' quality of life, both at work and away from it. On average, benefits constitute 42 percent of employers' payroll costs.[2] In return for providing them, employers generally expect employees to be supportive of the organization and to be productive. Employees have come to expect more and more benefits; they were once viewed as gifts from the employer, but have come to be perceived as rights that all employees should expect. They must be well designed and well communicated if the benefits program is to have any motivational value.

Information Technology and Employee Benefits

So many benefits are being offered to employees today that administering a benefits program can be both costly and time-consuming. Even small employers with thirty to forty employees find it cumbersome to keep track of which benefits employees are using and which ones they want to change. Even rather straightforward tasks, such as monitoring employees' sick leave, can become overwhelming as the organization grows.

A large majority of employers, both large and small, have begun using interactive employee benefit systems. Employees can now access their benefits package on the Internet with a couple of mouse clicks. This provides them with greater control and ownership of the benefits being offered to them. Part of the advantage of an Internet benefits system is that employees can obtain information on their own time.[3]

On-line benefits programs create a form of self-service administration. One intent of on-line programs is to eliminate the annual open enrolment period for various benefits; this provides greater flexibility in benefits selection. Interactive benefits programs offer significant savings in administration costs. Once an on-line system is operational, it is easy and inexpensive to adapt to employer and employee demands. However, security issues must always be addressed before benefits information is posted on-line.[4]

Perhaps no part of the HR function is more technologically advanced than benefits administration. A wide variety of software packages are now available that can oversee benefits administration in areas such as pensions, variable pay, worker's compensation, health benefits, and time-off programs. These programs are regularly described (and advertised) in HR journals like *Canadian HR Reporter* and *Human Resource Professional*. For employers who lack the real-time resources or expertise to manage benefits programs, software programs are a cost-effective way to do it.

WWW

Requirements for a Sound Benefits Program

Too often, a particular benefit is provided because other employers are doing it, because someone in authority thinks it's a good idea, or because there is union pressure. Designing a benefits program that will help both the organization and its employees involves certain considerations.

Establishing Specific Objectives

Like any other component of the HR program, an employee benefits program should be based on specific objectives. What these objectives are will depend on many factors, including these: the size of the firm; its location; its degree of unionization; its profitability; and industry patterns. Most important, these aims must be compatible with the organization's strategic compensation plan (see Chapter 9), including its philosophy and policies.

The main objectives of most benefits programs are:

- to improve employee satisfaction,
- to meet employee health and security requirements,
- to attract and motivate employees,
- to reduce turnover, *and*
- to maintain a favourable competitive position.

Furthermore, these objectives must be considered within the framework of cost containment—a major issue in today's programs.

Unless the organization plans to develop a flexible benefits plan (to be discussed later), it should work toward a uniform package of benefits. This involves carefully considering which benefits are possible (i.e., on the market), which ones management and employees would prefer to get; how much they would cost; and how much money is available for the total benefits package.

Allowing for Employee Input

Before a new benefit is introduced, the organization should find out from its employees whether they need it. Many organizations have established management–employee committees to administer, interpret, and oversee their benefits policies. Opinion surveys can be used to obtain employee input. When managers involve their employees in the design of benefits programs, it is more likely that employee wants will be satisfied. Pan Canadian Petroleum formed eleven focus groups of randomly selected employees to provide insights and valuable feedback on their pension investments.[5]

WWW

Modifying Employee Benefits

If they are to serve their intended purpose, employee benefits programs must reflect the social changes that Canada is constantly facing. Especially significant are changes in the composition of the workforce, which make it necessary to develop new types of benefits. For example, more and more employers are tailoring their benefit programs to be family-friendly. (Specific family-friendly benefits are discussed later in the chapter.) Another example is that more and more women are entering the workforce. Do they have children? Are they covered by a spouse's benefits? Questions like these must be asked when determining which benefits will be of most value to them.

Unfortunately, benefit plans sometimes offer little to employees, which makes it harder for the organization to attract and retain quality employees. Example: Many employers provide medical benefits in the form of dependants' coverage. Young and/or single workers are unlikely to see this as useful. Nor are these people likely to get excited about a defined-benefits pension program, however well designed it is (or how costly). Similarly, the employer's contribution to the pension plan for a 30-year-old employee is roughly one-fourth the contribution for a 50-year-old employee for the same amount of pension commencing at age 65. This difference in funds spent on older workers in effect discriminates against younger workers, although in legal terms it is not regarded as discriminatory. These examples illustrate the need for benefits programs that take into account the differing needs of a variety of workers.

Providing for Flexibility

Flexible benefits plans (cafeteria plans)

Benefit plans that enable individual employees to choose the benefits that are best suited to their particular needs

To accommodate the individual needs of employees, many organizations are embracing **flexible benefits plans**, also known as cafeteria plans. According to the *Compensation Planning Outlook 1998* report published by the Conference Board of Canada, 28 percent of respondents offer flexible benefits, nearly triple the number in 1990.[6] These plans enable individual employees to choose the benefits that are best suited to their particular needs. They also prevent certain benefits from being wasted on employees who have no need for them. Typically, employees are offered a basic or core benefits package of life and health insurance, sick leave, and vacation, plus a specified number of credits that they can use to "buy" whatever other benefits they need. Other benefit options might include prepaid legal services, financial planning, or long-term care insurance.[7]

www

Honeywell Canada considered three types of flexible benefits programs: cafeteria-style, whereby employees could choose any benefits they wanted; a module approach, whereby employees could select among prepackaged sets of benefits; and a core-plus-options plan, whereby employees could choose among options to augment a basic level of protection. Employees were able to select health and dental benefits that suited their life stages, and that matched well with the plans their spouses had. Figure 11.1 lists the most commonly cited advantages and disadvantages of flexible benefits programs. Because cafeteria plans are more complex, organizations often contract out the administration of them to a professional benefits vendor, which will charge a service or contract fee. Small firms in particular can benefit from these vendors. Benefits programs must be flexible enough to accommodate the changes in the laws and regulations that affect them. There are many consulting firms that specialize in benefits and that can help managers keep up with these changes.

FIGURE 11.1 *Flexible Benefits Plans: Advantages and Disdvantages*

ADVANTAGES

- Employees select benefits to match their individual needs.
- Benefit selections adapt to a constantly changing (diversified) workforce.
- Employees gain greater understanding of the benefits offered to them and the costs incurred.
- Employers maximize the psychological value of their benefits program by paying only for the highly desired benefits.
- Employers limit benefit costs by allowing employees to "buy" benefits only up to a maximum (defined) amount.
- Employers gain competitive advantage in the recruiting and retention of employees.

DISADVANTAGES

- Poor employee benefits selection results in unwanted financial costs.
- There are certain added costs to establishing and maintaining the flexible plan.
- Employees may choose benefits of high use to them that increase employer premium costs.

Communicating Employee Benefits Information

The true measure of a successful benefits program is how well the employees trust, understand, and appreciate it. Employers must carefully communicate information about complicated insurance and pension plans so that there is no misunderstanding about what the plans do and do not provide. Recent court cases in Canada have established that it is the employer's responsibility to properly inform and disclose information about benefits. In *Spinks vs Canada*, an employee was not advised of certain pension options when he started with a new employer—specifically, that he was eligible to purchase past service in connection with his prior employment. The Federal Court of Appeal ruled that the employee had been poorly advised. In other cases, such as *Schmidt vs Air Products of Canada*, the courts have ruled that employee brochures, which usually aren't considered to be legal documents, may in fact be legally binding.[8]

While it is important to communicate information about employee benefits, there is no legislation that mandates how this is to be done. Various provincial pension benefits acts and federal laws regulating pension benefits state that employers operating a pension plan must provide specific information to employees. However, there are differences between provinces in terms of what must be communicated. The sponsor of a registered retirement plan (RPP) has until six months after the end of the plan's fiscal year to provide active plan members with statements of their pension benefits. (Quebec regulations require annual pension statements for retired and deferred vested members.) The employee's name, date of birth, and date of hire must be included in the pension statement, along with the pension plan membership date, vesting date, and normal retirement date. Most provinces also require the name of the employee's spouse and/or pension plan beneficiary.[9]

Employers use a number of methods to communicate benefits to employees. In-house publications—which include employee handbooks and organization newsletters—are one popular way. Also, the topic is usually covered in new-hire orientation programs. Managers who are conducting orientations should be allowed plenty of time to inform new employees of the benefits program, and to answer any questions. Some employers summarize benefits information on a pay-cheque stub as a reminder to employees of their total compensation. Highlights in HRM 1 provides a list of recommendations for communicating benefits.

New self-service technologies have made it possible for employees to gather information about their benefits plans, enrol in their plans of choice, change their benefits coverage, or simply inquire about the status of their various benefit

Highlights in HRM

1   CRAFTING AN EFFECTIVE BENEFITS COMMUNICATION PROGRAM

A well-designed benefits communication program will greatly enhance employees' appreciation of their benefits while ensuring that employers receive the intended value of these offerings. An effective program provides information frequently to employees in a timely and cost-effective manner. Compensation specialists recommend the following when administering a benefits communication program.

IN BUILDING AN IDENTITY:
- Design materials that are eye-catching and of high interest to employees.
- Develop a graphic logo for all material.
- Identify a theme for the benefits program.

IN WRITING BENEFITS MATERIALS:
- Avoid complex language when describing benefits. Clear, concise, and understandable language is a must.
- Provide numerous examples to illustrate benefit specifics.
- Explain all benefits in an open and honest manner. Do not attempt to conceal unpleasant news.
- Explain the purpose behind the benefit and the value of the benefit to employees.

IN PUBLICIZING BENEFITS INFORMATION:
- Use all popular employee communication techniques.
- Maintain employee self-service (ESS) technology to disseminate benefits information and to update employee benefits selections.
- Use voice mail to send benefits information.
- Employ presentation software such as PowerPoint or Lotus Freelance to present information to groups of employees.
- Maintain a benefits hot line to answer employee questions.

WWW

accounts without ever contacting an HR representative.[10] Coopers & Lybrand uses a Benefits Information Line to provide its employees with instant access to a wide variety of HR and benefits information by telephone. Individual account information is available on entering a personal identification number (PIN). Other organizations use networked PCs or multimedia kiosks to the same purpose. At Nortel, 13,000 employees use an interactive voice response system to select their benefits. These latter approaches enable employees to click on icons to access different benefits and to type in new information to update their records. Once an update or change has been made, the new information is permanently entered into the organization's HR information system without the need for paperwork.

It is also important for each employee to have a current statement of the status of her or his benefits.[11] The usual means is the personalized computer-generated statement of benefits.

WWW

As the field of benefits becomes increasingly complex, and as employees become more sophisticated about financial planning, the need to hire and train benefits experts also grows. For those interested in specializing in this field, a good career move would be to become a certified employee benefit specialist (CEBS). In cooperation with the Wharton School at the University of Pennsylvania, Dalhousie University in Halifax sponsors a college-level program leading to the CEBS designation.[12] This ten-course program covers total compensation, health benefits, and strategic human resources.

Concerns of Management

Managing an employee benefits program requires close attention to many forces, which must be kept in balance if the program is to succeed. Management must consider union demands, the benefits other employers are offering, tax consequences, rising costs, and legal ramifications. Below, we briefly examine the last two concerns.

The rising cost of health care benefits has resulted in employers passing some of the costs on to employees in the form of higher deductibles or payroll deductions.

WWW

Significant Costs

According to KPMG's *20th Annual Employee Benefit Costs* survey (1996), the costs of employee benefits in that year averaged 41.8 percent of payroll.[13] Costs of benefits were higher in the public sector—45.8 compared to 34.9 percent. However, these benefit costs have dropped dramatically in the public sector, after years of unprecedented increases.

Many benefits represent a fixed rather than a variable cost, so management must decide whether it will be able to afford this cost in bad economic times. As managers can readily attest, the negative effects of discontinuing a benefit often outweigh any positive effects that accrued from providing it.

To soften any negative impact and to avoid unnecessary expense, many employers enlist the cooperation of employees in evaluating the importance of particular benefits. Also, more and more employers are requiring employees to pay part of the costs of certain benefits (e.g., through co-payments or higher deductibles). At all times, benefit plan administrators are expected to select vendors of benefit services that have the most to offer for the cost.

The escalating cost of health care benefits is a concern to employers, who must strike an appropriate balance between offering quality benefits and keeping costs under control. The shift in benefit planning from entitlement to self-responsibility is discussed in Reality Check.

The Conference Board of Canada has published a list of cost containment strategies, which include these:

- Contribution changes, such as increasing deductibles.
- Dollar limits, such as a dollar cap on specific benefits like eyeglasses.
- Coverage changes (e.g., limits on hospital upgrades).
- Benefit caps (e.g., on dispensing fees).
- Use of preferred providers and flexible benefits.[14]

EMPLOYEE BENEFITS REQUIRED BY LAW

Legally required employee benefits amount to 11.2 percent of the benefits packages that Canadian employers provide.[15] These benefits include employer contributions to the Canada and Quebec pension plans, unemployment insurance, workers' compensation insurance, and (in some provinces) provincial medicare.

Canada and Quebec Pension Plans (CPP/QPP)

The Canada and Quebec pension plans cover almost all Canadian employees between the ages of 18 and 65. (Certain migratory and casual workers who earn less than the specified amount may be excluded.) To receive a retirement benefit, an individual must apply to Human Resources Development Canada at least six months in advance of retirement.

Although similar in concept, the CPP and QPP differ in terms of how much they pay out to participants. Both plans require employers to match the contributions made by employees. The revenues generated by these contributions are used to pay three main types of benefits: retirement pensions, disability benefits, and survivors' benefits. Governments do not subsidize these plans; all contributions come from employers and employees. Self-employed individuals can also contribute to

Reality CHECK

BENEFIT PLANNING: FROM ENTITLEMENT TO SELF-RESPONSIBILITY

WWW

In recent years, we have witnessed major upheavals in the area of benefits. Never before have there been such large increases in the cost of providing benefits as senior executives in companies throughout Canada try to change the "entitlement mindset" so prevalent in employees. Human resources professionals and senior executives can no longer make decisions regarding benefit plans without the assistance of benefit consultants. We met with Daphne Woolf of William H. Mercer Limited to discuss trends in benefit coverage.

Woolf specializes in the design and implementation of flexible benefit plans, strategic planning as it relates to compensation and benefits, and workplace health promotion program design and monitoring. She provides companies with extensive experience in evaluating funding, administration, and utilization for the purpose of identifying ways to contain benefit plan costs. A visionary in her own right, she leads the national and central region task forces on flexible benefits for Mercer.

"First of all, we need to look at the drivers of change. We see four things happening: our demographics are changing as people age; we have double-income families and the workplace is becoming increasingly diverse; benefits are being taxed to greater extents; and human rights legislation is changing with respect to who should be covered. Due to the high costs of providing benefit coverage, we are seeing a shift in responsibility from the provinces to third parties and individuals. The provinces are covering less, and this trend will continue to grow. The final, most important, underlying issue is increased sensitivity to the magnitude of these trends and the resulting benefit cost impacts.

"The entitlement mindset stems from the fact that, fifteen years ago, benefits were considered fringe. Now they are viewed as part of total compensation, which is a change in mentality. Employers are starting to move away from this entitlement mindset to self-responsibility. Employees are not used to making their own health care decisions, and it is a challenge for employers to educate their employees sufficiently and sway them to a different way of thinking. As the population ages, employees' needs for benefits are increasing; at the same time, the quality of their benefits must decrease in response to the high costs. Based on some of our studies, what we are seeing for the first time is that employees are making employment decisions based on benefits. Employers look at dealing with these benefit trends by revisiting their philosophy and benefits objectives. For example, does an employer pay for smoking cessation, include high deductibles, offer choice, or provide coverage for dependents?

"We are seeing an increase in flexible benefit plans. Our belief is that in five years the majority of plans will be flexible, and an employer who waits may be disadvantaged. Employers are better off as flex leaders than flex followers. You want to create your own plan, not have to base your program design on what someone else has done. Now you can 'anti-select' the benefit costs of the spouse's plan, allowing your employee to 'cash out' or allocate flex credits to stock plans or an RRSP. In the future, however, employees and their dependents may not opt out of your plan, and this would potentially increase your costs. So going flex sooner than later, if it's in keeping with corporate objectives, makes sense for many employers who have employees with spouses who work elsewhere. It is going to be a much tougher sell in the future if employees don't learn what the costs are today—they'll still be thinking entitlement when they get older and their provincial medicare does not cover as much.

"Managers have to start watching the cost of illness and absenteeism and realize the lost production costs of paying for time off. These costs add to the overall cost of benefits and should be tied to compensation so that employees can appreciate those benefits. We are also moving toward managed care. We have to look at providing the same level of health care at the same cost. That means putting caps on dispensing fees where drugs are concerned and getting second opinions to ensure that unnecessary procedures are not being administered."

"Americans have moved to a two-tiered system, and Canada is not far behind. While this is not currently a problem, it will be soon. For instance, if a patient wants a second opinion for something serious such as cancer, he or she may have to wait to see another specialist. In a two-tiered system, the patient can pay to have a second opinion immediately. This would not be reimbursed by the provincial health plan. We are beginning to see the collapse of provincial medicare as we now know it."

"There is an increase in health promotion. We are talking about wellness programs, which may focus on stress reduction, fitness in the workplace, and smoking-cessation programs. Employers are seeing the value in keeping employees healthy and productive, that is, preventing the claims costs. In one of my presentations, 'Taking the Fluff Out of Health Promotion,' I specifically outline the advantages of introducing health promotion programs to target cost pressures within the organization. Employers can yield a favourable return on investment if they ensure the right steps are taken to implement health promotion to secure effective cost containment. We are also diverging from traditional medicine to naturopathy and other paramedic services."

"In essence, employers are revisiting the extension of benefits to part-timers, retirees, and dependents. There is a movement toward providing incentive-based benefits—that is, using benefits to reward performance—and, with this, bringing things back to the overall compensation strategy. Employee expectations have become unrealistic mainly because they have not been educated. Once informed, we find that employees become a valuable resource. They need to understand the numbers. Employee focus groups are fast becoming the way to heed the transition from entitlement mindset to self-responsibility."

"In closing, the trends are moving somewhere in the middle between the American health care system and Canada's. As we near the year 2000, flexible benefit plans will be the plan of choice so that educating the employee will be paramount if we are to move from an entitlement mindset to self-responsibility. Your plan should be devised considering an overall philosophy with particular attention to the strategic plan of your organization. Benefits can no longer be taken for granted as the costs of providing this commodity are at a premium. What constitutes benefits must be expanded beyond your basic dental, life insurance, and drug plans. Benefits strategies cannot be short term, but rather must be long range, and in this regard benefit consultants can provide value-added advice. Selecting the right consultant to work with you is just as important as determining your overall benefits philosophy. This philosophy is key to the design of your program as it sets the stage for what your benefit plan will entail."

the plan. With Canada's population aging, funds from the CPP will not be able to meet the needs of retirees unless those currently working, and their employers, significantly increase their contributions.

Canada has cross-border agreements with several countries to protect the acquired social security rights of people who have worked and lived in both countries, and who meet the minimum qualifications for benefits from either country. A contributor's rights to benefits under CPP or QPP are not affected or impaired in any way by a change of employment or residence in Canada. All Canadian workers have "universal portability"—that is, the right to claim benefit credits wherever they are employed in Canada.

Employment Insurance (EI)

Employment insurance (EI) benefits are payable to claimants who are unemployed and are actively seeking employment. A person who becomes unemployed is usually entitled to what most Canadians still call "Unemployment Insurance" (or "UI"), which was what this program used to be called. The new name reflects a change in focus from basic income support to active employment measures.[16]

The amount of benefit paid is determined by the number of hours of employment in the past year and the regional unemployment rate. At present, the weekly benefit is based on 55 percent of the claimant's average insured earnings for the last twenty insured weeks in the qualifying period. Individuals are entitled to unemployment insurance after they have contributed enough for a qualifying period and after a waiting period. The waiting period may vary with the individual's situation. Also, employees who resign from their job or who are terminated for cause may be ineligible for benefits unless they can prove there was no reasonable alternative to leaving their job.

Additional benefits may be extended for situations involving illness, injury, or quarantine, or for maternity, parental, or adoption leave. If an organization does not offer sick leave benefits, the employee may have to apply to EI for sick benefits. The benefit amount, which is calculated on the same basis as the regular benefit, varies across jurisdictions. Sickness or disability benefits are available for up to fifteen weeks. A combination of maternity, parental, or adoptive benefits may be available up to a cumulative maximum of thirty weeks.

Employees and employers both contribute to the EI fund. An EI premium reduction is available to employers who cover their employees under an approved wage-loss plan. The amount of the reduction depends on the supplement being given to the employee, and therefore varies from company to company. Work-sharing programs have recently come into existence as a means of reducing the overall burden on EI. Under work sharing, an organization reduces the workweek of all employees in a particular group instead of laying them off. The company pays for the time worked, and the employee draws EI for the rest of the workweek.

Workers' compensation insurance

Insurance provided to workers to defray the loss of income and cost of treatment resulting from work-related injuries or illness

Workers' Compensation Insurance

Workers' compensation insurance is based on the theory that compensation for work-related accidents and illnesses should be considered one of the costs of doing business and should ultimately be passed on to the consumer. Individual employees should not be required to bear the cost of their treatment or loss of income; nor should they be subjected to complicated, delaying, and expensive legal procedures.

Workers' compensation is a form of insurance. It was created by an act of Parliament to help workers injured on the job return to the workplace. Each provincial and territorial board is empowered by the relevant legislation to amend and collect assessments (i.e., insurance premiums), to determine the right to compensation, and to pay the amount due to the injured worker. This system of collective liability is compulsory. Employers' contributions are assessed as a percentage of their payroll. The percentage varies with the nature of the industry. For example, in a high-risk industry like mining, the assessment rates are higher than in knowledge-based industries.

Workers' compensation is based on the following principles:

- Employers share collective liability, though contributions may vary among employers in the same industry (e.g., some provinces punish employers who do not maintain a safe and healthy work environment by levying additional fines).
- Injured workers are compensated regardless of the financial status of the employer, and this compensation is based on loss of earnings.
- The system is no-fault and nonadversarial, and thus offers no recourse to the courts.

Benefits are paid out of an employer-financed fund and include medical expenses stemming from work-related injuries, survivors' benefits (including burial expenses and pensions), and wage-loss payments for temporary, total, or partial disability. Permanent disability benefits may be disbursed as a lump-sum payment or as a permanent disability pension with rehabilitation services. The amount paid depends on the employee's earnings and provincial legislation.

Employees cannot be required either to make contributions toward a workers' compensation fund or to waive their right to receive compensation benefits. Payments made to claimants are effectively nontaxable. Premiums paid for by the employer may be deducted as expenses and are not deemed a taxable benefit for employees.

About 1.2 million Canadians are injured at work every year. These injuries cost $7.5 billion, yet only $6.5 billion is collected from employers. These shortfalls have left workers' compensation boards with an unfunded liability of billions of dollars. Faced with this, boards across Canada are introducing experience-rating programs (see Chapter 12), and encouraging employers to introduce better prevention and claims management practices.[17]

Figure 11.2 lists the steps that an HR department can take to control workers' compensation costs.

Provincial Hospital and Medical Services

People who have been resident in a Canadian province for three months are eligible to receive health care benefits. Applications must be made and approval given before coverage starts. Benefits include services provided by physicians, surgeons, and other qualified health professionals; hospital services such as standard ward accommodation and laboratory and diagnostic procedures; and hospital-administered drugs. Many employers offer third-party benefit coverage, which entitles their employees to additional benefits such as semi-private or private accommoda-

---

FIGURE 11.2 *Reducing Worker's Compensation Costs: Key Areas*

1. Perform an audit to assess high-risk areas in the workplace.
2. Prevent injuries by ensuring proper ergonomic design of the workplace, effective assessment of job candidates, and worker training.
3. Provide to injured employees quality medical care from physicians with experience and preferably with training in occupational health.
4. Reduce litigation by ensuring effective communication between the employer and the injured worker.
5. Manage the care of the injured worker from time of injury until return to work. Keep a partially recovered employee at the worksite.[18]
6. Provide extensive worker training in all related health and safety areas.

---

tion, prescription drugs, private nursing, ambulance services, out-of-country medical expenses that exceed provincial limits, vision and dental care, and paramedic services. Depending on the employer, all or just a portion of the services may be covered.

The cost of providing health care has escalated to the point where major reform in Canada's health care system is becoming inevitable. For instance, in Toronto the number of people over the age of 85 is expected to double in the next ten years; this will impose a tremendous burden on the health care system.[19] Some observers fear the emergence of two-tiered medical care. If two-tier does come:

- patients with private health insurance will be able to jump waiting lists;
- doctors will be permitted to make arrangements with American insurance carriers to sell their "excess capacity," including some surgical procedures and the use of high-tech diagnostic tools such as CAT scans; *and*
- private companies will be allowed to offer a full range of supplementary health insurance.[20]

DISCRETIONARY MAJOR EMPLOYEE BENEFITS

Besides the mandated benefits, most employers offer other benefits such as health care and dental plans.

Health Care Benefits

The benefits receiving the most attention from employers today, owing to sharply rising costs and employee concerns, are health care benefits. In the past, health insurance plans covered only medical, surgical, and hospital expenses. Today employers are under pressure to include prescription drugs as well as dental, optical, and mental health care benefits in the packages they offer their workers.

Cost Containment

The growth in health care costs can be attributed to a number of factors, including the greater need for health care by an aging population, the costs associated with technological advances in medicine, the growing costs of health care labour, and the overuse of costly health care services.

The approaches used to contain the costs of health care benefits include reductions in coverage, increased deductibles or co-payments, and increased coordination of benefits to ensure that the same expense is not paid by more than one insurance reimbursement. A list of cost containment strategies is provided in Figure 11.3. Other cost containment efforts involve alternatives to traditional medical care: the use of health maintenance organizations and preferred providers, incentives for outpatient surgery and testing, and mandatory second opinions for surgical procedures. Some employers seek to control the costs of benefits by providing them only to full-time employees—a controversial practice (see Ethics in HRM). Cost containment strategies must be subject to a cost/benefit analysis. For example, although many employees use alternative health care therapies, there is little proof that these alternatives reduce health care costs.[21]

Employee assistance programs and wellness programs can help organizations cut the costs of health care benefits. Highlights in HRM 2 focuses on a team approach to cost reduction.

Other Health Benefits

In the past two decades, more and more employees have been receiving dental care insurance as a benefit. Besides their obvious purpose, dental plans encourage employees to receive regular dental attention. Typically, the insurance pays a portion of the charges and the subscriber pays the remainder.

Another fairly new benefit that many employers are offering is optical care. Typically, the coverage includes visual examinations and a percentage of the costs of lenses and frames.

FIGURE 11.3 *Cost Containment Strategies*

Employers can reduce the cost of benefits in the following ways:
1. **Education and Motivation**
   - Communicate the costs of benefits.
   - Provide incentives to employees to reduce costs.
   - Teach employees how to live healthy lifestyles, and how to plan for retirement.
2. **Change coverage**
   - Introduce dollar limits on benefits.
   - Eliminate duplicate coverage for spouses.
   - Remove upgrades.
   - Introduce minimum fees to be paid by employees.
3. **Change the system**
   - Form partnerships with pharmacies to provide discounts.
   - Move to defined contribution plans.
   - Move to a claims management approach, and audit claims.

Ethics in HRM

THE REAL VALUE OF A FULL-TIME JOB

Full-time workers get more pay (when you calculate hours worked and rate of pay per hour) and also more benefits. The differences are staggering, as the following table indicates:

BENEFIT	FULL-TIME WORKERS	PART TIME WORKERS
Employer pension plan	58%	19 %
Health care plan	68	18
Dental plan	63	16
Paid sick leave	66	18
Paid vacation leave	80	30

These differences have a profound impact on employees' lives: one in eight of Canada's 2.6 million part-time workers spend their spare time looking for full-time employment. If benefits are important to them, they should be looking for a large employer in an unionized environment. The probability of receiving benefits increases with the size of the employer. It also increases if the employer is unionized, and if the job is permanent rather than temporary.

All of this is a concern to the government, and should also concern taxpayers. Part-time workers are least able to afford their own benefits; as a result, society ends up paying for the services they need, such as health care and retirement plans, through social transfer payments. Should governments pass legislation to force employers to offer the same benefits to part-timers as full-timers? The Royal Bank of Canada now provides full benefits and bonuses to 7,500 part-time and casual workers.

Source: Bruce Little, "The Full-Scale Advantages of Full-Time Time Work," *The Globe and Mail*, July 14, 1997. Brenda Lipsett and Mark Reesor, "Job-Related Benefits for Employees," Human Resources Development Canada, June 1997.

Pay for Time Not Worked

The "pay for time not worked" category of benefits includes the following: statutory holiday pay and vacation pay; incentives and production bonuses; time off for bereavement, jury duty, and military duty; rest periods and coffee breaks; self-insured STD; and maternity benefits (which usually involve some form of salary continuance).

Vacations with Pay

It is generally agreed that vacation time is essential to the well-being of employees. Eligibility for vacations varies by industry, by locale, and by size of the organization. Systems are often set up so that the longer the employee has worked for the same organization, the more vacation time he or she gets (e.g., three weeks after seven years, four weeks after fifteen, five after twenty).

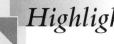

Highlights in HRM

2   A TEAM APPROACH TO COST CONTAINMENT

WWW

The University of New Brunswick (UNB) in Fredericton has long done what so many other organizations are only starting to do: it has used its employees to assist it in devising strategies to combat increases in benefit costs. In 1974, a Fringe Benefits Review Committee was established. According to Jim O'Sullivan, the university's vice-president of finance and administration, the committee was organized in "an effort to repair relations with angry faculty representatives after the university's board of governors was perceived to have unilaterally eliminated an existing benefit."

The committee, which comprises management as well as unionized and nonunionized employees, has the task of reviewing the university's group file, health, and long-term disability (LTD) plans. Although the board of governors still holds the final decision-making authority, the committee alone is responsible for making benefits recommendations and working out the details; its efforts have resulted in a $3.8 million benefits surplus.

For the past twenty years, the employees have shared the costs of the university's group insurance plan, thus allowing the university to maintain effective cost control and to plan redesigns. Because the plan costs are shared, employees are aware that increasing benefits will mean higher contributions for both sides. To keep LTD claims down, employees have allowed the university to follow up directly with workers on disability claims to help them return to work faster. UNB leads the way with the lowest claims among other universities with similar workforces. While for many other organizations the price tag for health care, drug, and dental benefits has grown annually, UNB has managed to hold benefit costs below the general rate of inflation. O'Sullivan attributes the savings to the cost-sharing partnership.

As in many other organizations, the employee assistance program is fully paid for by the employer. However, because the development of this program was discussed with the committee, employees played a major role in selling this plan. O'Sullivan believes that the plan is cost-effective in the long term. "Failure to seek treatment for personal problems," he notes, "would eventually affect job performance and lead to higher costs for health and LTD insurance."

The university has been self-insuring benefits, with a pay-as-you-go philosophy, since the 1970s. Commercial insurance is purchased only to provide protection against catastrophic losses. For example, the LTD plan is self-insured for the first ten years of any claim, after which commercial insurance coverage comes into effect.

Employer and employee representative groups each have control over their half share of surplus funds. Consideration has been given to contribution holidays or to implementing new benefits, but both sides, concerned that the good times could come to an end, have decided to act conservatively. The surplus funds are invested by the university's endowment fund investment managers; investment income is used to improve employees' benefits.

"I do believe we have developed a realistic balance between the operation of a responsive and competitive benefits package and the need to maintain effective cost controls," states O'Sullivan. "In this way, we have not only helped meet our overall financial objectives but have created positive spinoffs for labour–management relations generally."

As shown in Figure 11.4, European professional and managerial personnel tend to receive more vacation time than their Canadian, American, and Japanese counterparts. In most countries the government requires employers to guarantee vacation time to their workers; the United States and United Kingdom are exceptions to this.

Paid Holidays

Both hourly and salaried workers can expect to be paid for statutory holidays as designated by each province. The standard statutory holidays are New Year's Day, Good Friday, Canada Day (Memorial Day in Newfoundland), Labour Day, and Christmas Day. Other holidays commonly recognized by the various provinces are Victoria Day, Thanksgiving Day, and Remembrance Day. Some provinces have their own special statutory holidays. Many employers give workers an additional one to three personal days off (i.e., personal use days)

Sick Leave

Employees who cannot work because of illness or injury are compensated in various ways. Most public employees, and many in private firms—especially in white-collar jobs—receive a set number of sick leave days each year to cover such absences. Sometimes employees are permitted to accumulate the sick leave they do not use to cover prolonged absences. Accumulated vacation leave is sometimes treated as a source of income when sick leave benefits have been exhausted. Group insurance that provides income protection during a long-term disability is also

FIGURE 11.4 *Vacation Days: A Global Look*

COUNTRY	LEGAL MINIMUM	TYPICAL PRACTICE	PUBLIC HOLIDAYS
Brazil	22	22	11
Canada	10	20	11
France	25	25–30	13
Germany	18	30–33	13
Hong Kong	7	20–30	17
Japan	19	20	14
Mexico	14	15–20	19
Sweden	30	30–32	10
United Kingdom	0	25–30	9
United States	0	20	10

Source: William M. Mercer, Ltd. Data are for professional and managerial personnel.

becoming more common. Yet another alternative, depending on the situation, is workers' compensation insurance, which was discussed earlier in the chapter.

Severance Pay

An employee who is being terminated is sometimes given a one-term payment. Known as severance pay, it can amount to anywhere from a few days' wages to several months', with the exact payment depending on length of service. Employers that are downsizing often use severance pay to soften the impact of unexpected termination on employees.

Life Insurance

One of the oldest and most popular employee benefits is group term life insurance, which provides death benefits to beneficiaries and sometimes accidental death and dismemberment benefits as well.

Retirement Programs

Retirement is an important part of life and requires careful preparation. When convincing job applicants to come work for them, employers usually emphasize the retirement benefits that can be expected after a certain number of years of employment. As we noted earlier, it is common for each employee, once a year, to receive a personalized statement of benefits that contains information about projected retirement income from pensions and employee investment plans.

Retirement Policies

WWW

Although the usual mandatory retirement age in Canada is 65, an individual may retire at 55 and begin drawing a reduced pension from CPP/QPP as well as funds from other sources such as RRSPs. Alternatively, some individuals can work until 71, at which time they must retire. Statistics Canada reported that 61 is the average age of retirement, with women leaving at 58 and men at 62. The higher the household income, the lower the age of retirement.[22] Many are retiring because they have lost their jobs and cannot find other work. However, as we have seen, there is a growing trend for individuals in their golden years to take on part-time employment as a means of supplementing their income.

Silver handshake

An early retirement incentive in the form of increased pension benefits for several years or a cash bonus

To avoid making layoffs and to reduce salary and benefit costs, employers often encourage early retirement. This encouragement often takes the form of increased pension benefits or cash bonuses, sometimes referred to as the **silver handshake**. Some companies, including IBM Canada, have given generously to encourage the early retirement of workers. Ontario Hydro presented its employees with various options to retire early; these included an early retirement allowance, a voluntary separation allowance, a special retirement program, and a voluntary retirement program. The incentives succeeded; most employees with twenty-five years of service opted for the special retirement program.[23] An employer can offset the cost of retirement incentives by paying lower compensation to replacements and/or by reducing its workforce.

For employees, the main factors in a decision to retire early are health, personal finances, and job satisfaction. Lesser factors include an attractive pension and the possibility of future layoffs. Highlights in HRM 3 looks at the issues facing Canada's baby boomers, who are beginning to retire in record numbers.

Preretirement Programs

Most people are eager to retire; some are bitterly disappointed once they do. Some employers offer programs to help employees prepare for retirement. These programs typically include seminars and workshops, where lectures, videos, and printed materials are offered. Usually they cover topics such as how to live on a reduced, fixed income and how to cope with lost prestige, family conflict, and idleness. Also discussed are more concrete topics such as pension plans, health insurance coverage, retirement benefits and provincial health care, and personal financial planning.

WWW

At Consumers Gas, employees between 50 and 53 can attend, with their spouses, a three-day seminar that covers six subject areas: positive outlook, leisure time, health, home, financial planning, and estate planning. At other organizations, these programs have a more individual focus. CIBC, which has over 40,000 employees at 1,800 different locations, provides its employees with tools such as tapes, books, videos, and computer programs. The Retirement Council of Canada recommends that 1 percent of a company's pension program be earmarked for retirement planning programs.[24]

Highlights in HRM

3   LIVING FOREVER ON TODAY'S SALARIES

Canadians are living longer. Statistics Canada has estimated that by 2041 there will be almost 1.6 million Canadians aged 85 or over—four times the number in 1995. Seniors 65 and older will represent 8 percent of the total population. These facts raise a number of interesting benefits issues.

For example, how will these seniors support themselves? Only about half of all Canadians are covered by a pension plan. Furthermore, those who do have a plan will have lost it earlier than expected. The average age of retirement is dropping dramatically; it was 65 in the early 1970s, but is now 61. In the past several decades, there has been a steep decline in the number of men aged 55 to 64 in the labour force. In 1976, 74 percent of them were working; by 1995 it was only 54 percent. Some seniors top up their pensions through part-time work: 42 percent of Canadians 65 and over work part-time, compared to 13 percent of those aged 25 to 54.

A related issue is that in the future, because of health problems, 20 percent of those over 65 will not be able to take care of themselves. At the same time, there will not be enough nursing homes or hospitals to care for them. With government downloading the funding of these institutions, employers are soon going to have to provide benefits that will enable their employees to care for elders. These benefits may include referral services, paid family leave days, and perhaps on-site elder care facilities, such as are now being offered for children.

Source: *A Portrait of Seniors in Canada*, Statistics Canada, Catalogue: 80-519-XPE, Summer 1997.

WWW

Some organizations now offer retirement seminars to their younger employees as well. For instance, at Siemens Canada, employees as young as 35 are being offered the same financial sessions as employees 55 and over.

To help older workers get used to the idea of retirement, some organizations are experimenting with retirement rehearsal. Polaroid offers employees an opportunity to try out retirement through an unpaid three-month leave program. The company offers another program that permits employees to cut their hours gradually before retirement. Employees are paid only for hours worked, but receive full medical insurance and prorated pension credits. Most experts agree that preretirement planning is a much-needed, cost-effective employee benefit.[25]

Pension Plans

Originally, pensions were based on a *reward philosophy*; in other words, employers viewed pensions mainly as a reward to employees who stayed with them until retirement. Employees who quit or were terminated before retirement were not seen as deserving retirement benefits. Since then, most unions have negotiated vesting requirements into their contracts, and vesting has become required by law. Put another way, pensions are now based on an *earnings philosophy;* they are seen as deferred income that employees accumulate during their working lives; in other words, the pension belongs to the employee after a specified number of years of service, whether or not she or he remains with the employer until retirement.

Since the CPP/QPP legislation was enacted in 1966, pension plans have been used to supplement the protection provided by government-sponsored programs. Most private pension plans and a significant number of public plans now integrate their benefits with CPP/QPP benefits.

It is up to the employer whether to offer a pension plan. Because these plans are so expensive, companies are always looking for the least expensive ways to provide them to their employees.

Types of Pension Plans

Pensions can be categorized in two basic ways: according to contributions made by the employer, and according to the amount of pension benefits to be paid. In a **contributory plan**, contributions to a pension plan are made jointly by employees and employers. In a **noncontributory plan**, the contributions are made solely by the employer. Most plans in privately held organizations are contributory.

When pension plans are classified by the amount of pension benefits to be paid, there are two basic types: the defined benefit plan and the defined contribution plan. Under a **defined benefit plan**, the amount an employee is to receive on retirement is specifically set forth. This amount is usually based on the employee's years of service, average earnings during a specific period of time, and age at time of retirement. A variety of formulas exist for determining pension benefits; the one used most often is based on the employee's average earnings (usually over a three- to five-year period immediately preceding retirement) multiplied by the number of years of service with the organization. A deduction is then made for each year the retiree is under 65. As noted earlier, pension benefits are usually integrated with CPP/QPP. Very few employers introduce this type of plan, because it places them under the legal obligation to pay benefits regardless of the performance of the pension plan.

Contributory plan

A pension plan in which contributions are made jointly by employees and employers

Noncontributory plan

A pension plan in which contributions are made solely by the employer

Defined benefit plan

A pension plan in which the amount an employee is to receive on retirement is specifically set forth

Defined contribution plan

A pension plan that establishes the basis on which an employer will contribute to the pension fund

A **defined contribution plan** establishes the basis on which an employer will contribute to the pension fund. These plans come in a variety of forms: some involve profit sharing; others involve employers matching employee contributions; still others are employer-sponsored RRSP plans. The size of the pension the employee will get is determined by the funds in his or her account at the time of retirement and what retirement benefits (usually in the form of an annuity) these funds will purchase. These plans are not as predictable (i.e., secure) as defined benefit plans. However, even under defined benefit plans, retirees may not receive the benefits promised them if the plan is not adequately funded.

Defined benefit plans, with their fixed payouts, are falling out of use. They are less popular with employers nowadays because they cost more and because they require compliance with complicated government rules.[26] All new pension plans in Canada, such as those introduced by McMillan Bloedel and Molson Breweries, are defined contribution plans.

WWW

Registered retirement savings plans (RRSPs) have experienced tremendous growth in recent years because the funds in these plans are allowed to accumulate tax-free until they are withdrawn. RRSPs have annual contribution limits; also, if withdrawals are made from them before retirement, tax must be paid on them. Some employers offer group RRSPs, which have some advantages over individual RRSPs: they are deducted from payroll and have mass-purchasing power.

Federal Regulation of Pension Plans

Registered pension plans (RPPs) are subject to federal and provincial regulations. The federal Income Tax Act prescribes limits and standards that affect the amount of contributions that can be deducted from income; it also mandates how pension benefits can be taxed. (It is estimated that the government loses about $5 billion dollars a year in taxes because it does not tax private pension plans.) In the federal jurisdiction and most provincial ones, there are laws that state how pension plans must be operated. For example, the actuarial assumptions on which the funding is based must be certified by an actuary at specified intervals. An important issue to employees is vesting.

Vesting

A guarantee of accrued benefits to participants at retirement age, regardless of their employment status at the time

Vesting is a guarantee of accrued benefits to participants at retirement age, regardless of their employment status at that time. Vested benefits that have been earned by the employee cannot be revoked by the employer. Employees with two years of service in an organization are considered, in terms of their pension plans, fully vested and locked in.

Pension Portability

For a long time, most pension plans lacked portability; in other words, employees who changed jobs were unable to maintain equity in a single pension. Yet a large majority of Canadians (83 percent, according to one survey) wanted portability in their plans.[27] Unions addressed this concern by encouraging multiple-employer plans. These plans cover the employees of two or more unrelated organizations in accordance with a collective agreement. They are governed by boards of trustees on which both the employers and the union are represented. Multiple-employer plans tend to be found in industries in which few companies have enough employees to justify an individual plan. They are also found often in industries in which employment tends to be either seasonal or irregular. These plans are found in the following manufacturing sectors: apparel, printing, furniture, leather, and metalworking. They are also found in nonmanufacturing industries such as mining, construction, transport, entertainment, and private higher education.

Employees who leave an organization can leave their locked-in funds in their current pension plan, or they can transfer those funds into a locked in RRSP or into their new employer's pension plan (if one exists).

Pension Funds

A pension fund can be administered through a trusted plan or through an insured one. In a *trusted* plan, the pension contributions are placed in a trust fund. The fund is then invested and administered by trustees. The trustees are appointed by the employer; but if there is a union, the union sometimes appoints them. Contributions to an *insured* pension plan are used to purchase insurance annuities. These funds are administered by the insurance company that is providing the annuities.

Private and public pension funds constitute the largest pool of investment capital in the world, with over $4 trillion in assets. Canada's share is more than $1 trillion, and is expected to be $2.3 trillion by 2001.[28] Still, we cannot be complacent about the future. Government benefits such as CPP/QPP and Old Age Security will be stretched thin as baby boomers grow older, and some private pensions may be vulnerable to poorly performing investments. It should also be noted that the pension funds of some organizations are not adequate to cover their obligations.[29] Here is another interesting question: "Whose money is it?" When a pension fund has generated a surplus over plan (and many of them have), management tends to see this surplus as part of the organization's portfolio of assets; not, surprisingly, employees tend to view it as their own money. These legal and ethical issues have yet to be addressed.

EMPLOYEE SERVICES

WWW

Employee services, like other benefits, represent a cost to the employer. But they are often well worth the cost. More and more different services are being offered by employers to make life at work more rewarding and to enhance the well-being of employees. "Wellness is good for business," says Ann Coll of Husky Injection Molding Systems. The employees at Husky's plant in Bolton, Ontario, enjoy a subsidized cafeteria with organic vegetarian meals, a $500 stipend for vitamins, and a fitness centre that is open around the clock.

CREATING A FAMILY-FRIENDLY SETTING

WWW

Eddie Bauer, an outdoor clothing and equipment supplier, offers its employees take-out dinners and one paid "balance day" off a year. The Human Resources Professional Association of Ontario allows a half-day of paid leave for employee birthdays.[30] These organizations, and many others, are seeking to create a family-friendly organizational environment that allows employees to balance work and personal needs. A national survey conducted by the Conference Board of Canada found that 40 percent of employers are offering wellness programs, 35 percent some kind of child care assistance, 25 percent elder care assistance, and 11 percent stress management programs.[31] Programs like these help employees manage their time; employers benefit by attracting good workers and by reducing the var-

Many organizations have developed programs that emphasize regular exercise and wellness.

ious interruptions that affect workplace productivity.[32] Figure 11.5 lists some of the more popular employer-sponsored work/life benefits.

Employee Assistance Programs

Employee assistance programs (EAPs)

Services provided by employers to help workers cope with a wide variety of problems that interfere with the way they perform their jobs

To help workers cope with a wide variety of problems that interfere with their work performance, organizations have developed **employee assistance programs (EAPs)**. Typically, an EAP provides diagnosis, counselling, and referral

FIGURE 11.5 *Family-Friendly Benefits: Balancing Work and Home Needs*

- Child care/elder care referral services
- Time off for children's school activities
- Employer-paid on-site or near-site child care facilities
- Flexible work hours
- Employee-accumulated leave days for dependent care
- Subsidized temporary or emergency dependent care
- Extended leave policies for child/elder care
- Sick child programs (caregiver on call)
- Work-at-home arrangements/telecommuting
- Partial funding of child care costs

services for alcohol or drug problems, emotional problems, and financial or family crises. (EAPs will be discussed in more detail in Chapter 12.) It has been estimated that employees' stress adds as much as 8 percent to payroll costs. In 1990, 58 percent of organizations were offering assistance programs; by 1997, 81 percent were. The point of EAPs is to help employees solve their personal problems, or at least to prevent those problems from turning into crises that affect their ability to work productively. To handle crises, many EAPs offer twenty-four-hour hot lines.

Counselling Services

An important part of an EAP is the counselling services it provides. While most organizations expect managers to counsel subordinates, some employees will have problems that require professional counselling. Most organizations refer individual employees to outside services such as family counselling services, marriage counsellors, and mental health clinics. Some organizations have a clinical psychologist, counsellor, or comparable specialist on staff, to whom employees can be referred. About 80 percent of Canadian organizations offer employee assistance or family assistance programs.

Educational Assistance Plans

Educational assistance is yet another common employee benefit. The main purpose of this one is to help employees keep up to date with advances in their field; this will in turn help them rise in the organization. Usually the employer covers at least part of the cost of tuition, books, and related fees; the employee is required to pay for meals, transportation, and other expenses.

Child and Elder Care

Women with dependent children are entering the workforce in unprecedented numbers; this has led to an unprecedented demand for child care arrangements. Working parents used to have to make their own arrangements with sitters or with nursery schools. Nowadays many employers are offering related benefits, such as financial assistance, alternative work schedules, family leave, and on-site child care centres. On-site or near-site child care centres are the most visible, prestigious, and desired solution.[33]

WWW

Ontario Hydro has provided the space and is paying the occupancy costs for Hydro Kids. This program encompasses three on-site day care centres, which are open to company employees. These nonprofit centres are operated by the parents themselves, who hire the child care staff and manage day-to-day operations. Parents pay market rates for the child care services.[34] Ford Motor of Canada offers it employees as much as $2,000 a year in child care assistance.

Child care is "the new benefit of the 1990s," says the president of America West Airlines. "It is a critical need that companies that can afford it will meet because it is the right thing to do. Even companies that have limited means may be forced to support child care from a competitive standpoint, to attract, retain, and motivate personnel." A Conference Board of Canada study found that 25 percent of large organizations in this country offer information/referral services, 8 percent offer day care facilities, and 2 percent offer financial assistance.[35]

Flexible work arrangements allow a parent to be home to care personally for a sick child.

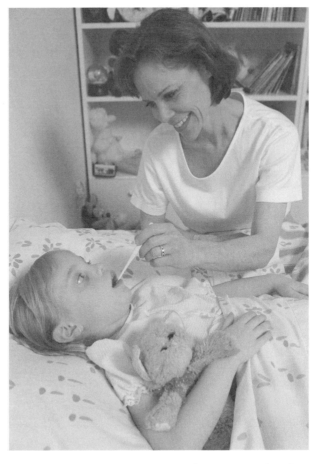

Responsibility for the care of aging parents and other relatives is another fact of life for more and more employees. By 2001, 5 million Canadians will be 65 or older. One million of them will have some sort of disability, and the facilities to care for them do not exist.[36] These seniors will have to be cared for by their children and relatives. The term **elder care**, as used in the context of employment, refers to situations where an employee provides care to an elderly relative while remaining actively at work. Most caregivers are women. The workplace consequences of all this have been described as follows:

> There is no doubt that elder care responsibilities detract from work efficiency: from time lost to take a parent to the doctor, to loss of concentration due to worry, work time being spent making care arrangements, never knowing when an emergency will occur, and calls from neighbours and relatives disrupting the workday. When combined, these responsibilities lead to a situation where neither the care giver nor employee role is filled adequately. Lost productivity due to absenteeism of those caring for elders can cost a 1,000 employee company without an elder care program as much as $400,000 per year. TransAmerica Corporation reported that 1,600 missed workdays per year were attributed to 22 percent of the employees who were caring for an elderly relative, for an annual loss to the corporation of $250,000. For larger companies, these costs can run into the millions.[37]

Elder care

Care provided to an elderly relative by an employee who remains actively at work

WWW

WWW

To reduce the negative effects of caregiving on productivity, organizations can offer elder care counselling, educational fairs and seminars, printed resources, support groups, and special flexible schedules and leaves of absence. Schering-Plough, a pharmaceuticals manufacturer, uses an 800 line for elder care referrals. IBM has established a nation-wide telephone network of more than 200 community-based referral agencies. Some employers band together for better elder care.

AT&T has given grants to community organizations to recruit, train, and manage elder care volunteers where its employees live and work. Travellers Corporation is part of a consortium of employers that trains family care workers; it also shares with employees the cost of three days' in-home care for family emergencies.[38] Interest in and demand for elder care programs will increase dramatically as baby boomers move into their early fifties and find themselves managing organizations and experiencing elder care problems with their own parents.[39]

Other Services

Some of the benefits and services that employers now offer could not have been imagined a few years ago. A few are becoming more or less standard. There are also unique ones that obviously grew out of specific concerns, needs, and interests. Among the latter are free baseball tickets for families and friends, summer boat cruises, and subsidized haircuts for MPs.

Legal Services

One of the fastest-growing employee benefits is the prepaid legal service plan. There are two basic types: access plans and comprehensive plans. *Access plans* provide free telephone or office consultation, and document review, as well as discounts on legal fees for more complex matters. *Comprehensive plans* cover other services such as representation in divorce cases, real estate transactions, and civil and criminal trials.

Financial Planning

One of the newer benefits is financial planning, which at present is being offered mainly to executives and middle managers. It will probably spread through organizations soon enough as part of flexible benefits programs. Financial planning programs cover investments, tax planning and management, estate planning, and similar.

Transportation Pooling

WWW

Commuting is often a serious issue for employees, many of whom spend considerable time and energy organizing car pools and scrambling for parking spaces. Many employers, including Caldwell Partners and Polo Ralph Lauren Canada, cover taxi expenses for employees whose working hours are long. Employer-organized van pooling is common among private and public organizations in metropolitan areas. Many employers report that tardiness and absenteeism are reduced by van pooling.

Purchasing Assistance

Some organizations help their employees buy merchandise more conveniently and at a discount. They do this in various ways. Many retailers have employee discount programs. Some employers procure certain items from other manufacturers and then offer them to their employees at a discount.

Credit Unions

Many organizations have credit unions that serve the financial needs of employees. These offer a variety of deposit and other banking services, and also make loans to their members. Although the employer may provide office space and a payroll deduction service, credit unions are operated by the employees under federal and state legislation and supervision.

Recreational and Social Services

Many organizations have sports programs for their workers. Participation is of course voluntary. Bowling, softball, golf, baseball, and tennis are often provided as intramural programs. Many organizations also subsidize employee teams in competitions with other local organizations. Memberships at health clubs and fitness centres, or discounts on memberships, are also popular offerings (see Chapter 12).

Organizations often arrange social functions for employees and their families. Employees should play a major role in the planning if these functions are to succeed. However, because of possible legal liability, the employer should retain control of all events associated with the organization. For example, employers can be held liable for injuries to third persons caused by an employee's actions arising from employment. "Employment" in this context can include attending a company party, if the employee was urged or obligated to attend it. Thus, an employee could be held responsible for an accident occurring while an employee is driving to or from an employer-sponsored event.

Emerging Benefits

The unique needs and lives of employees are compelling organizations to keep inventing new benefits. One that is suddenly gaining popularity is concierge service, which employees can use for help with everything from vacation planning to car repairs. Companies are also providing time off for community service or volunteer work; this has been said to improve both employee morale and the corporation's image, and to improve teamwork. It also makes for a healthier community where the organization is located. Many people own pets, and consider them part of the family, so pet insurance is becoming a popular benefit. Overall, these new benefits are aimed at saving time and enhancing the quality of life.

SUMMARY

Benefits are an established and integral part of the total compensation package. In order to have a sound benefits program, employers must consider certain fundamentals: the program must have specific objectives that are compatible with the organization's philosophy and policies; it must also be affordable. Through committees and surveys, the organization can develop a benefits package that meets its employees' needs. Under flexible benefit plans, employees can choose those benefits which are best suited to their individual needs. Employees have the most confidence in benefits programs when they are kept thoroughly informed of them through meetings, printed materials, and annual personalized statements of benefits.

Because many benefits represent a fixed cost, management must be cautious about taking on more benefit expense. More and more employers are requiring employees to pay part of the costs of certain benefits, and shopping around for benefit services that are competitively priced.

 A significant portion of the benefits packages provided by employers is legally required. Required benefits include employer contributions to retirement plans, employment insurance, and workers' compensation insurance.

 The cost of health care programs has become the major concern in the area of employee benefits. Health care costs can be contained by reducing coverage, by coordinating benefits, and by increasing deductibles. Employee assistance programs (EAPs) and wellness programs can also help cut the costs of health care benefits.

 Some benefits involve payments for time not worked; among these are vacations with pay, paid holidays, sick leave, and severance pay. Most Canadian workers receive 10 to 15 days' vacation leave plus statutory holidays. Besides vacation time, most employees—especially in white-collar jobs—receive a set number of sick leave days. Employees who are being terminated often receive severance pay in the form of a "one shot" payment.

 Currently, the average retirement age is 61. In most provinces the retirement age is 65, but more and more workers are choosing to retire earlier. Many employers provide incentives for early retirement in the form of increased pension benefits or cash bonuses. Some organizations now offer preretirement programs, which typically include seminars, workshops, and informational materials.

 Once a pension plan has been established, it is subject to federal and provincial regulation to ensure that benefits will be available when the employee retires. While two types of plans are available—defined benefit and defined contribution—most employers now opt for the latter. The amount an employee receives on retirement is based on years of service, average earnings, and age at time of retirement. Usually, pension benefits are integrated with CPP/QPP. Pension funds are administered through either a trustee or an insurance plan.

 Most employers now provide various service benefits. These often include EAPs, counselling services, educational assistance plans, child care, and elder care. There are many other possible ones, including food services, on-site health services, prepaid legal services, financial planning services, and recreational opportunities.

KEY TERMS

contributory plan	employee assistance programs	noncontributory plan
defined benefit plan	(EAPs)	silver handshake
defined contribution plan	flexible benefit plans (cafeteria	vesting
elder care	plans)	workers' compensation insurance

DISCUSSION QUESTIONS

1. You are a small employer wishing to establish a benefits program for your employees. What things should you consider to ensure that the program is a success for your employees?

2. Many organizations are concerned about the rising cost of employee benefits and question their value to the organization and to the employees.

    a. In your opinion, what benefits are of greatest value to employees? To the organization? Why?

    b. What can management do to increase the value to the organization of the benefits provided to employees?

3. Employers are required by law to provide specific benefits to employees. What laws mandate benefits to employees, and what are the provisions of those laws?

4. Identify and contrast the various ways employers can control the costs of health care.

5. Do you agree with the argument that the benefits for time not worked are the ones most readily available to reduce employer costs? Explain.

6. Employers used to prescribe a mandatory retirement age—usually 65. What do you think are the advantages and disadvantages of a mandatory retirement age? What factors may affect an individual's decision to retire at a particular time, and what factors may affect his or her ability to adjust to retirement?

7. Working in teams of three or four, list and discuss the various benefits offered by your employer (or former employer). How were the costs of these benefits paid for?

8. Assume your team has been hired as a benefits consultant by a small business with fifty to sixty employees. What benefits do you believe this employer should offer, given its limited resources? Explain why you would offer these benefits.

CASE 1

DO BENEFITS PAY?

Organizations are offering more and more benefits, not only in terms of *how much* coverage but also in terms of types. The number of vacation days and personal balance days provided to employees is increasing. As well, cell phones, laptops for home use, and financial counselling are becoming standard benefits, along with all the traditional ones.

    The benefits and perks offered by new-economy companies are especially innovative. They include meditation and nap rooms, massage therapy, gymnasiums with personal trainers, and laundry and concierge services. Free food is another popular perk, with companies supplying juice bars, bagels, fresh fruit, and cappuccino. Even the more traditonal companies are starting to offer benefits like these, in recognition of their appeal. Price Waterhouse Coopers has a concierge program that employees can use (at subsidized rates) to get their cars repaired or to pick up

WWW

dinner or dry cleaning. Many companies now offer sabbaticals to retain employees who want a break from work stress, or who want to travel or study.

Managers believe that benefits such as these help them hold on to prized employees. Some compensation experts disagree. "Benefits are not decisive in influencing employees to join the company," says one. The argument here is that base pay and incentive pay are the only ways to attract and motivate employees. Also, recruiters should not even discuss benefits, since they are a given, and don't vary much between companies. Most of the traditional benefits do not even interest young, mobile, and highly educated workers. These people are motivated by more challenge and more money, and by creating a culture in which work is fun.

Source: Adapted from R. Maxwell, "Companies Use Innovation to Combat Shortage," *Computer World Canada* 15, no. 3 (February 12, 1999): 45. L. Young, "Benefits Won't Bait Workers, Study Shows," *Canadian HR Reporter*, February 8, 1999: 1.

Questions

1. Do you think benefits attract, retain, and motivate employees?

2. If you were able to increase overall compensation by 5 percent in your organization, would you spend it on direct pay, incentive pay, or benefits?

3. Working in groups, devise the kind of benefits package that would motivate you to join an organization. Use **belcourt.nelson.com** to identify benefits that interest you, and cost them.

CASE 2

AWARD-WINNING BENEFITS COMMUNICATION

WWW

The Bank of Nova Scotia, which employs 27,000 people, has created a comprehensive benefits communication package that includes a video, software, magazines, leaders' guides, and plan booklets. This information is available in English, French, and braille. Because the bank's workforce is so diverse, much attention was paid to finding the right "voice." The bank finally decided on a friendly, conversational tone that was easy to understand. Employees were instrumental in designing the benefits program, providing input on everything, from how a flexible plan should be introduced to what the magazine's content should be.

The Bank of Canada also solicited input from its employees when designing a flexible benefits program. The employees even chose the program's name: À la Carte. The full communications package included posters, information bulletins, enrolment kits (program guides, enrolment worksheets, and information about the intranet-based flex calculator), and a communications survey. A benefits hotline was established, and special forums were arranged in which groups of employees could ask questions. The flex calculator, which enabled employees to determine different benefits scenarios and target coverage to meet their personal needs, was especially popular. The number of hits on this intranet-based feature averaged 18,000 a day during the launch phase of the communications plan. The HR team that devised the plan also handed out portfolios to employees in the lobby as they arrived for work.

The impact of the communications program was measured. Nine-tenths of employees indicated that they had a clear understanding of their choices, and three-tenths chose nonstandard packages. Nineteen out of twenty met the enrolment deadline.

Source: Adapted from two articles on the Benefits Canada website: **www.benefitscanada.com**.

Questions

1. Compare the launch of these two communication packages to the suggestions listed in Highlights in HRM 1.

2. Are face-to-face meetings a more effective communication tool than an intranet-based responsive site? Explain.

CAREER COUNSEL

Design your own benefits package by completing the Flexible Benefits exercise on the Managing Human Resources website (**belcourt.nelson.com**).

USING THE INTERNET

WWW

For information about the Certified Employee Benefit Specialist program at Dalhousie University, visit **www.dal.ca**.

A good benefits site is **www.benefitscanada.ca**.

For the most current information on employment insurance, visit Human Resources Development Canada's website **www.hrdc-grdc.ca**.

For a global compensation link providing current wage and benefits information and trends, visit **www.compensationlink.com**.

NOTES AND REFERENCES

1. Leslie, Young, "Benefits Won't Bait Workers," *Canadian HR Reporter*, February 8, 1999.

2. *KPMG 20th Annual Employee Benefit Costs* (Toronto: KPMG, 1996): Table 9.

3. Frank E. Kuzmits, "Communicating Benefits: A Double Click Away," *Compensation and Benefits Review* 30, no. 5 (September–October 1998): 60–4.

4. Jan Everett, "Internet Security," *Employee Benefits Journal* 23, no. 3 (September 1998): 14–18. See also Alan R. Parham, "Developing a Technology Policy," *Employee Benefits Journal* 23, no. 3. (September 1998): 3–5.

5. Dian Cohen, "Parallel Goals," *Benefits Canada* 22, no. 6 (June 1998): 98.

6. The cost of providing benefits to employees is a major concern of all employers. So it is not surprising that managers are constantly seeking innovative ways to contain or reduce these operating costs. See, for example, Joey J. Barber, "Lower Health Care Costs through Direct Contracting," *HRMagazine* 40, no. 9 (September 1995): 66; Charles R. Sundermeyer, "Employee Benefits Planning for Small Businesses," *Benefits Quarterly* 9, no. 4 (Fourth Quarter 1993): 78–84; and Lesley Alderman,

"Smart Ways to Maximize Your Company Benefits," *Money* 24, no. 1 (November 1994): 183–96.

7. Ronald W. Perry, and N. Joseph Cayer, "Cafeteria Style Health Plans in Municipal Govt.," *Public Personnel Management* 28, no. 1 (Spring 1999): 107–17.

8. "Communication Break Down: Employers Must Properly Inform Employees of Their Entitlement Benefits or Face Expensive and Time Consuming Court Challenges," *Benefits Canada* 21, no. 1 (January 1997): 27, 29.

9. M. Paterson, "Making a Statement: Are You Ready to Turn an Obligation into an Opportunity?" *Benefits Canada*, February 1995: 19–21.

10. Julie Amparano, "Human Resources Takes a Different Line," *Arizona Republic*, October 28, 1996: E1. See also James J. Moynihan and Kathryn Norman, "Better Benefit Administration through Electronic Data Interchange (EDI)," *Employee Benefits Journal* 19, no. 1 (March 1994): 30.

11. Jeffery M. Everson, "Effective Benefits Communication on a Shoestring Budget," *Employee Benefits Journal* 21, no. 4 (December 1996): 2–5.

12. For over forty years, benefits professionals have relied on the International Foundation of Employee Benefit Plans for education and information about employee benefits. This group's 35,000 members represent more than 7,400 trust funds, corporations, professional firms, and public employee funds throughout Canada and the United States as well as overseas. One of their many publications is a valuable reference book, *Employee Benefit Plans: A Glossary of Terms*, 8th ed, Brookfield, WI, International foundation of Employee Benefit Plans, 1993

13. "Cost of Individual Benefits Expressed as a Percentage of Payroll," *20th Survey of Employee Benefits Costs in Canada*, KPMG, Toronto, 1996. Table 9.

14. J. MacBride-King, "Managing Corporate Health Care," Conference Board of Canada, October 1995, Report 158–95: 10.

15. See note 13.

16. "FTNT Employment Insurance: More Than a New Name," *Work Life Report* 10, no. 2 (1996): 1–4, 5.

17. "Drafting the New Chapter: Workers' Compensation in Canada," *Risk Management* 43, no. 10 (October 1996): 16–22.

18. Robert J. McCunney and Cheryl Barbanel, "Auditing Workers' Compensation Claims Targets Expensive Injuries, Job Tasks," *Occupational Health and Safety* 32, no. 10 (October 1993): 75–84; Geoffrey Leavenworth, "Setting Standards for Workers' Comp," *Business & Health* 12, no. 10 (October 1994): 44–54.

19. Elaine Carey, "Rise in Over-80's Potential Health Disaster," *Toronto Star*, May 12, 1995: A1.

20. Murray Doben, "Medicare, the Market, and the Silence of the CEOs," *National Post,* May 1, 2000: C15.

21. Sonya Felix, "Healthy Alternative," *Benefits Canada* 2, no. 2 (February 1997): 47–50.

22. Dorothy Lipovenko, "Job Losses Force Early Retirement," *The Globe and Mail*, September 8, 1995: A8.

23. Doug Burn, "Wheel of Fortune: How Much Should an Organization Gamble on Early Retirement Planning?" *Human Resources Professional* 11, no. 4 (May 1994): 13–17.

24. David McCabe, "Retiring the Side: Approaches to Retirement Planning Range From the Conservative to the Revolutionary," *Human Resources Professional* 11, no. 4 (May 1994).

25. Catherine D. Fyock, "Crafting Secure Retirements," *HRMagazine* 35, no. 7 (July 1990): 30–3.

26. Larry Light, "The Power of the Pension Funds," *Business Week*, November 6, 1999: 154–8.

27. Bev Cline, "HR Professionals Find Challenges in Setting Up Pension Plans," *Human Resource Professional*, November 1997: 24.

28. Rick Drennan, "Global Warming," *Benefits Canada* 21, no. 6 (June 1997): 103.

29. Ellen E. Schultz, "Underfunded Pension Plan? Don't Panic Yet," *Wall Street Journal*, December 3, 1993: C1.

30. Carl Quintanilla, "Employers Get Creative as Workers Grapple with Family Issues," *Wall Street Journal*, September 17, 1996: A1. See also Keith H. Hammonds, "Balancing Work and Family," *Business Week* (September 16, 1996): 74–80.

31. Nathalie Borris Carlyle and Suzanne Payette, *Compensation Planning Outlook 1998*, Conference Board of Canada, October 1997.

32. "Employers Help Workers Achieve Balance in Life," *HRFocus* 75, no. 11 (November 1998): S3.

33. Elanna Yalow, "Corporate Child Care Helps Recruit and Retain Workers," *Personnel Journal* 69, no. 6 (June 1990): 48–55; Jennifer Haupt, "Employee Action Prompts Management to Respond to Work-and-Family Needs," *Personnel Journal* 72, no. 2 (February 1993): 96–107.

34. Sonya Felix, "Running on Empty," *Benefits Canada* 21, no. 16 (June 1997): 109–14.

35. See note 31.

36. Anita Elash, "Older and Needier," *Maclean's*, November 2, 1997: 64.

37. Elaine Davis and Mary Kay Krouse, "Elder Care Obligations Challenge the Next Generation," *HRMagazine* 41, no. 7 (July 1996): 98–103.

38. Sue Shellenbarger, "Firms Try Harder, but Often Fail, to Help Workers Cope with Elder-Care Problems," *Wall Street Journal*, June 23, 1993: B1.

39. Sue Shellenbarger, "The Aging of America Is Making Elder Care a Big Workplace Issue," *Wall Street Journal*, February 16, 1994: A1. See also Sue Shellenbarger, "With Elder Care Comes a Professional and Personal Crisis," *Wall Street Journal*, November 9, 1994: B1.

After studying this chapter, you should be able to

 Summarize the common elements of federal and provincial occupational health and safety legislation.

 Describe what management can do to create a safe work environment.

 Cite the measures that should be taken to control and eliminate health hazards.

 Describe the organizational services and programs for building better health.

 Explain the role of employee assistance programs in HRM.

 Describe methods for coping with stress.

HEALTH AND SAFETY

www

Occupational safety and health accidents are common, as well as costly to employers. In 1997, PCL Constructors Canada was fined $150,000 for failing to ensure that its workers were trained in the proper use of propane cylinders: an explosion at a construction site had caused the death of a PCL company foreman.[1] To prevent accidents such as these, employers are required by law to provide working conditions that are safe and healthy for their employees.

The laws safeguarding employees' physical and emotional well-being are certainly an incentive to establishing such programs; that being said, many employers would have them anyway, as a matter of simple morality. Furthermore, cost-oriented employers recognize how important it is to avoid accidents and illnesses whenever possible. The costs associated with sick leave, disability payments, workers' compensation, and replacement of employees who are injured or killed far exceed the costs of maintaining a safety and health program. Finally, accidents and illnesses attributable to the workplace can seriously damage both employee morale and the good will the organization enjoys in the community and in the business world.

Managers at all levels are expected to know and enforce their organization's safety and health standards. They must ensure a work environment that protects employees from physical hazards, unhealthy conditions, and the unsafe acts of other personnel. Effective safety and health programs preserve and sometimes even enhance the physical and emotional well-being of employees.

In this chapter we begin by discussing the legal requirements for safety and health. We then consider the process for creating a safe and healthy work environment. We end the chapter with a discussion of workplace stress.

HEALTH AND SAFETY: IT'S THE LAW

OBJECTIVE
1

The burden on the country's business community arising from workplace accidents and illnesses is staggering. Consider these facts:

- Across Canada, there is a workplace accident every nine seconds during working hours.
- About 800 workers are killed on the job every year.
- Roughly 60,000 Canadian workers suffer occupational injuries and illnesses.
- Canadian companies lose about 400,000 days a year, which costs them over $10 billion in lost wages, medical care, rehabilitation expenses, and disability pension payments.[2]

And, of course, there is no way to calculate the human suffering involved.

Occupational health and safety is regulated by the federal, provincial, and territorial governments. Statutes and standards vary slightly from jurisdiction to jurisdiction. Attempts have been made to harmonize the various acts and regulations. An **occupational injury** is any cut, fracture, sprain, or amputation resulting from a workplace accident. The worker's involvement in the accident can be direct, or the worker can simply be near enough to the accident to be injured as a result of it. An **occupational illness** is any condition or disorder (other than one resulting from an occupational injury) caused by the work environment. An occupational illness can be acute or chronic; it can result from inhaling, absorbing, ingesting, or directly contacting an illness-causing agent.

Occupational injury

Any cut, fracture, sprain, or amputation resulting from a workplace accident or from an exposure involving an accident in the work environment

Occupational illness

Any abnormal condition or disorder, other than one resulting from an occupational injury, caused by exposure to environmental factors associated with employment

Back injuries are the most common workplace injuries, followed by leg, arm, and finger injuries.[3] Repetitive strain injuries are the most common illness, followed by poisoning and chemical burns.[4]

Acts and Regulations

All HR managers should become familiar with the occupational health and safety laws that apply to their organization. The various acts and government departments that enforce the legislation are listed in Figure 12.1.

FIGURE 12.1 *Occupational Health and Safety in Canada*

JURISDICTION	LEGISLATION	ENFORCEMENT
Canada	Canada Labour Code, Regulations	Labour Canada
Alberta	Occupational Health and Safety Act	Department of Labour
British Columbia	Regulations under Workers' Compensation Act	Workers' Compensation Board
Manitoba	Workplace Safety and Health Act	Department of Environment and Workplace Health and Safety
New Brunswick	Occupational Health and Safety	Occupational Health and Safety Commission
Newfoundland	Occupational Health and Safety Act	Department of Labour
Nova Scotia	Occupational Health and Safety Act	Department of Labour
Ontario	Workplace Safety and Insurance Act	Ministry of Labour
Prince Edward Island	Occupational Health and Safety Act	Department of Fisheries and Labour
Quebec	Act respecting Occupational Health and Safety	Commission de la Santé et de la Sécurité du Travail
Saskatchewan	Occupational Health and Safety Act	Department of Labour
Northwest Territories	Safety Act	Commissioner NWT
Yukon	Occupational Health and Safety Act	Commissioner of the Yukon Territories; administered by the Workers' Compensation Board

Duties and Responsibilities

WWW

The fundamental duty of every employer is to take every reasonable precaution to ensure employee safety. The motivating forces behind workplace legislation were effectively articulated in the landmark case *Cory v. Wholesale Travel Group*:

> Regulatory legislation is essential to the operation of our complex industrial society; it plays a legitimate and vital role in protecting those who are most vulnerable and least able to protect themselves. The extent and importance of that role has increased continuously since the onset of the Industrial Revolution. Before effective workplace legislation was enacted, labourers—including children—worked unconscionably long hours in dangerous and unhealthy surroundings that evoke visions of Dante's inferno. It was regulatory legislation with its enforcement provisions which brought to an end the shameful situations that existed in mines, factories and workshops in the nineteenth century. The differential treatment of regulatory offences is justified by their common goal of protecting the vulnerable.

Duties of Employers

Besides providing a hazard-free workplace and complying with the applicable statutes and regulations, employers must inform their employees about safety and health requirements. Employers are also required to keep certain records, to compile an annual summary of work-related injuries and illnesses, and to ensure that supervisors are familiar with the work and its associated hazards (the supervisor, in

In certain environments, health and safety standards require the use of protective gear and equipment.

turn, must ensure that workers are aware of those hazards). An organization with many employees may have a full-time health and safety officer. The health and safety manager at the Peel Board of Education is profiled in Reality Check.

In all jurisdictions, employers are required to report to the Workers' Compensation Board accidents that cause injuries and diseases. Accidents resulting in death or critical injuries must be reported immediately; the accident must then be investigated and a written report submitted. In addition, employers must provide safety training and be prepared to discipline employees for failing to comply with safety rules. Employers are increasingly being required to prove due diligence. This includes establishing a comprehensive occupational health and safety management system; providing competent supervision, training, and instruction; and taking every reasonable precaution in the workplace for the health and safety of workers. Highlights in HRM 1 provides a list of health and safety procedures for new employees.

Duties of Workers

Employees are required to comply with all applicable acts and regulations, to report hazardous conditions or defective equipment, and to follow all employer safety and health rules and regulations, including those prescribing the use of protective equipment.

Workers have many rights that pertain to requesting and receiving information about safety and health conditions. They also have the right to refuse unsafe work without fear of reprisal. (Some professionals such as police, firefighters, teachers, and health care workers have only a limited right of refusal, the logic being that their work is inherently dangerous.) An employee who suspects that work conditions are hazardous can report this concern to his or her supervisor; this will trigger an investigation by the supervisor and a worker representative.

A work refusal investigation can result in either the employee's return to work or his or her continued refusal. In the latter case, the appropriate ministry is notified and an investigator is dispatched to the job site to provide a written decision. If a replacement worker is used, he or she must be notified of the previous employee's refusal to work.

Duties of Supervisors

A supervisor is generally defined as a person (with or without a title) who has charge of a workplace and authority over a worker. Occupational health and safety acts require supervisors to do the following: advise employees of potential workplace hazards; ensure that workers use or wear safety equipment, devices, or clothing; provide written instructions where applicable; and take every reasonable precaution to guarantee the safety of workers.

Duties of Joint Health and Safety Committees

Most jurisdictions require that health and safety committees be set up, with both union and management representation. The point of these joint committees is to establish a nonadversarial climate for creating safe and healthy workplaces. In Ontario, at least one management rep and one worker rep must be certified. The certification program provides training in the following subjects: safety laws, sanitation, general safety, rights and duties, and indoor air quality. Joint health and safety committees can reduce the number of occupational injuries and diseases.[5]

Reality CHECK

HEALTH AND SAFETY AT THE PEEL BOARD OF EDUCATION

WWW

Mary Smith, manager of health and safety for the Peel Board of Education, is dedicated to making the work environment safer and healthier. In the early 1970s she managed crews of workers on demolition sites in Ontario and saw first-hand the effects of ignorance of safety legislation. There were many tragic accidents. At that time, the laws covering occupational health and safety were enforced at the municipal level. Smith went on to become the first woman construction inspector for the Ontario Ministry of Labour. In the early 1980s she transferred to the Industrial Safety Division before moving on to the Ministry of the Environment, where she served as a laboratory safety officer. In 1986 the Peel Board of Education hired her to design and implement a health and safety program.

For the past decade Smith has worked hard to build a model program for the Peel board. A team of five ensures the safety of 10,000 employees. What makes her team unique, she feels, is that two people on it are worker representatives. This gives the program more credibility. As well, she and the safety officer do not sit on any joint health and safety committees, although they serve as a resource for them. According to Smith, this arrangement "keeps us at arm's length, bringing neutrality to the process. Our role is to support and be consultants to the system at all levels."

The health and safety team at the Peel board conducts inspections of 182 locations, responds to worker concerns, reviews accident reports, follows up on-site supervisor investigations, and liaises with various labour ministry inspectors. The team also maintains up-to-date chemical inventories and arranges for chemical disposal. Environmental legislation is followed scrupulously. Smith and her associates keep current by reading environmental health and safety journals, conducting literature searches, and watching developments in case law.

Smith describes the process involved in dealing with such issues as air quality, workplace violence, and ergonomics: "Many times there is a breakdown in communications and we need to find solutions. Employees just want to know you are listening, taking their concerns seriously, and trying to find solutions to their concerns. For example, if there is an air-quality concern that is brought to our attention we will work with the site manager or principal to help that person take the initial steps to investigate the situation. This may involve discussion with the worker and building occupants and having the plant maintenance staff ensure that the mechanical ventilation systems are functioning well. If all else fails, we involve an outside consultant. We set the mechanisms in place, but the supervisors actually take care of the issues."

A growing concern in schools is workplace violence. The Peel board is developing policies and procedures to address this concern. "Reviewing our statistics, we saw a growing trend in our workers' compensation claims, and we knew it was time to put some additional measures in place," Smith explains. Twenty-five percent of lost-time accidents for one worker group were mainly the result of violent incidents. Education and training for affected staff will include modules on health and safety rights and responsibilities, back care, and nonviolent intervention and restraint.

"In reviewing the Peel board successes, I must mention the development of the computerized Workplace Hazardous Material Information System (WHMIS), Vital Signs, that addresses both the legislated WHMIS training requirements and more importantly literacy in the workplace." Working in conjunction with the Peel board's Community Education Department, Smith and the health and safety officer contributed to the development of this program as technical consultants. The program won the 1992 OSH Award of Excellence. The honour is awarded annually at the OSH Conference sponsored by the Southam Corporation for, among other categories, the most innovative health and safety product or service. "Additionally, our 'train the trainer' programs have been successful in WHMIS as well as in asbestos management. In such a large workforce the health and safety department would require an enormous influx of additional staff in order to deliver safety training. The economics of a publicly funded institution demanded a different solution. Supervisors responsible for worker safety were trained to train in safety areas. The downside is that it is difficult to ensure a consistent message; the upside is the acceptance of responsibility for health and safety by the supervisor."

Government intervention can have a major impact on how health and safety is administered in each province. Smith believes strongly that government must take ultimate responsibility for setting health and safety regulations that will protect workers and for ensuring that employers comply with those regulations. Labour and management must work together and demand equal status as stakeholders in this process.

Penalties for Employer Noncompliance

The penalties for violating occupational health and safety regulations vary across provinces and territories. Most health and safety acts provide for fines up to $500,000, and offenders can be sent to jail. Kinross Gold was fined $500,000 for failing to ensure the safety of two miners killed on the job.[6] Under certain circumstances, the law provides for appeal by employers or employees.[7]

Workers' Compensation

Under workers' compensation, injured workers can receive benefits in the form of a cash payout (if the disability is permanent) or wage loss payments (if the worker can no longer earn the same amount of money). Unlimited medical aid is also provided, along with vocational rehabilitation, which includes physical, social, and psychological services. The goal is to return the employee to his or her job (or some modification thereof) as soon as possible.

Compensation has become a complex issue. The definitions of accidents and injuries have recently been expanded to include industrial diseases and stress. An **industrial disease** is a disease resulting from exposure to a substance relating to a particular process, trade, or occupation in industry. Cause and effect can be difficult to determine. Consider, for example, the case of a mine worker who has contracted a lung disease, but who also smokes heavily.

Equally problematic is compensation for stress. Stress-related disabilities are usually divided into three groups: physical injuries leading to mental disabilities (e.g., clinical depression after a serious accident); mental stress resulting in a phys-

Industrial disease

A disease resulting from exposure to a substance relating to a particular process, trade, or occupation in industry

Highlights in HRM

1   HEALTH AND SAFETY CHECKLIST FOR NEW EMPLOYEES

By the end of a new starter's first week, an employee should be familiar with the following health and safety procedures and issues:

1. **Fire Safety**
   - ✓ Identify the evacuation alarm sound.
   - ✓ Show his/her evacuation route and assembly point, and any alternative route.
   - ✓ Show where the extinguishers are in the work area.
   - ✓ Explain when water and other extinguishers can/cannot be used.
   - ✓ Show how to use extinguishers and what to do after use.
   - ✓ Show where the alarm point is and how to sound it.
   - ✓ Explain use of elevators and lifts in fire situation.

2. **Housekeeping and Access**
   - ✓ Explain reasons for maintaining clear access.
   - ✓ Explain hazards caused by obstructing gangways.

3. **Smoking**
   State where smoking is/is not allowed, and give reasons.

4. **Accidents and Abnormal Occurrence**
   - ✓ Explain reporting procedure and reasons.
   - ✓ Show the way to casualty (or first aid).
   - ✓ Explain action in case of serious injury to oneself or another.
   - ✓ Give two examples of abnormal occurrence.
   - ✓ Include any hazard special to the job.

5. **Lifting (manual handling)**
   - ✓ Demonstrate correct manual handling methods.

6. **Uniforms, Overalls**
   - ✓ Explain issue, care, and cleaning arrangements.

7. **Personal Clothing—Contamination**
   - ✓ Explain Action in the event of clothing being contaminated (give two examples).

8. **Protective Equipment**
   - ✓ Show how to wear equipment issued in department, and explain need for it.

9. **Personal Hygiene**
   - ✓ Explain reasons for attention to personal hygiene.
   - ✓ Give two examples of risk of cross-infection.
   - ✓ Explain why it is necessary to report contact with notifiable diseases, and give examples of diseases.

10. Absence
    ✓ Know what to do in the event of sickness or other absence.
    ✓ Know to consult Occupational Health staff.

11. Electrics
    ✓ Demonstrate checks required before using electrical equipment.
    ✓ Explain action if faults found.

12. Material Hazards
    ✓ Identify any dangerous materials or objects, and explain how to handle them.
    ✓ Supply workplace hazardous information sheets.

13. Chemical Hazards
    ✓ Demonstrate safe handling methods for: corrosive liquids, compressed gases, flammable solvents, other classes (appropriate to immediate workplace) (WHMIS).

14. Spillages
    ✓ Explain what must be done in the event of spillages.

15. Disposal
    ✓ Show waste/rubbish disposal system and explain hazards.

16. Machine Equipment Hazards
    ✓ Explain correct handling of equipment.
    ✓ Explain lock out/tagging procedures (appropriate to immediate workplace).

17. Health and Safety Management
    ✓ Explain the role of the Occupational Health Department.
    ✓ Identify the health and safety representatives and explain their roles.
    ✓ Explain the correct procedure if a hazard or problem in identified.
    ✓ Explain the functions of the safety committee.
    ✓ Describe the responsibilities of employees in health and safety.

Source: Adapted from: B. Pomfret, "Sound Employee Orientation Program Boosts Productivity and Safety," *Canadian HR Reporter*, January 25, 1999: 17. By permission of Carswell, Scarborough, Ontario: 1-800-387-5164.

ical disability (ulcers or migraines); and mental stress resulting in a mental condition (anxiety over workload or downsizing leading to depression). Most claims, it should be pointed out, result from accidents or injuries.

The emphasis in workers' compensation has been shifting away from simply making assessments and payments, toward creating safety-conscious environments where there will be fewer work-related accidents, disabilities, and diseases. In some industrial sectors, employers are working together to establish rules and training programs to further the cause of accident prevention.

CREATING A SAFE WORK ENVIRONMENT

As we have explained, the law requires employers to provide safe working conditions for their employees. To this end, most employers have a formal safety program. Typically, the HR department or the industrial relations department is responsible for this program. The success of a safety program depends heavily on the managers and supervisors of the operating departments. Usually, the role of the HR department is to coordinate the safety communication and training programs, maintain any safety records required by government regulations, and work closely with managers and supervisors to make the program a success.

Almost any organization with a formal safety program has an employee/management safety committee. On this sit representatives from management, from the various departments or manufacturing/service units, and from the employees themselves. Basically, these committees investigate accidents and help publicize the importance of safety rules.

Safety Motivation and Knowledge

Probably the key objective of any safety program is to motivate managers, supervisors, and employees to work safely. In one study conducted by the American Institute of Plant Engineers, "survey results showed a direct correlation between an increase in management's commitment to safety in the workplace and a decrease in accidents."[8] Where managers and supervisors fail to demonstrate awareness, their subordinates can hardly be expected to do so. Unfortunately, most managers and supervisors wear their "safety hats" far less often than their "production, quality control, and methods improvement hats." Other things are just as important as safety motivation: a knowledge of safety, and an understanding of where to place safety efforts. Training can help personnel at all levels understand the organization's policy on safety, its safety procedures, and its system for accountability.[9]

Safety begins with preparedness, as these employees demonstrate in this dress rehearsal.

Highlights in HRM

2   PAGE FROM A SAFETY AWARENESS PAMPHLET

HARD HAT CARE

Clean the shell of your hard hat at least once a month.

Your Checklist

❑ Make sure your hat fits right. There should be approximately 1" between the harness and the shell so air can circulate and keep your scalp cool. If your hat is too loose, it will fall off when you bend over. Too tight and it may cause headaches.

❑ Wear a color-coded hat if you need identification. Don't paint or scratch your hard hat to identify it.

❑ Add light-attracting tape to your hat if you work at night or in darkness. This will make it easier for others to see you.

❑ Clean the shell of your hard hat at least once a month to remove oil, grease, chemicals and sweat. Soak it for five minutes in mild detergent and water that's at least 140 degrees Fahrenheit (60 degrees Centigrade). Then wipe the hat and let the air dry it. Clean the hat according to the instructions provided.

❑ Take good care of your hat; don't drop it, throw it or drill holes in it.

❑ Sunlight and heat can rot the harness and straps. Don't leave your hard hat on the front or back window ledge of your car.

Source: Used by permission of the National Safety Council, Itasca, Illinois

WWW

The Manitoba Department of Labour reduced the number of injured worker claims by having the executive director of the provincial health and safety program call the CEOs of companies that were responsible for a disproportionate number of accidents, and telling them to fix the problem.

Promoting Safety Awareness

Most organizations have a safety awareness program that works through several different media—for example, safety lectures, commercially produced films, specially developed videocassettes, and pamphlets. All of these are useful for teaching and motivating employees to follow safe procedures at work.[10] A page from one of these pamphlets is shown in Highlights in HRM 2. Posters are often very effective because they can be displayed wherever workers are sure to see them.[11]

Interactive CD-ROM training is another excellent method for standardized safety, environmental, and health instruction.

Safety and TQM

Interestingly, the concepts that promote product and service quality through TQM are equally applicable to safety awareness programs. Thus, these concepts:

- Safety is a product that demands continuous improvement.
- A strong organizational culture will have zero tolerance for unsafe practices.
- Employees ought to be *safety empowered* (i.e., able to participate in forming safety policy, and to make in-field safety decisions).
- Safety management ought to be based on information, measurement, data, and analysis. In TQM safety terms, what gets measured gets managed and improved.[12]

The Key Role of the Supervisor

One of a supervisor's main responsibilities is to communicate to employees the need to work safely.[13] Beginning with orientation, safety should be emphasized continually. Potential hazards, proper work procedures, and the use of protective clothing and devices should be explained thoroughly. Furthermore, employees' understanding of all these things should be verified during training sessions, and employees should be encouraged to show some initiative in safety matters. Since training by itself does not ensure constant adherence to safe work practices, supervisors must observe employees at work and reinforce safe practices. Where unsafe acts are detected, supervisors should take immediate action to find the cause. Supervisors should also foster a team spirit of safety among the work group.

Safety Training Programs

The safety training programs found in many organizations cover first aid, defensive driving, accident prevention techniques, handling of hazardous materials, and emergency procedures. These programs emphasize the use of emergency first-aid equipment and personal safety equipment. Many organizations also provide training in off-the-job safety—at home, on the highway, and so on. Injuries and fatalities are much more common away from the job than on the job, and these off-the-job accidents also have an impact on employer costs for insurance premiums, wage continuation, and interrupted production. Safety is a core value at CN; each year the railway company spends $50 million on safety training.

WWW

As we discussed in Chapter 6, well-designed safety training programs begin with a needs assessment that identifies and prioritizes the safety needs of employees.[14] Safety needs have to do with the ability of employees to carry out their work safely, effectively, and in compliance with legal standards. After safety needs have been identified, key training objectives can be set for the workplace. For example, employees might be required to demonstrate the three necessary steps to take during a level 1 emergency spill. Training materials could then be developed to reinforce the training objectives.[15]

Motivating Safety through Incentives

An effective safety incentive program has many benefits. Employees suffer fewer accidents and injuries; they also think about safety more often. They perceive management as equally concerned about safety and as committed to enhancing it. As well, a successful incentive program can reduce workers' compensation premiums (see Chapter 11) and the costs associated with lost-time accidents.[16]

For safety programs to work, they must offer the right incentives. One authority suggests "surveying employees to find out their interests and what type of rewards would have the most value to them."[17] Also, a large number of employees should be in the running to earn safety awards. There are many workable incentives—for example, gift certificates, cash awards, trips, dinners, and gifts such as clothing or jewellery. Economy Carriers, based in Edmonton, offers an employee points program. It audits eighteen operational areas for safety; on the basis of that audit, employees accumulate safety points, which they can use for purchases. Two researchers looked at twenty-four studies where positive reinforcement and feedback were used to enhance safe behaviour. In all of the studies, incentives were found to improve safety conditions or reduce accidents.[18] Figure 12.2 provides the steps recommended for launching a successful safety incentive program.

Enforcement of Safety Rules

Specific rules and regulations concerning safety are communicated through supervisors, bulletin-board notices, employee handbooks, and signs attached to equipment. Safety rules are also emphasized during regular safety meetings, at employee orientations, and in manuals of standard operating procedures. These rules typically refer to the following types of employee behaviours:

- using proper safety devices
- using proper work procedures
- following good housekeeping practices
- complying with accident-and-injury reporting procedures
- wearing required safety clothing and equipment
- avoiding carelessness or horseplay

The penalties for violating safety rules are usually stated in the employee handbook. In the great majority of organizations, the penalties imposed on violators are the same as those imposed for violations of other rules. Typically, they include an oral or written warning for the first violation, suspension or disciplinary layoff for repeated violations, and, as a last resort, dismissal. However, for

---

FIGURE 12.2 *Steps in a Successful Safety Incentive Program*

- Obtain the full support and involvement of management by providing cost benefits.
- Review current injury and health statistics to determine where change is needed.
- Decide on a program of action and set an appropriate budget.
- Select a realistic safety goal such as reducing accidents by a set percentage, improving safety suggestions, or achieving a length of time without a lost-time injury. Communicate your objectives to everyone involved.
- Select incentive rewards on the basis of their attractiveness to employees and their fit with your budget.
- Develop a program that is both interesting and fun. Use kickoff meetings, posters, banners, quizzes, and/or games to spark employee interest. Give all employees a chance to win.
- Communicate continually the success of your program. Provide specific examples of positive changes in behaviour.
- Reward safety gains immediately. Providing rewards shortly after improvements reinforces changed behaviour and encourages additional support for the safety program.

---

serious violations—such as smoking around volatile substances—even a first offence may be just cause for termination.

Accident Investigations and Records

Every accident, even those considered minor, should be investigated by the supervisor and a member of the safety committee. This investigation may determine what caused the accident and reveal what corrections are needed to prevent it from happening again. Correction may require rearranging workstations, installing safety guards or controls, or, more often, giving employees additional safety training and reassessing their motivation for safety.

Employers are required to keep certain records and to compile and post annual summaries of work-related injuries and illnesses. From these records, organizations can compute their incidence rates (i.e., the number of injuries and illnesses per 100 full-time employees during a given year). The standard equation for computing the incidence rate is shown below; 200,000 constitutes the base for 100 full-time workers who work 40 hours a week, 50 weeks a year:

$$\text{Incidence rate} = \frac{\text{Number of injuries and illnesses} \times 200{,}000}{\text{Total hours worked by all employees during period covered}}$$

The same formula can be used to compute incidence rates for (1) the number of workdays lost because of injuries and illnesses, (2) the number of nonfatal injuries and illnesses without lost workdays, and (3) cases involving only injuries or only illnesses.

Incidence rates are useful for making comparisons between work groups, between departments, and between similar units in the same organization. They also provide a basis for making comparisons with other organizations doing sim-

Ethics in HRM

BURY THE RECORD

A supervisor was instructing a group of new recruits in the cleaning of metal parts in an assembly plant. She was attempting to demonstrate the cleaning technique to two employees at one workstation, while at another workstation another new employee was trying to clean the parts himself. The cleaning liquid was highly toxic. The employee felt restricted by his safety gloves and so removed them. His eyes started to water, and instinctively he rubbed them with his solution-soaked hands. The pain was overwhelming, and no water was immediately available with which he could rinse his eyes. The employee suffered some temporary vision loss.

Who is to blame? The worker who started to clean without receiving full instructions and without using the issued gloves? The supervisor who could have forbidden the worker to start work until she explained the safety aspects? Or the company that failed to post warning signs about the hazardous nature of the cleaning solvent and did not have an eye-washing facility available?

Because workplace accidents increase workers' compensation premiums and the number of inspections, the company had an interest in not reporting the accident. Furthermore, because the company had instituted a reward program that provided incentives to employees for accident-free days, even the employees did not want to report the accident. Thus the supervisor and the employees agreed to "bury the record." This is illegal. Another company was fined $600,000 for misleading the Workplace Health and Safety Insurance Board after it deliberately chose not to report that injured workers had missed time at work. What are the consequences of this decision?

WWW

ilar work. The occupational health and safety departments in each province and Human Resources Development Canada compile data that employers can use to measure their safety records against those of other organizations. As noted in Ethics in HRM, organizations that report and investigate their own accidents often face more inspections, higher insurance premiums, and possible lawsuits.

CREATING A HEALTHY WORK ENVIRONMENT

OBJECTIVE
3

Because workplace accidents are so immediate and dramatic in their impact, it often happens that managers and employees alike pay more attention to them than to more general health hazards. Yet it is essential that such hazards be identified and controlled. Attention should also be paid to illnesses and injuries that are *not* work–related and to their impact on the organization and its members. Special health programs can be developed to provide assistance to employees with health problems.

Largely because the public is growing more and more aware of the environment, factors in the workplace that affect health are receiving greater attention. The accelerating global threat of air and water pollution has made all of us pay more attention to the immediate environment in which we live and work. Newpapers often run articles about workers who have been exposed to potential dangers at work. All of this public concern, boosted by pressure from unions and the federal government, is driving employers to provide the safest and healthiest work environments possible.

Health Hazards and Issues

At one time health hazards were associated mainly with industrial jobs. In recent years, hazards in other sectors, such as in offices, health care facilities, and airports, have been recognized, and preventive methods have been adopted. Some of the more common preventions involve substituting materials, altering processes, enclosing or isolating processes, issuing protective equipment, and improving ventilation. It is also important for organizations to monitor general conditions with respect to sanitation, housekeeping, cleanliness, ventilation, water supply, pest control, and food handling.

Workplace Hazardous Materials Information Systems

In the belief that workers have the right to know about potential workplace hazards, industry, labour, and government have joined forces to develop a common information system for labelling hazardous substances. The workplace hazardous materials information system (WHMIS) is based on three elements:

Material Safety Data Sheets (MSDS)

Documents that contain vital information about hazardous substances

1. *Labels.* Labels are designed to alert the worker that the container holds a potentially hazardous substance. The two types of labels (supplier labels and workplace labels) must contain specified and regulated information, including product identifiers and data on safe handling and material safety. WHMIS class symbols and subclass designations are shown in Figure 12.3.

2. *Material Safety Data Sheets (MSDSs).* An MSDS identifies the product and its potentially hazardous ingredients, and suggests procedures for handling the product safely. The MSDS information must be comprehensive, current, and available in English and French.

3. *Training.* Workers must be trained to check for labels and to follow specific procedures for handling spills. Training workers is part of the due diligence required of employers; it also becomes an important factor in the event of a lawsuit. The Peel Board of Education in Ontario has developed a computer-based program to train workers in WHMIS. This program allows illiterate workers to respond to audio commands by touching the screen.

Indoor Air Quality

In an eight-hour workday, the average employee inhales over 3,000 litres of air—air that is often filled with vapours and particles, which are increasingly being blamed for a number of afflictions, from poor concentration to scarred lungs. After the energy crisis of the 1970s, commercial and some residential construction techniques were changed to increase the energy efficiency of heating, ventilating, and air-conditioning systems. This included sealing windows, reducing outside air, and in general "buttoning up" buildings. The result? The "sick building" phenomenon, with employees complaining of headaches, dizziness, disorientation, fatigue, and eye, ear, and throat irritation.[19]

FIGURE 12.3 *Class Symbols and Subclass Designations*

The subclass designations are shown below the class designation.

CLASS & SUBCLASS DESIGNATIONS

COMPRESSED GAS

FLAMMABLE AND
COMBUSTIBLE MATERIAL
Flammable Gas
Flammable Liquid
Flammable Solid
Flammable Aerosol
Reactive Flammable Material

OXIDIZING MATERIAL

POISONOUS AND
INFECTIOUS MATERIAL
Materials Causing
Immediate and
Serious Toxic Effects

Materials Causing
other Toxic Effects

Biohazardous
Infectious
Material

CORROSIVE MATERIAL

DANGEROUS REACTIVE
MATERIAL

Source: *Solvents in the Workplace*, Cat. No. B01230 (Toronto Industrial Accident Prevention Association, March

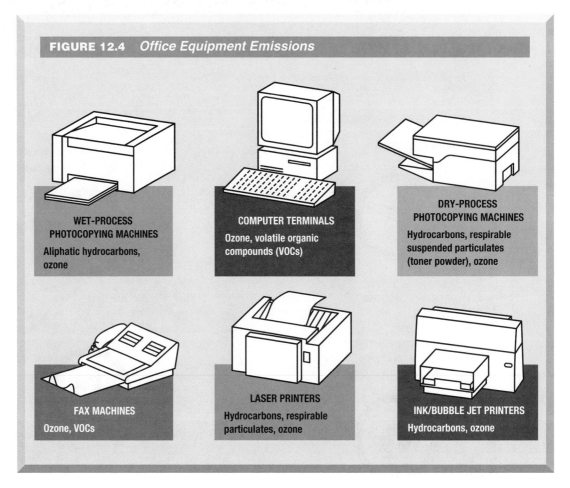

FIGURE 12.4 *Office Equipment Emissions*

WET-PROCESS PHOTOCOPYING MACHINES
Aliphatic hydrocarbons, ozone

COMPUTER TERMINALS
Ozone, volatile organic compounds (VOCs)

DRY-PROCESS PHOTOCOPYING MACHINES
Hydrocarbons, respirable suspended particulates (toner powder), ozone

FAX MACHINES
Ozone, VOCs

LASER PRINTERS
Hydrocarbons, respirable particulates, ozone

INK/BUBBLE JET PRINTERS
Hydrocarbons, ozone

Note: Health complaints include increased perception of headache, mucous imitation; eye, nose, and throat irritation; dry and tight facial skin.

Source: Adapted from Air and Energy Research, EPA.

There are four basic ways to overcome polluted buildings: (1) eliminate tobacco smoke, (2) provide adequate ventilation, (3) maintain the ventilating system, and (4) remove sources of pollution. Figure 12.4 shows the common sources of emissions released by office equipment. Study the figure carefully to gain a better understanding of the sources of irritants that can affect the well-being and job performance of office employees.

Tobacco smoke. Probably the most heated workplace health issue of the 1990s was smoking. Nonsmokers, fuelled by studies linking "passive smoking" (inhaling other people's smoke) with disease and death, and irritated by smoke getting in their eyes, noses, throats, and clothes, have been extremely vocal in demanding a smoke-free environment. The number of organizations restricting smoking in the workplace has risen dramatically, driven by legislation in most provinces. Employers that ban smoking no longer have to worry about related lawsuits. They also no longer have to install ventilating systems for smokers. Almost all large organizations and many smaller ones have initiated policies restricting smoking.

A British Columbia arbitrator has ruled recently that smoking is as addictive as cocaine and so constitutes a drug dependency. Under human rights legislation, employers may have to allow workers with a substance abuse problem to take a leave of absence to seek treatment. If nicotine addiction is accepted as a disability, companies may have to provide stop-smoking programs, and refrain from disciplining addicted employees who smoke. A 1997 Labour Canada study found that employees who smoke cost companies about $2,500 more per year (than non-smoking employees) in increased absenteeism, lost productivity, and increased health and life insurance premiums.[20] It has been documented that health care costs are higher for smokers; for this reason, some employers are charging smokers more for health insurance or are reducing their benefits. Many employers, however, prefer positive reinforcement through wellness programs to encourage employees to stop smoking.

Video Display Terminals

The almost universal use of computers and video display terminals (VDTs) in the workplace has generated intense debate over their possible hazards. Many fears about VDT use are now known to be unfounded, but there are still serious health complaints related to them. These complaints fall into four major groups:[21]

1. *Visual difficulties.* VDT operators often complain of blurred vision, sore eyes, burning and itching eyes, and glare.

2. *Radiation hazards.* Cataract formation and reproductive problems, including miscarriages and birth defects, have been attributed to VDT use, but the risks of exposure to VDT radiation have yet to be determined.

3. *Muscular aches and pains.* Pains in the back, neck, and shoulders are common complaints of VDT operators.

4. *Job stress.* Three-quarters of VDT users complain of eye strain, postural problems, noise, insufficient training, excessive workloads, and monotonous work.[22]

Dr. James Sheedy, a VDT and vision expert, offers these tips for minimizing the negative effects of computer use on the eyes and body:

- Place the computer screen four to nine inches below eye level.
- Keep the monitor directly in front of you.
- Sit in an adjustable-height chair and use a copyholder that attaches to both the desk and the monitor.
- Use a screen with adjustable brightness and contrast controls.
- Use shades or blinds to reduce the computer-screen glare created by window lighting.[23]

Repetitive Strain Injuries

Meat cutters, fish filleters, cooks, dental hygienists, textile workers, violinists, flight attendants, office workers at computer terminals, and others whose jobs require repetitive motion of the fingers, hands, or arms are reporting injuries in growing

Repetitive strain injuries (RSIs)

Injuries involving tendons of the fingers, hands, and arms that become inflamed from repeated stresses and strains

numbers. These injuries, known as **repetitive strain injuries (RSIs)**, involve inflammation of the tendons from repeated stresses and strains. One of the more common conditions is *carpal tunnel syndrome*, which is characterized by tingling or numbness in the fingers. It arises when a tunnel of bones and ligaments in the wrist narrows, thus pinching the nerves that reach the fingers and the ball of the thumb. Every year, 50 percent of all disability claims in Ontario, and 31 percent in British Columbia, are for RSI. The yearly cost is $2 billion. Minibreaks involving exercises (or even just changing position), properly designed workstations, and better-designed tools have all been found helpful in reducing RSI. These kinds of injuries often go away if they are caught and treated early. If they are not, months or years of treatment may be necessary, and possibly even surgical correction.[24]

AIDS

Provisions for communicable diseases such as herpes simplex (cold sores), influenza, athlete's foot, and AIDS (acquired immune deficiency syndrome) are covered in public health legislation, not occupational health and safety legislation. In recent years, few workplace issues have received as much attention as AIDS. Because so many legal and medical issues have come to surround AIDS, employers must be able to provide answers to everyone concerned.

Under public health and human rights laws, AIDS victims are likely to be considered disabled. This means that employers have no choice but to hire and/or retain people with AIDS who are able to perform the essential functions of the job. Under the same laws, employers must provide reasonable accommodation for people with AIDS through adjustments such as job restructuring, modified work schedules, and less rigid physical requirements.[25]

There is still no evidence that AIDS can be spread through casual contact in the typical workplace. Even so, one of the biggest problems employers face is other employees' fears of contracting it. It is important for employers to have programs in place to educate managers about how AIDS is transmitted, and to educate the entire workforce through newsletters, posters, and seminars.[26]

Because AIDS is still controversial, employers must make sure that managers and HR personnel are carefully briefed on all aspects of the issue; only then can they act in the best interests of all concerned. In the past several years, HR journals and health journals have published many articles that can be useful in developing reading files for the HR staff and for managerial and supervisory personnel. A comprehensive and widely distributed AIDS policy does much to reduce fears about this illness.[27]

Workplace Violence

Those working in health care, hospitality, retail sales, transportation, corrections, security, and police services are at the greatest risk of assault.[28] The Canadian Initiative on Workplace Violence surveyed more than two million employees and concluded that workplace violence is rising; in its definition of violence, it included physical attacks and psychological violence (harassment, bullying, mobbing, teasing and ridicule).[29]

Reducing Workplace Violence

A greater risk of being assaulted in the workplace is associated with the following: contact with the public; the exchange of money; the delivery of passengers, goods, or services; work in health care, social services, or criminal settings; and working alone or in small groups.[30] Employers are strongly advised to extend greater protection to these employees to whom these factors pertain.

At present, Saskatchewan and British Columbia are the only provinces with workplace violence regulations in place. Guidelines should include:

- Holding managers responsible for preventing acts of violence.
- Analyzing the workplace to uncover areas of potential violence.
- Preventing violence by designing safe workplaces and work practices.
- Providing violence prevention training.[31]

Employers can take specific actions to reduce workplace violence. For example, they can screen job applicants for the propensity to violence. For a negligible fee, small employers can use outside investigators to perform background checks.[32] Also, managers can be trained to recognize violence indicators (see Figure 12.5). Managers who are aware of threatening behaviours can intervene to prevent disruptive, abusive, or violent acts. Finally, organizations can establish formalized workplace prevention policies, informing employees that aggressive employee behaviour will not be tolerated. Highlights in HRM 3 describes one violence prevention policy.

FIGURE 12.5 *Violence Indicators: Know the Warning Signs*

Most people leave a trail of indicators before they become violent. Similarly, disgruntled former employees who commit acts of violence leave warning signs of their intent before and after termination. The following behaviours should be taken seriously when assessing situations of potential violence:

- Direct or veiled threatening statements.
- Recent performance declines, including concentration problems and excessive excuses.
- Prominent mood or behaviour changes.
- Preoccupation with guns, knives, or other weapons.
- Deliberate destruction of workplace equipment; sabotage.
- Fascination with stories of violence.
- Reckless or antisocial behaviour; evidence of prior assaultive behaviour.
- Aggressive behaviour or intimidating statements.
- Written messages of violent intent.
- Serious stress in personal life.
- Obsessive desire to harm a specific group or person.
- Violence against a family member.
- Substance abuse.

Source: Adapted from Christina McGovern, "Take Action, Heed Warnings to End Workplace Violence," *Occupational Health and Safety* 61, no 3 (March 1999): 61–3; Rebecca Speer, "Can Workplace Violence Be

Highlights in HRM

3   GARDEN FRESH'S WORKPLACE VIOLENCE PREVENTION POLICY

Garden Fresh is committed to conducting its operations in a safe manner. Consistent with this policy acts or threats (either verbal or implied) of physical violence, including intimidation, harassment, and/or coercion, which involve or affect Garden Fresh or which occur on Garden Fresh property will not be tolerated.

Acts or threats of violence include, but are not limited to, the following:

- All threats or acts of violence occurring on Garden Fresh premises, regardless of the relationship between Garden Fresh and the parties involved in the incident

- All threats or acts of violence occurring off of Garden Fresh premises involving someone who is acting in the capacity of a representative of the company

- All threats or acts of violence occurring off of Garden Fresh premises involving an employee of GFRC if the threats or acts affect the legitimate interests of Garden Fresh

- Any acts or threats resulting in the conviction of an employee or agent of Garden Fresh, or of an individual performing services for Garden Fresh on a contract or temporary basis, under any criminal code provision relating to violence or threats of violence which adversely affect the legitimate interests and goals of Garden Fresh.

Specific examples of conduct which may be considered threats or acts of violence include, but are not limited to, the following:

- Hitting or shoving an individual

- Threatening an individual or his/her family, friends or property with harm.

- The intentional destruction or threat of destruction of company property.

- Harassing or threatening phone calls.

- Harassing surveillance or stalking.

- The suggestion or intimation that violence is appropriate.

- Possession or use of firearms or weapons.

Garden Fresh's prohibition against threats and acts of violence applies to all persons involved in the company's operation, including Garden Fresh personnel contract and temporary workers, and anyone else on Garden Fresh property.

Violations of this policy by any individual on Garden Fresh's property by any individual acting as a representative of Garden Fresh while off of Garden Fresh property, or by an individual acting off of Garden Fresh's property when his/her actions affect the company's business interests will lead to disciplinary action (up to and including termination) and/or legal action as appropriate.

Employees should learn to recognize and respond to behaviors by potential perpetrators that may indicate a risk of violence.

Employees shall place safety as the highest concern, and shall report all acts or threats of violence immediately. Every employee and every person on Garden Fresh's property is encouraged to report incidents of threats or acts of physical violence of which he/she is aware. The report should be made to the Director of Human Resources, the reporting individual's immediate supervisor, or another supervisory employee if the immediate supervisor is not available.

It is the responsibility of managers and supervisors to make safety their highest concern. When made aware of a real or perceived threat of violence, management shall conduct a thorough investigation and take specific actions to help prevent acts of violence.

Nothing in this policy alters any other reporting obligation established by Garden Fresh policies or in state, federal, or other applicable law.

Source: Used with permission from Garden Fresh, 17180 Bernardo Drive, San Diego, Calif. 92128.

Violence Response Teams

Organizations like Allied Signal, Motorola, and Circle K Corporation have formal violence response teams. Home Depot has a crisis management team that arrives within one hour of an incident. These teams, composed of both hourly and managerial employees, conduct initial risk assessment surveys, develop action plans to respond to violent situations, and, importantly, perform crisis intervention during violent or potentially violent encounters. For example, a violence response team would investigate a threat reported by an employee. The team's mandate would be to gather facts about the threat and decide whether the organization should intervene.[33]

When the decision is to intervene—to try to defuse a volatile situation—the pointers provided in Figure 12.6 are sure to be helpful.

When violent incidents, such as leading to the death of a co-worker, happen at work, employees often experience shock, guilt, grief, apathy, resentment, cynicism, and a host of other emotions.[34] After a violent incident, employees become frightened and may not want to return to work.[35] Such incidents may require the violence response team to carry out crisis intervention through positive counselling techniques.

FIGURE 12.6 *Calming an Angry Employee*

If you try to defuse a tense situation, remember that anger frequently results from a person's feeling of being wronged, misunderstood, or unheard. Keep the following tips in mind to guide you:

- Confront the employee privately to prevent embarrassment.

- Don't lose your temper, overreact, or gesture aggressively; these will trigger a similar response in the employee.

- Listen without judgment. Many people simply want someone to hear what they have to say.

- Validate the employee's feelings or position. Say, "You have a good point," or agree that there is a problem.

- Help the employee save face during an anger situation. Don't pounce on a rash statement or pursue a muddled line of reasoning.

- If necessary, suggest a delay so that people can cool off. Say, "Let's meet at 2 p.m. to discuss this."

- Withdraw if necessary.

If you sense that the situation is escalating or if you are part of the employee's problem, offer to find someone else to help. Leave if the employee becomes so agitated that you become uneasy.

Source: Reprinted with permission from the Society for Human Reasource Management, Alexandria, VA.

Building Better Health

Many employers provide health services and have programs that encourage employees to improve their health habits. Better health not only benefits the individual, but also pays off for the organization in reduced absenteeism, increased efficiency, better morale, and other savings. A greater understanding of the close relationship between physical and emotional health and job performance has made broad health-building programs attractive to employers as well as to employees.

Health Services

Which health services employers provide is largely a function of size. Small organizations are likely to have only limited facilities, such as those required to handle first aid; many larger firms offer complete diagnostic, treatment, and emergency surgical services. Since employers are required to provide medical services after an injury, larger companies usually have nurses and physicians on full-time duty. Medium-size and smaller organizations will have one or more physicians on call.

We noted in Chapter 5 that some employers give medical examinations to prospective employees after a job offer has been made. The examination should include a medical history with specific reference to previous hazardous exposures. Exposure to hazards whose effects may be cumulative, such as noise, lead, and radiation, are especially relevant. For jobs involving unusual physical demands, the applicant's muscular development, flexibility, agility, range of motion, and cardiac and respiratory functions should be evaluated. Many organizations also give periodic examinations on a required or voluntary basis. Such examinations can help determine the effects of potential hazards in the workplace, and detect any health problems to which the employee's lifestyle or health habits may contribute.

Wellness Programs

WWW

Many organizations, such as Nortel and Labatt Breweries of Canada, have developed programs that emphasize regular exercise, proper nutrition, weight control, and the avoidance of substances harmful to health. Half the respondents to a Conference Board of Canada survey had a wellness program.[36] The employee health management program at Xerox includes cardiovascular fitness through aerobic exercises such as jogging, skipping rope, and racquet sports. The company gives its employees a publication called *Fitbook*, which provides instructions and illustrations for a variety of exercises. The book also includes chapters on the hazards of smoking and the effects of alcohol and drug abuse, facts on nutrition and weight control, and guidelines for managing stress and learning to relax.[37] Many smaller organizations distribute wellness literature obtained from various sources.[38]

WWW

Wellness programs are popular, and produce measurable cost savings. Wellness efforts are especially effective when organizations target their wellness initiatives at specific health risks such as high cholesterol or blood pressure counts, high body-fat levels, and smoking. Thanks to FitWorks, Pacific Bell's wellness program, employees achieved a 20 percent reduction in cardiovascular risks in two years. Charles Schwab and Co. attributes its reduction in heart disease to its Pro-Fit wellness program.[39] Figure 12.7 gives ten tips for launching a successful wellness program, even on a limited budget.

OBJECTIVE 5

Employee Assistance Programs

Health encompasses both the emotional and the physical aspects of one's life. Emotional problems, personal crises, alcoholism, and drug abuse are considered personal matters; however, they become organizational problems when they affect behaviour at work and interfere with job performance. One-third of working Canadians will suffer temporary emotional problems at one time or another; for one-fifth of employees, this suffering will be severe enough to cause injuries, absenteeism, or reduced productivity.[40] This is why four in ten Canadian employers offer some kind of employee assistance program (EAP).[41] Typically, such a program refers employees

---

FIGURE 12.7 *Tips for Starting a Successful Wellness Program*

1. Conduct a health risk assessment of employees.

2. Determine where medically related money is spent.

3. Include family members and retirees in wellness instruction.

4. Provide nutritional advice from a registered dietitian.

5. Include healthy, low-fat choices among snacks and meals provided in cafeterias and through vending machines.

6. Eliminate smoking from the work setting.

7. Negotiate discounts from area health clubs.

8. Start a health and fitness newsletter.

9. Focus on reducing one or two high-risk factors among employees.

Source: Copyright 2000, Steelcase Inc. Reprinted with permission.

---

in need of assistance to in-house counsellors or outside professionals. Supervisors are often given training and policy guidance in the type of help they can offer their subordinates. In contracting with professional counsellors outside the organization, the HR department needs to give special attention to their credentials, cost, accountability, and service capabilities.[42] Research suggests that for every dollar employers spend on EAPs, they receive a three- to-seven dollar return in productivity gains.[43]

Personal Crises

The most prevalent problems among employees are personal crises involving marital, family, financial, or legal matters. These problems often come to a supervisor's attention. Usually the supervisor can provide the best help simply by being understanding and supportive and by helping the individual find the type of assistance he or she needs. Often, in-house counselling or referral to an outside professional is recommended. In recent years, crisis hotlines have been set up in many communities to provide counselling by telephone for those too distraught to wait for an appointment with a counsellor.

Emotional Problems

While personal crises are typically fraught with emotion, most of them are resolved in a reasonable period of time, and the troubled individual's equilibrium is restored. However, a small percentage of employees—roughly 3 percent on average—will have emotional problems serious enough to require professional treatment. Whether these individuals will be able to perform their jobs must be determined on an individual basis. In reviewing cases like this, the organization should pay special attention to workplace safety factors, since there is general agreement that emotional disturbance is the primary or secondary factor in a large proportion of industrial accidents and violence.

Unfortunately, when personal crises linger, stress and tension may cause or intensify mood disorders such as depression. **Depression** is the decrease in functional activity accompanied by symptoms of low spirits, gloominess, and sadness. The Canadian Mental Health Association estimates that depression costs employers nearly $4 billion a year when lost productivity, absenteeism, and health care expenses are taken into account.[44] With available treatment, however, 70 percent of afflicted individuals will significantly improve, usually within a matter of weeks.[45]

Depression lowers individual productivity, causes morale problems, increases absenteeism, and contributes to substance abuse, so it is important for managers to identify signs of depression on the job and learn to deal with depressed employees.[46] The most likely workplace signs of depression are decreased energy, concentration and memory problems, guilt feelings, irritability, and chronic aches and pains that don't respond to treatment. Highlights in HRM 4 lists the symptoms of depression. When dealing with a depressed employee, managers and supervisors are encouraged to show concern for the person's problem, to listen actively, and—if the depression persists—to suggest professional help. Under no circumstances should a manager attempt to play amateur psychologist and try to diagnose an employee's condition. Mood disorders, like depression, are complex in nature and do not lend themselves to quick diagnoses.[47]

Alcoholism

Business and industry lose billions each year because of alcoholism. According to a Conference Board of Canada report, the total social cost of alcohol abuse in 1992 in Ontario alone was $4.3 billion.[48] Alcoholism affects workers in every occupational category, both blue-collar and white-collar.[49] Survey and workforce studies have shown a correlation between alcohol abuse and increases in workers' compensation claims, insurance payouts, lost productivity, and theft.[50]

Employers must recognize that alcoholism is a disease that follows a rather predictable course. Armed with this knowledge, they can take specific actions to deal with employees who are showing symptoms of the disease at particular stages of its progression. Alcoholism typically begins with social drinking getting out of control. As the disease progresses, the alcoholic loses control over how much he or she

Depression

Negative emotional state marked by feelings of low spirits, gloominess, sadness, and loss of pleasure in ordinary activities

WWW

Highlights in HRM

4 DEPRESSION IN THE WORKPLACE

When a depressed mood persists for a few weeks, deepens, and eventually starts interfering with work and other aspects of everyday life, it has likely become an illness—or a clinical depression. In the workplace, a person with depression will exhibit many of the following signs:

RECOGNIZING DEPRESSION

Personal Changes

- Irritability, hostility
- Hopelessness, despair
- Slowness of speech
- Chronic fatigue
- Withdrawal from or extreme dependency on others
- Alcohol or drug abuse

Workplace Changes

- Difficulty in making decisions
- Decreased productivity
- Inability to concentrate
- Decline in dependability
- Unusual increase in errors in work
- Accident proneness
- Frequent tardiness, increased "sick" days
- Lack of enthusiasm for work

Someone who has been experiencing many of these signs for a few weeks or more should seek help immediately.

Source: Canadian Mental Health Association, National Office, 2160 Yonge St., Toronto M4S 2Z3 (416) 484-7750.

drinks and eventually cannot keep from drinking, even at inappropriate times. The person resorts to denial to avoid facing the problems created by the abuse of alcohol and often blames others for these problems. The first step in helping the alcoholic is to awaken the person to the reality of the situation at hand.[51]

To identify alcoholism as early as possible, it is essential that supervisors monitor the performance of all personnel regularly and systematically. A supervisor should carefully document evidence of declining performance on the job and then confront the employee with unequivocal proof that the job is suffering. The employee should be assured that help will be made available without penalty. Since the evaluations are made solely in terms of lagging job performance, a supervisor can avoid any mention of alcoholism and allow such employees to seek aid as they would for any other problem. Disciplinary action can be taken against employees who refuse to take advantage of this assistance or whose performance does not improve with repeated warnings. Between 70 and 80 percent of employees accept the offer to get help and resolve their problems. It is important for employers to recognize, however, that in discharge cases brought by alcoholic employees, arbitrators look at on-the-job alcoholism as a sickness, not as a disciplinary matter.

Abuse of Illegal Drugs

The abuse of drugs by employees is one of the major employment issues today. Drug abuse is now a national problem and has spread to every industry, occupation, and employee level. Estimates of the costs of substance abuse by employees vary considerably. Besides lost productivity, there are the costs of increased numbers of accidents and injuries, and rising rates of employee theft. The costs of substance abuse can have a dramatic impact on the bottom line. To date, there are no provincial or federal laws prohibiting drug testing by employers.

While attention is usually focused on the abuse of illegal drugs, it should be noted that the abuse of legal drugs can also pose a problem for employees. Employees who abuse legal drugs—that is, those prescribed by physicians—often do not realize they have become addicted, or that their behaviour has changed as a result of their addiction. Also, managers should be aware that some employees may be taking legal sedatives or stimulants as part of their medical treatment and that their behaviour at work may be affected by their use of these drugs.[52] A standard reference book of legal drugs is the Physicians' Desk Reference (PDR).[53]

THE MANAGEMENT OF STRESS

Many jobs require employees to adjust to conditions that place unusual demands on them. In time these demands create stresses that can affect the health of employees as well as their productivity and satisfaction. Fortunately, employers are making more effort to identify stressors and prevent undue stress on the job. To protect the well-being of their employees and to reduce the costs to their organizations, they will have to do even more of this. One study of group disability insurers found that mental and nervous claims accounted for 30 percent of long-term disability claims.[54]

What Is Stress?

Stress

Any adjustive demand caused by physical, mental, or emotional factors that requires coping behaviour

Eustress

Positive stress that accompanies achievement and exhilaration

Distress

Harmful stress characterized by a loss of feelings of security and adequacy

Alarm reaction

Response to stress that basically involves an elevated heart rate, increased respiration, elevated levels of adrenaline in the blood, and increased blood pressure

Stress is any demand on the individual that requires coping behaviour. Stress has two basic sources: physical activity, and mental or emotional activity. Psychologists distinguish between positive and negative stress, even though the biochemical reactions to them are the same. **Eustress** is positive stress; it accompanies achievement and exhilaration. Eustress is the stress of meeting challenges such as those found in managerial, technical, or public contact jobs. Eustress is regarded as a beneficial force that helps us forge ahead against obstacles. What is harmful is **distress**. Stress becomes distress when we begin to feel inadequate and insecure. Helplessness, desperation, and disappointment turn stress into distress.

In a stressful situation, the entire body mobilizes to meet the requirements of "fight or flight." The sympathetic nervous system in effect orders the endocrine glands to begin releasing hormones; these place the body on a "war footing." This response, commonly referred to as the **alarm reaction**, involves an elevated heart rate, increased respiration, elevated levels of adrenaline in the blood, and increased blood pressure. It persists until the person has judged that the threat to his or her well-being has receded. If distress persists long enough, it can result in fatigue, exhaustion, and even physical and/or emotional breakdown. Stress has been linked to heart disease, and also to hypertension (high blood pressure). High blood pressure is the most common cause of strokes.[55]

Job-Related Stress

The body experiences a certain degree of stress (either eustress or distress) in all situations; here we are concerned mainly with the stress related to work settings. This is where management can take preventive action.

Sources of Job-Related Stress

WWW

Work is the leading cause of stress in Canada. According to a study by the Conference Board of Canada, almost half of all Canadians say that they are experiencing high or moderate levels of stress. This stress has many causes, including a heavy work load, organizational restructuring, and the demands of balancing work with life outside work. Linda Duxbury at Carleton University and Chris Higgins at the University of Western Ontario both found that nearly 20 million workdays are lost each year due to conflicts between work and family.[56] Disagreements with managers or fellow employees are another common cause of distress. Others are having little or no say about how a job is performed, lack of communication on the job, and lack of recognition for work done well. Even more minor irritants such as lack of privacy, unappealing music, and excessive noise can be distressing.

Figure 12.8 lists the results from one study of the sources of stress among Canadian workers.

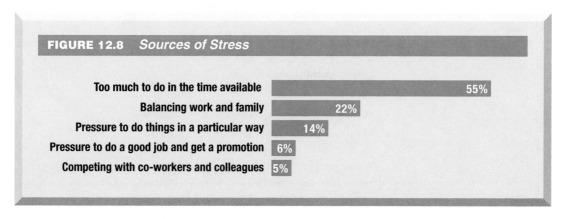

FIGURE 12.8   *Sources of Stress*

Too much to do in the time available — 55%
Balancing work and family — 22%
Pressure to do things in a particular way — 14%
Pressure to do a good job and get a promotion — 6%
Competing with co-workers and colleagues — 5%

Source: I. Ross and G. MacDonald, "Scars from Stress Cut Deep in the Workplace," *The Globe and Mail*, October 9, 1997: B16.

Burnout

Burnout

Most severe stage of distress, manifesting itself in depression, frustration, and loss of productivity

Burnout is the most severe stage of distress. Career burnout generally occurs when a person begins questioning his or her own personal values. Quite simply, the individual no longer feels that what he or she is doing is important. Depression, frustration, and loss of productivity are all symptoms of burnout. The root cause of burnout is a lack of personal fulfilment in the job, or a lack of positive feedback about performance.[57] In organizations that have downsized, the remaining employees can experience burnout because the demand is on them to perform more work with fewer co-workers. Overachievers can experience burnout when they realize that their work goals are unattainable. Employees in high-tech industries face conditions—a high-pressure atmosphere combined with an "all work, no play" lifestyle—that make them especially susceptible to burnout.

Coping with Stress

The issue of stress on the job has received considerable attention in the media. In the past decade, workers' compensation claims for mental stress have mushroomed because of (1) the growing number of employees in service jobs, where the work is more mental than manual, (2) the repetitive nature of tasks, (3) the trend toward seeking compensation for mental as well as physical injuries, and (4) the receptivity of the courts to such cases.[58]

Action to alleviate organizational stress must begin with managers learning to recognize the universal symptoms of work stress, as well as the stressful situations particular to their work units. Major stressors include the following:

- Responsibility without authority
- Lack of means to voice complaints
- Prejudice because of age, gender, race, or religion
- Poor working conditions
- Inadequate recognition
- Fuzzy job description or chain of command
- Unfriendly interpersonal relationships[59]

Many employers have developed stress management programs to teach employees how to minimize the negative effects of job-related stress. A typical program includes instruction in the following: relaxation techniques, coping skills, listening skills, methods of dealing with difficult people, time management, and assertiveness. The purpose of all of these is to help break the tension that accompanies stress situations, and to help participants achieve greater control of their lives. Other techniques for reducing stress focus on the organization itself: clarifying the employee's work role, redesigning and enriching jobs, correcting physical factors in the environment, and handling interpersonal factors more effectively.[60] BC Tel has developed a software program to help its 14,000 employees manage stress. Wilson Banwell, the largest psychological service in Canada, has made on-line counselling available for its clients. Figure 12.9 shows the results of one study of stress management techniques commonly used by Canadian workers.

WWW

The number and severity of organizational stressors can be reduced; even so, everyone encounters situations that can be described as distressful. Those in good physical health are generally better able to cope with the stressors they encounter. Figure 12.10 describes several ways to resolve job-related stress.

Before concluding this discussion, we should observe that stress that is harmful to some employees may be healthy for others. Most executives learn to handle distress effectively and find that it actually stimulates better performance. (Highlights in HRM 5 describes how Michael Cowpland of Corel Corp. thrives on stress.) However, there will always be those who are unable to handle stress and need help coping with it. All people, young and old alike, are interested in developing habits that will enable them to lead happier and more productive lives. This will benefit them as individuals, and the organizations where they work, and society in general, where people are becoming more and more interdependent.

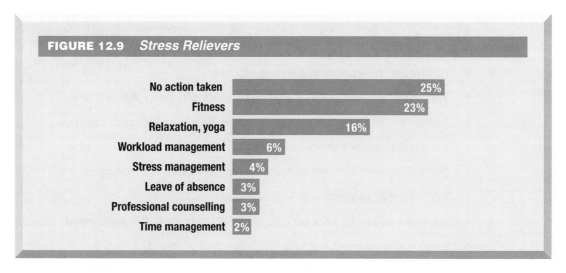

FIGURE 12.9 *Stress Relievers*

No action taken	25%
Fitness	23%
Relaxation, yoga	16%
Workload management	6%
Stress management	4%
Leave of absence	3%
Professional counselling	3%
Time management	2%

Source: I. Ross and G. MacDonald, "Scars from Stress Cut Deep in the Workplace," *The Globe and Mail*, October 9, 1997: B16.

Highlights in HRM

5   PERSONAL POWER

WWW

Michael Cowpland, chairman, president, and CEO of software giant Corel Corp., was known for his hands-on management style—for becoming involved in every decision and having few middle managers. Virtually everyone in his company reported to him. He had no secretary and answered and returned his own mail. Cowpland regularly worked eighty-hour weeks. He read fifty industry magazines in one week (he was beyond speed-reading and into hyper-reading, he said). He played tennis five times a week, and squash three times, and watched a wall of sixteen televisions all at the same time. He handled stress well. According to one stress researcher, the only factor that has any significant impact on a person's ability to withstand work pressure is "personal power"— having control over your time, resources, important information, work load, and so on. It is not the volume of work or work demands that makes people sick; it is the extent to which they can control it. Michael Cowpland was an example of a man who controls his work environment.

Sources: "Racquet Scientist," *Canadian Business*, June 1995; P. Froiland, "What Cures Job Stress?" *Training*, December 1993: 32–6.

FIGURE 12.10 *Tips for Reducing Job-Related Stress*

- Build rewarding relationships with co-workers.
- Talk openly with managers or employees about job or personal concerns.
- Prepare for the future by keeping abreast of likely changes in job demands.
- Don't greatly exceed your skills and abilities.
- Set realistic deadlines; negotiate reasonable deadlines with managers.
- Act now on problems or concerns of importance.
- Designate dedicated work periods during which interruptions are avoided.
- When feeling stressed, find time for detachment or relaxation.
- Don't let trivial items take on importance; handle them quickly or assign them to others.
- Take short breaks from your work area as a change of pace.

SUMMARY

 Occupational health and safety legislation is designed to ensure, as far as is possible, safe and healthful working conditions for all working people. In general, it extends to all employers and employees. Occupational health and safety acts set standards, ensure employer and employee compliance, and provide safety and health consultation and training where needed. Both employers and employees have certain responsibilities and rights under these acts. Employers are required to provide a hazard-free work environment; they must also keep employees informed about legislative requirements and insist that they use protective equipment when necessary. In addition, employers are required to keep employees informed of hazardous substances and to instruct them in avoiding the dangers these present. Employees, for their part, are required to comply with safety standards, to report hazardous conditions, and to follow all employer safety and health regulations.

 To provide safe working conditions for their employees, employers typically establish a formal program that, in the great majority of organizations, is under the direction of the HR manager. The program may have many facets, including providing safety knowledge and motivating employees to use it, making employees aware of the need for safety, and rewarding them for safe behaviour. Such incentives as praise, public recognition, and awards are used to involve employees in the safety program. By law, records must be kept of accident investigations; these provide data that can be used to create a safer work environment.

 Job conditions that are dangerous to the health of employees are now receiving much more attention than in the past. There is special concern for toxic chemicals, which are proliferating at a rapid rate, and many of which lurk in the body for years without outward symptoms. Health hazards other than those found in industrial processing operations—indoor air pollution, video display terminals, repetitive strain injuries, and the like—present special problems that must be addressed. Today tobacco smoke is rarely tolerated in the work environment. While there is no evidence that AIDs can be spread through casual contact in the workplace, employers have found that it is important to educate managers and employees about AIDs and to assist those who are afflicted.

 Besides providing safer and healthier work environments, many employers have established programs that encourage employees to improve their health habits. Some of the larger employers have opened primary care clinics for employees and their dependents to provide better health care service and reduce costs. Wellness programs that emphasize exercise, nutrition, weight control, and avoidance of harmful substances serve employees at all organizational levels.

 Almost all large organizations and many smaller ones have found that employee assistance programs benefit all concerned. Emotional problems, personal crises, alcoholism, and drug abuse are often viewed as personal matters; yet it is clear that they affect behaviour at work and interfere with job performance. An employee assistance program typically provides professional assistance by in-house counsellors or outside professionals where needed. In contracting with professionals outside the organization, the HR department should pay special attention to their credentials.

 An important dimension to health and safety is the stress that comes from physical activity and mental or emotional activity. Stress is an integral part of being alive; however, when it turns into distress it becomes harmful. Many sources of stress are job-related. Employers can develop stress management programs to help employees learn to cope with stress. Organizations are well advised to redesign and enrich jobs, clarify their employees' work roles, and correct any physical shortcomings in the environment; these can all help reduce stress on the job.

KEY TERMS

alarm reaction
burnout
depression
eustress

distress
industrial disease
Material Safety Data Sheet
    (MSDS)

occupational illness
occupational injury
repetitive strain injuries (RSIs)
stress

DISCUSSION QUESTIONS

1. What effects have occupational health and safety laws had on employer and employee behaviour?

2. What steps should management take to increase motivation for safety?

3. An unhealthy work environment can lower productivity, contribute to low morale, and increase medical and workers' compensation costs. Working individually or in teams, list specific ways that managers can

a. Improve indoor air quality

b. Reduce the harmful effects of VDTs

c. Address employees' fears about AIDS.

4. Medical professionals say that to live a healthier life, we need to identify those things we currently do that either impede or contribute to our health. Prepare lists of your own healthy and unhealthy activities. Discuss with others ways to develop a lifetime program for a healthy lifestyle.

5. What behaviours would suggest that a worker is under the influence of drugs?

6. In groups, identify the sources of stress in your life by consulting the Career Counsel website.

a. In what ways does this stress affect you? your employer?

b. What can managers and supervisors do to make the workplace less stressful?

c. Debate this resolution: "Managing stress is the responsibility of the employee."

PREVENTING REPETITIVE-STRAIN INJURIES AT CTAL

Repetitive strain injuries (RSIs) have been with us for centuries, under names like "carpet layers' knees" and "postman's shoulders." People who use computer keyboards for long stretches of time are especially prone to carpal tunnel syndrome, a condition characterized by numbness, pain, and tingling in the fingers and sometimes a burning or tingling sensation in the shoulder and arm. If left untreated, this condition can have serious long-term consequences for employees.

WWW

At Canadian Tire Acceptance Limited (CTAL) in Welland, Ontario, about 80 percent of the employees—many of them data entry workers—regularly use personal computers. In response to employee complaints of stiffness and pain, management hired an outside consultant, who determined that nearly 60 percent of CTAL's workforce was experiencing symptoms of RSI. Of that number, about half had seen a health care professional about the problem.

To prevent future injuries, CTAL modified its workstations and introduced a system under which job duties were rotated. At counselling and group sessions, employees learned how to identify risk factors and how to prevent RSIs through correct posture and optimum work habits. Wellness programs emphasizing fitness and nutrition were also part of the RSI prevention program. Employees who had reported RSI symptoms were linked with an occupational therapist who helped them manage the symptoms.

The RSI prevention program worked. No RSIs were reported in 1996, and 90 percent of those employees who required the services of an occupational therapist returned to work and remain productive. CTAL has saved at least three dollars for every dollar spent on the program.

Sources: L. Ramsay, "Working Pains," *Financial Post*, May 23, 1997: 4; "The Case for Integration," *Occupational Health and Safety* 12, no. 7 (1997): 68, 70; "CTAL Sheds Light on Repetitive Strain Dilemma," *Canadian Occupational Safety* 13, no. 1 (January–February 1997): 2.

Questions

1. The number of reported RSIs is increasing in most workplaces. Explain why.

2. What reasons might employees have for not reporting RSI symptoms?

3. Which aspect(s) of the above program do you think had the greatest effect?

CASE 2   WORKPLACE SAFETY AND YOUNG WORKERS

Young workers are 70 percent more likely to have a workplace injury than any other group.

About 95 percent of these young workers are men. This means that one in eleven young men can expect to suffer a workplace injury. Typically, these young men are employed at small manufacturing businesses, fast food restaurants, convenience stores, and warehouses. The accidents happen within the first six months on the job. These young men lose fingers while slicing meat at the deli counter, are crushed by equipment they do not know how to operate, are electrocuted on metal ladders that touch hydro poles, or are burned handling chemicals with no protective equipment. The top five causes of injuries to young workers are slips and falls, overexertion, being struck by an object, exposure to toxic chemicals, and burns.

Young workers do receive some safety training, but it is not enough. About 30 percent of teenagers receive first aid and CPR in their safety training, but most learn nothing about the law, their rights, hazards on the job, or safety management. Young workers are especially vulnerable because they feel invincible and lack experience. Most will not ask for safety training because they are unaware of risks, anxious to please, or fearful of losing their jobs.

Many provinces, recognizing these risks, have added health and safety training to the high school curriculum. Most such programs discuss workplace hazards, employer rights and responsibilities, health and safety laws, and the workers' right of refusal. Alberta has the most advanced training course for young workers in Canada: Job Safety Skills, which consists of 75 hours of instruction, divided into three modules:

- personal safety management (first aid, back care, safety and the law)
- workplace safety practices (ergonomics, confined space entry, transportation of dangerous goods, and farm safety)
- safety management systems (loss control, accident investigation, and a mock workshop in which students develop an entire safety program)

Source: Adapted from L. Ramsay, "Work Can Kill You," *National Post*, September 27, 1999: C12; L. Young, "Young Workers: Changing the Face of Safety," *Occupational Health and Safety* 14, no. 4, June–July 1998: 24–30; Anonymous, "Workplace Safety" *The Globe and Mail*, Friday, May 12, 2000.

Questions

1. Why are there more workplace injuries among those aged 16 to 25?

2. By law, workplace safety is the responsibility of the employer and employee. Why have nearly all provinces created courses in occupational health and safety as part of the high school curriculum? Should these be mandatory courses or electives?

3. Check the website of the Industrial Accident Prevention Association **www.iapa.on.ca**, which has excellent information on OH&S training programs. Design a training program that an employer could provide to young workers.

CAREER COUNSEL

The Job Stress Assessment on the Managing Human Resources website (**bel-court.nelson.com**) is designed to help you measure the amount of stress you are experiencing. Visit this site to measure your stress level and learn about strategies for managing stress.

USING THE INTERNET

WWW

The Canada Labour Congress site is worth visiting: **www.clc.ctc.ca/health-safety**.

The Canada Safety Council website (**www.safety-council.org/index.htm**) provides resources to assist in the development of a safe work environment.

The Industrial Accident Prevention Association (IAPA) (**www.iapa.on.ca**) offers six diploma programs for workers, supervisors, managers, and health and safety representatives. Course topics include health and safety legislation, hazard identification, and workplace inspection.

Unions have made health and safety a priority, and it is important for HR professionals to have a union perspective on health and safety. The Canadian Auto Workers website provides this perspective at **www.caw.ca**.

Visit the website of the Canadian Centre for Occupational Health and Safety for links to information about current issues (**www.ccohs.ca**). There is good information about indoor air quality on this site.

You can test your knowledge of WHIMIS at **www.whimis.net**.

All the provincial Occupational Health and Safety websites can be visited through **www.canoshweb.org**.

For current statistical information on occupational health and safety, check out **info.load-otea.hrdc-drhc.gc.ca/~oshweb/homeen.shtml**.

The Canadian Centre for Occupational Health and Safety (**www.ccohs.ca**) is an excellent site for links to government programs and legislation.

A good site for OHS information for employers is Employers Online (**employers.gc.ca**). Click on "Human Resource," then "Occupational Health and Safety."

The Nova Scotia Department of Environment and Labour (**www.gov.ns.ca/enla**) provides a comprehensive list of publications, including committee reports and news releases.

The Canadian Iniative on Workplace Violence (**www.workplaceviolence.ca**) publishes studies on the effects of workplace violence on productivity, and has suggestions for policies in the workplace. You can also find guidelines to reduce workplace violence at **www.opm.gov**, where you can download a copy of "Dealing with Workplace Violence: A Guide for Agency Planners."

NOTES AND REFERENCES

1. B. Sutton, "PCL Constructors Canada Inc. Fined $150,000," News Release 97-61, Ministry of Labour, October 21, 1997.

2. *Occupational Injuries and Their Cost in Canada 1998-1999*, Human Resources Development Canada, 1999, Canada Labour Congress website, **www.clsc–ctc.ca/health-safety.** Anonymous, "Statistics Grim but Improving," *Occupational Health & Safety* 15, no. 2 (March 1999): 10.

3. Statistics Canada, *Work Injuries 1991–1993*, Cat. No. 72–208 (Ottawa: Ministry of Supply and Services, 1994).

4. T. Van Alpen, "New Epidemic in the Workplace? RSI Pains, Strains and Computers," *Toronto Star*, April 17, 1995: B1, B3.

5. G.K. Bryce and P. Manga, "The Effectiveness of Health and Safety Committees," *Industrial Relations* 40, no. 2 (1985): 257–83.

6. Canadian Press newswire "Mining Company Fined $500,000 for Deaths of Two Miners," March 22, 2000.

7. Check the website of your province's occupational health and safety agency (see Figure 12.1).

8. "Workplace Accidents Decrease as Safety Commitment Increases," *HRFocus* 71, no. 9 (September 1994): 16.

9. Dan Petersen, *Safety Management—A Human Approach*, 2nd ed. (Riverside, N.J.: Aloray, 1988), 33–6.

10. Stephen G. Minter, "Safety Training That Sticks," *Occupational Hazards* 58, no. 7 (June 1996): 36.

11. Kaija Leena Saarela, "A Poster Campaign for Improving Safety on Shipyard Scaffolds," *Journal of Safety Research* 20 (1989): 177–85.

12. Michael B. Weinstein, "Improving Safety Programs through Total Quality," *Occupational Hazards* 58, no. 8 (August 1996): 42–6.

13. F. David Pierce, "10 Rules for Better Communication," *Occupational Hazards* 58, no. 5 (May 1996): 78–80.

14. Ann Boyce, "Effective Training Begins with Needs Assessment," *Occupational Health and Safety* 65, no. 8 (August 1996): 72–3. See also Stephen G. Minter, "Safety Training That Sticks," *Occupational Hazards* 58, no. 7 (July 1996): 36.

15. For more information about safety training programs, see J. Montgomery, *Occupational Health and Safety* (Scarborough, Ont.: ITP Nelson, 1996).

16. Jerry Laws, "The Power of Incentives," *Occupational Health and Safety* 65, no. 1 (January 1996): 25–8.

17. S.L. Smith, "Reaping the Rewards of Safety Incentives," *Occupational Hazards* 58, no. 1 (January 1996): 100. See also "Choosing the Right Incentive Reward," *Occupational Hazard* 58, no. 3 (March 1996): 63–5.

18. R. Bruce McAffee and Ashley R. Winn, "The Use of Incentives/Feedback to Enhance Work Place Safety: A Critique of the Literature," *Journal of Safety Research* 20 (1989): 7–19. See also Thomas R. Krause, John H. Hidley, and Stanley J. Hodson, "Broad-Based Changes in Behavior Key to Improving Safety Culture," *Occupational Health and Safety* 59, no. 7 (July 1990): 31–7, 50; Matthew P. Weinstock, "Rewarding Safety," *Occupational Hazards* 56, no. 3 (March 1994): 73–6.

19. Paul H. Marshall, "Addressing Indoor Air Quality Concerns," *Occupational Hazards* 58, no. 1 (January 1996): 83–5. See also Amal Kumar Naj, "Squabbles Delay Cure of ''Sick' Office Buildings," *Wall Street Journal*, October 26, 1995: B1; Joe E. Beck, "It's Time for a Breath of Fresh Air," *Occupational Health and Safety* 65, no. 2 (February 1996): 26–7.

20. D. Dyck, "Wrapping Up the Wellness Package," *Benefits Canada* 23, no. 1 (January 1999): 16–20.

21. J.A. Savage, "Are Computer Terminals Zapping Workers' Health?" *Business and Society Review* 84 (Winter 1993): 41–3.

22. *BNA Policy and Practice Series—Personnel Management* (Washington, D.C.: Bureau of National Affairs, 1988), 247:164.

23. "An Ounce of Prevention for Eye Strain," *HRFocus* 72, no. 11 (November 1995): 18. See also "Laptop Fitness," *HRFocus* 73, no. 9 (September 1996): 18.

24. Elizabeth Sheley, "Preventing Repetitive Motion Injuries," *HRMagazine* 40, no. 10 (October 1995): 57–60.

25. Linda C. Kramer, "Legal and Ethical Issues Affect Conduct Towards AIDS Sufferers," *Occupational Health and Safety* 59, no. 1 (January 1990): 49–50, 57.

26. Eileen Oswald, "Workplace AIDs/HIV: Are You Immune?" *Occupational Health and Safety* 65, no. 4 (April 1996): 39–40.

27. "As AIDS Cases Increase, So Does the Number of Corporate Policies," *HRFocus* 72, no. 2 (February 1995): 8.

28. Neil Boyd, "Violence in the Workplace in British Columbia: A Preliminary Investigation," *Canadian Criminal Justice Association* 37, no. 4 (November 1995): 491–519.

29. D. Brown, "Canadian Workplace Violence on the Rise" *Canadian HR Reporter*, May 22, 2000.

30. Stephen C. Yohay and Melissa L. Peppe, "Workplace Violence: Employer Responsibilities and Liabilities," *Occupational Hazards* 58, no. 7 (July 1996): 21–6.

31. "Preventing On-the-Job Violence," *HRFocus* 73, no. 8 (August 1996): 19. See also Gary R. Vandenbos and Elizabeth Q. Bulatao, *Violence on the Job: Identifying Risks and Developing Solutions* (Washington, D.C.: American Psychological Association, 1996): 4.

32. Michael Barrier, "The Enemy Within," *EAP Digest* 15, no. 4 (May–June 1995): 18–23. See also James O. Vigneau, "To Catch a Thief … and Other Workplace Investigations," *HRMagazine* 40, no. 1 (January 1995): 90–5.

33. Charles E. Labig, "Forming a Violence Response Team," *HRFocus* 72, no. 8 (August 1995): 15–16. See also Jacqueline Jacques, "Taking Crises Step-by-Step," *EAP Digest* 15, no. 5 (July–August 1995): 28–31; Geoffrey Luce, "When Seconds Count," *EAP Digest* 16, no. 4 (May–June 1996): 16–18.

34. Helen Frank Bensimon, "Violence in the Workplace," *Training and Development Journal* 5 (January 1994): 27–32. See also Marianne L. McManus, "When a Co-Worker Dies on Duty," *EAP Digest* 12, no. 4 (May–June 1992): 39.

35. Linda Thornburg, "When Violence Hits Business," *HRMagazine* 38, no. 7 (July 1993): 40–5.

36. D. Brown, "Wellness Programs Mo Magic Cure," *Canadian HR Reporter*, October 4, 1999: 2

37. Paul L. Cerrato, "Employee Health: Not Just a Fringe Benefit," *Business and Health* 13, no. 11 (November 1995): 21–6.

38. *Wellness Resources*, Association for Worksite Health Promotion, 60 Revere Dr., Suite 500, Northbrook, Ill. 60062, (847) 480-9574; Department of Health and Human Services, Office of Disease Prevention and Health Promotion, Washington, D.C. 20201, (202) 401-7780; National Wellness Institute, 1045 Clark St., Suite 210, P.O. Box 827, Stevens Point, Wisc. 54481-0828, (715) 342-2969; American Institute for Preventive Medicine, 30445 Northwestern Highway, Suite 350, Farmington Hills, Mich. 48334, (810) 539-1800.

39. "How Heart Disease Prevention Helped Two Employers," *Heart Disease Prevention* 13, no. 12 (December 1995): 26–30. See also "Workplace Prevention: The State of the Nation," Heart Disease Prevention 13, no. 12 (December 1995): 20–3; Nancy Ann Jeffrey, "Wellness Plans Try to Target the Not-So-Well," *Wall Street Journal*, June 20, 1996: B1.

40. P. Smith, "Stress out! " *Benefits Canada* 23, no. 11 (November 1999): 115–17.

41. J. Crocker, "Exposing the EAP," *Benefits Canada* 17, no. 9 (October 1993): 29–31.

42. *BNA Bulletin to Management* 40, no. 6 (February 9, 1989): 44. See also Ellen E. Schultz, "If You Use Firm's Counselors, Remember Your Secrets Could Be Used against You," *Wall Street Journal*, May 26, 1994: C1; Jerry Beilinson, "Are EAPs the Answer?" *Personnel* 68, no. 1 (January 1991): 3–4.

43. W. Koteff, "Duelling Roles," *Benefits Canada* 18, no. 11 (December 1994): 26–7.

44. S. Felix, "The Gloom Doom," *Benefits Canada* 21, no. 1 (January 1997): 32–7.

45. "More Businesses Helping Workers Deal with the Blues," *Sacramento Bee*, April 21, 1996: Section D.

46. David Chaudron, "Mood Disorders: Warning Signs and Action Steps," *HRFocus* 71, no. 10 (October 1994): 9.

47. Sandra Turner, "Identifying Depression in the Workplace," *HRMagazine* 40, no. 10 (October 1995): 82–4.

48. Shahid Alvi, "Corporate Responses to Substance Abuse in the Workplace," Conference Board of Canada Report 87-–92, Ottawa, 1993.

49. Jim Castelli, "Addiction," *HRMagazine* 35, no. 4 (April 1990): 55–8.

50. B. Butler, "Alcohol and Drug Testing in Canada: Do You Have a Right to Test? Do You Have a Right Not To?" *Occupational Health and Safety* 13, no. 1 (January–February 1997): 28–31.

51. Jonathan A. Segal, "An Employer's Right with Alcoholic Employees," *EAP Digest* 16, no. 4 (May–June 1996): 26–9.

52. Michael E. Cavanagh, "Abuse of Legal Drugs," *Personnel Journal* 69, no. 3 (March 1990): 124–8; Helene Cooper, "Warning: Americans Overuse Over-the-Counter Drugs," *Wall Street Journal*, January 11, 1994: B1. For details on one company's drug rehabilitation program, see Cheryl Thieme, "Better-Bilt Building a Substance Abuse Program That Works," *Personnel Journal* 69, no. 8 (August 1990): 52–8.

53. The *Physicians' Desk Reference* is published annually. The 1997 edition is the 51st edition.

54. P. Wysong, "Dealing with Disability Early," *Canadian Healthcare Manager* 5, no. 2 (February–March 1998): 28–30.

55. *USA Today*, April 11, 1990: A1.

56. Dianne Dyck, "Make Your Workplace Family Friendly," *Canadian HR Reporter*, December 13, 1999: G5.

57. Cynthia L. Cordes and Thomas W. Dougherty, "A Review and Integration of Research on Job Burnout," *The Academy of Management Review* 18, no. 4 (October 1993): 621–56.

58. Karen E. Semenuk, "Stress Test," *EAP Digest* 16, no. 6 (September–October 1996): 20–1.

59. Laurel Coppersmith, "Whose Problem Is It, Anyway?" *EAP Digest* 15, no. 5 (July–August 1995): 19. See also Steven L. Sauter and Lawrence R. Murphy, eds., *Organizational Risk Factors of Job Stress* (Hyattsville, Md.: American Psychological Association, 1995).

60. Lawrence R. Murphy, Joseph J. Hurrell, Steven L. Sauter, and Gwendolyn Puryear Keita, eds., *Job Stress Interventions* (Hyattsville, Md.: American Psychological Association, 1995).

…

EMPLOYEE RIGHTS

AND DISCIPLINE

After studying this chapter, you
should be able to

OBJECTIVE **1**

*Explain statutory rights,
contractual rights, and due
process.*

OBJECTIVE **2**

*Identify the job expectancy
rights of employees.*

OBJECTIVE **3**

*Explain the process for
establishing disciplinary
policies, including the
proper implementation of
organizational rules.*

OBJECTIVE **4**

*Discuss what discipline
means, and how to
investigate a disciplinary
problem.*

OBJECTIVE **5**

*Explain two approaches to
disciplinary action.*

OBJECTIVE **6**

*Identify the different types
of alternative
dispute-resolution
procedures.*

OBJECTIVE **7**

*Discuss the role of ethics
in the management of
human resources.*

I n this chapter we discuss employee rights, workplace privacy, and employee discipline. Managers are discovering that the right to discipline and discharge employees—a traditional responsibility of management—has become more difficult to exercise now that employment protection rights have been strengthened.[1] Also, most managers and supervisors find disciplining employees a difficult and unpleasant task; many of them report that taking disciplinary action against employees is the most stressful duty they perform. Balancing employee rights and employee discipline is not easy, but it is a universal requirement, and critical to good management.

The rising importance of employee rights issues has led to an increase in the number of lawsuits filed by employees. For this reason, in this chapter we discuss alternative dispute resolution systems as means of fostering organizational justice. Because disciplinary actions are subject to challenge and possible reversal through government agencies or the courts, managers should strive to prevent the need for such action. However, when disciplinary action can no longer be avoided, that action should be taken in accordance with carefully developed HR policies and practices. Since ethics is an important element of organizational justice, we conclude this chapter with a discussion of ethics in employee relations.

In a discussion of organizational discipline, the role of counselling in achieving individual and organizational objectives deserves special attention. This is why we have provided an appendix to this chapter that reviews counselling techniques.

EMPLOYEE RIGHTS

OBJECTIVE 1

Employee rights

Guarantees of fair treatment from employers, especially regarding an employee's right to privacy

Various human rights laws, wage and hour regulations, and safety and health laws have secured basic employee rights and brought many improvements to the workplace. Employee rights litigation has now shifted to workplace issues such as the following: the right of employees to protest unfair disciplinary action, to refuse to take drug tests, to review their personnel files, to challenge employer searches and surveillance, and to receive advance notice of plant closings.[2]

Society is always changing, and so is the business sector, and employee rights change along with both. **Employee rights** can be defined as the guarantees of fair treatment that employees expect in regard to their status in the workplace.[3] These expectations become rights when they are granted to employees by the courts, by legislatures, or by employers. Employee rights often involve the employer's alleged invasion of an employee's right to privacy. Unfortunately, the distinction between an employee's legal right to privacy and the moral or personal right to privacy is not always clear. The confusion is due to the lack of a comprehensive and consistent body of privacy protection law.

Balanced against employee rights is the employer's responsibility to provide (a) a safe workplace for employees, and at the same time, (b) safe goods and services of high quality to consumers. Suppose an employee who uses drugs chooses to exercise his or her privacy right and refuses to submit to a drug test. If that employee produces a faulty product as a result of drug impairment, the employer can be held liable for any harm caused by that product. So employers must exercise reasonable care when hiring and training employees and assigning jobs to them. Employers who fail to exercise reasonable care can be held negligent by outside parties or by other employees for injuries resulting from a dishonest, unfit, or

Negligence

Failure to provide reasonable care where such failure results in injury to consumers or other employees

incompetent employee.[4] In law, **negligence** is the failure to use a reasonable amount of care where such failure results in injury to another person.

It is in situations like this that employee rights and employer responsibilities come most sharply into conflict. An organization that fails to honour employee rights can get caught up in costly lawsuits that damage both its reputation and the morale of its workers. But litigation can be started just as easily by employee groups who see their safety and welfare being threatened, and by consumers who are unhappy with the products and services the organization provides. This conflict is illustrated in one of the cases described in Reality Check. For the rest of this section, we will discuss various rights that employees have come to expect in the workplace.

Employment Protection Rights

It is not surprising that employees regard their jobs as an established right—a right that should not be taken away without just cause.[5] People's personal well-being relies heavily on being able to work. This line of reasoning has led to the emergence of three legal considerations regarding job security: statutory rights, contractual rights, and due process.

Statutory Rights

Statutory rights

Rights that derive from legislation

Statutory rights are rights that derive from legislation. As we saw in Chapter 2, employment equity legislation protects employees from discrimination on the basis of grounds such as age, sex, and race. On Prince Edward Island, 314 seasonal workers received compensation from the Tory government after it was determined that they had been fired because of their political affiliation.[6] Pay equity legislation addresses inequities in how men and women are compensated; occupational health and safety legislation attempts to ensure safe and healthful working conditions; labour relations laws give employees the right to form and belong to unions, and to bargain for better working conditions (see Chapter 14).

WWW

Contractual Rights

Contractual rights

Rights that derive from contracts

In contrast to statutory rights, **contractual rights** are derived from contracts. A contract is a legally binding agreement; if one party breaches the contract, a remedy can be sought through the courts. Formal contracts between employers and full-time employees are rare; however, they are standard practice for contingent workers, a growing segment of the Canadian labour force. A contract that outlines what constitutes fair notice and justification for dismissal, and that includes clauses about nonsolicitation and noncompetition, provides employers with greater flexibility but tends to limit the rights of employees and to reduce their opportunities for making a living after they have left the company. An organization should not ask an employee to sign a contract after beginning work; the courts tend to see this as unilaterally trying to change the unwritten employment contract.

Not all contracts are written. An *implied* contract can arise when an employer extends to an employee a promise of some form of job security. Implied contractual rights can be based on oral or written statements; those statements can be made during the pre-employment process or after the hire. Promises of job security are sometimes contained in employee handbooks, HR manuals, or employment applications. Whether promises of job security are explicit or implicit, the

Reality CHECK

TWO CASES OF EMPLOYEE RIGHTS LITIGATION

WWW

Brian Smeenk is a management-side labour lawyer with the law firm of McCarthy Tétrault. For this specialist in employment and labour law, two issues stand out:

"A hot issue continues to be termination. The *Wallace v. United Grain Growers* decision has added new complexity to the concept of reasonable notice. Formerly, employers could calculate what constituted reasonable notice by looking at factors such as age, length of service, position, and salary. But the Wallace decision added another factor: Did the employer behave fairly during the termination and preceding it? In the Wallace case, the employer was found to have acted in bad faith. They had alleged cause for his dismissal, even though there were no grounds for doing so. They had misled him about how secure his job was. As a result, the Supreme Court of Canada ruled that the normal entitlement to reasonable notice, which the lower court had assessed at fifteen months, should be increased to twenty-four months. The court awarded Wallace damages in the amount of his salary and benefits for the longer period.

"One of the toughest issues facing employers in the rights area is discrimination on the basis of disability. Disability is so difficult to define, and it is even more difficult to draw the line between the employee's right to accommodation and the employer's right to run a business. Let me give you a fascinating case. A pharmaceutical company manages a number of employees, with science credentials, involved in testing products. One scientist was experiencing psychiatric problems (paranoid schizophrenia) and was having trouble functioning at work. The employer arranged for psychiatric assistance at the Clarke Institute, and the scientist was cleared to return to work. However, her work was substandard. The scientist maintained that her work was substandard because others were tampering with her work. After receiving warnings and counselling, she knew her job was in trouble. She said she couldn't take the pressure and that if she lost her job, she would commit suicide, taking her son with her. To signal her intent, she slit her wrists in her boss's office, but the cuts were not serious and she survived. The workplace was on edge. All her co-workers were seriously concerned about her safety, and their safety, as the materials they handled were hazardous.

"Management wanted to either terminate her or arrange for a disability leave. However, her doctor would not certify her as disabled. If management terminated her, they risked being faced with a human rights complaint alleging discrimination on the basis of a mental disability, with no attempt to accommodate. The key questions were: Does she have a right to be accommodated? Does this cause undue hardship to the employer? Could the employer win a case based on the argument that accommodation would cause undue hardship? What if her colleagues' fears are not supported by the medical evidence?"

courts tend to rule that they are binding. In this regard, *Wallace v. United Grain Growers* was an important case. Wallace had been seduced by assurances of job security until retirement to leave his employer of twenty-five years and join a Winnipeg

WWW

printing firm owned by United Grain Growers. Then Wallace was dismissed abruptly by his new employer. He was later awarded damages by the Supreme Court of Canada. In another case, the court found that an employer made misleading representations of a job, that the employee believed these representations, and that he suffered damages as a result of believing them. The employer was found liable. In its decision, the court stated that it is the duty of employers to ensure that the information about a job is accurate.[7]

In the following circumstances, an implied contract may become binding:

- Employees are told their jobs are secure as long as they perform satisfactorily and are loyal to the organization.
- The employee handbook states that employees will not be terminated without the right of defence or access to an appeal procedure (i.e., due process).
- An employee is persuaded to leave another organization by promises of higher wages and benefits; the hiring company then reneges after hiring that person.

To reduce their vulnerability to implied contract lawsuits, employers can do the following:

1. Train supervisors and managers not to imply contract benefits in conversations with new or present employees.

2. Include in employment offers a statement that the employee may voluntarily terminate employment with proper notice, and that the employee may be dismissed by the employer at any time and for a justified reason (just cause). The language in this statement must be appropriate, clear, and easily understood.

3. Explain the nature of the employment relationship in documents—for example, in employee handbooks, employment applications, and letters of employment.

4. Have written proof that employees have read all the documents pertaining to the employment relationship.

Due Process

Due process

Employee's right to present his or her position during a disciplinary action

Management has traditionally possessed the right to direct employees and to take corrective action when needed. Nevertheless, many people also believe that a job is the property right of an employee and that the loss of employment has such serious consequences that employees should not lose their jobs without the protection of due process. Managers normally define **due process** as the employee's right to be heard through the employer's own complaint procedure.[8] However, proactive employers will also incorporate the following principles—or rights—in their interpretation of due process:

1. The right to know job expectations and the consequences of not fulfilling those expectations.

2. The right to consistent and predictable management action for the violation of rules.

3. The right to fair discipline based on facts, the right to question those facts, and the right to present a defence.

4. The right to appeal disciplinary action.

5. The right to progressive discipline.

Employment Rights Not a Guarantee

Although employees may have cause to regard their jobs as an established right, there is no legal protection affording employees a permanent or continuous job. Furthermore, in general terms, due process does not guarantee employment to workers. However, the concepts of due process and of job-as-right do obligate managers to treat their employees fairly, equitably, and consistently.[9] Employees *do* have the right to sound employment practices, and to be treated as individuals of dignity and substantial worth.

In Canada, in absence of a formal contract specifying the duration of employment, the employment relationship is construed as ongoing. Thus, even when employment is not necessarily considered to be permanent, the employer must provide reasonable notice as well as grounds for termination. In the United States the *employment-at-will* principle assumes that an employee has a right to sever the employment relationship for a better job opportunity or for other personal reasons. Likewise, an employer is free to terminate the employment relationship at any time—and without notice—for any reason, no reason, or even a bad reason.[10] In essence, employees are said to work "at the will" of the employer. The employment-at-will relationship is created when an employee agrees to work for an employer for an unspecified period of time. Since the employment is of an indefinite duration, it can, in general, be terminated at the whim of either party. This freedom includes the right of management to unilaterally determine the conditions of employment and to make personnel decisions.

Wrongful Dismissal

An employer can dismiss an employee—that is, terminate the employment relationship—for just cause. To do so, the employer must document and prove serious misconduct or incompetence on the part of the employee. In recent years more and more employees have sued their former employers for "wrongful or unjust dismissal." One comprehensive study of wrongful dismissal suits found that employers won 40 percent of the time when the charge was dishonesty, theft, substance abuse, or abusive behaviour; 54 percent of the time when the charge was insubordination; 65 percent of the time when the charge was conflict of interest or competing with the employer; and just 25 percent of the time when the charge was poor performance.[11]

Managers, with the help of the HR department, must be able to document that the performance problems were brought to the attention of the employee and that sufficient time, training, and assistance was given to improve the weak performance. To help avoid charges of wrongful dismissal, HR specialists recommend that employers follow the tips provided in Figure 13.1. Also, Highlights in HRM 1 describes how employees can challenge a just cause case.

Constructive dismissal

Changing an employee's working conditions such that compensation, status, or prestige is reduced

Constructive Dismissal

In 1997 the Supreme Court of Canada set the standard for **constructive dismissal**. Constructive dismissal has occurred when an employer changes an employee's working conditions in such a way that compensation, status, or prestige

---

FIGURE 13.1 *Tips to Avoid Wrongful Employment Termination Lawsuits*

- *Terminate an employee only if there is an articulated reason.* An employer should have clearly articulated, easily understandable reasons for discharging an employee. The reasons should be stated as objectively as possible and should reflect company rules, policies, and practices.
- *Set and follow termination rules and schedules.* Make sure every termination follows a documented set of procedures. Procedures can be from an employee handbook, a supervisory manual, or even an intra-office memorandum. Before terminating, give employees notices of unsatisfactory performance and improvement opportunities through a system of warnings and suspensions.
- *Document all performance problems.* A lack of documented problems in an employee's personnel record may be used as circumstantial evidence of pretextual discharge if the employee is "suddenly" discharged.
- *Be consistent with employees in similar situations.* Document reasons given for all disciplinary actions, even if they do not lead to termination. Terminated employees may claim that exception-to-the-rule cases are discriminatory. Detailed documentation will help employers explain why these "exceptions" did not warrant termination.

WWW

is reduced. The changes must be substantive—that is, they must affect pay, reporting relationships, responsibilities, and location; they cannot be trivial (e.g., minor changes in working hours). Even if the employee agrees to the changed conditions (the only other option might be unemployment) or resigns, the court considers him or her to have been dismissed.[12]

Two cases illustrate the concept. One involved a Royal Trust regional manager who was earning about $150,000 in base salary and commissions when his job was eliminated. He was offered the position of branch manager at the company's least profitable branch, where his income would have been based solely on commissions (he had held a similar position about four promotions earlier). The court ruled that he had been constructively dismissed and awarded him damages and legal costs. In another case, Embassy Cleaners changed the working conditions of a presser, resulting in a more physically demanding job, an earlier start time (6:00 a.m. instead of 7:30 a.m.), a change in the work week from five to six days, and a change from hourly wages to piecework. The court ruled that these changes constituted a fundamental breach of contract and hence constructive dismissal.[13]

In an nonunion context, employers can give notice of future changes in compensation, benefits, incentives, working hours, location, and so on as long as they provide actual notice equivalent to that given for dismissal.

Job Expectancy Rights

Once hired, employees expect certain rights associated with fair and equitable employment. Employee rights on the job relate to these issues, among others: substance abuse and drug testing, privacy, plant closing notification, and just cause disciplinary and discharge procedures.

Highlights in HRM

1   FIRING BACK!

Once you have received either verbal or written warnings about performance, a decision has usually been made to fire you. What can you do? Writing back, picking holes in the accusations, is the least effective defence. Using the same weapons as management, you must prove that the just cause will not hold.

Harold Leavitt, a legal expert on dismissal, offers the following advice:

- Establish in writing that you were unaware of the standards of performance or conduct. You can argue that the standards are new or were not part of the initial job offer, position description, performance evaluations, or previous warnings. The company must prove that you were grossly incompetent, so any letters of praise or good performance review should be used. Any aspects of performance that may override the weak areas should be noted. For example, if you are being dismissed for poor communication skills but your productivity figures are increasing, this should be documented. As soon as you commence employment, start a file containing all performance evaluations; letters of praise from customers, co-workers, internal clients, and supervisors; and all other examples of performance achievements. Establish a paper trail of good performance.
- Argue that the company, while complaining about poor performance, has not stated specifically what is required to improve performance.
- Assert that you were not given the time, training, assistance, or learning opportunities necessary to improve performance.
- Establish, if true, that the employer hired you knowing that you did not possess the necessary skills. Note any understanding that you would receive the appropriate training.
- State, if applicable, that the skills desired now were not part of your original job description.
- Attribute your poor performance to factors outside your control, such as a decline in sales in all regions, or poorly priced products, or a temporary illness. If possible, establish that the company contributed to the performance problem by failing to respond to your (documented) suggestions for improvement.

Leavitt further advises that letters and all other documentation be written with the assistance of a specialist. In the end, you may not get your job back, but if successful you can expect an attractive severance package.

Source: Howard Leavitt, "How Employees Can Fight Firing for Just Cause," *Toronto Star*, August 17, 1992: C1.

Substance Abuse and Drug Testing

The impact on employers of employee drug abuse is staggering. It is estimated that drug abuse by employees costs Canadian employers an estimated $4.1 billion a year for alcohol, $6.8 billion for tobacco, and $823.1 million for illicit drugs—a total of $11.8 billion in productivity losses. That represents 1.7 percent of the gross domestic product, or $414 per capita.[14] Most human rights commissions see drug and alcohol as dependencies; it follows that testing for these dependencies is a form of discrimination.[15] Compared with nonabusing employees, substance abusers have been found to

- take three times as much sick leave;
- file five times more workers' compensation claims;
- have four times more accidents on the job; *and*
- make twice as many mistakes.[16]

In these litigious times, an employer's failure to ensure a safe and drug-free workplace can result in astronomical liability claims when consumers are injured because of a negligent employee or faulty product.[17] The Canadian government has not introduced legislation on drug testing; such legislation does exist south of the border.[18] Companies that do use drug testing are faced with high costs ($15–$45 for each test), error rates as high as 40 percent, and employee resistance.[19] At the same time, companies with drug-testing policies report reductions in absenteeism, sick days, and accidents. Some of the issues surrounding drug testing are discussed in Highlights in HRM 2.

Employee Searches and Surveillance

It is estimated that 33 percent of American workers steal from their employers and that roughly 20 percent of all American businesses fail because of internal theft.[20] Loss prevention experts in Canada estimate that $2 million a day is lost in the grocery business alone as a result of theft.[21] Employers can minimize the risk of employee theft by following the guidelines provided in Figure 13.2.

WWW

Where work rules providing for inspections have been put into effect, employees have no reasonable expectation of privacy: they must comply with probable cause searches by employers. And they can be appropriately disciplined—most likely for insubordination—for refusing to comply with search requests. Albert Pendergast, senior vice-president for human resources at Master Card International, says, "We've taken the position that we want a clean company and that we aren't going to tolerate white-collar crime."[22]

Managers must be diligent when conducting employee searches. Improper searches can lead to employee lawsuits charging the employer with invasion of privacy, defamation of character, and negligent infliction of emotional distress. Employers are advised to develop an HR search policy based on the following guidelines:[23]

1. The search policy should be widely publicized and should advocate a probable or compelling reason for the search.

2. The search policy should be applied in a reasonable, evenhanded manner.

3. Where possible, searches should be conducted in private.

4. The employer should attempt to obtain the employee's consent prior to the search.

Highlights in HRM

2 RIDING HIGH

WWW

The debate over performance-enhancing (or -diminishing) drugs reached new levels at the 1998 Winter Olympics in Japan when Ross Rebagliati found his gold medal in snowboarding in jeopardy after testing positive for marijuana. At most companies in Canada, if Rebagliati had been an employee he would not have been tested for drugs, and would not have been fired for testing positive. Drug-testing laws in Canada are very strict; testing is allowed only in jobs where safety is a critical issue, as it is at Ontario Hydro's nuclear power plants. Greyhound Canada in Calgary does random drug tests on bus drivers who are bidding for routes to the United States, where drug testing in the transportation sector is mandatory.

The Addiction Research Foundation points out that while drug tests show that drugs have been used, they do not indicate the level of impairment and therefore whether the user is "under the influence." Also, drugs such as cocaine take only three days to clear the body, whereas others such as marijuana can take three weeks. The inability to prove impaired performance, coupled with concerns about people's right to privacy, has made the courts hesitant to give companies the authority to conduct random drug tests, or to ask employees if they have a history of substance abuse.

One advertising agency tolerates the use of drugs on the grounds that "ad people tend to be creative and live on the edge." However, most companies suspecting substance abuse would take immediate action (e.g., referral to an employee assistance program), and resort to discharge or extended disability leave if the employee's performance continued to deteriorate.

Source: M. Gibb-Clark and E. Church, "Pot Policing Fails the Workplace Test," *The Globe and Mail*, February 12, 1998: B16. Reprinted with permission from The Globe and Mail.

5. The search should be conducted in a humane and discreet manner to avoid inflicting emotional distress.

6. The penalty for refusing to consent to a search should be specified.

WWW

It is not uncommon for employers to monitor the conduct of employees through surveillance techniques. Managers sometimes act as stationary surveillance covers or as moving surveillance covers, following the subject from point to point.[24] Employers are permitted to use electronic surveillance equipment that provides photographic or video images. General Electric has installed tiny fish-eye lenses behind pinholes in walls and ceilings to observe employees suspected of crimes. DuPont uses long-distance cameras to monitor its loading docks. One of the most common means of electronic surveillance by employers is telephone surveillance to ensure that customer requests are handled properly or to prevent theft.

Federal legislation relating to privacy includes the 1982 Privacy Act, which prohibits the indiscriminate use of personal information, and the 1983 Access to

> **FIGURE 13.2** *Tips for Reducing the Risk of Employee Theft*
>
> Employers lose over 1 percent of annual revenues as a result of "inventory shrinkage"—that is, employee and customer theft. Thieves are like good customers: if they like what they get, they'll come back for more. The key to preventing loss through employee theft is to break up the employee dishonesty triangle—opportunity, rationalization, and financial need. Experts recommend the following strategies for decreasing employee theft:
>
> - Install security cameras that can tilt, scan, and zoom.
> - Tag products to minimize "sweethearting"—a practice in which the cashier does not scan a product that a friend or accomplice is checking out. The tags are deactivated when they are scanned; if they aren't, an alarm sounds.
> - Scrutinize job application forms. Be on the alert for lack of references, skipped portions of the form, conflicting dates of employment, lack of explanation for leaving old jobs, and long gaps between jobs.
> - Check references thoroughly.
> - Limit access to the cash office. Keep the door locked, and have employees store personal belongings elsewhere.
>
> **Source:** "Security Measures: How to Arrest Shrinkage in Your Store," *Canadian Grocer* 111, no. 5 (May 1997): 19–20; "Tough Policies Minimize Shrink," *Canadian Grocer* 107, no. 12 (December 1993): 10, 37.

Information Act, which gives employees the right to examine their personnel files. Employers have the right to monitor employees, provided they do so for compelling business reasons and provided that the employees have been told that their calls will be monitored.[25] While employees can sue for invasion of privacy, the courts have held that to win damages, the employee must show that the reasonable expectation of privacy outweighed the organization's reason for surveillance.[26] In 1997 a company fired an employee after videotaping him sleeping on the job. The tape was ruled admissible as evidence.[27] Ethics in HRM highlights some of these issues.

Access to Personnel Files

The information kept in personnel files can have a significant impact (positive or negative) on the career development of employees. Personnel files are usually kept by the HR department and typically contain performance appraisals, salary notices, investigatory reports, credit checks, criminal records, test scores, and family data. Errors and/or omissions in personnel files can create employment or personal hardships; so can access to those files by unauthorized persons.[28] In compliance with the Access to Information Act, most employers allow employees to see their personnel files. Employment professionals recommend that organizations develop a policy on employee files that covers, as a minimum, the points noted in Figure 13.3.[29]

Ethics in HRM

SUPERVISING OR SUPER-SPYING?

Cameras monitor much of our everyday life, often without our knowledge. Surveillance systems may be monitoring you as you leave the lobby of your apartment building, as you enter the underground garage, as you drive on the highway to work, as you purchase a coffee at the variety store, and even at some workplaces. Pinhole cameras the size of a quarter can fit into a picture on the wall, a telephone, or a ceiling device that looks like a water sprinkler. They can catch an employee loading up on office supplies; they can even determine whether the employee is using chat lines or the Internet for personal reasons. Some employers keep records of the calls employees make, and their duration. A standard feature on network management software enables the administrator to pull up the screen of any employee on the network.

Employees who work as customer representatives, handling sixty to eighty calls a day, may have their conversations monitored by supervisors or a trainer to ensure that the information given is accurate and that service standards are maintained. At one firm that raises money for charities, employees are required to make 8,500 keystrokes an hour; failure to achieve this standard is noted electronically. (Distractions are minimized by covering windows, forbidding conversation unrelated to business, and facing all desks in the same direction.) Eight cameras are capable of zooming in on any desk, in case any employee is displaying materials unrelated to work.

Even babysitters and nannies are being targeted for electronic monitoring. Cameras hidden in books watch the children and the babysitter or nanny while anxious parents are at work. Parents insist that this surveillance enables them to ensure the safety and emotional security of their children; babysitters and nannies are outraged at the lack of trust and invasion of their privacy.

WWW

According to a national director with the Canadian Union of Postal Workers, "Surveillance and monitoring is really about power, and the uneven levels of power in the workplace. If it is abused by employers, then it really becomes a powerful weapon that is used to control the behaviour of workers, or as a source of discipline." A 1994 study concluded that electronic monitoring can create adverse working conditions that lead to stress, anxiety, depression, anger, and fatigue.

Would you work differently if you knew that your performance was continually being monitored? Is it ethical for employers monitor their employees in this way?

Sources: J. Powell, "Keeping an Eye on the Workplace," *Financial Post*, September 6, 1997: 24; M. Gooderham, "Rise in Technology Lets Everyone Be a Spy," *The Globe and Mail*, June 7, 1995: A1; A.M. Stewart, "For a Nervous Breakdown, Please Press One," *The Globe and Mail*, June 1, 1994: A25; G. Arnaut, "Electronic Big Brother Is on the Job," *The Globe and Mail*, October 22, 1996: C1; R. Fulford, "Tolerating Electronic Sweatshops," *The Globe and Mail*, December 14, 1994: C1.

As a means of electronic security, this hand scanner device reads a person's palm once a code is entered on the keypad.

FIGURE 13.3 *Personnel Files: Policy Guidelines*

- Ensure compliance with applicable laws.
- Define exactly what information is to be kept in employee files.
- Develop different categories of personnel information, depending on legal requirements and organizational needs.
- Specify where, when, how, and under what circumstances employees may review or copy their files.
- Identify company individuals allowed to view personnel files.
- Prohibit the collection of information that could be viewed as discriminatory or could form the basis for an invasion-of-privacy suit.
- Audit employment records on a regular basis to remove irrelevant, outdated, or inaccurate information.

E-Mail and Voice Mail Privacy

The benefits of e-mail and voice mail are many; they provide instant delivery of messages, they facilitate teamwork, they increase time efficiency, they offer access to global information, and they promote flexible work arrangements.[30] Unfortunately, the growth of HR information systems can create privacy problems by making personnel information more accessible to those with prying eyes, or to "hackers" who might use the information inappropriately. Messages can be read or heard, and deleted messages can be retrieved. Even log-on IDs and passwords do not prevent unauthorized access to computers by nonprivileged users.[31] Moreover, messages can be forwarded, replicated, and printed with ease. Employees have used e-mail to steal company information and to harass co-workers.[32]

High technology has created tensions between employee privacy and the employer's need to know. Employees often assume that their right to privacy extends to e-mail and voice mail messages; in fact, it does not. While there are few laws or court cases governing e-mail or voice mail monitoring, those that exist grant to employers the right to monitor materials created, received, or sent for business-related reasons.[33] Employers are strongly encouraged to develop clear policies and guidelines relating to how e-mail and voice mail are to be used, including when and under what conditions employees can be monitored (see Figure 13.4).[34] Only about 5 percent of Canadian companies have such policies in place, compared with about 40 percent of American companies.[35] Where e-mail and voice mail policies do exist, employees should be required to sign a form indicating that they have read and understand the policy.

Employee Conduct Outside the Workplace

Consider the following situation. On Monday morning the owner of ABC Corporation reads in the newspaper that a company employee has been charged

FIGURE 13.4 *E-Mail and Voice Mail: Policy Guidelines*

- Ensure compliance with federal and provincial legislation.
- Specify the circumstances, if any, under which the system can be used for personal business.
- Specify that confidential information not be sent on the network.
- Set forth the conditions under which monitoring will be done—by whom, how often, and with what notification to employees.
- Specify that e-mail and voice mail information be sent only to users who need it for business purposes.
- Expressly prohibit use of e-mail or voice mail to harass others or to send anonymous messages.
- Make clear that employees have no privacy rights in any material delivered or received through e-mail or voice mail.
- Specify that employees who violate the policy are subject to discipline, including dismissal.

with robbery and assault on a local convenience store owner. The employee has been released pending trial. A phone call to the employee's supervisor reveals that the employee has reported to work. What should the owner do?

According to legal authorities, the off-duty behaviour of employees is not subject to employer disciplinary action. Organizations that want to discipline employees for off-duty misconduct must establish that the misconduct had a clear negative effect on other employees or the organization. This might be established where the off-duty misconduct (e.g., child molestation) obviously disrupted the workplace. Or where the public nature of the employee's job (e.g., police officer or firefighter) created an image problem for the organization. Generally, however, little of what an employee does outside the workplace bears discipline by the employer.[36]

Workplace romances pose multiple dilemmas for organizations. Power differentials are often a factor (as between a manager and his secretary, or a new employee and a co-worker with a lot of seniority). When a power-differentiated romance goes sour, charges of sexual harassment can easily arise.[37] Behaviour that was acceptable in a consensual relationship between employees can quickly evolve into harassment when one party to the relationship stops welcoming the conduct. Such romances can also be sources of workplace violence (i.e., jilted lover arrives at work with a weapon).

Furthermore, workplace romances can lead to charges of favouritism. When an employee involved in office romance with a superior gets preferential treatment, charges of "reverse harassment" can easily arise. Workplace romances can create morale problems—jealousy, resentment, hard feelings, and so on—when other employees feel unfairly treated. Romances involving supervisors and their underlings can have profound effects on organizational operations and productivity.[38] One study found that despite all this, only 6 percent of surveyed organizations had a policy on employee dating or fraternization.[39]

Genetic Testing

With advances in genetics, it is now possible to identify the genetic basis for human diseases and illnesses.

Genetic findings present opportunities for individualized prevention strategies and early detection and treatment. Unfortunately, the knowledge gained through genetic testing can also be used discreetly by employers to discriminate against or stigmatize individuals who are applying for employment or are currently employed. For example, genetic testing can identify an individual's risk of developing common diseases and disorders such as cancer, heart disease, and diabetes. Diseases like these can raise employment costs (e.g., recruitment, training, and medical costs).

Employers must remember that there is no scientific evidence linking unexpressed genetic factors to an individual's ability to perform a job. There are few federal or state laws, or court decisions, governing the use by employers of genetic information. So we caution employers about gathering genetic data, whatever its intended purpose.

Plant Closing Notification

Thousands of jobs have been lost in Canada as a result of plant closings. These shutdowns can devastate not merely individual employees but entire communities. It has been estimated that for every 100 jobs lost from a plant closing, the local community loses 200 to 300 jobs through ripple effects. Several provincial governments have passed legislation preventing employers from unilaterally closing or relocating their facilities. For example, Ontario has passed legislation that requires organizations with fewer then 50 employees to give four weeks' notice of any closure; organizations with more than 500 employees must give sixteen weeks' notice.[40]

DISCIPLINARY POLICIES AND PROCEDURES

The right of managers to discipline and discharge employees is becoming more and more limited. For this reason, managers at all levels must thoroughly understand discipline procedures. Any disciplinary action taken against an employee must be for justifiable reasons, and must follow carefully thought-out guidelines. These guidelines should help managers carry out an onerous duty, and should ensure that employees are being treated fairly and constructively. Equally important, these guidelines should help prevent disciplinary actions from being voided or reversed through the appeal system.

Figure 13.5 shows one disciplinary model, which consists of steps that must be carried out to ensure enforceable decisions.

A major responsibility of the HR department is to develop disciplinary policies and procedures. (Top management will then have to approve them.) The development process must involve the supervisors and managers who have to carry out the policies. Their experience can make the disciplinary policy more effective, as well as more consistent throughout the organization.   The HR department is also responsible for ensuring that disciplinary policies—and any disciplinary actions taken against employees—are consistent with collective agreements (where they exist) and conform with current law.

The primary responsibility for preventing or correcting disciplinary problems rests with the employee's immediate supervisor. This person is in the best position to observe unsatisfactory behaviour or performance and to discuss these matters with the employee. Discussion is often all that is needed to correct the problem; when it is, disciplinary action is then unnecessary. When disciplinary action *is*

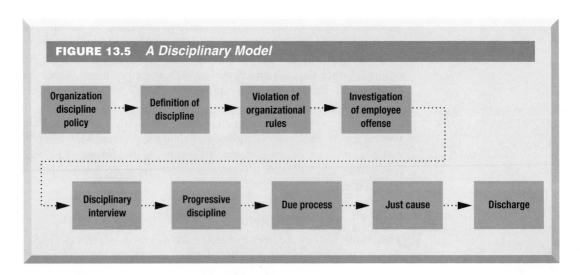

FIGURE 13.5   *A Disciplinary Model*

required, the supervisor should strive for a problem-solving attitude. The causes underlying the problem are as important as the problem itself, and if the problem is not to recur, those causes must be understood. It is often difficult for supervisors to be objective about employee infractions. But if supervisors can maintain a problem-solving stance, they are likely to come up with a diagnosis that is nearer the truth than would be possible if they were to use the approach of a trial lawyer.

The Results of Inaction

Figure 13.6 lists the more common disciplinary problems identified by managers. Failure to take disciplinary action in any of these areas will only make the problem worse.[41] Failure to act implies that the performance of the employee concerned has been satisfactory. If disciplinary action is eventually taken, the delay will make it more difficult to justify the action if it is appealed. In defending against such an appeal, the employer is likely to be asked why the employee who had not been performing or behaving satisfactorily was kept on the payroll. An even more damaging question: "Why did that employee receive satisfactory performance ratings [or perhaps even merit raises]?"[42]

Contradictions in practice like these can only help employees successfully challenge management's corrective actions. Unfortunately, some supervisors begin building a case to justify their corrective actions only after they have decided that a particular employee should be dismissed. Supervisors often give the following reasons for failing to impose a disciplinary penalty:

1. Since they hadn't documented earlier actions, no record existed on which to base any later actions.

2. They believed they would receive little or no support from higher management for the disciplinary action.

3. They were uncertain of the facts underlying the situation that required disciplinary action.

4. Because they had failed to discipline employees in the past for a certain infraction, they had no choice (for the sake of consistency) but to forgo current disciplinary action.

5. They wanted to be liked.

Setting Organizational Rules

WWW

Establishing an effective disciplinary system begins with setting organizational rules. These rules tell employees what type of behaviour the employer expects. Organizations as diverse as Gerber Products, Wal-Mart, and Pitney Bowes have written rules of conduct. Following are suggestions for establishing organizational rules:

1. Rules should be widely disseminated and known to all employees. It should not be assumed that employees know all the rules.

2. Rules should be reviewed periodically—perhaps annually—especially those rules critical to work success.

3. The reasons for a rule should always be explained. Acceptance of an organizational rule is greater when employees understand the reasons behind it.

FIGURE 13.6 *Common Disciplinary Problems*

ATTENDANCE PROBLEMS

- Unexcused absence
- Chronic absenteeism
- Unexcused/excessive tardiness
- Leaving without permission

DISHONESTY AND RELATED PROBLEMS

- Theft
- Falsifying employment application
- Wilfully damaging organizational property
- Punching another employee's time card
- Falsifying work records

WORK PERFORMANCE PROBLEMS

- Failure to complete work assignments
- Producing substandard products or services
- Failure to meet established production requirements

ON-THE-JOB BEHAVIOUR PROBLEMS

- Intoxication at work
- Insubordination
- Horseplay
- Smoking in unauthorized places
- Fighting
- Gambling
- Failure to use safety devices
- Falure to report injuries
- Carelessness
- Sleeping on the job
- Using abusive or threatening behaviour with supervisors
- Possession of narcotics or alcohol
- Possession of firearms or other weapons
- Sexual harassment

4. Rules should always be written. Ambiguity should be avoided, since this can result in different interpretations of the rules by different supervisors.

5. Rules must be reasonable, and must relate to the safe and efficient operation of the organization. Rules should not be made simply because of personal likes or dislikes.

6. If management has been lax in enforcing a rule, the rule must be restated, along with the consequences for its violation, before disciplinary action can begin.

7. Have employees sign that they have read and understand the organizational rules.

Disciplinary action should never be thought of as punishment. Discipline can embody a penalty as a means of obtaining a desired result; however, punishment should not be the intent of disciplinary action. Rather, the whole point of discipline must be to improve the employee's future behaviour. To apply discipline in any other way—as punishment or for revenge—can only invite problems for management, including possible wrongful dismissal suits.

When seeking reasons for weak performance, supervisors must keep in mind that employees may not be aware of certain work rules. Before starting any disciplinary action, it is essential that supervisors determine whether they have carefully and thoroughly oriented their employees to the rules and regulations relating to their jobs. In fact, the proper communication of organizational rules and regulations is so important that labour arbitrators cite neglect in communicating rules as a major reason for reversing the disciplinary action taken against an employee.[43]

The Hot-Stove Approach to Rule Enforcement

Hot stove rule

Rule of discipline that can be compared with a hot stove in that it gives warning, is effective immediately, is enforced consistently, and applies to all employees in an impersonal and unbiased way

Whatever the reason for the disciplinary action, it should be taken as soon as possible after the infraction, once a complete investigation has been conducted. HR professionals often use the **hot stove rule** to explain the correct application of discipline. A hot stove gives warning that it should not be touched. Those who ignore the warning and touch it are assured of being burned. The punishment is an immediate and direct consequence of breaking the rule never to touch a hot stove. Likewise, a work rule should apply to all employees and should be enforced consistently and in an impersonal and unbiased way. Employees should know the consequences of violating the rule, so that it has preventive value.

Defining Discipline

Discipline

(1) Treatment that punishes; (2) orderly behaviour in an organizational setting; or (3) training that molds and strengthens desirable conduct—or corrects undesirable conduct—and develops self-control

In management seminars conducted by the authors of this text, when managers are asked to define the word "discipline," their most frequent response is that discipline means punishment. Although this answer is not incorrect, it is only one of three possible meanings. As normally defined, **discipline** has these meanings:

1. Treatment that punishes

2. Orderly behaviour in an organizational setting

3. Training that molds and strengthens desirable conduct—or corrects undesirable conduct—and develops self-control

To some managers, discipline is synonymous with force. They equate the term with punishing employees who violate rules or regulations. Other managers think of discipline as a general state of affairs—a state of orderliness in which employees conduct themselves according to standards of acceptable behaviour. Discipline viewed in this manner can be considered positive when employees willingly practice self-control and respect organizational rules.

The third definition considers discipline a management tool for correcting undesirable employee performance. Discipline is applied as a constructive means of getting employees to conform to acceptable standards of performance. Goodyear Aerospace defines the term "discipline" in its policy manual as training that "corrects, molds, or perfects knowledge, attitudes, behavior, or conduct." It is not the only organization to perceive discipline in this way. Discipline when seen in this light is much more than punishment for offences—it corrects poor employee performance. As these organizations emphasize, discipline should be seen as a method of training employees to perform better or to improve their job attitudes or work behaviour.[44]

Investigating the Disciplinary Problem

It's a rare manager who has a good, intuitive sense of how to investigate employee misconduct. Too often, investigations are conducted in a haphazard manner; worse, they overlook one or more investigative concerns. When conducting an employee investigation, managers must be objective and avoid the assumptions, suppositions, and biases that often surround discipline cases. Figure 13.7 lists seven questions to consider when investigating an employee offence. Attending to all seven will help ensure a full and fair investigation, and provide reliable information free from personal prejudice.

Documentation of Employee Misconduct

"It's too complicated." "I just didn't take time to do it." "I have more important things to do." Managers who have failed to document employee misconduct often resort to these excuses. But the most significant reason for inadequate documentation is that managers have no idea of what constitutes good documentation. When managers fail to record employee misconduct accurately, later disciplinary actions are more easily reversed. It follows that maintaining complete and accurate work records is an essential part of an effective disciplinary system.[45] For documentation to be complete, it must include the following eight items:

1. Date, time, and location of the incident(s).

2. Negative performance or behaviour exhibited by the employee (i.e., the problem).

3. The consequences of that action or behaviour on the employee's overall work performance and/or on the operations of the employee's work unit.

4. Prior discussion(s) with the employee about the problem.

5. Disciplinary action to be taken, and the specific improvement expected.

6. Consequences if improvement is not made, and a follow-up date.

7. The employee's reaction to the supervisor's attempt to change behaviour.

8. The names of witnesses to the incident (if appropriate).

When preparing documentation, it is important for the manager to record the incident immediately after the infraction takes place, when the memory of it is still fresh, and to ensure that the record is complete and accurate. The documentation need not be lengthy, but it must include the eight points in the above list. A manager's records of employee misconduct are considered business documents, and as such they are admissible as evidence in arbitration hearings, administrative proceedings, and courts of law.[46]

FIGURE 13.7 *Considerations in Disciplinary Investigations*

1. In very specific terms, what is the offence charged?
   - Is management sure it fully understands the charge against the employee?
   - Was the employee really terminated for insubordination, or did the employee merely refuse a request by management?
2. Did the employee know he or she was doing something wrong?
   - What rule or provision was violated?
   - How would the employee know of the existence of the rule?
   - Was the employee warned of the consequence?
3. Is the employee guilty?
   - What are the sources of facts?
   - Is there direct or only indirect evidence of guilt?
   - Has anyone talked to the employee to hear his or her side of the situation?
4. Are there extenuating circumstances?
   - Were conflicting orders given by different supervisors?
   - Does anybody have reason to want to "get" this employee?
   - Was the employee provoked by a manager or another employee?
5. Has the rule been uniformly enforced?
   - Have all managers applied the rule consistently?
   - What punishment did previous offenders receive?
   - Were any other employees involved in this offence?
6. Is the offence related to the workplace?
   - Is there evidence that the offence hurt the organization?
   - Is management making a moral judgment or a business judgment?
7. What is the employee's past work record?
   - How many years of service has the employee given the organization?
   - How many years or months has the employee held the present job?
   - What is the employee's personnel record as a whole, especially his or her disciplinary record?

The Investigative Interview

Before any disciplinary action is taken, an investigative interview should be conducted to make sure the employee is fully aware of the offence. This interview is necessary because the supervisor's perceptions of the employee's behaviour may not be entirely accurate. The interview should concentrate on how the offence violated the performance standards of the job. It should avoid getting into personalities or areas unrelated to job performance. Most important, the employee must be given a full opportunity to explain his or her side of the issue so that any deficiencies for which the organization may be responsible are revealed.

Approaches to Disciplinary Action

If a thorough investigation shows that an employee has violated some organization rule, disciplinary action must be taken. Two approaches to disciplinary action are *progressive* discipline and *positive* discipline.

A disciplinary investigation requires accurate and complete documentation.

Progressive discipline

Application of corrective measures by increasing degrees

Progressive Discipline

Generally, discipline is imposed in a progressive manner. **Progressive discipline** involves applying corrective measures by increasing degrees. It is designed to motivate the employee to correct his or her misconduct voluntarily. It is intended to nip problems in the bud, using only as much corrective action as necessary. The sequence and severity of the disciplinary action will vary with the type of offence and the circumstances surrounding it. Since each situation is unique, a number of factors must be considered in determining how severe a disciplinary action should be. Some of the factors to consider were listed in Figure 13.7.

The typical progressive discipline procedure has these four steps: (1) an oral warning (or counselling) that subsequent unsatisfactory behaviour or performance will not be tolerated; (2) a written warning; (3) a suspension without pay; and (4) dismissal.[47] The progressive discipline process used by Samaritan Health System is described in Highlights in HRM 3. The "capital punishment" of discharge is seen as a last resort. Organizations usually apply lesser forms of disciplinary action for less severe performance problems. Managers must remember that three important things happen when progressive discipline is applied properly:

1. Employees always know where they stand regarding offences.

2. Employees know what improvement is expected of them.

3. Employees understand what will happen next if improvement is not made.

Positive Discipline

Positive (or nonpunitive) discipline

System of discipline that focuses on the early correction of employee misconduct, with the employee taking total responsibility for correcting the problem

Progressive discipline is the most popular approach to correcting employee misconduct. However, some managers have begun questioning its logic and noting certain flaws in it—for example, its intimidating and adversarial nature. As a result, some organizations are now using an approach called **positive (or nonpunitive) discipline**. Positive discipline is based on the concept that employees must assume responsibility for their personal conduct and job performance.[48] Highlights in HRM 4 outlines Volkswagen Canada's positive discipline program.

Positive discipline requires a cooperative environment in which the employee and the supervisor can engage in joint problem solving to resolve incidents of

Highlights in HRM

3   THE SAMARITAN HEALTH SYSTEM CORRECTIVE ACTION PROCESS

When corrective action is necessary, managers should take the lowest-level action possible to correct the problem, even if that means repeating a step taken earlier. Samaritan believes that a progressive corrective action process is in the best interests of the employee and Samaritan. Progressive corrective action is not intended to be punishment, but rather to impress on the employee the need for improvement. All facts, including length of service, previous performance, and attendance, will be considered.

An informal counselling with the employee may be all that is necessary to correct performance or attendance problems, and should be used before corrective action is taken. This is an opportunity to discuss with the employee the problem, the resources available to him or her, and the ways to resolve the problem:

- *Step 1: Verbal warning.* Discuss the problem with the employee, pointing out what is needed to correct the problem. Be clear with the employee by saying, "This is a verbal warning," and by indicating that a written warning will result if performance or attendance is not improved as expected. This action should be documented and kept in the supervisor's file for future reference. No record of this warning is to be placed in the employee's official personnel record.

- *Step 2: Written warning.* If sufficient improvement is not observed in performance or attendance after the verbal warning is issued, a written warning is to follow. The problem and the relevant facts should be described on the corrective action form. The employee must be told that if performance or attendance does not improve, further corrective action will be taken in the form of a final written warning or a suspension. A record of this warning should be placed in the employee's personnel record.

- *Step 3: Final written warning or suspension.* If sufficient improvement is not observed after the written warning, the supervisor should proceed to a final written warning or suspension. A suspension can be for one to three days, and in the progressive action process is always without pay. Employees should be advised that the suspension is the last step before discharge and that they should use the time away from work to decide whether they can correct their performance or attendance problem. Employees should be told that a final written warning is the final step before discharge. Suspensions and final written warnings are to be documented with relevant information (including the dates of previous corrective action steps) on the corrective action form.

- *Step 4: Discharge.* Before making the final decision to terminate, the supervisor should discuss with the employee the issue or incident that has led to the decision to discharge him or her. If the employee gives information that needs to be investigated, the supervisor should take time to do so. If there is no new information, the human resources department should be consulted prior to discharging the employee. A Notice of Discharge form should be completed at the time the employee is discharged.

The statement on the form should document the dates of the verbal, written, and final written warnings and the decree of suspension. It should also address the particular events that have brought about this decision, as well as any other actions that have been taken or suggested to the employee to assist in the correction of the problem.

IMMEDIATE ACTION

Occasionally an infraction is so severe that immediate corrective action, up to and including termination, may appear to be warranted. If it is necessary to remove an employee from the work area, suspend him or her immediately, pending an investigation, which should not last more than a few days. There is no reason to terminate an employee "on the spot." The investigation may reveal that disciplinary action was not appropriate. In such cases the employee will be paid for the days of suspension.

Source: Adapted from *Samaritan Employee Handbook and Management Guideline*. Used with permission of Samaritan Health System, Phoenix, Ariz.

Highlights in HRM

4   VOLKSWAGEN CANADA'S POSITIVE DISCIPLINE PROGRAM

Positive discipline is a method for attempting to solve employee problems before they develop into serious situations. It treats employees as adults and emphasizes turning inappropriate behaviour around instead of punishing employees every time they do something wrong. Positive discipline relies on frontline coaching and counselling to help employees identify inappropriate behaviour; it also suggests ways of turning that behaviour around. Positive discipline allows supervisors to treat their fellow employees in a fair and consistent manner. Most employees will respond to coaching and counselling. For employees who do not correct their behaviour—or who are involved in an incident so serious that coaching or counselling is deemed inappropriate—there are steps in place to impress on every employee the seriousness of their actions and the consequences of continued poor behaviour. The following is a general outline of the program:

There are five general methods used in the Positive Discipline Program:

- Coaching and Counselling
- Step 1: Verbal Reminder
- Step 2: Written Warning
- Step 3: Decision Making
- Step 4: Termination

There are three categories of work rule violations:

- Work Performance
- Attendance
- Misconduct

There are three degrees of severity of workplace violations:

- Minor
- Major
- Grave

There are two other major ingredients of the Positive Discipline Program:

- Praise
- Goal Setting

GUIDELINES

- The union, if requested, may be involved in every step of the discipline process, but must be involved in step 1 and higher.
- An employee may, under certain circumstances, be sent home with or without pay pending an investigation into the incident. The union should be involved in any investigation into serious incidents.
- Counselling should be the preferred method of correcting behaviour when a problem first appears.
- Praise should be used often, whenever an employee has corrected a potential problem, had a step deactivated, performed beyond his/her normal duties, or any other time the supervisor feels it is appropriate. This praise should be done both orally and in writing.
- Goal setting should be used at every step in the disciplinary process in order to ensure both the supervisor and the employee know exactly what is expected of them.
- This program is aimed at those very few employees who insist on conducting themselves in an inappropriate manner. The vast majority of our employees may never have to encounter the various steps of this program.

TIME LIMITS

The time periods in which satisfactory performance must be maintained before a disciplinary step is considered inactive are:

- Step 1   6 months
- Step 2   9 month
- Step 3   12 months

NOTE

This quick reference guide is meant to give you a brief overview of the program and should not be considered to be the total program or have all the answers. For a full explanation of the program, please refer to the Positive Discipline Program manual.

WORKPLACE VIOLATIONS

- For an employee with no active discipline on record, the appropriate level of discipline for each degree of seriousness is set out below:

Minor: Verbal reminder or written warning
Major: Written warning or decision-making leave
Grave: Decision-making leave or discharge

- A range of disciplinary responses is provided here, as specific incidents may vary in severity. These work rule violations are not intended to be a total list. Discipline may be imposed for offences not included above.

Violations	Relative Degree of Seriousness
AWOL (1 day—including scheduled overtime shifts)	Minor
Lateness	Minor
Safety rule violations	Minor
Failure to report injury/accident	Minor
Unexcused absences	Minor
Unauthorized distribution of literature	Minor
Leaving workstation early, or without authorization	Minor
Creating or contributing to unsanitary conditions	Minor
Reading on the job	Minor
Extended coffee/lunch breaks	Minor
Soliciting	Minor
Insufficient quantity	Minor
Excessive waste	Minor
Verbal abuse (profanity)	Minor
Smoking in unauthorized areas	Minor
Insubordination	Major
Sleeping on the job	Major
Leaving plant early or without permission	Major
Reporting for work in an unfit condition	Major
AWOL (2 days)	Major
Excessive error	Major
Poor quality	Major
Assault or threat of assault	Grave
Sexual/workplace assault	Grave
Work refusal (except OHSA)	Grave
Illegal weapons on premises	Grave
Possession, distribution, consumption of alcohol or drugs on company property	Grave
Theft	Grave
Fighting	Grave
Deliberate destruction of company property	Grave
Misrepresentation, altering, or forging company, medical or WCB forms	Grave
Initiating, encouraging or participating in a walkout or work stoppage	Grave
Violations of safety rules that could inflict serious consequences	Grave
AWOL (3 days or more)	Grave

Source: Donald McQuirter, Manager of Human Resources, Volkswagen Canada Inc.

employee irresponsibility. This approach focuses on the early correction of misconduct, with the employee taking total responsibility for resolving the problem. Nothing is imposed by management; all solutions and affirmations are reached jointly. HR managers often describe positive discipline as "nonpunitive discipline that replaces threats and punishment with encouragement."[49]

Figure 13.8 illustrates the procedure for implementing positive discipline. While positive discipline seems similar to progressive discipline, it emphazes reminding employees rather than reprimanding them. The technique is implemented in three steps:[50]

- The employee and the supervisor confer with each other, with the goal of finding a solution to the problem through discussion. It should end with the employee making an oral agreement to improve performance. The supervisor does not reprimand the employee or threaten further disciplinary action. The supervisor can document this conference, but a written record of this meeting is not placed in the employee's file unless the misconduct occurs again.
- If the employee does not improve after this first step, the supervisor holds a second conference with the employee to determine why the solution agreed to in the first conference did not work. At this stage, a written reminder is given to the employee. This document states the new or repeated solution to the problem, and affirms that improvement is the responsibility of the employee and a condition of continued employment.
- If both conferences fail to produce the desired results, the employee is given a one-day decision-making leave (a paid leave). The purpose of this paid leave is for the employee to decide whether he or she wishes to

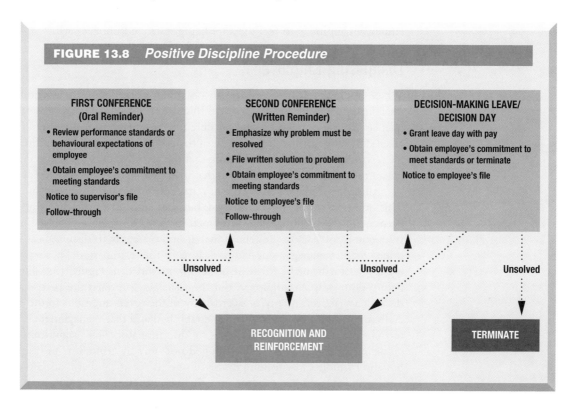

FIGURE 13.8 *Positive Discipline Procedure*

FIRST CONFERENCE
(Oral Reminder)
- Review performance standards or behavioural expectations of employee
- Obtain employee's commitment to meeting standards

Notice to supervisor's file

Follow-through

SECOND CONFERENCE
(Written Reminder)
- Emphasize why problem must be resolved
- File written solution to problem
- Obtain employee's commitment to meeting standards

Notice to employee's file

Follow-through

DECISION-MAKING LEAVE/
DECISION DAY
- Grant leave day with pay
- Obtain employee's commitment to meet standards or terminate

Notice to employee's file

Unsolved Unsolved Unsolved

RECOGNITION AND REINFORCEMENT

TERMINATE

continue working for the organization. The organization pays for this leave to demonstrate its desire to retain the person. Also, paying for the leave eliminates the negative effects for the employee of losing a day's pay. Employees who are given decision-making leave are instructed to return the following day with a decision either to make a total commitment to improve performance or to quit the organization. If a commitment is not made, the employee is dismissed on the assumption that he or she lacked responsibility toward the organization.[51]

Compiling a Disciplinary Record

When applying either progressive or positive discipline, it is important for managers to maintain complete records of each step of the procedure. An employee who fails to meet the obligation of a disciplinary step should be given a warning, and the warning should be documented by the manager. A copy of this warning is usually placed in the employee's personnel file. Usually, after an established period—often six months—the warning is removed, provided it has served its purpose. Otherwise it remains in the file to serve as evidence should a more severe penalty become necessary later.

An employee's personnel file contains the employee's complete work history. It serves as a basis for determining and supporting disciplinary action and for evaluating the organization's disciplinary policies and procedures. Maintenance of proper records also provides management with valuable information about the soundness of its rules and regulations. Those rules that are violated most frequently should receive particular attention, because the need for them may no longer exist or some change may be required to facilitate their enforcement. A rule that has little or no demonstrable value should be revised or rescinded. Otherwise employees are likely to feel they are being restricted unnecessarily.

Dismissing Employees

When employees fail to conform to organizational rules and regulations, the final disciplinary action in many cases is dismissal. Since dismissal has such serious consequences for the employee—and possibly for the organization—it should be undertaken only after a painstaking review of the case. An employee who is fired may well file a wrongful dismissal suit claiming that the termination was "without just or sufficient cause," the implication being that management did not extend fair treatment.

All of this demands that we ask: What constitutes fair treatment of employees? This question is not easily answered, but standards governing just cause dismissal do exist, in the form of rules developed in the field of labour arbitration.[52] These rules consist of a set of guidelines that arbitrators apply to dismissal cases to determine whether management had just cause for the termination. These guidelines are usually set forth in the form of questions, provided in Figure 13.9. For example, before dismissing an employee, did the manager forewarn the person of possible disciplinary action? A "no" answer to any of the seven questions in the figure generally means that just cause was not established and that management's decision to terminate was arbitrary, capricious, or discriminatory. The significance of these guidelines is that they are being applied not only by arbitrators in dismissal cases, but also by judges in wrongful dismissal suits. It is critical that managers at all levels understand the just cause guidelines, including their proper application.[53]

FIGURE 13.9 *"Just Cause" Dismissal Guidelines*

1. Did the organization forewarn the employee of the possible disciplinary consequences of his or her action?
2. Were management's requirements of the employee reasonable in relation to the orderly, efficient, and safe operation of the organization's business?
3. Did management, before discharging the employee, make a reasonable effort to establish that the employee's performance was unsatisfactory?
4. Was the organization's investigation conducted in a fair and objective manner?
5. Did the investigation produce sufficient evidence or proof of guilt as charged?
6. Has management treated this employee under its rules, orders, and penalties as it has other employees in similar circumstances?
7. Did the discharge fit the misconduct, considering the seriousness of the proven offence, the employee's service record, and any mitigating circumstances?

Informing the Employee

Whatever the reasons for dismissal, it should be done with personal consideration for the employee affected. Every effort should be made to ease the trauma a dismissal creates. The employee must be informed honestly yet tactfully of the exact reasons for the action. This candour can help the employee face the problem and adjust to it in a constructive manner.

Managers may wish to discuss, and even rehearse, with their peers the upcoming termination meeting. This practice can ensure that all important points are covered while giving confidence to the manager. While managers agree that there is no single right way to conduct a dismissal meeting, the following guidelines will help make the discussion more effective:

1. Come to the point within the first two or three minutes, and list in a logical order all reasons for the termination.

2. Be straightforward and firm, yet tactful, and remain resolute in your decision.

3. Make the discussion private, businesslike, and fairly brief.

4. Avoid making accusations against the employee and injecting personal feelings into the discussion.

5. Avoid bringing up any personality differences between you and the employee.

6. Provide any information concerning severance pay and the status of benefits and coverage.

7. Explain how you will handle employment inquiries from future employers.

Termination meetings should be held in a neutral location, such as a conference room, so that the manager can leave if the meeting gets out of control. The prudent manager will also have determined, prior to the termination decision, that the dismissal does not violate any legal rights the employee may have.

Finally, when the terminated employee is escorted off the premises, the removal must not serve to defame the employee. Managers should not give peers the impression that the terminated employee was dishonest or untrustworthy. Increasingly, terminated employees are pursuing lawsuits that go beyond the issue of whether their dismissal was for business-related reasons.[54]

Providing Outplacement Assistance

Employers often use employment agencies to help dismissed employees locate new jobs. This assistance is especially likely to be provided for managers of long tenure. Sometimes it is also provided for employees being laid off as a result of organizational rightsizing or restructuring, or because they don't fit a changed corporate identity.[55] Often, a termination under such conditions is not called a discharge, but rather an *outplacement*.

Managers note the following reasons for providing outplacement services: concern for the well-being of employees, protection against potential lawsuits, competition from other organizations offering such services, and the effect on the morale of remaining employees. Outplacement consultants assist employees being terminated in a number of ways—for example, by reducing their anger and grief and by helping them regain self-confidence as they begin searching in earnest for new work. Many terminated workers will have been out of the job market for some time and so lack the knowledge and skills they need to look for a new job. Outplacement specialists can coach them as they develop contacts, seek out job openings, attend employment interviews, and negotiate salaries.

APPEALING DISCIPLINARY ACTIONS

More and more organizations are taking steps to protect employees from arbitrary and inequitable treatment by their supervisors. The emphasis in this effort is on creating a climate in which employees can voice their dissatisfaction with their superiors without fear of reprisal—and know they can do so. This safeguard can be provided by implementing a formal procedure for appealing disciplinary actions.

Alternative Dispute-Resolution Mechanisms

Alternative dispute resolution (ADR)

Term applied to different types of employee complaint or dispute resolution procedures

Where a workforce is unionized, grievance procedures are almost always stated in the collective agreement. In nonunion organizations, **alternative dispute resolution (ADR)** procedures are a relatively recent development.[56] The employer's interest stems from the desire to meet employees' expectations for fair treatment in the workplace and to guarantee them due process. The hope is to minimize discrimination claims and wrongful dismissal suits.

Some organizations champion these procedures as means for employees to communicate upwards and as ways to gauge the temperament of the workforce. Others view these systems as a way to resolve minor problems before they mushroom into major issues. Below we describe the following appeal procedures: the step review system, the peer review system, the use of hearing officers, the open door policy, the use of an ombudsman, and arbitration.

Step Review Systems

Step review system

System for reviewing employee complaints and disputes by successively higher levels of management

As Figure 13.10 illustrates, a **step review** system is based on a pre-established set of steps—normally four. Under these, the employee's complaint is reviewed by successively higher levels of management. These procedures are patterned after the union grievance systems we will discuss in Chapter 15. For example, they normally require that the employee's complaint be formalized as a written statement. At each step, managers are required to provide a full response to the complaint within a specified time—perhaps three to five working days.

An employee is sometimes allowed to bypass the meeting with the immediate supervisor if he or she fears reprisal from this person. Unlike appeal systems in unionized organizations, nonunion appeal procedures ordinarily do not provide for a neutral third party (such as an arbitrator) to serve as the judge of last resort.[57] In most step review systems, the president, the CEO, the vice-president, or the HR director acts as the final authority, and this person's decision cannot be appealed. Some organizations help employees prepare their complaint cases. For example, an employee who wishes it may be able to get advice and counsel from a designated person in the HR department before discussing the issue with management.

Unfortunately, step review systems sometimes don't work as intended. Employees may believe that management is slow in responding to complaints, or that management's responses often do not solve problems. Furthermore, employees may believe that regardless of policies forbidding reprisal, supervisors will still hold it against them if they exercise their rights as spelled out in the step review system. These concerns do not mean that all step review systems are ineffective, only that management must take special precautions to ensure that the systems provide the benefits intended. We offer the following suggestions for making step review systems successful:

1. Consult employees when designing the complaint system. Commitment to the process is enhanced when employees participate in its design.

2. Train supervisors in handling complaints.

3. Handle complaints in a timely manner.

4. Make sure all employees know how to use the complaint procedure, and encourage them to use the system when they feel aggrieved.

5. Handle cases in a fair manner, and assure employees that they need not fear reprisal for filing complaints.

Peer Review Systems

Peer review system

System for reviewing employee complaints that utilizes a group composed of equal numbers of employee representatives and management appointees

A **peer review system**, also called a complaint committee, is composed of equal numbers of employee representatives and management appointees. Employee

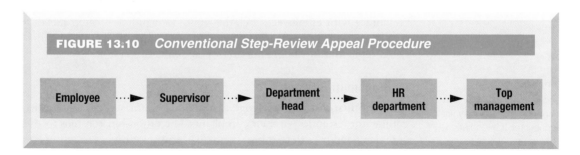

FIGURE 13.10   *Conventional Step-Review Appeal Procedure*

Employee ····▶ Supervisor ····▶ Department head ····▶ HR department ····▶ Top management

representatives are usually elected by secret ballot by their co-workers for rotating terms; management representatives are assigned, also on a rotating basis.[58] A peer review system functions as a jury in the sense that its members weigh evidence, consider arguments, and, after deliberation, vote independently to render a final decision.[59]

One benefit of the peer review system is that employees tend to have faith in it. The peer review system can be used as the only method for resolving employee complaints, or it can be used in conjunction with a step review system. When the two systems are used together, an employee who is not satisfied with management's action at, say, step 1 or 2 in the step review system, can submit the complaint to the peer review committee for final resolution. Darden Industries, which owns the Red Lobster and Olive Garden restaurant chains, uses a peer review system.

WWW

Use of a Hearing Officer

Hearing officers

People who work full-time for the organization but who assume a neutral role when deciding cases between aggrieved employees and management

This procedure is found almost exclusively in large organizations, sometimes in union environments. **Hearing officers** are full-time employees of the organization; however, they function independently from other managers and occupy a special place in the organization's hierarchy. To succeed, employees must perceive them as neutral, highly competent, and totally unbiased in handling complaints. They hear cases on request—almost always the employee's request. After considering the evidence and the facts presented, they render decisions or awards, which are usually final and binding on both sides. Like the peer review system, the hearing officer system can be used by itself or as part of a step review procedure.

Open Door Policy

Open door policy

Policy of settling grievances that identifies various levels of management above the immediate supervisor for employee contact

The open door policy is an old standby for settling employee complaints. In fact, most managers, whether or not their organization has adopted a formal open door policy, profess to maintain one for their employees. The traditional **open door policy** identifies various levels of management above the immediate supervisor that an aggrieved employee may contact; the levels may extend as high as a vice-president, president, or CEO. Typically, the person who acts as "the court of last resort" is the HR director or a senior staff member.

Two common complaints against an open door policy are that managers are unwilling to listen honestly to employee complaints, and that workers are reluctant to approach managers with their complaints. As one employee once told the authors of this text, "My manager has an open door policy but the door is only open one inch." Obviously, this employee felt he had little opportunity to get through to his manager. This system has other problems as well. It generally fails to guarantee consistent decision making, since what is fair to one manager may seem unfair to another. Higher-level managers tend to support supervisors for fear of undermining their authority. And as a system of justice, open door policies lack credibility with employees. Still, the open door policy is often successful when it is supported by all levels of management and when management works to maintain a reputation for being fair and open-minded.[60]

Ombudsman System

Ombudsman

Designated individual from whom employees may seek counsel for the resolution of their complaints

An **ombudsman** is a designated individual from whom employees may seek counsel for resolution of their complaints. The ombudsman listens to an employee's complaint and tries to resolve it by mediating a solution between the employee and the supervisor. This individual works cooperatively with both sides to reach a settlement, often employing a clinical approach to problem solving. Since the ombudsman has no authority to finalize a solution to the problem, compromises are highly likely, and all concerned tend to feel satisfied with the outcome.

Ombudsmen must be able to operate in an atmosphere of confidentiality that does not threaten the security of the managers or subordinates who are involved in a complaint. While ombudsmen do not have power to overrule decisions made by an employee's supervisor, they should be able to appeal the decision up the line if they believe an employee is not being treated fairly. Ombudsmen help employees achieve equity; they also provide management with a check on itself.

Arbitration

WWW

At the 1996 Summer Olympics, the athletes were required by the International Olympic Committee (IOC) to agree to take any Olympic dispute (including those over drug testing) to a special arbitration panel for a binding decision. The point of this was to avoid costly and disruptive battles in U.S. courts.[61]

In the same vein, private employers may require employees to submit their employment disputes to binding arbitration. (Arbitration is discussed in depth in Chapter 15.) Arbitration is used mainly to resolve discrimination suits relating to age, gender, sexual harassment, and race.[62] Arbitration can save litigation costs and avoid time delays and unfavourable publicity. However, to ensure that their arbitration policies are legal, employers must:

- have a clear, well-defined, and widely communicated arbitration policy;
- specify those topics subject to arbitration;
- inform employees of the rights they are relinquishing by signing an arbitration agreement;
- provide a procedurally fair arbitration system; *and*
- allow for the nonbiased selection of an arbitrator or arbitration panel.[63]

ORGANIZATIONAL ETHICS IN EMPLOYEE RELATIONS

OBJECTIVE 7

Throughout this text we have emphasized the legal requirements of HRM. Laws and court decisions affect all aspects of employment—recruitment, selection, performance appraisal, safety and health, labour relations, and testing. Managers must comply with governmental regulations to establish an environment free from litigation.

However, beyond what is required by the law is the question of organizational ethics and the ethical—or unethical—behaviour engaged in by managers. **Ethics** can be defined as a set of standards of acceptable conduct and moral judgment. Ethics provides cultural guidelines—both organizational and societal—that help differentiate proper from improper conduct. Ethics, like the law, permeates all aspects of the employment relationship. For example, managers may adhere to the organization's objective of hiring more members of designated groups, but how those employees are supervised and treated once employed gets to the issue of managerial ethics. We have presented Ethics in HRM boxes in each chapter of this book to illustrate the complexity of ethical dilemmas.

Law and ethics are two completely different aspects of the manager's job. Ethical dilemmas always arise when employees are being supervised. An ethical organization is distinguished from an unethical one by how it treats its employees.

Ethics

Set of standards of conduct and moral judgments that help determine right and wrong behaviour

In our view, an ethical organization is one that recognizes and values the contributions of its employees and respects their personal rights.

Many organizations have a code of ethics that governs relations with employees and the public at large. This written code focuses attention on ethical values and provides a basis for the organization, and individual managers, to evaluate their plans and actions. HR departments have been given a greater role in communicating the organization's values and standards, monitoring compliance with its code of ethics, and enforcing those standards throughout the organization. Organizations now have ethics committees and ethics ombudsmen to provide training in ethics to employees. The goal of ethics training is to reduce unethical behaviour and adverse publicity; to gain a strategic advantage; but most of all, to treat employees in a fair and equitable manner, recognizing them as productive members of the organization.

SUMMARY

OBJECTIVE 1 Both employees and employers have rights and expectations in the employment relationship. The due process right of employees is the right for them to express their views concerning an incident; statutory and contractual rights have to do with the rights of employees and employers to terminate the employment relationship. Under the implied contract concept, an employer's oral or written statements may form a contractual obligation that can preclude the automatic termination of employees.

OBJECTIVE 2 Once employed, employees expect certain rights regarding fair and equitable treatment on the job. These rights extend over such issues as substance abuse and drug testing, searches and surveillance, off-duty privacy, e-mail and voice mail privacy, and plant closing notification.

OBJECTIVE 3 The HR department, in combination with other managers, should establish disciplinary policies. This will help employees accept discipline and ensure its consistent application. Disciplinary rules and procedures should be written down, widely known, explained to employees, and reviewed on a regular basis. The rules must relate to the safe and efficient operation of the organization. When managers fail to enforce rules, they must re-emphasize those rules and their enforcement before disciplining an employee.

OBJECTIVE 4 The term "discipline" has three meanings: punishment, orderly behaviour, and the training of employee conduct. Discipline should correct undesirable employee behaviour and instill in the employee a desire for self-control. Discipline can be constructive only when managers conduct a complete and unbiased investigation of employee misconduct. The investigation of employee misconduct begins with proper documentation. When managers are investigating employee problems they must establish precisely what the employee did, whether the employee knew about the rule that was violated, and any extenuating circumstances. Disciplinary rules must be uniformly enforced. The past work record of the employee must be considered in any disciplinary procedure.

OBJECTIVE 5 There are two approaches to discipline: progressive and positive. Progressive discipline follows a series of steps based on increasingly strong corrective action. The corrective action applied should match the severity of the employee misconduct. Positive discipline is a cooperative approach and is based on reminders; employees accept responsibility for the desired improvement. The focus is on coping with the unsatisfactory performance and dissatisfactions of employees before the problems become major.

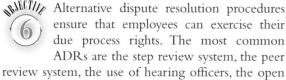 Alternative dispute resolution procedures ensure that employees can exercise their due process rights. The most common ADRs are the step review system, the peer review system, the use of hearing officers, the open door system, the ombudsman system, and arbitration.

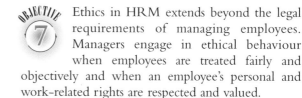 Ethics in HRM extends beyond the legal requirements of managing employees. Managers engage in ethical behaviour when employees are treated fairly and objectively and when an employee's personal and work-related rights are respected and valued.

KEY TERMS

alternative dispute resolution (ADR)
constructive dismissal
contractual rights
discipline
due process
employee rights

ethics
hearing officer
hot stove rule
negligence
ombudsman
open door policy

per review system
positive (or nonpunitive) discipline
progressive discipline
statutory rights
step review system

DISCUSSION QUESTIONS

 1. Do you have a right to your job? Discuss with reference to statutory rights, contractual rights, and due process.

 2. Describe a situation in which electronic monitoring of employees would be justified. Discuss any potential problems that might result from the monitoring.

 3. If you were asked to develop a policy on discipline, what topics would you cover in the policy?

 4. What should be the purpose of an investigative interview, and what approach should be taken in conducting it?

 5. Discuss why documentation is so important to the disciplinary process. What constitutes correct documentation?

 6. Describe progressive and positive discipline, noting the differences between these two approaches.

 7. What do you think would constitute an effective ADR system? What benefits would you expect from such a system? If you were asked to rule on a dismissal case, what facts would you analyze in deciding whether to uphold or reverse the employer's action?

 8. Working by yourself, or in a team, identify ethical dilemmas that could arise in the HR areas of selection, performance appraisal, safety and health, privacy rights, and compensation.

 9. In groups, discuss whether the following situations are fair or not fair:

a. Zabeen was using the company Internet to locate a nursing home for her increasingly handicapped father. Her supervisor observed this, and verified it with the Information Technology unit. Zabeen was given a written reprimand. Meanwhile, Sonia used the company telephone to do her personal banking and bill paying, and was not reprimanded.

b. Anthony spent his lunch hour at the gym, following a strenuous workout program with a personal trainer.

Meanwhile, Nicholas met his friends for lunch, sharing several beers at the local pub. Both employees felt fatigued in the afternoon, and their diminished productivity was noticed by their supervisor. Nicholas was asked to meet with his supervisor to review performance standards, and received a verbal warning. Anthony was not.

CASE 1

IMPROVING PERFORMANCE THROUGH A PROGRESSIVE DISCIPLINE POLICY

WWW

Simon Ouellet, former President of the Human Resources Professionals Association of Ontario, started his new job as Vice-President, Human Resources, at Fantom Technologies in November 1998. Fantom is a manufacturer of state-of-the-art floor care products, based in southern Ontario.

One of the first issues he faced was an unacceptable absenteeism rate. There were about 250 employees on the three assembly lines, operating two shifts a day. The average employee was absent 13 or 14 days a year. The benchmark for other manufacturing sites was 8 or 9 days. Simon calculated that Fantom was employing between 30 and 35 extra people to cover absences. This hurt the bottom line.

A related problem was punctuality. Employees were habitually 5 or 10 minutes late on their shifts. In a white-collar environment with flextime, this would not have been as critical. But tardiness in this situation meant that the assembly line could not operate, and that the other employees on the three lines were forced to remain idle.

The solution was to develop a system of progressive discipline. Simon prepared a simple two-page policy. Page 1 dealt with culpable absenteeism—the behaviour in the control of employees such as arriving late, leaving work without permission, calling in sick but playing golf, and so on. Page 2 dealt with legitimate or innocent absences. Simon met with the unions and notified them that this policy would come into effect as of December 1998. All employees started at zero absences at this time.

The policy assumed that all absences were innocent. However, if an employee was absent five times in a twelve-month period, the supervisor met with that employee to express concern over the absences and to identify any need for counselling or assistance. The goal of the meeting was to express legitimate concerns, reinforce that the employee was needed, and ensure that the employee accepted responsibility for managing his or her own attendance. Following this meeting, if the employee had fewer than two absences in the ensuing six months, the employee was no longer part of the program. However, if the absence pattern continued, the employee was counselled a second and third time. If no improvements resulted, a level 4 employment status review was conducted. This was done on a case-by-case basis. For example, a frequently absent employee with twenty-eight years of good service would be treated differently from another employee with the same absenteeism record but only two years of employment.

The results were impressive. About 70 employees entered the program. Of these, 8 to 10 advanced to step 2, two to step 3, and none to step 4. The absenteeism rate dropped to an average of less than ten days, and punctuality was no longer an issue. Labour costs were reduced, because it meant that twenty fewer employees were needed.

Questions

1. "The policy assumed that all absences were innocent." What do you think this means?

2. The policy was active as of November 1998, and all employees were treated equally from that date, regardless of their previous absenteeism records. Was this fair?

3. Could a policy of this type be developed to manage student punctuality and absenteeism?

CASE 2

PRIVACY IN THE WORKPLACE

There are two sides to the issue of workplace privacy. The employee side suggests that employees have the right to privacy and that employers should respect and trust their employees. The employer side returns that the workplace is a public environment and that the organization is responsible for the actions of its employees, and for their interactions with clients, visitors, and other employees.

More than 40 percent of companies monitor e-mail, voice mail, and employee computer use. Most employee monitoring is perfectly legal. The general legal view is that computers, telephones, and so on are company property, and that employees should not be using them for personal reasons. Companies can trace deleted e-mails and voice mails; special software can track Internet use; and wireless video cameras are small enough to look like pagers. More and more employees are using technology, and this makes it even easier to monitor their work. Even Bill Gates was caught: his private e-mails were used in the Microsoft antitrust hearings in the United States. Organizations monitor employees in order to deter crime, protect business secrets, and ensure a safe and equitable workplace.

A major reason for monitoring is to ensure that employees are actually working. Most employees waste at least a little time each day, however innocently. One company used a software tracking system to identify a group of employees who were selling Amway products from work. Another manager watched in horror as one of his top employees was led away by police, who had tracked his illegal activity (child pornography) through his e-mail address, which contained the company name.

Some employers have abused their right to monitor employees—for example, by videotaping them in washrooms, or hiring investigators to follow them. Another problem is the inferential misuse of the information obtained. For example, an employee may be visiting sites on suicide, AIDS, or substance abuse while doing research for a university paper. Employers may falsely infer from this that the individual is personally affected by these issues.

Privacy policies should inform employees that they are being monitored. If not, the company risks violating a section of the Criminal Code that prohibits "interception of private communication."

Questions

1. Employers do not have policies on using the telephone at work. They do not tell employees that they will be checking the fax machine for incidences of personal use. Why, then, do employers need to develop policies on monitoring the use of e-mail and the Internet?

2. Few studies have considered the impact of monitoring on employee behaviour. Does it reduce crime, and make workplaces safer and more productive? Or does it increase stress, and result in an adversarial relationship?

3. Go to the website of HR online (**www.hronline.com/lib/netpolicy.htm**). Develop an Internet and e-mail monitoring policy for your organization.

CAREER COUNSEL

Visit the Managing Human Resources website (**belcourt.nelson.com**) for tips on negotiating a formal employment contract.

USING THE INTERNET

WWW

Have you ever been curious about employee rights in other countries? Visit **www.hmso.gov.uk/acts/acts1996.htm** to read Great Britain's Employment Rights Act of 1996, straight from Her Majesty's Stationery Office.

The laws that have been discussed in this chapter can be found on the website of Canada Law Book (**www.canadalawbook.ca**).

The Canadian Centre on Substance Abuse (**www.ccsa.ca**) is a nonprofit organization that works to minimize the harm associated with the abuse of alcohol, tobacco, and various drugs. Its site has many articles on workplace drug abuse.

ADR and mediation resources are available at **www.adrr.com**. Also, visit the Arbitration and Mediation Institute of Ontario (**www.amio.org**), the Arbitration and Mediation Institute of Canada (**www.amic.org**), and the Network for Conflict Resolution (**www.nicr.ca**).

NOTES AND REFERENCES

1. M. Wolpert, "Front Page News," *Benefits Canada* 20, no. 2 (February 1996): 21–5.

2. James W. Hunt and Patricia K. Strongin, *The Law of the Workplace: Rights of Employers and Employees* (Washington, D.C.: Bureau of National Affairs, 1994).

3. Alfred G. Felio, *Primer on Individual Employee Rights* (Washington, D.C.: Bureau of National Affairs, 1996).

4. Donald H. Weiss, "How to Avoid Negligent Hiring Law Suits," *Supervisory Management* 36, no. 6 (June 1991): 6.

5. Samuel Greengard, "Privacy: Entitlement or Illusion?" *Personnel Journal* 75, no. 5 (May 1996): 74–88. See also James R. Redeker, *Employee Discipline: Policies and Practices* (Washington, D.C.: Bureau of National Affairs, 1989): 21. This book has an excellent discussion of the rights and responsibilities of employers and employees in the employment relationship; it also provides a comprehensive discussion of employee discipline.

6. K. Cox, "PEI to Pay Damages to 314 Workers Fired by Tories," *The Globe and Mail*, November 27, 1997: A4.

7. K. Makin, "Insensitive Firings Not Tolerated: Supreme Court Decision Will Aid Future Victims of Wrongful Dismissal, Lawyers Say," *The Globe and Mail*, October 31, 1997: A4; D. Johnston, "Promises, Promises: the Case of *Queen versus Cognos*," *Law Now* 22, no. 3 (December 1997, January 1998): 16–18.

8. Robert S. Seeley, "Corporate Due Process," *HRMagazine* 37, no. 7 (July 1992): 46–9.

9. Redeker, *Employee Discipline*, 25–38.

10. Christopher Bouvier, "Why At-Will Employment Is Dying," *Personnel Journal* 75, no. 5 (May 1996): 123–8. See also Marvin J. Levine, "The Erosion of the Employment-at-Will Doctrine: Recent Developments," *Labor Law Journal* 45, no. 2 (February 1994): 79–89.

11. T. Wagar, "Wrongful Dismissal: Perception vs. Reality," *Human Resources Professional* 8, no. 10 (1996).

12. J. Carlisle, "Court Sets Standard for Constructive Dismissal," *Financial Post*, April 29, 1997: 14.

13. J. Melnitizer, "*Ciciretto vs Embassy Cleaners*," *Workplace News* 5, no. 2 (February 1999): 1.

14. *Canadian Profile 1999, Substance Abuse and the Workplace*, Canadian Centre on Substance Abuse **www.ccsa.ca/cp1999work.html**.

15. Ontario Human Rights Commission, *Policy on Drug and Alcohol Testing* **www.ohrc.onc.ca/english/publications/drug_alcohol_testing_eng.html**.

16. *Drug-Free Workplace: Back on Track* (Virginia Beach, Va.: Coastal Human Resources, 1993): 3.

17. Edward J. Miller, "Investigating in a Drug-Free Workplace," *HRMagazine* 36, no. 5 (May 1991): 48–51.

18. B. Butler, "Alcohol and Drug Testing in Canada: Do You Have a Right To Test? Do You Have a Right Not To?" *Occupational Health and Safety* 13, no. 1 (January–February 1997): 28–31.

19. K. Hefner and S. Garland, "Testing for Drug Use: Handle With Care," *Business Week*, March 28, 1985: 65.

20. Samuel Greengard, "Theft Control Starts with HR Strategies," *Personnel Journal* 72, no. 4 (April 1993): 81–91.

21. "Tough Policies Minimize Shrink," *Canadian Grocer* 107, no. 12 (December 1993): 10, 37.

22. Greengard, "Theft Control": 81.

23. Robert L. Brady, "Workplace Searches: Avoid Legal Problems," *HRFocus* 72, no. 4 (April 1995): 18.

24. James D. Vigneau, "To Catch a Thief . . . and Other Workplace Investigations," *HRMgazine* 40, no. 1 (January 1995): 92–3.

25. Jennifer J. Laabs, "Surveillance: Tool or Trap?" *Personnel Journal* 71, no. 6 (June 1992): 102.

26. Ann K. Bradley, "An Employer's Perception on Monitoring Telemarketing Calls: Invasion of Privacy or Legitimate Business Practice?" *Labor Law Journal* 42, no. 5 (May 1991): 259–73.

27. Carlisle, "Videotape Can Be Used as Evidence in Civil Court," *Financial Post* , May, 27, 1997.

28. Dan Wise, "Private Matters," *Business and Health* 13, no. 2 (February 1995): 22–8.

29. Robert L. Brady, "Personnel Files: Keep Your Policies Updated," *HRFocus* 72, no. 2 (February 1995): 18. See also Brenda Paik Sunoo, "When to View Personnel Files," *Personnel Journal* 7, no. 7 (July 1996): 92; Donald J. McNerney, "Setting Boundaries in the Information Age," *HRFocus* 71, no. 12 (December 1994): 1.

30. Richard Behar, "Who's Reading Your E-Mail?" *Fortune*, February 3, 1997, 57–70; Richard F. Federico and James M. Bowley, "The Great E-Mail Debate," *HRMagazine* 41, no. 1 (January 1996): 67–72.

31. Kathy J. Lang and Elaine Davis, "Personnel E-Mail: An Employee Benefit Causing Increasing Privacy Concerns," *Employee Benefits Journal* 22, no. 2 (June 1996): 30–3.

32. K. Sibley, "The E-mail Dilemma: To Spy or Not to Spy?" *Computing Canada*, March 31, 1997: 14.

33. Don A. Cozzetto and Thomas B. Pedeliski, "Privacy and the Workplace," *Public Personnel Administration* 16, no. 2 (Spring 1996): 21–31. See also Donald H. Seifman and Craig W. Trepanier, "Evolution of the Paperless Office: Legal Issues Arising Out of Technology in the Workplace," *Employee Relations Law Journal* 21, no. 3 (Winter 1995–96): 5–15.

34. Robert L. Brady, "Electronic Mail: Drafting a Policy," *HRFocus* 72, no. 10 (October 1995): 19.

35. G. Arnaut, "Electronic Big Brother is on the Job," *The Globe and Mail*, October 22, 1996: C1.

36. Rosalyn L. Wilcots, "Employee Discipline for Off-Duty Conduct: Constitutional Challenges and the Public

Policy Exception," *Labor Law Journal* 46, no. 1 (January 1995): 3–16; Steve Bergsman, "Employee Misconduct Outside the Workplace," *HRMagazine* 36, no. 3 (March 1991): 62.

37. Melinda Socol Herbst, "Employers May Police Some Workplace Romances," *The National Law Journal*, February 26, 1996: C19; Douglas Massengill and Donald J. Petersen, "Legal Challenges to No Fraternization Rules," *Labor Law Journal* 46, no. 7 (July 1995): 429–35.

38. Dean J. Schaner, "Romance in the Workplace: Should Employers Act as Chaperones?" *Employee Relations Law Journal* 20, no. 1 (Summer 1994): 47–67.

39. Sharon Clinebell, Lynn Hoffman, and John Kilpatrick, "Office Romances: Rights and Liabilities," *HRFocus* 72, no. 3 (March 1995): 19.

40. "Termination and Layoff," *The Employer's Guide to the Employment Standards Act* (Ontario: Queen's Printer, 1997).

41. Catherine M. Petrini, ed., "Help for Discipline Dodgers," *Training and Development* 47, no. 5 (May 1993): 19–22.

42. Gary Bielous, "The Five Worst Discipline Mistakes," *Supervisory Management* 40, no. 1 (January 1995): 14–15.

43. Caleb S. Atwood, "Discharge Now, Pay Later? Establishing Reasonable Rules Can Keep You Out of Hot Water," *Personnel Administrator* 34, no. 8 (August 1989): 92–3.

44. Donald C. Mosley, Leon C. Megginson, and Paul H. Pietri, *Supervisory Management: The Art of Developing and Empowering People*, 4th ed. (Cincinnati: South-Western, 1997).

45. Cecily A. Waterman and Teresa A. Maginn, "Investigating Suspect Employees," *HRMagazine* 38, no. 1 (January 1993): 85–7.

46. Rebecca K. Spar, "Keeping Internal Investigations Confidential," *HRMagazine* 41, no. 1 (January 1996): 33–6.

47. Jeffrey A. Mello, "The Fine Art of the Reprimand: Using Criticism to Enhance Commitment, Motivation, and Performance," *Employment Relations Today* 22, no. 4 (Winter 1995): 19–27.

48. Readers interested in the pioneering work on positive discipline should see James R. Redeker, "Discipline, Part 1: Progressive Systems Work Only by Accident," *Personnel* 62, no. 10 (October 1985): 8–12; James R. Redeker, "Discipline, Part 2: The Nonpunitive Approach Works by Design," *Personnel* 62, no. 11 (November 1985): 7–14. See also Alan W. Bryant, "Replacing Punitive Discipline with a Positive Approach," *Personnel Administrator* 29, no. 2 (February 1984): 79–87.

49. Dick Grove, *Discipline without Punishment* (New York: American Management Association, 1996).

50. Chimezie A.B. Osigweh, Yg and William R. Hutchison, "Positive Discipline," *Human Resources Management* 28, no. 3 (Fall 1989): 367–83. See also Redeker, *Employee Discipline*.

51. Brenda Paik Sunoo, "Positive Discipline: Sending the Right or Wrong Message?" *Personnel Journal* 75, no. 8 (August 1996): 109–10.

52. Adolph M. Koven and Susan N. Smith, *Just Cause: The Seven Tests*, 2nd ed. (Washington, D.C.: Bureau of National Affairs, 1992).

53. For an expanded discussion of just cause, see Frank Elkouri and Edna Asher Elkouri, *How Arbitration Works*, 4th ed. (Washington, D.C.: Bureau of National Affairs, 1985), 650–54.

54. John E. Lyncheski, "Mishandling Terminations Causes Legal Nightmares," *HRMagazine* 40, no. 5 (May 1995): 25–30.

55. Lewis Newman, "Outplacement the Right Way," *Personnel Administrator* 34, no. 2 (February 1989): 83–6.

56. Susan E. Klein, "AAA President Slate Focuses on ADR Challenges," *Dispute Resolution Journal* 51, no. 2–3 (April 1996): 29–33, 130–5.

57. Douglas M. McCabe, "Corporate Nonunion Grievance Arbitration Systems: A Procedural Analysis," *Labor Law Journal* 40, no. 7 (July 1989): 432–7.

58. Mary Helen Yarborough, "Use Peer Review for Conflict Resolution," *HRFocus* 71, no. 10 (October 1994): 21.

59. Douglas M. McCabe, *Corporate Nonunion Complaint Procedures and Systems* (New York: Praeger, 1988): 9. See also Dawn Anfuso, "Coors Taps Employee Judgement," *Personnel Journal* 13, no. 2 (February 1994): 50.

60. Antonio Ruiz-Quintanilla and Donna Blancero, "Open Door Policies: Measuring Impact Using Attitude Surveys," *Human Resource Management* 35, no. 3 (Fall 1996): 269–89.

61. Norm Frauenheim, "Clause Alarms Athletes," *Arizona Republic*, May 10, 1996: C1.

62. Stuart L. Bass, "Recent Court Decisions Expand Role of Arbitration in Harassment and Other Title VII Cases," *Labor Law Journal* 46, no. 1 (January 1995): 38–46; Patrick J. Cihon, "Recent Developments in the Arbitration of Employment Discrimination Claims," *Labor Law Journal* 46, no. 10 (October 1995): 587–96; Lamont E. Stallworth and Linda K. Stroh, "Who Is Seeking to Use ADR and Why Do They Choose to Do So?" *Dispute Resolution Journal* 51, no. 1 (January–March 1996): 30–8; Kathryn M. Werdegar, "The Courts and Private ADR: Partners in Serving Justice," *Dispute Resolution Journal* 51, no. 2–3 (April 1996): 52–5.

63. George W. Bohlander, Robert J. Deeny, and Mishka L. Marshall, "Alternative Dispute Resolution Policies: Current Procedural and Administrative Issues," *Labor Law Journal* 47, no. 9 (September 1996): 619–26; Thomas R. Kelly and Danielle L. Berke, "What's New in ADR?" *HRFocus* 73, no. 4 (April 1996): 15.

THE MANAGER AS COUNSELLOR

Without question, employee counselling is an important part of a manager's job. Disciplinary interviews are often restricted to obtaining and giving specific information; in contrast, counselling involves a dynamic relationship between two parties in which one person is free to discuss needs, feelings, and problems for the purpose of obtaining help. Counselling involves many variables on both sides of the relationship (see Figure 13.A). The relationship is the chief means of meshing the helpee's problems with the counsel of the helper. Counselling can help employees with their personal problems—poor health, drug or alcohol abuse, family concerns, or financial difficulties; it can also help them deal with their job-related complaints or performance problems. The most effective way to reduce complaints is to encourage them to be brought out into the open.

Nature of the Relationship

Counselling does not take place in a vacuum: it occurs in the context of the relationship between the two parties. In organizations, authority affects that relationship. For example, an employee is not free to ignore a supervisor's help in work-related matters; whereas in the counselling relationship, he or she is—the helper is advising the helpee, not instructing. Another factor in the counselling relationship is confidentiality. Generally, what takes place in a counselling relationship is expected not to go beyond the two parties involved. There are times, however, when certain types of information must be reported—for example, if serious harm to others might result if it is not. Another factor that can affect the relationship is the manager's degree of commitment to help.

Counselling Techniques

All of us have a natural tendency to judge, to evaluate, to approve or disapprove. Sometimes we do these things prematurely on the basis of our preconceived assumptions; when we do, we are reducing our ability to communicate effectively. One way to avoid premature judgments is through a counselling technique called *active listening*. Active listening involves trying to understand what the other person is thinking by allowing this person to explain his or her perspective more fully without interrupting, or asking questions, or introducing new topics. The supervisor should maintain eye contact and should be relaxed and attentive to what the employee says or is trying to say.

Active listening is always important. It is absolutely essential when:

- we do not understand how the other person feels, and we need to understand the person's perspective;
- we believe that what is being said is not as important as what is *not* being said; *and*
- the other person is so confused that a clear message cannot be communicated.

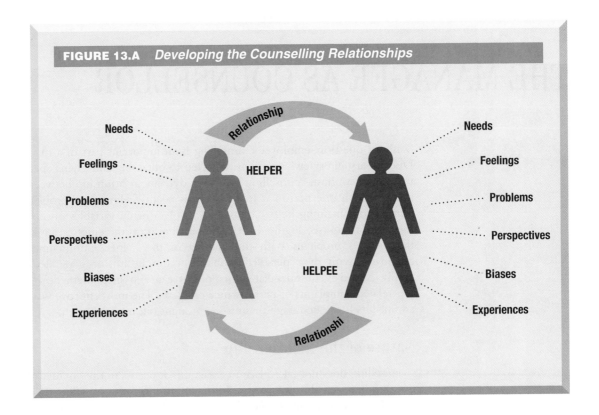

FIGURE 13.A   *Developing the Counselling Relationships*

Besides listening actively, a manager will use a technique known as *reflecting feelings*. This involves expressing—in somewhat different words—the employee's feelings, whether stated or implied. The goal is to focus on feelings rather than content, to bring vaguely expressed feelings into clearer focus, and to help the person talk about his or her feelings.

Examples of this technique include the use of comments such as "You resent the way the boss treats you," and "You feel that you deserve more recognition from the company." This technique is especially useful in the early stages of counselling. It is the standard procedure in nondirective counselling, a type of counselling we will discuss later.

Another good approach is to ask questions that will help the person understand his or her problem. Generally, these questions should be open-ended—that is, they should require more than yes or no answers. Thus, "Tell me more about your experiences with Mr. Jones." The questions should lead to clarification for the employee rather than information for the supervisor. Open-ended questions leave the employee free to take the interview in the direction that will do the most for him or her.

Counselling Approaches

There are many approaches to counselling, but they all depend on active listening. Sometimes the problem can be solved simply by furnishing information or advice. More often, however, the problem cannot be solved easily, because of frustrations or conflicts, and because the helpee is consumed with strong feelings such as fear, confusion, and hostility. A manager, therefore, needs to learn to use whatever approach seems to work at the time. Flexibility is a key part of counselling.

Directive Counselling

In directive counselling, the manager attempts to control (directly or indirectly) the topics the employee is talking about; and describes the choices the employee faces; and/or advises the employee what to do. It is very often appropriate for the supervisor to provide information and advice in areas where he or she is knowledgeable and experienced, especially if that information and/or advice is sought. However, where there are choices to be made and frustration and/or conflict are apparent, the directive approach should be avoided.

Nondirective Counselling

In nondirective counselling, the employee is allowed maximum freedom to determine the course of the interview. Nonevaluative listening is important here; it is the primary technique in nondirective counselling. Fundamentally, this approach involves listening, with understanding and without criticism or appraisal, to the problem as the employee describes it. This encourages the employee to express feelings without fear of shame, embarrassment, or reprisal.

The nondirective approach encourages free expression, which tends to reduce tensions and frustrations. The employee who has had an opportunity to release pent-up feelings is usually in a better position to view the problem more objectively and with a problem-solving attitude. The permissive atmosphere provides the employee with space to work through the entanglements of the problem and to see it in a clearer perspective. This increases the likelihood of reaching a desirable solution.

Participative Counselling

The directive and nondirective approaches that have just been described are obviously at the extremes of a continuum. Professional counsellors tend to stay at one end or the other of the continuum; in contrast, most managers vary their approach during a first session and/or in subsequent sessions. Many choose a middle-of-the-road approach in which both parties work together in planning how a particular problem will be analyzed and solved. This approach, which some refer to as participative counselling, is especially suitable in work organizations.

Many of the problems that managers and supervisors are concerned with require not only that the subordinates' feelings be recognized, but also that subordinates be made aware of and adhere to management's expectations that they be productive, responsible, and cooperative. On the other side of the coin, most people with problems would prefer to be actively involved in the solution once they see that there is a positive course of action available. In many work situations where counselling will be used, the participative approach is recommended in working with an individual over a period of time. However, at different times in the course of a single session, it may be advisable to be both directive and nondirective.

When Counselling Doesn't Work

Counselling by managers will not always achieve the goals it sets. When it doesn't, the employee may have to be disciplined or transferred.

The manager or supervisor may not have the skill or time to handle the more complex personal problems of employees. Sometimes the supervisor will have little or no influence over the problem area, as in the employee's family relationships. At these times it may be advisable for the supervisor to recommend that the employee see a professional counsellor. So there should be an established system for making referrals to trained counsellors. Usually it is the HR department that handles referrals to these professionals.

THE DYNAMICS OF

LABOUR RELATIONS

After studying this chapter, you should be able to

OBJECTIVE 1

Identify and explain the federal and provincial legislation that provides the framework for labour relations.

OBJECTIVE 2

Cite the reasons employees join unions.

OBJECTIVE 3

Describe the process by which unions organize employees and gain recognition as their bargaining agent.

OBJECTIVE 4

Describe the overall structure of the labour movement and the functions labour unions perform at the national and local levels.

OBJECTIVE 5

Describe the differences between private sector and public sector labour relations.

OBJECTIVE 6

Discuss some of the effects that changing conditions are having on labour organizations.

S ay the word "union" and most people will have some opinion, positive or negative, about Canadian labour organizations. To some, the word evokes images of labour–management unrest—grievances, strikes, picketing, boycotts. To others, the word represents industrial democracy, fairness, opportunity, and equal representation. Many feel that unions create an adversarial relationship between employees and managers.

Regardless of attitudes toward them, since the mid-1800s unions have been an important force shaping legislation, political thought, and organizational practices in Canada. Unions are still of interest today because of how they influence labour legislation, organizational productivity and competitiveness, and HR policies and practices. Like business organizations themselves, unions are changing both their operations and their philosophy. Labour–management cooperative programs, company buyouts by unions, and labour's increased interest in global trade are evidence of labour's new role in society.

Though unions have a long history, the intricacies of labour relations are unfamiliar to many individuals. This chapter describes government regulation of labour relations, the labour relations process, the reasons why workers join labour organizations, the structure and leadership of labour unions, and contemporary challenges to labour organizations.

Unions and other labour organizations can affect significantly the ability of managers to direct and control the various functions of HRM. Examples: union seniority provisions in the labour contract often influence who is selected for job promotions or training programs; pay rates may be determined through union negotiations; and unions may impose restrictions on management's employee appraisal methods. In light of all this, it is essential that managers understand how unions operate and be thoroughly familiar with the growing body of law governing labour relations. Labour relations is a highly specialized function of HRM to which managers must give appropriate consideration. Before reading further, test your knowledge of labour relations law by answering the questions in Highlights in HRM 1. (The correct answers are provided at the end of the chapter.)

GOVERNMENT REGULATION OF LABOUR RELATIONS

OBJECTIVE 1

Unions have a long history in North America, and the regulations governing labour relations have been evolving for just as long. In the early years, employers strongly opposed the growth of unions, and attempted to block them through the courts (e.g., through court orders forbidding picketing or strikes) and by devices such as the "yellow dog contract." A yellow dog contract was an anti-union tactic by which employees bound themselves not to join a union while working for the employer. Employers also used strikebreakers, blacklists, and various economic strong-arm tactics to defend themselves against unionization.

Today's labour relations laws try to create an environment where both unions and employers can discharge their respective rights and responsibilities. When you understand labour relations laws, you will understand how union–management relations operate in Canada.

Highlights in HRM

1   TEST YOUR LABOUR RELATIONS KNOW-HOW

1. During a labour organizing drive, supervisors questioned individual employees about their union beliefs. Was this questioning permissible?

Yes_____ No _____

2. While an organizing drive was under way, an employer agreed—as a social gesture—to furnish refreshments at a holiday party. Was the employer acting within the law?

Yes_____ No _____

3. A company distributed to other anti-union employers in the area a list of job applicants known to be union supporters. Was the distribution unlawful?

Yes_____ No _____

4. During a union organizing drive, the owner of Servo Pipe promised her employees a wage increase if they would vote against the union. Can the owner legally make this promise to her employees?

Yes_____ No _____

5. John Green, a maintenance engineer, has a poor work record. Management wishes to terminate his employment; however, Green is a union steward and is highly critical of the company. Can management legally discharge this employee?

Yes_____ No_____

Labour Relations Legislation

Labour relations in Canada is regulated by a multiplicity of federal and provincial laws. There are specific laws, or acts, for different sectors, industries, and workers. It is a highly decentralized system. For example, interprovincial transportation and communications are under federal jurisdiction, while manufacturing and mining are provincial. However, 90 percent of workers are governed by provincial legislation.

The Industrial Relations Disputes and Investigation Act

The Industrial Relations Disputes and Investigation Act (1948) specified the right of workers to join unions, allowed unions to be certified as bargaining agents by a labour relations board, required management to recognize a certified union as the exclusive bargaining agent for a group of employees, required both unions and management to negotiate in good faith, outlined unfair labour practices by both unions and management, and created a two-stage compulsory conciliation process that was mandatory before strikes or lockouts became legal.[1]

The federal government later incorporated these rights into a more comprehensive piece of legislation known as the Canada Labour Code. At the same time, the Canada Labour Relations Board (LRB) was established to administer and enforce the code. Similarly, each province has a labour relations board that administers labour law. (The exception is Quebec, which has a labour court and commissioners.) The members of these boards are government appointees. The LRB is generally autonomous from the federal government, and has representatives from both labour and management. The duties of the LRB include:

- administrating the statutory procedures for the acquisition, transfer, and termination of bargaining rights;
- hearing complaints related to unfair labour practices;
- determining whether bargaining was done in good faith; *and*
- remedying violations of collective bargaining legislation.[2]

THE LABOUR RELATIONS PROCESS

Labour relations process

Logical sequence of four events: (1) workers desire collective representation, (2) union begins its organizing campaign, (3) collective negotiations lead to a contract, and (4) the contract is administered

Individual employees usually have little power in their relations with employers. The treatment and benefits they receive depend in large part on how their employers view their worth to the organization. Of course, if they believe they are not being treated fairly, they have the option of quitting. However, employees can also correct this situation by organizing and bargaining with the employer collectively. When employees pursue this direction, the labour relations process begins. As Figure 14.1 illustrates, the **labour relations process** consists of a logical sequence of four events: (1) workers desire collective representation, (2) union

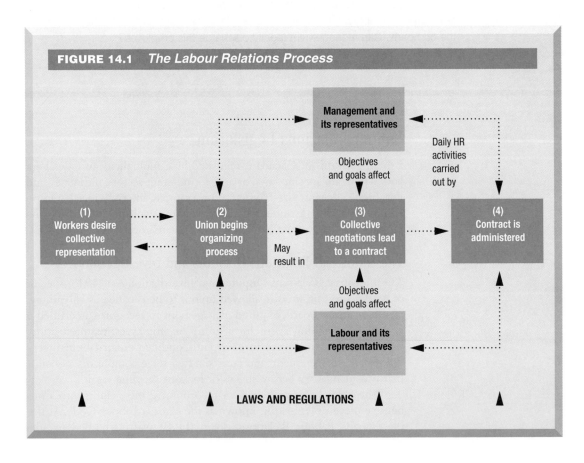

FIGURE 14.1   *The Labour Relations Process*

begins its organizing campaign, (3) collective negotiations lead to a contract, and (4) the contract is administered. Laws and administrative rulings influence each of these separate events by granting special privileges to, or imposing defined constraints on, workers, managers, and union officials.[3]

Why Employees Unionize

Most of the research on why employees unionize relates to blue-collar employees in the private sector. These studies generally conclude that employees unionize as a result of economic need, and/or because of general dissatisfaction with managerial practices, and/or as a way to fulfil social and status needs. In short, employees see unionism as a means to achieve results they cannot achieve acting individually.[4] As Highlights in HRM 2 illustrates, some segments of the labour force are, for a variety of reasons, highly resistant to unionization.

It should be pointed out that some employees join unions because of union shop provisions. A **union shop** is a provision in the collective agreement that requires employees to join as a condition of their employment. Compulsory union membership is being challenged in Quebec, where a group is invoking the Charter of Rights and Freedoms to argue that while Canadians have a right to associate, they should have a right to not associate.

Union shop

Provision of the collective agreement that requires employees to join the union as a condition of their employment

---

Highlights in HRM

2   HOMEWORKERS: CANADA'S INVISIBLE LABOUR FORCE

Rosanna Gonzalez (not her real name) works in the basement of her home in a small room crowded with industrial sewing machines. Rosanna is in the process of making 410 sweatshirts. To meet her deadline she will have to put in forty hours of work in two days. There is no natural light in the airless basement room, no way to escape the flying dust and thread particles. Last week the assignment was T-shirts. Rosanna received 38 cents per shirt. She can churn one out in five minutes, but even at that speed, she still earns only about $4.50 per hour—the minimum wage a decade ago.

In most provinces the law requires that homeworkers be paid at least one dollar above minimum wage to compensate them for the use of space and equipment in their homes. But enforcement of the law is rare. Canadians are quick to condemn working conditions in Third World countries, yet they are notably silent about abuses in their own country. Joining a union is a traditional response to abysmal working conditions. For homeworkers, unionization is a remote possibility at best. These individuals (most of whom speak no English) work in scattered and unlicensed locations and are usually unaware of their rights. Those who are aware are afraid that if they complain, they will suffer retribution at the hands of the retailers, contractors, and subcontractors they do business with. These women have few employment options and are often the sole providers for their children. For them the choice is clear: put up with the exploitation, or don't work at all.

Economic Needs

Whether or not a union will become the bargaining agent for a group of employees depends in part on the employees' degree of dissatisfaction (if any) with their employment conditions. It also depends on whether the employees perceive a union as likely to improve these conditions. Dissatisfaction with wages, benefits, and working conditions is the strongest reason for joining a union. This point is continually driven home by research studies, which have found that the expectations on unions are highest regarding the "bread and butter" issues of collective bargaining.[5] Unions are built on these traditional issues of wages and benefits.

Dissatisfaction with Management

Employees may seek unionization when they perceive that managerial practices regarding promotions, transfers, shift assignments, and the like are being administered unfairly. Employees cite management favouritism as a major reason for joining unions. This is especially true when the favouritism concerns the HR areas of discipline, promotions, and wage increases.

As we have noted throughout this book, today's employees are better educated than those of the past, and they often want to be more involved in decisions affecting their jobs. Chapter 3 discussed the concept of employee empowerment and highlighted various employee involvement techniques. The failure of employers to involve employees in decisions affecting their welfare may encourage union membership. It is widely believed that managers often begin empowerment programs as a means to avoid collective action by employees. In one organizing effort by the United Auto Workers at a Nissan plant, the union lost the election because workers were satisfied with the voice in decision making that Nissan's participatory style of management gave them.

Social and Status Concerns

Employees whose needs for status and recognition are being frustrated may join a union as a means of satisfying these needs. Through their union, they have an opportunity to fraternize with other employees who have similar desires, interests, problems, and gripes. Joining the union also enables them to use their leadership talents.

The limited studies conducted on employee unionization in the public sector generally have found that public employees unionize for about the same reasons as their private sector counterparts. In other words, higher wages and benefits, job security, and protection against arbitrary and unfair management treatment are primary motives for unionization among public sector employees.[6] In the final analysis, the deciding factor is likely to be whether employees perceive that the benefits of joining a union outweigh the costs associated with membership.

Organizing Campaigns

A formal organizing campaign can be started by a union organizer or by employees acting on their own behalf. Contrary to popular belief, most organizing campaigns are begun by employees rather than by union organizers. However, large national unions like the Canadian Auto Workers, the United Brotherhood of Carpenters, the United Steelworkers, and the Teamsters have formal organizing departments that identify organizing opportunities and launch organizing campaigns.

WWW

The CAW is Canada's largest private sector union with 238,000 members.

These campaigns can be expensive, so union leaders carefully evaluate their chances of success and the possible benefits to be gained from their efforts. Important in this evaluation is the employer's vulnerability to unionization. Union leaders also consider the effect that allowing an employer to remain nonunion may have on the strength of their union in the area. A nonunion employer can impair a union's efforts to standardize employment conditions within an industry or geographic area; it can also weaken the union's bargaining power with employers it has unionized.

Organizing Steps

The typical organizing campaign normally follows these steps:

1. Employee/union contact

2. Initial organizational meeting

3. Formation of an in-house organizing committee

4. Application to labour relations board

5. Issuance of certificate by labour relations board

6. Election of bargaining committee and contract negotiations

Step 1. The first step begins when employees and union officials make contact to explore the possibility of unionization. During these discussions, the employees investigate the advantages of representation, and union officials begin to gather information on employee needs, problems, and grievances. Union organizers also seek specific information about the employer's financial health, supervisory style, and organizational policies and practices. To win employee support, union organizers must build a case against the employer and for the union. Typically there are signs, reported in Highlights in HRM 3, that an organizing drive is occurring.

Highlights in HRM

3   IS A UNION BEING ORGANIZED?

Senior management is sometimes the last to know that a union has targeted the company. Often the process starts after employees call a union with complaints and want to understand their legal rights and responsibilities. Listed below are a few common signs that an organization drive is happening:

- Unusual employee behaviour of any kind
- An increase in the number of complaints about working conditions
- Demands for detailed information about employment policies
- Gatherings of employees that appear larger in number than usual, or that involve employees whose jobs are unrelated, or who would usually have no common interests
- Changes in how employees interact their supervisors
- The presence of union leaflets or other union material

Note also that most organizing drives take place inside the company.

Authorization card

A statement signed by an employee authorizing a union to act as his or her representative for the purposes of collective bargaining

Step 2. As the organizing campaign gathers momentum, the organizer will schedule an initial union meeting to attract more supporters. The organizer will use the information gathered during step 1 to address the employees' needs and explain how the union can meet them. Organizational meetings serve two other purposes: they identify employees who can help the organizer direct the campaign, and they establish communication chains that will reach all employees.

Step 3. The third important step in the organizing drive is to form an in-house organizing committee comprising employees who are willing to provide leadership to the campaign. The committee's role is to interest other employees in joining the union and in supporting its campaign. An important task for the committee is to have employees sign **authorization cards** indicating their willingness to be represented by a labour union in collective bargaining with their employer. The number of signed authorization cards demonstrates the potential strength of the labour union. Legislation across Canada states that a union must have a majority of employees as members in a bargaining unit before it can apply for a certification election. Most jurisdictions now interpret this to mean that at least 50 percent of those voting constitute a majority. In Manitoba a union is now automatically certified if 65 percent of employees sign union cards; in Alberta the figure is 40 percent. In other words, those who do not cast ballots are not assumed to be voting against the certification of the union. Union membership cards, once signed, are confidential, and only the labour relations board has access to them.

Step 4. Application is made to the appropriate labour relations board. In Canada, most unions are certified without a vote if the labour relations board finds that the union has the support of the majority of the employees, based on the number of signed cards.

Step 5. The labour relations board reviews the application, and a certificate is issued. This certificate allows the union to represent the employees as a recognized union under provincial labour relations legislation.

Step 6. Once the certification is issued, the bargaining committee is elected by secret ballot. A national representative works with the bargaining committee to negotiate a collective agreement with the company. The committee is often assisted by specialists in benefits and health and safety.

Employer Tactics

Employers must not interfere with the labour relations process of certification. They are prohibited by law from dismissing, disciplining, or threatening employees for exercising their right to form a union. Employers cannot promise better conditions, such as increased vacation days, if the employees vote for no union or choose one union over another. They cannot unilaterally change wages and working conditions during certification proceedings or during collective bargaining. Like unions, they must bargain in good faith, meaning that they must demonstrate a commitment to bargain seriously and fairly. In addition, they cannot participate in the formation, selection, or support of unions representing employees (see Figure 14.2).

WWW

None of these prohibitions prevents an employer from making the case that the employees have the right not to join a union and that they can deal directly with the employer on any issue. When Wal-Mart consolidated its entry into Canada by buying 122 nonunionized Woolco stores, the company was widely viewed as anti-union. However, Wal-Mart spokespeople insist that they are not

---

FIGURE 14.2 *Employer "Don'ts" During Union Organizing Campaigns*

Union organizing drives are emotionally charged events. Furthermore, labour law, LRB rulings, and court decisions greatly affect the behaviour and actions of management and union representatives. During the drive, managers and supervisors should avoid the following:

- Attending union meetings, spying on employee–union gatherings, and questioning employees about the content of union meetings.
- Questioning present or current employees about their union sentiments—especially about how they might vote in a union election.
- Threatening or terminating employees for their union support or beliefs.
- Changing the working conditions of employees because they actively work for the union or simply support its ideals.
- Supplying the names, addresses, and phone numbers of employees to union representatives or other employees sympathetic to the union.
- Promising employees improvements in working conditions (e.g., wage increases, benefit improvements, etc.) if they vote against the union.
- Accepting or reviewing union authorization cards or pro-union petitions, since employees' names are listed on these documents.

WWW

anti-union, but rather "pro-associate" (the Wal-Mart term for the retail sales clerk). During an organizing drive by the United Food and Commercial Workers Union, Wal-Mart's managers stated that they believed strongly in their people, would take care of them, and were ready to listen and to discuss any issue.[7]

Employers' attempts to influence employees are scrutinized closely by officials of the organizing union and by the labour relations board. In one case, an employer interfered with the organizing process, and the union was automatically recognized by the labour board, even though only 5 percent of the employees had signed authorization cards.[8]

Union Tactics

Unions also have a duty to act in accordance with labour legislation. Unions are prohibited from interfering with the formation of an employer's organization. They cannot intimidate or coerce employees to become or remain members of a union. Nor can they force employers to dismiss, discipline, or discriminate against nonunion employees. They must provide fair representation for all employees in the **bargaining unit**, whether in collective bargaining or in grievance procedure cases. Unions cannot engage in activities such as strikes before the expiration of the union contract.

Any of the prohibited activities noted above for both employers and unions are considered **unfair labour practices (ULPs)**. Charges of ULPs are registered with the labour relations board, whose duty it is to enforce the Industrial Relations Disputes and Investigations Act (IRDI).

How Employees Become Unionized

The procedures for union certification vary across Canadian jurisdictions. As mentioned earlier, the common practice is for unions to present documentation to the appropriate labour relations board for certification. The labour relations board must certify a union before it can act as a bargaining unit for a group of employees. In order to acquire certification, the union must demonstrate that it has obtained the minimum level of membership support required by the labour relations board. Usually, the union provides evidence by submitting signed authorization cards and proof that initiation dues or fees have been paid.[9] Recognition of a union can be obtained through voluntary recognition, or regular certification, or a prehearing vote.

Employer Recognition

Any employer, except those in Quebec, can voluntarily recognize and accept a union. This rarely happens, except in the construction industry, where there is a great reliance on union hiring halls.

Regular Certification

The regular certification process begins with the union submitting the required evidence of minimum membership to the labour relations board. Generally, if an applicant union can demonstrate that it has sufficient support in the proposed bargaining unit, labour boards may grant certification on that basis. (However, with changes in government, labour relations legislation is often reformed. Therefore, requirements for granting certification may change.) The labour relations board can order a representative vote if a sizable minority of workers have indicated either support or opposition to the unionization. Then a formal election is held.

Bargaining unit

Group of two or more employees who share common employment interests and conditions and may reasonably be grouped together for purposes of collective bargaining

Unfair labour practices (ULPs)

Specific employer and union illegal practices that operate to deny employees their rights and benefits under federal and provincial labour law

Prehearing Votes

If there is evidence of irregularities, such as unfair labour practices during the organizing drive, a prehearing vote may be taken. The purpose of this vote is to establish the level of support among the workers. In jurisdictions where a prehearing vote is allowed, the labour relations board will conduct the vote and seal the ballots pending the outcome of the investigation. If the labour relations board determines that the employees support the union, it will certify the union. Failure to reach the required proportional support could result in decertification of the union.

Decertification

All legislation allows for the decertification of unions under certain conditions. If the majority of employees indicate that they do not want to be represented by the union, or that they want to be represented by another union, or if the union has failed to bargain, an application for decertification can be made to the labour relations board. If a collective agreement has been reached with the employer, this application can be made only at specified times, such as a few months before the agreement expires. The application for decertification can be initiated by either the employees or the employer if the union fails to bargain.

Contract Negotiation

Once a bargaining unit has been certified by the labour relations board, the employer and the union are legally obligated to bargain in good faith over the terms and conditions of a collective agreement. Usually the terms of a collective agreement apply for a minimum of one year and a maximum of three years. As the contract expiry date approaches, either party must notify the other of its intention to bargain for a renewal collective agreement or contract negotiation.

Impact of Unionization on Managers

The unionization of employees can affect managers in several ways. Perhaps most significantly, it can affect management's prerogatives in making decisions about employees. Also, unionization can restrict management's freedom to formulate HR policy unilaterally and can challenge the authority of supervisors.

Challenges to Management Prerogatives

Typically, unions will try to achieve greater participation in management decisions that affect their members. These decisions often involve issues such as the subcontracting of work, productivity standards, and job content. Employers quite naturally seek to claim that these decisions are **management prerogatives**—decisions they have an exclusive right to make. However, these prerogatives can be challenged and eroded by the union. They can be challenged at the bargaining table, through the grievance procedure, and through strikes.

Loss of Supervisory Authority

At a labour–management conference, a union official commented, "Contract terms covering wages, benefits, job security, and working hours are of major importance to our membership." However, for managers and supervisors, the union's impact is

Management prerogatives

Decisions regarding organizational operations over which management claims exclusive rights

felt mainly at the operating level (the shop floor or office facility), where the terms of the collective agreement are implemented on a daily basis. For example, these terms can determine how employees can be directed and how they can be disciplined. When disciplining employees, supervisors must be certain they can demonstrate just cause (see Chapter 13), because their actions can be challenged by the union, and the supervisor called as a defendant during a grievance hearing. If the challenge is upheld, the supervisor's effectiveness in coping with later disciplinary problems may be impaired. Also, specific contract language can reduce the supervisor's ability to manage in such areas as scheduling, training, performance evaluation, and promotions.

STRUCTURES, FUNCTIONS, AND LEADERSHIP OF LABOUR UNIONS

WWW

Craft unions

Unions that represent skilled craft workers

Industrial unions

Unions that represent all workers—skilled, semiskilled, unskilled— employed along industry lines

Employee associations

Labour organizations that represent various groups of professional and white-collar employees in labour–management relations

Unions that represent skilled craft workers, such as carpenters and masons, are called **craft unions**. Craft unions include the International Brotherhood of Electrical Workers, the United Brotherhood of Carpenters and Joiners of America, and the United Association of Journeymen and Apprentices of the Plumbing and Pipefitting Industry. Unions that represent unskilled and semiskilled workers employed along industry lines are known as **industrial unions**. The Canadian Union of Postal Workers is an industrial union, as are the United Steelworkers of America, the Office and Professional Employees International Union, and the Ontario Secondary School Teachers' Federation. While the distinction between craft and industrial unions still exists, technological changes and competition among unions for members have done much to reduce it. Today, skilled and unskilled workers, white-collar and blue-collar workers, and professional groups are being represented by both types of unions.

Besides unions, there are also **employee associations**, which represent various groups of professional and white-collar employees. Examples of employee associations include the Federation of Quebec Nurses and the Alberta Teachers' Association. In competing with unions, these associations may function as unions and become just as aggressive as unions in representing their members.

Regardless of their type, labour organizations are diverse organizations. Each will have its own structure, objectives, and methods of governance. Most researchers when describing labour organizations divide them into three levels: (1) central labour congresses, (2) international and national unions, and (3) local unions belonging to a parent national or international union. Each level has its own reason for existence and its own operating policies and procedures.

Structures, Functions, and Leadership of the Canadian Labour Congress

WWW

The Canadian Labour Congress (CLC) is a central federation of unions. As Figure 14.3 illustrates, the CLC is similar in structure to the American Federation of Labor and Congress of Industrial Organizations (AFL-CIO). The two organizations operate independently, although many local unions are members of both organizations.

The CLC represents most of the unions in Canada. Its total membership in 2000 was 2.3 million Canadians.[10] Because of its size and resources, the CLC is consid-

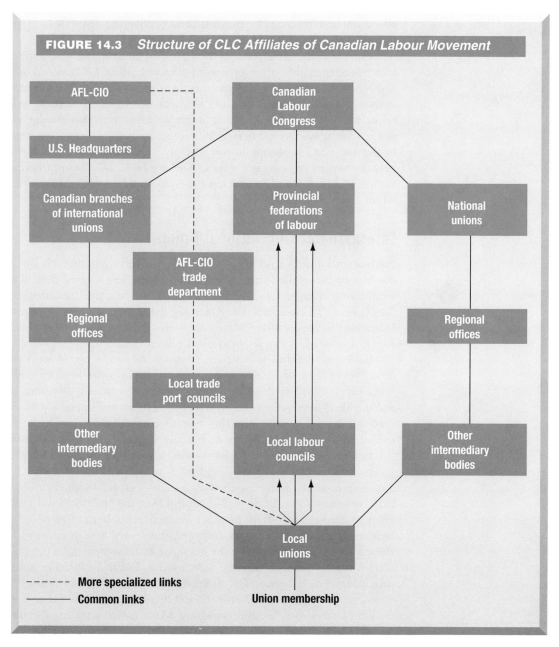

FIGURE 14.3   *Structure of CLC Affiliates of Canadian Labour Movement*

Source: John Crispo, *International Unionism* (Toronto: McGraw-Hill Ryerson, 1967): 167.

ered the most influential labour federation in Canada. It is mainly a service organization representing over 90 international and national unions; these finance the CLC through dues based on membership size. Like the AFL–CIO, the CLC attempts to influence legislation and promote programs that are of interest to labour. It does this by lobbying, resolving jurisdictional disputes, maintaining ethical standards, providing education and training to its members, conducting research, and representing Canadian interests in the international labour movement.

Every year the CLC presents the Canadian government with a memorandum, which is often critical of government policy (e.g., the CLC opposed both the FTA and NAFTA). This memo outlines various objectives that the CLC thinks the government should pursue. The CLC issues press releases in reaction to changes in economic indicators such as the unemployment rate. Knowledge and service workers are nowadays being targeted more heavily for certification, and as a result of this the CLC is playing an increasingly important role in refereeing disputes between unions competing for these workers. The CLC does not have any formal authority over its members and must align its members in common causes by consensus and moral suasion.

International and National Unions

WWW

International unions tend to be affiliates of American unions, with headquarters in the United States. The large membership base offers a good deal of leverage to local unions engaged in strike action. The merger of three international unions—the United Steelworkers of America, the United Auto Workers, and the International Association of Machinists—into the largest industrial union in North America resulted in a strike fund of $1 billion.[11]

Both international and national unions are made up of local unions. The objectives of these "umbrella" unions are to help organize local unions, to provide strike support, and to assist local unions with negotiations, grievance procedures, and the like. These unions also represent their members' interests with internal and external constituents. By ensuring that all employers pay similar wages to their unionized workers, they also remove higher wages as a competitive disadvantage.[12]

In Canada, most of the decision-making authority in national unions is vested in the local unions or at the bargaining unit level. This is often referred to as *bottom-up unionism*. Many international unions, especially craft unions, are more likely to retain a greater degree of control over the affairs of local unions. This is often referred to as *top-down unionism*. The officers of both types of union typically include a president, a secretary-treasurer, and several vice-presidents, all officially elected. These officers make up the executive board, which is the top policymaking body. A typical national structure is depicted in Figure 14.4. Other positions at the national level include lawyer, economist, statistician, and public relations officer. An economics director gathers, analyzes, and disseminates economic and other information of value in collective bargaining. Many national unions also have an education director, whose job is to provide training for local union officers and stewards. The structure of the Canadian Auto Workers, the largest private sector union, is described in Reality Check.

International and national unions often have social and political objectives outside their traditional goal of representing member interests. This contentious issue is discussed in Ethics in HRM.

Local Unions

Employees of any organization can form their own union, with no affiliation to a national or international union. In situations like this, the local is the union. However, most local unions are members of national or international unions or the

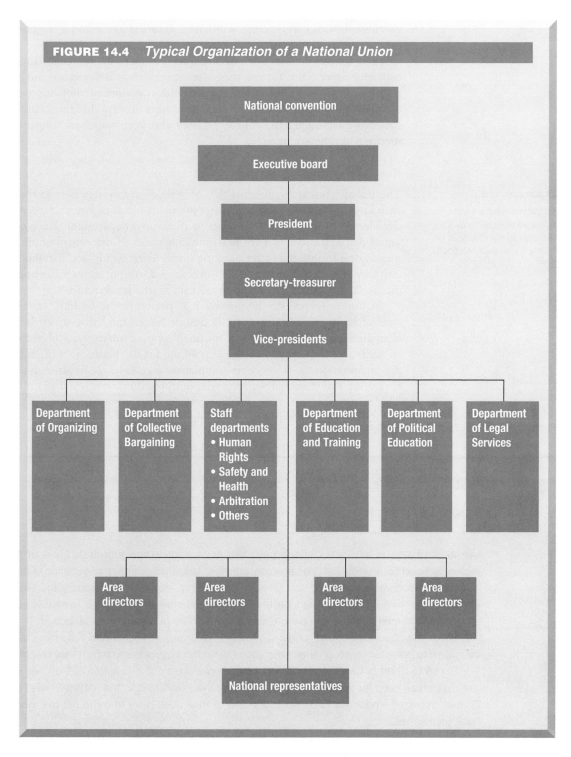

FIGURE 14.4   *Typical Organization of a National Union*

Canadian Labour Congress, which make available to them financial resources and advice. There are an estimated 13,000 locals in Canada.

Each dues-paying member has one vote and can participate in the election of the officials. Smaller unions typically have a president, a secretary-treasurer, and an executive board. Larger locals will have a business agent and a negotiating committee and/or a grievance committee.

The officers of a local union are usually responsible for negotiating the local collective agreement, for ensuring the agreement is adhered to, and for investigating and processing member grievances. Most important, they help prevent their members from being treated by their employers in ways that run counter to management-established HR policies.[13] They also keep members informed through meetings and newsletters.

Role of the Union Steward

Union steward

Employee who as a nonpaid union official represents the interests of members in their relations with management

The **union steward** represents the interests of union members in their relations with immediate supervisors and other members of management. Stewards are usually elected by the union members in their own department and serve without union pay. Since stewards are full-time employees of the organization, they often spend considerable time after working hours investigating and handling members' problems. When stewards represent members during grievance meetings on organizational time, their lost earnings are paid by the local union.

A union steward can be viewed as a "person in the middle," caught between conflicting interests and groups. It cannot be assumed that stewards will always champion union members and routinely oppose managerial objectives. Union stewards are often insightful people working for the betterment of employees and the organization. So supervisors and managers at all levels are strongly encouraged to develop a professional working relationship with stewards and all union officials. This relationship can have a major bearing on union–management cooperation and on the efficiency and morale of the workforce.[14]

Ethics in HRM

UNION DUES

Members of unions and associations pay dues to support union activities. Most of this money is used to finance traditional union activities such as contract negotiation, labour market and economic research, and grievance handling. However, sometimes the union, especially at the international or national level, dedicates some of these funds to causes such as opposing human rights violations in China or supporting gun control in Canada.

Union members challenged, under the Canadian Charter of Rights and Freedoms, their obligation to contribute through their union dues to political causes with which they disagree. The Supreme Court of Canada ruled (1) that trade unions are not in violation of the Charter if they use union dues for purposes other than collective bargaining in the narrow sense, and (2) that unionized workers who object to the use of their dues have to try to get the money back themselves.

Should union dues be allocated for purposes other than those related directly to contract negotiation and collective bargaining?

Sources: P.E. Larson, "Fighting for Labour," *Canadian Business Review* 13, no. 4 (Winter 1986): 8–12; P. Poiter, "Court Dashes Labour's Hope of More Rights," *The Globe and Mail*, June 28, 1991: A5.

Reality CHECK

THE CANADIAN AUTO WORKERS

Buzz Hargrove, president of the Canadian Auto Workers, oversees the operations of Canada's largest private sector union. The CAW was established in 1985 after breaking away from its American affiliate, the United Auto Workers. Membership has since increased from 118,000 to 238,000 through mergers with twenty other unions, including Mine Mill Workers, the Canadian Brotherhood of Railway Transportation, and General Workers. In an interview, Hargrove explained the CAW structure.

"Our union is a centrally directed organization. The CAW council meets three times a year with our national workplace representatives to openly discuss issues and establish policies that affect our members. The policy issues include social, collective bargaining, economic, or international issues. Whatever could possibly affect our workers is discussed. This is referred to as an 'accountability session.' We are the only union that discusses matters with our local leadership on a national basis so frequently. Working collectively as a team brings the issues to the forefront of all our representatives' minds, and makes us a more solid force to better represent our members. The real strength in our union is this ability we have to bring local leadership together with the national leadership to collectively debate issues that affect our membership.

"Every three years we hold a conference to discuss collective bargaining and political education issues. At this conference we develop our collective bargaining objectives—such as wages, pensions, benefits, work hours, job creation, equality, and diversity—for the next three years. Through our strong representation of women, we have been able to better understand their issues and represent them more fairly than we had in the past. We also hold our constitutional convention every three years, where elections of union officers takes place.

"The strength of our structure is built around the auto industry. When we win concessions through these negotiations, there is a spin-off effect felt throughout the entire union. We often help other workers who are represented in other unions win rights because we instil confidence in all workers that certain issues can be won.

"Our members join unions for different reasons. Some members want their earnings levels to increase. Others feel that earning respect for their years of service is important. For others union membership may be centred on equality issues, or affordable housing, or child care arrangements. However, the majority of our members are realistic about what they can expect in their own set of negotiations.

"I am personally concerned that we have lost some of our political base over the past few years. Our members are not listening to social issues such as employment equity or same-sex spousal coverage, or issues like gun control. On a national basis, we supported gun control, but a number of our members did not agree, and we have been debating the issue for a long time.

"The future of the CAW is to increase the size of our union by signing on new members and more union mergers. There are a lot of smaller unions that do not have the resources to represent their membership appropriately; by pooling resources, they will be better represented. We also can't keep increasing our member dues. Our members have been faced with large tax increases and they just can't make any more financial sacrifices. The manufacturing sector will remain an important target, since we believe that it will continue to grow over the next few decades. The service sector will be another target. Key to these strategies will be the rebuilding of our political base in Canada and finding means to bring our members around to the concepts of equity and diversity."

The Canadian Auto Workers website is **www.caw.ca**.

Role of the Business Agent

Business agent

Normally a paid labour official responsible for negotiating and administering the collective agreement and working to resolve union members' problems

Negotiating and administering the collective agreement and working to resolve problems arising in connection with it are major responsibilities of the **business agent**. In performing these duties, business agents must be all things to all people in their unions. They are often required to assume the role of counsellor in helping union members with both personal and job-related problems. They are also expected to dispose satisfactorily of the members' grievances that cannot be settled by the union stewards. Administering the daily affairs of the local union is another significant part of the business agent's job.

Union Leadership Approaches and Philosophies

To evaluate the role of union leaders accurately, one must have some understanding of union politics. The leaders of many national unions have developed political machines that enable them to perpetuate themselves in office. For the leaders of local unions, tenure is less secure. In a local union the officers, by federal law, must run for re-election at least every third year. If they are to remain in office, they must be able to convince a majority of the members that they are serving them effectively.

Union leaders occupy positions of power in their organizations; that being said, rank-and-file members often have a powerful influence over them, especially when it comes to negotiating and administering the collective agreement. It is important for managers to understand that union officials are elected to office and, like any political officials, must be responsive to their constituents' views. A union leader who ignores the demands of union members risks (1) being voted out of office, (2) having members vote the union out as their bargaining agent, (3) having members refuse to ratify the union agreement, or (4) having members engage in wildcat strikes or work stoppages.

Business unionism

Term applied to the goals of labour organizations, which collectively bargain for improvements in wages, hours, job security, and working conditions

To be effective leaders, union officials must pay constant attention to the philosophy and general goals of the labour movement. **Business unionism** is a general term referring to the goals of many labour organizations: increased pay and benefits, job security, and improved working conditions. Furthermore, union leaders also know that unions must address the broader social, economic, and legislative issues of concern to members.[15] The CAW continually lobbies for protective legislation favourable to the auto industry. The CLC has been an active promoter of women's issues and policies favouring job creation over deficit reduction. Finally, as part of Canada's adjustment to global competition, union leaders have been active in working with managers to make their respective industries more competitive.

LABOUR RELATIONS IN THE PUBLIC SECTOR

Collective bargaining among federal, provincial, and municipal government employees, and among employees in parapublic agencies (private agencies or branches of the government acting as extensions of government programs), has increased dramatically since the 1960s. Over 75 percent of all public employees are now unionized.[16] The three largest unions in Canada represent public sector employees. The Canadian Union of Public Employees (CUPE) is the largest union in Canada, with 486,656 members. The second-largest union, with 325,000 members, is the National Union of Provincial Government Employees (NUPGE). The largest union representing employees at the federal level is the Public Service Alliance of Canada (PSAC), with 150,000 members. PSAC comprises seventeen different unions representing various groups such as the Professional Institute of the Public Service of Canada (PIPS), the Economists, Sociologists and Statisticians Associations (ESSA), and the Air Traffic Controllers.[17] Growth in these unions is threatened by increased cost-cutting efforts of governments at all levels, resulting in employee reductions.

WWW

While public sector collective bargaining is quite similar to bargaining in the private sector, there are a number of differences worth noting. Below, we explore these differences in three contexts: (1) legislation governing collective bargaining in the public sector, (2) the political nature of the labour–management relationship, and (3) public sector strikes.

Public Sector Legislation

WWW

The Public Service Staff Relations Act (PSSRA) grants to federal civil servants bargaining rights, including the right to strike and the right to bargain for improvements in wages, hours, and working conditions. The PSSRA created the Public Service Staff Relations Board, which, like the labour relations boards governing the private sector, is responsible for certifying unions as bargaining agents and for resolving conflicts. Differences between the labour relations boards and the PSSRB are discussed later in the chapter.

At the provincial level, labour legislation applies to both sectors, public *and* private. For example, the Quebec Labour Code, the Saskatchewan Trade Union Act, and the British Columbia Industrial Relations Act apply to both sectors. Other jurisdictions may operate under more than one piece of legislation; in Ontario, for example, seven different statutes are operative. Some statutes cover more than one sector; in New Brunswick, for instance, statutes cover hospitals, schools, and public utilities.

Political Nature of the Labour–Management Relationship

Government employees are not able to negotiate with their employers on the same basis as their counterparts in private organizations. It is doubtful that they will ever be able to do so because of inherent differences between the public and private sectors.

Nurses often have different interests when negotiating their collective agreements.

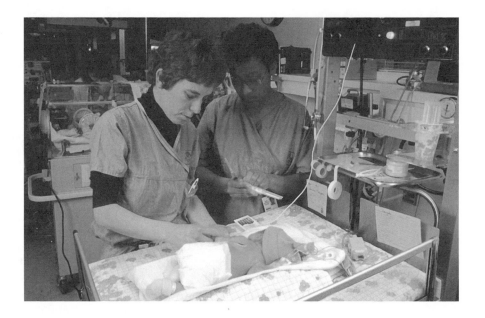

One of the significant differences is that labour relations in the private sector has an economic foundation, whereas in government its foundation tends to be political. Since private employers must stay in business in order to sell their goods or services, their employees are not likely to make demands that could bankrupt them. A strike in the private sector is a test of the employer's economic staying power, and usually the employer's customers have alternative sources of supply. Governments, on the other hand, must stay in business because alternative services are usually not available.

Another difference between the public and private sectors relates to the source of management authority. In a private organization, authority flows downwards from the board of directors and, ultimately, from the shareholders. In contrast, authority in the public sector flows upward from the public at large to their elected representatives and to the appointed or elected managers. It follows that public employees can exert influence not only as union members but also as pressure groups and voting citizens.[18]

Strikes in the Public Sector

Strikes by government employees create a problem for lawmakers and for the general public. Because many of the services that government employees provide, such as policing and firefighting, are considered essential to the well-being of the public, public policy is opposed to strikes by these people. However, various provincial legislatures have granted public employees the right to strike. Where striking is permitted, the right is limited to specific groups of employees—those performing nonessential services—and the strike cannot endanger the public's health, safety, or welfare. Public sector unions contend, however, that denying them the same right to strike as employees in the private sector greatly reduces their power during collective bargaining.

Compulsory binding arbitration

Binding method of resolving collective bargaining deadlocks by a neutral third party

Final offer arbitration

Method of resolving collective bargaining deadlocks whereby the arbitrator has no power to compromise but must select one or another of the final offers submitted by the two parties

One test of unions' right to strike was when the federal government, under provisions in the Public Service Staff Relations Act, attempted to designate all air traffic controllers as essential, even though the parties had previously agreed that all commercial flights would be cancelled in the event of a strike by controllers. The dispute went all the way to the Supreme Court, which ruled in favour of the government and, furthermore, gave the government the authority to determine the necessary level of service. The federal government ultimately declared that 100 percent of the bargaining unit were essential employees.

Public employees who perform essential services do in fact strike. Teachers, sanitation employees, police, transit employees, firefighters, and postal employees have all engaged in strike action. To avoid potentially critical situations, various arbitration methods are used for resolving collective bargaining deadlocks in the public sector. One is **compulsory binding arbitration** for employees such as police officers, firefighters, and others in jobs where strikes cannot be tolerated. Another method is **final offer arbitration**, under which the arbitrator must select one or the other of the final offers submitted by the disputing parties. With this method, the arbitrator's award is more likely to go to the party whose final bargaining offer has moved the closest to a reasonable settlement. The government can also enact back-to-work legislation, an option being used with increasing frequency.

CONTEMPORARY CHALLENGES TO LABOUR ORGANIZATIONS

Among the challenges facing labour organizations today are the changing nature of work and workers, political/legislative changes, and a new model of human resources management.

The Changing Nature of Work

Improvements in computer technology and highly automated operating systems have lowered the demand for certain types of employees in many different sectors, from manufacturing to services. The decline in membership in the auto, steel, rubber, and transportation unions reflects this fact. Unions have not been able to capitalize on the rapid growth in the service sector. Many businesses in this sector are small firms employing nontraditional workers. It is easier to organize one manufacturing plant of 500 employees than it is to organize 10 small business with 50 employees each.

Overall, more work is being done by contract, part-time, teleworking employees, and unions have not succeeded in organizing these types of employees.[19] Technological advances have also diminished the effectiveness of strikes, because highly automated organizations are capable of maintaining satisfactory levels of operation with minimum staffing levels during work stoppages.

The demographic profile of workers, and thus of union members, is also changing. Nowadays, nearly half of all union members are women. Also, the average age of union members is increasing (along with the average age of Canadians generally). The average union member is four years older than the average nonunionized employee, and the rate of unionization has declined among younger workers. Except in the public service sector, the unionized segment of the workforce is less educated; a disproportionate number of union members lack a high school education.[20] Unions have had to allocate time and money to organize the new workers (i.e., those in professional and white-collar occupations) in their new workplaces.

At one time, white-collar employees tended to identify with owners or managers, in the sense that they perceived themselves as enjoying certain privileges (e.g., not having to punch a time clock) and socioeconomic status that blue-collar workers did not. As well, the improvements in working conditions that union members had to fight to win, generally were extended to the white-collar group without any need for collective action on their part. Also, the high turnover among clerical workers made it harder to organize them. For these reasons, and because union drives to organize white-collar employees were not attuned psychologically to their needs and thinking, white-collar employees have been slow to unionize. In recent years, however, growth in the size of private organizations has tended to depersonalize the work of white-collar groups and to isolate them from management. The lack of job security during layoffs, and growing difficulties in grievance resolution, have pushed white-collar workers toward unionization.

In response to these changes, unions are stepping up their efforts to organize white-collar workers. Some unions are targeting the financial sectors, including banking and insurance. Other unions are recruiting employees of small businesses and employees in the so-called pink-collar ghetto—a term describing low-paying clerical and sales positions traditionally held by women. Unions are also capitalizing on new health and safety issues in white-collar jobs, such as the effects of working at video display terminals or working with potentially hazardous substances.

Political/Legislative

Union density—the percentage of the labour force that belongs to unions—in Canada is double that of the United States (about 30 percent to 15 percent). This does not mean that unions enjoy greater public support in Canada. The density figure, which has remained remarkably stable for several decades, can be attributed to the existence of political parties, such as the New Democratic Party, that are favourable to unions. The rise of political parties that favour the "business agenda" will result in changes such as the repeal of legislation banning replacement workers during strikes. The second factor in the rate of unionization is legislation, which in Canada tends to protect labour unions. Most notably, the legislation favouring certification is one of the principal reasons for union stability.

Innovative Workplace Practices

Employers are moving from a control-oriented system, in which the goals are to reduce labour costs and ensure worker compliance, to a new model of human resources management. Under this emerging model, employers attempt to obtain the commitment of workers to organizational goals, and support participation, empowerment, incentives, and profit sharing.

Organizations have been undertaking experiments in workplace restructuring that affect how work is organized and allocated. The "autonomic" workplace, where employees are given a high degree of autonomy, and where performance is monitored and either rewarded or disciplined, may alter union–management relationships. The workplace structures that are emerging in this type of workplace include semiautonomous work teams that determine work allocation, pace, skill upgrades, and the like. This kind of structure changes the role of the supervisor by reducing the need for rules, regulations, and close supervision. Pay in these environments is sometimes contingent on performance, and profit sharing and gain-sharing are increasing.

WWW

Critics argue that innovative workplace practices undermine union power by co-opting employees and aligning employee interests with management interests. However, one survey has reported that workplace reorganization has had mainly neutral effects on local unions. Some unions have reported more input into decision making and less militant members. One example of an innovative approach to the workplace that has yielded impressive results is the one created by unions and management at the highly automated Shell Canada plant in Sarnia, Ontario, where multiskilled workers are responsible for planning, scheduling, hiring, and training, and are compensated according to knowledge and skill. The result is higher output, low absenteeism, fewer grievances, and excellent product quality. The plant is seen as a model of a new approach to working life.

Employers have recognized the advantages of building an empowered and committed workforce. Highlights in HRM 4 lists the key strategies identified by HR specialists to reduce workers' motivation to join unions. Since these strategies are under the direct control of management, they can be used to help discourage or prevent unionization.

Highlights in HRM

4 STRATEGIES TO REMAIN UNION-FREE

- Offer competitive wages and benefits based on labour market comparisons and salary and benefit surveys.
- Train supervisors in progressive human relations skills, including employee motivation, job design, and employment law.
- Institute formal procedures to resolve employee complaints and grievances; these may include peer review committees, step review complaint systems, or open door policies.
- Involve employees in work decisions affecting job performance or the quality or quantity of the product or service provided.
- Give attention to employee growth and development needs; recognize that the workforce is growing older, more female, more vocal, better educated, less patient, and more demanding.
- Draft HR policies that reflect legal safeguards and that are fair and equitable in employment conditions such as discipline, promotions, training, and layoffs.

The best work environment, and the least receptive to unionization, is one that treats the individual with respect, dignity, and fairness, while encouraging participation in decision making.

SUMMARY

 Labour relations legislation in Canada recognizes the right of employees to form and join unions, and prohibits both unions and employers from engaging in unfair labour practices. Provincial labour relations laws are administered and enforced by labour relations boards.

 Studies show that workers unionize for different economic, psychological, and social reasons. Some employees join unions because they are required to do so; most belong to unions in the belief that unions help them improve their wages, benefits, and working conditions. Employee unionization is driven mainly by dissatisfaction with managerial practices and procedures.

 Unions carry out formal organizing campaigns to solicit employee support. In most jurisdictions, if more than 50 percent of those voting in the election vote for the union, the union will file an application with the labour relations board for approval of the union as the certified bargaining agent. If the labour relations board feels that there were irregularities in the application process, it has the power to call for a vote.

 There are three branches to the Canadian labour movement: (1) the national labour federations, such as the Canadian Labour Congress, a federation to which national

and international unions can elect to belong; (2) international and national unions; and (3) local unions chartered by the various national and international labour organizations. National and international unions and their locals carry out various functions for members. These include negotiating contracts, handling grievances, training union officials, offering social functions, and providing legal and political activity.

 Labour relations laws for the public sector differ from those for the private sector. For example, many public employees—especially those designated as providing essential services—are denied the right to strike. Also, collective bargaining in the private sector has an economic base, whereas in the public sector the base is often political. In the private sector, authority flows downwards along clear lines of responsibility; in the public sector, authority flows upwards and is much fuzzier.

 Challenges facing union leaders today include the changing nature of work and workers, political and legislative changes, and changing relations resulting from innovative work practices.

KEY TERMS

authorization card
bargaining unit
business agent
business unionism
compulsory binding arbitration

craft unions
employee associations
final offer arbitration
industrial unions
labour relations process

management prerogatives
unfair labour practices (ULPs)
union shop
union steward

DISCUSSION QUESTIONS

1. Describe how labour relations are regulated at the federal and provincial levels.

2. Contrast the arguments concerning union membership that are likely to be presented by a union with those likely to be presented by an employer.

3. Which unfair labour practices apply to (1) unions and (2) employers?

4. What are the functions of national unions and local unions?

5. What arguments would public sector managers put forth in opposition to unionization?

6. There has been a substantial increase (some estimate 40 percent) in the number of individuals who are self-employed. Some see this as a positive sign (i.e., of an increase in entrepreneurial activity): others see it as a response to the lack of permanent employment opportunities. The labour laws in each province effectively ignore independent workers. For many of them, wages (i.e., contract rates) are low, working conditions are difficult, and income security does not exist. Prepare to debate solutions to this issue, taking one of two sides: "Governments should change labour laws to recognize and protect self-employed workers," *or,* "Unions should organize these independent contractors and fight for better treatment."

CASE 1 NORTHERN CORPORATION: THE ORGANIZING DRIVE

Jean Lipski, HR director for Northern Corporation, had little experience with unions in general and no specific experience with union organizing campaigns. Unfortunately for her, the Brotherhood of Machine Engineers, Local 1463, began an organizing drive against Northern on June 1. At first, the union confined its efforts to passing out flyers about an organizational meeting; however, by June 10 it was obvious that employee support for the union was growing and that union campaigning had greatly intensified. The question faced by Lipski was no longer, "Should Northern do something?" but rather, "What should Northern do?" It was obvious to Lipski that the union was committing itself to an all-out effort to unionize Northern's employees. Supervisors reported to her that union supporters were passing out authorization cards in order to petition the labour relations board for a certification election.

Questions

1. Since the job of a labour organizer is to build a case for the union and against the company, what information about the organization do you think the union organizer would like to have?

2. What should Northern do—both strategically and tactically—to defeat the organizing drive? Be specific.

3. List things that managers should *not* do lest they commit unfair labour practices.

CASE 2

WAL-MART STORE IN WINDSOR, ONTARIO

In 1997, Wal-Mart was operating over 2,600 stores in the United States, Canada, Mexico, Brazil, China, and other countries.

Wal-Mart tries to distinguish itself from other retailers by its culture. For example, it calls its workers "associates," not employees. Every day at 8:45 a.m., a compulsory meeting is held at each store during which company managers share financial information and performance targets and respond to questions. The meeting ends with the Wal-Mart cheer. The company operates an open door policy, whereby any employee can talk to any member of management about issues, and receive answers, without being threatened with reprisal. The sundown rule ensures that management responds to the questions before sundown the same day.

The first Wal-Mart store ever to be unionized was in Windsor, Ontario, where the United Steelworkers (Retail and Wholesale Division) was certified by the Ontario Labour Relations Board. On April 14, 1997, the United Steelworkers began their organizing drive. On April 26, the store manager became aware that associates were being approached to sign unionization cards. The district manager was told of the organizing drive, and the next morning attended the morning meeting. The district manager asked the associates why they would want to join a union, and spent the day circulating through the store to discuss their problems or concerns. By April 27, eighty-four associates had signed cards. On April 29, an associate asked to speak at the morning meeting, and there expressed her opposition to the union, ending with the statement, "A union will only cause discontentment in our store, and I assure you as I am standing here, Wal-Mart will not put up with it." (Management did not ask, nor did the associate reveal, why she wanted to speak.) An inside organizer was prevented from responding because it was 9:00 a.m. and customers were waiting to enter the store.

Between May 4 and May 9, Wal-Mart managers—including managers from outside the store—responded to questions placed in a question-and-answer box, and to those raised while they wandered about the store. Most of the questions focused on compensation and hours of work. However, one associate testified that one manager said that things would change if the employees were unionized—for example, the profit-sharing plan would be revoked. During one meeting, the managers were asked if the store would close; they replied, "It would be inappropriate for your company to comment on what it will or will not do if the store is unionized."

On May 9, the union lost the vote, with 151 employees voting against it, and 43 voting for it.

The Ontario Labour Relations Board nontheless certified the union, because the employer violated the Labour Relations Act by not disassociating itself from the remarks made by the associate at the meeting; by not allowing the inside organizer to respond; by subtly threatening job security; and by allowing outside managers in the store from May 4 to 9. The OLRB stated that the union had 84 cards signed before the managers' visits, and a week later, this support had dropped. A second vote would not change the outcome, because the threat to job security could not be erased from employees' minds.

The legislation that allows the OLRB to overturn a certification board has now been changed.

Sources: Adapted from J. Hobel, "Allegation of Union Vote Rigging Investigated at Wal-Mart," *Canadian HR Reporter*, September 20, 1999: 1, 19. Anonymous, "Employer Interference: the Wal-Mart Case," *Worklife Report* 11, no. 2: 1–4.

Questions

1. What were the rights of Wal-Mart, the employer, during the organizing drive?

2. The certification of Wal-Mart was hailed by labour as a milestone event. Why?

3. Why would the United Steelworkers attempt to organize a retailer?

CAREER COUNSEL

For feedback on how you handle conflict, complete the Managing Conflict Questionnaire on the Managing Human Resources website (**belcourt.nelson.com**).

USING THE INTERNET

WWW

Every large union maintains an Internet site: for the Canadian Union of Public Employees (CUPE), visit **www.cupe.ca**; for the National Union of Public and General Employees (NUPGE), **www.nupge.ca**; for the Public Service Alliance of Canada (PSAC), **www.psac.com**; for the Canadian Auto Workers (CAW), **www.caw.ca**; and for the Canadian Labour Congress (CLC), **www.clc-ctc.ca**. This last one has links too nearly every union in Canada.

Private sector bargaining legislation can be found at the Human Resources Development Canada website, **www.hrdc-chrc.ca**.

NOTES AND REFERENCES

1. C. Heron, *The Canadian Labour Movement, A Short History* (Toronto: James Lorimer & Company, 1989).
2. J.C. Anderson, M. Gunderson, and A. Ponak, *Union–Management Relations in Canada*, 2nd ed. (Don Mills, Ont.: Addison-Wesley, 1989).
3. Readers interested in reading more about the labour relations process can consult J. Godard, *Industrial Relations: The Economy and Society* (Toronto: McGraw-Hill Ryerson, 1994); and Anderson, Gunderson, and Ponak, *Union–Management Relations in Canada*.
4. Robert R. Sinclair and Lois E. Tetrick, "Social Exchange and Union Commitment: A Comparison of Union Instrumentality and Union Support Perceptions," *Journal of Organizational Behavior* 16, no. 6 (November 1995): 669–79.
5. John A. Fossum, *Labor Relations: Development, Structure, Process*, 6th ed. (Homewood, Ill.: Irwin, 1995): 3.
6. Marc G. Singer and Thomas Li-Ping Tang, "Factors Related to Perceived Organizational Instrumentality," *Journal of Collective Negotiations in the Public Sector* 25, no. 3 (1996): 271–85.
7. J. Heinz, "Union Attempts to Organize Wal-Mart Stores in Ontario," *The Globe and Mail*, June 3, 1995: B3.
8. Discussion with CAW business representative, July 1995.
9. Canada Labour Relations Board regulations and Ontario Labour Relations Act.
10. **www.clc-ctc.ca**
11. T.V. Alphen, "Unions Eye Blockbuster Merger Plan," *Toronto Star*, July 28, 1995: A3.
12. Godard, *Industrial Relations*, 228.
13. E. Kevin Kelloway and Julian Barling, "Members' Participation in Local Union Activities: Measurement, Prediction, and Replication," *Journal of Applied Psychology* 78, no. 2 (April 1993): 262–78.
14. Researchers have discussed the erosion of union steward power in contract administration. The loss of power has been attributed to bureaucratization and centralization of labour relations activity within both unions and management hierarchies. While no one doubts the influence— positive or negative—that stewards can have on labour–management relations, the shifting power of the steward is important in deciding labour–management controversies. See Patricia A. Simpson, "A Preliminary Investigation of Determinants of Local Union Steward Power," *Labor Studies Journal* 18, no. 2 (Summer 1993): 51–67.
15. Aaron Bernstein, "Labor's Modest Quid Pro Quo," *Business Week*, November 11, 1996, 38.
16. Visit these websites: **www.cupe.ca**; **www.nupge.ca**; **www.psac.com**; and **www.clc-ctc.ca**.
17. Ibid.
18. Harvey C. Katz and Thomas A. Kochan, *An Introduction to Collective Bargaining and Industrial Relations* (New York: McGraw-Hill, 1992), 372–73.
19. J. Barling, E.K. Kelloway, and S. Harvey, "Changing Employee Relations: What Can Unions Do?" *Canadian Psychology*, May 1998: 124–32.
20. Galarnau, D. "Unionized Workers," *Perspectives*, Spring 1996: 43–52.

ANSWERS TO HIGHLIGHTS IN HRM 1

1. **No.** Individual questioning of employees about their union membership or activities is unlawful.

2. **Yes.** However, this must be part of normal conduct, and cannot be interpreted as a gesture to buy votes.

3. **Yes.** Blacklisting of job applications or employees is against labour law.

4. **No.** During an organizing drive, an employer cannot promise improvements in wages or benefits as a means of defeating the union.

5. **Yes.** Employees can be disciplined or discharged for work-related misconduct but not solely because of their union affiliations or union sentiments.

COLLECTIVE BARGAINING AND CONTRACT ADMINISTRATION

After studying this chapter, you should be able to

OBJECTIVE **1**

Discuss the bargaining process and the bargaining goals and strategies of a union and an employer.

OBJECTIVE **2**

Describe the forms of bargaining power that a union and an employer may utilize to enforce their bargaining demands.

OBJECTIVE **3**

Cite the principal methods by which bargaining deadlocks can be resolved.

OBJECTIVE **4**

Give examples of current collective bargaining trends.

OBJECTIVE **5**

Identify the major provisions of a collective agreement, and describe the issue of management rights.

OBJECTIVE **6**

Describe a typical grievance procedure.

OBJECTIVE **7**

Explain the basis for arbitration awards.

N egotiating is a large part of daily life. We negotiate when buying a car or a home, and sometimes when setting our salary. Researchers studying the art of negotiation note that the basic techniques of negotiating are applicable to a variety of bargaining arrangements, including labour negotiations. So while this chapter focuses on labour–management negotiations, remember that the bargaining principles we discuss here are appropriate to many different situations.

After a labour organization has won bargaining rights for employees, it has two main functions: to negotiate the collective agreement, and to resolve members' grievances through arbitration. Interestingly, according to labour law, once a union has been certified to negotiate for its bargaining unit members, it must represent everyone in the unit equally, both those who have joined the union and those who have chosen not to. The collective agreement that ultimately is negotiated establishes the wages, hours, employee benefits, job security, and other conditions under which represented employees agree to work.

This chapter is important because it explains how labour and management reach agreements. An organization's negotiators must arrive at an agreement with the union that will allow the employer to remain competitive. And it must be possible to administer the agreement with a minimum of conflict, so that managers can continue to manage.

THE BARGAINING PROCESS

Collective bargaining process

Process of negotiating a collective agreement, including the use of economic pressures by both parties

Those unfamiliar with contract negotiations often imagine the process as an emotional conflict between labour and management, complete with marathon sessions, fist pounding, and smoke-filled rooms. Actually, negotiating a collective agreement involves long hours of extensive preparation combined with diplomatic manoeuvring and the development of bargaining strategies. Furthermore, negotiation is only one part of the **collective bargaining process** (see Figure 15.1). Collective bargaining sometimes involves various forms of economic arm-twisting: strikes and boycotts by the union, or lockouts, plant closures, and the use of replacement labour ("scabs," in the union vernacular) by the employer. Besides all this, either or both parties may seek support for its position from the courts and from the public at large.

Preparing for Negotiations

Preparing for negotiations includes assembling data to support bargaining proposals, forming the bargaining team, and planning the strategy. All of these steps make it possible to conduct collective bargaining on an orderly, factual, and positive basis, and increase the likelihood of achieving the desired goals. Negotiators often develop a bargaining book that serves as a cross-reference file for determining which contract clauses would be affected by a demand. The bargaining book also contains a general history of the contract terms and their relative importance to management.[1] Assuming that the collective agreement is not the first one to be negotiated by the parties, preparation for negotiations ideally should start soon after the current agreement has been signed. This allows negotiators to review and diagnose mistakes made during past negotiations, while they are still fresh in their minds.

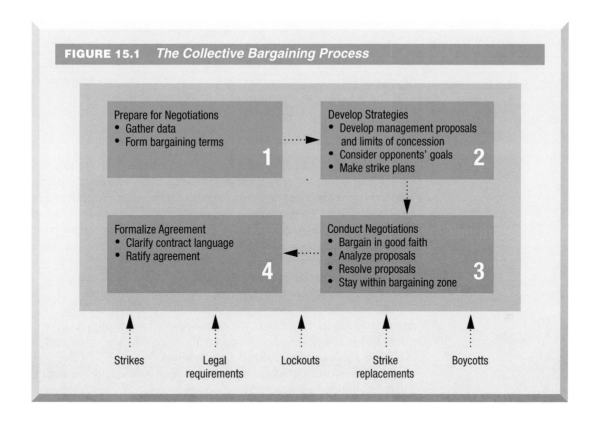

FIGURE 15.1 *The Collective Bargaining Process*

Prepare for Negotiations
- Gather data
- Form bargaining terms

1

Develop Strategies
- Develop management proposals and limits of concession
- Consider opponents' goals
- Make strike plans

2

Formalize Agreement
- Clarify contract language
- Ratify agreement

4

Conduct Negotiations
- Bargain in good faith
- Analyze proposals
- Resolve proposals
- Stay within bargaining zone

3

Strikes   Legal requirements   Lockouts   Strike replacements   Boycotts

Gathering Bargaining Data

Internal data on grievances, disciplinary actions, transfers and promotions, layoffs, overtime, past arbitration awards, and wage payments will help the employer formulate its bargaining position. The supervisors and managers who must live with and administer the collective agreement can be vital sources of ideas about changes to make in the next agreement. Through their contact with union members and representatives, they have first-hand knowledge of the changes that union negotiators are likely to propose.

WWW

Data obtained from government sources—Statistics Canada, the Bureau of Labour Information, and the like—can provide support to the employer's position during negotiations. Information from *The Globe and Mail* and from Conference Board of Canada publications can also be useful. These sources offer information on general economic conditions and cost-of-living trends, and on geographical wage rates for a wide range of occupations.

When negotiating contracts, union bargainers talk about "taking wages out of competition." This refers to negotiating similar contract provisions—especially relating to wages and benefits—with different companies in order to prevent one employer from having a favourable labour cost advantage over another. **Pattern bargaining** allows unions to show their members that the wages and benefits they are receiving are in line with those of employees doing like work; at the same time, it provides employers with assurances that their labour costs are comparable with those of their competitors.[2] Example: the Canadian Auto Workers negotiates similar contract provisions for workers at Ford, General Motors, and Chrysler. Pattern

Pattern bargaining

Bargaining in which unions negotiate provisions covering wages and other benefits that are similar to those provided in other agreements existing in the industry or region

bargaining also minimizes political problems within unions.[3] Quite naturally, employers try to keep a lid on increases by pointing out that other employers are paying lower compensation costs. Other collective agreements establish a pattern, which one side or the other may use to support its own bargaining position. While pattern bargaining has lost much of its prominence at the national level, at the local and regional levels it still plays a significant part in collective bargaining.

Bargaining Teams

Usually, each side will have four to six representatives at the negotiating table. Exactly how many, and who those people are, will depend on past practices and on what the teams are trying to achieve. The chief negotiator for management will be the vice-president or manager for labour or industrial relations; the chief negotiator for the union will be the local union president or union business agent. Management's team will usually include representatives from accounting or finance, operations, employment, legal, and training. The local union president will probably be supported by the chief steward, various local union vice-presidents, and a representative from the national union.

Many negotiators, over a period of time, acquire the ability "to read their opponents' minds," to anticipate their actions and reactions. Inexperienced negotiators bargaining for the first time may misinterpret their opponents' actions and statements and unintentionally cause a deadlock.

The initial meeting of the bargaining teams is especially important because it establishes the climate for the negotiations to come. A cordial attitude, with perhaps the injection of a little humour, can do much to ease tensions and help the negotiations start smoothly. The point of this attitudinal structuring is to change the attitudes of the parties toward each other, often with the objective of persuading one side to accept the other side's demands.[4]

Developing Bargaining Strategies

Negotiators for the employer should develop a bargaining strategy in writing. This plan should consider the proposals the union is likely to submit, based on its most recent agreements with other employers and the demands that remain unsatisfied from previous negotiations. It should also consider the union's goals and the extent to which it may be willing to make concessions or to resort to strike action in order to achieve these goals.

At a minimum, the employer's bargaining strategy must include the following:

- Likely union proposals, and management responses to them.
- Management demands, limits to concessions, and anticipated union responses.
- A database to support management's bargaining proposals and to counteract union demands.
- A contingency operating plan, should employees strike.

Certain elements of strategy are common to both the employer and the union. Generally, both sides start out demanding more than they expect to get. This approach provides room for concessions. Also, each party usually avoids giving up the maximum it is capable of conceding, in order to allow for further concessions, if these are needed to break a bargaining deadlock.

Conducting the Negotiations

The following factors tend to make each bargaining situation unique: the economic climate the two sides are facing, the experience and personalities of the negotiators, the goals the two sides are seeking to achieve, and the relative strengths of the two sides' positions. Some collective agreements can be negotiated informally in a few hours, especially if the contract is short and the terms are not too complex. Other agreements, such as those negotiated with large organizations like the National Hockey League and Stelco, require months to negotiate.

WWW

Bargaining in Good Faith

Once a union has been recognized as the representative for employees, the employer is obligated to negotiate in good faith with the union's representatives over conditions of employment. Good faith requires the employer's negotiators to meet with their union counterparts at a reasonable time and place to discuss these conditions. It requires also that the proposals submitted by each party be realistic. In discussing the other party's proposals, each side must offer reasonable counterproposals for those it is unwilling to accept.[5] Also, neither party can engage in **surface bargaining**—the process of going through the motions with no intention of making meaningful concessions.[6] Furthermore, an employer cannot end-run the bargaining process by making an offer directly to the employees.

When an employer argues a financial inability-to-pay position during negotiations, the duty to bargain in good faith requires it to provide relevant financial information to the union as proof that the claim is legitimate.[7] Finally, both parties must sign the written document containing the agreement reached through negotiations. Figure 15.2 offers several prevalent examples of bad faith employer bargaining.

Surface bargaining

Process of going through the motions of bargaining with no intention of making meaningful concessions

Analyzing the Proposals

In some ways, the negotiation of a collective agreement is similar to a poker game, in that each side attempts to determine its opponent's position without revealing its own. Usually, each party tries to avoid disclosing the relative importance it attaches to a proposal so that it will not be forced to pay a higher price for its acceptance. Salespeople will try to get a higher price for a product when they think

---

FIGURE 15.2 *Examples of Bad Faith Employer Bargaining*

- Using delaying tactics such as frequent postponements of bargaining sessions.
- Withdrawing concessions previously granted.
- Insisting that the union stop striking before resuming negotiations.
- Unilaterally changing bargaining topics.
- Negotiating with individual employees rather than with bargaining unit representatives.
- Engaging in mere surface bargaining rather than honest negotiations.
- Refusing to meet with duly appointed or elected union representatives.

the prospective buyer strongly desires it; in the same vein, negotiators will try to extract greater concessions for the proposals the other side wants most.

Astute negotiators know that for both sides, some demands will be more important than others, whether this is for economic or political reasons. It follows that the proposals each side submits generally can be divided into three categories: those it feels it must achieve, those it only hopes to achieve, and those it is submitting mainly for trading purposes. When discussing proposals, the bargainers will constantly try to determine how deeply the other side is committed to its demands. The ability to accurately gauge "commitment" to various proposals can spell the difference between an agreement and a bargaining impasse.

Resolving the Proposals

Regardless of its degree of importance, every proposal submitted must be resolved before the agreement can be finalized. A proposal can be withdrawn, or accepted by the other side in its entirety, or accepted in some compromise form.

Bargaining zone

Area within which the union and the employer are willing to concede when bargaining.

In a frequently cited model, Ross Stagner and Hjalmar Rosen refer the concept of a **bargaining zone**. In some bargaining situations, such as the one illustrated in Figure 15.3, the solution desired by one party may exceed the limits of the other party. If it does, that solution is outside the bargaining zone. If that party refuses to modify its demands sufficiently to bring them within the bargaining zone, or if the opposing party refuses to extend its limit to accommodate the demands of the other party, a bargaining deadlock will result.[8] Example: When bargaining a wage increase for employees, if the union's bottom limit is a 4 percent increase and management's top limit is 6 percent, an acceptable range—the bargaining zone (4 to 6 percent)—is available to both parties. But if management's top limit is only 3 percent, a bargaining zone is not available to either side, and a deadlock is likely to occur. Figure 15.3 is based on the Stagner and Rosen's original model and shows that as bargaining takes place, several important variables affect whether the negotiators will be able to reach agreement within the bargaining zone.

Formalizing the Agreement

The negotiators having finally agreed on contract terms, those terms must be reduced to clear contract wording. This is a difficult task, since the language of labour relations can be unintentionally confusing. Phrases like "just cause discharge," "emergency conditions," and "a day's work" are inherently muddy. For example, if an employee works seven hours of an eight-hour shift, and then goes home with the permission of the supervisor, has the individual technically completed "a day's work" according to the language of the agreement? When ambiguity creeps into a collective agreement, arbitration may be required to resolve the dispute.

Before negotiated contracts—called tentative agreements—become binding, they must be ratified (i.e., approved) by the members of the local. The bylaws of a local may state that a tentative agreement becomes binding only when, say, 75 percent of the members vote for acceptance. If the tentative agreement is not approved, the parties will have to return to the bargaining table.

Nonadversarial Bargaining

Sometimes, labour–management negotiations are characterized as adversarial. With adversarial bargaining, negotiators start with defined positions; then, through deferral, persuasion, trade, or power, the parties work toward resolving individual bargaining demands. In traditional bargaining, with its give-and-take philosophy, the results may or may not be to the complete satisfaction of one or both parties. In fact, when one side feels it has received "the short end of the stick," bitter feelings may persist for the life of the agreement. One labour negotiator notes: "Adversarial bargaining does little to establish a long-term positive relationship based on open communications and trust. By its nature, it leads to suspicion and compromise."[9] To overcome these negative feelings, labour and management practitioners may follow a nonadversarial approach. Figure 15.4 contrasts adversarial and nonadversarial bargaining.

Nonadversarial bargaining, also called interest-based bargaining (IBB), emphasizes identifying mutual interests rather than resolving specific bargaining

Nonadversarial bargaining (IBB)

Problem-solving bargaining based on a win–win philosophy and the development of a positive long-term relationship

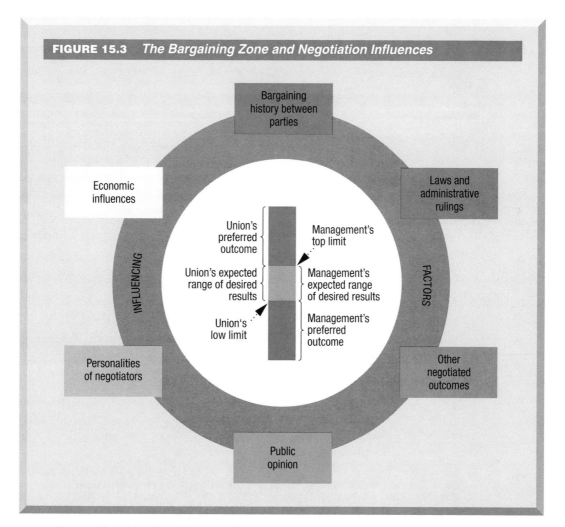

FIGURE 15.3 *The Bargaining Zone and Negotiation Influences*

Source: Adapted from Ross Stagner and Hjalmar Rosen, *Psychology of Union-Management Relations* (Belmont, CA: Wadsworth Publishing, 1965): 96. Adapted with permission from BrooksCole Publishing Co.

FIGURE 15.4 ·Adversarial vs. Nonadversarial Bargaining

ADVERSARIAL

- Discredit opponent's position; attack individuals.

- Present and defend position, provide supporting materials.

- Continually insist on predetermined bargaining positions.

- Negotiate to obtain outcomes for your own best interest.

- Use power, pressure, deferral to obtain desired solutions.

NONADVERSARIAL

- Address mutual problems and concerns, focus on specific issues—not on individuals or past conflicts.

- Explore interests of joint concern; clearly define mutual issues.

- Be open-minded to possibilities and/or future opportunities; satisfy others' interests as well as your own.

- Work toward satisfying the interests of all concerned.

- Define acceptable solutions measured against jointly developed standards; use consensus decision making to reach solutions.

Source: *Interest-Based Negotiations: Participants' Handbook* (Washington, D.C.: Federal Mediation and Conciliation Service, 1998). Reprinted with permission.

---

demands.[10] IBB is "a problem-solving process conducted in a principled way that creates effective solutions while improving the bargaining relationship."[11] Nonadversarial bargaining focuses on discovering mutual bargaining interests with the intent of formulating options and solutions for mutual gain.[12]

Specifically, during negotiations the parties will:

- present an issue (a topic for discussion) and interests (concerns about an issue);
- brainstorm options to resolve interests;
- establish a set of standards to evaluate the options;
- evaluate options relative to standards; *and*
- select the most appropriate option, and reduce it to writing.

IBB is unique in philosophy and process, and also in the tools it uses. Instead of relying on proposals and counterproposals to reach agreement (as with adversarial negotiations), the participants use brainstorming, consensus decision-making, active listening, process checking, and matrix building to settle issues (see Highlights in HRM 1). An underlying goal of nonadversarial bargaining is to foster a relationship based on trust, understanding, and mutual respect. Wilfrid Laurier University in Kitchener-Waterloo, Ontario, used an IBB process to negotiate a landmark five-year deal.

WWW

The Union's Power in Collective Bargaining

OBJECTIVE 2

During negotiations it is necessary for each party to retreat from its original position to the point where an agreement can be achieved. Otherwise, the negotiations

Highlights in HRM

1   THE TOOLS AND TECHNIQUES OF INTEREST-BASED BARGAINING

BRAINSTORMING

Brainstorming is used to develop creative and innovative ideas. All team members contribute suggestions in a round-robin fashion while a recorder captures ideas without criticism. Brainstorming allows novel ideas to surface, enlarges the pool of ideas (including unfamiliar ones), encourages synergy, and discourages evaluation. Brainstorming leaps the boundaries of logical thinking and transcends tradition, precedent, time, staff, and resource constraints.

CONSENSUS DECISION-MAKING

Consensus decision-making involves finding a solution acceptable enough that all negotiators can support the decision to some degree. Consensus decision-making does not require unanimity, nor does it invoke majority vote. Rather, it encourages total participation in a give-and-take exchange of thoughts and opinions. Differences are debated, and compromises are made. Consensus decision-making is useful for establishing ground rules, formulating standards, arriving at solutions, and developing a joint statement.

ACTIVE LISTENING

Active listening refers to the ability to listen effectively and to understand not only words but also the emotions and body language of the speaker. It encourages the listener to ask questions to verify or expand on the information received. Active listening is especially useful when selecting an issue, discussing interests, defining standards, and communicating results to constituents.

PROCESS CHECKING

Process checking allows for the monitoring of adherence to the IBB process and the interactions of negotiators. It gives team members a structured opportunity to share observations about the negotiations. Process checking prevents negative behaviour from becoming ingrained in the bargaining process. It is employed when a team member perceives that ground rules are being violated or when negotiators are not following the IBB process.

RECORDING

Recording is the writing of spoken ideas on a flip chart for all to view. It is used to capture ground rules, issues and interests, and proposed options, standards, and solutions. Recording helps preserve language and the meaning of oral statements; it also creates joint ownership of ideas.

MATRIX BUILDING

Matrix building helps participants evaluate options against standards. In a matrix formulation, columns represent standards and rows represent options. Negotiators place a "yes" or "no" in each matrix square depending on whether the option satisfies the standards under review.

will become deadlocked, and the union may decide to use its economic clout to achieve its demands. The only other alternative to this is for the union members to continue working without a collective agreement after the old one has expired. The union can exercise its economic power by striking or picketing, or by boycotting the employer's products and encouraging others to do likewise. As managers well know, the mere threat to engage in such activities is a form of pressure.

Striking the Employer

WWW

A strike is the refusal of a group of employees to perform their jobs. Strikes account for only a small portion of total workdays lost in industry each year; however, when they do take place they are a costly and emotional event for all concerned. According to the Canadian Federation of Independent Business, the 1997 strike at Canada Post cost small and medium-sized businesses around $200 million per day.[13] Unions usually seek strike authorization from their members as a bargaining lever to gain concessions that will make a strike unnecessary. A vote by the members to strike does not mean they actually want or expect to go out on strike. Rather, it is intended as a vote of confidence to strengthen the position of their leaders at the bargaining table.

Of critical importance is whether the employer will be able to continue operating using supervisory and nonstriking personnel and replacement workers.[14] Highly automated organizations tend to have fewer employees and so are more likely to continue operating through supervisors and managers. In highly automated telephone companies, most services can be maintained by supervisors during a strike. According to one authority, "Because of technological change, striking in many industries no longer has the effect of curtailing the employer's operations significantly."[15] The greater the ability of the employer to continue operating, the smaller the union's chances of achieving its demands through a strike.[16]

The number of work stoppages involving 500 or more workers declined from 66 in 1990 to 53 in 1999.[17] Roughly nine in ten collective agreements are settled without a strike. HRM practitioners attribute the decline in strikes to a decrease in employee support and public tolerance for strikes. Unfortunately, Canada leads the G7 nations in workdays lost due to strikes and lockouts.[18]

Picketing the Employer

When a union goes on strike, it places people at the entrances to the business to publicize the dispute and to discourage people from entering the premises. Even when the picketers represent only a small proportion of employees, they can shut down the entire organization if enough of the nonstriking employees refuse to cross their picket line (these latter are "sympathy strikers"). Also, because unionized workers often refuse to cross another union's picket line, the pickets may prevent delivery trucks and railcars from entering the business.

If a strike fails to stop an employer's operations, the picket line may serve as more than a passive weapon. Employees who try to cross the line may be subjected to verbal insults and even physical violence. Mass picketing, in which large groups of pickets try to block the path of people trying to enter the premises, may also be used. However, it is illegal for picketers to use physical force or incite violence, and their resorting to either can do their cause more harm than good.

Boycotting the Employer

Boycott

Union tactic to encourage others to refuse to patronize an employer

Another economic weapon of unions is the **boycott**, which is a refusal to patronize the employer.

In a *primary boycott*, the union asks its members and/or customers not to patronize the business; for example, production employees on strike against a hand tool manufacturer might picket a retail store that sells the tools made by the struck employer.[19] Usually this type of boycott is legal, as long as the union is advising consumers to boycott the tools and not the neutral store. The union may go a step farther, however, and try to induce third parties—mainly the suppliers of the struck employer—to refrain from doing business with the employer with whom it has a dispute. This type of boycott, called a *secondary boycott*, is generally illegal.

The Employer's Power in Collective Bargaining

In collective bargaining, the employer's power rests largely in its right to shut down the organization or certain of its operations. The employer can transfer these operations to other locations, or it can subcontract them to other employers through outsourcing. General Motors outsources to foreign manufacturers many of the parts it uses to build its North American cars. In exercising their economic freedom, however, employers must be careful that their actions are not interpreted by labour relations boards as attempts to avoid bargaining with the union.

Operating During Strikes

When negotiations become deadlocked, typically it is the union that *acts* and the employer that *reacts*. In reacting, the employer must balance the cost of taking a strike against the short- and long-term costs of agreeing to union demands. It must also consider how long operations may have to be suspended, and how long both it and the union will be able to endure a strike. An employer that decides to accept a strike must then decide whether to continue operating during the strike (if it is possible to do so).

Picketing is used by unions to publicize their disputes and discourage people from entering the premises.

Nowadays, organizations seem more willing than they used to be to face a strike. Several reasons for this have been advanced:

1. Union members seem less willing to support strike activity. Put another way, unions are finding it harder to maintain solidarity among their members.

2. Because organizations are being forced to reduce labour costs to meet domestic and global competition, unions have no choice but to accept lower wages and benefits.

3. Technological advances are making it easier for employers to operate during a strike.

4. Organizations are finding it easier to obtain favourable (often concessionary) contracts.

WWW

In some jurisdictions, employers face restrictions to their right to hire replacement workers. Quebec and British Columbia have "anti-scab" laws that forbid the use of replacement workers during a strike. In the 1980s the use of "scabs" at Canada Post and Gainers Meats created a great deal of anger among picketing workers. Employers have the right to dismiss workers who engage in sabotage or violence during a strike.

Once a strike has been settled, the workers are entitled to return to their jobs, though not necessarily their previous positions. The right to return to work is often an issue to be negotiated. Although laws vary, employees are often required to submit in writing their intention to return to their jobs once a strike is finalized.

Using the Lockout

Lockout

Strategy by which the employer denies employees the opportunity to work by closing its operations

A **lockout** involves the employer closing down its operations on its own initiative. It is rarely resorted to. Employees may lock out their workers to break a bargaining impasse, or to combat a union slowdown, or to end violence or property damage relating to a labour dispute.

Under Labour Relations Board provisions everywhere in Canada, an employer cannot begin a lockout within a set number of hours (between 48 and 72) before a strike vote. Lockouts affect nonstriking workers. For example, when miners at Inco are locked out, administrative work ceases and office personnel are locked out or laid off. The employer is often reluctant to resort to a lockout, because of the damage it can do to its image by denying work to its regular employees.

OBJECTIVE 3

Resolving Bargaining Deadlocks

When a strike or a lockout occurs, both parties are soon affected by it. The employer suffers a loss of profits and customers, and possibly of public good will. The union members suffer a loss of income that is likely to be only partially offset by strike benefits and outside income. The union's leaders run many risks: of losing members, being voted out of office, losing public support, and/or having the members vote to decertify. As the losses to each side mount, both sides face increasing pressure to reach a settlement.

Mediation and Arbitration

When the disputing parties cannot resolve a deadlock, a third party may be called in to help. In most jurisdictions some type of conciliation is compulsory before a legal strike or lockout. The conciliator, appointed by the provincial labour ministry, tries to help the two sides reach a workable agreement. If this effort doesn't succeed, a report is filed with the ministry, which may (albeit rarely) appoint a conciliation board that accepts presentations from both parties and makes nonbinding formal recommendations. If after all this a settlement still can't be reached, a strike is permitted. (In Manitoba, Alberta, Saskatchewan, and Quebec, strikes are permissible during conciliation.) This two-stage conciliation process is usually reserved for highly visible disputes in which a strike would have significant social and economic consequences.

Mediation is similar to conciliation, with two main differences: it is voluntary (the two parties contract a neutral third party to help them), and the mediator assumes a more active role in the negotiations. A **mediator** serves mainly as a fact finder and to open up channels of communication between the parties. Typically, the mediator meets with one party and then the other for the purpose of suggesting compromises or recommending concessions. Mediators have no authority to force either side toward an agreement. They must use their communication skills and the power of persuasion to help the parties resolve their differences in such a way that both save face.[20]

Arbitration is the only form of third-party resolution that results in binding recommendations. An **arbitrator** assumes the role of decision maker and determines what the settlement between the two parties should look like. In other words, the arbitrator writes a final contract that the two parties must accept. Arbitration is not often used to settle private sector bargaining disputes.

Interest arbitration is often used to resolve deadlocks in the essential service sectors of the public service. As noted earlier, strikes are prohibited in these sectors. Because one or both parties are generally reluctant to give a third party the power to make the settlement for them, a mediator typically is used to break the deadlock and to help the parties reach agreement. Once an agreement is concluded, an arbitrator may be called on to resolve disputes over how the agreement is being administered. This is called *rights arbitration* or *grievance arbitration*, which will be discussed shortly.

Mediator

Third party in a labour dispute who meets with one party and then the other in order to suggest compromise solutions or to recommend concessions

Arbitrator

Neutral third party who resolves a labour dispute by issuing a final decision in an agreement

Interest arbitration

Determination of a collective bargaining agreement by an arbitrator

TRENDS IN COLLECTIVE BARGAINING

Managers see the late 1990s and beyond as a period of great importance to labour–management relations. Innovative workplace practices, advances in technology, and continued competitive pressures are having their impact. The Conference Board of Canada's *Industrial Relations Outlook 2000* predicts that strategic alliances, cooperation, and partnering will be necessary because of increasing competitiveness and globalization. These conditions will affect the attitudes and objectives of both employers and unions in collective bargaining. They will also influence the climate in which bargaining occurs and the bargaining power each side is able to exercise.

Changes in Collective Bargaining Relationships

Traditionally, the collective bargaining relationship between employers and unions has been adversarial. Organized labour has held the view that though the employer is responsible for managing the organization, unions have the right to challenge certain actions of management. It also has taken the position that employers are obligated to operate their organizations in such a manner that the employees are adequately compensated. Moreover, organized labour maintains that union members should not be expected to subsidize poor management by accepting less than their full entitlement.

Fortunately, labour organizations are coming to recognize the danger of making demands that will create economic hardship for employers. However, this has not stopped them from bargaining for what they consider to be fair agreements for their members. While the goal of organized labour has always been to improve workers' economic and working conditions, large layoffs caused by economic downturns and domestic and global competition have resulted in both sides changing their goals and tactics. We are seeing a gradual movement away from direct conflict and toward labour–management accommodation.

Facilitating Union-Management Cooperation

WWW

Improving union–management cooperation generally requires a restructuring of attitudes by both managers and union officials and members. John Calhoun Wells, director of the Federal Mediation and Conciliation Service, notes: "This cooperative model emphasizes trust, common ground, sharing of information, joint problem solving, risk taking, and innovation."[21] Joint labour–management committees are concerned not only with ensuring that regulatory standards are met, but also with working together to bring about innovations in areas ranging from product development to customer service.[22]

WWW

The Federal Mediation and Conciliation Service is responsible for fostering positive relations between trade unions and employers in federal jurisdiction industries in Canada. The crisis of survival has forced unions, their members, and management to make concessions at the bargaining table and to collaborate in finding solutions that will ensure survival. If cooperation is to continue after the crisis has passed, however, it will have to rest on a solid foundation. For example, it has been noted that cooperation lasts only as long as both sides embrace a systems approach grounded in developmental activities.[23] Also, union–management cooperation programs have a greater chance for success when the two sides jointly establish goals and philosophies for mutual gain. Highlights in HRM 2 shows the jointly written statement of purpose and values of the collective agreement developed by Volkswagen Canada and the National Automobile, Aerospace and Agricultural Implement Workers Union of Canada.

When building a cooperative environment, it is especially important that union members believe that management is sincerely interested in their personal well-being.[24] Also, a review of meaningful labour–management cooperative endeavours strongly suggests that success depends on an open and honest style of communication. Furthermore, both supervisors and employees must be trained in participative approaches to problem resolution. At Algoma Steel in Sault Ste. Marie, Ontario, hundreds of workers and managers who attended problem-solving workshops applied their new skills and succeeded in reducing the number of outstanding grievances from 500 to 3.[25]

Highlights in HRM

2   SAMPLE OF A JOINTLY WRITTEN STATEMENT OF PURPOSE AND VALUES

COLLECTIVE AGREEMENT
BETWEEN:
VOLKSWAGEN CANADA INC
BARRIE, ONTARIO
(hereinafter called "the Company")
AND
NATIONAL AUTOMOBILE, AEROSPACE AND AGRICULTURAL
IMPLEMENT WORKERS UNION OF CANADA (CAW-CANADA)
AND ITS LOCAL 1991
(hereinafter referred to as "the Union")

PURPOSE AND VALUES OF AGREEMENT

It is the mutual desire of the parties hereto to foster a progressive, equal, just, proactive and harmonious relationship. These principles and goals are consistent with the corporation's mission of becoming the leading organization in Canada measured in terms of customer satisfaction.

The parties recognize that attainment of these goals, coupled with continuing mutual effort, open communication, safe and fair working conditions, should provide the highest degree of job security possible in a market driven economy. To help ensure success, the parties further recognize that:

The field of labour relations is an evolutionary process which can be improved as a result of mutual trust and respect, common purpose, and a positive workplace environment;

A co-operative workplace environment will help provide a strong foundation for achieving high operational efficiency and productivity, and higher product quality, together with employee satisfaction and job security;

By achieving these goals, the Company may enhance and improve its position in the global market, and be better able to continue to provide stable employment, equitable treatment, a congenial working environment, a safe workplace with fair compensation recognizing the employees' contribution to the overall success of the enterprise, and a social commitment to the community.

The culture of the plant will be based on co-operation, mutual trust and respect, and the recognition and preservation of the established values: putting people first; a belief in unparalleled customer care; the fostering of innovation; and a belief in providing real value in everything we do.

The Company and Union agree that if these endeavours are to be a success, labour and management must work together. To attain these goals, all employees share in the common endeavour with the following responsibilities:

- Support and abide by reasonable standards of conduct and attendance policies;
- Promote good housekeeping and maintain a safe work environment;
- Support and promote efficient work processes;
- Strive to achieve quality goals and endeavour to improve quality standards.

In order to develop and maintain flexibility of the workforce, while at the same time developing the ability and interest of the individual employee, the parties are committed to a continuous learning and development process for the employees. This process will include multi-job training, involvement in group decision-making processes to discuss better ways to produce products, and group efforts based on employees' active and voluntary participation and familiarization on matters such as quality, safety, increasing productivity, increasing work efficiency, and enhancement of the work environment. The parties have agreed to co-operate in the implementation of these activities and to encourage employee participation.

Source: Donald McQuirter, Manager of Human Resources, Volkswagen Canada Inc.

Definition and Forms of Cooperation

Labour–management programs can take any form of bargaining or joint discussions. However, the objective is always to improve the well-being of both parties. The purpose and structure of cooperative endeavours depend largely on the needs and goals of the parties. Area-wide labour–management committees are jointly sponsored organizations operating on a regional or industry basis. Their purpose is to identify common problems—job security and reduced profits, for two examples—and to make joint efforts to resolve them. Shop committees, department committees, and employee involvement groups are examples of union–management efforts at the operating level. The participatory management approach adopted by BPCO of Pont-Rouge, Quebec, has resulted in increased productivity and cost savings, as well as a climate in which "people ... try to find solutions to their problems together."[26]

Concessionary Bargaining

Economic adversity and competition motivate a concessionary bargaining stance by management. Concessions sought by managers have been fairly consistent across industries and are directed toward (1) limiting, freezing, or lowering compensation payments and (2) increasing productivity. To gain wage concessions, employers may offer gainsharing plans (see Chapter 10) that link compensation to productivity or sales. Profit sharing and stock ownership are other plans being offered to motivate employees and reward improvements in performance.

Restrictive work rules are especially troublesome to employers because in this age of technology, these rules are detrimental to productivity.[27] Unions may make concessions relating to reductions in job classifications and the loosening of restrictions on work tasks. In return for these, they will probably demand enhanced job security for their members.[28] Unions are also likely to demand provisions restricting the transfer of work, the outsourcing of work (subcontracting), and the closing of plants by employers.[29] Advance notice of shutdowns, and severance pay and transfer rights for displaced employees, will also be high on the "want lists" of

Replacing traditional labour, robotic welder arms work on the frame of an automobile.

union negotiators. For employees likely to be replaced by technology, unions will bargain for retraining and skills-upgrading programs.

A troubled financial condition may not always bring forth the desired concessions. While union leaders often recognize when an organization is in financial crisis, their willingness to make concessions typically depends on (1) a positive labour–management relationship and (2) management's credibility with them. Union officers, who tend to question the need for concessions, may consider management demands for concessions as mere opportunism.

THE COLLECTIVE AGREEMENT

After an agreement has been reached, it must be put in writing, ratified by the union membership, and signed by the representatives of both parties. The scope of the agreement (and the length of the written document) will vary with the size of the employer and the length of the bargaining relationship. Highlights in HRM 3 shows some of the major articles in a collective agreement; it also provides examples of some new and progressive contract clauses.[30] Two important items in any collective agreement pertain to the issue of management rights and to the forms of security afforded the union.

The Issue of Management Rights

Management rights have to do with conditions of employment over which management is able to exercise exclusive jurisdiction. Since almost every management right can be and has been challenged successfully by unions, the determination of these rights ultimately depends on the relative bargaining power of the two parties. Furthermore, to achieve union cooperation or concessions, employers have had to relinquish some of these time-honoured rights.

Highlights in HRM

3   ITEMS IN A COLLECTIVE AGREEMENT

TYPICAL CLAUSES WILL COVER

- Wages
- Vacations
- Holidays
- Work schedules
- Management rights
- Union security
- Transfers
- Discipline

- Grievance procedures
- No strike/no lockout clause
- Overtime
- Safety procedures
- Severance pay
- Seniority
- Pensions and benefits
- Outsourcing

PROGRESSIVE CLAUSES WILL COVER

- Employee access to records
- Limitations on use of performance evaluation
- Elder care leave
- Flexible medical spending accounts
- Protection against hazards of technology equipment (VDTs)
- Limitations against electronic monitoring
- Bilingual stipends
- Domestic partnership benefits

Residual Rights

Residual rights

Concept that management's authority is supreme in all matters except those it has expressly conceded to the union in the collective agreement

In the collective agreement, management rights are often treated as **residual rights** or as **defined rights**. The residual rights concept holds that "management's authority is supreme in all matters except those it has expressly conceded in the collective agreement, or in those areas where its authority is restricted by law. Put another way, management does not look to the collective agreement to ascertain its rights; it looks to the agreement to find out which and how much of its rights and powers it has conceded outright or agreed to share with the union."[31]

Residual rights typically include the right of management to determine the product it will produce and/or to select production equipment and procedures. Employers that subscribe to the residual rights concept prefer not to mention management rights in the collective agreement on the grounds that they already possess such rights. To mention them might create an issue with the union.

Defined Rights

Defined rights

Concept that management's authority should be expressly defined and clarified in the collective agreement

The defined rights concept is about reinforcing management's rights and clarifying what those are. This reduces confusion and misunderstandings and reminds union officers, union stewards, and employees that management never relinquishes its right to operate the organization. A defined right might include the right of management to take disciplinary action against problem employees. The great majority of collective agreements have provisions covering management rights. The following is an example of a general statement defining management rights in one collective agreement:

> It is agreed that the company possesses all of the rights, powers, privileges, and authority it had prior to the execution of this agreement; and nothing in this agreement shall be construed to limit the company in any way in the exercise of the regular and customary functions of management and the operation of its business, except as it may be specifically relinquished or modified herein by an express provision of this agreement.[32]

Forms of Union Security

When a labour organization is certified by a labour relations board as the exclusive bargaining representative for all employees in a bargaining unit, by law it must represent all employees in the unit, nonunion and union members alike. In exchange for this, union officials will seek to negotiate some form of compulsory membership as a condition of employment. Union officials argue that compulsory membership precludes the possibility that some employees will receive the benefits of unionization without paying their share of the costs. These employees are generally referred to as *free riders*. A standard union security provision is dues checkoff, which makes the employer responsible for withholding union dues from the paycheques of union members who agree to such a deduction.

Other common forms of union security found in collective agreements include the following:

1. The *closed shop*—employers will hire only union members.

2. The *union shop*—any employee not a union member upon employment must join the union within thirty days or be terminated.

3. The *agency shop*—union membership is voluntary; however, all bargaining unit members must pay union dues and fees.

4. The *maintenance-of-membership shop*—employees who voluntarily join a union must maintain membership for the life of the agreement; however, membership withdrawal is possible during a designated escape period.

5. The *open shop*—employees can join the union or not, and nonmembers do not pay union dues.

6. The *modified union shop*—new workers must join the union, and current union members must remain in the union; however, established employees who are nonunion are entitled to remain so.

Few issues in collective bargaining are more controversial than the negotiation of these agreements. Closed shop clauses are rare. They are also perhaps the most adversarial, because they require employers to recruit employees from a union hiring hall. The advantages and disadvantages of closed shop arrangements are the subject of Ethics in HRM.

Working in conjunction with the union shop clause are the various seniority provisions of the collective agreement. Unions prefer that many personnel decisions (promotions, job transfers, shift assignments, vacations) be based on seniority. This criterion limits the discretion of managers to make such decisions on the basis of merit.

ADMINISTRATION OF THE COLLECTIVE AGREEMENT

As mentioned earlier, negotiation of the collective agreement is usually the most publicized and critical aspect of labour relations. Strike deadlines, press conferences, and employee picketing help create this image. Nevertheless, as managers in

---

Ethics in HRM

UNION SECURITY CLAUSES

Early in the history of labour relations, a "yellow dog contract" was the employer's way of preventing employees from joining a union. The closed shop clause in collective agreements is the union's way of requiring employees to join a union. Closed shop clauses are found in 2 percent of agreements (excluding the construction industry), maintenance-of-membership clauses in 4 percent, union shop clauses in 23 percent, and modified union shop clauses in 21 percent. Unions argue that compulsory membership is necessary because unions provide an indivisible service (i.e., workers benefit from the agreements whether they pay for them or not). If these free riders could benefit without paying dues, the union's position would be weakened as other workers chose the same strategy. Also, the union has more control over members than nonmembers during situations such as strikes. Through the use of hiring halls, unions can control the labour supply and ensure that senior employees are not replaced by more junior ones, that laid-off workers are rehired, and that pro-union members are rehired.

Employers resist closed shop arrangements. Although hiring halls can be viewed as a free placement service, employers contend that the workers sent may not be the ones they would have chosen. Also, those workers who can't obtain union membership are prevented from working. In 1988 the owners of a crane rental company challenged the use of closed shops in Ontario. Their grandson was prevented from working for them because the collective agreement required union membership, and the only way to become a member was to take an apprenticeship course. The judge upheld the provision, pointing out that the grandson could work for another crane rental company that did not have this provision.

Is it unfair to restrict people's right to work by making them join unions? If workers have the right to join a union, should they also have the right not to join? Alternatively, is it fair that some employees can be free riders?

Source: A.W.J. Craig and N.A. Solomon, *The System of Industrial Relations in Canada*, 4th ed. (Scarborough, Ont.: Prentice-Hall Canada, 1993).

unionized organizations know, the bulk of labour relations activity is found in the day-to-day administration of the agreement. As Reality Check illustrates, no agreement could possibly anticipate all the forms that disputes can take. In addition, once the agreement is signed each side will naturally interpret ambiguous clauses to its own advantage. These differences are traditionally resolved through the grievance procedure.

Reality CHECK

COLLECTIVE BARGAINING AT ROGERS COMMUNICATIONS

WWW

"Crafting the collective agreement is a most exacting and most challenging process," says Carol Gibson, vice-president of human resources at Rogers Communications in Vancouver. "I have to manage the tension between what the company wants, what the employees want, and what the employees want as represented by their unions. These words then have to be interpreted by a third party—the arbitrator—who has a different kind of power than a judge. There is no recourse if the arbitrator does not understand the intent of the agreement."

The time frame for negotiating a collective agreement varies considerably. "The last one took eighteen months for a four-year agreement," Gibson recalls, "and before it was officially ratified, I had begun preparing for the next round by starting a file. The collective agreement is a living document, always subject to interpretation and potential for conflict and change. A clause can lie dormant for years, because we haven't had to apply it or we have only applied it in one way. Then business circumstances change or a new manager reads it in a different way and there is a desire to test its intent. The result is often a grievance. A number of grievances or difficulties in interpretation will lead us to renegotiate that clause in the next round."

This happened in the most recent round of negotiations. The communications industry is a stable industry, where the average length of employment is sixteen years and the average age is forty-five. But Rogers was dealing with the International Brotherhood of Electrical Workers (IBEW), a union that has traditionally supplied electricians to the construction industry, which is notably unstable. As a result of the instability, all construction companies used union hiring halls to recruit employees. These halls would send two to three employees for a job, selected on the basis of who you know. Gibson felt this had to change.

"We wanted to select on specific criteria, on qualifications such as skills and abilities, because we are a high-tech industry. But this is a big issue for unions, because they get a lot of power from their hiring halls. Employees also liked the union hiring halls, because their children or relatives could get hired. They saw it as security for their children. In addition, employees have a strong commitment to the union, which was responsible for getting them their jobs. The hiring hall was an emotional issue. We wanted to not use the hiring halls, and the union resisted. In the end, we locked them out for nine months and forced them to negotiate."

Negotiated Grievance Procedures

Grievance procedure

Formal procedure that provides for the union to represent members and nonmembers in processing a grievance

The **grievance procedure** typically provides for the union to represent the interests of its members (and nonmembers as well) in processing a grievance. It is considered by some authorities to be the heart of the bargaining agreement—the safety valve that gives flexibility to the entire system of collective bargaining.[33] When negotiating a grievance procedure, one important concern for both sides is how effectively the system will serve the needs of employees and management. A well-written grievance procedure allows grievances to be processed expeditiously and with as little red tape as possible. It also fosters cooperation, not conflict, between the employer and the union.

Grievance procedures are negotiated to address the organization's structure and labour–management philosophy and the specific desires of the parties. Thus, no two systems are the same. That being said, there are plenty of common elements among systems. For example, grievance procedures usually specify how the grievance is to be initiated, the number and timing of steps in the procedure, and the identity of representatives from each side who are to be involved in the hearings at each step (see Figure 15.5). When a grievance cannot be resolved at one of the

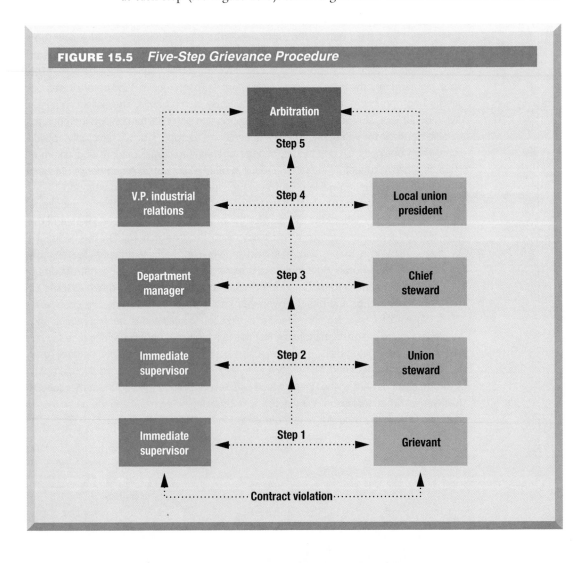

FIGURE 15.5 *Five-Step Grievance Procedure*

Arbitration — Step 5

V.P. industrial relations — Step 4 — Local union president

Department manager — Step 3 — Chief steward

Immediate supervisor — Step 2 — Union steward

Immediate supervisor — Step 1 — Grievant

Contract violation

specified steps, most agreements provide for the grievance to be submitted to a third party—usually an arbitrator—whose decision is final. It is not the function of an arbitrator to help the two parties reach a compromise solution. Rather, it is the arbitrator's job to mandate how the grievance will be resolved.

Initiating the Formal Grievance

For an employee's grievance to be considered formally, it must be expressed orally and/or in writing—ideally to the employee's immediate supervisor. If the employee feels unable to communicate effectively with the supervisor, the grievance can be taken to the union steward, who will discuss it with the supervisor. Since grievances are often the result of an oversight or a misunderstanding, many of them can be resolved at this point. Whether the grievance will be resolved at the initial step will depend on the supervisor's ability and willingness to discuss the problem with the employee and the steward. Supervisors should be given formal training in resolving grievances. This training should familiarize them with the terms of the collective agreement and help them develop problem-solving skills.

In some situations, a satisfactory solution may not be possible at the first step because there are legitimate differences of opinion between the employee and the supervisor, or because the supervisor does not have the authority to take the action required to satisfy the grievant.[34] Personality conflicts, prejudices, stubbornness, too much emotion, and other factors can also prevent a satisfactory solution at this step.

Preparing the Grievance Statement

Most collective agreements require that grievances carried beyond the initial step be stated in writing. A written statement reduces the likelihood that different versions of the grievance will arise because of lapses in memory.[35] It also forces the employee to think more objectively about the grievance. Grievances that stem from trivial complaints or feelings of hostility are less likely to be pursued beyond the first step if they are put in writing.

Grievance Resolution

Grievance resolution

Process where a neutral third party assists in the resolution of an employee grievance

For a grievance to be resolved successfully, representatives of both management and the union must be able to discuss the problem in a rational and objective manner. A grievance should not be approached as something to be won or lost. Rather, both sides must view the situation as an attempt to solve a human relations problem. If the conflict cannot be resolved, all collective agreements in Canadian jurisdictions contain a provision for arbitration, or **grievance resolution**. Only about 2 percent of grievances reach the arbitration stage.[36] An arbitrator or an arbitration board or panel (consisting of a union nominee, a management nominee, and a neutral chair) hears the case and submits a decision, including the rationale. The decision is final, and the parties are legally bound to accept the decision unless there is a serious concern over the arbitrator's competence or integrity.

Expedited arbitration

An agreement to bypass some steps in the grievance process

One criticism of the arbitration process is that it is slow (up to one year) and costly. One solution is **expedited arbitration**, which is an agreement to bypass some steps in the grievance process when the issue is especially important or urgent, as in the case of employee dismissals. The United Steelworkers of America and the International Nickel Company of Canada use expedited arbitration in their Sudbury and Port Colborne operations.

WWW

Grievance Arbitration

The point of **grievance arbitration** is to resolve a grievance that the union and the employer have been unable to resolve by themselves. As mentioned earlier, arbitration is performed by a neutral third party (an arbitrator or impartial umpire). This third party's decision dictates how the grievance is to be settled. Both parties are required to comply with the decision.[37] Even when one of the parties believes the arbitrator's award is unfair, unwise, or inconsistent with the collective agreement, that party may have no alternative but to comply with the decision.

Sources of Arbitrators

The arbitrator must be acceptable to both disputing parties. An arbitrator who is retained on a permanent basis to resolve all grievances arising under an agreement has the advantage of being familiar with the agreement and the labour–management relationship. Most grievances, however, are resolved by arbitrators appointed on an ad hoc basis. If both parties are satisfied with an arbitrator's performance, that person may be called on to resolve subsequent grievances.[38]

Many collective agreements include a list of mutually acceptable arbitrators. In the absence of such a list, the Federal Mediation Conciliation Service or the provincial labour relations board can provide one. If the two parties cannot agree on an arbitrator, the labour relations board may appoint one. Typically, arbitrators are professionals such as professors, lawyers, or retired government labour arbitrators. Because of their professional backgrounds, they tend to be identified with neither labour nor management and are therefore perceived as neutral.

The Decision to Arbitrate

In deciding whether to use arbitration, each party must weigh the costs involved against the importance of the case and the prospects of gaining a favourable award. Logic dictates that neither party will allow a case to go to arbitration if there is little possibility of gaining a favourable award. But there may be other reasons to advance a grievance. For example, it is not unusual for a union to take a weak case to arbitration in order to demonstrate to the members that the union is willing to exhaust every remedy in looking out for their interests. Also, union officers are not likely to refuse to take to arbitration the grievances of members who are popular or politically powerful in the union, even when their cases are weak. Moreover, unions have a legal obligation to provide assistance to members who are pursuing grievances. Because members can bring suit against their unions for failing to process their grievances adequately, many union officers are reluctant to refuse taking even weak grievances to arbitration.

In the same vein, management may allow a weak case to go to arbitration to demonstrate to the union officers that management "cannot be pushed around." Also, middle managers may be reluctant to risk the displeasure of senior managers by stating that a certain HR policy is unworkable or unsound. Stubbornness and mutual antagonism have forced many grievances into arbitration; sometimes one party is unwilling to make concessions, even when it knows it is in the wrong.

The Arbitration Process

The issues to be resolved through arbitration are sometimes described in a formal statement known as a **submission to arbitrate**. The two parties make a joint submission to the arbitrator indicating the rationale for the grievance. The submission to arbitrate must state the nature of the dispute with reference to the section of the collective agreement that allegedly has been breached. The statement might read: "Was the three-day suspension of Alex Hayden for just cause? If not, what is the appropriate remedy?" Grievable issues can also be presented orally to the arbitrator by the two parties at the beginning of the hearing. If minutes and memoranda covering the meetings held at earlier stages of the grievance procedure have been prepared, these are sometimes submitted prior to the formal hearing, to acquaint the arbitrator with the issues.

It is the responsibility of the arbitrator to ensure that each side receives a fair hearing and has the opportunity to present all of the facts it considers pertinent. The procedures for conducting arbitration hearings, and the restrictions as to what evidence can be introduced, are more flexible than in a court of law. For example, hearsay evidence can be introduced, as long as it is considered as such when evaluated with the other evidence presented. The main purpose of the hearing is to help the arbitrator obtain the facts necessary to resolve the problem, which is approached as a human relations problem rather than a legal one. To this end, the arbitrator has the right to question witnesses and to request additional facts from either party.

Depending on the importance of the case, the hearings can be informal or highly formal—almost as formal as in a court trial. If one of the parties wishes it, or if both do, or if the arbitrator does, a court reporter may be present during the hearing to prepare a transcript. After conducting the hearing and receiving post-hearing briefs (should the parties choose to submit them), the arbitrator usually has thirty days to consider the evidence and prepare a decision. However, extensions beyond this period are not uncommon. In most labour contracts, the parties split the arbitration costs.

The Arbitration Award

The **arbitration award** should include not only the arbitrator's decision but also the reasons for it. The reasons for the decision often provide guidance for interpreting the collective agreement and for resolving any future disputes. They can also lessen the disappointment of the unsuccessful party, and protect the self-esteem of those who represented that individual. In short, tact and objective reasoning can do much to reduce disappointment and hard feelings. The foundation for an arbitrator's decision is the collective agreement and the rights it establishes for each party.

In many grievances, such as those involving employee performance or behaviour on the job, the arbitrator must determine whether the evidence supports the employer's action against the grievant. The evidence must also show that the employee was accorded the right of due process (i.e., the employee's right to be informed of unsatisfactory performance and to respond to accusations of it). Under most collective agreements the employer must have just cause (i.e., a good reason) for the actions it takes, and those actions must be supported by the evidence presented.

If the arbitrator concludes that the employee was accorded due process and that disciplinary action was for just cause, the severity of the penalty will then be assessed. When the evidence supports the discipline imposed by the employer, the arbitrator will probably let the discipline stand intact. However, it is within the arbitrator's power to reduce the penalty, unless that power is denied by the submission agreement. For example, it is not uncommon for the arbitrator to reduce

Arbitration award

Final and binding award issued by an arbitrator in a labour–management dispute

a discharge to a suspension without pay for the period the grievant has been off the payroll.

It is important to note that arbitration awards do not establish precedents for future cases. In practice, however, past arbitration awards have some influence on the decision of the arbitrator, who may seek guidance from decisions of other arbitrators in somewhat similar cases. Therefore, when preparing arbitration cases, managers may choose to review decisions compiled and published by the labour relations boards in each province and by the Canadian Industrial Relations Board (CIRB) at **www.cirb-ccri.gc.ca/eng/headnotes.html**.

WWW

How Arbitrators Decide Cases

Because of the importance of arbitration to resolving grievances, the process by which arbitrators make decisions and the factors that influence those decisions are of continuing interest to managers. Typically, arbitrators consider four factors when deciding cases:

1. The wording of the collective agreement (or employment policy, in nonunionized organizations).

2. The submission agreement as presented to the arbitrator.

3. Testimony and evidence offered during the hearing.

4. The arbitration criteria or standards (i.e., similar to standards of common law) against which cases are judged.

For example, when deciding the case of an employee discharged for absenteeism, the arbitrator would consider these factors separately and/or jointly. Arbitrators are constrained to decide cases on the basis of the wording of the collective agreement and the facts, testimony, and evidence presented at the hearing.

Since most arbitrated grievances are about discipline or dismissal, it is worth trying to understand what makes arbitrators overturn managers in these cases. In one study, five reasons accounted for over 70 percent of all reversal cases:

- The evidence did not support the charge of wrongdoing.
- The evidence supported the charge, but there were mitigating circumstances.
- Management committed procedural errors that prejudiced the grievant's rights.
- The rule was fair, but punishment for its infraction was harsh.
- Management was partly at fault.[39]

Arbitration is not an exact science; in fact, the decisions of arbitrators can be rather subjective. Arbitrators can and do interpret contract language differently (e.g., What does "just cause dismissal" actually mean?); they assign varying degrees of importance to testimony and evidence; they judge the truthfulness of witnesses differently; and they give arbitration standards greater or lesser weight as they apply to facts of the case. These things all inject subjectivity into the decision-making process.

SUMMARY

 Negotiating a collective agreement is a detailed process. Each side prepares a list of proposals and tries to anticipate those of the other side. Bargaining teams are selected, and all proposals are analyzed to determine their impact on and cost to the organization. Negotiators on both sides must be sensitive to current bargaining patterns in the industry, general cost-of-living trends, and geographical wage differentials. Managers seek to retain control over operations and to minimize costs. Union negotiators focus their demands on improved wages, hours, and working conditions. An agreement is reached when both sides compromise their original positions and final terms fall within the limits of the parties' bargaining zone.

 The collective bargaining process includes not only the actual negotiations but also the power tactics used to support negotiating demands. When negotiations become deadlocked, bargaining becomes a power struggle to force concessions needed to break the deadlock. The union's power in collective bargaining comes from its ability to picket, strike, or boycott the employer. The employer's power during negotiations comes from its ability to lock out employees or to continue to operate during a strike using managerial or replacement employees.

 Mediation is the principal means of resolving negotiating deadlocks. Mediators seek to assist the negotiators by opening up lines of communication between the parties and by offering suggestions to resolve deadlocked proposals. In some situations, interest arbitration is employed to finalize the collective agreement. Interest arbitration is rarely used in the private sector; however, it is used often in the public sector, where unions are largely prohibited from striking.

 In the 1990s, several trends have arisen in labour relations. These include attempts to instil more cooperation in labour–management endeavours and to bargain in less adversarial ways. Management has used concessionary bargaining to minimize or reduce labour costs and to improve workplace productivity. When employers have sought concessions, unions have stressed employee retraining and job security.

 The typical collective agreement contains many provisions governing the relationship between labour and management. The major areas of interest concern wages (rates of pay, overtime differentials, holiday pay), hours (shift times, days of work), and working conditions (safety issues, performance standards, retraining). To managers the issue of management rights is especially important. In their view, management's authority is supreme for all issues except those shared with the union through the collective agreement.

 Differences between labour and management are usually resolved through the grievance procedure. Grievance procedures are negotiated and thus reflect the needs and wishes of both parties. The typical grievance procedure consists of three, four, or five steps, with each step having specific filing and reply times. Higher-level managers and union officials become involved in disputes at the higher steps of the grievance procedure. The final step of the grievance procedure may be arbitration. Arbitrators render final decisions to problems not resolved at lower grievance steps.

 A submission to arbitrate is a statement of the issue to be resolved through arbitration. It is simply the problem the parties wish to have settled. The arbitrator must base the arbitration award on four factors: the contents of the collective agreement, the submission agreement as written, testimony and evidence obtained at the hearing, and various arbitration standards developed over time to help resolve different types of labour–management disputes. Arbitration is not an exact science, since arbitrators will give varying degrees of importance to the evidence and criteria by which disputes are resolved.

KEY TERMS

arbitration award
arbitrator
bargaining zone
boycott
collective bargaining process
defined rights

expedited arbitration
lockout
mediator
grievance arbitration
grievance procedure
grievance resolution

interest arbitration
nonadversarial bargaining (IBB)
pattern bargaining
residual rights
submission to arbitrate
surface bargaining

DISCUSSION QUESTIONS

 1. Of what significance is the bargaining zone when negotiations are being conducted? What are some influences affecting negotiated outcomes?

 2. Why might an employer be willing to face a strike that could result in a loss of customers and profits?

 3. How does mediation differ from arbitration? In what situations is each of these processes most likely to be used?

 4. What are some of the bargaining concessions generally sought by employers and unions in return for the concessions they may grant?

 5. At an election conducted among the twenty employees of the Exclusive Jewellery Store, all but two voted in favour of the Jewellery Workers Union, which subsequently was certified as their bargaining agent. In negotiating its first agreement, the union demanded that it be granted a union shop. The two employees who had voted against the union then informed the management that they would quit rather than join. Unfortunately for the store, the two employees were the store's most valu-

able—skilled gem cutters who would be difficult to replace. What position should the store take with regard to the demand for a union shop?

 6. Why might a union or an employer allow a weak grievance to go to arbitration?

 7. The dismissal of an employee for poor work performance is scheduled for an arbitration hearing. What arguments is each side likely to put forward to support its case?

8. A group of students wants a Burger King fast food franchise on their university campus. University administrators want a healthy food place on campus. Resources allow for only one food outlet. Divide the class into bargaining teams, with one team representing the students, and the other team representing the university administrators. (If there is another issue at your campus, use the real and current issue instead). After the groups have started bargaining, consult the Career Counsel website to assess the negotiating styles employed by each team.

CASE 1

TUNED IN OR TURNED OFF?

For nine years, the use of personal radios while working was an accepted practice at Vision-Trax Industries. Then Vision-Trax moved to a new location where an open-space design permitted close employee contact. Unfortunately, the new design also created more noise. So the employees were told that all personal radios and cassettes, even those with earphones, would no longer be permitted. On behalf of her employees, the union steward filed a grievance that resulted in arbitration.

At the hearing, the union argued these points:

- Employees' use of personal radios and cassette players is a right granted by the contract. The agreement specifically states that any right not mentioned in the contract, but in existence prior to the contract, is to remain in effect.
- The use of earphones eliminates the noise concerns of managers and other employees.
- There has been no loss of productivity relating to the use of radios and cassette players.

During its presentation at the arbitration hearing, the company made these arguments:

- The rule prohibiting use of radios is consistent with management's right to run the organization in an efficient and effective manner.
- Employees had been warned that excessive noise could result in radios and cassette recorders being banned. When noise levels were not reduced, the new rule was put in effect.
- Excessive radio noise can cause safety problems, including personal arguments between employees.
- The wearing of earphones presents an unprofessional appearance to visitors and customers.

Source: Adapted from "Tuned-in Employees," *Supervisory Management* 40, no. 4 (April 1995): 6.

Questions

1. Which arguments should receive more weight—those based on the contract or those alleging other concerns? Or should both types of arguments be given equal weight? Explain.

2. How important is the company's argument that radios present an unprofessional appearance? Explain.

3. If you were the arbitrator, how would you rule in this case? Explain.

CASE 2

DON'T I DESERVE A SECOND CHANCE?

At the arbitration hearing, both parties were adamant. Nancy McCormick, manager for All-Freight Storage, argued that the grievant, Tom Benedict, had been justly terminated for knowingly and willingly falsifying his employment application—a direct violation of company policy and the employee handbook. In his defence, Benedict argued that he had been a good employee during his seven years of employment. Furthermore, at the time of his hiring, he was in desperate need of a job to support himself and his family.

The submission agreement governing the case read, "It is the employer's position that just cause existed for the discharge of Mr. Tom Benedict and the penalty was appropriate for the offense committed." Additionally, the employer introduced into evidence the company handbook, which defined just cause termination as follows:

"Just cause shall serve as the basis for disciplinary action and includes, but is not limited to: dishonesty, inefficiency, unprofessional conduct, failure to report absences, falsification of records, violation of company policy, destruction of property, or possession or being under the influence of alcohol or narcotics."

Benedict was hired as inventory control clerk on November 7, 1992, a position he held until he was terminated on October 25, 1999. According to McCormick's testimony, the position of inventory control clerk required a high degree of honesty and integrity. Benedict's performance evaluations showed him to be an average employee, although he had received several disciplinary warnings for poor attendance and one three-day suspension for an "inventory control error."

Benedict's termination related to the concealment of his criminal record. When filling out his employment application in 1992, he had checked "no" in a box on the form asking whether he had ever been convicted of a felony or misdemeanor, other than minor violations. On the application was a statement that applicants were required to sign. It stated: "I understand the truth of my answers is a condition of employment, and that any misrepresentation or omission of facts on this application may cause dismissal." Benedict signed and dated the application October 22, 1992.

In September 1999, All-Freight Storage learned through a recently hired security guard that before Benedict was hired in 1992, he had served seven years in the federal prison system for four separate felony convictions for grand theft. He had been released from prison six months before being hired by All-Freight Storage. The security guard had once worked as a guard for the Correctional Service of Canada.

At arbitration, Benedict readily admitted that he had falsified his employment application. His reason was his desperate need for employment and the likelihood that the company would not have hired him had he revealed his criminal record. Since his release from prison he'd had no further felony or misdemeanor convictions. Interestingly, in some jurisdictions—including the one in which Benedict was working—the law allows criminal records to be sealed a certain number of years after incarceration or completion of probation. Benedict failed to apply for this benefit.

Source: Adapted from an arbitration heard by Dr. Marcus Miller, December 1999. All names are fictitious.

Questions

1. Which arguments should be given more weight: those based on company policy, the employee handbook, and the application form, or the mitigating arguments offered by the grievant? Explain.

2. How important is it that Benedict's felony conviction bear a relationship to the position of inventory control clerk? Explain.

3. If you were the arbitrator, how would you rule in this situation? Explain in full.

CAREER COUNSEL

Visit the Managing Human Resources website (**belcourt.nelson.com**) to learn about six common negotiating strategies and how they can be used in salary negotiations.

USING THE INTERNET

WWW

Information about the Federal Mediation and Conciliation Service can be found at **www.labour.hrdc-drhc.gc.ca/doc/fmcs-sfmc/eng/about.cfm**. This site also provides links to provincial labour relations contacts.

Arbitration decisions can be found at **www.quicklaw.com/en/home.html**.

Software is available to examine the impact of management and union proposals before, during, and after collective bargaining. Samples can be found at **www.bargaining power.com**.

The Canadian Industrial Relations Board (**www.cirb-ccri/gc.ca/eng/main.html**) is an independent, representational, quasi-judicial tribunal responsible for interpreting and administering parts of the Canada Labour Code.

Two centres in Canada conduct tracking research on union–management relations. Visit their websites: Queen's University Industrial Relations Centre (**qsilver.queensu.ca/irl**) and the Centre for Labour-Management Studies (**clams.ubc.ca/collective**).

NOTES AND REFERENCES

1. John A. Fossum, *Labor Relations: Development, Structure, Process*, 6th ed. (Homewood, Ill.: BPI-Irwin, 1995): 278.
2. Daniel Q. Mills, *Labor–Management Relations*, 5th ed. (New York: McGraw-Hill, 1994).
3. John W. Budd, "The Internal Union Political Imperative for UAW Pattern Bargaining," *Journal of Labor Research* 16, no. 1 (Winter 1995): 43–53.
4. For the original description of attitudinal structuring, see Richard E. Walton and Robert B. McKersie, *A Behavioral Theory of Labor Negotiations* (New York: McGraw-Hill, 1965). This book is considered a classic in the labour relations field.
5. James G. Baker, "Negotiating a Collective Bargaining Agreement: Law and Strategy—A Short Course for Non-Labor Lawyers," *Labor Law Journal* 47, no. 4 (April 1996): 253–67.
6. J. Godard, *Industrial Relations: The Economy and Society* (Toronto: McGraw-Hill Ryerson, 1994).
7. Employers who refuse to pay union demands are not legally required to provide financial data to union repre-

sentatives. The requirement to provide financial data would normally arise where an employer asserts during negotiations that it cannot survive if it agrees to union wage proposals or that it has no operating profit.

8. Ross Stagner and Hjalmar Rosen, *Psychology of Union–Management Relations* (Belmont, Calif.: Wadsworth, 1965): 95–7. This is another classic in the field of labour–management relations.

9. Conversation with Joe Stanley, July 23, 1999, Phoenix, Arizona.

10. George W. Bohlander and Jim Naber, "Non-adversarial Negotiations: The FMCS Interest-Based Bargaining Program," *Journal of Collective Negotiations in the Public Sector,* 28, no. 1, 1999.

11. *Interest-Based Negotiations: Participants' Guidebook* (Washington, D.C.: Federal Mediation and Conciliation Service, 1998).

12. Victor G. Devinatz, "What Do We Know about Mutual Gains Bargaining among Educators?" *Journal of Collective Bargaining in the Public Sector* 27, no. 2 (1998): 79–91.

13. "Strike Costs," *The Globe and Mail*, November 26, 1997: B18.

14. John W. Budd, "Canadian Strike Replacement Legislation and Collective Bargaining Lessons for the United States," *Industrial Relations* 35, no. 2 (April 1996): 245–60.

15. "Strikes Fall to 50-Year Low as Job Insecurities Increase," *New York Times National*, January 29, 1996: A1.

16. Brenda Paik Sunoo and Jennifer J. Laabs, "Winning Strategies for Outsourcing Contracts," *Personnel Journal* 13, no. 3 (March 1994): 69.

17. "Chronological Perspective on Work Stoppages in Canada," *Workplace Information Directorate*, Labour Branch, Human Resources Development Canada, 2000.

18. M. MacKinnon, "Canada Leads G7 in Time Lost to Strikes," *The Globe and Mail*, April 5, 1999: B1.

19. Margot Hornblower, "Picking a New Fight," *Time*, November 25, 1996: 64–5.

20. Deborah M. Kolb, *When Talk Works: Profiles of Mediators* (San Francisco: Jossey-Bass, 1994). See also Sam Kagel and Kathy Kelly, *The Anatomy of Mediation: What Makes It Work* (Washington, D.C.: Bureau of National Affairs, 1989).

21. John Calhoun Wells, "Conflictive Partnership: A Strategy for Real World Labor–Management Cooperation," *Labor Law Journal* 47, no. 8 (August 1996): 484–92; Owen E. Herrnstadt, "Labor–Management Cooperation: Is Management Ready?" *Labor Law Journal* 46, no. 10 (October 1995): 636–8.

22. *Workplace Innovations Overview 1994*, Bureau of Labour Information, Human Resources Development Canada, 1994.

23. ill Kriesky and Edwin Brown, "The Union Role in Labor–Management Cooperation: A Case Study at the Boise Cascade Company's Jackson Mill," *Labor Studies Journal* 18, no. 3 (Fall 1993): 17–32.

24. Tom Juravich, "Empirical Research on Employee Involvement: A Critical Review for Labor," *Labor Studies Journal* 21, no. 2 (Summer 1996): 52–66; Douglas M. McCabe, "Labor–Management Cooperation: A Business Ethics and Business–Government Relations Perspective," *Labor Law Journal* 47, no. 8 (August 1996): 467–78.

25. V. Galt, "Algoma Reinvents Labour Relations," *The Globe and Mail*, April 21, 1995: B1.

26. Ruth Chamberlain, "Innovative Workplace Practices: Case Studies, BPCO Participatory Management Approach," *Collective Bargaining Review*, Workplace Information Directorate, Labour Branch, Human Resources Development Canada, June 1997: 93–8.

27. "GM, UAW Battle over Staffing Levels As Auto Maker Faces Pressure to Trim," *Wall Street Journal*, August 5, 1996: A3.

28. Peter Nulty, "Look What the Unions Want Now," *Fortune*, February 1993, 128–35.

29. William Symonds and Kathleen Kerwin, "So Much for Hardball," *Business Week*, November 4, 1996: 48; Angelo B. Henderson, "Chrysler Finds Peaceful Way to Labor Pact," *Wall Street Journal*, March 25, 1996: A10.

30. Joan E. Pynes, "The Two Faces of Unions," *Journal of Collective Negotiations in the Public Sector* 25, no. 1 (Spring 1996): 31–43.

31. For an expanded discussion of management's residual rights, termed "reserved rights" in the United States, see Paul Prasow and Edward Peters, *Arbitration and Collective Bargaining*, 2nd ed. (New York: McGraw-Hill, 1983): 33–4. This book is considered an authority on management rights issues.

32. Labor agreement, Wabash Fibre Box Company and Paperworkers.

33. *Grievance Guide*, 9th ed. (Washington, D.C.: BNA Books, 1995). See also Frank Elkouri and Edna Asher Elkouri, *How Arbitration Works*, 4th ed. (Washington, D.C.: Bureau of National Affairs, 1985), 153. This book continues to be a leading reference on the topic of arbitration and the resolution of grievances.

34. David Meyer, "The Political Effects of Grievance Handling by Stewards in a Local Union," *Journal of Labor Research* 15, no. 1 (Winter 1994): 33.

35. Michael J. Duane, "To Grieve or Not to Grieve: Why Reduce It to Writing?" *Public Personnel Management* 20, no. 1 (Spring 1991): 83–8.

36. J. Gandz and J.D. Whitehead, "Grievances and Their Resolution," in M. Gunderson et al., eds., *Union Management Relations in Canada*, 2nd ed. (Don Mills, Ont.: Addison-Wesley, 1989).

37. Fred Witney and Benjamin J. Taylor, *Labor Relations Law*, 7th ed. (Englewood Cliffs, N.J.: Prentice-Hall, 1995), 44. Arbitration awards are not final in all cases. They may be overturned through the judicial process if it can be shown

that the arbitrator was prejudiced or failed to render an award based on the essence of the agreement.

38. Some labour agreements call for the use of arbitration boards to resolve employee grievances. Arbitration boards, which can be temporary or permanent, are composed of one or more members chosen by management and an equal number chosen by labour. A neutral member serves as chair. See Peter A. Veglahn, "Grievance Arbitration by Arbitration Boards: A Survey of the Parties," *Arbitration Journal* 42, no. 2 (July 1987): 47–53.

39. Donna Blancero and George W. Bohlander, "Minimizing Arbitrator Reversals in Discipline and Discharge Cases," *Labor Law Journal* 46, no. 10 (October 1995): 616–21. See also George W. Bohlander and Donna Blancero, "A Study of Reversal Determinants in Discipline and Discharge Arbitration Awards: The Impact of Just Cause Standards," *Labor Studies Journal* 21, no. 3 (Fall 1996): 3–18.

INTERNATIONAL HUMAN RESOURCES MANAGEMENT

After studying this chapter, you should be able to

OBJECTIVE 1

Identify the types of organizational forms used for competing internationally.

OBJECTIVE 2

Explain how domestic and international HRM differ.

OBJECTIVE 3

Discuss the staffing process for individuals working internationally.

OBJECTIVE 4

Identify the unique training needs for international assignees.

OBJECTIVE 5

Reconcile the difficulties of home country and host country performance appraisals.

OBJECTIVE 6

Identify the characteristics of a good international compensation plan.

OBJECTIVE 7

Explain the major differences between Canadian and European labour relations.

I n the first chapter of this textbook we said that one of the chief forces driving HRM today was the globalization of business. According to the Ottawa-based Export Development Corporation (EDC), exports now account for 43 percent of GDP in Canada—up from 27 percent in 1986—and the amount of capital Canadian companies have invested internationally has grown by 75 percent in the past decade. While estimates vary, approximately 70 to 85 percent of the Canadian economy today is affected by international competition. And as we move rapidly toward a more global economy, many organizations are reassessing their approaches to human resource management. To a large degree, the challenge of managing across borders boils down to the philosophies and systems we use to manage people.[1]

The importance of globalization notwithstanding, we have—for the most part—emphasized HRM practices and systems as they exist in Canada. This is not so much an oversight on our part as it is a deliberate pedagogical choice. The topic of international HRM is so important that we wanted to dedicate an entire chapter to it. Our thinking is that now that you have read (and hopefully discussed) some of the best practices for managing people at work, it may be time for you to see how some of these HRM systems change when you begin to manage people in the international arena. Much of what has been discussed throughout this text can be applied to international operations, provided you are sensitive to the requirements of the particular international setting.

We start with a brief introduction to international business firms. In many important respects, how a company organizes its international operations will affect the managerial and human resources issues it faces. We then briefly describe some of the environmental factors that also affect the work managers do in a global setting. Just as with domestic operations, the dimensions of the environment have a strong influence on how HRM decisions are made. A large part of this chapter deals with the various HR activities involved in recruiting, selecting, developing, and compensating employees who work in international settings.

MANAGING ACROSS BORDERS

International Corporation

Domestic firm that uses its existing capabilities to move into overseas markets

Multinational corporation (MNC)

Firm with independent business units operating in multiple countries

International businesses can take several different forms. A large percentage carry on with only limited facilities and representation in foreign countries. Others, especially *Fortune 500* corporations, have extensive facilities and personnel in various countries of the world. Managing these resources effectively, and integrating their activities to achieve global advantage, is a challenge to the leaders of these companies.

Figure 16.1 shows four basic types of organizations and how they differ in the degree to which their international activities are *separated* to respond to the local regions and *integrated* to achieve global efficiencies. The **international corporation** is essentially a domestic firm that builds on its existing capabilities to penetrate overseas markets. Companies such as Honda, General Electric, and Procter & Gamble used this approach to gain access to Europe; essentially, they have adapted existing products for overseas markets without changing much else about their normal operations.[2]

A **multinational corporation (MNC)** is a more complex form and usually has fully autonomous units operating in multiple countries. Shell, Phillips, and ITT are three typical MNCs. These companies have traditionally given their foreign

FIGURE 16.1   *Types of Organizations*

	Low LOCAL RESPONSIVENESS High	
High	**GLOBAL** Views the world as a single market; operations are controlled centrally from the corporate office.	**TRANSNATIONAL** Specialized facilities permit local responsiveness; complex coordination mechanisms provide global integration.
Low	**INTERNATIONAL** Uses existing capabilities to expand into foreign markets.	**MULTINATIONAL** Several subsidiaries operating as stand-alone business units in multiple countries.

GLOBAL EFFICIENCY (High / Low, vertical axis)

Global corporation

Firm that has integrated worldwide operations through a centralized home office

Transnational corporation

Firm that attempts to balance local responsiveness and global scale via a network of specialized operating units.

WWW

subsidiaries a great deal of latitude to address local issues such as consumer preferences, political pressures, and economic trends in different regions of the world. Often these subsidiaries are run as independent companies, without much integration. The **global corporation**, on the other hand, can be viewed as a multinational firm that maintains control of operations back in the home office. Japanese companies such as Matsushita and NEC tend to treat the world market as a unified whole, and try to combine activities in each country to maximize efficiency on a global scale. These companies operate much like domestic firms, except that they view the entire world as their marketplace.

Finally, a **transnational corporation** attempts to achieve the local responsiveness of an MNC while also achieving the efficiencies of a global firm. To balance this "global/local" dilemma, a transnational uses a network structure that coordinates specialized facilities positioned around the world. Under this flexible structure, a transnational provides autonomy to independent country operations but brings these separate activities together into an integrated whole. For most companies, the transnational form represents an ideal rather than a reality.[3] Thomson Corp, with US$4.5 billion in foreign sales, has been rated by the United Nations as the most transnational firm on the planet. Also listed are Montreal's Seagram Corporation (13) and Alcan Aluminum (15).[4]

Although various forms of organization exist, in this chapter we will generally refer to any company that conducts business outside its home country as an international business. Canada, of course, has no monopoly on international business. International enterprises are found throughout the world. In fact, some European and Pacific Rim companies have been conducting business on an international basis much longer than their Canadian counterparts. The close proximity of European countries, for example, makes them likely candidates for international trade. Figure 16.2 shows the headquarters locations of the top fifty corporations in the world.[5]

These companies are in a strong position to affect the world economy in the following ways:

FIGURE 16.2 *The Top 50 Companies*

COMPANY	HDQUTS	SALES 1998	COMPANY	HDQUTS	SALES 1998
1. General Motors	U.S.	161,315	26. Matsushita	Japan	59,771
2. DaimlerChrysler	Germany	154,615	27. Philip Morris	U.S.	57,813
3. Ford Motor	U.S.	144,418	28. Ing Group	Netherlands	56,468
4. Wal-Mart Stores	U.S.	139,208	29. Boeing	U.S.	56,154
5. Mitsui	Japan	109,373	30. AT&T	U.S.	53,588
6. Itochu	Japan	108,749	31. Sony	Japan	53,156
7. Mitsubishi	Japan	107,184	32. Metro	Germany	52,126
8. Exxon	U.S.	100,697	33. Nissan Motor	Japan	51,478
9. General Electric	U.S.	100,469	34. Fiat	Italy	50,999
10. Toyota Motor	Japan	99,740	35. Bank of America	U.S.	50,777
11. Royal Dutch/Shell	U.K./Neth.	93,692	36. Nestle	Switzerland	49,504
12. Marubeni	Japan	93,568	37. Credit Suisse	Switzerland	49,143
13. Sumitomo	Japan	89,020	38. Honda Motor	Japan	48,747
14. IBM	U.S.	81,667	39. Assicurazioni Generali	Italy	48,478
15. Axa	France	78,729	40. Mobil	U.S.	47,678
16. Citigroup	U.S.	76,431	41. Hewlett-Packard	U.S.	47,061
17. Volkswagen	Germany	76,306	42. Deutsche Bank	Germany	45,165
18. Nippon T&T	Japan	76,118	43. Unilever	U.K./Neth.	44,908
19. BP Amoco	U.K.	68,304	44. State Farm Insurance	U.S.	44,620
20. Nissho Iwai	Japan	67,741	45. Dai-Ichi Insurance	Japan	44,485
21. Nippon Life Insurance	Japan	66,299	46. Veba Group	Germany	43,407
22. Siemens	Germany	66,037	47. HSBC Holdings	U.K.	43,338
23. Allianz	Germany	64,874	48. Toshiba	Japan	41,471
24. Hitachi	Japan	62,409	49. Renault	France	41,353
25. U.S. Postal Service	U.S.	60,072	50. Sears Roebuck	U.S.	41,332

Source: Adapted from *The Wall Street Journal, Business Week,* and other company documents.

1. Their production and distribution extend beyond national boundaries, making it easier for them to transfer technology.
2. They have direct investments in many countries, affecting the balance of payments.

3. They have a political impact that leads to cooperation among countries and to the breaking down of barriers of nationalism.

WWW

Despite the success of well-known Canadian companies such as Bombardier, CanWest, and Nortel, Canadian companies are not expanding globally as rapidly as those of other countries. Canada has only 1,800 transnational corporations, compared to Denmark's 5,000 and Switzerland's 4,500.[6]

How Does the Global Environment Influence Management?

In Chapter 1 we highlighted some of the global trends affecting human resource management. One of the major economic issues we discussed was the creation of free trade zones within Europe, North America, and the Pacific Rim. Figure 16.3 shows a map of the fifteen member countries of the European Union (EU), which has the goal of facilitating the flow of goods, services, capital, and human resources across national borders in Europe in much the same way as they cross provincial borders in Canada.[7] Despite the political and legal obstacles to unification, most

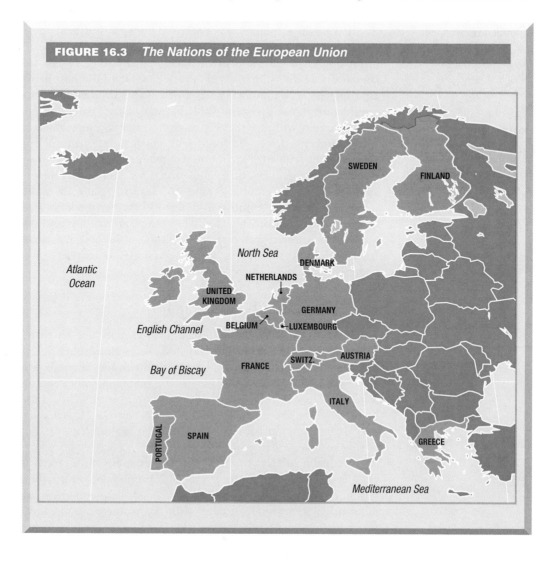

FIGURE 16.3   *The Nations of the European Union*

observers agree that ultimately the EU will become a unified buying and selling power that will compete as a major economic player with North America and Japan. Highlights in HRM 1 describes some of the effects that unification may have on HRM practices within Europe.

A similar transition has been happening within North America with the passage of NAFTA (see Chapter 1). Some alarmists feared that NAFTA would lead to a loss of jobs in Canada. However, a recent report by the U.S. Department of Commerce on the merits of NAFTA shows that job growth has surged in all three North American countries: in the United States there has been a 7 percent increase (12.8 million jobs), in Canada there has been a 10.1 percent increase (1.3 million jobs), and in Mexico there has been a 22 percent increase (2.2 million jobs).[8]

WWW

Many global companies are also fully engaged in Asia. Although the focus for many years has been on Japan, companies are now operating in a broader range of Asian countries such as Korea, Vietnam, Taiwan, Malaysia, and China (including Hong Kong). For example, Motorola has invested $1.2 billion in China, and its annual sales in that country are more than $3.2 billion (almost 12 percent of its worldwide revenue). Nike also does a good deal of business in Asia; the stories of its mismanagement in Vietnam and China are now well known.[9]

Cultural environmnent

Communications, religion, values and ideologies, education and social structure of a country

Beyond the economic issues of world trade, the **cultural environment** (communications, religion, values and ideologies, education, and social structure) has a major impact on decisions in an international setting. Figure 16.4 illustrates the complexity of the cultural environment in which HR must be managed. By recognizing and accommodating a country's social structure, taboos, rituals, attitudes toward time, kinship systems, and the many other components listed in Figure 16.4, managers will pave the way toward greater harmony and achievement in the **host country**—that is, the country in which an international business operates.

Host country

Country in which an international corporation operates

Different cultural environments require different approaches to human resources management. Strategies, structures, and management styles that are appropriate in one cultural setting may lead to failure in another. Managers at Coca-Cola are quite sensitive to differences among the more than 200 countries in which their company operates. They point out that forging effective relations is a matter of accurate perception, sound diagnosis, and appropriate adaptation.[10] Later in this chapter we will discuss several HR issues related to adapting to different cultural environments.

OBJECTIVE ②

Domestic versus International HRM

Canadian corporations have internationalized more quickly than the HRM profession itself. Executives in the very best companies around the world still lament that their HR policies have not kept pace with the demands of global competition. And unfortunately, the academic community has not been an especially good source of answers to international HRM problems. While various journals on international business have published articles on HRM over the years, it was not until 1990 that a journal specifically devoted to this area—the *International Journal of Human Resource Management*—was started.[11]

International HRM differs from domestic HRM in several ways. In the first place, it necessarily places more emphasis on functions and activities such as relocation, orientation, and translation services to help employees adapt to new and different environments. Assistance with tax matters, banking, investment management, home rental while on assignment, and coordination of home visits is also

Highlights in HRM

1   HR ISSUES OF A UNIFIED EUROPE

STAFFING

Unification provides workers the right to move freely throughout Europe and opens labour markets on a pan-European basis. However, unemployment rates vary dramatically across countries throughout Europe. For example, Spain's unemployment rate is improving but still hovers around 18 percent, while countries such as Norway enjoy employment rates around 3 percent. Many of these differences reflect the existence of hard-core unemployed, a problem due to many factors, including political systems, sociocultural differences, and worker training. In some cases, unemployment is the result of racial discrimination. Managers must overcome these problems to take advantage of the labour markets that have been opened to them.

The EU prohibits discrimination against workers and unions. However, while member countries are required to interpret national law in light of EU directives, most companies are still trying to reconcile EU policies with laws in their home countries.

TRAINING AND DEVELOPMENT

It has not been easy bringing education up-to-date to prepare Europe's youth and to eliminate the bottlenecks that already exist in many advanced industries. Under a unified Europe, every worker is guaranteed access to vocational training. However, training experts fear that attempts to improve vocational training standards across the European Union will fail unless standards of quality are assured. Germany remains a model of apprenticeship programs and worker development. Firms in other countries are struggling to create transnational employability in the face of inadequate training regulation. Meanwhile, there is a need for "Euroexecutives"—those who speak many languages, are mobile, and are experienced at managing a multicultural workforce.

PRODUCTIVITY

To be competitive in a global economy, Europeans must increase their level of productivity. Europeans on average work fewer hours, take longer vacations, and enjoy far more social entitlements than do their counterparts in North America and Asia. In contrast to the ten vacation days that American employees receive, in the United Kingdom, France, and the Netherlands workers receive about twenty-five days of paid vacation, and workers in Sweden and Austria receive thirty. In many countries, these periods are established by law and must be reconciled in a unified Europe.

COMPENSATION AND BENEFITS

Wages also differ substantially across countries throughout Europe. Workers in industrialized countries such as Germany and Switzerland receive an average hourly rate of about $28. Workers in Greece and Portugal, in contrast, have hourly wages between $5 and $9. Market forces are diminishing these differences somewhat, but to be competitive, companies need to bring compensation levels further in line with productivity.

Although pay discrimination is prohibited by law, women workers still tend to be in low-paying jobs. Because of this, the European Commission has proposed "codes of practice on equal pay for work of equal value," similar to comparable worth in the United States.

In addition to wage issues, the EU has also addressed issues related to benefits. Under EU mandate, all workers have the right to social security benefits regardless of occupation or employer. In addition, even persons who have been unable to enter the workforce are given basic social assistance. Several directives on occupational safety and health establish minimal standards throughout Europe.

LABOUR RELATIONS

In the past, powerful trade unions have fiercely defended social benefits. In a unified Europe, unions retain collective bargaining rights laid out under the host country's laws and the right to be consulted regarding company decisions. Stimulating economic growth to create jobs may mean eliminating rigid work rules and softening policies related to social benefits. Union leaders have promised to fight these initiatives.

Sources: James C. Cooper and Kathleen Madigan, "Growth Has Joblessness on the Run," *Business Week,* July 5, 1999, 21; Xan Smiley, "Survey: The Nordic Countries: Well-Oiled Independence," *Economist,* January 23, 1999, N13–N15; "Special Article: Crisis in Brussels: Europe Has to Scratch Its Head," *Economist,* March 20, 1999, 21–27; "Paying Dues: Once a Big Muscle of German Industry, Unions See It All Sag," *Wall Street Journal,* November 29, 1999, A-1, A-18; Mike Leat, *Human Resource Issues of the European Union* (London: Financial Times Management, 1998); Andrew Martin and George Ross, eds., *The Brave New World of European Labor* (Oxford, England: Berghahn Books, 1999); David Fairlamb, Carol Matlack, John Rossant, Stephen Baker, Gail Edmondson, and Jack Ewing, "Europe's Big Chance," *Business Week,* September 27, 1999, 62; Jennie Walsh, "No Stamp for Passport to EU Training," *People Management* 4, no. 12 (June 11, 1998):15.

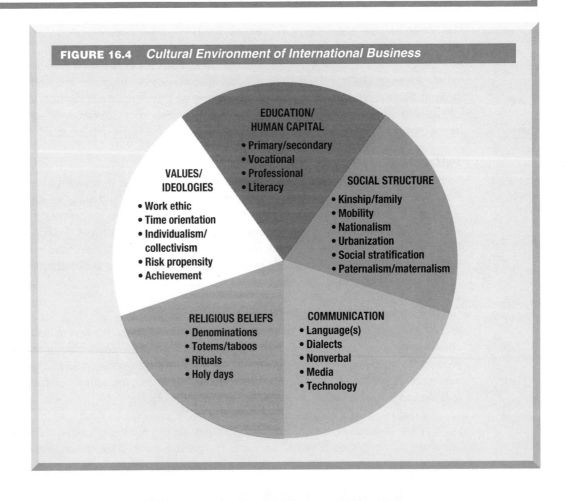

FIGURE 16.4   *Cultural Environment of International Business*

WWW

usually provided by the HR department. Most larger corporations have a full-time staff of HR managers devoted solely to assisting globalization. McDonald's, for example, has a team of HR directors who travel around the world to help country managers stay updated on international concerns, policies, and programs.

Coca-Cola provides support to its army of HR professionals working around the world. There is a core HR group in the company's Atlanta headquarters that holds a two-week HR orientation twice a year for the international HR staff. This program helps international HR practitioners share information about HR philosophies, programs and policies established either in Coca-Cola's headquarters or another part of the world that can be successfully adopted by others. The program also provides a foundation for an HR network within Coca-Cola that helps participants get a broader view of the company's activities.[12]

The HR department in an overseas unit must be especially responsive to the cultural, political, and legal environments. Companies such as Shell, Xerox, Levi Strauss, Digital, and Honeywell have made a special effort to create codes of conduct for their employees throughout the world, with the goal of ensuring that standards of ethical and legal behaviour are known and understood. Pepsico has taken a similar approach to ensuring that company values are reinforced (even while recognizing the need for adapting to local cultures). The company has four core criteria that are viewed as essential in worldwide recruiting efforts: (1) personal integrity, (2) a drive for results, (3) respect for others, and (4) capability.[13]

INTERNATIONAL STAFFING

OBJECTIVE
3

International management poses many problems in addition to those faced by a domestic operation. Because of geographic distance and a lack of close, day-to-day relationships with headquarters in the home country, problems must often be resolved with little or no counsel or assistance from others. It is essential, therefore, that special attention be paid to the staffing practices of overseas units.

There are three sources of staffing for international operations. *First*, the company can send people from its home country. These employees are often referred to as **expatriates**, or **home country nationals**. *Second*, it can hire **host country nationals** (i.e., natives of the host country) to do the managing. *Third*, it can hire **third country nationals**, natives of a country other than the home country or the host country.

Each of these three sources of overseas workers provides certain advantages and certain disadvantages. Some of the more important advantages are presented in Figure 16.5. Most corporations use all three sources to staff their multinational operations, although some companies exhibit a distinct bias for one or another of the three sources.[14]

As shown in Figure 16.6, at early stages of international expansion, organizations often send home country expatriates to establish activities (especially in less developed countries) and to work with local governments. At later stages of internationalization, there is typically a steady shift toward the use of host country nationals. There are three reasons for this trend:

1. Hiring local citizens is less costly, because the company does not have to worry about the costs of home leaves, transportation, and special schooling allowances.

Expatriates (home country nationals)

Employees from the home country who are sent on international assignment

Host country nationals

Natives of the host county

Third country nationals

Natives of a country other than the home country or the host country

---

FIGURE 16.5 *Comparison of Advantages in Sources of Overseas Managers*

HOST COUNTRY NATIONALS	HOME COUNTRY NATIONALS (EXPATRIATES)	THIRD COUNTRY NATIONALS
Less cost	Talent available within company	Broad experience
Preference of host country governments	Greater control	International outlook
Intimate knowledge of environment and culture	Company experience	Multilingualism
Language facility	Mobility	
	Experience provided to corporate executives	

---

2. Since local governments usually want good jobs for their citizens, foreign employers may be required to hire them.

3. Using local talent avoids the problem of employees having to adjust to the culture.

WWW

Recently, there has also been a trend away from using only expatriates for top management positions. Canadian companies often want to be viewed as true international citizens. To reduce the strong influence of the home country, more and more companies are changing their staffing policies with the goal of replacing North American expatriates with local managers. In Honeywell's European Division, twelve of the top executive positions are held by non–North Americans.[15]

Companies such as Pepsi-Cola, ABB, and IBM have strong regional organizations and tend to hire third country nationals as well as host country nationals. These companies tend to use expatriates only when they need specific sets of skills or when individuals in the host country require development. American-based companies in particular have tended over the years to use more third country nationals.[16]

It should be recognized that while top managers may prefer one source of employees over another, the host country may restrict their choices and require them to employ host country nationals. These restrictions take various forms, including administrative or legislative decrees and behind-the-scenes arm-twisting.

Recruitment

In general terms, employee recruitment is subject to more government regulation in other countries than it is in Canada. These regulations cover a broad spectrum of issues—for example, some cover procedures for recruiting employees; others govern the employment of foreign labour; still others require the employment of the physically disabled, or war veterans, or displaced persons. Many Central American countries have stringent regulations about the number of foreigners that can be employed as a percentage of the total workforce. Virtually all countries have work permit or visa restrictions that apply to foreigners. A **work permit**, or **work certificate**, is a document issued by a government granting authority to a foreign individual to seek employment in that government's country.[17]

Work permit (work certificate)

Government document granting a foreign individual the right to seek employment

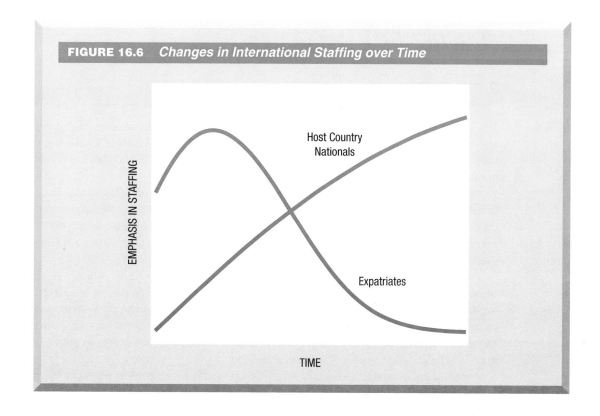

FIGURE 16.6   *Changes in International Staffing over Time*

MNCs tend to use the same kinds of internal and external recruitment sources as in their home countries. At the executive level, companies use search firms such as Korn/Ferry and Heidrick & Struggles. At lower levels, more informal approaches tend to be useful. Unskilled labour tends to be readily available in a developing country; it is harder to find skilled workers. Many employers have learned that the best way to find workers in these countries is through referrals and radio announcements, because many people lack sufficient reading or writing skills.

Many countries have laws requiring that locals be hired if adequate numbers of skilled people are available. In these situations, recruiting is limited to a restricted population. Specific exceptions are granted (officially or unofficially) for contrary cases (e.g., for Mexican and Jamican farmworkers in Canada, and for Italian, Spanish, Greek, and Turkish workers in Germany and the Benelux countries). Read Highlights in HRM 2 to learn why the hospitality industry in Canada employs foreign workers. Foreign workers invited into a country to perform needed labour are usually referred to as **guest workers**. The employment of non-nationals may result in lower direct labour costs; however, indirect costs—language training, health services, recruitment, transportation, and so on—may be substantial.[18]

WWW

Guest workers

Foreign workers invited in to perform needed labour

Selection

As you might imagine, selection practices vary around the world. In Canada, managers tend to emphasize merit, with the best-qualified person getting the job. In other countries, firms tend to hire on the basis of family ties, social status, language, and common origin. The candidate who satisfies these criteria may get the job

Highlights in HRM

2 IMPORTING CULTURE

The Inn at Manitou in Ontario's Muskoka District has a staff of about seventy, half of whom are not Canadian. The decision to recruit outside Canada for this Relais et Chateux luxury hotel and spa was made after years of trying to find Canadian workers and train them to offer the type of service that a luxury inn must offer.

Ben Wise, the Inn's owner, gives several reasons for employing non-Canadians. The first is culture: "We hire Europeans, who have a culture of hospitality. To serve people is not perceived by Europeans to be denigrating. Canadians berate the job of a waiter, saying that they are not waiters, but on their way to be stockbrokers. Being a waiter is a profession in Europe. Chefs are celebrities in Europe."

In Europe, jobs in the hospitality sector are seen as professions for which extensive training is necessary. Europeans arrive at Wise's inn with four to five years of training and experience at some of the best hotels. Canadian candidates cannot compete. Wise tried to train Canadians, but four weeks of on-the-job training could not match the extensive training Europeans receive. Besides, he didn't think it was fair to ask the inn's clients to put up with the mistakes and deficiencies of workers in training.

Another reason was the seasonal nature of the hospitality industry in Muskoka District: "Canadians have a summer job mentality to these positions. Consequently, a report on their performance is of no value to them. There is little we can do to motivate them to meet our service expectations. Europeans are serious. Their future employment depends on our performance evaluations and our references."

So each year The Inn at Manitou places ads in trade magazines, screens hundreds of applicants, interviews and selects those with training and experience at the best resorts and hotels, and finally arranges work permits for the lucky thirty. Why lucky? "Canada has a fascinating appeal for Europeans, especially the French, who must have all read books about a charming little cabin in the woods, with mountains, space, and fresh water."

WWW

even if otherwise unqualified. This is beginning to change; more and more organizations in other countries are realizing that they must start hiring those most qualified. Reality Check profiles John Young, Executive VP Human Resources, Four Seasons, and the issues he faces.

The Selection Process

The selection process for international assignments should emphasize different employment factors, depending on the extent of contact that employees will have with the local culture and the degree to which the foreign environment differs from the home environment. For example, if the job involves extensive contacts with the community—as with a CEO—this factor should be given appropriate weight. The magnitude of differences between the political, legal, socioeconomic, and cultural systems of the host country and those of the home country should also be assessed.[19]

Reality CHECK

SELECTING FOR SERVICE

Four Seasons Hotels, with a staff of over 25,000, manages fifty hotels and luxury resorts around the world, from Bali to Boston. The Four Seasons brand is synonymous with luxury and first-class service standards. The execution of the strategy of being the best in the world starts with leaders who are passionate about the corporation's customer service and employee relations values. These leaders can take a concept such as, "We will deliver exceptional personal service" and paint a picture for employees that is clear and motivational and that results in the delivery of that exceptional personal service.

Does the perception of service excellence depend on the country or culture in which Four Seasons operates? John Young, executive vice-president of human resources, states that the Four Seasons guest is typically a sophisticated global traveller who has acquired a sensitivity to differences in culture without negative preconceptions. Nevertheless, Four Seasons trains service staff to be sensitive to guests' needs and to minimize or avoid culture and language problems. For example, in Asia, when an English-speaking guest gives a food or beverage order, the service staff are trained to repeat the order. This is done not only to prevent a potential service error, but to avoid loss of face for the employee. In North America, a repetition of the order would be seen as redundant.

So that employees can meet these high performance expectations, Four Seasons selects employees based on their service attitudes. Candidates for employment must undergo four behaviourally based interviews (including one with the general manager) to determine their service attitudes and current skills and knowledge. As Young says: "Customer service is the heart and soul of our business, and we need to assess if a candidate has sensitivity to the needs and wants of others. Of course, we also look at high levels of knowledge, skill, and experience, but these can be trained. We continuously adapt our service to match guest needs. For example, many years ago, in our Seattle hotel, one of the valet parking attendants noted that on weekends our guests were disproportionately families with children. On his own initiative, he put chocolate chip cookies and milk in cars that he was returning to these departing guests. They loved it. This practice has now become one of Four Seasons' standards."

Four Seasons does not have a rigid formula for selecting home country nationals or expatriates for any given country. The ratios depend on three factors: regulations, economics, and corporate management development needs. Young continues: "For example, Indonesia used to have a rule that no more than three expatriates could be employed per hotel. So we set expatriate reduction targets to meet this regulation. Economically it made sense for us, since an expatriate general manager could cost us as much as seventy-five or eighty local employees. And finally, we will choose candidates based on their need for global exposure and professional development, to match our targeted needs for international expansion.

"Our biggest challenge in international HR now is management development in the context of our growth plans. We need to develop culturally appropriate leadership in preparation for specific new locations on a defined time line. If we cannot find managers who can speak the language, and understand the culture, then our ability to grow is limited. Recently we opened a hotel in Puerto Vallarta. We found a Spanish-speaking general manager from Colombia who, over time, was able to integrate the Four Seasons way of doing business with the Mexican culture. Business culture in Mexico tends to be very rule and policy driven. Employees continuously asked, 'What is the policy ...' in HR, sales, everything." Over time, the general manager learned to deal with the questions by no longer looking to home office for all the rules, but by asking himself and his team, 'What should the rule be in our situation?'

"We cannot just hire the management talent we want from other sectors or hotel chains on short lead time, because of differences in operating standards and corporate culture. For example, we were opening a hotel with a general manager recruited from Hilton International. As he toured the new facility with Issy Sharp, our founder and CEO, the general manager said that the lounge facilities ought to be larger. He explained that this would make guests more comfortable while waiting for their dinner reservations. Issy replied, 'At Four Seasons our guests do not wait for their reservations.' These cultural differences, across countries, across sectors, and across competitors, underline the importance of our investing the time and effort in developing our own management talent, which is culturally and linguistically fluent, mobile, and imbued with our service culture."

This attention to the selection and development of high-performance employees has resulted in Four Seasons being named by *Fortune* magazine one of the 100 best employers for three consecutive years. Consequently, Four Seasons is now able to attract more and better applicants. Four Seasons is also widely recognized as the best luxury hotel chain in the world. Furthermore, The turnover rate at Four Seasons is one of the lowest in the hospitality sector. Even those employees who have left are often recaptured as they elect to return to the kind of culture that treats them as they treat the guests.

If the candidate for expatriation is willing to live and work in a foreign environment, an evaluation of his or her tolerance for cultural differences should be obtained. On the other hand, if local nationals have the technical competence to carry out the job successfully, they should be considered carefully for the job before the firm launches a search (at home) for a candidate. As stated earlier, most corporations realize the advantages to be gained by staffing international operations with host country nationals wherever possible.

Selecting home country and third country nationals requires that more factors be considered than in selecting host country nationals. While the latter must of course possess managerial abilities and the necessary technical skills, they have the advantage of familiarity with the physical and cultural environment and the language of the host country. The discussion that follows will focus on the selection of expatriate managers from the home country.

Selecting Expatriates

One of the toughest jobs facing many organizations is finding employees who can meet the demands of working in a foreign environment. There are several steps involved in selecting individuals for an international assignment. The sequencing of these activities can make a big difference.

Step One: Self-selection. Employees should begin the process years in advance by thinking about their career goals and their interest in international work. By beginning with self-selection, companies can avoid forcing otherwise promising employees into international assignments where they would be unhappy and

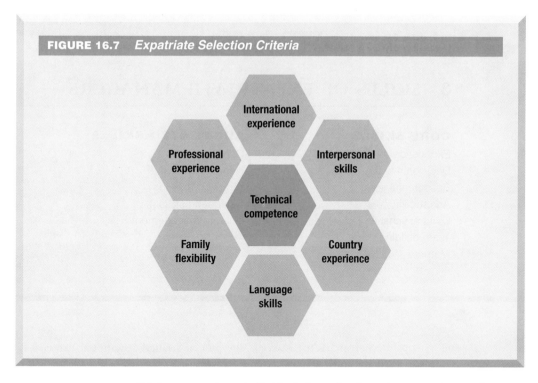

FIGURE 16.7   *Expatriate Selection Criteria*

WWW

Core skills

Skills considered critical to an employee's success abroad

Augmented skills

Skills helpful to facilitating the efforts of expatriate managers

Failure rate

Percentage of expatriates who do not perform satisfactorily

unsuccessful. In cases where individuals have families, decisions about relocation are more complicated. Employees should seek out information to help them predict their chances of success living abroad. Companies such as EDS and Deloitte and Touche give the self-selection instruments to their employees to help them think through the pros and cons of international assignments.

Step Two: Create a candidate pool. After employees have self-selected, organizations can begin putting together a database of candidates for international assignments. Information on the database might include availability, languages, country preferences, and skills.

Step Three: Assess core skills. From the shortlist of potential candidates, managers can assess each candidate on technical and managerial readiness relative to the needs of the assignment. Although many factors determine success abroad, the initial focus should be on the requirements of the job.

Step Four: Assess augmented skills and attributes. As shown in Figure 16.7, expatriate selection decisions are typically driven by technical competence as well as professional and international experience. In addition, more and more organizations have begun considering an individual's ability to adapt to different environments. Satisfactory adjustment depends on flexibility, emotional maturity and stability, empathy for the culture, language and communication skills, resourcefulness and initiative, and diplomatic skills.[20]

To be more specific, companies such as Colgate-Palmolive, Whirlpool, and Dow Chemical have identified a set of **core skills** that they view as critical for success abroad, and a set of **augmented skills** that facilitate the efforts of expatriate managers. These skills and their managerial implications are shown in Highlights in HRM 3. It is worth noting that many of these skills are not significantly different from those required for managerial success at home.

These efforts to improve the selection process have often been helpful; unfortunately, the **failure rate** among expatriates continues to run between 25 and 50

Highlights in HRM

3 SKILLS OF EXPATRIATE MANAGERS

CORE SKILLS
Experience
Decision making
Resourcefulness
Adaptability
Cultural sensivity
Team building
Maturity

AUGMENTED SKILLS
Compute skills
Negotiation skills
Strategic thinking
Delegation skills
Change management

percent. What is worse, the cost of a failed assignment can rise as high as US$2.1 million.[21] Figure 16.8 shows the major causes of expatriate assignment failure. By far the biggest factor is the spouse's inability to adjust to new surroundings.[22]

Women Going Abroad

Traditionally, companies have been hesitant to send women on overseas assignments. Executives either mistakenly assume that women do not want international assignments, or assume that host country nationals are prejudiced against women. The reality is that women want international assignments at least as often as men. And while locals may be prejudiced against women in their own country, they view women first as foreigners (*gaijin* in Japanese) and only second as women. In sum, the cultural barriers that typically constrain women in a male-dominated societies may not totally apply in the case of expatriates.

When women have been given international assignments, they generally have performed quite well. Female expatriates succeed around 97 percent of the time, which is far more often than men.[23] Ironically, women expatriates attribute at least part of their success to their gender. Because locals are aware of how unusual it is for a woman to be given a foreign assignment, they often assume that the company would not have sent a woman unless she was the very best. Also, because women expatriates are a novelty (especially in managerial positions), they are very visible and distinctive. In many cases they even receive preferential treatment not extended to their male colleagues. For these reasons, female expatriates are expected to increase in numbers over the next five years, according to a survey of corporate relocation consultants in North America, Europe and Asia.[24]

Transnational teams

Teams composed of members of multiple nationalities working on projects that span multiple countries

Staffing Transnational Teams

More and more companies are using transnational teams to conduct international business. **Transnational teams** are composed of members of multiple nationalities working on projects that span multiple countries.[25] These teams are especially

FIGURE 16.8 *Why Expatriate Assignments Fail: Most Frequently Cited to Least Frequently Cited Reasons*

- Family adjustment
  - Lifestyle issues
    - Expatriate work adjustment
      - Wrong candidate
        - Performance
          - Other opportunity
            - Business reasons
              - Repatriation issues

Source: Donald McNerney, "Global Staffing: Some Common Problems—and Solutions," *HRFocus*, June 1996, 6. Reproduced with permission of copyright owner. Further reproduction prohibited.

useful for performing tasks that the firm as a whole is not yet structured to accomplish. For example, they may be used to transcend the existing organizational structure to customize a strategy for different geographic regions, transfer technology from one part of the world to another, and communicate between headquarters and subsidiaries in different countries.

The fundamental task in forming a transnational team is assembling the right group of people who can work together effectively to accomplish the goals of the team. Many companies try to build variety into their teams in order to maximize responsiveness to the special needs of different countries. When Heineken formed a transnational team to consolidate its production facilities, it made certain that the members were drawn from each major region in Europe. Team members tended to have specialized skills, and additional members were added only if they offered unique skills that added value to the team.

WWW

Selection Methods

The methods of selection most commonly used by corporations operating internationally are interviews, assessment centres, and tests. Some companies interview only the candidate. Others interview both the candidate and the spouse; this is evidence that companies are increasingly acknowledging the importance of the spouse's adjustment to the manager's performance abroad. The impact of this factor in selection and expatriation decisions raises some interesting issues about validity, fairness, and discrimination.

TRAINING AND DEVELOPMENT

Although companies try to recruit and select the very best people for international work, they must often provide some type of training to achieve the desired level of performance. Over time, given the rapidity of change in an international setting, employees may also need to upgrade their skills as they continue on the job. This training can be provided within the organization or outside it in some type of educational setting.

Skills of the Global Manager

If businesses are to be managed effectively in an international setting, managers need to be educated and trained in global management skills. Levi Strauss has identified the following six skill categories for the **global manager**:

- Ability to seize strategic opportunities
- Ability to manage highly decentralized organizations
- Awareness of global issues
- Sensitivity to issues of diversity
- Competence in interpersonal relations
- Skill in building community[26]

Corporations that are serious about succeeding in global business are tackling these problems head-on by providing intensive training. Companies such as AMP, Texas Instruments, Procter & Gamble, Bechtel, and others with large international staffs carefully prepare their employees for overseas assignments. The biggest mistake managers can make is to assume that people are the same everywhere. An organization that makes a concerted effort to ensure that its employees understand and respect cultural differences will be rewarded through reduced costs and increased sales and productivity.[27]

Global manager

Manager equipped to run a global business

WWW

International assignments provide an employee with a set of experiences that are uniquely beneficial to both the individual and the firm.

Content of Training Programs

Training and development programs that prepare employees to work internationally have four essential elements: (1) language training, (2) cultural training, (3) career development, and (4) personal and family life.[28]

Language Training

It is very difficult to communicate with people who have a different language and a different cultural orientation. Most executives agree that it is among the biggest problems for the foreign business traveller. Even with an interpreter, much is missed.[29]

WWW

When ARCO Products began exploring potential business opportunities in China, its HR department set up a language training class (with the help of Berlitz International) in conversational Mandarin Chinese.[30] While foreign language fluency is important in all aspects of international business, only a small percentage of Canadians are skilled in a language other than English. Students who plan careers in international business should start learning one or more foreign languages as early as possible. The Schulich School of Business at York University requires a high level of oral proficiency in a language of specialization for its International Master of Business Administration (IMBA) program, and offers noncredit language courses that expose students to business practices in the countries and regions where these languages are spoken.

Fortunately for most Canadians, English is the lingua franca of the international business community. Especially when many people from different countries are working together, English is usually the designated language for meetings and formal discourse. Although English is a required subject in many foreign schools, students may not learn to use it effectively. Many companies provide instruction in English for those who are required to use English in their jobs.

Learning the language is only part of communicating in another culture. One must also learn how the people think and act in their relations with others. The following list illustrates the complexities of the communication process in international business.

1. In England, to "table" a subject means to put it on the table for present discussion. In North America, it means to postpone discussion of a subject, perhaps indefinitely.

2. In North America, information flows to a manager. In cultures where authority is centralized (Europe and South America), the manager must take the initiative to seek out the information.

3. Getting straight to the point is uniquely North American. Europeans, Arabs, and many others resent this directness in communication.

4. In Japan, there are sixteen ways to avoid saying "no."

5. When something is "inconvenient" to the Chinese, it is most likely downright impossible.

6. In most foreign countries, expressions of anger are unacceptable; in some places, public display of anger is taboo.

7. The typical North American must learn to treat silences as "communication spaces" and not interrupt them.

8. In general, North Americans must learn to avoid gesturing with the hand.

To understand the communication process, you must pay attention to non-verbal communication. Highlights in HRM 4 illustrates that some of our everyday gestures have very different meanings in other cultures. In summary, when you leave Canada, you must remember that perfectly appropriate behaviour in one country can lead to an embarrassing situation in another.

Since factors other than language are also important, those working internationally need to know as much as possible about (1) the place where they are going, (2) their own culture, and (3) the history, values, and dynamics of their own organization. Figure 16.9 offers an overview of what you need to study for an international assignment.

Cultural Training

Cross-cultural differences are one of the most elusive aspects of international business. Most people are generally unaware of their own culturally conditioned behaviour, and tend to react negatively to tastes and behaviours that deviate from those of their own culture.

Managerial attitudes and behaviours are influenced in large part by the society in which managers have received their education and training. Similarly, employees' reactions are the result of cultural conditioning. Each culture has its own expectations of managers and employees. For example, what one culture encourages as participative management another might see as managerial incompetence.[31] Succeeding as a manager depends on being able to understand how things are usually done, and on recognizing that changes cannot be made abruptly without considerable resistance, and possibly antagonism, on the part of local nationals. Next, we discuss some of the areas in which there are often significant cultural differences between countries.

Cross-cultural studies have shown repeatedly that nations tend to cluster according to similarities in certain cultural dimensions such as work goals, values, needs, and job attitudes. Simcha Ronen and Oded Shenkar did a meta-analysis of eight studies of cultural differences, and grouped countries into the clusters shown in Figure 16.10. Countries with higher per capita GDPs relative to others are placed closer to the centre.

Ronen and Shenkar point out that while evidence favouring the grouping of countries into Anglo, Germanic, Nordic, Latin European, and Latin American clusters seems quite strong, clusters encompassing the Far Eastern and Arab countries are ill defined and require further research, as do clusters of countries classified as independent. Many areas, such as Africa, have not been studied much at all. It should also be noted that the clusters presented in Figure 16.10 do not include Russia and the former satellites of the ex-Soviet Union.[32]

Studying cultural differences can help managers identify and understand work attitudes and motivation in other cultures. In Japan, employees are more likely to feel strongly loyal to their company, although recent reports suggest this may be changing. Canadians feel less loyalty to their organization than Japanese. Latin Americans tend to work not for a company but for an individual manager. Thus, managers in Latin American countries can encourage performance only through

Highlights in HRM

4   NONVERBAL COMMUNICATIONS IN DIFFERENT CULTURES

CALLING A WAITER

In North America, a common way to call a waiter is to point upward with the forefinger. In Asia, a raised forefinger is used to call a dog or other animal. To get the attention of a Japanese waiter, extend the arm upward, palm down, and flutter the fingers. In Africa, knock on the table. In the Middle East, clap your hands.

INSULTS

In Arab countries, showing the soles of your shoes is an insult. Also, an Arab may insult a person by holding a hand in front of the person's face.

A-OKAY GESTURE

In North America, using the index finger and the thumb to form an "o" while extending the rest of the fingers is a gesture meaning okay or fine. In Japan, however, the same gesture means money. Nodding your head in agreement if a Japanese uses this sign during the discussion could mean you are expected to give him some cash. And in Brazil the same gesture is considered a seductive sign to a woman and an insult to a man.

EYE CONTACT

In Western and Arab cultures, prolonged eye contact with a person is acceptable. In Japan, on the other hand, holding the gaze of another

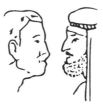

person is considered rude. The Japanese generally focus on a person's neck or tie knot.

HANDSHAKE AND TOUCHING

In most countries, the handshake is an acceptable form of greeting. In the Middle East and other Islamic countries, however, the left hand is considered the toilet hand and is thought to be unclean. Only the right hand should be used for touching.

SCRATCHING THE HEAD

In most Western countries, scratching the head is inter-preted as lack of understanding or non-comprehension. To the Japanese, it indicates anger.

INDICATING "NO"

In most parts of the world, shaking the head left and right is the most common way to say no. But among the Arabs, and in parts of Greece, Yugoslavia, Bulgaria, and Turkey, a person says no by tossing the head to the side, sometimes clicking the tongue at the same time. In Japan, no can also be said by moving the right hand back and forth.

AGREEMENT

In addition to saying yes, Africans will hold an open palm perpendicular to the ground and pound it with the other fist to emphasize "agreed." Arabs will clasp their hands together, forefin-gers pointed outward, to indi-cate agreement.

Source: S. Hawkins, *International Management* 38, no. 9 (September 1983): 49. Copyright © 1983 by Reed Business Information Ltd. Reprinted with permission.

FIGURE 16.9 *Preparing for an International Assignment*

To prepare for an international assignment, one should become acquainted with the following aspects of the host country:

1. Social and business etiquette
2. History and folklore
3. Current affairs, including relations between the host country and Canada
4. Cultural values and priorities
5. Geography, especially its major cities
6. Sources of pride and great achievements of the culture
7. Religion and the role of religion in daily life
8. Political structure and current players
9. Practical matters such as currency, transportation, time zones, hours of business
10. The language

personal influence, by working with group members as individuals. In North America, competition is fierce within organizations; in Japan, Taiwan, and other Asian countries, cooperation is more the underlying philosophy.[33]

One of the important dimensions of leadership, in both domestic and international situations, is the degree to which managers invite employees to participate in decision making. While it is difficult to find hard data on employee participation across different countries, careful observers report that North American managers are about in the middle on the continuum between autocratic to democratic decision-making styles. Scandinavian and Australian managers also appear to be in the middle. South American and European managers—especially those from France, Germany, and Italy—are toward the autocratic end of the continuum; Japanese managers are at the most participatory end. Because Far Eastern cultures and religions tend to emphasize harmony, group decision making predominates in that region.[34]

Ethics in HRM describes the difficulties we can encounter when judging cultural practices on the basis of Canadian moral and legal standards.

Assessing and Tracking Career Development

International assignments offer definite developmental and career advantages. For example, they tend to increase the employee's responsibilities and influence within the corporation. They also provide the employee with unique experiences that both benefit the firm and foster personal growth. International assignments enhance the employee's understanding of the global marketplace and provide opportunities to work on projects that are important to the organization.[35]

An employee should ask two key questions about the employer before accepting an overseas post:

- Do the organization's senior executives view the firm's international business as critical to its operations?

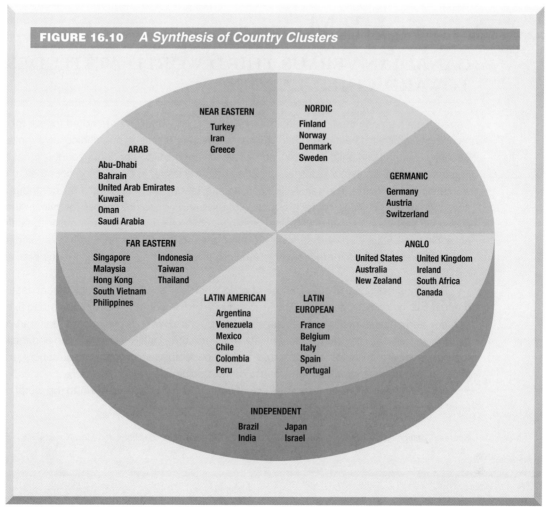

FIGURE 16.10 *A Synthesis of Country Clusters*

Source: Simcha Ronen and Oded Shenkar, "Clustering Countries on Attitudinal Dimensions: A Review and Synthesis," *Academy of Management Review* 10, no. 3 (July 1985): 435–54. Copyright Academy of Management Review. Reprinted with permission.

- How many of the organization's top executives have worked overseas, and do they consider it important for employees to have overseas experience?

WWW

At Dow Chemical, fourteen members of the firm's twenty-two-member management committee, including the CEO, have had overseas assignments. To ensure appropriate career development, Dow appoints what their expatriates refer to as "godfathers"; usually, these are high-level managers who act as stateside contacts for information about organizational changes, job opportunities, and anything related to salary and compensation. At Exxon, employees are given a general idea of what they can expect after an overseas assignment even before they leave to assume it. This helps smooths the transition, and makes it possible for them to continue enhancing their careers. Colgate-Palmolive and Ciba-Geigy make special efforts to stay in touch with expatriates while they are abroad. Colgate's division executives and other corporate staff make regular visits to international transferees.[36]

Ethics in HRM

CANADIAN VERSUS THIRD WORLD ATTITUDES TOWARD CHILD LABOUR

Canadians are among the first to deplore the use of child labour. We are noted for our media campaigns against it, and our child impact assessments affect our choice of suppliers. Because we don't use child labourers ourselves, we are quick to condemn countries that do. Foreigners resent it when Westerners preach about the issue. In developing countries, child workers are the norm. The family is seen as the labour unit, with children contributing, according to their abilities, to the production of food and goods or services for sale. In these countries, there is no social welfare or insurance: children's earnings often make the difference between starvation and survival. Furthermore, school is not an alternative for many child labourers. Schools for those who can afford them are often crowded, ill-equipped, and harsh in their treatment of children.

Programs designed to stop the use of child labourers, such as the child impact assessment, result in cosmetic changes. These changes in turn encourage corruption among fixers, brokers, and consultants, which results in child labourers being driven into the underground economy where they are at the mercy of labour contractors. Until Westerners can understand the culture of Third World countries, and the deeply embedded roots of child labour, their interventions and sanctions will only cause more problems.

Do you agree that labour practices in one country should not be subject to the moral and legal standards of other countries?

Source: Mohammad Qadeer, "Why the Third World Needs Child Labour," *The Globe and Mail*, November 7, 1997, A8.

Repatriation

Process of employee transition home from an international assignment

WWW

More and more companies, including Monsanto, 3M, Digital, and GTE, are developing programs specifically to facilitate **repatriation**—that is, to help employees make the transition back home. Readjusting to life at home can be more difficult than adjusting to a foreign assignment. Through such programs, employees learn how much the expatriate experience may have changed them and their families. Monsanto's program is also designed to smooth the employee's return to the home organization and to help ensure that the expatriate's knowledge and experience are fully utilized. In one component, returning expatriates get the chance to showcase their new knowledge in debriefing sessions.[37] A repatriation checklist is shown in Highlights in HRM 5. Expatriates may find it worthwhile to visit the Expatriate Forum website (**www.expatforum.com**).

Unfortunately, not all companies have career development programs for repatriating employees. Several recent studies have found that most companies do not do an effective job of repatriation. For example:

- Only about one-third of companies have a repatriation plan in place before the expatriate leaves home.
- Another one-third typically don't begin formal repatriation discussions until two to six months before the end of the assignment.
- The remaining one-third never have a repatriation discussion at all.

Highlights in HRM

5 REPATRIATION CHECKLIST

For employees returning from an overseas assignment, there are guidelines to help make their homecoming easier. Remember, planning for repatriation begins even before a person leaves to go overseas. Then there are things to take care of during their stint abroad, and finally, there are some important things to be considered when they come home.

BEFORE THEY GO

- Make sure you have clearly identified a need for the international assignment. Don't send somebody abroad unnecessarily. Develop a clear set of objectives and expectations.
- Make certain that your selection procedures are valid. Select the employee and also look at the family situation.
- Provide (or fund) language and cultural training for the employee and the employee's family.
- Offer counselling and career assistance for the spouse.
- Establish career planning systems that reward international assignments.

WHILE THEY ARE AWAY

- Jointly establish a developmental plan that focuses on competency development.
- Tie performance objectives to the developmental plan.
- Identify mentors who can act as liaisons and support persons from home.
- Keep communications open so that the expatriate is aware of job openings and opportunities.
- Arrange for frequent visits back home (for the employee and the family). Make certain they do not lose touch with friends and relatives.

WHEN THEY COME BACK HOME

- Throw a "welcome home" party.
- Offer counselling to ease the transition.
- Arrange conferences and presentations to make certain that knowledge and skills acquired away from home are identified and disseminated.
- Get feedback from the employee and the family about how well the organization handled the repatriation process.

Sources: Adapted from Bennet & Associates, Price Waterhouse; Charlene Marmer Solomon, "Repatriation Planning Checklist," *Personnel Journal* 14, no. 1 (January 1995): 32.

Not surprisingly, employees often lament that their organizations are vague about repatriation, about their new role in the company, and about their career progression. Far too often, employees return home after a few years and find that the firm has no position for them and that they no longer know anyone who can help them. Employees often feel that their firms play down their difficulties in readjusting to life back in the home country. Even when employees have been repatriated successfully, their companies often do not fully utilize the knowledge, understanding, and skills they developed overseas. And even though many managers take international assignments to gain advancement, the evidence suggests that only a fraction are actually promoted on their return; in fact, many employees end up in lower-level jobs on their return from overseas. This hurts the employee, and it may hurt just as much the firm's chances of using that employee's expertise to gain competitive advantage. Expatriates sometimes leave their company within a year or two of returning home.[38]

Managing Personal and Family Life

As noted earlier, one of the most common reasons why an employee fails to complete an international assignment is personal and family stress. **Culture shock** is the perceptual stress experienced by people who settle overseas for extended periods. It is caused by the piling up of hundreds of jarring and disorienting incidents—being unable to communicate, having trouble getting the telephone to work, being unable to read the street signs, and a myriad of other everyday matters that are no problem at home. Minor frustrations soon become catastrophic events, and the employee feels helpless and drained, both emotionally and physically.

Culture shock

Perceptual stress experienced by people who settle overseas

In Chapter 7 we noted that more and more employers are helping two-career couples find suitable employment in the same location. To accommodate dual-career partnerships, some employers are helping the spouses of international transferees to find jobs—albeit on an informal basis. Other companies are offering more formal programs to assist expatriate couples—for example, career- and life-planning counselling, continuing education, intercompany networks to identify job openings, and job-hunting and fact-finding trips. A company may even create a job for the spouse, though this is hardly usual. The types of relocation assistance provided to spouses include the following: reimbursing the costs of résumé preparation and career counselling; circulating spousal résumés to other companies in the area; retaining an employment agency; funding employment search trips; and reimbursing the spouse for lost income.[39] The available evidence suggests that while a spouse's career may create some problems initially, in the long run it actually may help smooth the expatriate's adjustment.[40]

Training Methods

A host of training methods are available to prepare an individual for an international assignment. Unfortunately, the overwhelming majority of companies provide only superficial preparation for their employees. Lack of training is one of the principal causes of failure among employees working internationally.

Often the employee and his or her family can learn much about the host country—about its culture, geography, social and political history, climate, food, and so on—through books, lectures, and videotapes. However, this minimal exposure cannot fully prepare the employee and family for a foreign assignment.

Training methods such as sensitivity training (which focuses on learning at the affective level) can do a great deal to reduce ethnic prejudices. The U.S. Peace Corps uses sensitivity training supplemented by field experiences. Field experience can sometimes be obtained in a nearby "microculture" where similarities exist.

Companies often send employees on temporary assignments—lasting, say, a few months—to encourage shared learning. These temporary assignments are probably too short for employees to completely absorb the nuances of a culture; even so, companies such as AMP and Texas Instruments use them to help employees gather new ideas and learn technologies in other regions.[41]

Overseas assignments can last for years. Fuji-Xerox sent fifteen of its most experienced engineers from Tokyo to a Xerox facility in Webster, New York, on a five-year assignment. For that long a time, these engineers worked with a team of American engineers to develop the "world" copier. By working together on such an extended basis, the American and Japanese employees learned from one another both the technical and the cultural requirements for a continued joint venture.[42]

WWW

Developing Local Resources

Most companies have found that good training programs help them attract needed employees from the host countries. In less developed countries especially, individuals are quite eager to receive the training they need to improve their work skills. Often, however, a company's human capital investment does not pay off. For example, it is very common for locally owned firms to hire away workers who have been trained by foreign-owned organizations.

Apprenticeship Training

A major source of trained labour in European nations is apprenticeship training programs (see Chapter 6). On the whole, apprenticeship training is better in

Language training is an essential element to prepare employees to work internationally.

Europe than in Canada. In Europe, a dual-track system of education directs many young people into vocational training. The German system of apprenticeship training, one of the best in Europe, provides training for office and shop jobs under a three-way responsibility contract between the apprentice, his or her parents, and the organization. At the end of their training, apprentices can work for any employer; usually, however, they receive seniority credit with the firm that trained them if they remain in it.

Management Development

Various Canadian organizations offer management development programs, and foreign nationals have generally welcomed the training they receive through these. The Chinese have entered into partnerships with McGill University to customize training experiences to the specific needs of expatriate managers and foreign nationals.

PERFORMANCE

As we noted earlier, employees often accept international assignments because they know they will acquire skills and experiences that will increase their value. That being said, one of the biggest problems organizations face in managing their overseas people is that performance is so difficult to evaluate from a distance. Also, the very notion of performance evaluation betrays a North American mindset in which the individual is paramount; this can cause problems in Asian countries such as China, Japan, and Korea, and in eastern European countries such as Hungary and the Czech Republic. Difficulties in performance appraisal may be one of the biggest reasons why failure rates are so high among expatriates, and why international assignments can derail careers instead of enhancing them.[43]

Who Should Appraise Performance?

An individual working internationally often has at least two allegiances: one to his or her home country (i.e., the office that made the assignment), and the other to the country where he or she is presently working. Superiors in each location often have different information about the employee's performance, and may also have very different expectations about what constitutes good performance. For these reasons, the multirater (360 degree) approach to appraisal is gaining favour among global firms (see Chapter 8).[44]

Home Country Evaluations

Domestic managers often cannot understand expatriates' experiences, or value them, or accurately measure their contribution to the organization. Physical distance poses severe communication problems for expatriates and home country managers. Both expatriates and domestic managers tend to focus on their own local issues rather than coordinate their efforts across time zones and national borders. As a result, communication suffers. Information technology has improved this situation, and it is far easier to communicate globally today than it was just a few years ago.[45] But even when expatriates contact their home country offices, it is often not to converse with their superiors; more likely it is to talk with peers and others in the organization.

Host Country Evaluations

Local managers often have the most accurate picture of an expatriate's performance; after all, they are in the best position to observe effective and ineffective behaviour. Even so, host country evaluations have their own drawbacks. The local culture may influence the manager's perceptions of the employee's performance. For example, and as we noted earlier, participative decision-making can be viewed either positively or negatively, depending on the culture. Cultural biases like these may not have any bearing on an individual's true level of effectiveness. Also, local managers often don't have enough perspective on the entire organization to know how well an individual is really contributing to the firm as a whole.

Given the pros and cons of home country and host country evaluations, most observers agree that performance evaluations should try to balance the two sources of appraisal information.[46] Although host country employees are in a good position to view day-to-day activities, in many situations the individual is still formally tied to the home office. Because promotion, pay, and other administrative decisions lead back there, the written evaluation is usually handled by the home country manager. Nevertheless, that appraisal should be written only after extensive consultation with the host country manager. Multiple sources of appraisal information can be invaluable for providing independent points of view, especially for people working on teams (see Chapter 8). If there is much concern about cultural bias, it may be possible to have people of the same nationality as the expatriate conduct the appraisal.

Adjusting Performance Criteria

Whether an employee succeeds or fails overseas depends on a host of technical and personal factors. Many of these factors should be considered in developing a broader set of performance criteria.

Augmenting Job Duties

Obviously, the goals and responsibilities inherent in the job assignment are among the most important criteria used to evaluate an individual's performance. However, because of the difficulties in observing, documenting, and interpreting performance information in an international setting, superiors often resort to "easy" criteria such as productivity, profits, and market share. These criteria may be valid, but they are still deficient if they do not capture the full range of the expatriate's responsibilities. Other, more subtle factors should also be considered as well. An expatriate is often an ambassador for the company, and a significant part of almost any overseas job is cultivating relationships with the host country's citizens.

Individual Learning

Any foreign assignment involves learning. As one might guess, it is much easier to adjust to similar cultures than to dissimilar ones. A Canadian can usually travel to the United Kingdom or Australia and work with the locals almost immediately. Send that same individual to Hungary or Malaysia and the learning curve is steeper. The expatriate's adjustment period may be even longer if the company has not yet established a good base of operations in the region. The first individuals transferred to a country have no one to show them the ropes or to explain local customs. Even relatively simple activities such as navigating the rapid transit system can seem insurmountable.

Organizational Learning

Bottom-line measures of performance may not fully convey how much the employee has learned from a foreign assignment. Yet learning may be among the very most important reasons for sending an individual overseas, especially at early stages of internationalization and during joint ventures.[47] Even if superiors do acknowledge the level of learning, they often use it only as an excuse for less-than-desired performance, rather than treating it as a valuable outcome in itself. What they fail to recognize is that knowledge gained, if it is shared, can speed the adjustment process for others. If the learning is not shared, each new employee sent to the region may have to go through the same cycle of adjustment.

Providing Feedback

Performance feedback in an international setting is clearly a two-way street. The home country and host country superiors may tell an expatriate how well he or she is doing; at the same time, it is important for expatriates to provide feedback regarding the support they are receiving and the obstacles they are facing, and to offer suggestions about the assignment. More than almost any other employees, expatriates are in a strong position to evaluate their own performance.

Furthermore, expatriates should be debriefed immediately on returning home. Repatriation interviews serve several purposes:

- They help expatriates re-establish old ties with the home organization, and may help set new career paths.
- They address technical issues related to the job assignment itself.
- They address general issues relating to the company's overseas commitments, such as how relationships between the home and host countries should be handled.
- They provide insights about the region that can be incorporated into training programs for future expatriates.

COMPENSATION

One of the most complex areas of international HRM is compensation. Different countries have different norms for employee compensation. Managers should consider carefully the use of incentives and rewards as motivators in foreign countries. For Canadians, while nonfinancial incentives such as prestige, independence, and influence may be motivators, money is likely to be the driving force. Other cultures are more likely to emphasize respect, family, job security, a satisfying personal life, social acceptance, advancement, or power. Since there are many alternatives to money, the rule is to match the reward with the values of the culture. Figure 16.11 shows how pay plans can vary with one cultural dimension: individualism. In individualistic cultures such as Canada, pay plans often focus on individual performance and achievement. In collectively oriented cultures such as Japan and Taiwan, pay plans focus more on internal equity and personal needs.[48]

A good guiding philosophy when designing pay systems is "think globally and act locally." In other words, executives should try to create a pay plan that supports the overall strategy of the organization but is flexible enough that policies and programs can be customized for specific locations. Next we briefly discuss compensa-

FIGURE 16.11 *Individualism and Compensation Strategies*

DOMINANT VALUES	CORPORATE FEATURES	COMPENSATION STRATEGIES	SAMPLE COUNTRIES
HIGH • Personal accomplishment • Selfishness • Independence • Individual attributions • Internal locus of control • Belief in creating one's own destiny • Utilitarian relationship with employee	• Organizations not compelled to care for employees' total well-being • Employees look after individual interests • Explicit systems of control necessary to ensure compliance and prevent wide deviation from organizational norms	• Performance-based pay utilized • Individual achievement rewarded • External equity emphasized • Extrinsic rewards are important indicators of personal success • Attempts made to isolate individual contributions (i.e., who did what) • Emphasis on short-term objectives	• Canada • United States • Great Britain • New Zealand
LOW • Team accomplishment • Sacrifice for others • Dependence on social unit • Group attributions • External locus of control • Belief in the hand of fate • Moral relationship with employees	• Organizations committed to a high level of involvement in worker's personal lives • Loyalty to the firm is critical • Normative, rather than formal, systems of control to ensure compliance	• Group-based performance is important criterion • Seniority-based pay utilized • Intrinsic rewards essential • Internal equity key in guiding pay policies • Personal need (e.g., number of children) affects pay received	• Singapore • South Korea • Indonesia • Japan

(Left axis label: INDIVIDUALISM)

Source: L. R. Gomez-Mejia and T. Welbourne, "Compensation Strategies in a Global Context," *Human Resources Planning* 14, no. 1 (1991): 29–41.

tion practices for host country employees and managers; then we consider how to compensate expatriates.

Compensation of Host Country Employees

As shown in in Figure 16.12, hourly wage rates vary dramatically from country to country. Labour costs are one of the biggest motivators for international expansion, but there are many managerial and administrative issues that must be addressed when an organization establishes operations overseas.

Host country employees are generally paid on the basis of either productivity, or time spent on the job, or a combination of the two. In industrialized countries, pay is generally by the hour; in developing countries, by the day. The piece rate method is quite common. In some countries, including Japan, seniority does much to determine employees' pay rates. When companies commence operations in a

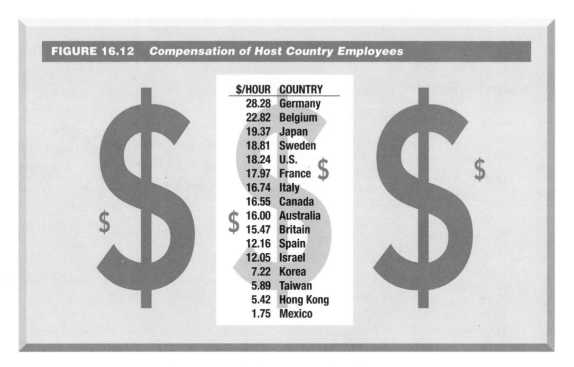

FIGURE 16.12 *Compensation of Host Country Employees*

$/HOUR	COUNTRY
28.28	Germany
22.82	Belgium
19.37	Japan
18.81	Sweden
18.24	U.S.
17.97	France
16.74	Italy
16.55	Canada
16.00	Australia
15.47	Britain
12.16	Spain
12.05	Israel
7.22	Korea
5.89	Taiwan
5.42	Hong Kong
1.75	Mexico

foreign country, they usually set their wage rates at or slightly higher than the prevailing wage for local companies. Eventually, though, they are urged to conform to local practices to avoid "upsetting" local compensation practices.

Employee benefits in other countries are often costlier than in Canada. In France, benefits are about 70 percent of wages; in Italy, 92 percent; in Canada, 40 to 50 percent. In Canada many benefits are awarded to employees by employers; in other industrialized countries most of them are legislated or ordered by governments. Some of these plans are changing. Defined contribution plans are on the rise; sex equality is becoming important; and stock ownership plans are being tried.[49]

In Italy, Japan, and some other countries, it is customary to add semiannual or annual lump sum payments equal to one or two months' pay. These payments are not seen as profit sharing but rather as an integral part of the basic pay package. Profit sharing is legally required in certain industries in Mexico, Peru, Pakistan, India, and Egypt (among the developing countries) and in France (among the industrialized countries). Compensation patterns in eastern Europe are in flux as these countries make the adjustment to capitalism.

Compensation of Host Country Managers

At one time, the remuneration of host country managers was ruled by local salary levels. However, increased competition among different companies with subsidiaries in the same country has led to a gradual upgrading of host country managers' salaries. Among international firms there has been an overall narrowing of the salary gap between host country managers and expatriates. A recent survey of twenty-six countries by Wyatt Company found that on average, firms in Japan ($387,000), Mexico ($277,000), Argentina ($229,000), Switzerland ($213,000), and Hong Kong ($206,000) all paid managers more than firms in the United States ($195,000).[50]

WWW

Compensation of Expatriate Managers

Compensation plans for expatriate managers must be competitive, cost-effective, motivating, fair, consistent with international financial management, and easy to understand, administer, and communicate. To be effective, an international compensation program must do the following:

- Provide an incentive to leave the home country.
- Allow for maintaining a North American standard of living.
- Facilitate re-entry into Canada.
- Provide for the education of children.
- Allow for maintaining relationships with family, friends, and business associates.[51]

Balance sheet approach

Compensation system designed to match the purchasing power of a person's home country

The expatriate compensation programs used by over 90 percent of American-based international organizations rest on the **balance sheet approach**. Such systems are designed to equalize the purchasing power of employees in comparable positions living overseas and in the home country, and also to provide incentives to offset qualitative differences between assignment locations.[52] The balance sheet approach generally comprises the following steps:

Step 1: Calculate Base Pay. Begin with the home-based gross income, including bonuses. Deduct taxes and pension contributions.

Step 2: Cost of Living Allowance (COLA). Add or subtract a cost-of-living allowance to the base pay. Typically, companies don't subtract when the international assignment has a lower cost of living. Instead, they allow the expatriate to benefit from the negative differential. Often a housing allowance is added in here as well.

Step 3: Add Incentive Premiums. General mobility premiums and hardship premiums compensate expatriates for separation from family, friends, and domestic support systems. These premiums usually amount to 15 percent of base salary.

Step 4: Add Assistance Programs. These additions are often used to cover added costs such as moving and storage, automobile, and education expenses.

The differentials element is intended to correct for the higher costs of overseas goods and services so that in relation to their domestic peers, expatriates neither gain purchasing power nor lose it. The calculations for arriving at a total differential figure are complex, but in general, the cost typically runs between 3 and 5 times the home country salary.

INTERNATIONAL ORGANIZATIONS AND LABOUR RELATIONS

Labour relations in other countries differ significantly from those in Canada. These differences relate not only to the collective bargaining process but also to political and legal conditions. To give a basic idea about labour–management relations in an international setting, we will consider four key areas: (1) the role of unions in different countries, (2) collective bargaining in other countries, (3) international labour organizations, and (4) the extent of labour participation in management.

The Role of Unions

Unions play different roles in different countries. Various factors are at work here: the level of per capita labour income, mobility between management and labour, the homogeneity of labour (racial, religious, social class), and the level of employment. All of these factors and others determine whether the union will have the strength it needs to represent labour effectively. In countries with relatively high unemployment, low pay levels, and no union funds for welfare, unions are often driven into alliances with other organizations such as political parties, churches, and governments. This is in marked contrast to Canada, where the union is selected by the majority of voting employees and bargains only with the employer, not with other institutions.

Even in the major industrial countries, there are great national differences with respect to (1) the level at which bargaining takes place (national, industry, or workplace), (2) the degree of centralization of union–management relations, (3) the scope of bargaining, (4) the degree of government intervention, and (5) the degree of unionization.

Labour relations in Europe differ from those in Canada in a number of significant ways:

1. In Europe, organizations typically negotiate with the union at the national level, through an employer association. The resulting agreement establishes certain minimum conditions of employment, which are often augmented through negotiations with the union at the company level.

2. In many European countries, unions have more political power than in Canada. As a result, when employers deal with the union they are, in effect, dealing indirectly with the government. In some countries the unions are allied with one particular political party; in other countries the situation is more complex, and they are predominantly but not exclusively aligned with one party.

3. There is a greater tendency in Europe for salaried employees, including those at the management level, to be unionized—quite often in a union of their own.[53]

European countries are facing the realities of globalization. Especially in Germany and the United Kingdom, unions have been losing some of their power. The power of the unions to gain high wages and enforce rigid labour rules for their members has been blamed for damaging the competitiveness of European companies. As the power of unions declines a little, workers are becoming less inclined to make constant demands for higher wages. The trend has been to demand other forms of compensation, such as improved benefits or greater participation in company decision making.[54] Various approaches to participation will be discussed later.

Collective Bargaining in Other Countries

We discussed in Chapter 15 how the collective bargaining process is usually carried out in Canada. Other countries do things very differently, especially with regard to the role that government plays. For example, in the United Kingdom and

France, government intervenes in all aspects of collective bargaining. Government involvement is only natural when some sectors of industry are nationalized. In countries where industry is more heavily nationalized, government involvement is more routinely accepted, even by nonnationalized companies. At Renault, which is owned by the French government, unions use political pressure when bargaining with managers, who are essentially government employees. The resulting contract then sets the standard for other firms. In developing countries it is common for government representatives to be present during bargaining sessions to ensure that unions with relatively uneducated leaders are not disadvantaged in bargaining with management representatives.

International Labour Organizations

WWW

International corporations can choose the countries in which they wish to establish subsidiaries; it follows that they will select those countries which have the most to offer. Certainly, the availability of inexpensive labour is a factor that most strategists consider. By coordinating their resources—including human resources—and their production facilities, companies operate from a position of strength. International unions, such as the United Auto Workers, have found it difficult to achieve the same sort of international influence. Those that have been successful operate in countries that are similar, such as Canada and the United States.

The most active of the international union organizations has been the International Confederation of Free Trade Unions (ICFTU), headquartered in Brussels. Cooperating with the ICFTU are some twenty international trade secretariats (ITSs), which are really international federations of national trade unions operating in the same or related industries. From the point of view of management, the significance of the ITSs is that behind local unions may be the expertise and resources of an ITS. Another active and influential organization is the International Labor Organization (ILO), a specialized agency of the United Nations. It does considerable international research and endorses standards for various working conditions, referred to collectively as the International Labor Code. At various times and places this code may be quoted to management as international labour standards to which employers are expected to conform.[55]

Labour Participation in Management

In many European countries, provisions for employee representation are established by law. An employer may be legally required to provide for employee representation on safety and hygiene committees, on worker councils, and even on boards of directors. While their responsibilities vary from country to country, worker councils basically provide a communication channel between employers and workers. The legal codes that set forth the functions of worker councils in France are very detailed. Councils are generally concerned with grievances, problems of individual employees, internal regulations, and matters affecting employee welfare.

A higher form of worker participation in management is found in Germany, where representation of labour on the board of directors of a company is

Codetermination

Representation of labour on the board of directors of a company

required by law. This arrangement is known as **codetermination** and often by its German name, *Mitbestimmung*. While sometimes puzzling to outsiders, the system is fairly simple: company shareholders and employees are required to be represented in equal numbers on the supervisory boards of all corporations with more than 2,000 employees. Power is generally left with the shareholders, and shareholders are generally assured the chairmanship. Other European countries and Japan either have or are considering minority board participation.[56]

Each of these differences makes managing human resources in an international context more challenging. But the crux of the issue in designing HR systems is not choosing one approach that will meet all the demands of international business. Instead, organizations facing global competition must balance multiple approaches and make their policies flexible enough to accommodate differences across national borders. Throughout this book we have noted that different situations call for different approaches to managing people, and nowhere is this point more clearly evident than in international HRM.

SUMMARY

OBJECTIVE 1
There are four basic ways to organize for global competition: (1) the international corporation is essentially a domestic firm that has leveraged its existing capabilities to penetrate overseas markets; (2) the multinational corporation has fully autonomous units operating in multiple countries to address local issues; (3) the global corporation has a world view but controls all international operations from its home office; and (4) the transnational corporation uses a network structure to balance global and local concerns.

OBJECTIVE 2
International HRM places greater emphasis on a number of responsibilities and functions, such as relocation, orientation, and translation services, to help employees adapt to a new and different environment outside their own country.

OBJECTIVE 3
Because of the special demands made on managers with international assignments, many factors must be considered in their selection and development. Hiring host country nationals or third country nationals automatically avoids many potential problems, but expatriate managers are sometimes preferable. Selecting the latter involves carefully evaluating the personal characteristics of the candidate and his or her spouse.

OBJECTIVE 4
Once an individual is selected, an intensive training and development program is essential to qualify that person for the assignment. Wherever possible, development should extend beyond information and orientation training to include sensitivity training and field experiences that will enable the manager to understand cultural differences better. Those in charge of the international program should provide the help needed to protect managers from career development risks, re-entry problems, and culture shock.

OBJECTIVE 5
Home country managers often have formal responsibility for individuals on foreign assignment, but they may not be able to fully understand expatriate experiences because geographical distances pose severe communication problems. Host country managers may be in the best position to observe day-to-day performance, but may be biased by cultural factors and may not have a view of the organization as a whole. To balance the pros and cons of home country and host country evaluations, performance evaluations should combine the two sources of appraisal information.

Compensation systems should support the overall strategic intent of the organization but be customized for local conditions. Especially for expatriates, compensation plans must provide an incentive to leave Canada; enable maintenance of an equivalent standard of living; facilitate repatriation; provide for the education of children; and make it possible to maintain relationships with family, friends, and business associates.

 In many European countries—Germany, for one—employee representation is established by law. Organizations typically negotiate the agreement with the union at a national level, often with government intervention. Since European unions have been in existence longer than their Canadian counterparts, they have more legitimacy and much more political power. In Europe, it is more likely for salaried employees and managers to be unionized.

KEY TERMS

augmented skills
balance sheet approach
codetermination
core skills
cultural environment
culture shock
expatriates, or home country
    nationals

failure rate
global corporation
global manager
guest workers
host country
host country nationals
international corporation

multinational corporation
    (MNC)
repatriation
third country nationals
transnational corporation
transnational teams
work permit (work certificate)

DISCUSSION QUESTIONS

 1. What do you think are the major HR issues that must be addressed as an organization moves from an international form to a multinational, to a global, and to a transnational form?

 2. In recent years we have observed an increase in foreign investment in Canada, to the point where 35 percent of total corporate revenue generated in Canada in 1997 was by foreign-controlled companies. What effect is this degree of foreign ownership likely to have on HRM in Canada?

 3. If you were starting now to plan for a career in international HRM, what steps would you take to prepare yourself?

 4. Describe the effects that different components of the cultural environment can have on HRM in an international firm.

 5. Pizza Hut is opening new restaurants in Europe every day, it seems. If you were in charge, would you use expatriate managers or host country nationals in staffing the new facilities? Explain your thinking.

6. In what ways are Canadian managers likely to experience difficulties in their relations with employees in foreign operations? How can these difficulties be minimized?

 7. This chapter strongly emphasizes the role of the spouse in the success of an overseas manager. What steps should management take to increase the likelihood of a successful experience for all parties involved?

 **8.** Talk with a foreign student on your campus. Ask about his or her experience with culture shock on first arriving in Canada. What did you learn from your discussion?

 9. If learning (both individual and organizational) is an important outcome of an overseas assignment, how can this be worked into a performance appraisal system? How would a manager assess individual and organizational learning?

 10. If the cost of living is lower in a foreign country than in Canada, should expatriates be paid less than they would be at home? Explain.

 11. What are the main differences between labour/management relations in Europe and those in Canada?

 12. Do you believe that codetermination will ever become popular in Canada? Explain.

CASE 1   DEVELOPING A GLOBAL WORKFORCE AT NORTEL

Nortel won a 1999 award for the "best global company" in the communication sector. Nortel focuses on the high-growth opportunities generated by the Internet revolution and by the explosive growth of e-business. This company delivers the high-performance networks that underpin the new global economy. For the most current information on the company, consult **www.nortelnetworks.com**.

The expatriate population of Nortel has increased rapidly, with hundreds employees on long-term international assignments (three to five years) and hundreds more on short-term assignments. These employees are entering new markets or expanding existing markets, and Nortel views them not just as employees, but as ambassadors to its customers and suppliers and to the communities in which they live and work. To prepare them for their international assignments, Nortel has developed a training program.

The program grew out of concerns that the expats and their families were not well enough prepared for international assignments. They had problems dealing with how business was being done in their host countries (in particular, with the change in pace). There were also problems with day-to-day living issues—with a new language and new customs, culture, and so on. Discontented employees were demanding better pay, housing, and benefits.

The training program, developed with a selected service provider, Family Guidance International (FGI), had three phases:

1. *Predeparture assessment and preparation.* Candidates for international assignments were required to meet with a counsellor, who assessed them for the risks associated with international assignments, and who provided them and their families with information about the country. Risks included marital conflict, negative attitudes toward the host country, health concerns, and dependency problems. This phase sometimes helped candidates self-screen themselves. It also alleviated their anxieties about the placement.

2. *International Employee Assistance Program.* The objective of this program was to prepare assignees for the culture shock they would soon be facing. They were given tips on how to adapt to daily life, and information on the country's history, politics, and culture. In addition, they were given basic language skills. This program was customized for each family.

3. *Repatriation counselling.* This program was designed to ease the return home of the expat and the family.

Overall, the program has been a success. Over 90 percent of the candidates are recommended for assignments, and employees are recommending the program to those considering international assignments. The orientation program, given close to the departure date, has been rated as very relevant by participants, even after three months on the job. A security module has been added to deal with employee concerns about their safety while on assignment.

Source: Adapted from S.R. Fishman, "Developing a Global Workforce," *Canadian Business Review* 21, no. 1 (Spring 1996): 18–21.

Questions

1. What are the chief human resource challenges that Nortel faces as a global organization?

2. What value is gained from mandating an assessment and orientation program for international candidates?

3. If you were designing phase 3, the repatriation program, what would you include as objectives and content?

CASE 2

CULTURAL CONUNDRUM

Anna had enjoyed great success in the Toronto office of a global company. When she was offered an assignment in Tokyo, she approached the job with the full confidence of her employer that she could oversee the reorganization of the subsidiary. By asking her extensive network of colleagues about Japan, she learned a few tips. For example, she learned that when a Japanese businessman hands you his business card, it is proper to read the card before taking it, and to never throw it on the desk. Even with these tips, however, Anna's assignment was heading toward failure.

After six months she was very discouraged, and when she returned home for Christmas she reported the following problems:

*   Although everyone spoke English, there were communication problems.
*   Everything took too long to complete, with deadlines missed and employees not following schedules.
*   Although she asked her employees for feedback and information, and received promises that these would be forthcoming, no data arrived.

The company's response was to give her cross-cultural training. Anna learned the following:

- In Japanese culture, group identity supersedes individual identities. Loyalty is to the group, and criticisms of performance are taboo. Group meetings are the norm, and one-on-one meetings designed to elicit feedback make employees very uncomfortable.
- Japanese culture is based on hierarchy and is organized to recognize the power differentials between superiors and subordinates. Japanese workers do not expect to have input into decisions; their only expectation is to be told what to do. If forced to participate in decision making, the typical Japanese will avoid uncertainty by accumulating every possible item of information to support the decision.
- Japan is a masculine society, and women are employed in low-status positions. Anna's credibility as a decision maker would be questioned, and male employees would be uncomfortable working for her.

The communication problems only compounded the difficulty of the situation. Yes, the employees spoke English. But there were cultural differences. To a direct request to meet a deadline that they perceived as impossible, employees would save face (for themselves and for the person making the request) by saying that they would do their best. Saying "no" is not part of Japanese culture.

Anna made the mistake of tranferring her management style, which was successful in Toronto, to Tokyo without understanding the cultural differences.

Source: Adapted from Z. Fedder, "Same Language, Different Meanings," *Canadian HR Reporter* 13, no. 11 (June 5, 2000): 9, 13; S. McKay, "Women Going Global," *Financial Post Magazine*, December 1998: 38–54.

Questions

1. Exactly what preparation should Anna's company have given her before she started her assignment?

2. In general, what should a candidate for an international assignment do to prepare for a job, in the absence of company orientation and training?

3. Many believe that women on international assignments prove to be very effective, because they are both task oriented (a North American cultural imperative) and relationship oriented (an important attribute in Asian and other cultures). Why did these two sets of skills not help Anna?

CAREER COUNSEL

Take the Culture Quiz on the Managing Human Resources website (**belcourt.nelson.com**) to assess your sensitivity to other cultures.

USING THE INTERNET

WWW

Europa, the website of the European Union (**www.europa.eu.int**) is filled with details about the EU's goals and policies.

To find out the salary a manager would need to receive to maintain his/her real current income while working in a foreign city, see the international calculator at **www.homefair.com**.

NOTES AND REFERENCES

1. Peter Dowling, Denice E. Welch, and Randall S. Schuler, *International Human Resource Management: Managing People in a Multinational Context* (Cincinnati: South-Western, 1998); Nancy J. Adler, *International Dimensions of Organizational Behavior* (Cincinnati: South-Western, 1997); Michael S. Schell and Charlene Marmer Solomon, "Global Culture: Who's the Gatekeeper?" *Workforce* 76, no. 11 (Nov 1997): 35-9.

2. Christopher A. Bartlett and Sumatra Ghoshal, *Managing Across Borders: The Transnational Solution* (Boston: Harvard Business School Press, 1998).

3. Scott A. Snell, Charles C. Snow, Sue Canney Davison, and Donald C. Hambrick, "Designing and Supporting Transnational Teams: The Human Resource Agenda," *Human Resource Management* 37, no. 2: 147-58. See also Charles C. Snow, Scott A. Snell, Sue Canney Davison, and Donald C. Hambrick, "Use Transnational Teams to Globalize Your Company," *Organizational Dynamics* (Spring 1996): 50-67.

4. S. McKay, "Canadians Competing Outside Canada," *Financial Post, Special Report*, 35th edition, June 3, 1999: 86.

5. Jeremy Kahn, "The *Fortune* Global 5 Hundred: The World's Largest Corporations," *Fortune* 140, no. 3 (August 2, 1999): 144-6; 'Country by Country," *Business Week* 3586 (July 13, 1998): 54.

6. K. Kidd, "Outward Bound: Canadian Firms Quietly Conquering the World," *Globe and Mail Report on Business*, August, 8; 1997.

7. Bill Emmott, "The 20th Century: Free to be European," *The Economist* 352, no. 8136 (September 11, 1999): S21-3.

8. Tom Bagsarian, 'Nafta at 5: A boon for Customers," *Iron Age New Steel* 15, no. 10 (September 1999): 18-22; "The Real NAFTA Winner," *Business Week* 3648 (September 27, 1999): 34.

9. Jeremy Kahn, "China's Tough Markets," *Fortune* 140, no. 7 (October 11, 1999): 282; Charlene Marmer Solomon, "The Big Question," *Workforce, Special Supplement* (July 1997): 10-16; Philip Knight, "Global Manufacturing: The

Nike Story Is Just Good Business," *Vital Speeches of the Day* 64, no. 20 (August 1, 1998): 637-40.

10. Stephen J Mezias, Ya-Ru Chen, and Patrice Murphy, "Toto, I Don't Think We're in Kansas Anymore: Some Footnotes to Cross-Cultural Research," *Journal of Management Inquiry* 8 no. 3 (September 1999): 323-3; Pan Suk Kim, 'Globalization of Human Resource Management: A Cross-Cultural Perspective for the Public Sector," *Public Personnel Management* 28, no. 2 (Summer 1999): 227-34; David Veale, Lynn Oliver, and Kees van Langen, "Three Coca-Cola Perspectives on International Management Styles," *Academy of Management Executive* 9, no. 3 (August 1995): 74-7.

11. Interested readers can access this journal online at **www.journals.routledge.com/hr/hrtext.htm**.

12. Maali H Ashamalla, "International Human Resource Management Practices: The Challenge of Expatriation," *Competitiveness Review* 8, no. 2 (1998): 54-65.

13. Readers interested in codes of conduct and other ethical issues pertaining to international business can read the following: Janice M. Beyer and David Nino, "Ethics and Cultures in International Business," *Journal of Management Inquiry* 8, no. 3 (September 1999): 287-97; Ronald Berenbeim, "The Divergence of a Global Economy: One Company, One Market, One Code, One World," *Vital Speeches of the Day* 65, no. 22 (September 1, 1999): 696-8; Larry R. Smeltzer and Marianne M. Jennings, "Why an International Code of Business Ethics Would Be Good for Business," *Journal of Business Ethics* 17. no. 1 (January 1998): 57-66. See also Charlene Marmer Solomon, "Put Your Ethics to a Global Test," *Personnel Journal* 75, no. 1 (January 1996): 66-74; David J. Cherrington and Laura Zaugg Middleton, "An Introduction to Global Business Issues," *HRMmagazine* 40, no. 6 (June 1995): 124-30; Rochelle Kopp, "International Human Resource Policies and Practices in Japanese, European, and United States Multinationals," *Human Resource Management* 33, no. 4 (Winter 1994): 581-99; "Global Companies Reexamine Corporate Culture," *Personnel Journal* (August 1994): 12-13.

14. Rosalie L. Tung, "American Expatriates Abroad: From Neophytes to Cosmopolitans," *Journal of World Business* 33, no. 2 (Summer 1998): 125–44; Calvin Reynolds, "Strategic Employment of Third Country Nationals," *Human Resource Planning* 20, no. 1 (1997): 33–93; Donald McNerney, "Global Staffing: Some Common Problems—and Solutions," *HRFocus, June* 1996: 1, 4–6.

15. Charlene Marmer Solomon, "Staff Selection Impacts Global Success," *Personnel Journal* 73, no. 1 (January 1994): 88–99; Cecil G. Howard, "Profile of the 21st-Century Expatriate Manager," *HRMagazine* 37, no. 6 (June 1992): 93–100.

16. Calvin Reynolds, "Strategic Employment of Third Country Nationals," *Human Resource Planning* 20, no. 1 (1997): 33–93; Dawn Anfuso, "Coca-Cola's Staffing Philosophy Supports Its Global Strategy," *Personnel Journal* 73, no. 11 (November 1994): 116.

17. Valerie Frazee, "Expert Help for Dual-Career Spouses," *Workforce* 4, no. 2 (March 1999): 18–20; "On the Border," *Government Executive* 31 no. 2 (February 1999): 101–4.

18. Barb Cole-Gomolski, "A Whole New Ball Game for High-Tech Guest Workers," *Computerworld* 32, no. 47 (November 23, 1998): 24; Stuart Rosewarne, "The Globalization and Liberalization of Asian Labor Markets," *The World Economy* 21, no. 7 (September 1998): 963–79; Jennifer Hunt, "Japan's 'Guest Workers': Issues and Public Policies," *Industrial and Labor Relations Review* 48, no. 4 (July 1995): 863–64.

19. John P. Harrison and Alfons Westgeest, "Developing a Globally Savvy Staff," *Association Management* 51, no. 2 (February 1999): 58–64; Ingemar Torbiorn, "Staffing for International Operations," *Human Resource Management Journal* 7, no. 3 (1997): 42–52.

20. Allan Halcrow, "Expats: The Squandered Resource," *Workforce* 78, no. 4 (April 1999): 42–8; Valerie Frazee, "Selecting Global Assignees," *Workforce* 3, no. 4 (July 1998): 28–30.

21. Allan Halcrow, "Expats: The Squandered Resource," *Workforce* 78, no. 4 (April 1999): 42–8; "Expat Assignments: Key Is Preparedness," *HRFocus* 75, no. 9 (September 1998): 2; Reyer A. Swaak, "Expatriate Failures: Too Many, Too Much Cost, Too Little Planning," *Compensation and Benefits Review* 27, no. 6 (November–December 1995): 47–55.

22. Carl Quintanilla, "The Number One Reason Overseas Assignments Fail: The Spouse Hates It," *Wall Street Journal,* January 7, 1997: A1.

23. Michael Harvey and Danielle Wiese, "The Dual-Career Couple: Female Expatriates and Male Trailing Spouses," *Thunderbird International Business Review* 40, no. 4 (July–August 1998): 359–88; "Women Managers in Asia," *Training and Development* 50, no. 4 (April 1996): 37; Sully Taylor and Nancy Napier, "Working in Japan: Lessons from Women Expatriates," *Sloan Management Review* 37, no. 3 (Spring 1996): 76–84.

24. Anonymous, "Movers and Shakers," *CMA Management* 73, no. 4 (May 1999): 33–5.

25. Snell et al., "Designing and Supporting Transnational Teams."

26. "What Does It Take to Be a Global Manager?" *Quality* 37, no. 3 (March 1998): 34; Sheila Rothwell, "Leadership Development and International HRM," *Manager Update* 4, no. 4 (Summer 1993): 20–32.

27. Cynthia L. Kemper, "Global Training's Critical Success Factors," *Training & Development* 52, no. 2 (February 1998): 35–7; Margaret Kaeter, "International Development," *Training* 32, no. 5 (May 1995): S23–9.

28. Valerie Frazee, "Send Your Expats Prepared for Success," *Workforce* 4, no. 2 (March 1999): 6–8; Janet D. Lein and Nichole L. Sisco, "Language and Cross-Cultural Training for Expatriate Employees: A Comparison between the U.S. and Germany," *The Journal of Language for International Business* 10, no. 2 (Glendale, 1999): 47–59.

29. Managers who are interested in setting up a language-training program or who wish to evaluate commercially available language-training programs should consult the "Standard Guide for Use-Oriented Foreign Language Instruction." The seven-page guide is put out by the American Society for Testing and Materials (ASTM) (**www.astm.org**).

30. Stephen Dolainski, "Language Training Improves Global Business at ARCO," *Workforce* 76, no. 2 (February 1997): 38; Kathryn Tyler, "Targeted Language Training Is Best Bargain," *HRMagazine* 43, no. 1 (January 1998): 61–4; Tom Lester, "Pulling Down the Language Barrier," *International Management* 49, no. 6 (July–August 1994): 42–4; Robert McGarvey and Scott Smith, "Speaking in Tongues," *Training* 31, no. 1 (January 1994): 113–16. See also Stephen H. Wildstrom, "Log On—and Learn a Language," *Business Week*, January 22, 1996" 22.

31. Neil J. Simon, "Competitive Intelligence Personnel: Requirements for the Multicultural Organization," *Competitive Intelligence Magazine* 2, no. 1 (January–March 1999): 43–4; Abbas J. Ali, Ahmed A. Azim, and Krish S. Krishnan, "Expatriates and Host Country Nationals: Managerial Values and Decision Styles," *Leadership and Organization Development Journal* 16, no. 6 (1995): 27–34; Dean B. McFarlan, Paul D. Sweeney, and John L. Cotton, "Attitudes toward Employee Participation in Decision-Making: A Comparison of European and American Managers in a United States Multinational Company," *Human Resource Management* 31, no. 4 (Winter 1992): 363–83.

32. Readers interested in HR-related issues for managing in Russia should see the following: Carl Fey, Pontus Engstrom and Ingmar Bjorkman, "Doing Business in Russia: Effective Human Resource Management Practices for Foreign Firms in Russia," *Organizational Dynamics* 28, no. 2 (Autumn 1999): 69–74; Ruth May, Carol Bormann Young, and Donna Ledgerwood, "Lessons from Russian Human Resource Management Experience," *European Management Journal* 16, no. 4 (August 1998): 447–59; Martha Cooley, "HR in Russia:

Training for Long-Term Success," *HRMagazine* 42, no. 12 (December 1997): 98–106.

33. Mike Bendixen and Bruce Burger, 'Cross-Cultural Management Philosophies," *Journal of Business Research* 42, no. 2 (June 1998): 107–14; Clifford C. Hebard, "Managing Effectively in Asia," *Training and Development* 74, no. 12 (December 1995): 113–17.

34. Geert Hofstede, "Cultural Constraints in Management Theories," *Academy of Management Executive* 7, no. 1 (February 1993): 81–94. See also Fons Trompenaars, *Riding the Waves of Culture: Understanding Cultural Diversity in Business* (London: Economist Books, 1993).

35. William E. Franklin, 'Careers in International Business: Five Ideas or Principles," *Vital Speeches of the Day* 64, no. 23 (September 15, 1998): 719–21; Ronald Mortensen, 'Beyond the Fence Line," *HRMagazine* 42, no. 11 (November 1997): 100–9.

36. Mary A. Scelba, "Developing an Effective Repatriation Process at Chubb and Sons Inc.," *Employee Relations Today* 22, no. 4 (Winter 1995–96): 55–61; "What You Thought," *Personnel Journal* 75, no. 6 (June 1996): 16; Kenton J. Klaus, "How to Establish an Effective Expatriate Program—Best Practices in International Assignment Administration," *Employment Relations Today* 22, no. 1 (Spring 1995): 59–70.

37. Sherrie Zhan, "Smooth Moves," *World Trade* 12, no. 7 (July 1999): 62–4; Charlene Marmer Solomon, "Repatriation: Up, Down, or Out?" *Personnel Journal* 74, 1 (January 1995): 28–30.

38. Lance J. Richards, 'Hiring Multicultural Vagabonds," *Workforce* 3, no. 6 (November 1998): 28–30; Allan Halcrow, "Expats: The Squandered Resource," *Workforce* 78, no. 4 (April 1999): 42–8. Also see, J. Stewart Black and Mark E. Mendenhall, *Global Assignments: Successfully Expatriating and Repatriating International Managers* (San Francisco: Jossey-Bass, 1992); Solomon, "Repatriation," 28–30.

39. A. Bross, A. Churchill, and J. Zifkin, 'Cross-Cultural Training: Issues to Consider During Implementation," *HR Reporter* 13, no. 11 (June 5, 2000): 10–12.

40. Stephen S. McIntosh, "Breaking Through Culture Shock: What You Need to Succeed in International Business," *HRMagazine* 44, no. 6 (June 1999): 184–6; Michael G. Harvey and M. Ronald Buckley, 'The Process for Developing an International Program for Dual-Career Couples," *Human Resource Management Review* 8, no. 1 (Spring 1998): 99–123; Nancy Carter, "Solve the Dual-Career Challenge," *Workforce* 2, no. 4 (October 1997): 21–2; Charlene Marmer Solomon, "One Assignment, Two Lives," *Personnel Journal* 75, no. 5 (May 1996): 36–47.

41. Nancy Adler, *International Dimensions of Organizational Behavior* (Cincinnati: South-Western Publishing, 1997).

42. Snell et al., "Designing and Supporting Transnational Teams."

43. Paul Y. Huo and Mary Ann Von Glinow, "On Transplanting Human Resource Practices to China: A Culture Driven Approach," *International Journal of Manpower* 16, no. 9 (1995): 3–15; Robert C. Kovach, Jr.,

"Matching Assumptions to Environment in the Transfer of Management Practices: Performance Appraisal in Hungary," *International Studies of Management and Organization* 24, no. 4 (Winter 1994–95): 83–99; Gary Oddou and Mark Mendenhall, "Expatriate Performance Appraisal: Problems and Solutions," in Mendenhall and Oddou, eds. *Readings and Cases,* 399–410.

44. Charlene Marmer Solomon, "How Does Your Global Talent Measure Up?" *Personnel Journal* 73, no. 10 (October 1994): 96–108.

45. "10 tips for Expatriate Management," *HRFocus* 75, no. 3 (March 1998): S8; M.G. Martinsons, 'Human Resource Management Applications of Knowledge-Based Systems," *International Journal of Information Management* 17. no. 1 (February 1997): 35–53.

46. Michael Harvey, 'Focusing the International Personnel Performance Appraisal Process," *Human Resource Development Quarterly* 8, no. 1 (Spring 1997): 41°62.

47. Andrew C. Inkpen, "Learning and Knowledge Acquisition through International Strategic Alliances," *The Academy of Management Executive* 12, no. 4 (November 1998): 69–80; Oded Shenkar and Jiatao Li, "Knowledge Search in International Cooperative Ventures," *Organization Science* 10, no. 2 (March–April 1999): 134–43. Charlene Marmer Solomon, "Return on Investment," *Workforce* 2, no. 4 (October 1997): 12–18; Dianne J. Cyr and Susan C. Schneider, "Implications for Learning: Human Resource Management in East-West Joint Ventures," *Organizational Studies* 17, no. 2 (1996): 207–26; Igor Gurkov and Yaroslav Kuz Minov, "Organizational Learning in Russian Privatized Enterprises: The Beginning of Strategic Change," *International Studies of Management and Organization* 25, no. 4 (Winter 1995–96): 91–117.

48. Timothy D. Dwyer, "Trends in Global Compensation," *Compensation and Benefits Review* 31, no. 4 (July–August 1999): 48–53; George Milkovich and Matt Bloom, "Rethinking International Compensation," *Compensation and Benefits Review* 30, no. 1 (Janunary–February 1998): 15–23; "Japanese Companies Can't Seem to Adjust to U.S. Pay Practices," *HRFocus* 72, no. 2 (February 1995): 14.

49. Mark Sullivan, "European Benefit Issues: Costs to the Multinational Employers," *Compensation and Benefits Management* 12, no. 2 (Spring 1996): 54–60; "Becoming a Global Company: The Implications for the Benefits Department," *Employee Benefit Plan Review* 50, no. 8 (February 1996): 40–4; Jim McKay, "Benefit Trends in Europe," *Employee Benefits* 19, no. 1 (March 1994): 25–9.

50. Jacqueline M. Graves, "U.S. Managers Rank Sixth in Pay," *Fortune,* January 16, 1995: 18; 'Want the Big Bucks? Head East—Far East," *Personnel Journal,* April 1995: 26.

51. Carolyn Gould, "Expat Pay Plans Suffer Cutbacks," *Workforce* 78, no. 9 (September 1999): 40–6; Carolyn Gould, 'What's the Latest in Global Compensation?" *Workforce,* supplement (July 1997): 17–21; Ranae M. Hyer, "Executive Compensation in the International Arena:

Back to the Basics," *Compensation and Benefits Review* 25, no. 2 (March–April 1993): 49–54.

52. Valerie Frazee, 'Is the Balance Sheet Right for Your Expats?" *Workforce* 77, no. 9 (September 1998): 19–26; Carolyn Gould, "What's the Latest in Global Compensation?" *Workforce*, supplement (July 1997): 17–21.

53. Andrew Martin and George Ross (eds.), *The Brave New World of European Labor : European Trade Unions at the Millennium* (Oxford, UK: Berghahn Books, 1999); Haknoh Kim, "Constructing European Collective Bargaining," *Economic and Industrial Democracy* 20, no. 3 (August 1999): 393–426.

54. "Paying Dues: Once the Big Muscle of German Industry, Unions See It All Sag," *Wall Street Journal* 234, no. 105 (November 29, 1999): A1, 18; Bernard Ebbinyhaus, Jelle Visser, and Bernard Ebbinghaus, *Development of Trade Unions in Western Europe: 1945–1995* (New York: Grove's

Dictionaries, Inc., 1999); "Looking for Work: In Employment Policy, America and Europe Make a Sharp Contrast," *Wall Street Journal*, March 14, 1994: A1; 'Payroll Policy: Unlike Rest of Europe, Britain Is Creating Jobs, but They Pay Poorly," *Wall Street Journal*, March 28, 1994: A1.

55. Interested readers can find more information about international trade unions by going to **www.icftu.org**, the website for the ICFTU, and **www.ilo.org**, for the ILO.

56. Anke Hassel, "The Erosion of the German System of Industrial Relations," *British Journal of Industrial Relations* 37, no. 3 (September 1999): 483–505; Manfred Schumann, "'Mitbestimmung'—A German Model for Social Peace," *World Trade* 9, no. 4 (April 1996): 9; Klas Levinson, "Codetermination in Sweden: From Separation to Integration," *Economic and Industrial Democracy* 17, no. 1 (February 1996): 131–42.

After studying this chapter, you should be able to

Discuss the underlying principles of high-performance work systems.

Identify the components that make up a high-performance work system.

Describe how the components fit together and support strategy.

Recommend processes for implementing high-performance work systems.

Discuss the outcomes for both employees and the organization.

Explain how the principles of high-performance work systems apply to small and medium-sized organizations as well as large ones.

WWW

This chapter is available on the Managing Human Resources Website (belcourt.nelson.com).

CREATING HIGH-PERFORMANCE WORK SYSTEMS

 COMPREHENSIVE CASES

CASE 1

THE MEASUREMENT OF HUMAN CAPITAL

The Office of the Auditor General of British Columbia recognized that human capital is critically important to the delivery of high-quality service to the province's citizens. So it set out to measure whether training and development (T&D) were being used to increase human capital in the B.C. public service. As a first step it defined human capital as the collective brainpower in an organization. This brainpower consists of:

- *facts* acquired through informal and formal education;
- *skills* gained through training and practice;
- *experience* gained through reflection on past successes and mistakes;
- *value judgments* based on individual perceptions; *and*
- *social networks* developed through relationships with co-workers, colleagues, and customers.

The audit took several measures, including a large-scale survey of a random sample of full-time employees, and an in-depth audit of three ministries. Some of the data generated by this audit :

- 36 percent of government employees had received no formal training.
- The average B.C. government employee received 17 hours of training (compared to a Canadian benchmark of 29 hours).
- Less than 1 percent of payroll was spent on training (compared to the 4 percent that the best employers spend).
- 40 percent of employees had had their jobs redefined.
- 43 percent of senior managers would reach fifty-five in the next five years and be eligible to retire.
- 33 percent of employees with less than one year of employment did not feel they had been trained properly to carry out their duties.

The audit revealed that most T&D decisions were based on requests made from individual employees, and that most programs they attended consisted of one- and two-day courses outside the organization. It had never been ascertained whether these courses increased employees' skills or helped the organization achieve its goals. There was no way knowing how effective this training was; nor was there any accounting for T&D expenditures.

Government employees generally believed that training was of great value to them and their organizations. Paradoxically, they also believed that they weren't being supported in their work; and only half thought they had the tools and resources they needed to do their jobs. (A full copy of the report is available at **www.oag.bc.ca**.)

Source: Adapted from J. McCannel & L. McAdams, "The Learning Culture in the Public Service," *Public Sector Management* 11, no. 1 (2000); **www.ipaciapc.ca**.

Questions

1. B.C.'s Auditor General wanted to measure the provincial public service's human capital and the strategic role that T&D played in its development. Did it succeed? Explain.

2. Develop some benchmark statistics on T&D. To start, consult any book on benchmarking human resources (e.g., Jac Fitz Ens, *The ROI of Human Capital*, McGraw-Hill Ryerson, 2000); or, at your school's library, search databases for journal and newspaper articles that provide these statistics.

3. Using your answers from 1 and 2, prepare a plan that addresses the following three of the report's findings:

   - *Finding 1.* The British Columbia Public Service is facing urgent human capital issues that threaten the effectiveness and quality of government services.
   - *Finding 2.* The British Columbia Public Service lacks a human resource strategy to guide its investment in training and development.
   - *Finding 3.* The B.C. Public Service has made minimal commitment to training and developing its employees to maintain an effective workforce.

CASE 2

WOMEN IN A MEN'S WORLD

Attempts to integrate women into jobs traditionally held by men, such as combat positions and tree planting, have regularly been frustrated. There are many obstacles to integration, including these:

- Men and women have different physical abilities. However, those who advocate integrating women into traditional sectors question the need for physical ability. Most jobs in the Canadian military do not require long periods of grinding physical labour. How much muscle does it take to drive a tank? The problem here is that driving is not the driver's sole task. When a tank breaks down, the driver has to perform other tasks, such as lifting links (which weigh 110 pounds) and loading turrets (which weigh 80 pounds each).
- Women may not want traditional male jobs. The recruiting campaigns for the Canadian military emphasize travel and adventure and show women wearing make-up. The reality is boot camp, and the make-up is more likely to be green combat paint. No woman who has served a full term in the Canadian infantry has ever signed up for a second one.
- Roles for women are limited by the stereotypes that attach to jobs. For example, tree planting is characterized by a hierarchical social structure: foremen (with years of experience) are at the top; below them are "highballers" (highest performance; most experience); then, at the bottom, are the "lowballers" (least productive). Women tree planters who can keep up with the highballers are still ranked as lowballers and forced to take orders from both highballers and foremen. They are valued not for their high productivity but rather for their ability to provide emotional support (i.e., to exude a calming influence and be "motherly").
- Women tree planters are also valued as sexual partners. Crew foremen have been known to hire women for the benefit of the crew—"to keep morale up." Foremen whose sexual advances were rejected often became threatening and verbally abusive. Most of the women quit.

- Men in traditionally male jobs often refuse to accept female counterparts because they don't think women can keep up to the work's physical demands (i.e., they lack strength and stamina). They're concerned about their safety and security on the job. At the same time, supervisors can be reluctant to push women to meet the job's standards, in case they are accused of harassment.

Source: Adapted from J. Clark, "The More Lady You Are, the More They Treat You Like a Lady," *Canadian Woman Studies* 18, no. 1 (Spring 1998): 82–5; Donna Laframboise, "Looking, Desperately for a Few Good Women," *National Post,* December 4, 1999: B7.

Questions

1. Although the average woman may not be able to do the same physical labour as the average man, some women can outperform some men. Should physical standards be lowered to accommodate the average woman (e.g., women should do fifteen sit ups, men nineteen)? Should women applicants receive additional training or assistance so that they can succeed at the same rates as men? Divide into teams and debate these issues.

2. Women applying to serve in the Canadian military are often more intelligent and better educated than the men candidates. Is this an argument for a gender division of labour (i.e., men do the physical work, and women do the mental work)?

3. Discuss ways to overcome the obstacles to integrating women in male-dominated occupations.

CASE 3   JOB ANALYSIS AND HIRING DECISIONS AT OVANIA CHEMICAL

COMPANY BACKGROUND

Ovania Chemical Corporation is a specialty chemicals producer. Its core product is polyethylene terephthalate (PET) thermoplastic resins, which are used mainly to make containers and packages for bottled water, soft drinks, foods, and pharmaceuticals. Ovania is one of the smaller chemical producers but has competed successfully in its niche. In recent years, technological advances have shaken up the industry, and like other firms in it, Ovania is modernizing its facilities. Not surprisingly, the company has had to redesign its employees' jobs as a result. In fact, in the past three years those jobs have changed drastically. Following is an example, from Ovania's Boucherville plant.

SYSTEM ANALYZER

Because chemical production is such a complex process, workers are needed who can monitor all of the individual steps and procedures simultaneously. This is what system analyzers do. It is one of the most prestigious nonmanagerial jobs in the entire plant, and its importance is likely to grow.

The position was once classified as semiskilled (i.e., maintenance technician); however, with automation, the requirements for the job are expanding dramatically. A system analyzer will soon have to know pneumatics, hydraulics, information technology, programming, and electrical wiring. Ovania has estimated that within two years, a system analyzer's tasks, duties, and responsibilities will have changed by over 70 percent. The three men who currently hold the position admit that they will soon be unable to perform their duties adequately. For these reasons, the decision has been made to recruit three new people for the position.

JOB ANALYSIS AND NEW POSITION ANALYSIS

The manager of Ovania's Boucherville plant, Pierre Landry, the HR manager, Emily Bouchard, and two senior engineers, Jeet Singh and David Parizeau, formed a selection committee. With the help of two consultants, they have just completed a job analysis for the changed position of system analyzer. They have had to project into the future regarding the specific requirements of the job, but feel that their conclusions are quite justifiable. **Figure 3A** lists the major performance dimensions of the job; it also indicates the specific tasks that will be characteristic of each dimension.

The selection committee has drawn from this list of tasks to arrive at a set of personal qualities that system analyzers will need. These qualities include the twelve abilities shown in **Figure 3B.** Beside each ability are numbers corresponding to the tasks to which it is related (see **Figure 3A**). The abilities marked with an asterisk (★) are considered by the committee to be "critical." Any applicant not scoring well on each of the critical dimensions will be considered unqualified for the job.

ANTICIPATED SELECTION PROCESS

The committee hopes to acquire "new blood" for the redesigned system analyzer job; this will entail recruiting outside the organization for the best talent available. Yet as a matter of policy, management is strongly committed to promoting from within. After careful deliberation, the committee has decided to recruit both inside and outside Ovania for the new position. It has also decided to encourage the current system analyzers in particular to "reapply" for the job.

Because the changes in the position will not be in place for two more years, the committee is being very careful not to include in the selection battery any skills or knowledge that could reasonably be trained within that two-year period. Only aptitude or ability factors have been incorporated into the selection process; achievement tests have not been.

In a private session, some of the committee members admit candidly that they seriously doubt whether any women or minority members currently in the relevant labour market have the credentials to compete for the position. The three system analyzers presently employed are white males. However, because Ovania Chemical has a rather unenviable history of employment discrimination charges, the decision has been made to do no unnecessary prescreening of applicants' qualifications, previous experience, and so on. It is hoped that this strategy will encourage minorities and women to apply for the new positions, whatever their past employment history.

There is some concern that Ovania will be accused of prejudice if women or members of minority groups are hired for the jobs. Word through the grapevine is that many do not consider these people suitable for such a prestigious position. Moreover, several comments have been heard that a woman would not get down into the treatment tanks to check gauge readings. All of these factors, taken together, are making for a very sensitive selection process. Ovania's managers, however, are committed to making the procedures and decisions fair and objective.

The job is posted, and fifty-six employees apply for the new position of system analyzer. Twenty-one are women; fifteen belong to visible minorities. Only two of the three current system analyzers have reapplied for the new position. The company had decided that a total score of 800 on the twelve tests would be the cutoff score for an applicant to be seriously considered for the position. This criterion has resulted in a pool of twenty primary candidates (see **Figure 3C**). Note that although each of the aptitude tests has been published, standardized (100 points possible for each test), and validated on other jobs, there are no normative or validity data for the specific job of system analyzer. This means that the test battery can be defended solely on the basis of content validity. The selection committee is having a difficult time arriving at a method for combining the multiple predictors to reach the final cutoff scores.

Questions

1. How would you go about conducting a job analysis for a job that does not yet exist?

2. Do you think the abilities chosen for selection are content valid? What other kinds of predictors might be generally useful for employee selection?

3. What reasons did the selection committee have for selecting only those factors which could not be acquired through a two-year training program?

4. Should the concern for women getting down into the dirty treatment tanks have been a selection issue? How might you include this factor in a selection battery?

5. For the abilities termed "critical," what score should someone receive in order to be considered scoring "well" on that test? How should the test scores be combined (e.g., compensatory, multiple hurdle, combination)?

6. Which three candidates seem most qualified? What are your reservations, if any, about this recommendation?

7. Would this test battery and selection procedure be defensible in court?

FIGURE 3A *Performance Dimensions (Duties and Tasks)*

MAINTAINING SPARES AND SUPPLIES

1. Anticipates future need for parts and supplies and orders them.
2. Stocks parts and supplies in an orderly fashion.
3. Maintains and calibrates test equipment.

TROUBLESHOOTING

4. Applies calibration standards to verify operation by subjecting the system to known standards.
5. Decides whether the problem is in the sensor, in the processor, in the process stream, and/or in the sample system.
6. Uses troubleshooting guides in system manuals to determine the problem area.
7. Uses test equipment to diagnose the problem.
8. Makes a general visual inspection of the analyzer system as a first troubleshooting step.
9. Replaces components such as printed circuit boards and sensors to see if the problem can be alleviated.

HANDLING REVISIONS AND NEW INSTALLATIONS

10. Makes minor piping changes such as size, routing, and additional filters.
11. Makes minor electrical changes such as installing switches and wires and making terminal changes.
12. Uses common pipefitting tools.
13. Uses common electrical tools.
14. Reads installation drawings.

RECORD KEEPING

15. Maintains system files showing historical record of work on each system.
16. Maintains loop files that show the application of the system.
17. Updates piping and instrument drawings if any changes are made.
18. Maintains Environment Canada records and logbooks.
19. Disassembles analyzers to perform repairs on-site or back in the shop.
20. Replaces damaged parts such as filters, electronic components, light sources, lenses, sensors, and values.
21. Uses diagnostic equipment such as oscilloscopes, ohmmeters, and decade boxes.
22. Tests and calibrates repaired equipment to ensure that it works properly.
23. Reads and follows written procedures from manuals.

ROUTING MAINTENANCE

24. Observes indicators on systems to ensure that there is proper operation.
25. Adds reagents to systems.
26. Decides whether the system or the lab results are correct regarding results (i.e., resolves discrepancies between lab and analyzer results).
27. Performs calibrations.

FIGURE 3B Abilities and Tasks

Numbers represent tasks cited in Figure 3A. Asterisks indicate abilities considered critical by the committee.

SKILLS	TASK NUMBERS
*Finger dexterity	3, 4, 7, 9, 10, 11, 12, 13, 19, 20, 21, 22, 25, 27
*Mechanical comprehension	3, 5, 6, 8, 9, 10, 12, 13, 7, 14, 19, 20, 22, 23, 24, 27, 11, 17
*Numerical ability	11, 3, 4, 24, 10, 21, 12, 13, 14, 27
*Spatial ability	2, 4, 5, 9, 10, 11, 14, 19, 20
*Visual pursuit	3, 4, 5, 6, 7, 8, 9, 10, 11, 14, 16, 17, 19, 20, 21, 22, 27
*Detection	2, 3, 5, 6, 8, 9, 10, 14, 19, 20, 23, 7
Oral comprehension	1, 2, 5, 6, 26, 7, 8, 9, 19, 21, 25
Written comprehension	1, 15, 16, 17, 18
Deductive reasoning	1, 5, 3, 6, 7, 8, 9, 10, 11, 19, 21, 20, 22, 2, 26, 27
Inductive reasoning	1, 3, 5, 6, 7, 8, 9, 10, 11, 19, 21, 20, 22, 2, 26, 27
Reading comprehension	3, 6, 14, 7, 22, 23, 21, 9, 27
Reading scales and tables	3, 4, 7, 8, 9, 21, 23, 24, 27, 2, 6, 14

FIGURE 3C Primary Pool of Candidates

Name	Race	Sex	E/I	Test Scores														
				Finger dexterity	Mechanical comprehension	Numerical ability	Spatial ability	Visual pursuit	Detection	Oral comprehension	Written comprehension	Deductive reasoning	Inductive reasoning	Reading comprehension	Reading scales and tables			
Bohlander, G.	W	M	E	67	78	74	70	76	62	80	69	71	76	78	82	=	883
Baldwin, T.	W	M	I	83	76	78	76	69	71	90	70	74	72	88	92	=	941
Beliveau, D.	W	M	E	92	62	88	89	96	85	90	94	93	89	97	87	=	1062
Buffett, J.	B	M	E	87	97	89	61	94	93	75	90	85	96	85	80	=	1032
Denny, A.	B	F	I	92	88	72	72	78	79	69	76	81	83	81	78	=	949
Egan, M.	W	F	E	93	80	76	98	76	88	93	92	93	78	81	92	=	884
Groulx, D.	W	F	I	82	82	79	75	77	73	72	80	81	77	70	80	=	856
Haney, H.	W	M	E	82	76	76	71	69	80	62	76	75	74	78	67	=	810

Kight, G.	W	F	E	65	75	72	67	80	74	62	47	66	67	60	80	=	815
Lalonde, S.	W	M	E	82	87	85	85	83	88	81	80	80	83	84	80	=	998
Laukitis, T.	B	F	E	87	97	63	89	93	90	91	85	86	96	88	89	=	1054
Lesko, B.J.	B	F	I	83	84	89	91	80	82	86	88	85	84	90	89	=	1031
Roth, D.	B	M	I	80	60	67	66	67	62	74	80	67	72	75	66	=	835
Sara, E.	W	F	I	89	91	77	93	90	91	88	78	98	80	80	76	=	1021
Sherman, A.	W	F	I	91	82	78	93	92	94	89	77	95	77	81	92	=	1041
Singh, C.	W	F	E	76	72	78	81	80	72	73	77	75	79	82	82	=	927
Snell, J.	W	M	E	80	85	84	81	81	80	89	88	84	86	81	82	=	1001
Timothy, S.	W	F	E	82	78	76	71	69	80	62	76	76	70	71	67	=	878
Whitney, J.	W	M	I	67	71	70	76	76	62	81	69	71	76	78	82	=	815
Yee, P.	W	M	I	80	60	57	56	57	62	74	80	69	72	75	65	=	887

CASE 4

MICROSOFT—HIRING THE SUPERSMART

At Microsoft, the pre-eminent software developer based in Redmond, Washington, human resources are truly the company's most important asset. Working on the cutting edge of technology in a fast-paced industry, Microsoft's top managers are quick to acknowledge that their success rests mainly on the intellectual talents of their employees. Essentially, Microsoft depends on employees who are learners rather than knowers. Microsoft wants people who understand current technology, who ask questions, and who have the potential to continue learning about technological changes. Microsoft wants its people to be able to think flexibly so that they can adapt to changes in the industry. For these reasons, the software company makes significant effort to ensure that it has the right people in its organization. It does this mainly through innovative recruitment and selection techniques.

Like most organizations, Microsoft relies on a variety of tools to reach potential applicants. It places ads in newspapers, accepts applications on its Microsoft World Wide Web page, and recruits at college and university job fairs. To complement these basic practices, Microsoft has also developed hiring techniques that reflect its reputation for creativity and innovation.

All applicants, regardless of recruitment source, go through a rigorous screening process. This is a major task, when you consider that Microsoft receives approximately 12,000 résumés a month. Each résumé is logged into a computer database, which recruiters sort through, using keyword searches that indicate skills and abilities valuable to Microsoft.

The present employees are heavily involved in the recruitment process. To help match prospective employees with Microsoft, recruiters are involved in business meetings and solicit feedback from current employees throughout the organization about their needs. As a result, the recruiters are familiar with the needs of each position. Because Microsoft's goal is to have the smartest employees possible, whatever their previous experiences, background, and education, the top managers also get involved in recruiting. Even Bill Gates, the highly visible CEO, has been known to call potential employees to let them know that Microsoft is interested in bringing them on board.

Microsoft's selection techniques are equally creative. The company does not place a lot of emphasis on traditional selection tests, and recruiters do not usually conduct reference checks or drug tests. Instead, after sorting through résumés and identifying potential employees, recruiters schedule candidates for intensive interview sessions. Interviews do not focus on verifying information or seeking answers to basic questions; they are intended mainly to get a sense of how potential employees think and learn. For instance, an interviewer might ask an applicant how much water flows through the Mississippi on a daily basis, or why manhole covers are round. The interviewers are not looking for correct answers; instead, they are trying to gauge an applicant's ability to solve problems, by examining how the applicant thinks and what information the applicant requests.

Do these recruiting and selection practices work for Microsoft? It seems they do. The applicants who are selected seem to be a good fit for this company. Indeed, the turnover rate for employees is roughly 7 percent a year—far below the industry average. Microsoft is always looking for potential employees who will continually advance the organization. By pushing employees and recruiters to challenge interviewees to assess their true capabilities and potential, Microsoft continually recruits the best talent it can get.

Sources: Ron Lieber, "Wired for Hiring: Microsoft's Slick Recruiting Machine," *Fortune,* February 5, 1996: 123–4; George Taninecz, "In Search of Creative Sparks," *Industry Week,* December 4, 1995: 43–7; Stuart J. Johnston, "Microsoft Scrambles to Find 'Brightest,'" *Computerworld*, February 20, 1995: 32; Randall E. Stross, "Microsoft's Big Advantage—Hiring Only the Supersmart," *Fortune,* November 25, 1996: 159–62.

Questions

1. What are the costs and benefits associated with using such innovative hiring techniques?

2. How successfully would these practices transfer to other firms in the same industry? How successfully would these practices transfer to firms in other industries?

3. What type of training, career development, performance appraisal, and compensation initiatives should Microsoft use to complement its unique hiring practices?

CASE 5

RECRUITMENT AND SELECTION AT THE PUBLIC SERVICE COMMISSION

Each year, Canada's Public Service Commission (PSC) conducts a postsecondary recruitment campaign aimed at bringing qualified university graduates into Canada's public service. These recruitment efforts focus on filling high-demand entry-level positions. At present, government departments are in particular need of human resource professionals, lawyers, internal auditors and financial officers, mathematical statisticians, economists, engineers, computer systems analysts, and foreign service officers.

Staff in regional PSC offices assess completed application forms to determine whether applicants possess the required skills and abilities. The names of those who do are added to a database of qualified people. The PSC also administers mandatory tests. For example, potential financial officers and internal auditors are required to take the General Competency Test, Level 2 (GCT2); applicants for the foreign service must take the Foreign Service Knowledge Test (FSKT) and a written communication test. After the testing phase has been completed, the PSC refers successful candidates to the individual hiring departments, which conduct structured interviews and make final selections.

The PSC also recruits candidates for two developmental programs: the Management Trainee Program (MTP) and the Accelerated Economist Training Program (AETP). Here the selection process is somewhat more complex.

The MTP is designed to replenish the pool of public service managers. Over five years, university graduates receive the training they need to function as middle managers. There are four steps in the selection process. First, applicants are screened on the basis of their application forms, their résumés, and transcripts of their grades. HR specialists use these documents to evaluate factors such as the applicant's written communication skills. Those who are successful at this first stage are invited to an interview that lasts about one hour and is designed to assess management potential, verbal communication and interpersonal skills, and qualities such as motivation and judgment.

Candidates who pass the interview undergo a one-day assessment conducted by psychologists, who use recognized methods to measure six management skills: communication, behavioural flexibility, action management, leadership, interpersonal relations, and thinking. Simulations, task forces, and structured interviews are among the tools used. The final phase, final selection, involves compiling the results of the previous three stages and arriving at a shortlist. Candidates on this list are referred to participating departments, which make the final selections. A formal letter of offer is then sent to successful candidates.

The two-year AETP is designed to give individuals with master's degrees in economics or business administration an opportunity to develop their policy analysis skills. As with the MTP, there is a four-step selection process, and participants are trained to function at the middle-management level in the federal public service.

Sources: Interview with Peter Corner and Leslie Goddard, conducted by Deborah M. Zinni in June 1995 and November 1997; *Communiqué: Perspectives in Staffing,* Ottawa: Public Service Commission, October 1992, September 1993, and November 1993.

Questions

1. In what ways does the PSC's postsecondary recruitment campaign differ from recruitment drives initiated in the private sector?

2. In what ways might the recruitment process be improved?

3. In what ways might the selection process for the MTP and AETP be improved?

CASE 6

THE TRAINING AND DEVELOPMENT DILEMMA AT WHITNEY AND COMPANY

COMPANY BACKGROUND

Whitney and Company is a global management consulting firm that has been growing rapidly. The firm, which is headquartered in Chicago, provides comprehensive business planning and analysis as well as consulting in operational and technical areas such as finance, operations, and information technology. Its client list includes medium-sized firms, but its growth tends to focus on *Fortune* 1000 companies. Whitney contracts include manufacturing and service organizations as well as government, health care, and religious organizations. The firm has offices in twenty-four American cities and offices in sixteen other countries. Whitney employs nearly 27,000 people, the vast majority of whom are young, aggressive professionals.

In light of the tremendous growth of the consulting industry, Whitney has ambitious plans for expanding the firm. Estimates are that in the next five years alone it will need 1,200 new managers and about 200 new partners. Because Whitney maintains a policy of promoting from within, these people will come mainly from the ranks of entry-level employees. There is plenty of incentive for these young professionals to do well; starting salaries for partners average $250,000 (although individuals usually don't reach partner status until they have been with the firm for ten years).

TRAINING AND DEVELOPMENT

Given the critical importance of professional talent, Whitney has invested millions of dollars over the years in in-house educational and training facilities that are now the envy of the industry. The keystone of this effort is the luxurious Corporate Education and Development Center (CEDC) in St. Charles, Illinois, thirty minutes west of Chicago. The 100-acre centre provides living and meeting accommodations for approximately 500 people and has an impressive array of classrooms, conference rooms, libraries, and even a television studio. The centre has nearly fifty instructors on staff, most of them field managers, who rotate on a two-year basis into the CEDC.

Every new Whitney employee spends two weeks at CEDC before going on to three additional months of training at one of nine other regional facilities (Atlanta, Boston, Cleveland, Chicago, Dallas, Denver, Los Angeles, Seattle, New York City). All told, Whitney spends almost $3,500 per employee for training and education each year.

Most of this investment is in technical and systems training for entry-level consultants. Beyond this, employees receive extensive training in the specific industries in which they will be working (e.g., oil and gas, telecommunications, banking, health care). Senior managers are profoundly aware that Whitney's public image is largely a function of the actions and work quality of its first-level associates. Executives clearly recognize the importance of an expert workforce, and spare no expense in this regard.

EMPLOYEE PERFORMANCE

Whitney offers many opportunities to its employees and spends a great deal of money on professional development; but it also expects a great deal back. It is not at all uncommon for beginning associates to work seventy-hour weeks, especially in the first two years. The travel is often gruelling, and so are the schedules, and the rewards for the first few years do not usually reflect this effort. Starting salaries are generally in the mid-$40,000s, and benefits are only average for a firm of Whitney's size and reputation. As indicated earlier, the real payoffs come with the achievement of partner status, but not much earlier.

Yet Whitney has little trouble attracting very aggressive, energetic employees—generally right out of university—who are eager "to pay their dues" for success in a major firm. Some clients, especially in the health care industry, have been put off by this aggressiveness, which strikes them as boorish and callous. Some clients have even stopped doing business with Whitney, not because they question Whitney's expertise, but because of the "fast-in, fast-out style of big-time consulting." Whitney employees usually learn to interpret the subtleties of client needs; occasionally (and increasingly), employees have been let go because of their poor interpersonal skills.

Considering how important interpersonal skills are for Whitney, some of the training staff have suggested that more attention should be paid to that part of initial staff development. However, past additions to training in customer relations have not been well received. Also, more and more senior partners are coming to believe that too much is already being spent on education and training, since so many of those trained employees subsequently leave to take jobs with other companies.

The facts in this regard are clear. Only about 50 percent of new hires stay with Whitney beyond their first five years, and around 90 percent of employees leave the firm within ten. Most of these people either start their own firms or go to work for one of Whitney's clients. (Whitney doesn't fire many people.) Many people think this turnover rate is terribly detrimental to the success of Whitney, especially given the huge expense of training and development. Many others, however, feel that the departures are inevitable, given Whitney's promotion-from-within policies. Some feel the turnover actually helps business, since those who go to work for other companies often convince them to become clients of Whitney—the logic being that former employees are familiar with Whitney's procedures and generally will have respect for the quality of the firm's work.

THE TRAINING AND DEVELOPMENT DILEMMA

Not surprisingly, debate is growing regarding the role and importance of education and training at Whitney and Company. It is very difficult to know which parts of the current programs are good and which are not. Likewise, it is difficult to determine whether additional training is needed. As Anthony Blaine, one of the training directors, summarized it: "For years we've been throwing tons of training at these people, but we aren't sure if it's the right kind, if it's too much, or even if they're catching what we're throwing. We've got to start coming up with some good questions, and then figure out some pretty intelligent answers."

Questions

1. What could Whitney do to enhance the value of training?

2. Is the company using the most effective techniques, especially with regard to training for client and customer service? What changes in techniques would you recommend?

3. How should Whitney decide specifically who needs training? Is it advisable, even cost-efficient, to send everyone through the program?

4. How can Whitney determine whether its education and training programs are of sufficient utility? How would you specifically evaluate the programs?

CASE 7

REALIGNING HR PRACTICES AT EGAN'S CLOTHIERS

As of the end of 2000, revenues at Egan's Clothiers have increased 21 percent over 1999, and at a compounded rate of 24 percent over the past five years. That's the good news. The bad news is that costs have risen even more quickly and chewed into the company's gross margins. As a consequence, Egan's profitability (measured as return on sales and return on net assets) has actually fallen by 14 percent over the past three years.

Because the retail industry in general has been enjoying growth due to a healthy economy, this drop in profitability at Egan's is especially worrisome. In fact, according to Egan's CFO, Richard Coyle, if something isn't done immediately to control material and labour costs, as well as administrative expenses, the company may need to restructure its operations. In the short run, Coyle, company president Karen Egan, and vice-president of HR Jim Rooney have put an indefinite freeze on all hiring. They are also considering laying off nearly one-quarter of Egan's sales staff and are weighing the benefits of cutting back on HR-related expenses such as training. Compared to others in the industry, their labour costs are very high.

COMPANY BACKGROUND

Egan's opened its first store in 1958. The company grew rapidly in the 1980s and now operates a chain of thirty-four medium-sized stores. Since the beginning, most Egan's customers have been middle- and upper-middle-class families purchasing sportswear, dresswear, and fashion accessories. The company has a strong reputation for quality and customer service. Besides thirty-four stores, the company also maintains two distribution centres and an administrative office. It has roughly 2,400 people on the payroll: 15 executives, 40 staff specialists, 40 store managers, 215 sales managers, 250 administrative personnel, 1,600 salespeople, and 240 distribution workers. At present, only the employees at the distribution centres are unionized. It is no secret that Egan's managers have been working very hard recently to keep current labour organizing activities to a minimum. Especially in these times of growth and change, management perceives unionism as a threat to the company's success. In this regard, the HR office has been called on to conduct a program audit of the company's various HR practices. The purpose of this audit is to assess the impact of HR policies and practices on employee outcomes (e.g., performance, satisfaction, absenteeism, turnover). The corollary objective of this audit is to identify specific problem areas where policy adjustments may be necessary. The final report to the executive staff will include the HR department's evaluation of current problems, as well as recommendations for implementing changes in HR practices.

HUMAN RESOURCES MANAGEMENT HISTORY

Over the past five years, Egan's has made several changes in its HR policies. In part this has been to forestall unionization efforts; but mainly it is a reflection of Egan's long-held belief that success in retailing depends on the competencies and efforts of its employees.

Egan's commitment to HR is demonstrated by the fact that in 1998 it spent $1.3 million on an intranet-based human resources information system (HRIS). The HRIS has successfully automated most employment records (job titles, salary information, sales levels, attendance, demographics, etc.), and connects each of the retail stores, distribution centres, and executive offices. To ensure that its workers are highly skilled, the company has established selection standards that are substantially higher than those of its competitors. Other retail companies typically hire inexperienced high school students; Egan's generally hires only people with some retailing or sales experience. Also, for the past five years Egan's has maintained an ongoing training program to help its salespeople improve their retail selling skills (RSSs) and customer service. This program has cost roughly $750,000 a year. While these policies have increased overall labour costs, Egan's managers believe firmly that the added expense is well justified in the long run. However, recently even the strongest proponents of HR have been wondering, given the company's current financial picture, whether it might not be wiser to cut back on training.

By far the most complex and volatile HR issues at Egan's relate to promotions and salary increases. Because the company promotes from within and distributes raises on a company-wide basis, comparisons generally have to be made across employees in different jobs and departments. To forestall accusations of subjectivity and bias, Egan's links these rewards to objective measures of performance. Specifically, instead of utilizing managers' subjective evaluations of employee performance, the company maintains ongoing sales records for each of its employees through the HRIS. On the basis of this information, each department manager assigns each employee to one of five categories:

Superior—top 10 percent

Very good—next 20 percent

Good—middle 40 percent

Fair—lower 20 percent

Poor—lowest 10 percent

Administrative decisions are then made across departments, utilizing these standardized distributions. To provide constant feedback to each employee concerning his or her relative performance, data are updated and posted daily. The point of this system is to motivate employees and to ensure that they are not surprised when the semiannual performance appraisal interviews are conducted. It is interesting that since this system has been put in place, not one formal complaint has been registered regarding salary or promotion decisions. However, the sales managers themselves have sometimes mentioned that they don't feel as comfortable now that they are required to assign employees to the "fair" and "poor" categories.

HR OUTCOMES

Despite management's concerted efforts to establish a first-rate HR system, the company is facing several troubling issues. Its HR practices are not working the way it had hoped. For example, complaints have been heard recently that employees have not been as patient or courteous with customers as they should be. This was best summarized by Paul Kelly, a store manager: "My people are beating up the clientele in order to make a sale—the very opposite of what the RSS program trains them to do." This deterioration in customer service is frustrating to management, since the RSS training has been effective in the past. Also, intense competition is developing within departments. While rivalries *between* departments have always been viewed as normal and healthy, this lack of cohesiveness within departments is seen as a problem.

Also, Egan's has been plagued with increases in lost and damaged merchandise. Management attributes this to the fact that storage rooms are disorganized and unkempt. This is in sharp contrast to the selling floors, which have remained fairly well orderly and uncluttered. Nevertheless, inventory costs have been increasing at an alarming rate.

Everyone has noticed that something is wrong. But the patterns are perplexing. Absenteeism has decreased by 23 percent, yet employee turnover has actually increased from 13 to over 29 percent, so labour costs have increased overall. Unfortunately, it is the very good to superior employees who are leaving; they account for 43 percent of turnover.

Egan's executives are understandably concerned about these trends. The success of the company and its reputation for quality and service depend on solid investments in HR to ensure the best possible workforce. However, the expenses are eroding the company's profits, and worse, it looks now like these investments are not paying off.

Questions

1. What overall changes could you recommend to the executive team at Egan's in regard to their HR practices?

2. What are the pros and cons of Egan's performance appraisal system? Do you think it identifies the best employees? Do you think it helps employees develop so as to perform the best they can?

3. Can increased sales be linked directly and/or indirectly to the appraisal system? How about some of the other performance effects? How would you change the system?

4. How do you account for the fact that absenteeism has decreased at Egan's while turnover has increased?

CASE 8

THE LAYOFF OF PAUL DOUGHERTY—A MANAGER'S TOUGH DECISION

Applied Technologies (ApTech), with fifty-five employees, provides tech support to larger firms. When ApTech was founded twelve years ago, it faced almost no competition and the growth possibilities seemed limitless. However, over the past five years the company has experienced slow growth and diminished profitability. As the industry prospered, more companies entered the market and competition increased. In addition, with advances in computer and software technology, fewer companies are requesting tech support from contractors. This has become especially apparent in the computer graphics area. Requests for traditional graphics support services from other companies have declined over 20 percent in the past year alone.

Beverly Meyers, ApTech's manager for computer graphics, and Mike Peterson, the company's founder and owner, recently began meeting to discuss what they need to do to improve the company's performance. Both Meyers and Peterson know that something must change, and after a series of long discussions they have determined that Meyers's unit must shift its emphasis. Specifically, her unit must move away from providing only computer graphics support and toward providing a greater degree of customer service along with some basic computer support.

Meyers must restructure her unit and lay off one of her four employees. This decision is especially difficult because all four workers are good employees and get along very well. In determining which of the employees will be laid off, she reviews their personnel files:

- Paul Dougherty is married and has two children in high school. His wife works evenings as an assistant manager at a local department store to help make ends meet. Dougherty has been with ApTech for just over eight years. He was hired during a period of growth in computer graphics support during the late 1980s and has been a good performer on the job. His work is not the best among the four employees, but he is consistent and never complains about his workload.
- Shannon Wall is a single mother with a child in elementary school. Wall came to ApTech a year after Dougherty as a highly recruited graphic design specialist, after earning both a bachelor's and a master's degree in graphic design from a well-respected university. Meyers has high expectations for Wall, but her performance has slipped in the past twenty-four months. The rumour around the office is that she has recently gone through a tough divorce and is in counselling to deal with her problems. Despite her decline in performance, Meyers still thinks Wall has the most potential of her four employees.
- Teresa Livingstone is a dedicated worker; in fact, everyone says she is "married to her job." She has been known to put in twenty hours of work on weekends to make sure that her work is up to date. Livingstone has a university degree in marketing with a minor in graphic design. Though her computer graphics skills are not as strong as those of the other three employees, she has a comprehensive understanding of the marketing side of the business, is capable of bringing in customers, and consistently meets her performance expectations.
- Greg Stevens came to ApTech two years ago directly out of university, where he completed an undergraduate degree in computer graphics. Though Stevens started rather slowly, once he settled into his role at ApTech his performance took off. In fact, he has been the top performer of the four workers for the past year-and-a-half. Although his performance is exceptional, Stevens does not take the marketing side of the business as seriously as he should. In sum, his potential to bring in new business is not as strong as his ability to do the work once a contract has been negotiated.

After reviewing the personnel information for each of her four employees, Meyers has decided to lay off Paul Dougherty. She has also committed herself to helping him find another job. Though it was not an easy decision to make, she feels confident that she has made the right one.

	SENIORITY, YEARS	COMPENSATION	1995	PERFORMANCE 1996	1997	1998
Paul Dougherty	8	$36,500	Average	Average	Good	Average
Shannon Wall	7	$40,500	High	Good	Average	Low
Teresa Livingstone	3	$34,000	Poor	Average	Average	
Greg Stevens	2	$32,500	Good	High		

QUESTIONS

1. What criteria should be used to determine whom to lay off? What emphasis, if any, should be given to factors that aren't job related, such as personal problems or a spouse's need to work? Explain.

2. Do you agree with Meyers's decision to lay off Paul Dougherty? Whom would you have laid off in this situation? Explain your position.

3. Are there any potential legal implications to Meyers's decision? Explain.

CASE 9

A BUSINESS CASE FOR WELLNESS

An organization's first efforts in occupational health and safety may be as simple as providing a first aid kit. As the organization grows, it typically adds to this by providing referral services for medical and psychological help. Still later it may take on full-time staff dedicated to the well-being of employees.

Especially in industries where it is difficult to attract and retain employees, organizations offer a variety of wellness programs, including social weekends, stretch breaks, and classes in relaxation, nutrition, and weight management. Any of Nortel's 3,500 employees can take advantage of twenty health-related programs. Nortel has built a 4,200-square-foot wellness centre that contains a library of books and tapes, three multimedia stations, two relaxation areas with massage chairs, a workout room, a back care clinic, four physio treatment rooms, two examination rooms, and offices for occupational health nurses, a physician, and administrative staff. A 16,000-square-foot fitness centre with a staff of seven completes the wellness program. Nortel's programs are based on a needs assessment survey that the company sent to 2,800 of its employees. The workers' needs were matched with Nortel's core values, goals, and objectives.

Why did Nortel go to this trouble? Partly because wellness programs have been associated in various studies with higher morale and increased productivity, and, it is hoped, improved profits. There is also hard evidence that wellness programs reduce casual absenteeism, short- and long-term disability, and costs for drug claims. A study done by Canada Life Assurance company and the University of Toronto found a three-to-one ROI associated with wellness programs. BCT Telus spent around $1.5 million on a wellness program in 1998 and saw returns of $4.5

million. Husky Oil spent $4.2 million in 1998 on health and safety and achieved savings through reduced absenteeism, accidents, and so on of $9 million. As well, programs such as child care and fitness centres are a means for recruiting and retaining employees. MDS Nordian in Kanata, Ontario, credits its wellness program for the following results:

- A turnover rate of 6 percent, compared to the benchmark of 10 percent.
- A decline in annual sick day use from 5.5 days in 1993 to 3 days.
- A reduction in lost-time injuries to an all-time low of 0.25 injuries per 100 person years.

Organizations can reduce the costs of wellness programs by partnering with other organizations. In this vein, public agencies such as the Cancer Society have mandates to educate the public and are willing to supply information and speakers free of charge. Nortel reduces costs and increases the commitment of its employees by charging user fees for fitness sessions (which do not cover the program's costs).

Source: Adapted from R. Wayman, "Wellness Workout," *Benefits Canada* 22, no. 1 (January 1998): 24–30; L. Young, "Integrated Wellness at Husky Makes for Real Savings," *Canadian HR Reporter,* February 28, 2000: 8; L. Young, "Health Workplace Keeps in Touch with Employees," *Canadian HR Reporter,* February 28, 2000: 9.

Questions

1. Is an employee's mental and physical health the responsibility of the employer?

2. Wellness programs have resulted in employer benefits, such as reduced absenteeism and accidents, and employee benefits, such as increased health. Should employers consider making wellness programs mandatory?

3. In teams, draft a proposal for establishing a wellness program in your organization. Develop it as a PowerPoint presentation for your organization's managers. Have some of you play these different roles: CEO, and vice-presidents of Human Resources, Finance, Production, and Marketing. Will the CEO decide "go" or "no go"?

CASE 10   TRANSFORMING LABOUR RELATIONS AT ALGOMA STEEL

In 1991, employees at Algoma Steel, Canada's third-largest steel producer, concluded the largest worker buyout in the history of North American business. As majority shareholders, Algoma employees elected four new members to the thirteen-member board of directors, and had a strong influence on the election of another seven members. The buyout ushered in a new era of management–union cooperation.

Before 1991, labour relations at Algoma had been bitterly adversarial. The unions viewed management as uncaring autocrats, while management viewed the unions as rigid and bullying. In the early stages of the union–management relationship, success was defined as parties from each side being able to sit in the same room without resorting to physical violence. The turnaround in labour relations at

Algoma began only when both sides recognized the damage that the hostile climate was inflicting on the bottom line.

Today's labour–management partnership is driven by mutual respect and a spirit of cooperation that extends from the joint steering committee (on which representatives of both management and labour serve as co-chairs) to the shop floor, where workers are grouped into employee participation units (EPUs). Worker empowerment is based on the idea that employees know best how to run the workplace. Workers are encouraged to submit their ideas to the EPUs. Over one four-month period, employee suggestions saved the company $1.2 million. In addition, employees share in the profits (in 1994, they pocketed an extra $400 each), and are involved in decision making in areas that were once the exclusive domain of management, such as flexibility, hiring, and training. As Denis Desjardins, coordinator of Algoma's employee participation program, says, "It's a fabulous opportunity. Every worker thinks, 'If only I could change things around here.' Now they have the chance."

The sea change in labour relations at Algoma is reaping substantial benefits for the company. Profits and productivity are up, grievances are down, and all those workers who were laid off after Algoma's near-bankruptcy in 1991 have been recalled.

Sources: K. Mark, "Buyout and the Bottom Line," *Human Resources Professional,* April 1995: 17–19; M. Lowe, "Steel Resolve," *Financial Post Magazine,* April 1995: 20–4; and V. Galt, "Algoma Reinvents Labour Relations," *The Globe and Mail,* April 21, 1995: B1.

Questions

1. Which aspects of Algoma's labour–management partnership do you think contributed the most to the company's turnaround?

2. What kinds of training would both management and labour need to assist them in developing and maintaining a cooperative relationship?

3. Assume that Algoma's profitability suffers as a result of a major decline in steel prices. How might each side in the labour–management partnership respond to the crisis?

CTV VIDEO CASES

CHAPTER 1: THE CHALLENGE OF HUMAN RESOURCES MANAGEMENT

Brain Drain

Glenn Wong of Electronic Arts Inc. and John Izzo, author of "Values Shift," comment on the so-called "brain drain" and it effects on keeping workers in Canada. Wong's company is 700 strong with plans to hire another 200 workers. He says the company pays competitive salaries, stock options, and attractive benefit plans including fitness centre memberships to keep people working in a motivating environment. Izzo says financial consideration is only one aspect of the problem of keeping talent in Canada and that an exciting work atmosphere is a large draw for talent workers, an aspect he says many Canadian companies are not focusing on enough. However, both speakers concede that the Canadian tax situation is a barrier to keeping talented workers in Canada.

1. What kinds of programs can Canadian companies undertake to keep their talent workers?

2. What can an HR department do to retain valued employees?

Nortel Announces Cuts to Its Workforce

Nortel cut 4,000 jobs, or about 4 percent of its workforce, in North America (1,000 jobs cut in Canada), mostly in the phone service areas, in an attempt to "streamline" its operations. The company says it will ultimately increase jobs in the areas of Internet and fibre optics to maintain overall employment levels. These increases are in the company's "high growth" sectors.

1. How much effect will the stock market have on employment levels at Nortel?

2. Will Nortel's efforts to streamline operations ultimately lead to a smaller workforce?

3. What is the impact on recruitment when a company announces substantial cuts to its workforce?

CHAPTER 2: EQUITY AND DIVERSITY IN HUMAN RESOURCES MANAGEMENT

Military Subs Now Open to Women

The Canadian navy has finally ended segregation of the sexes on submarines with the opening of Canada's newest submarines, which have separate dressing rooms and toilets, though not separate sleeping quarters. Women were integrated into the surface fleet in the late 1970s, but it is only now that women are allowed to serve on submarines. In a military survey, 67 percent of submariners opposed allowing women on subs; the main concerns being lack of privacy, sexual temptation, and fear of harassment charges. Critics say the decision was not based on the operational requirements of the military, but on political correctness. Proponents say that concerns come only from old, macho attitudes, since there haven't been problems on surface ships that have been integrated.

1. What are the benefits of desegregating the navy, or any other company that uses segregation? What are the drawbacks?

2. Discuss the things an HR department can do to help a situation like the one in this video.

HRC Accuses U of T of Racism

The Ontario Human Rights Commission accepted Dr. Kin-Yip Chun's claim that he was fired because of racial discrimination by the University of Toronto. To complicate matters, Chun claims that he almost lost his children when the university complained to the Children's Aid Society, simply because he complained of unfair treatment. Though the university admits that Chun was exploited during his nine years of employment, it is not ready to give him a position or back pay since it says there is no evidence of racial discrimination in this case. Dr. Chun fights on for justice.

1. What would you do as an employer to avoid complaints like this?

2. Should the university accept blame and give Chun his job back?

3. What other information do you think is necessary to make a judgment in this case?

Supreme Court Order Will Protect Alberta's Gays

An Alberta teacher was fired from his position after members of the school found out he was gay. The teacher spent seven years fighting the Supreme Court after he found out that the law did not protect against discrimination. The SCC ordered Alberta to change its human rights code to include protection for gays. Many opposing the decision believe that Alberta should have the right to make its own laws and not have them imposed by Supreme Court appointees.

1. Do you think the Supreme Court should have the authority to overrule provincial law?

2. What reason can a governing body provide for the lack of protection the law gave in this case? What would happen if it was a for-profit company that had these allegations made against it?

CHAPTER 3: JOB REQUIREMENTS AND EMPLOYEE CONTRIBUTIONS

Nortel's Innovative User-friendly Plant

Nortel transformed one of its manufacturing plants in Brampton, Ontario, into a high-tech office of the future. In this single-storey, worldwide headquarters facility for Nortel, workers can rent videos, do their banking, buy magazines, and go to restaurants, all within the walls of one office building. Departments are organized like neighbourhoods, with street names guiding you where to go, since the plant is so big it would be about 50 stories high if it were built up instead of out. The setting is casual; workers and managers say this informal setting makes people more innovative and productive.

1. Do you think the Nortel headquarters facility truly is a vision of the future? Or is it a misguided attempt to placate workers in these times of high demand for high-tech workers?

2. Will a work environment like this one help workers increase their contributions to their companies?

3. How much does a job environment like this one change the job requirements for the jobs?

Suspend Without Pay Senator Thompson

In a first for the Canadian Parliament, a member has been suspended without pay for poor attendance. Andrew Thompson missed a Special Senate Rules Committee meeting called to ask him about his abysmal attendance record over the years, though he faxed his regrets from his winter home in Mexico. He claims he was unable to attend the meeting due to poor health. Thompson has been in attendance at the senate only 14 times since 1990 and was held in contempt of the senate.

1. Has Senator Thompson been fulfilling the requirements of his job?

2. What should an employer do when it feels an employee's contributions are not what were expected?

CHAPTER 4: HUMAN RESOURCES PLANNING AND RECRUITMENT

High-tech Companies Steal Competitor's Staff

With the competition for high-tech workers intense, companies have altered their recruitment strategies. Zero Knowledge followed an employee's suggestion and put an advertising billboard on the back of a flatbed truck to create a mobile recruitment message. It was often parked right in front of a competitor's office.

1. What can a company do to attract and retain employees in high demand industries such as information technology?

2. Which recruitment channels do you think will be more effective for high-tech positions?

Seniors Continuing to Work

Though many Canadian companies have a mandatory retirement at age 65 policy, some are finding it beneficial to waive this policy to keep productive, older workers. This video shows an engineer working full-time under his company's work-at-home option, which allows him to continue working even though his health wouldn't allow him to go to the office every day. Keeping older workers on staff is smart business.

1. How can a company keep its more productive older workers while trying to rid itself of less productive workers and maintain a discrimination-free environment?

2. Which recruitment channels do you think will be more effective to attract older workers?

Autoworkers Unemployed

Early 2001 figures showed flat growth in Canadian jobs; they also showed that 9,100 jobs were lost in manufacturing. These figures did not include recent layoffs and job losses in the auto industry such as in Barrie, Ontario, where a large auto parts plant went bankrupt, putting 500 people out of work. A manufacturing recession is predicted for Canada. With auto sales down 20 percent, it is expected that 20 percent of manufacturing jobs will be lost at least temporarily.

1. How could HR planning have helped with the manufacturing job loss predicament shown in this video?

2. Is the loss of jobs a normal part of planning in the auto industry?

Nursing Association Predicts Shortages

One in three graduating nurses in Canada either quit or moved to the United States within three years of graduation. In addition to overwork, the biggest reason was low wages, evidenced by a drop in average earnings from $36,876 in 1988 to $31,200 in 1997. Combine this drop with a rise in salary in the United States, and it isn't difficult to see why nurses don't stay in Canada to work.

1. How can hospitals retain their nurses?

2. Will different recruitment strategies help in this situation?

CHAPTER 5: SELECTION

Employee Checks

Vincent Tsang, a partner with Infocheck Ltd., talks about his company's line of work: performing employee checks to examine a job applicant's honesty. He says over 33 percent of people applying for jobs lie on their résumés or somehow give false information about themselves. He says it is vital that all employees have their credentials examined, since many people even lie about the level of education they have. He advocates that companies get consent to perform a background check, check the applicant's true education level, get in touch with at least three references, and establish the referees' credibility. It seems that some people even list friends as references instead of actual employment references in an effort to outfox potential employers.

1. Though Tsang says it is worth the money to have a company like his perform checks on potential employees, do you think most companies will undertake this effort as part of their selection system? Why or why not?

2. What other ways can a company examine the integrity of potential employees?

CHAPTER 6: TRAINING

Employee Training

Jim Clemmer, author of "Growing the Distance," offers his views on why the effects of training are not as strong as they should be. He says training programs often are not connected to the job to which the trainee will return. Clemmer also believes that managers should deliver training programs to "practise what they preach" and to increase attendance and attention. Training programs should be synchronized with corporate practices, strategy, and culture to increase training benefits to individuals. The least effective training programs are those that are not applied enough and that focus on theory too much, he says.

1. How can one develop an effective training program that does not focus too much on theory? Is this possible?

2. Can managers be expected to build and implement a training program effectively?

Youth Trained as Street Mechanics

A Toronto car retailer is taking in young males from shelters to train as mechanic apprentices. Apprentices work alongside a mentor, keep journals, and have their performance evaluated weekly. After three months of instruction, they are ready to set out on their own.

1. What are the pros and cons of using apprenticeships as training programs?

2. Evaluate the alternatives to this training program for mechanics.

CHAPTER 7: CAREER DEVELOPMENT

Mentoring a Growing Business Trend

This video shows different types of mentoring programs. In one type, a retired businessman volunteers his time to help young entrepreneurs he met at a university's program navigate the storms of business. We hear that there are mentoring programs for women and minorities, and that some companies even have internal mentorship programs due to their popularity.

1. What are the pros and cons of a mentoring program?

2. What is the incentive for a mentor to help someone in a mentoring program?

Female CEO Micheline Bouchard

Only twelve CEOs and only 12 percent of senior managers in Canada are women. Micheline Bouchard, the CEO of Motorola Canada, says the glass ceiling is getting higher, but it is still present. Women are typically not given the opportunities to move up the corporate ranks, and it will be twenty years before the attitudes of male senior managers change enough to stop holding women back.

1. Is their any rational basis for the presence of the glass ceiling for women?

2. What can an HR department do to increase the career development opportunities for women and minorities?

Search Guides Expand Market

A Montreal company, begun by two young men as an outgrowth of a school project, produces career guides in print and on CD-ROMs and websites. Some of the books help students pick the right school, while others help people find a new job. The company currently operates only in Quebec, but it has plans to expand to the rest of Canada, beginning in Ontario.

1. How much can a published career guide help people with their career development?

CHAPTER 8: APPRAISING AND IMPROVING PERFORMANCE

Company Offers Bonus for Employees Who Aren't Absent

In Alberta, 4,500 workers are part of the largest construction site in Canada. Absenteeism was an enormous problem for the company, which faced an 11 percent absentee rate in the summer, or almost 500 workers absent on any given day. The company has taken an innovative approach to combat this problem: it puts the names of all workers who weren't absent each week into a lottery for four weekly prizes of $5,000 each. At the end of the year, anyone who hasn't missed any days of work is put into a lottery for a chance at $1,000,000. The company says that absenteeism has dropped by 60 percent due to the lottery, and that the costs of the lottery are more than made up for by people being on the job.

1. Do you think an incentive program like this will work in the long term? Why or why not?

2. Will a bonus program for attendance have any effect on improving the performance of employees? Why or why not?

CHAPTER 9: MANAGING COMPENSATION

Native Bands Question Chiefs' Salaries

Two East Coast native reserves are questioning their chiefs' salaries. One chief makes at least $120,000 tax free per year, while the other is reported to have received over $416,000 in the past fourteen months while making $140,000 per year in salary. People on the reserves are living in poverty and are calling for more accountability.

1. Native band chiefs can be viewed as the top managers, even the CEOs, of their bands. What are the implications of high CEO salary levels for workers in companies?

2. What do you think is an appropriate worker-to-CEO ratio of pay? Why?

Labour Tribunal Rules EI Penalizes Stay-At-Home Moms

A Winnipeg labour tribunal ruled that when a mother works part-time because of her unpaid parental responsibilities, she should not receive inferior employment insurance coverage. Women who work part-time rarely work enough hours to qualify for EI benefits, but they are required to pay premiums nonetheless. This ruling opens the doors for thousands of women to reapply for EI benefits who have been turned down in the past.

1. Should EI premiums be collected from all workers? What are the ramifications of not collecting premiums from some, but collecting from others?

2. How might this ruling affect how a company manages its compensation system?

Civil Servants and Pay Equity

After a sixteen-year battle with the federal government over pay equity, 230,000 mostly female civil servants received a $3.6 billion settlement. The settlement is to cover years of wage discrimination against women and will average $20,000 to $30,000 per person. The government agreed with the principle of pay equity, but disagreed with the methods used to determine pay equity among federal employees.

1. What is pay equity, and how can the people who wrote the laws governing it not be in compliance?

2. How does a company determine whether it is in compliance with pay equity legislation?

CHAPTER 10: INCENTIVE REWARDS

Companies Give Perks to Keep Employees

Signing bonuses, higher salaries, in-house gyms, massages, dry cleaning, shoe cleaning services, and casual dress are among the perks being offered to employees in an attempt to retain employees, increase company loyalty, and make workers feel they are part of a "family."

1. Will this type of incentive increase company loyalty and reduce turnover?

2. Which perks should an HR department focus on when developing incentive reward plans?

Retailers Find Ways to Lure and Keep Workers

Many employers were scrambling to find enough retail staff to cope with the busy Christmas season in 2000. With a booming economy and plenty of jobs, workers could afford to be choosy. In Ontario, where the minimum wage is $6.85 an hour, retailers and store owners had to come up with more incentives to attract employees. Some incentives mentioned by those interviewed on this segment were a 25 percent wage increase and a $500 bonus paid to each employee who recruited another new worker who stayed on the job at least six months. The restaurant industry is particularly hard hit in times like these, when job seekers are in the driver's seat. It has a 75 percent per year turnover rate.

1. With unemployment at such low levels, what else can employers offering entry level jobs do to retain employees?

2. Is it worthwhile to keep these employees, or is it just as beneficial to simply hire new workers as needed?

Royal Bank Shareholders Upset with Stock Options

Major Royal Bank shareholders such as the Ontario Teachers Pension Plan want stock options tied to performance for senior executives. A proposal to do so was voted down at the annual meeting, the main reason being competitiveness. Executives warn that without stock option plans, companies cannot be competitive in recruiting and maintaining top managers in the current global economy.

1. Are senior executive pay plans that include stock options the best way to build incentive reward plans?

2. What other options could be used effectively to recruit and retain top managers?

CHAPTER 11: EMPLOYEE BENEFITS

Woman with Chronic Fatigue Syndrome Disability

A recent court ruling has declared that chronic fatigue syndrome is an illness and not a psychiatric disability. It ruled that an Alberta woman should receive long-term disability benefits since her disability caused her to quit her job. About 30,000 Canadians battle chronic fatigue, and an expert in this area says these people will be the victors in getting their disability recognized as a physical ailment.

1. Should companies make sure that disabilities such as chronic fatigue syndrome are covered in their insurance company's benefit plans?

2. What are the costs and benefits of including such disabilities in company benefit plans?

Bereavement Benefits for Grieving Workers

Bereavement benefits are one workplace benefit that has little legislation guiding it. Some companies offer plane tickets and as much time as needed before returning to work, while others do nothing. Three days off for bereavement is what the Canadian Labour Code suggests, but this amount is seen as too little time, and it is not required to be given except in Quebec. Groups such as Bereaved Families of Ontario are calling for a national policy to increase bereavement leave time to recognize the different needs in our diverse cultures.

1. What are the implications of increased bereavement benefits for workers?

2. Will such a benefit be a useful tool in recruiting and retaining valued workers?

Lavish Employment Benefits

Many companies are phasing out traditional benefit plans and replacing them with plans that are more valued by workers. Among the most popular newer benefits are health programs such as on-site fitness centres, adjustable pension plans, stock options, and flexible work hours. Other benefits such as office valet services are being implemented to increase office efficiency. These benefits are seen as recruitment tools and are designed to keep employees who would otherwise have quit.

1. Which of the newer benefits such as valet services do you find most attractive? Will the presence of these benefits draw you to a company as an employee and keep you there?

2. How can a company afford to offer lavish benefit plans?

CHAPTER 12: HEALTH AND SAFETY

Coming Back to Work After an Illness

An innovative way to get sick or injured workers back on the job is to bring them back slowly. One woman, coming back from a two-year absence caused by chronic fatigue syndrome, worked two hours per day for a week, then three per day for a week, and so on until she was back up to full-time hours. Fewer than one in five Canadian companies offer such a program—a fact that is peculiar, since sick pay costs billions per year.

1. Can companies afford to take back workers before they are ready to work full-time?

2. What are the implications of having some people working full hours and others working less than full hours?

Teenager Dies from Fall at Construction Site

A fourteen-year-old died when he fell five stories on a construction site where he had worked only two days. Since businesses often don't give due diligence to safety on the job, the responsibility of parents is said to be of utmost importance, especially in jobs where there are serious safety concerns. Parents cannot assume that all job sites are safe for their children. Advances are being made in some provinces toward workplace safety, including health and safety training in high schools.

1. How can companies increase health and safety on the job?

2. Should there be minimum age restrictions for people taking jobs? How about in industries where there are more accidents and safety concerns?

Health Risks for Sedentary Workers

Nearly 15 percent of workers are not getting enough exercise and are labelled "desk potatoes." The Health Council of Canada is asking employers to make time for employees to exercise more. One idea is to provide tax breaks for companies for the costs associated with fitness plans. Some companies are finding that exercise areas with showers and change rooms are a good investment that pays off in lower absenteeism and turnover.

1. Do companies have an obligation to provide their workers with company-sponsored ways to stay fit?

2. Can employer-sponsored fitness programs lower absenteeism and turnover?

CHAPTER 13: EMPLOYEE RIGHTS AND DISCIPLINE

Work Rage: Canadians on the Edge

A recent poll of Canadians indicates that 63 percent feel at least as much stress as they did five years ago, and that most stress is job-related. This video shows workplace stress and how a couple decided that work was too much for them to handle. The work environment has changed through such things as downsizing and company restructuring, which force workers to do more in less time. The result is higher stress levels.

1. What is the employer's responsibility in dealing with work stress?

2. Are employee's rights being infringed when companies ask them to do more work in less time?

Woman Nearly Fired for Having TB

A woman who contracted tuberculosis by helping Kosovo refugees initially was fired because coworkers and customers were concerned about the risks involved in coming in contact with her. Her company clarified her dismissal by saying it placed her on "compassionate leave" with pay until the end of the month. Experts on TB say the woman cannot infect others since she only has tuberculosis infection, not the disease.

1. What are the options available to a company in a case like this?

2. What obligations do both the company and the worker have in a case like this?

Judith Lapierre Claims Sexual Harassment

A Canadian woman was locked in a space capsule for 100 days with seven male Russian scientists to study human behaviour in a scientific study on confinement. She claims that one of the males tried to forcibly kiss her twice out of the range of on-board cameras. Russian officials say it was a "misunderstanding," though they disciplined one of the scientists. She is concerned that this event will hamper her in her goal of becoming an astronaut. Keeping males and females in close quarters was an issue that she and Canadian officials didn't think would arise in this study.

1. What could be the "misunderstanding" the Russian officials say was the reason for this harassment?

2. What is sexual harassment? Does this video show a case of sexual harassment?

CHAPTER 14: THE DYNAMICS OF LABOUR RELATIONS

Strikes Affecting Services across Canada

This video clip shows strike activity all across Canada. In it 20,000 public servants on strike shut down almost everything in Newfoundland in their quest for "respect" and higher pay. In Ontario, Petro Canada employees went on strike for better pensions. Transit was shut down for over a month in Calgary, where the government has handed out over $1 million in taxi chips to low income earners. Vancouver and Victoria transit workers went on strike for better pay too, rounding out this report of strike activity from coast to coast.

1. Most of the strikes in this video are in the public sector. What differences arise with a strike in the public sector as opposed to a strike in the private sector?

2. What can authorities do to avoid strikes in the public sector?

3. What is the problem in Canada as indicated by increased strike activity compared to strike rates in other countries?

Air Canada Pilots Agree to Nonbinding Mediation

The management of Air Canada and the pilots' union agreed to nonbinding mediation as suggested by the federal labour minister. Job security and salary increases were the biggest issues in this contract impasse. Frustrated fliers felt that service is poorer and prices are higher since the merger of Air Canada and Canadian Airlines. This had improved business for companies like Canada 3000.

1. Do you think one side or the other is in a position of power in this impasse?

2. What can an impartial mediator do in contract negotiations like this one?

Leaders Try New Strategies for Workers of the Future

Nearly half of Canada's 3.6 million union members are over 45. It has been suggested that unions should target younger people in industries like high-tech. However, these workers have turned their backs on unions. Labour leaders have tried to attract young people through a variety of methods, including holding a youth festival in Toronto. One of the successes that the union movement points to is that almost half of union members are now women—a much higher ratio than in the past.

1. Are unions needed today in industries such as high-tech? Has unionization seen its better days?

2. What can unions offer young people to convince them of the need for a union?

CHAPTER 15: COLLECTIVE BARGAINING AND CONTRACT ADMINISTRATION

CAW & Daimler Chrysler

A worker at the Brampton, Ontario, Daimler Chrysler plant and a CAW union official are interviewed about the impending layoff of up to 2,700 employees. The union blames the company for poor planning resulting in a surplus of vehicles. Now there will be layoffs at least until the excess inventory has shrunk. The interviewer asks the worker if he thinks his $25 per hour salary has anything to do with the layoffs. Both he and the union official say the layoffs are due to Daimler Chrysler simply building too many vehicles. The union official reveals that the union will be trying to convince about 500 workers close to retirement to take early retirement to allow the younger workers to keep working.

1. With just the information from this video, what kinds of items do you think will be negotiated in the next auto workers' contract with Daimler Chrysler?

2. Contract clauses to increase job security are very popular in unionized environments, especially in cyclical industries such as the auto industry. Evaluate the pros and cons of increased job security for both the company and the workers.

CHAPTER 16: INTERNATIONAL HUMAN RESOURCES MANAGEMENT

Canadian Diplomatic Foreign Service Officers on Strike

Canada's foreign service officers picketed the foreign affairs headquarters to publicize their demands for higher salaries. Salaries range from $36,000 to $69,000. They were frozen for six years before the government offered a 2 percent raise, a raise rejected by diplomats as an insult. Though the jobs themselves are interesting, they say that they need higher pay, since often their spouses can't work and their children must go to foreign schools. High-profile support comes from Kim Campbell, former prime minister, who is a diplomat in Los Angeles. She says her receptionist makes more than her immigration officer, and this is unacceptable.

1. With an increasing emphasis on global operations, many firms will have employees working abroad. What kinds of issues arise with placements abroad?

2. What can a company do to make foreign placements enticing to employees?

Search Continues for Canadian Hostages

Eight Canadians—seven oil company workers and an aid worker from Montreal—were abducted in Ecuador near the Colombian border. It was not clear what the kidnappers wanted since they didn't make their demands known. The oil workers had armed guards and the company would not have sent the workers if it had known it was a dangerous area. The Foreign Affairs department had been warning Canadians not to travel to this area for the past two months, but the head of the company did not find out about this until after his employees had been kidnapped.

1. What kinds of policies can an HR department establish to avoid a situation like this?

CHAPTER 17: CREATING HIGH-PERFORMANCE WORK SYSTEMS

Top Employers

The author of a book called *Canada's Top 100 Employers* explains how he compiled his list of good companies to work for. He talked to the companies to inventory the practices they used to attract and retain workers. He examined the companies' "extras," for example, the physical work environment, the benefit packages, vacation time, and the role the company takes in the wider community. There are lists in the book sorting the companies by industry, and suggesting which companies are better places to work for women, and which are best for visible minorities. All of these companies go the extra mile to attract and retain workers and treat their employees well.

1. What would cause a company to examine its benefit package and offer some of the more exotic options to its employees? Do these options make a company a high-performance work system?

2. What do you think makes a company a top company to work for?

GLOSSARY

Achievement tests Measures of what a person knows or can do right now.

Alarm reaction Response to stress that basically involves an elevated heart rate, increased respiration, elevated levels of adrenaline in the blood, and increased blood pressure.

Alternative dispute resolution (ADR) Term applied to different types of employee complaint or dispute resolution procedures.

Apprenticeship training System of training in which a worker entering the skill trades is given thorough instruction and experience, both on and off the job, in the practical and theoretical aspects of the work.

Aptitude tests Measures of a person's capacity to learn or acquire skills.

Arbitration award Final and binding award issued by an arbitrator in a labour management dispute.

Arbitrator Third party who resolves a labour dispute by issuing a final decision in an agreement.

Assessment centre Process by which individuals are evaluated as they participate in a series of situations that resemble what they might be called upon to handle on the job.

Attitude survey Technique used to elicit employee views in order to make decisions and/or initiate change.

Attrition A natural departure of employees from organizations through quits, retirements, and deaths.

Augmented skills Skills helpful in facilitating the efforts of expatriate managers.

Authorization card A statement signed by an employee authorizing a union to act as his or her representative for the purposes of collective bargaining.

Balance sheet approach Compensation system designed to match the purchasing power of a person's home country.

Bargaining unit Group of two or more employees who share common employment interests and conditions and may reasonably be grouped together for purposes of collective bargaining.

Bargaining zone Area within which the union and the employer are willing to concede when bargaining.

Behaviour modelling Approach that demonstrates desired behaviour and gives trainees the chance to practise and role-play those behaviours and receive feedback.

Behaviour modification Technique that operates on the principle that behaviour that is rewarded, or positively reinforced, will be exhibited more frequently in the future, whereas behaviour that is penalized or unrewarded will decrease in frequency.

Behaviour observation scale (BOS) A behavioural approach to performance appraisal that measures the frequency of observed behaviour.

Behavioural description interview (BDI) An interview in which an applicant is asked questions about what he or she actually did in a given situation.

Behaviourally anchored rating scale (BARS) A behavioural approach to performance appraisal that consists of a series of vertical scales, one for each important dimension of job performance.

Benchmarking Process of measuring one's own services and practices against the recognized leaders in order to identify areas for improvement.

Bona fide occupational qualification (BFOQ) A justifiable reason for discrimination based on business reasons of safety or effectiveness.

Bonus Incentive payment that is supplemental to the base wage.

Boycott Union tactic that encourages others to refuse to patronize an employer.

Burnout Most severe stage of distress, manifesting itself in depression, frustration, and loss of productivity.

Business agent Normally a paid labour official responsible for negotiating and administering the collective agreement and working to resolve union members' problems.

Business unionism Term applied to the goals of labour organizations, which collectively bargain for improvements in wages, hours, job security, and working conditions.

Career counselling Process of discussing with employees their current job activities and performance, their personal job and career goals, their personal skills, and suitable career development objectives.

Career curves (maturity curves) Experience or performance bases for providing salary increases for professional employees.

Career paths Lines of advancement in an occupational field within an organization.

Career plateau Situation in which for either organizational or personal reasons the probability of moving up the career ladder is low.

Codetermination Representation of labour on the board of directors of a company.

Collective bargaining process Process of negotiating a collective agreement, including the use of economic pressures by both parties.

Combined salary and commission plan Compensation plan that includes a straight salary and a commission.

Comparable value The concept that male and female jobs that are dissimilar, but equal in terms of worth to the employer, should be paid the same.

Compensatory model Selection decision model in which a high score in one area can make up for a low score in another area.

Competency assessment Analysis of the sets of skills and knowledge needed for decision-oriented and knowledge-intensive jobs.

Compulsory binding arbitration Binding method of resolving collective bargaining deadlocks by a neutral third party.

Computer-assisted instruction (CAI) System that delivers instructional material directly through a computer terminal in an interactive format.

Computer-managed instruction (CMI) System normally employed in conjunction with CAI that uses a computer to generate and score tests and to determine the level of training proficiency.

Concentration Term applied to designated groups whose numbers in a particular occupation or level are high relative to their numbers in the labour market.

Concurrent validity The extent to which test scores (or other predictor information) match criterion data obtained at about the same time from current employees.

Construct validity The extent to which a selection tool measures a theoretical construct or trait.

Constructive dismissal Changing an employee's working conditions such that compensation, status, or prestige is reduced.

Consumer price index (CPI) Measure of the average change in prices over time in a fixed "market basket" of goods and services.

Content validity The extent to which a selection instrument, such as a test, adequately samples the knowledge and skills needed to perform a particular job.

Contractual rights Rights that derive from contracts.

Contrast error Performance rating error in which an employee's evaluation is biased either upward or downward because of comparison with another employee just previously evaluated.

Contributory plan A pension plan where contributions are made jointly by employees and employers.

Cooperative training Training program that combines practical on-the-job experience with formal educational classes.

Core competencies Integrated knowledge sets within an organization that distinguish it from its competitors and deliver value to customers.

Core skills Skills considered critical in an employee's success abroad.

Craft unions Unions that represent skilled craft workers.

Criterion-related validity The extent to which a selection tool predicts, or significantly correlates with, important elements of work behaviour.

Critical incident Unusual event that denotes superior or inferior employee performance in some part of the job.

Critical incident method Job analysis method by which important job tasks are identified for job success.

Cross-training Training of employees in jobs in areas closely related to their own.

Cross-validation Verifying the results obtained from a validation study by administering a test or test battery to a different sample (drawn from the same population).

Cultural audits Audit of the culture and quality of work life in an organization.

Cultural environment Language, religion, values, attitudes, education, social organization, technology, politics, and laws of a country.

Culture shock Perceptual stress experienced by people who settle overseas.

Customer appraisal Performance appraisal, which, like team appraisal, is based on TQM concepts and seeks evaluation from both internal and external customers.

Defined benefit plan A pension plan in which the amount an employee is to receive on retirement is specifically set forth.

Defined contribution plan A pension plan that establishes the basis on which an employer will contribute to the pension fund.

Defined rights Concept that management's authority should be expressly defined and clarified in the collective agreement.

Depression Negative emotional state marked by feelings of low spirits, gloominess, sadness, and loss of pleasure in ordinary activities.

Designated groups Women, visible minorities, Aboriginal peoples, and persons with disabilities who have been disadvantaged in employment.

Differential piece rate Compensation rate under which employees whose production exceeds the output receive a higher rate for all of their work than the rate paid to those who do not exceed the standard amount.

Discipline (1) Treatment that punishes; (2) orderly behaviour in an organizational setting; or (3) training that moulds and strengthens desirable conduct—or corrects undesirable conduct—and develops self-control.

Distress Harmful stress characterized by a loss of feelings of security and adequacy.

Diversity management The optimization of an organization's multicultural workforce in order to reach business objectives.

Downsizing The planned elimination of jobs.

Dual-career partnerships Couples in which both members follow their own careers and actively support each other's career development.

Due process Employee's right to present his or her position during a disciplinary procedure.

Earnings-at-risk incentive plans Incentive pay plans placing a portion of the employee's base pay at risk, but giving the opportunity to earn income above base pay when goals are met or exceeded.

Elder care Care provided to an elderly relative by an employee who remains actively at work.

Employee assistance programs (EAPS) Services provided by employers to help workers cope with a wide variety of problems that interfere with the way they perform their jobs.

Employee associations Labour organizations that represent various groups of professional and white-collar employees in labour–management relations.

Employee empowerment A technique of involving employees in their work through a process of inclusion.

Employee involvement groups (EIGs) Groups of employees who meet to resolve problems or offer suggestions for organizational improvement.

Employee leasing Process of dismissing employees who are then hired by a leasing company (which handles all HR-related activities and contracting with that company to lease back the employees).

Employee rights Guarantees of fair treatment from employers, especially regarding an employee's right to privacy.

Employee stock ownership plans (ESOPs) Stock plans in which an organization contributes shares of its stock to an established trust for the purpose of stock purchases by its employees.

Employee teams An employee contributions technique whereby work functions are structured for groups rather than for individuals and team members are given discretion in matters traditionally considered management prerogatives.

Employment equity The employment of individuals in a fair and nonbiased manner.

Entrepreneur One who starts, organizes, manages, and assumes responsibility for a business or other enterprise.

Ergonomics An interdisciplinary approach to designing equipment and systems that can be easily and efficiently used by human beings.

Error of central tendency Performance rating error in which all employees are rated about average.

Escalator clauses Clauses in collective agreements that provide for quarterly cost-of-living adjustments in wages, basing the adjustments on changes in the consumer price index.

Essay method A trait approach to performance appraisal that requires the rater to compose a statement describing employee behaviour.

Ethics Set of standards of conduct and moral judgments that help determine right and wrong behaviour.

Eustress Positive stress that accompanies achievement and exhilaration.

Expatriates (home country nationals) Employees from a home country who are sent on international assignment.

Expedited arbitration An agreement to bypass some steps in the grievance process.

Factor comparison system Job evaluation system that permits the evaluation process to be accomplished on a factor-by-factor basis by developing a factor comparison scale.

Failure rate Percentage of expatriates who do not perform satisfactorily.

Fast track program Program that encourages young managers with high potential to remain with an organization by letting them advance more rapidly than those with less potential.

Final offer arbitration Method of resolving collective bargaining deadlocks whereby the arbitrator has no power to compromise but must select one or another of the final offers submitted by the two parties.

Flexible benefits plans (cafeteria plans) Benefit plans that enable individual employees to choose the benefits that are best suited to their particular needs.

Flextime Flexible working hours that permit employees the option of choosing daily starting and quitting times, provided that they work a set number of hours per day or week.

Flow data Data that provide a profile of the employment decisions affecting designated groups.

Forced-choice method A trait approach to performance appraisal that requires the rater to choose from statements designed to distinguish between successful and unsuccessful performance.

Functional job analysis (FJA) Quantitative approach to job analysis that utilizes a compiled inventory of the various functions or work activities that can make up any job and that assumes that each job involves three broad worker functions: (1) data, (2) people, and (3) things.

Gainsharing plans Programs under which both employees and the organization share the financial gains according to a predetermined formula that reflects improved productivity and profitability.

Global corporation Firm that has integrated worldwide operations through a centralized home office.

Global manager Manager equipped to run a global business.

Globalization Trend toward opening up foreign markets to international trade and investment.

Graphic rating-scale method A trait approach to performance appraisal whereby each employee is rated according to a scale of characteristics.

Grievance arbitration The use of a neutral third party to resolve disagreements between union and management.

Grievance procedure Formal procedure that provides for the union to represent members and non-members in processing a grievance.

Grievance resolution Process where a neutral third party assists in the resolution of an employee grievance.

Guest workers Foreign workers invited to perform needed labour.

Hay profile method Job evaluation technique using three factors—knowledge, mental activity, and accountability—to evaluate executive and managerial positions.

Hearing officer People who work full-time for the organization but who assume a neutral role when deciding cases between aggrieved employees and management.

High-performance work system (HPWS) A specific combination of HR practices, work structures, and process that maximizes employee knowledge, skill, commitment, and flexibility.

Hiring freeze A practice whereby new workers are not hired as planned, or workers who have left the organization are not replaced.

Horizontal fit Situation in which all the internal elements of the work system complement and reinforce one another.

Host country Country in which an international corporation operates.

Host country nationals Natives of the host country.

Hot stove rule Rule of discipline that can be compared with a hot stove in that it gives warning, is effective immediately, is enforced consistently, and applies to all employees in an impersonal and unbiased way.

Hourly work Work paid on an hourly basis.

Human capital The knowledge, skills, and abilities of individuals that have economic value to an organization.

Human resources information system (HRIS) Computerized system that provides current and accurate data for purposes of control and decision-making.

Human resources management (HRM) A set of interrelated functions and processes whose goal is to attract, socialize, motivate, maintain, and retain an organization's employees.

Human resources planning (HRP) The process of anticipating and making provision for the movement of people into, within, and out of an organization.

Improshare Gainsharing program under which bonuses are based on the overall productivity of the work.

In-basket training Assessment centre process for evaluating trainees by simulating a real-life work situation.

Increases in real wages Wage increases larger than rise in the consumer price index.

Industrial disease A disease resulting from particular process, trade, or occupation in industry.

Industrial engineering A field of study concerned with analyzing work methods and establishing time standards.

Industrial unions Unions that represent all workers—skilled, semiskilled, unskilled—employed along industry lines.

Instructional objectives Desired outcomes of a training program.

Interest arbitration Determination of a collective bargaining agreement by an arbitrator.

International corporation Domestic firm that uses its existing capabilities to move into overseas markets.

Internship programs Programs jointly sponsored by colleges, universities, and other organizations that offer students the opportunity to gain real-life experience while allowing them to find out how they will perform in work organizations.

Job A group of related activities and duties.

Job analysis Process of obtaining information about jobs by determining what the duties, tasks, or activities associated with those jobs are.

Job characteristics model Job design that purports that three factors (meaningful work, responsibility for work outcomes, and knowledge of the results of the work performed) result in improved work performance, increased internal motivation, and lower absenteeism and turnover.

Job classification system System of job evaluation by which jobs are classified and grouped according to a series of predetermined wage grades.

Job description Statement of the tasks, duties, and responsibilities of a job to be performed.

Job design Outgrowth of job analysis that improves jobs through technological and human considerations in order to enhance organization efficiency and employee job satisfaction.

Job enrichment Enhancing a job by adding more meaningful tasks and duties to make the work more rewarding or satisfying.

Job evaluation Systematic process of determining the relative worth of jobs in order to establish which jobs should be paid more than others within an organization.

Job posting and bidding Posting vacancy notices and maintaining lists of employees looking for upgraded positions.

Job progressions Hierarchy of jobs a new employee might experience, ranging from a starting job to jobs that successively require more knowledge and/or skill.

Job ranking system Simplest and oldest system of job evaluation by which jobs are arrayed on the basis of their relative worth.

Job specification Statement of the needed knowledge, skills, and abilities of the person who is to perform the job.

Knowledge workers Workers whose responsibilities extend beyond the physical execution of work to include decision making, problem solving, and trouble shooting.

Labour market The area from which applicants are to be recruited.

Labour relations process Logical sequence of four events: (1) workers desire collective representation, (2) union begins its organizing campaign, (3) collective negotiations lead to a contract, and (4) the contract is administered.

Leaderless group discussion Assessment centre process that places trainees in a conference setting to discuss an assigned topic, either with or without designated group roles.

Leniency or strictness error Performance rating error in which the appraiser tends to give employees either unusually high or unusually low ratings.

Lockout Strategy by which the employer denies employees the opportunity to work by closing its operations.

Lump-sum merit program Program under which employees receive a year-end merit payment, which is not added to their base pay.

Management by objectives (MBO) Philosophy of management that rates performance on the basis of employee achievement of goals set by mutual agreement of employee and manager.

Management forecasts The opinions (judgments) of supervisors, department managers, and others knowledgeable about the organization's future employment needs.

Management prerogatives Decisions regarding organizational operations over which management claims exclusive rights.

Manager and/or supervisor appraisal Performance appraisal done by an employee's manager and often reviewed by a manager one level higher.

Managing diversity Being aware of characteristics common to employees, while also managing employees as individuals.

Markov analysis Method for tracking the pattern of employee movements through various jobs.

Material Safety Data Sheets (MSDS) Documents that contain vital information about hazardous substances.

Mediator Third party in a labour dispute who meets with one party and then the other in order to suggest compromise solutions or to recommend concessions.

Mentoring functions Functions concerned with the career advancement and psychological aspects of the person being mentored.

Mentors Managers who coach, advise, and encourage individuals of lesser rank.

Merit guidelines Guidelines for awarding merit raises that are tied to performance objectives.

Mixed-standard scale method A trait approach to performance appraisal similar to other scale methods but based on comparison with (better than, equal to, or worse than) a standard.

Multinational corporation (MNC) Firm with independent business units operating in multiple countries

Multiple cutoff model Selection decision model that requires an applicant to achieve some minimum level of proficiency on all selection dimensions.

Multiple hurdle model A sequential strategy in which only the applicants with the highest scores at an initial test stage go on to subsequent stages.

Negligence Failure to provide reasonable care when such failure results in injury to consumers or other employees.

Nepotism A preference for hiring relatives of current employees.

Nonadversial bargaining Problem-solving bargaining based on a win-win philosophy and the development of a positive long-term relationship.

Noncontributory plan A pension plan where contributions are made solely by the employer.

Nondirective interview An interview in which the applicant is allowed the maximum amount of freedom in determining the course of the discussion, while the interviewer carefully refrains from influencing the applicant's remarks.

Occupational illness Any abnormal condition or disorder, other than one resulting from an occupational injury, caused by exposure to environmental factors associated with employment.

Occupational injury Any cut, fracture, sprain, or amputation resulting from a workplace accident or from an exposure involving an accident in the work environment.

Ombudsman Designated individual from whom employees may seek counsel for the resolution of their complaints.

On-the-job training (OJT) Method by which employees are given hands-on experience with instructions from their supervisor or other trainer.

Open door policy Policy of settling grievances that identifies various levels of management above the immediate supervisor for employee contact.

Organization analysis Examination of the environment, strategies, and resources of the organization to determine where training emphasis should be placed.

Organizational capability The capacity to act and change in pursuit of sustainable competitive advantage.

Orientation Formal process of familiarizing a new employee with the organization, the new job, and the new work unit.

Outplacement services Services provided by organizations to help terminated employees find a new job.

Outsourcing Contracting outside the organization to have work done that formerly was done by internal employees.

Panel interview An interview in which a board of interviewers questions and observes a single candidate.

Pattern bargaining Bargaining in which unions negotiate provisions for wages and other benefits that are similar to those provided in other agreements existing in the industry or region.

Pay equity An employee's perception that compensation received is equal to the value of the work performed.

Pay for performance standard Standard by which managers tie compensation to employee effort and performance.

Pay grades Groups of jobs within a particular class that are paid the same rate or rate range.

Peer appraisal Performance appraisal done by one's fellow employees, generally on forms that are compiled into a single profile for use in the performance interview conducted by the employee's manager.

Peer review system System for reviewing employee complaints that utilizes a group composed of equal numbers of employee representatives and management appointees.

Perquisites Special benefits given to executives; often referred to as perks.

Person analysis Determination of the specific individuals who need training.

Piecework Work paid according to the number of units produced.

Point system Quantitative job evaluation procedure that determines the relative value of a job by the total points assigned to it.

Position The duties and responsibilities performed by only one employee.

Position analysis questionnaire (PAQ) Questionnaire covering 194 different tasks that, by means of a five-point scale, seeks to determine the degree to which different tasks are involved in performing a particular job.

Positive (or nonpunitive) discipline System of discipline that focuses on the early correction of employee misconduct, with the employee taking total responsibility for correcting the problem.

Predictive validity The extent to which applicants' test scores match criterion data obtained from those applicants/employees who have been on the job for some indefinite period.

Proactive change Change initiated to take advantage of targeted opportunities.

Profit sharing Any procedure by which an employer pays, or makes available to all regular employees, in addition to base pay, special current or deferred sums based on the profits of the enterprise.

Progressive discipline Application of corrective measures by increasing degrees.

Promotion Change of assignment to a job at a higher level in the organization.

Reactive change Change that occurs after external forces have already affected performance.

Real wages Wage increases larger than rises in the consumer price index; that is, the real earning power of wages.

Realistic job preview Informing applicants about all aspects of the job, both desirable and undesirable.

Reasonable accommodation Attempt by employers to adjust the working conditions or schedules of employees with disabilities or religious preferences.

Recency error Performance rating error in which the appraisal is based largely on the employee's most recent behaviour rather than on behaviour throughout the appraisal period.

Re-engineering Fundamental rethinking and radical redesign of business processes to achieve dramatic improvements in cost, quality, service, and speed.

Reliability The degree to which interviews, tests, and other selection procedures yield comparable data over time and alternative measures.

Relocation services Services provided to an employee who is transferred to a new location.

Repatriation Process of employee transition home from an international assignment.

Repetitive-strain injuries (RSIs) Injuries involving tendons of the fingers, hands, and arms that become inflamed from repeated stresses and strains.

Replacement charts Listings of current jobholders and persons who are potential replacements if an opening occurs.

Residual rights Concept that management's authority is supreme in all matters except those it has expressly conceded to the union in the collective agreement.

Restructuring Any major change that occurs within an organization. It may be the result of acquisitions, retrenchments, mergers, leveraged buyouts, divestitures, plant closures or relocations, and bankruptcies.

Reverse discrimination Giving preference to members of designated groups to the extent that nonmembers become the subjects of discrimination.

Rucker Plan Bonus incentive plan based on the historical relationship between the total earnings of hourly employees and the production value created by the employees.

Scanlon Plan Bonus incentive plan using employee and management committees to gain cost-reduction improvements.

Selection The process of choosing individuals who have relevant qualifications to fill existing or projected job openings.

Selection ratio The number of job applicants compared with the number of persons hired.

Self-appraisal Performance appraisal done by the employee being evaluated, generally on an appraisal form completed by the employee prior to the performance review.

Severance pay A lump-sum payment given to terminated employees.

Sexual harassment Unwelcome advances, requests for sexual favours, and other verbal or physical conduct of a sexual nature in the working environment.

Silver handshake An early-retirement incentive in the form of increased pension benefits for several years or a cash bonus.

Similar-to-me error Performance rating error in which an appraiser inflates the evaluation of an employee because of a mutual personal connection.

Situational interview An interview in which an applicant is given a hypothetical incident and asked how he or she would respond to it.

Skill-based pay Pay based on how many skills employees have or how many jobs they can perform. Also referred to as knowledge-based pay.

Skill inventories Files of employee education, experience, interests, skills, etc., that allow managers to quickly match job openings with employee backgrounds.

Spot bonus Unplanned bonus given for employee effort unrelated to an established performance measure.

Staffing tables Graphic representations of all organizational jobs, along with the numbers of employees currently occupying those jobs and future (monthly or yearly) employment requirements.

Standard hour plan Incentive plan that sets rates based on the completion of a job in a predetermined standard time.

Statutory rights Rights that derive from legislation.

Step review system System for reviewing employee complaints and disputes by successively higher levels of management.

Stock data Data showing the status of designated groups in occupational categories and compensation level.

Straight commission plan Compensation plan based on a percentage of sales.

Straight piecework Incentive plan under which employees receive a certain rate for each unit produced.

Straight salary plan Compensation plan that permits salespeople to be paid for performing various duties that are not reflected immediately in their sales volume.

Stress Any adjustive demand caused by physical, mental, or emotional factors that requires coping behaviour.

Structured interview An interview in which a set of standardized questions having an established set of answers is used.

Submission to arbitrate Statement that describes the issues to be resolved through arbitration.

Subordinate appraisal Performance appraisal of a superior by an employee, which is more appropriate for developmental than for administrative purposes.

Succession planning The process of identifying, developing, and tracking key individuals for executive positions.

Suggestion system Technique used to stimulate participation in upward communication.

Supplemental unemployment benefits (SUBs) A plan that enables an employee who is laid off to draw, in addition to state unemployment compensation, weekly benefits from the employer that are paid from a fund created for this purpose.

Surface bargaining Process of going through the motions of bargaining with no intention of making meaningful concessions.

Systemic discrimination The exclusion of certain groups through the application of employment policies or practices based on criteria that are not job-related.

Task analysis Process of determining what the content of a training program should be on the basis of a study of the tasks and duties involved in the job.

Team appraisal Performance appraisal, based on TQM concepts, that recognizes team accomplishment rather than individual performance.

Team or group incentive plan Compensation plan where all team members receive an incentive bonus payment when production or service standards are met or exceeded.

Telecommuting Use of microcomputers, networks, and other communications technology such as fax machines to do work in the home that is traditionally done in the workplace.

Termination Practice initiated by an employer to separate an employee from the organization permanently.

Third-country nationals Natives of a country other than the home country or the host country.

Total quality management (TQM) A set of principles and practices whose core ideas include understanding customer needs, doing things right the first time, and striving for continuous improvement.

Trainee readiness The trainee's maturity and experience.

Transfer of training Effective application of principles learned to what is required on the job.

Transfer Placement of an individual in another job for which the duties, responsibilities, status, and remuneration are approximately equal to those of the previous job.

Transnational corporation Firm that attempts to balance local responsiveness and global scale via a network of specialized operating units.

Transnational teams Teams composed of members of multiple nationalities working on projects that span multiple countries.

Trend analysis A quantitative approach to forecasting labour demand based on an organizational index such as sales.

Two-tier wage system Compensation plan that pays newly hired employees less than present employees performing the same or similar jobs.

Underutilization Term applied to designated groups that are not utilized or represented in the employer's workforce proportional to their numbers in the labour market.

Unfair labour practices (ULPs) Specific employer and union illegal practices that operate to deny

employees their rights and benefits under federal and provincial labour law.

Union shop Provision of the collective agreement that requires employees to join the union as a condition for their employment.

Union steward Employee who as a nonpaid union official represents the interests of members in their relations with management.

Validity generalization The extent to which validity coefficients can be generalized across situations.

Validity How well a test or selection procedure measures a person's attributes.

Vertical fit Situation in which the work system supports the organization's goals and strategies.

Vesting A guarantee of accrued benefits to participants at retirement age, regardless of their employment status at that time.

Virtual teams Teams that use advantage telecommunications technology to link their members, who can be anywhere in the world.

Wage and salary survey Survey of the wages paid to employees of other employers in the surveying organization's relevant labour market.

Wage curve Curve in a scattergram representing the relationship between relative worth of jobs and wage rates.

Wage rate compression Compression of differentials between job classes, particularly the differential between hourly workers and their managers.

Work permit (work certificate) Government document granting a foreign individual the right to seek employment.

Workers' compensation insurance Insurance provided to workers to defray the loss of income and cost of treatment resulting from work-related injuries or illness.

Yield ratio The percentage of applicants from a recruitment source that make it to the next stage of the selection process.

LIST OF WEB SITES

Chapter 1

3M	http://www.3m.com/intl/CA/english/
Academy of Management Executive	http://www3.oup.co.uk/acadme/
Aetna	http://www.aetna.com/index1.htm
Air Canada	http://www.aircanada.ca/
Alcoa	http://www.alcoa.com/
Algoma Steel	http://www.algoma.com/
Asia Pacific Economic Cooperation (APEC)	http://www.apecsec.org.sg/
AT&T Canada	http://www.attcanada.com/
Avis	http://www.avis.com/
Bank of Montreal	http://www.bmo.com/
BC Telecom	http://www.telus.com/cgi-ebs/homepage.jsp
Bell Canada	http://www.bell.ca/home.asp
Canada Post Corporation	http://www.canadapost.ca/
Canada Trustco	http://www.td.com/
Canadian HR Reporter	http://www.hrreporter.com/
Canon Corporation	http://www.canon.ca/
Chevron	http://www.chevron.ca/
Chrysler Canada	http://www.daimlerchrysler.ca/
Clarica	http://www.clarica.com/
Commerce Clearing House	http://www.ca.cch.com/aboutframe.asp
Corel	http://www3.corel.com/cgi-bin/gx.cgi/ AppLogic+FTContentServer?pagename=Corel/Index
Days Inn Hotels	http://www.daysinn.com/ctg/cgi-bin/DaysInn
Deloitte & Touche	http://www.deloitte.ca/
Disney	http://disney.go.com/park/homepage/today/ flash/index.html?clk=1004398
Dow Corning Corporation	http://www.dowcorning.thomasregister.com/ olc/dowcorning/home.htm
European Union (EU)	http://europa.eu.int/
Federal Express Canada	http://www.fedex.com/ca_english/
Ford	http://www.ford.ca/
General Electric	http://www.ge.com/canada/
Hewlett-Packard Canada	http://welcome.hp.com/country/ca/eng/welcome.htm
Honeywell Limited	http://www.honeywell.ca/
Hughes Space & Communications Company	http://www.hughespace.com/home.html
Human Resources Professionals Association of Ontario (HRPAO)	http://www.hrpao.org/index1.asp
IBM	http://www.ibm.com/ca/en/
John Deere Limited Canada	http://www.deere.com/deerecom/_Deere+Worldwide/default.htm
K Mart	http://www.bluelight.com/?c=KMART/
Kenworth	http://www.kenworth.com/1000_hom.asp

L.L. Bean	http://www.llbean.com/
Levi Strauss	http://www.levistrauss.com/
McDonald's	http://www.mcdonalds.com/countries/canada/
McKinsey	http://www.mckinsey.com/
Merck	http://www.merck.com/
Microsoft	http://www.microsoft.com/canada/default.asp
Motorola	http://canada.motorola.com/asp/english/english.asp
National Quality Institute	http://www.nqi.ca/
Nygard International	http://www.nygard.com/http://www.hughespace.com/home.html
ORTECH Corporation	http://www.ortech.ca/
PepsiCo	http://www.pepsico.com/
Price Waterhouse Coopers	http://www.pwcglobal.com/ca/eng/main/home/
Skandia Insurance	http://www.skandia.com/
SNC Lavalin	http://www.snc-lavalin.com/
St. Mary's University	http://www.stmarys.ca/
Statistics Canada	http://www.statcan.ca/
Sun Microsystems	http://www.sun.com/
The Bay	http://www.hbc.com/hbconline/home.asp?langid=EN
Trans Alta	http://www.transalta.com/website2001/ tawebsite.nsf/.frmHome?OpenForm
USA Today	http://www.usatoday.com/weather/wfront.htm
Workforce Solutions (WFS)	http://www.workforceinc.com/
Xerox Canada	http://www.fujixerox.co.jp/eng/index.html

Chapter 2

Amdahl Canada Limited	http://www.amdahl.com/about/locations/
Apple Computer	http://www.apple.com/
B.C. Government and Service Employees Union	http://www.bcgeu.bc.ca/
B.C. Hydro	http://eww.bchydro.bc.ca/
Bank of Montreal	http://www.bmo.com/
Bank of Nova Scotia	http://www.scotiabank.ca/
Cartierville	http://www.radq.gouv.qc.ca/ institutions_inscrites/application_asp/fedmtlou.htm
City of Calgary	http://www.gov.calgary.ab.ca/
City of Toronto	http://www.city.toronto.on.ca/
CN	http://www.cn.ca/
Conference Board of Canada	http://www.conferenceboard.ca/
Connaught Laboratories	http://www.aventispasteur.com/canada/
Department of National Defense	http://www.dnd.ca/
Digital Equipment of Canada	http://www.compaq.ca/
Ebco	http://www.ebco.com/
Human Resources Development Canada	http://www.hrdc-drhc.gc.ca/
Imperial Oil	http://www.imperialoil.ca/
Levi Strauss & Co. (Canada)	http://www.us.levi.com/ussites/levi/templates/l_splash.html
Magna International	http://www.magnaint.com/
McDonald's Restaurants of Canada	http://www.mcdonalds.com/
National Bank of Canada	http://www.nbc.ca/

Ontario College of Art	http://www.ocad.on.ca/
Pratt & Whitney	http://www.pratt-whitney.com/
Public Service Commissions	http://www.psc-cfp.gc.ca/
Quebecor Printing Inc.	http://www.quebecorworld.com/
Rogers Communications	http://www.rogers.com/
Royal Bank Financial Group	http://www.royalbank.com/
Simon Fraser University	http://www.sfu.ca/index2.htm
SNC-Lavalin	http://www.snc-lavalin.com/
Sunnybrook Health Science Centre	http://www.sunnybrookandwomens.on.ca/
The Canadian Armed Forces	http://www.recruiting.dnd.ca/
The Canadian Human Rights Commission (CHRC)	http://www.chrc-ccdp.ca/
University of Victoria	http://www.uvic.ca/
Warner-Lambert	http://www.pfizer.com/find/wlindex.html
York University	http://www.yorku.ca

Chapter 3

Abitibi-Consolidated	http://www.abicon.com/
Arthur D. Little	http://www.adlittle.com/
Bank of Montreal	http://www.bmo.com/
Bell Canada	http://www.bell.ca/
Canadian Marconi Company	http://www.cmcelectronics.ca/main.html
Canadian Technology Human Resources Board	http://www.cthrb.ca/
Chrysler Corporation	http://www.daimlerchrysler.com/index_e.htm
CIBC	http://www.cibc.com/
City of Calgary	http://www.gov.calgary.ab.ca/
City of Vancouver	http://www.city.vancouver.bc.ca/
Dictionary of Occupational Titles (DOT)	http://www.immigration-usa.com/dot_index.html
Dofasco Inc.	http://www.dofasco.ca/
Ducks Unlimited Canada	http://www.ducks.ca/
Eastman Kodak Company	http://www.kodak.com/
Federal Express	http://www.fedex.com/
General Motors of Canada	http://www.gmcanada.com/
Hay McBer	http://trgmcber.haygroup.com/
Hewitt Associates	http://was.hewitt.com/hewitt/
HR Magazine	http://www.shrm.org/hrmagazine/
Manulife Financial	http://www.manulife.com/
National Occupation Classification	http://www.worklogic.com:81/noc/
Personnel	http://www.workforce.com/
Royal Bank Financial Group	http://www.royalbank.com/
Royal Bank of Canada	http://www.royalbank.com/
Shell Oil	http://www.shell.com/
Sunnybrook Health Science Centre	http://www.sunnybrookandwomens.on.ca/
Telus	http://www.telus.com/
Toronto Star	http://www.thestar.com/
Vancouver City Savings	http://www.vancity.com/
Vancouver Fire Department	http://www.city.vancouver.bc.ca/fire/

Workforce	http://www.workforce.com/
Work-Life Harmony Enterprises	http://www.worklifeharmony.com/index2.html
Xerox Canada	http://www.xerox.ca/
Zero Knowledge Systems	http://www.zeroknowledge.com/

Chapter 4

Bata Ltd.	http://www.bata.com/main.html
Bell Canada	http://www.bell.ca/
Bell Mobility	http://www.bellmobility.ca/
Blue Jays	http://www.bluejays.ca/
BMO	http://www.bmo.com/
British Petroleum	http://www.bpamoco.com/
Canada Post Corporation	http://www.canadapost.ca/
CBC	http://www.cbc.ca/
CIBC	http://www.cibc.com/
CN Rail	http://www.cn.ca/
Conference Board of Canada	http://www.conferenceboard.ca/
Dofasco Inc.	http://www.dofasco.ca/
Dow	http://www.dow.com/
Dunlop Slazenger Corporation	http://www.dunlopsports.com/
DuPont Canada	http://www.dupont.ca/
Dylex	http://www.dylex.com/
Ford	http://www.ford.com/
GE	http://www.ge.com/
General Motors of Canada	http://www.gmcanada.com/
Government of Canada	http://canada.gc.ca/
Hewlett-Packard	http://www.hp.com/
Human Resources Development Canada	http://www.hrdc-drhc.gc.ca/
Human Resources Professional Association of Ontario	http://www.hrpao.org/index1.asp
Humber College	http://www.humberc.on.ca/
IBM	http://www.ibm.com/
JobShark	http://www.jobshark.com/
Lucent Canada	http://www.lucent.com/intl/americas/canada.html
Maxfli	http://www.maxfli.com/
McDonald's	http://www.mcdonalds.com/
McKinsey and Company	http://www.mckinsey.com/
Molson Canada	http://www.molson.com/
Nortel	http://www.nortelnetworks.com/index.html
Ontario Hydro	http://www.opg.com/
Petro-Canada	http://www.petro-canada.ca/
Public Service Alliance of Canada (PSAC)	http://www.psac.com/
Royal Bank Financial Group	http://www.royalbank.com/
Safeway	http://www.safeway.com/
Scotia Bank	http://www.scotiabank.com/
Second Cup	http://www.secondcup.com/
Shell Canada	http://www.shell.com/

Shell Oil	http://www.shell.com/
Star Data Systems	http://www.stardata.com/
Statistics Canada	http://www.statcan.ca/
Steelcase Canada	http://www.steelcase.com/
Tim Hortons	http://www.timhortons.com/
TOSI	http://www.tosi.com/
Trent University	http://www.trentu.ca/
United Food and Commercial Workers Union	http://www.ufcw.org/
University of Toronto	http://www.utoronto.ca/
Wilfrid Laurier University	http://www.wlu.ca/
William M. Mercer	http://www.mercer.com/
Xerox	http://www.fujixerox.co.jp/eng/

Chapter 5

Bell Canada	http://www.bell.ca/
Bourgault Industries	http://www.bourgault.com/
Canadian Human Rights Commission (CHRC)	http://www.chrc-ccdp.ca/
Canadian Pacific	http://www.cpr.ca/internet/CprPortal.asp
Federal Transport Department	http://www.tc.gc.ca/
Imperial Oil	http://www.imperialoil.ca/
KPMG	http://www.kpmg.ca/english/
McDonald's	http://www.mcdonalds.com/
Mitsubishi	http://www.mitsubishi.com/
Nordstrom	http://store.nordstrom.com/content/pub/help/help.asp
Payless ShoeSource	http://www.payless.com/
RCMP	http://www.rcmp-grc.gc.ca/
Sobey's	http://www.sobeysweb.com/
Society for Human Resource Management (SHRM)	http://www.shrm.org/
The Bay	http://www.hbc.com/
The Canadian Civil Liberties Association	http://www.ccla.org/
The Canadian Forces	http://www.dnd.ca/
The Canadian Security Intelligence Service	http://www.csis-scrs.gc.ca/
Toronto-Dominion Bank	http://www.tdbank.ca/
Weyerhauser Company	http://www.weyerhaeuser.com/
Zellers	http://www.hbc.com/zellers/

Chapter 6

American Society for Training and Development (ASTD)	http://www.astd.org/
AT&T Canada	http://www.attcanada.com/
British Columbia Institute of Technology (BCIT)	http://www.lib.bcit.ca/l1.htm
CAE Electronics	http://www.cae.com/home.html

Cambrian College	http://www.cambrianc.on.ca/
Centennial College	http://www.cencol.on.ca/
Centre for Addiction and Mental Health	http://www.camh.net/
Chateau Whistler	http://www.whistler.worldweb.com/ Whistler/WheretoStay/HotelsMotels/4-1934.html
Church of Scientology	http://www.scientology.org/
CIBC	http://www.cibc.com/
Coca-Cola	http://www.cocacola.com/
Conference Board of Canada	http://www.conferenceboard.ca/
Connaught Laboratories	http://www.aventispasteur.com/
CPR	http://www.cpr.ca/internet/CprPortal.asp
Dofasco	http://www.dofasco.ca/
Domino's Pizza	http://www.dominos.com/
Ernst & Young	http://www.ey.com/global/gcr.nsf/Canada/Welcome_2
Ford	http://www.ford.com/
FORDSTAR	http://members.aol.com/_ht_a/abox316/page2/report.pdf
General Electric	http://www.ge.com/
Humber College	http://www.humberc.on.ca/
Janssen-Ortho	http://www.janssen-ortho.com/JOI/eng_intro.html
Ministry of Education and Training	http://www.edu.gov.on.ca/
Molson Breweries	http://www.molson.com/
Polaroid	http://www.polaroid.com/
ReMax	http://www.remax.com/
Rogers Communications	http://www.rogers.com/
Ryerson Polytechnic University	http://www.ryerson.ca/
SaskTel	http://www.sasktel.com/
Seagulls Pewter and Silversmiths	http://www.seagullpewter.com/
TD Bank	http://www.tdbank.ca/
Union Carbide	http://www.unioncarbide.com/
United Technologies	http://www.utc.com/
Xerox Canada	http://www.xerox.ca/

Chapter 7

Alco Railings	http://www.alpro.com/alco.htm
AT&T	http://www.att.com/
Bank of Montreal	http://www.bmo.com/
BC Tel	http://www.telus.com/
Career Edge	http://www.careeredge.org/
DMR Consulting	http://www.dmr.ca/corporatif/en/
General Electric	http://www.ge.com/
General Motors of Canada	http://www.gmcanada.com/
Human Resources Development Canada (HRDC)	http://www.hrdc-drhc.gc.ca/
IBM	http://www.ibm.com/
Imperial Oil	http://www.imperialoil.ca/
Intel	http://www.intel.com/
KPMG	http://www.kpmg.ca/english/
Marriott Corporation	http://www.marriott.com/

McKinsey and Company	http://www.mckinsey.com/
Ontario Hydro	http://www.ontariopowergeneration.com/
Ontario Public Service	http://www.gojobs.gov.on.ca/mbs/gojobs/gojobs.nsf/GOjobsHome
Proctor and Gamble	http://www.pg.com/
Public Service Commission	http://www.psc-cfp.gc.ca/
Royal Bank of Canada	http://www.royalbank.com/
Sears	http://www.sears.ca/
Statistics Canada	http://www.statcan.ca/
University of Toronto	http://www.utoronto.ca/
Xenova Corporation	http://www.xenova.co.uk/
Xerox	http://www.xerox.ca/

Chapter 8

3M	http://www.3m.com/
Arthur Anderson	http://www.arthurandersen.com/
AT&T	http://www.att.com/
Avenor	http://www.bowater.com/main.html
Bank of Montreal	http://www.bmo.com/
Canadian Institute of Chartered Accountants	http://www.cica.ca/
Canadian Pacific Hotels	http://www.fairmont.com/FA/CDA/Home/CDHomepage/0,2592,,00.html
Coopers & Lybrand	http://www.pwcglobal.com/gx/eng/main/home/
Deloitte & Touche	http://www.deloitte.ca/
Dominion Directory	http://www.dominioninfo.com/specialproducts.html
Ernst & Young	http://www.ey.com/global/gcr.nsf/Canada/Welcome_2
General Electric	http://www.ge.com/
Intel	http://www.intel.com
Johnson & Johnson Advanced Behavioural Technology (JJABT)	http://www.quality.org/tqmbbs/tools-techs/360pa.txt
KPMG	http://www.kpmg.ca/english/
Langley Memorial Hospital	http://www.southfraserhealth.com/Site_Map.asp
Levi Strauss	http://www.levistrauss.com/
Merrill Lynch	http://www.ml.com/
Monsanto	http://www.monsanto.com/
Motorola	http://www.motorola.com/
Ontario Ministry of Northern Development and Mines	http://www.gov.on.ca/MNDM/MINES/mmdhpge.htm
Peat Marwick	http://www.kpmg.ca/english/
Price Waterhouse	http://www.pwcglobal.com/gx/eng/main/home/
Proctor & Gamble	http://www.pg.com/
Rubbermaid	http://www.rubbermaid.com/

Chapter 9

American Association of Industrial Management	http://www.aaimmgmtassoc.org/
American Compensation Association	http://www.acaonline.org/
Boeing	http://www.boeing.com/

Canada Post Corporation	http://www.canadapost.ca/
CIBC	http://www.cibc.com/
City of Mississauga	http://www.city.mississauga.on.ca/
Conference Board of Canada	http://www.conferenceboard.ca/
Durham College	http://www.durhamc.on.ca/
Federal Business Development Bank	http://www.bdc.ca/
Frito-Lay	http://www.fritolay.com/
Hay	http://www.haygroup.com/about.asp
Hewlett-Packard	http://www.hp.com/
Honeywell	http://www.honeywell.com/
Human Resources Development Canada	http://www.hrdc-drhc.gc.ca/
Human Resources Professionals Association of Ontario	http://www.hrpao.org/
Mercer Management Consulting	http://www.mercermc.com/ defaultFlash.asp?Section=&Path=&Tier=
Northern Telecom	http://www.nortelnetworks.com/
Performance Sports	http://www.performance-ski.com/
Robert Half Canada	http://www.roberthalf.com/
Sherwin-Williams	http://www.sherwin.com/default.asp
Star Data Systems	http://www.stardata.com/
Statistics Canada	http://www.statcan.ca/
TPF & C	http://www.towers.com/towers/
Watson Wyatt Worldwide	http://www.watsonwyatt.com/

Chapter 10

AT&T Network Systems	http://www.atnetindia.net/
AT&T Universal Card	http://www.att.com/ucs/
Barrick Gold Corporation	http://www.barrick.com/
BCE	http://www.bce.ca/
BFGoodrich	http://www.bfgoodrich.com/
Borders	http://www.borders.com/
Canadian Airlines	http://www.aircanada.ca/
Canadian Tire	http://www.canadiantire.ca/intro/homepage.jsp?ASSORT MENT%3C%3East_id=166971&bmUID=989864015882
CIBC	http://www.cibc.com/
Conference Board of Canada	http://www.conferenceboard.ca/
Delta Airlines	http://www.delta.com/home/index.jsp
Delta Inns	http://www.deltahotels.com/
Derivion	http://www.derivion.com/
Dofasco	http://www.dofasco.ca/
Federal Express	http://www.fedex.com/
Granite Rock	http://www.graniterock.com/
IBM Canada	http://www.can.ibm.com/
IBM Rochester	http://www-3.ibm.com/employment/us/virtualtour/rch_main.html
KPMG	http://www.kpmg.ca/english/
Lincoln Electric Company	http://www.lincolnelectric.com/corporate/career/default.asp
MacDonald Dettwiler & Associates	http://www.mda.ca/
McGraw-Edison	http://www.cooperlighting.com/brands/mcgraw-edison/

Ontario Securities Commission	http://www.osc.gov.on.ca/
Potlatch Corporation	http://www.potlatchcorp.com/
Price Waterhouse Coopers	http://www.pwcglobal.com/gx/eng/main/home/
Royal Bank of Canada	http://www.royalbank.com/
Saturn Corporation	http://www.saturn.com/
Sears	http://www.sears.com/
Sears Canada	http://www.sears.ca/
Securities and Exchange Commission (SEC)	http://www.sec.gov/
Star Data Systems	http://www.stardata.com/
Starbucks	http://www.starbucks.com/
Steelcase	http://www.steelcase.com/
Sun Life of Canada	http://www.sunlife.com/
Taco Bell Corporation	http://www.tacobell.com/
Toronto Stock Exchange	http://www.tse.com/
Towers Perrin	http://www.towersperrin.com/
Xaloy Corporation	http://www.xaloy.com/tdframe1_1.htm
Xerox	http://www.fujixerox.co.jp/indexEn.html

Chapter 11

America West Airlines	http://www.americawest.com/
AT&T	http://www.att.com/
Bank of Canada	http://www.bank-banque-canada.ca/
Bank of Nova Scotia	http://www.scotiabank.ca/
Caldwell Partners	http://www.caldwell.ca/
CEBS	http://www.ifebp.org/cebs/cebscanada/default.asp
CIBC	http://www.cibc.com/
Conference Board of Canada	http://www.conferenceboard.ca/
Consumers Gas	http://www.cgc.enbridge.com/
Coopers & Lybrand	http://www.pwcglobal.com/gx/eng/main/home/
Dalhousie University	http://www.dal.ca/
Eddie Bauer	http://www.eddiebauer.com/
Ford Canada	http://www.ford.ca/
Honeywell Canada	http://www.honeywell.com/
HR Reporter	http://www.hrreporter.com/
Human Resource Professional	http://www.hrprofessional.org/
Human Resources Professionals Association of Ontario	http://www.hrpao.org/
Husky Injection Molding Systems	http://www.husky.ca/
IBM Canada	http://www.can.ibm.com/
IBM	http://www.ibm.com/
KPMG	http://www.kpmg.ca/english/
McMillan Bloedel	http://www.weyerhaeuser.com/
Molson Breweries	http://www.molson.com/
Nortel	http://www.nortelnetworks.com/index.html
Ontario Hydro	http://www.ontariopowergeneration.com/
Pan Canadian Petroleum	http://www.pcp.ca/index_java.html
Polaroid	http://www.polaroid.com/
Polo Ralph Lauren Canada	http://www.canadaoneoutlets.com/stores/prl.html

Price Waterhouse Coopers — http://www.pwcglobal.com/gx/eng/main/home/
Schering-Plough — http://www.sch-plough.com/
Siemens Canada — http://www.siemens.ca/
Statistics Canada — http://www.statcan.ca/
TransAmerica Corporation — http://www.transamerica.com/
University of New Brunswick — http://www.unb.ca/
Wharton School at the University of
Pennsylvania — http://www.wharton.upenn.edu/
William M. Mercer Limited — http://www.wmmercer.com/

Chapter 12

Allied Signal — http://www.alliedsignal.com/
American Institute of Plant Engineers — http://www.google.com/url?sa=U&start=1&q=http://
www.ocec.org/ memsoc/aipe.html&e=42
BC Tel — http://www.telus.com/
Canadian Mental Health Association — http://www.cmha.ca/
Canadian Tire Acceptance Limited
(CTAL) — http://cantire2.canadiantire.ca/CTenglish/locate/niagara.html
Carleton University — http://www.carleton.ca/
Charles Schwab and Co. — http://www.schwab.com/
Circle K Corporation — http://circlekservice.com/
CN — http://www.cn.ca/
Conference Board of Canada — http://www.conferenceboard.ca/
Corel Corp. — http://www.corel.com/
FitWorks — http://www.fitworks.com/
Home Depot — http://www.homedepot.com/home.html
Human Resources Development
Canada — http://www.hrdc-drhc.gc.ca/
Labatt Breweries of Canada — http://www.labatt.com/
Manitoba Department of Labour — http://www.gov.mb.ca/labour/
Motorola — http://www.motorola.com/
Nortel — http://www.nortelnetworks.com/
Ontario Ministry of Labour — http://www.gov.on.ca/LAB/main.htm
Pacific Bell — http://www.pacbell.com/
PCL Constructors Canada — http://www.pcl.com/
Peel Board of Education — http://www.peel.edu.on.ca/
University of Western Ontario — http://www.uwo.ca/
Wholesale Travel Group — http://www.wholesaletravel.com/
Wilson Banwell — http://www.wilsonbanwell.com/
Xerox — http://www.fujixerox.co.jp/indexEn.html

Chapter 13

Addiction Research Foundation — http://www.arf.org/
Canadian Union of Postal Workers — http://www.cupw-sttp.org/
Clarke Institute — http://www2.camh.net/CLARKEPages/about_the_clarke/
welcome.html
DuPont — http://www.dupont.com/
Fantom Technologies — http://www.fantom.com/

General Electric	http://wwrincew.ge.com/
Gerber Products	http://www.gerber.com/
Greyhound Canada	http://www.greyhound.ca/
Human Resources Professionals Association of Ontario	http://www.hrpao.org/
International Olympic Committee (IOC)	http://www.olympic.org/
Master Card International	http://www.mastercard.com/
McCarthy Tetrault	http://www.mccarthy.ca/
Ontario Hydro	http://www.ontariopowergeneration.com/
Pitney Bowes	http://www.pitneybowes.com/cgi-bin/pb.dll/ home/index.jsp?homepg=index_flash
Prince Edward Island	http://www.gov.pe.ca/
Red Lobster	http://www.redlobster.com/index.asp
Royal Trust	http://www.royalbank.com/rt-wealth/
Supreme Court of Canada	http://www.lexum.umontreal.ca/csc-scc/en/
United Grain Growers	http://www.ugg.com/
Volkswagen Canada	http://www.vw.com/
Wal-Mart	http://www.walmartstores.com/

Chapter 14

Air Traffic Controllers	http://www.natca.org/
Alberta Teachers' Association	http://www.teachers.ab.ca/
American Federation of Labor and Congress of Industrial Organizations (AFL-CIO)	http://www.aflcio.org/home.htm
Canadian Auto Workers	http://www.caw.ca/
Canadian Labour Congress (CLC)	http://www.clc-ctc.ca/
Canadian Union of Postal Workers	http://www.cupw-sttp.org/
Canadian Union of Public Employees (CUPE)	http://www.cupe.ca/
Federation of Quebec Nurses	http://www.fiiq.qc.ca/
International Association of Machinists	http://www.iamaw.org/
International Brotherhood of Electrical Workers Union	http://ibew.org/
National Union of Provincial Government Employees (NUPGE)	http://www.nupge.ca/
Ontario Secondary School Teachers' Federation	http://www.osstf.on.ca/
Professional Employees International Union	http://www.opeiu.org/
Public Service Alliance of Canada (PSAC)	http://www.psac.com/home-e.htm
Public Service Staff Relations Board	http://www.pssrb-crtfp.gc.ca/
Shell Canada	http://www.shell.ca/
Teamsters	http://www.teamster.org/

United Association of Journeymen
and Apprentices of the Plumbing and
Pipefitting Industry   http://www.ua.org/
United Auto Workers   http://www.uaw.org/
United Brotherhood of Carpenters
and Joiners of America   http://www.necarpenters.org/UBC.htm
United Food and Commercial
Workers Union   http://www.ufcw.org/
United Steelworkers of America   http://www.uswa.org/
Wal-Mart   http://www.walmartstores.com/

Chapter 15

Algoma Steel   http://www.algoma.com/
Canada Post Corporation   http://www.canadapost.ca/
Canadian Auto Workers   http://www.caw.ca/
Canadian Federation of Independent
Business   http://www.cfib.ca/
Canadian Industrial Relations Board   http://www.cirb-ccri.gc.ca/
Chrysler   http://www.daimlerchrysler.com/
Conference Board of Canada   http://www.conferenceboard.ca/
Federal Mediation and Conciliation
Service   http://www.fmcs.gov/
Ford   http://www.ford.com/
General Motors   http://www.gm.com/
International Nickel Company of
Canada   http://www.inco.com/
National Hockey League   http://www.nhl.com/
Rogers Communications   http://www.rogers.com/
Statistics Canada   http://www.statcan.ca/
Stelco   http://www.stelco.com/
The Globe and Mail   http://www.theglobeandmail.com/
United Steelworkers   http://www.uswa.org/
Volkswagen Canada   http://www.vw.com/
Wilfrid Laurier University   http://www.wlu.ca/

Chapter 16

3M   http://www.3m.com/
ABB   http://www.abb.com/
Alcan Aluminum   http://www.alcan.com/
AMP   http://www.amp.com/
ARCO   http://www.arcogas.com/gas/index.html
Bechtel   http://www.bechtel.com/
Berlitz International   http://www.berlitz.com/
Bombardier   http://www.bombardier.com/
CanWest   http://www.canwestglobal.com/
Ciba-Geigy   http://www.novartis.com/

Coca-Cola	http://www.cocacola.com/
Colgate-Palmolive	http://www.colgate.com/
Deloitte & Touche	http://www.deloitte.ca/
Digital	http://www.compaq.com/
Dow Chemical	http://www.dow.com/
EDS	http://www.eds.com/
Expatriate Forum	http://www.expatforum.com/
Export Development Corporation (EDC)	http://www.edc-see.ca/
Exxon	http://www.exxon.com/
Four Seasons	http://www.fourseasons.com/
Fuji-Xerox	http://www.fujixerox.co.jp/indexEn.html
General Electric	http://www.ge.com/
GTE	http://www.gte.com/
Heidrick & Struggles	http://www.heidrick.com/
Heineken	http://www.heineken.com/
Honda	http://www.honda.com/
Honeywell	http://www.honeywell.com/
IBM	http://www.ibm.com/
International Confederation of Free Trade Unions (ICFTU)	http://www.icftu.org/
International Labor Organization (ILO)	http://www.ilo.org/
ITT	http://www.ittind.com/
Korn/Ferry	http://www.kornferry.com/
Levi Strauss	http://www.levistrauss.com/
Matsushita	http://www.panasonic.com/
McDonald's	http://www.mcdonalds.com/
McGill University	http://www.mcgill.ca/
Monsanto	http://www.monsanto.com/
Motorola	http://www.motorola.com/
NEC	http://www.nec.com/
Nike	http://www.nike.com/
Nortel	http://www.nortelnetworks.com/
PepsiCo	http://www.pepsico.com/
Pepsi-Cola	http://www.pepsico.com/pepsicocareers/02_pepsi.html
Phillips	http://www.phillips.com/
Proctor & Gamble	http://www.pg.com/
Schulich School of Business at York University	http://dr.ssb.yorku.ca/ssb.nsf?open
Seagram Corporation	http://www.seagram.com/
Shell	http://www.shell.com/
Texas Instruments	http://www.ti.com/
Thomson Corp.	http://www.thomson.com/
United Auto Workers	http://www.uaw.org/
Whirlpool	http://www.whirlpool.com/
Wyatt Company	http://www.watsonwyatt.com/
Xerox	http://www.fujixerox.co.jp/indexEn.html

Chapter 17

American Express	http://www.americanexpress.com/
American Society for Training and Development (ASTD)	http://www.astd.org/
Ames Rubber Corporation	http://www.amesrubber.com/totalqlt.htm
Ashton Photo	http://www.ashtonphoto.com/
Colgate-Palmolive	http://www.colgate.com/
Connor Formed Metal Products	http://www.devicelink.com/company/mem/co/13/1385.html
Doubletree Hotels	http://www.doubletreehotels.com/
Eastman Chemical Company	http://www.eastman.com/
Federal Express	http://www.fedex.com/
Ford	http://www.ford.com/
General Motors' Saturn	http://www.saturn.com/
Granite Rock	http://www.graniterock.com/
Harley Davidson	http://www.harley-davidson.com/
Honeywell	http://www.honeywell.com/
Kodak	http://www.kodak.com/
MacMillan Bloedel	http://www.weyerhaeuser.com/
Macy's/Bullocks	http://www.macys.com/
Manitoba Telephone System	http://www.mts.mb.ca/
Merck	http://www.merck.com/
Microsoft	http://www.microsoft.com/
Monsanto	http://www.monsanto.com/
Nissan	http://www.nissan-usa.com/
Northern Telecom	http://www.nortelnetworks.com/
Nucor Steel	http://www.nucor.com/
One Valley Bank	http://www.onevalley.com/
Reebok International	http://www.reebok.com/
Schindler Elevator	http://www.schindler.com/
Shell Canada	http://www.shell.ca/
Southwest Airlines	http://www.iflyswa.com/
Texas Instruments	http://www.ti.com/
The Ohio CBU	http://www.cbu.edu/Alumni/profiles00.html
TriHealth System	http://www.trihealth.com/trihealth/trihealth/history/vision_takes_shape.htm
TRW	http://www.trw.com/
University of Southern California	http://www.usc.edu/
Wal-Mart	http://www.walmartstores.com/
Weyerhauser	http://www.weyerhaeuser.com/
Xaloy	http://www.xaloy.com/
Xerox	http://www.xerox.com/go/xrx/template/013.jsp

NAME INDEX

ORGANIZATION INDEX

SUBJECT INDEX

PHOTO CREDITS